All Roads
Lead to
BAGHDAD

$\cancel{X}$ 68484322

For sale by the Superintendent of Documents, U.S. Government Office
Internet: bookstore.gpo.gov Phone: toll free (866) 512-1800: DC area (202)512-1800
Fax: (202) 512-2250 Mail: Stop SSOP. Washington, DC 20402-00001

ISBN-13: 978-0-16-075364-0
ISBN-10: 0-16-075364-3

All Roads
Lead to
BAGHDAD

Army Special Operations Forces in Iraq

Charles H. Briscoe, Kenneth Finlayson, Robert W. Jones Jr., Cherilyn A. Walley,
A. Dwayne Aaron, Michael R. Mullins, James A. Schroder

USASOC History Office
Fort Bragg, North Carolina

UNITED STATES SPECIAL OPERATIONS COMMAND
OFFICE OF THE COMMANDER
7701 TAMPA POINT BOULEVARD
MACDILL AIR FORCE BASE, FLORIDA 33621-5323

UNITED STATES SPECIAL OPERATIONS COMMAND FOREWORD

Army Special Operations were a dynamic force in the US-led offensive to remove the regime of Saddam Hussein from power in Iraq and to capture Baghdad during Operation IRAQI FREEDOM, our nation's second campaign in the Global War on Terrorism. Special Operations warriors spearheaded the ground invasion of Iraq on 19 March 2003 little more than a year after they had forced the collapse of the Taliban regime in Afghanistan and shattered al-Qaeda forces. These stories of courageous Army Special Operations soldiers and airmen remind us of the vital role they played, and how much they accomplished in those first months in Iraq. Their sacrifices and contributions have brought honor to our great country and demonstrate pride in their profession.

All Roads Lead to Baghdad is the Army Special Operations story of the major combat operations in Iraq. It is one of night air attacks swarming the frontier posts and anti-aircraft artillery systems and daring long-range infiltrations of Special Forces "A" teams by Night Stalkers of the 160th Special Operations Aviation Regiment. Rangers parachute and helicopter assault deep behind Iraqi lines with Psychological Operations and Civil Affairs tactical teams. Signal and Support Soldiers make it possible. This was the Army SOF team that united Joint conventional elements and Coalition allies to overwhelm Iraqi forces, collapsing a tyrant's regime and bringing freedom to an oppressed people.

Just as Army Special Operations Forces made the difference in Operation ENDURING FREEDOM in Afghanistan, these forces were again the catalysts to success in Operation IRAQI FREEDOM. The essence of Special Operations is small, well-trained teams of intrepid warriors that have the skills, talent, and overwhelming will to succeed. Their stories, told here in *All Roads Lead to Baghdad*, highlight why Army Special Operations Forces have not only a glorious past, but a very bright future.

Bryan D. Brown
General, U.S. Army
Commander

USASOC FOREWORD

All Roads Lead to Baghdad is the story of Operation IRAQI FREE-DOM, the second Army Special Operations campaign in America's Global War on Terrorism. Much like its predecessor *Weapon of Choice* explained what Army SOF soldiers accomplished in Operation ENDURING FREEDOM in Afghanistan, this book shows how Army Special Operations supported a US-led conventional air and ground offensive to collapse the regime of Saddam Hussein and capture Baghdad. Army SOF performed its traditional role, serving as a dynamic force-multiplier, in support of the major offensive effort. Army Special Operations Forces were responsible for three fronts in the US Central Command campaign against Iraq—the SCUD/WMD hunt and UW mission in West, the Kurdish unconventional warfare mission in the North, and the PSYOP mission. And, they directly supported the other two fronts—the Air campaign and Ground offensive to seize Baghdad.

Army Special Operations Forces spearheaded ground operations in Iraq. Special Forces teams assigned special reconnaissance missions were infiltrated into the Karbala Gap by the 160th Special Operations Aviation Regiment while other Night Stalkers attacked border posts and anti-aircraft artillery systems. The 75th Rangers assaulted by parachute and helicopter deep inside Iraq after Psychological Operations had broadcast and dropped leaflets all over the country. Signalers, Support, and Civil Affairs soldiers rounded out the ARSOF team. The stories of Army SOF soldiers best explain their missions and what they succeeded in accomplishing. Just like it was for Afghanistan, the ARSOF successes can be directly attributed to mid-grade officers and sergeants leading small operational teams and aircrews. These young warriors—whether in operational, staff, or support elements—made the difficult appear routine because they are well-disciplined, highly motivated, and very innovative professionals.

All Roads Lead to Baghdad is the second book in the USASOC-sponsored Army SOF History series. It is current operations history that covers the entire spectrum of Army Special Operations Forces and benefits not only the "Force," but the Army and other services. This is your story and it is one that you can be justly proud of today. This book is dedicated to those fallen comrades whose lives enabled the oppressed to know freedom and liberty.

Philip R. Kensinger, Jr.
Lieutenant General, U.S. Army
Commanding Officer

Contents

List of Figures

Acknowledgments

All Roads Lead to Baghdad is a history of the Army special operations forces during Operation IRAQI FREEDOM, the second major campaign in America's Global War on Terrorism since terrorist-piloted airliners crashed into the Twin Towers in New York City and the Pentagon on 11 September 2001. It covers the role of Army SOF in support of U.S. Central Command offensive combat operations to topple the regime of Saddam Hussein in Iraq from the planning in late spring 2002 through June 2003. The mission of the U.S. Army Special Operations Command History Office, much like it had been for Afghanistan, was "to capture the current operations history of the Army SOF soldiers fighting the war in Iraq." It entailed writing a second unclassified, well-documented history of current operations. Fortunately, the Afghanistan and Philippines projects had "paved the way" for the commanders and staff of USASOC, the supported headquarters, U.S. Central Command, U.S. Special Operations Command, Joint Special Operations Command, and the Special Operations Command Central. The staff review process for current operations history based on classified sources ("sanitization") is tedious, but absolutely necessary. The Global War on Terrorism is ongoing and Army SOF soldiers are still engaged in combat in Afghanistan and Iraq. It was a team effort that made the campaign issue of *Veritas*, "ARSOF in Iraq," and this latest book, *All Roads Lead to Baghdad: Army Special Operations Forces in Iraq,* possible.

Sincere special thanks are due a myriad of people who provided encouragement, counsel, assistance "above and beyond," and support necessary to get *All Roads Lead to Baghdad* funded, written, formatted, approved, published, and distributed to the Army special operations soldiers, the "heart and soul" of ARSOF. In the USASOC History Office, Mr. Earl J. Moniz, information technician and producer of the ARSOF history poster series, compiled, scanned, and organized photographs, PSYOP leaflets, and the supporting material, and Ms. Wendy Nielsen, *Veritas* managing editor and designer, raised format and quality standards "several notches" for this book. U.S. Army Reserve LTC Robert W. Jones Jr., an author, arranged the 126th Military History Detachment (Massachusetts Army National Guard) deployment to cover Civil Affairs and Psychological Operations in Iraq: MAJ Paul Landry, SFC Daniel Moriarty, SSG Patrick Jennings, and SGT Landon Mavrelis. Two active duty Special Forces soldiers were part of the USASOC history team that visited Iraq—CW4 Yul Yurcaba and SGM Mike Barnes—to conduct field interviews. The historians appreciated that Ms. Cynthia Hayden, ARSOF

Archivist, shared her area; that Ms. Monet McKinzie provided willing administrative assistance and humor; that Ms. Connie Moralez-Piper assisted with research; and that Mr. Erdie Picart managed the physical security.

All Roads Lead to Baghdad would not have been possible without the total cooperation and support of the Army SOF soldiers and unit leadership. Without classified interviews there would simply be no "personality" in this history. The subtle nuances and context are critical to presenting current operations history. It helped immensely that *Weapon of Choice* demonstrated the value of the ARSOF history program to soldiers and commanders. It also showed that views voiced to USASOC historians in confidence would be respected. To all interviewed, thanks for the candor, patience, interest, and support in capturing and preserving Army SOF history.

Those on the USASOC, U.S. Army Special Forces Command, U.S. Army Civil Affairs and Psychological Operations Command, and U.S. Army John F. Kennedy Special Warfare Center and School staffs who deserve special mention are: **USASOC**—COL Ives Fontaine, COL Charles Cleveland, and COL Andrew Milani, Chiefs of Staff and major proponents of the project; LTC Edward McHale, LTC Hank Dodge, and LTC Adam Loveless, ACS; Mr. Charles Pimble, SGS; Ms. Connie Wicker, Mrs. Irma Winbush, and Mr. Mike Kunik; COL Steve Kilgore, MAJ Chris Valentino, and CPT Elizabeth Allen (manuscript reader) of the SJA; Ms. Jane Sutherlin, Ms. Sandra Aman, Ms. Karen Glass, and Ms. Ella Porter of DCS, Acquisition & Contracting; CW5 Russ Vona, Ms. Ruth Crumley, and Ms. Doris Taylor of DCS, G-1; Ms. Mavis Muldrow of CPAC, Fort Bragg; Mr. John Green, Ms. Sally Hurt, Mr. Dan Brand, Mr. John Watkins, Ms. Mary Mehan (manuscript reader), Mr. Ed Nelson, Mr. Lynn Kirkland, and Ms. Sarah Fields of the DCS, G-2; COL James Holloway, COL Walter Herd, LTC Earle Hudson, LTC David Duffy, MAJ Andy Nichols, MSG Frank Rossi, Mr. Robin McDonald (manuscript reader), and Ms. Sharon Smith of the DCS, G-3; COL Steve Pelley of the DCS, G-4; COL Philip McGhee, LTC Christopher White, LTC Darrell Brimberry, Ms. Becky Mauldin, Ms. Rose Reid, Mr. Greg Parks, and Ms. Robin Jones of the DCS, Comptroller; Mr. Dorsey Mellott and MSG Charles Koonce of the CIO/G-6; MAJ Donald Davis of the DCS, Engineer; LTC Tom Brew of the DCS, SOA; MAJ Fred O'Donnell and Mr. Randall Wilkie of the ACE; LTC Hans Bush and Mr. Walt Sokalski of the DCS, PA; LTC Gary Barnes, Australian LNO; MAJ James Spivey, SFC Theodore Dennis Jr., and SSG James H. Simon III of the USASOC Headquarters Company; **USASFC**—COL Manny Diemer, Deputy Commander, COL John Knie, Chief of Staff, Mr. James Hargraves (manuscript reader) and Mr. Chris Crain of the G-3; **USACAPOC**—Ms. Connie Almueti and COL Ferdinand Irizarry of the G-3; **USAJFKSWCS**—COL Richard Helfer, COL Michael Rose, and COL Joe Smith, Chiefs of Staff; and Mr. Jerry Steelman, editor, *Special Warfare* magazine.

At **USSOCOM**—special thanks to the USSOCOM History Office: Dr. John Partin, Command Historian; Ms. Gaea D. Levy, Archivist; and the historians who worked in Iraq: Col Dennis P. Mroczkowski, U.S. Marine Corps Reserve, LtCol Rick Perkins, U.S. Marine Corps Reserve, LTC John Katz, U.S. Army Reserve,

LtCol Nate Lowrey, U.S. Marine Corps Reserve, MAJ Mike Schellhammer, U.S. Army Reserve, Maj David Crist, U.S. Marine Corps Reserve, and LTC Michael A. Ceroli, U.S. Army; LTC Edward Nye and Ms. Jennifer Whittle, PAO. At **SOC-CENT**—COL Patrick Higgins, J-3, MAJ Frank Fahringer, COL Jerry Vaughn, LCDR Kevin Aandahl, PAO, LCDR Gregory Bart, Legal Advisor, CSM Jay Lovelace, MAJ Reid Webber, and LTC Jack Kaplan, Headquarters' Commandant, for facilitating entrance and exit, providing weapons, ammunition, body armor, and NBC gear to the USASOC History team. At **CJSOTF-AP**—COL Hector Pagan, LTC Kirk Burton, LTC John Chin, and MAJ Chad Reiman who arranged to get us to Kirkuk and all over Baghdad. At **JSOC**—Mr. Steve Cage and Mr. James Kelliher (manuscript readers).

Carol Rippey and Tad Sifeis, Armed Forces Information Service, Alexandria, Virginia, as they did for *Weapon of Choice*, provided the USASOC historians with CDs of *The Early Bird*. The September 2001–May 2002 coverage proved invaluable. Photos by the Department of Defense Joint Combat Camera teams were appreciated. ANTEON, Inc., Fayetteville, North Carolina, provided three top quality retired Army special operations officers with academic degrees and experience to serve as the contract historians for this project.

And finally, accolades are due Dr. Kenneth Finlayson, Dr. Cherilyn A. Walley, LTC Robert W. Jones Jr., LTC Katherine P. Rhine, Mr. Earl J. Moniz, and Ms. Wendy Nielsen of the USASOC History staff for editing and producing a top quality manuscript for *All Roads Lead to Baghdad* in a timely manner.

While the other authors and I sincerely appreciate the help provided by everyone who contributed to this book, as senior writer and editor, I assume responsibility for errors of fact, identification, and conclusion.

C.H. Briscoe

xxvi

Introduction

The purpose of this book is to explain what the various Army special operations elements accomplished during the U.S.-led Coalition offensive to collapse the regime of Saddam Hussein in Iraq called Operation IRAQI FREEDOM. The successes achieved by Army special operations forces elements, just like Afghanistan, were directly attributable to majors and below. How they "fixed" large Iraqi forces in the north, how they got Kurdish peshmerga units to attack Iraqi mechanized regiments and divisions, how they neutralized SCUD missile threats in the western desert, and how they gained Iraqi tribal support is best accomplished by letting Army SOF soldiers describe the latest action or activity while it was still quite vivid. This is a better approach than an account by a historian composed in the comfort of peace five to ten years afterward. While this book provides only a five-month "snapshot" of the planning, preparations, and offensive operations in Iraq, it covers that phase when ARSOF was the most active. Major combat operations ended in less than five weeks, almost two months sooner than initially anticipated.

While *All Roads Lead to Baghdad* was written to capture the history of the Army special operations forces in Iraq and the primary audience—the "bulls eye"—is ARSOF soldiers, outer rings of the "target" were taken into account. There had to be some appeal to the rest of the Army, family members, veterans, and the general public. It had to be well documented to stand the test of time. Declassification will be a long time coming, but researchers will then discover that this book provided better than 90 percent "official ground truth" when it was published.

The great majority of *All Roads Lead to Baghdad* was prepared using classified materials as primary sources. The classified parts of narrative and vignettes were carefully "sanitized" by the writers. They were staffed through the U.S. Army Special Operations Command Deputy Chiefs of Staff, G-2 (security) and G-3 (operations), and Joint Special Operations Command for approval before being sent out to the field for editorial comments/corrections. Classified reviews, staffing, and command approval before publication, while tedious, are critical elements of the process of writing current operations history because the Global War on Terrorism is still ongoing. Combat operations are being conducted by ARSOF soldiers in support of Operation IRAQI FREEDOM in Iraq and Operation ENDURING FREEDOM in Afghanistan today. The U.S. Army Special Operations Command, sponsor of the ARSOF history program, will not put these Army SOF soldiers "at risk."

Since publishing *Weapon of Choice: ARSOF in Afghanistan* in October 2003, the "rules of engagement" for the ARSOF history writers were modified. Army SOF soldiers, majors and below will have pseudonyms based on legal guidance and regulatory policy. An asterisk by the name in the text indicates a pseudonym has been used. It will also be noted in the endnotes and the index. In lieu of photographs with "blacked out" eyes, electronic "blurring" will be used. Maps not created by staff members and photographs used are from U.S. Government sources (USASOC History Office Files) to avoid copyright use fees. Sensitive classified parts were "sanitized" based on very specific security guidelines, hence special forces elements are not always Special Forces and some forward bases are identified regionally instead of specifically. None of the tape or digitally recorded interviews will be transcribed because official field personnel interviewed did not sign permissions to release statements. All materials used for this project will be treated as sensitive, limited access, non-releasable, classified draft documents.

Following publication of *All Roads Lead to Baghdad,* a limited access classified annex will be prepared. This will contain true names for pseudonyms and by endnote, specify classified documents, briefings, and after action reports used to corroborate those references. The classified annex will be strictly controlled by USASOC and will not be available to researchers who do not have appropriate security clearances, access to special programs, and a bona fide "need to know."

Acronyms are a spawn of the Information Age. Today, all organizations, government and civilian, businesses, and professions to include sports have their own lexicons. The media adopts them to lend credence to its around-the-clock presentations. The military is no exception. So, IGNORE the acronyms. There will not be a test at the end of the book. Instead, read the narrative and focus on the soldiers' stories—the vignettes. They are the essence.

The selected historical vignettes tell the ARSOF in Iraq story. Unit actions and activities are presented when they appear in the chronological order of the war. For example, the Combined Joint Special Operations Task Force–West activities appear first because CJSOTF-North is still trying to gets its forces into northern Iraq when the SOF war begins. An events time-line (with ARSOF actions highlighted) first appears on the page bottoms of Chapter 4. The soldier stories explain how they prepared for missions, the skill sets and tactics, some of the capabilities of SOF-unique equipment, how success was determined, and what they were trying to achieve. Consider all these aspects and the strength of ARSOF will be revealed—highly trained, motivated, and dedicated soldiers. While technology is important to SOF, individual soldiers and small elements make the difference. Like it was in Afghanistan, the credit for the successes in Iraq belongs to the majors, captains, warrant officers, sergeants and enlisted soldiers on the Army SOF tactical teams, aircrews, and support units.

Within security constraints there was a conscious effort to present an equitable sampling of stories that covered all ARSOF elements. Complete coverage of all participating teams was impossible. The Special Operations Command Central, Special Forces group commanders, and ARSOF regimental commanders identified their "best" stories to the history writers. The stories selected were taken from those available to demonstrate a capability, illustrate an activity, or explain a combat mission in detail. Every interview provided context for the writers whether it became a vignette or not. Multiple views—top, middle, bottom, and Coalition—were sought to gain perspective. These vignettes were based primarily on classified field interviews, after-action reports, personal journals, and operations center logs. Secondary sources from *The Early Bird* (Armed Forces Information Service) were used, but for this most recent current operations history, several hundred digital and tape-recorded interviews of soldiers (generals to privates) serving on tactical teams or as commanders and staff in the SOF headquarters were the most valuable. These interviews gave "personality" to the history and added realism. Where there were minor differences between accounts provided by a tactical team "on the ground" and Headquarters' files, cross-referencing corroborated the most reliable story. In the interest of producing timely history while the war was "still fresh," any unresolved discrepancies were addressed by the project director (USASOC historian) who evaluated the importance, relevance, and whether the issues contributed to, or confused the subject. This book only covers ARSOF actions in Iraq through June 2003.

The purpose of *All Roads Lead to Baghdad* is not to resolve Army special operations doctrinal issues nor to clarify military definitions, rather to provoke discussion and promote analysis and comparisons. Questions, issues, or concerns about how and why ARSOF elements were employed by the CJSOTFs and tactics, techniques, and procedures should be sent to the U.S. Army John F. Kennedy Special Warfare Center and School, proponent for Army SOF doctrine, and to U.S. Joint Forces Command, the proponent for joint doctrine.

This project is not intended to be the definitive history of the unconventional war in Iraq. That war is still ongoing. It is a "snapshot" history of ARSOF current operations in IRAQI FREEDOM from the late spring 2002 into the summer 2003. The command decision to have professional historians with ARSOF experience capture the history of current operations in Iraq is evidence that it was not intended to be a public relations piece. The conduct of combat operations in war rarely models the planning and preparations beforehand. Elaborate campaign plans and detailed operations orders often "go to the winds" when the fighting starts. Intelligence estimates of the enemy's strengths and weakness are found to be "full of holes." Confusion abounds. Combined these factors are referred to as the "fog of war" and negative aspects rarely appear in after action reports. The writing team, composed of ARSOF veterans, accepted these elements as "givens." When everything goes according to plan, professional soldiers consider it to be an anomaly. Foremost in the minds of the veteran writers surrounded by ARSOF soldiers was the sports adage: "It's easy to fool the fans, but you can't fool the players." If today's troops (70 percent of whom are already veterans) accept the history with minimal grumbling (following the age-old military premise that if soldiers aren't complaining, there's something wrong), then the public has a good product.

All Roads Lead to Baghdad begins by answering the contextual questions: What is Iraq and why Iraq? Then, the reader is given a brief ethnic, cultural, and political history of Iraq and Saddam Hussein is profiled. Iraq and Saddam became synonymous when the United States defended Kuwait in the first Gulf War (1990–1991). The post-war period discussion extends into Operation ENDURING FREEDOM in Afghanistan. The contingency planning against Iraq undertaken by various commands is followed by the Army and joint SOF preparations for a second major campaign in the Global War on Terrorism. Special Operations Command Central established two Combined Joint Special Operations Task Forces and a Naval Task Force to execute the SOF campaign in support of 1003V, the U.S. Central Command offensive operation to topple the regime of Saddam Hussein in Iraq. Because Army SOF is supporting the conventional air and ground attacks, the ARSOF stories regularly follow a sequential big picture overview of the war.

Since Operation IRAQI FREEDOM is still ongoing, the concluding remarks will be a short summary of ARSOF activities through June 2003. That summary will be followed by Observations and Reflections based on official documents and interviews with soldiers at all levels and with the Coalition allies. The reflections are non-attributable assessments made by active and retired ARSOF officers who participated in the war and the Operation IRAQI FREEDOM history project.

Chapter One

Why Iraq?

T HE PURPOSE OF THIS chapter is to provide context by answering two basic questions. The first is simply, "What is there about this Iraq?" A fact book-style presentation provides critical specifics about the country of Iraq. The encyclopedic facts range from size to population to ethnic group demography to terrain to industry and gross national product to communications. More details about the history of Iraq are provided after the second question is answered. Since this book is a military history of the war against Iraq, the second question, "Why Iraq?" is best explained by the threat Iraq posed to the United States in its Global War on Terrorism. A general Iraqi order of battle also includes the paramilitary "wild cards" on the field—the Iranian Mujahedin-e Khalq brigade, the Ansar al-Islam, Sunni terrorists, the Saddam Fedayeen loyalist fanatics, and the Badr Corps of Shia defectors from the Iraqi army. A thumbnail history of Iraq covering the ancient Sunni-Shia split and the Kurdish role centers on three constants: nepotism, oil, and the continual struggle for power. The history of Iraq and Saddam Hussein became synonymous in 1975, when he assumed the leadership of the Baath Party. This section concludes with a culture-based psychological profile of Saddam.

IRAQ

Figure 1.1 Republic of Iraq flag.

Country Name	Republic of Iraq
Capital	Baghdad
Location	Middle East—bordered by Turkey to the north, Iran to the east, the Persian Gulf and Kuwait to the southeast, Saudi Arabia to the south, and Jordan and Syria to the west
Size	approximately 437,072 sq km (slightly larger than California)
Time Zone	Zulu plus 3 = U.S. Eastern Standard Time plus eight hours
Population	approximately 24,510,000 in 2002 (a little more than the combined populations of Texas and Oklahoma)
Population density	Slightly over 70 percent of the population lives in urban areas concentrated in the Tigris-Euphrates flood plain
Population of major cities	Baghdad 5,000,000 Basra 1,500,000 Mosul 1,200,000 Kirkuk 535,000
Language	Arabic (official language) spoken by 80 percent of the population; 15 percent speak Kurdish (official language in Kurdish areas)
Literacy rate	58 percent (male 70 percent, female 45 percent)
Ethnic groups	Arab 75–80 percent, Kurdish 15–20 percent, other 5 percent
Religion	Islam (official) 97 percent; Islamic sects: Shia 60–65 percent, Sunni 32–35 percent, Christian or other 3 percent
Climate	hot, dry season May–October; mild, wet season November–April
Terrain	desert in west and southwest, mountains in north and northeast, plains in center, and marshes in east, center, and south
Arable land	13.15 percent
Natural hazards	violent dust storms, sandstorms, floods during winter rains and early spring
Major ports	Basra and Umm Qasr
Major airports	Baghdad International Airport Basra International Airport

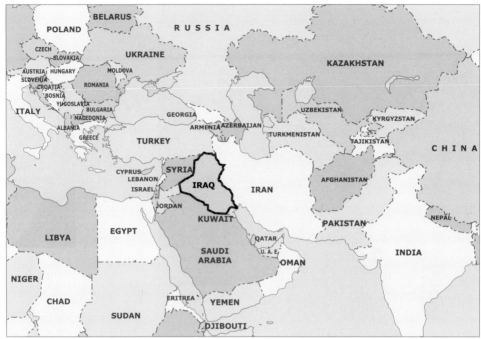

Figure 1.2 Map of area surrounding Iraq.

Currency	Dinar; exchange rate was 2,000 Iraqi Dinar to one U.S. dollar in August 2002
Purchasing power parity	U.S. $57 billion
Real growth rate	15 percent
Per capita:	U.S. $2,500
Industries	petroleum, chemicals, textiles, construction materials, and food processing
Exports	U.S. $21,800,000,000
Commodities	crude and refined oil products (estimated 20 percent of world's known reserves), fertilizer, and sulfur
Exports to	Russia, France, Switzerland, and China
Imports	U.S. $13,800,000,000
Commodities	Manufactured goods, food, and medicine
Imports from	Egypt, Russia, France, and Vietnam
Communications	Radio is the most effective means of mass communication. Two Baghdad radio stations are capable of broadcasting nation-wide. Two television networks broadcast from the major cities. All of the major newspaper presses are located in Baghdad.

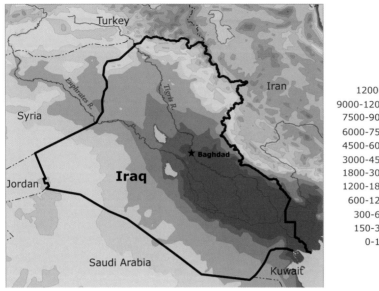
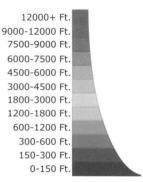

	12000+ Ft.
	9000-12000 Ft.
	7500-9000 Ft.
	6000-7500 Ft.
	4500-6000 Ft.
	3000-4500 Ft.
	1800-3000 Ft.
	1200-1800 Ft.
	600-1200 Ft.
	300-600 Ft.
	150-300 Ft.
	0-150 Ft.

Figure 1.3 Relief map of Iraq.

THE THREAT

At the beginning of 2003, Saddam Hussein was not a toothless lion. Although the 1990–1991 Gulf War had reduced the Iraqi Army and Air Force to 60 percent strength and had left all but nine ships of the Iraqi Navy on the bottom of the sea, the Iraqi military was still the dominant force in the Persian Gulf. Iraqi regular armed forces numbered around 400,000 (U.S. armed forces = 1.4 million) and could swell to double that number with reserves. Coalition Forces Special Operations Component Command estimated the Iraqi order of battle to be seventeen Regular Army divisions and six Republican Guard divisions, with 5,800 armored vehicles and 200 aircraft. There were wild cards on the battlefield as well.[1]

Pro-Saddam irregular forces included the Mujahedin-e Khalq, a well-trained and equipped mechanized brigade of more than 5,000 Iranian dissidents operating in eastern Iraq. Ansar al-Islam, a Sunni Kurd terrorist group funded by al-Qaeda, was based on the northeastern Iraq-Iran border where they confronted the Kurds. The Saddam Fedayeen, almost 40,000 loyalist fanatics controlled by Saddam's eldest son Uday, were the force by which Saddam controlled the Iraqi military. They posed considerable problems for the Coalition forces because they could blend in with the civilian population. Opposing Saddam, but still a threat to Coalition forces was the Badr Corps,

Fedayee
(plural fedayeen)
"One who sacrifices himself." Term came into use in 1955 to describe Arab commandos conducting cross-border raids against the fledgling state of Israel.

composed of several thousand Shia defectors from the Iraqi army in southern and western Iraq.

Iraq's capability to conduct offensive operations against the U.S. forces was severely constrained by Coalition airpower. But if invaded, its air defense network and weapons of mass destruction could cause significant damage to attacking forces. The Iraqi air defense forces—armed with Russian, French, and Italian-made surface-to-air missiles, anti-aircraft guns, and electronic jamming systems—were organized into a densely interlocking network around the cities of Baghdad, Basra, Mosul, and Kirkuk. United Nations inspection teams had found and destroyed some of Saddam's weapons of mass destruction capabilities after the Gulf War. Israeli intelligence estimated that Iraq still had hidden five to ten surface-to-surface tactical ballistic missile launchers and thirty medium-range missiles, capable of carrying chemical or biological warheads. British intelligence reports stated that Iraqi scientists were working to extend the ranges of liquid and solid propellant short-range ballistic missiles beyond the restrictions imposed by the United Nations. Strategic assessments by American and British intelligence agencies concluded that Saddam had been working to improve and increase his weapons of mass destruction capabilities during the four years that he had banned UN security inspectors. Saddam had shown no reluctance to use chemical agents against his people—as witnessed in the 1988 attacks on the Kurds. It was logical to conclude that, given the opportunity, he would use chemical and/or biological agents against invading forces.[2]

Iraqi Armed Forces (2002 estimates)

Armor	1400 newer model tanks (about half T-72, with the rest a mix purchased from various countries or captured during the war with Iran)
	1200 older model Soviet-bloc tanks
	400 older model French and Soviet-bloc Armored Reconnaissance Vehicles
	900 various-model BMP (Soviet-bloc armored infantry fighting vehicles)
Army Aircraft	100 attack helicopters
	275 transport helicopters
Air Force Aircraft	325 Soviet-bloc, French, and Chinese combat aircraft
	2 tankers
	unknown number of transport aircraft (jet and propeller)

Air strength estimates varied greatly between intelligence-gathering sources. Most sources agreed that no more than 60 percent of the available aircraft were combat-capable.

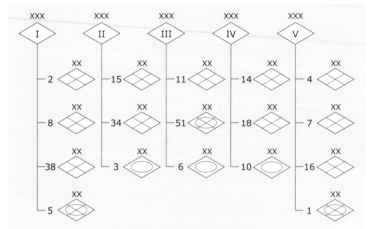

Regular Army Brigades

2nd Infantry Div	2nd, 4th, and 36th Infantry Bdes
8th Infantry Div	22nd, 44th, and 48th Bdes
38th Infantry Div	130th, 847th, and 848th Infantry Bdes
5th Mechanized Div Bde	15th and 20th Mechanized Bdes and 26th Armored
15 Infantry Div	76th, 104th, and 436th Infantry Bdes
34th Infantry Div	90th, 502nd, and 504th Infantry Bdes
3rd Armored Div	6th and 12th Armored Bdes and 8th Mechanized Bde
11th Infantry Div	23rd, 45th, and 47th Infantry Bdes
51st Mechanized Div	31st and 32nd Mechanized Bdes, 41st Armored Bde
6th Armored Div	30th and 70th Armored Bdes and 25th Mechanized Bde
14th Infantry Div	14th, 18th, and 426th Infantry Bdes
18th Infantry Div	95th, 422nd, and 704th Infantry Bdes
10th Armored Div	17th and 42nd Armored Bdes, 25th Mechanized Bde
4th Infantry Div	5th, 29th, and 96th Infantry Bdes
7th Infantry Div	38th, 39th, and 116th Infantry Bdes
16th Infantry Div	108th, 505th, and 606th Infantry Bdes
1st Mechanized Div	1st and 27th Mechanized Bdes and 34th Armored Bde

Figure 1.4 Iraqi Order of Battle

THUMBNAIL HISTORY OF IRAQ

During the post-World War I dismemberment of the Ottoman Empire, an almost landlocked country a little larger than California was carved out of the former provinces of Baghdad, Basra, and Mosul to form Iraq. For six centuries, the country's importance was its geographical location as the center of the trade and communications routes between west and east. The discovery of oil in Baku, Azerbaijan, in 1870, and a like discovery in Masjid-i-Sulaiman, Persia (Iran), in 1908, raised international interest in the Middle East. Twenty years after major oil deposits were discovered near Kirkuk in 1927, the field had produced over 100 million tons (roughly 733 million barrels) of oil. By then oil had become a vital international commodity, but before proceeding further the ancient roots of Iraq should be addressed.[3]

ANCIENT IRAQI HISTORY—FADED GLORY

Biblical tradition designated this area between the Tigris and Euphrates rivers as Mesopotamia, the location of the Garden of Eden. As early as the eighth century, Persian and Arab maps labeled it al-'Iraq (the riverbanks). To understand the Iraqi mind, one must accept that what is seen now is not all there is. In many respects, Iraq today is a result of the Mongol invasion in the thirteenth century. Saddam Hussein al-Tikriti was convinced that the blood of King Nebuchadnezzar, the scourge of the Assyrians, flowed in his veins.[4]

Figure 1.5 Lion statue. *Ancient Babylonian lion statue from the time of Nebuchadnezzar. The lion is standing over a freshly-killed man.*

The inhabitants of Iraq are descendants of conquerors and kings. In the period 5,000 B.C. to 1258 A.D., numerous advances in culture, religion, engineering, literature, and agriculture came from the Fertile Crescent. As the cradle of civilization, this region was the birthplace of the patriarch Abraham and the home and kingdom of the powerful ancient Sumerians, who developed the earliest known forms of writing and astronomy and irrigated their crops. A few centuries later, Babylonian King Hammurabi developed one of the earliest legal codes. King Nebuchadnezzar, the last and the greatest native Mesopotamian monarch was a successful warrior and prolific architect. He rebuilt Babylon and designed its Hanging Gardens. Nebuchadnezzar defeated the Assyrians and then destroyed Jerusalem and sacked the Temple of Solomon.[5]

Persians (from modern-day Iran), Greeks, and Parthians held parts of Iraq until Arab Muslim armies conquered the region in 650 A.D., eighteen years after the death of the prophet Mohammed. Under Islamic rule, Baghdad became the capital of the Abbisid Caliphate, whose dominion stretched from Spain and Morocco in the west, included Tunisia, Egypt, Arabia, Mesopotamia, and Persia, to as far east as Afghanistan and as far north as Kyrgyzstan. Arabic culture, philosophy, literature, and science flourished. Baghdad, as the economic connectivity between Asia and the Mediterranean, was at the center. However, in 1258, the Abbisid Caliphate and the Mesopotamian civilization was brought to its knees by the Mongols, who ruthlessly killed large segments of the population, destroyed its cities, and smashed the irrigation systems for farming—elements of life that directly contradicted their nomadic view of life. The social, political, and economic fabric of Iraq disintegrated. This wholesale disruption of life led to one of the prevailing schisms in Iraqi society.[6]

THE SUNNI-SHIA SPLIT AND OTTOMAN RULE

Shiism as practiced by Iraqis is a relatively new development, and has been heavily influenced by Arab tribal values of manhood, courage, and honor. This differentiates the Iraqi form of the sect from Iranian Shiism, which developed over centuries without persecution, and emphasized mystical and otherworldly values such as the reward martyrs would reap in Paradise. The twin themes common to both Iraqi and Iranian Shia are martyrdom and unjust treatment at the hands of Sunnis.[9]

Less than a generation after Mohammed's death, Muslims split into two groups over who the rightful heir to the caliphate was. The Shia party, based in Iraq, lost its bid when its leaders Ali and Husain were slain. The Sunni party, centered in Damascus, Syria, became the dominant sect of Islam. In 1514, the Ottoman Turks conquered Iraq to secure a buffer zone against Iran. The Turks divided Iraq into three provinces: Mosul, Baghdad, and Basra. During the four hundred years of Ottoman rule, Persian Shia and Turkish Sunni battled for dominance.[7]

Tribal Iraqis began to shed their Sunni beliefs en masse about 1831, and converted to Shia Islam mainly in response to the Sunni-dominated government and the tax system. The Shia felt that by rejecting the state-controlled religion as illegitimate, taxes, and conscription could be ignored. The minority Sunnis remained the ruling elite, while the lower class majority became solidly and stubbornly Shia.[8]

KURDISTAN—A LAND THAT ISN'T

Kurdistan refers to the Kurdish tribal homelands in the mountains of northern Iraq bordering northwestern Iran, southeastern Turkey, and the northeastern tip of Syria. The Kurds are mountain-dwelling nomads. The majority of them are Sunni Muslims, but there are significant populations of Shia Muslims, Christians, and Yazidis—a mix of paganism, mystic Zoroastrianism, and ancient Christianity. The essence of the Kurdish story is a deep desire for autonomy hindered by the absence of unifying leaders to make autonomy possible. One of the major objections neighboring countries have to a sovereign Kurdistan is the fear that its existence would encourage Kurdish revolts within their states. Iraq has always been unwilling to cede the oil-rich region surrounding Kirkuk to an independent Kurdish nation.

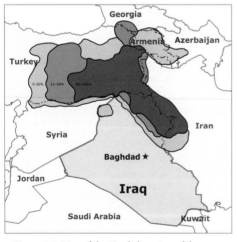

Figure 1.6 Map of the Kurdish region of the Middle East.

Iran supported the Kurdish rebellion against the Baathist regime in 1974. But when Saddam Hussein promised the Shah of Iran that he would not permit Kurdish autonomy in 1975, the support vanished. This accord led to Saddam's slaughter of the Kurds. During the Iraq-Iran war, the Kurds with Iranian assistance revolted again. Towards the end of the war when Iraq was losing badly, Saddam sent a relative, Hassan al-Majid ("Chemical Ali"), to terrorize the Kurds by gassing large numbers of men, women, and children in their remote villages. The Anfal campaign was like Adolf Hitler's final solution: an attempt to eliminate the Kurds in Iraq.

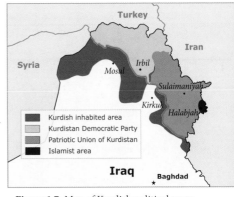

Figure 1.7 Map of Kurdish political areas.

In 1991, after the Gulf War, the Kurds again rebelled unsuccessfully. This time the United States intervened with Operation PROVIDE COMFORT to establish safe havens for Kurdish refugees and enforced a no-fly zone over their territory in Iraq. The Kurds essentially control their own lands. However, peacetime unity still eludes them. The two major competing Kurdish political parties are the Kurdistan Democratic Party and the Patriotic Union of Kurdistan. In Operation IRAQI FREEDOM, Kurdish freedom fighters (peshmerga) agreed to join Coalition forces to defeat Saddam.

IT COMES DOWN TO OIL

At the turn of the 19th century, the powers of Europe developed commercial interests in Iraq, the vital link in east–west trade and communications routes. Great Britain sought a connection to its eastern empire in India. Germany won the railroad concession from the Ottoman Turks in 1899 and began steamship service to the Persian Gulf in 1906. With the Suez Canal open, Kaiser Wilhelm had rapid access to the east via the Mediterranean Sea.[10]

The 1908 discovery of oil in southwestern Iran made Iraq a lucrative target for exploration. Several nations began negotiating with the Ottoman Empire for access rights. Though no discovery of consequence occurred in Iraq until 1927, the British Navy's conversion from coal to oil made British dominance of the Middle East oil fields a strategic necessity. Thus, when the Turks entered World War I on the side of the Germans in 1914, the British seized the province of Basra, to secure their access to the Persian Gulf. During World War I, Great Britain expanded its control of Iraq to include all three Ottoman provinces—Basra, Baghdad, and Mosul. In April 1920, it was logical for the

Peshmerga *"Those who face death."* *The term used by the Kurds to refer to freedom fighters. These trained armed retainers are generally affiliated with the political parties or prominent personalities in the Kurdish independence movement. They often wear traditional Kurdish garb, the baggy shar-wall trousers, plain jacket and a colorful sash.*

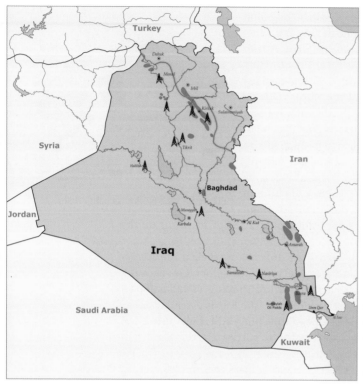

Figure 1.8 Map of major Iraqi oil fields and refineries.

League of Nations to place Iraq under British mandate.[11]

Iraqis did not take well to the mandate. Within two months, armed rebellion broke out in Baghdad and spread throughout the mid-Euphrates region west to Najaf and Karbala. Although suppressed within a few months, the revolt was immortalized in the mythology of the Iraqi nationalism. Anyone who claimed a part in the revolt could use that for political gain. Having learned that direct rule was not acceptable, the British created a new Iraqi government and organized a native army led by minority Sunni and Kurds. The enlisted soldiers were mostly Shia tribesmen. This practice continued the Ottoman tradition of a minority Sunni leadership over the majority Shia.[12]

In March 1921, Winston Churchill brought the new Iraqi leaders to the Cairo Conference during which the Western Powers decided to establish a monarchy in Iraq. The throne was offered to Amir Faisal, a well-educated Syrian Arab who claimed descent from the prophet Mohammed. According to British standards that included compliancy, Faisal had impeccable credentials. The Iraqi people, however, were nonplussed; the Kurds disliked his Arab background; the majority Shia population resented that he was Sunni; and the minority Iraqi Sunni regarded him as an outsider. The twelve-year reign of Amir Faisal was marked by constant uncertainty and infighting.[13]

Oil had a role in the boundaries of Iraq. Mosul Province in the north was a Kurdish stronghold. The original British intent was to permit an autonomous state, but they could find no Kurdish leader strong enough to control the diverse population. International squabbling allowed Ataturk to take over Kurdish territories in eastern Turkey. This prompted the British to keep Mosul Province in Iraq, to serve as a northern buffer against the Turks and the Bolsheviks in the northwest. The openly stated goal was to eventually unify the northern (now Turkish) and southern (Iraqi) Kurdish territories into an autonomous Kurdistan. But, the discovery of oil in Kirkuk in 1923, cemented the Iraqi border. British interest in Kurdish autonomy dwindled.[14]

For the next nine years, 1923–1932, the Iraqis, Kurds, British, and Turks wrestled over oil revenues from Mosul Province and Kurdish autonomy. On 13 October 1932, when Iraq was granted sovereignty and admitted to the League of Nations, the nation was a political mess. The nouveau-riche city-dwellers, sheiks, tribesmen, the Sunni Iraqi officers corps, and the large Kurdish and Assyrian minority groups all wanted a voice in the new government and access to oil profits. The weak monarchy inherited from the British could not hold up to the demands of a new Iraq. The next twenty-eight years saw ethnic revolts, tribal rebellions, two military coups-d'état, another British invasion, a second attempt at a monarchy, and the imposition of martial law. Finally, on 14 July 1958, a military coup eliminated the monarchy. The young king and his regent were killed. The coup leaders severed all ties to Great Britain. This set the stage for Saddam Hussein to rise to power in Iraq.[15]

THE RISE AND FALL OF SADDAM HUSSEIN

Saddam Hussein was born on 28 April 1937, near the city of Tikrit, about 200 kilometers north of Baghdad on the Tigris River. At age 20, he applied for but failed to gain entry into the prestigious Baghdad Military Academy, most likely because he only had an elementary school education. The Baath Party in Baghdad had no education requirements for membership. In 1959, Saddam was a participant in the failed assassination attempt on Iraqi leader General Abdul Karim Qasim. While exiled to Egypt, Saddam finished high school. After a coup brought the Baath Party to power, Saddam returned in 1963 to join the party leadership. Six months later, the Arif regime deposed the Baath Party and Saddam was arrested in the round up of Baath Party members. While imprisoned for two years, he was elected dep-

Figure 1.9 Saddam the Hero. *Monument to Saddam Hussein outside one of the headquarters buildings at Tallil Air Base.*

uty secretary general of the Baath Party. When Saddam managed to escape from prison in 1967, he immediately began planning a second Baath coup. This 1968 coup was successful. Saddam's relative, General Ahmed Hassan al-Bakr, became president and chairman of the Revolutionary Command Council. Saddam was selected to be the internal security chief. In this position he removed non-Baathists from positions of power by forced retirement, exile, imprisonment, and execution. That same year Saddam graduated from law school.

Figure 1.10 Family portrait in marble. *Brigadier General James Parker stands in front of a marble portrait of Saddam's family in Qusay's palace. Notably missing are Saddam's other two daughters and their now-late husbands, Hussein Kamel Hasan al-Majid and his brother Saddam Kamel, who defected in 1995. All were later murdered at Saddam's behest. Qusay was Saddam Hussein's youngest son. (In a different palace, another marble family portrait originally had the entire family. After 1995, the offending members were sandblasted off the wall.)*

A year later, he became the deputy chairman and vice president of the Revolutionary Command Council. He remained in charge of internal security and intelligence and built his power base through intrigue and murder. Three years later, in 1972, Saddam went public by leading the move to nationalize the Iraqi oil fields. This bold maneuver increased Iraqi oil revenues eight-fold in three years and established Saddam as the leader of the Baath Party in 1975.[16]

When the Kurds revolted in 1974, Saddam reacted ruthlessly, launching a genocidal war against them. To end Iranian support to the Kurds, Saddam pre-empted President Bakr and signed the Algiers Accord. This transferred the disputed Kurdish territory to Iran. After dealing with the Kurds, Saddam ordered purges and mass deportations of Shia from Iraq. To crown this effort, he deported the Shia Ayatollah Khomeini in 1978. That done, Saddam began purging Iraqi Communists and closing all party offices. These moves were designed to put him in a position of absolute power.

In July 1979, Saddam forced General Bakr out of office and placed him under house arrest. When Saddam was sworn in, it was as president of the Republic of Iraq, chairman of the Revolutionary Command Council, secretary-general of the Baath Party Regional Command, prime minister, and commander-in-chief of the armed forces. After purging the Baath Party and army of all but those loyal only to him, he began installing his relatives in key positions. On 17 September 1980, Saddam terminated the Algiers Accord with Iran, provoking an eight-year war. Late in the Iran war, Saddam initiated the Anfal extermination campaign by gassing Kurdish villagers along the Turkish border with chemicals.

By 1990, the combination of the Iran-Iraq war and nepotistic economic practices had nearly bankrupted Iraq. With the war with Iran at an end, Saddam looked south for money. He invaded and occupied Kuwait on the premise that the Gulf country was the nineteenth province of Iraq. Following UN sanctions, the U.S.-led Coalition of more than thirty-four countries began aerial bombardment in January 1991, the start of Operation DESERT STORM.[17]

On 24 February 1991, the U.S.-led Coalition ground offensive drove the Iraqis from Kuwait in less than one hundred hours. President George Bush chose to allow Saddam to remain in office to preclude more upheaval in the Middle East. The UN-imposed sanctions required a drawdown of Iraqi military defense, including weapons of mass destruction. Throughout the sanction period, Saddam continued to build palaces while the Iraqi economy declined. Operation PROVIDE COMFORT established safe havens for the Kurds after another failed revolt.

In 1996, the United Nations renewed its Oil-for-Food program offer to Iraq. This time Saddam agreed to it hoping that the sanctions would be lifted. The only Iraqis to receive humanitarian aid were those that had ingratiated themselves to Saddam. In the midst of the Oil-for-Food program, Saddam began to offer Russia and France oil development deals. Continuing to defy the UN sanctions, Saddam ejected the UN Security Council arms inspectors in 1998. The United States and Great Britain responded with air strikes (Operation DESERT FOX). In 2001, Saddam refused to re-admit UN weapons inspectors. After repeated attempts by the United Nations to break the deadlock on 17 March 2003, President George W. Bush gave Saddam and his sons an ultimatum: leave Iraq within forty-eight hours or Coalition forces would attack. Saddam refused and Operation IRAQI FREEDOM began on 19 March. His reign of terror ended with the fall of Baghdad in April 2003. Saddam was ultimately captured by U.S. forces on 13 December 2004 and imprisoned. How Saddam Hussein came to power and managed to control the Iraqi populace for twenty years cannot be fully appreciated without a psychological profile of his personality.[18]

THE MAN WHO WOULD BE KING

Iraqis, since the time of the Sumerians, have venerated the cult of the "great man." Over the centuries, Mesopotamian kings and conquerors proclaimed themselves "Kings of the World." Saddam Hussein followed suit, styling himself Iraq's "Hero President," demanding absolute obedience and delivering swift and brutal punishment to those who opposed him. "Myself and my brother against the world" is an old tribal proverb that underlies the Iraqi mindset. Traditionally, power and wealth are kept within the extended family. Patron-client relationships and obligations include exacting vengeance on anyone who offends clan honor. The practice of power retention by murder prevented national unity among the ethnic and religious groups of Iraq, but served Saddam well.[19]

Lieutenant Colonel John Chin, the staff psychologist for Combined Joint Special Operations Task Force–West, developed a psychological profile of Saddam Hussein based on culture that succinctly described the man:

> *Born into poverty, Saddam was raised in a dysfunctional, abusive family with no father and a suicidal mother who had tried to abort him. After meeting a cousin his age that could read, Saddam decided he deserved an education. He ran away from home at age ten and lived with his uncle Kairallah, a radical Baathist who had spent five years in prison for agitating against the monarchy. Kairallah sent him to primary school and taught Saddam Baath ideology and tales of Mesopotamian greatness.*
>
> *Some of the dominant personality traits resulting from his youth are mistrust and rage toward anyone he perceives more powerful than he. He sees himself as a hero with a vision, assuming that everyone else adores him and shares his dream—but he does not trust anyone other than his closest family members—and even they have to undergo loyalty tests. He despises the fact that he suffered as a child. As a result, he is aggressively ruthless and sadistic, enjoying the power to make others suffer. However, he is not a madman—he is paranoid, manipulative, narcissistic, and utterly devoid of conscience—U.S. psychologists who have studied him believe Saddam Hussein is in touch with reality.*[20]

Saddam considers himself to be Nebuchadnezzar's successor—a historical association that bonds the hearts of Arabs, because that emperor conquered Jerusalem in 586 B.C. In a desperate attempt to shatter the multinational Coalition in the Gulf War, Saddam ordered SCUD missiles fired on Israel. With U.S. Patriot counter-missile batteries protecting Tel Aviv and Jerusalem, Israel did not respond militarily. When Ariel Sharon was elected Prime Minister of Israel in 2001, Saddam announced that seven million Iraqis had formed a "Jerusalem Army" to follow him in a march on Israel to liberate their Palestinian brothers.[21]

Figure 1.11 Interior palace view. *Ornate interior of one of Saddam's palaces. The frieze in the background shows Nebuchadnezzar (seated).*

Saddam Hussein had intentionally modeled himself after the Mesopotamian king, even to the point of building palaces countrywide that rivaled those of Nebuchadnezzar. Atop ancient bricks inscribed with Nebuchadnezzar's name and his exploits, Iraqi workmen laid new bricks exalting Saddam Hussein as the "protector of Iraq, who rebuilt civilization and rebuilt Babylon." Saddam built about seventy palaces—all incredibly ostentatious and self-aggrandizing—while Iraqi infrastructure was imploding, the economy was collapsing, and Iraqi people were starving.[22]

In his eyes, and in the eyes of many Arabs, Saddam remained, bloodied but still standing, victorious after the "Mother of all Battles"—Operation DESERT STORM. President George H. W. Bush, the leader of the most powerful nation in the world, might have defeated the Iraqi military, but he did not remove Saddam Hussein from power. Ergo, Saddam had ultimately won the war.

It was completely logical then, when Saddam refused to respond to President George W. Bush's ultimatum in March 2003. In the Arab mind, the father and the son are the same. Therefore, Saddam fully expected to outlast the American military. He was convinced that the U.S. and Coalition forces would quit and he would re-emerge again, as Iraq's Hero-President. As history showed, Saddam was wrong.

The answers to "What is there about this Iraq?" and "Why Iraq?" provide context and background to explain why Iraq posed a significant threat to the United States. While the United Nations sought to gain access to Iraq to determine whether the regime of Saddam Hussein possessed weapons of mass destruction, the U.S. regional military combatant command, U.S. Central Command, began reviewing its contingency plans. The following chapter explains

POLITICAL PARTIES IN IRAQ

Kurdistan Democratic Party

KDP. Kurdish secessionist party led by Massoud Barzani. Tribal-based, with a large militia (peshmerga).

Patriotic Union of Kurdistan

PUK. Leftist splinter party of KDP led by Jalal Talabani and urban intelligentsia.

Iraqi National Congress

INC. Opposition group based in Kurdistan and London, sponsored by the United States and United Kingdom. Chaired by Ahmed Chalabi.

Supreme Council for the Islamic Revolution in Iraq

SCIRI. Iranian-backed organization of anti-Saddam Shias. Its military arm is the Badr Corps.

Baath Party

Arab Socialist Renaissance Party. Originally a pan-Arab nationalist movement, the party came briefly to power in Iraq in 1963, but was overthrown within six months. Re-organized and dominated by Tikritis, with Saddam Hussein as a primary figure, the Baath Party seized power again in 1968, and remained Saddam's party of power until his capture in 2004. The party was disbanded when the United States removed Saddam from power in 2003.

the planning efforts of those commands that affected Army special operations forces—from Special Operations Command Central and Special Operations Command Europe to the Special Forces groups involved—in the war against Iraq.

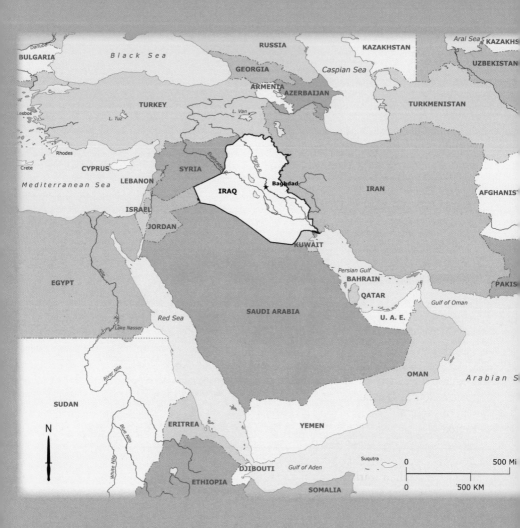

Chapter Two

Planning for War

*I*N RESPONSE TO THE terrorist attacks of 11 September 2001, President George W. Bush declared a Global War on Terrorism. Intelligence sources revealed that the 11 September terrorist attacks on America had been organized, funded, and directed by Osama bin Laden, leader of the international terrorist organization al-Qaeda. When the radical Muslim Taliban government of Afghanistan refused to surrender bin Laden, to whom it had granted asylum, a U.S.-led Coalition vowed to dismantle the Taliban regime and destroy al-Qaeda forces throughout the world. Advised and assisted by U.S. Army special operations forces, the Northern Alliance of Afghan warlords began offensive operations in Afghanistan in November 2001, launching America's first campaign against worldwide terrorism: Operation ENDURING FREEDOM.[1]

CONVENTIONAL PLANNING

U.S. Central Command planners began seriously developing military options for Iraq three short months after Operation ENDURING FREEDOM began. President Bush and Secretary of Defense Donald Rumsfeld realized that the Global War on Terrorism could not be waged in Afghanistan alone; terrorists would not restrict themselves to a single battlefield, so neither could the United States and its allies. One of their deepest fears was that terrorists harbored by Saddam Hussein would obtain weapons of mass destruction that Iraq still possessed after years of United Nation sanctions and arms inspections. Intelligence sources verified Saddam's contact with terrorist elements. The dictator's use of weapons of mass destruction against the Iranians and Kurds indicated that he would not be reluctant to employ them against the West.

PLAN 1003

Figure 2.1 CENT-COM logo.

At Rumsfeld's behest, U.S. Central Command commander General Tommy Franks began to review the assumptions of Contingency Plan 1003, the U.S. military's regional war plan for the Middle East. In a series of meetings held between Franks and Rumsfeld in December 2001, Plan 1003 was reconceptualized and revised to capitalize on the strengths of the modern U.S. military. The key to Franks' approach was joint operations—full integration of the Army, Navy, Air Force, and Marines. While the military had been moving in that direction for years, and had recently proven the advantages of such an approach in Afghanistan, the United States had never conducted joint operations on the level Franks envisioned.[2]

While the State Department pursued diplomatic options to neutralize or contain Saddam, Franks and his staff formulated the operational concept for CENTCOM's strategy against Iraq and Saddam Hussein. Franks created a matrix showing how military capabilities—"lines of operation"—intersected with Saddam's bases of power—"slices." While the matrix would change as the plan devel-

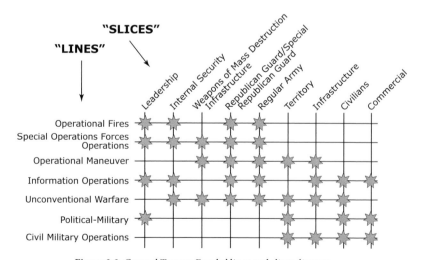

Figure 2.2 General Tommy Franks' lines and slices diagram.

oped, his 8 December 2001 sketch contained the primary goals of the campaign and the military tools to be used.[3]

PHASES

By the end of December 2001, CENTCOM planners had identified four phases to support the operational concept, although the timelines for each phase remained elastic. The original phases indicated that by the end of *Phase I–Preparation*, a Coalition of international support would be formed and troops would be flowing into staging bases in the region. *Phase II–Shape the Battlespace* projected that an air campaign would precede ground operations, much like in the Gulf War. Plans and timelines for this phase drastically changed over the fifteen months between Franks' initial briefing to President Bush and D-DAY. *Phase III–Decisive Operations* would be concluded once

> **OPLAN 1003V PHASES**
>
> Phase I — Preparation
> Phase II — Shape the Battlespace
> Phase III — Decisive Operations
> Phase IV — Stability Operations

the campaign's two primary goals had been accomplished: regime forces had been defeated or surrendered, and the leadership was neutralized—dead, captured, or marginalized. The timeline for *Phase IV– Post-Hostility or Stability Operations* was the most nebulous, although everybody involved realized that rebuilding the country would take longer than dismantling the regime.[4]

PLAN 1003V

President Bush accepted Franks' Concept of Operations for war against Iraq and Rumsfeld confirmed his tenure at CENTCOM for another year. With the approval of the service chiefs, CENTCOM planners began developing Operation Plan 1003v—the revised plan for war with Iraq—in January 2002. The first task was to figure out how and when to build sufficient forces in the region to actually carry out operations against Saddam's regime. The old Plan 1003 called for a huge buildup of troops and equipment before operations began. While this "Generated Start" option was viable, planners also developed an alternative, which they dubbed "Running Start."[5]

GENERATED START

Preparations for Generated Start were already underway and the entire timeline for the Iraq campaign was beginning to compress by the time Franks briefed Rumsfeld on the force buildup options on 1 February 2003. Franks already had his commanders improving their bases in the region as well as pre-positioning equipment in theater. Under Generated Start, ground forces would continue to flow into position while Phase II air operations were conducted. The timeline projected that G-DAY—the day ground forces attacked—would be forty-five days after A-DAY—the day air strikes began. More ground forces would continue to flow in after G-DAY as well, and the buildup would continue into Phase IV.[6]

Running Start

After Franks briefed the Generated Start concept to Rumsfeld, he presented his preferred option: Running Start. Under this plan, the air and ground campaigns would begin simultaneously—a decidedly unconventional approach for U.S. military planners. A key component of the Running Start concept was that instead of a large buildup of forces in anticipation of attack, follow-on forces would continue deploying even as the campaign began. Further expanding the plan beyond the conventional realm, Running Start depended extensively on special operations forces for its success. The SOF teams would need to locate and disable missile launchers in the western desert to prevent Iraq from attacking Israel, which would undoubtedly trigger a religious war of disastrous proportion. SOF would also need to prevent the destruction of the oil fields and dams to preclude environmental and economic disaster.[7]

Buildup

Key to both operational start concepts was the buildup of a critical mass of forces within the region without Saddam realizing that the United States was posturing for war. Such a discovery might prematurely trigger conflict, since diplomatic efforts to prevent war were ongoing. By the time Franks briefed the National Security Council a second time on Plan 1003 in August 2002, the buildup had already begun. Capitalizing on Saddam's weak international intelligence system, the military started flowing forces and equipment into the region under the guise of training rotations and international exercises. Kuwait, Qatar, and Oman were willing hosts to U.S. forces; Jordan and Saudi Arabia permitted previously scheduled exercises and promised not to expel forces already inside their countries; and State Department and military officials were negotiating with Turkey to allow the U.S. forces to stage from that country.[8]

The successful pre-positioning of forces and equipment caused CENTCOM planners to compress the campaign timeline even more. The first forty-five days would consist of air and SOF operations while conventional forces continued to deploy into theater. Initial combat operations would take another ninety days, and Phase III–Decisive Operations were predicted to last no longer than ninety days. Phase

IV was still an unknown quantity, though it was projected to be long. The variant option had been approved, but Franks was moving closer toward launching the air and ground war simultaneously.[9]

FIVE FRONTS

In September, Franks presented Rumsfeld and Secretary of State Colin Powell with the planning team's ideas for the actual attack on Iraq. The planners wanted to completely isolate the regime and confront it from as many directions as possible. The five-front concept was a far cry from the plan Powell helped execute in the Gulf War, but Franks believed it capitalized on the strengths of the modern military and its ability to conduct joint operations. The concept, which soon became the actual plan for Operation IRAQI FREEDOM, placed SOF in key roles. Special Forces would work with Kurdish forces in northern Iraq and also keep Iraqi units along the Green Line occupied. SOF teams would also infiltrate the western desert and secure what Franks referred to as the "SCUD baskets." Information Operations, which also relied heavily on SOF, would confront the regime and Iraqi citizens from above by distributing leaflets and interjecting broadcasts on Iraqi networks. Only two of the five fronts relied primarily on conventional forces—the air campaign against Baghdad and the ground attack from Kuwait north toward Baghdad—but SOF were integrated into both.[10]

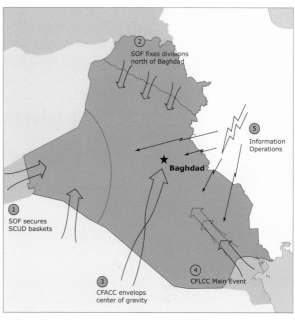

Figure 2.3 Map of General Tommy Franks' five fronts.

RESOLVE

On 12 September 2002, President Bush addressed the United Nations and outlined the history of Saddam Hussein's belligerence and potential threat to the United States and the world. The UN Security Council adopted Resolution 1441 on 8 November 2002, censuring Iraq for failing to comply with past resolutions, impeding arms inspections, and proliferating weapons of mass destruction and long-range missiles. "Serious consequences" were threatened if Iraq did not reform its ways. Unwilling to wait for international consensus, the U.S. Congress issued a joint resolution on 2 October 2002 authorizing the President to use force against Iraq if Saddam did not comply. By then, the U.S. military was well on its way to applying that force decisively and effectively.[11]

PLANNING

When Army Special Operations Forces began planning for Operation IRAQI FREEDOM, it was already heavily engaged in other operations throughout the world in support of the Global War on Terrorism. These existing obligations determined how the ARSOF community was able to organize and prepare for a second war. From personnel to ammunition, military assets were tight, but time was even tighter.

REGIONAL COMMANDS

While CENTCOM prosecuted the war in Afghanistan, Secretary of Defense Rumsfeld asked other combatant commands to develop regional campaign plans in support of the Global War on Terrorism. The U.S. European Command shifted the emphasis of its peacekeeping mission in the Balkans to the fight against terrorism. EUCOM also intensified its focus on Muslim countries in the Horn of Africa region. For its part, the U.S. Southern Command was already decisively engaged in countering drug-related terrorism in Colombia and the Andean region.

The U.S. Pacific Command focused on the criminal/terrorist Abu Sayaf Group, which was responsible for kidnapping U.S. citizens in the Philippines. Abu Sayaf Group terrorist activities were linked to Mu'ammar Qaddafi in Libya as well as to Jemaah Islamiyah in Indonesia, the latter led by a brother-in-law of Osama bin Laden. In response to the Abu Sayaf Group terrorist threat, Pacific Command significantly expanded the scope of the newly revived combined U.S.-Philippines Exercise Balikatan. Joint Task Force 510 was deployed to

Figure 2.4 1st SFG beret flash.

Mindanao, Philippines, with the 1st SFG command group serving as the Army special operations task force. Two Special Forces battalions were assigned major training and advisory roles with the Philippine Army and Marine forces combating the Abu Sayaf Group on Basilan Island. The well-publicized rescue of Martin and Gracia Burnham was an ancillary mission to the major training effort.[12]

AFGHANISTAN

By the time Balikatan 02 was in full swing in the Philippines, Combined Joint Special Operations Task Force–North in Uzbekistan had used the 5th Special Forces Group teams to direct air strikes against Taliban and al-Qaeda forces, enabling Northern Alliance warlords to affect the collapse of the Taliban regime. Civil Affairs and Psychological Operations teams worked to build confidence in U.S.-led Coalition forces, and the State Department focused its efforts on establishing an interim Afghanistan authority to maintain order and to govern the country. Conventional U.S. ground forces were brought into Afghanistan to stabilize conditions countrywide, while Special Forces worked to organize and train a national Afghan military. ARSOF obligations in Afghanistan were ongoing and continued to take their toll.

Figure 2.5 Task Force Dagger Afghanistan logo.

RESOURCING

MATERIEL

March 2002's Operation ANACONDA (one of the larger operations in Operation ENDURING FREEDOM) was successful, although at a heavy materiel price for ARSOF. The primary helicopter workhorses used in the high mountainous terrain of northern Afghanistan—the air-refuelable MH-47E Chinooks of the 160th Special Operations Aviation Regiment—proved to be vulnerable after all: two aircraft were shot down in the mountains, and another was severely battle-damaged. Just days before ANACONDA, another MH-47E helicopter crashed into the sea off the Philippines. While the rest of the Army possessed Chinooks, those of the 160th SOAR were specially outfitted for special operations missions and could not easily be replaced. As ARSOF participated in continued fighting in Afghanistan, the U.S. Army Special Operations Command began to manage this critical aviation resource intensely.

Emergency appropriations had not solved all the equipment, munitions, and personnel problems associated with Operation ENDURING FREEDOM, let alone supported preparations for another war. The American industrial base to support its military forces had been severely reduced by congressionally mandated force reductions and base closures, especially after the Gulf War. Commercial ammunition manufacturing capabilities and military munitions storage areas had been constructed to support the monthly needs of a peacetime Army, not prolonged campaigns against hostile forces in which the United States was now involved. Industry could not quickly retool and realign to meet the military's increased requirements. As a result, the military had to wage war as if it were conducting peacetime training—with strict ammunition forecasting and accountability. International competition for high-tech individual combat equipment critical to special operations personnel (such as night vision goggles, secure radios, satellite communications, and lightweight body armor) also delayed replacement and fielding of equipment to units preparing for combat.

PERSONNEL

With significant ARSOF elements already committed to Afghanistan, the Philippines, the Balkans, and Colombia, every command that had ARSOF units—U.S. Special Operations Command, U.S. Army Special Operations Command, the U.S. Army Reserve, the National Guard Bureau, and several state adjutants general—faced major resourcing challenges. Although it was most definitely a war, the Global War on Terrorism was being fought under peacetime constraints. National Guard and Reserve units were only at 70–80 percent operational readiness due to the level of funding the Department of Defense had accorded them for years. These readiness levels could not be increased in a matter of mere months. Because all four branches of the American military are strictly volunteer organizations, efforts to suddenly increase recruiting and training not only had to overcome problems related to money, but also the population's willingness to serve in the military.

INTERNATIONAL GOODWILL

The international mood regarding the United States and its defense policies also affected ARSOF's preparation and planning for Operation IRAQI FREEDOM. Euphoria induced by the rapid victory in Afghanistan led many U.S. government officials and military leaders to overlook changing national attitudes toward supporting the American-led Global War on Terrorism. As Washington officials sought United Nations support to take action against Iraq for possessing weapons of mass destruction, most international supporters of the war in Afghanistan declined to support a second conflict. The only powerful countries willing to commit military forces to a U.S.-led Coalition effort were Great Britain and Australia. The reluctance of regional allies to become openly involved in or to further support military operations against terrorism made forward basing of troops difficult. Basing rights, military overflight authorities, temporary access to airfields, and border crossings all became hot issues directly affecting ARSOF operations.

SOCCENT PLANNING

Special Operations Command Central was unable to begin planning for Operation IRAQI FREEDOM until March 2002. Lieutenant General James McNeill of XVIII Airborne Corps took charge of operations in Afghanistan in March, relieving SOCCENT of tactical command of special operations forces in CENTCOM (elements of the 3rd and 20th Special Forces Groups). At that point, Rear Admiral Albert Calland and the SOCCENT staff joined the ongoing CENTCOM planning efforts for possible war with Iraq. Fortunately, the late start did not put SOCCENT planners behind, since ARSOF's role in the various versions of 1003 remained constant.

Figure 2.6 SOCCENT shoulder patch.

MISSIONS

SOCCENT had three major missions in the pending operation in Iraq. Its first mission was to support the Coalition Forces Air Component Command–orchestrated hunt for SCUDS in the western desert. The second was to support the Coalition Forces Land Component Command ground campaign directed at Baghdad by leveraging Kurdish combat power in northern Iraq to occupy the Iraqi forces there and prevent their reinforcement of the Iraqi Army around Baghdad. The third mission was to organize and employ Iraqi regime opposition groups in the south. Several tasks inherent in these missions included attacking and fixing Iraqi forces, seizing key infrastructure (bridges, passes, and oil fields), and preventing the destruction of critical nodes (dams above Baghdad and bridges spanning the Tigris and Euphrates Rivers) along lines of communication to be used by Coalition Forces Land Component Command forces to rapidly advance on the Iraqi capital.[13]

Figure 2.7 Brigadier General Gary Harrell.

PLANNING

When Army Brigadier General Gary Harrell took command of SOCCENT in June 2002, planning for IRAQI FREEDOM began in earnest. Harrell's own assessment was that "SOF planning to that point had been quite rudimentary. The [Special Operations Command] had to get serious about Iraq. A concept had to be prepared and guidance had to be given to the units. We were going to write a SOF campaign plan."[14]

Harrell also intended to fight the next campaign in theater; in Afghanistan, he had witnessed how important it was to have the special operations commander in theater and actively engaged in the joint SOF fight. Harrell and Brigadier General Mike Jones, the new commander of Special Operations Command Europe, had served

Figure 2.8 Brigadier General Mike Jones.

together as assistant division commanders for Major General Franklin Hagenbeck of Task Force Mountain during the heavy fighting that took place in Operation ANACONDA. The professional bond Harrell and Jones forged during ANACONDA would prove invaluable in IRAQI FREEDOM.[15]

PSYCHOLOGICAL OPERATIONS

Figure 2.9 JPOTF logo.

Although the Department of Defense and CENTCOM began revising Plan 1003 in January 2002, the early SOCCENT planning effort was limited at best. Only force-listed elements of 1003 (those units specifically named as part of the plan) were invited to send unit planners to Tampa, Florida, where revisions to the plan were being made—leaving out most of ARSOF. Having demonstrated its value in Afghanistan, however, Psychological Operations planners did get an early start on the Iraq planning. The Joint Psychological Operations Task Force formed around the 8th PSYOP Battalion staff was located near CENTCOM headquarters. Embedded in the regional command staff shortly after 11 September 2001, the JPOTF enjoyed good access to the intelligence and operations staffs, as well as to General Franks. JPOTF Commander Lieutenant Colonel Steve Herzig was able to task an entire company of the 8th PSYOP Battalion to focus on Iraq.[16]

CIVIL AFFAIRS

Civil Affairs did not enjoy the same confidence from CENTCOM. Only one of the four Civil Affairs officers on the Coalition Forces Land Component Command Civil Affairs operational planning staff at Camp Doha, Kuwait, was "read on" to 1003 planning; he was tasked to write the draft Civil Affairs Annex G. Meanwhile, seventy senior Army Reserve officers were mobilized and sent to CENTCOM in late spring 2002 to write the Civil Affairs campaign plan for Iraq. SOCCENT did not write a Civil Affairs plan to support the SOF campaign because neither the draft Annex G nor the CENTCOM campaign plan was ever approved. The absence of approved CENTCOM Civil Affairs guidance plagued the supporting headquarters of ARSOF throughout IRAQI FREEDOM. Fortunately, the warfighting roles were better defined.[17]

By mid-summer 2002, CENTCOM had granted increased access to 1003V planning and efforts at all levels of SOF expanded considerably. Previously left out, those units not force-listed yet considered potential assets for IRAQI FREEDOM were invited to send planners to SOCCENT. The JPOTF dispatched small PSYOP planning support elements to the Special Forces groups and the 75th Ranger Regiment. Although low-level planning went forward without a hitch, planning at higher levels was complicated by regional combatant command relationships.[18]

EUCOM'S ROLE

While Iraq was clearly in the CENTCOM area of operations, key staging areas for the northern campaign—first Turkey, and then Romania—were in European Command's area of responsibility. The two regional commands could not help but approach the problem from different perspectives based on their separate locations and responsibilities. CENTCOM was responsible for actually prosecuting the war, while EUCOM would support the CENTCOM effort with troops, equipment, and forward staging bases. EUCOM always knew that following any action against Iraq, EUCOM—not CENTCOM—would have to "live" with European countries bordering Iraq and deal with any resulting backlash. Because Secretary of Defense Rumsfeld never specified that CENTCOM would be the *supported* combatant command and EUCOM would be *supporting*, EUCOM also sought appropriate combat missions for its forces and resources. Any special operations forces EUCOM might lend CENTCOM would have to walk a fine line between the two commands. EUCOM-allocated ARSOF solved this problem by focusing all its attention on guidance from SOCCENT.

Figure 2.10 Map of CENTCOM's area of responsibility.

SPECIAL OPERATIONS COMMAND EUROPE

In his new post as commander of Special Operations Command Europe, General Jones was quickly reminded that EUCOM was a long-established joint regional headquarters; the combatant commander was dual-hatted as the supreme allied commander, Europe. The EUCOM deputy commander and the EUCOM staff in Stuttgart, Germany, were effectively in charge of all U.S. forces in Europe. Thus, in addition to being a EUCOM component commander, the SOCEUR commander was also expected to be the special operations advisor to the deputy commander, and the senior SOF staff officer of the headquarters. By summer, it became very evident that Jones had to "get on the EUCOM staff team" or else his role as the special operations commander would be marginalized: "My personal goal was

Figure 2.11 Map of EUCOM's area of responsibility.

Figure 2.12 SOC-EUR shoulder patch.

to make the EUCOM/CENTCOM special operations forces relationship in northern Iraq transparent." That philosophy was key to SOCCENT's planning efforts; 1003V required military overflights of a number of NATO countries, presumed that U.S. forces would forward base in Turkey, and involved EUCOM theater-allocated forces. The relationship formed in Afghanistan between Jones and Harrell served them well as they conferred daily about regional developments that might impact the special operations campaign supporting 1003V.[19]

TURKEY

The unconventional warfare mission in Iraq also required extensive coordination with other U.S. and allied government elements. Authorities had to be granted and permissions received in order to conduct an effective unconventional warfare campaign. Since a later NATO role in Iraq was anticipated, Lieutenant General Colby Broadwater, commander of NATO's Central Army Group and the Allied Command Europe quick reaction force, was designated as EUCOM's principal emissary in U.S.-Turkish military negotiations. Broadwater would spend almost six months shuttling between Brussels, Belgium; Stuttgart and Heidelberg, Germany; and Ankara, Turkey, making arrangements key to 1003V. Turkey was understandably concerned about the infringements on national sovereignty posed by the debarkation and cross-country transit of a U.S. mechanized division on its way to invade a bordering nation. Turkey also worried about potential future retaliation by Iraq and by Arab terrorists for granting such permission, and the threat posed by a possible independent Kurdish state that controlled the oil fields of northern Iraq. All were issues difficult for U.S. diplomats and military leaders to dismiss, and the outcome of negotiations would have considerable impact on SOF planning and operations.

Figure 2.13 Lieutenant General Colby Broadwater.

ARMY SOF'S MISSIONS

Examining its responsibilities for IRAQI FREEDOM, SOCCENT determined that two Combined Joint Special Operations Task Forces and a Naval Task Force along the southern coast of Iraq would prosecute the special operations campaign in support of 1003V. CJSOTF-NORTH would be responsible for northern Iraq and the Kurdish forces, and CJSOTF-WEST would suppress the SCUD missile threat in the western and southern deserts of Iraq and organize resistance among the Shia. The Naval Task Force would secure Iraqi oil and gas platforms from sabotage as well as capture the facilities at Al Faw and Umm Qasr. All three efforts supported the CENTCOM conventional forces, whose primary objective was Baghdad—the center of gravity for Saddam Hussein and his regime.

5TH SPECIAL FORCES GROUP

The CENTCOM-oriented 5th Special Forces Group had a significant role in Plan 1003V, as it had during DESERT STORM. Still, the Army corps headquarters assuming command of Afghanistan wanted to maintain a full complement of Army special operations forces in that country, the 5th SFG could not fulfill both obligations. Having been released from its on-order contingency mission in the Horn of Africa, the 3rd SFG assumed the ARSOF mission in Afghanistan, freeing the 5th SFG to prepare for Iraq. In Afghanistan, the unconventional warfare campaign was replaced by counterinsurgency operations against the remaining Taliban and al-Qaeda elements. As the most mobile Special Forces element, the 5th SFG left its organic military and civilian vehicles and heavy weapon systems for the 3rd SFG's use in Afghanistan.

Figure 2.14 CJSOTF-Afghanistan logo.

In the late summer of 2002, SOCCENT assumed the entire western desert mission in Iraq, which was subsequently assigned to the 5th SFG. British and Australian elements were transferred to JSOTF-west, making it a Combined JSOTF. SOCCENT modified the JSOTF-west Joint Manning Document and embedded Australian and British officers; Colonel John Mulholland had an Australian as his deputy, and a British officer serving as the operations officer. Once the manning issues had been resolved, CJSOTF-west turned its attention to its own area of operations. The SCUD threat was the number one priority of the intelligence community; also crucial was the question of whether the Shia would revolt again after the debacle in 1991. In addition, the CJSOTF-west staff had to evaluate the Iraqi military architecture in the south based on a sadly out-of-date Iraqi Order of Battle.[20]

Figure 2.15 Colonel John Mulholland and Secretary of Defense Donald Rumsfeld in Afghanistan.

10TH SPECIAL FORCES GROUP

Colonel Mulholland's 5th SFG was force-listed in the original 1003 plan and was, therefore, guaranteed a role in 1003V. The CENTCOM plan called for two Special Forces groups. The 10th SFG commander Colonel Charles Cleveland lobbied for the 10th SFG to fill the second mission. His justifications were solid: the 1st SFG was committed to Exercise Balikatan 02 in the Philippines, the 7th SFG was committed to Colombia, and the 3rd SFG was in charge of CJSOTF-Afghanistan. His group was not only available, but also had the current experience. The 10th SFG participated in Operation PROVIDE COMFORT (providing humanitarian aid to the Kurds) in 1991, had recently conducted a joint combined training exercise in the Middle East, and had just con-

Figure 2.16 Colonel Charles Cleveland.

cluded JSOTF operations based on a northern Iraq mission scenario in Joint Training Exercise Flintlock Reborn.[21]

Shortly after taking command of the 10th SFG in July 2001, Colonel Cleveland announced his intent to exercise the group headquarters overseas as a JSOTF according to EUCOM Operations Plan 2929. Cleveland understood that resources would be a problem, and envisioned creating this JSOTF under SOCEUR by blending the 10th SFG headquarters and its support elements with those of the Air Force's 352nd Special Operations Group staff and its communications suite. Having received approval for his plan from the commander of U.S. Army Special Forces Command, Major General Geoffrey Lambert, the 10th SFG staff began planning and coordinating in late summer 2001 to execute Flintlock Reborn in the spring of 2002.

Due to the U.S. Army Special Operations Command's reprioritization of funding and equipment fielding to support Operation ENDURING FREEDOM, Special Forces Command tasked the 10th SFG to provide winter warfare training to the 5th SFG. Afterward, the 10th SFG transferred its winter warfare gear (from snowshoes to snowmobiles) to the 5th SFG. As with all SFGs in the command, the 10th SFG had also attached personnel with critical skills to the 5th SFG for its mission in Afghanistan. Undaunted by these commitments, Cleveland committed the majority of his fiscal year 2002 budget to fund Flintlock Reborn, and asked Special Operations Command, Joint Forces Command to provide JSOTF training to his staff.[22]

Having made a "pact of sorts" with Colonel O.G. Mannon, the 352nd Special Operations Group commander, to integrate his staff and communications suite with the 10th SFG headquarters to form a JSOTF for Flintlock Reborn, Cleveland chose twenty 352nd SOG officers to be integrated into the JSOTF and establish a habitual relationship with the 10th SFG. The 352nd SOG was involved in aerial resupply of SOF teams in Afghanistan and had based out of Turkey for that mission. The resupply mission was reduced in February 2002, thereby allowing the 352nd to participate in Flintlock Reborn. The arrangement between the 10th SFG and the 352nd SOG was made possible by the support of Brigadier General Leslie Fuller, commander of SOCEUR during that time.[23]

To fund and schedule his plan, Cleveland took advantage of a joint combined exercise for training in Turkey and garnered additional funds from a rarely conducted U.S.-Israeli SOF exchange, with the concurrence of General Lambert and the CENTCOM joint exercises officer. To kick off Flintlock Reborn in April 2002, the 10th SFG and the 352nd SOG established a JSOTF in Stuttgart. One Special Forces battalion located its forward operating base in Stuttgart, while another established its forward operating base in Turkey to direct the combined U.S.-Turkish special forces training exercise. The JSOTF then executed a northern Iraq scenario and mission profile. As agreed, Special Operations Command, Joint Forces Command provided trainers/mentors to review joint staff procedures and effect technology transfers within the JSOTF. In the course of the exercise, the Army and Air Force staffs coalesced into an effective JSOTF. Thus, the 10th SFG was exercising as a JSOTF while the 3rd SFG with 20th SFG augmentees was operating as the CJSOTF-Afghanistan in Bagram. The 10th SFG now had the most current experience in the region. [24]

Having supported Cleveland in training as JSOTF, General Lambert petitioned SOCCENT and SOCEUR to give the SOF mission in northern Iraq to the 10th SFG. He attached the 3rd Battalion, 3rd SFG, to the 10th SFG to give it a mobile heavy weapons capability. SOCEUR retained the 1st Battalion of 10th SFG to handle regional contingencies, and using C Company, 2nd Battalion, 20th SFG, to "round-out" the 10th SFG's 3rd Battalion for 1003V, the 10th SFG could still provide a Special Forces company to Kosovo for peacekeeping. "It took some juggling to balance worldwide commitments, but it got the 10th into the fight," commented Lambert afterward. [25]

Figure 2.17 Major General Geoffrey Lambert.

Finally receiving the sought-after order to support 1003V, Cleveland headed to Tampa.

> *After attending several SOCCENT planning sessions, it was pretty evident that the SOF fight in the north would be very different than Colonel Mulholland's in the west and Captain Bob Harward's fight in the south. I did not need the [special operations commander] to write my campaign plan. One of my battalion commanders, Lieutenant Colonel Kenneth Tovo, was a recent [School for Advanced Military Studies] graduate. With him as the primary architect, and with some outside assistance, we prepared the Task Force Viking campaign plan while keeping track of the 4th [Infantry Division] planning. We attended the daily [tactical operations center] update briefs of the 3rd Brigade Combat Team at Fort Carson. During JTX Flintlock Reborn, the JSOTF carefully evaluated the major Turkish lines of communication into Iraq. I did not think that the 4th [Infantry Division] would get into the fight going overland through Turkey. The primary ingress was a two-lane highway with numerous bridges. Though they could accommodate some armored traffic, the roads and bridges had not been built to support the movement of a U.S. mechanized division. Knowing this, I decided to plan my fight as if SOF would be the only force in northern Iraq. And, that proved to be wise. Still, I sent a mobilized [Army Reserve Special Forces] lieutenant colonel to Fort Hood, Texas, as a permanent liaison officer to the 4th ID headquarters, and even provided a*

Figure 2.18 Original 10th SFG distinctive unit insignia with Trojan Horse.

SOCCE [Special Operations Command and Control Ele-
ment] to go through a warfighting exercise with them."[26]

THE "TYRANNY OF TIME"

The time and distance between headquarters planning the fight,
Army and special operations headquarters providing resources, and
combat units preparing for war made coordination difficult and kept
operational planners hopping when suspenses for critical decisions
negated responses from the field. Some units were simply too late with
their input. The 5th and 10th SFGs were allocated to different combatant commands—CENTCOM and EUCOM—which made coordination
with higher headquarters difficult. In addition, ARSOF had other units
scattered around the globe, answering to commands in still other
locations. The 5th SFG was stationed at Fort Campbell, Kentucky, and
operated on Central Standard Time, while the 10th SFG headquarters
and two of its battalions were based at Fort Carson, and functioned
on Mountain Standard Time. The 75th Ranger Regiment and the 3rd
Ranger Battalion based at Fort Benning, Georgia, and the 1st Ranger
Battalion in Savannah, Georgia, were both on Eastern Standard Time.
But the 2nd Ranger Battalion was at Fort Lewis, Washington, which

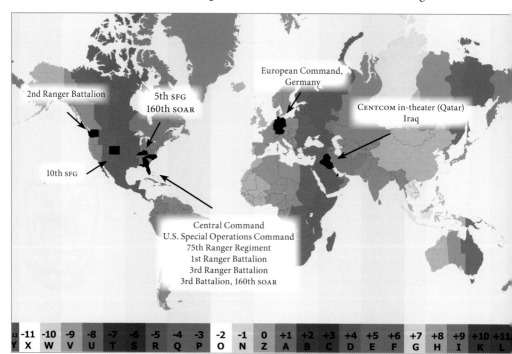

Figure 2.19 Map showing Colonel Charles Cleveland's tyranny of time. *Large time zone differences contributed to planning difficulties.*

was on Pacific Standard Time. The 160th SOAR and two of its battalions were located at Fort Campbell, but its 3rd Battalion was in Savannah. CENTCOM and the U.S. Special Operations Command were both located in Tampa, but CENTCOM's in-theater headquarters was located in Qatar—eight hours ahead of Eastern Standard Time; and EUCOM was headquartered in Stuttgart, which was five hours ahead of Tampa. At times it was impossible to contribute to or influence a decision before the planning matrix reached fruition. Cleveland referred to this dilemma as the "tyranny of time."[27]

Prior obligations and complicated circumstances provided the context in which commanders at all levels began planning for Operation IRAQI FREEDOM. ARSOF units were already committed to operations in Afghanistan, the Balkans, Colombia, and the Philippines, limiting the forces available for operations against Iraq. Operation ENDURING FREEDOM revealed that the ability of U.S. industry to provide wartime levels of materiel had been severely degraded by more than a decade of Department of Defense budget cuts and drawdowns. Early planners discovered that politics would play a large part in IRAQI FREEDOM, as international support for a campaign against Saddam Hussein was slow in coming, and negotiations with Turkey became bogged down over issues of sovereignty and regional concerns. Command relationships within the U.S. military and the SOF components also had to be ironed out before effective planning could take place.

As IRAQI FREEDOM planning overlapped preparations, the various SOF commands and elements confronted a variety of challenges. Time and distance continued to complicate planning and coordination efforts. Funding and equipment issues became significant factors in readying units for war—especially for the 5th SFG. Finally, the availability of trained personnel became an overarching concern for all commands; the call up of Reservists and Guardsmen revealed systemic problems in the mobilization system, and training of all personnel took valuable time and resources. In typical SOF fashion, however, these challenges and more were met with competence and ingenuity.

3

Preparing for War

O NCE IT BECAME OBVIOUS that the United States might go to war against Iraq, the military began to prepare in earnest. Central Command's Contingency Plan 1003 had been available since soon after the Gulf War, so it took no stretch of the imagination to assume it would provide at least a starting point for planners. Conventional and special operations units included in 1003's Time-Phased Force Deployment List assumed they would take part in any future war with Iraq, and began to prepare accordingly. Units not force-listed in 1003 had no such guarantee, and their efforts were correspondingly less aggressive. Army special operations forces preparations were affected by those of Special Operations Command Central, which was in turn affected by CENTCOM's preparations.

CONVENTIONAL PREPARATIONS

By November 2002, the National Security Council had settled on General Tommy Franks' Hybrid variant of Contingency Plan 1003—1003v. Finding a middle ground between the ponderous Generated Start and the aggressive Running Start variations, the 1003 Hybrid—which became 1003 Victor (1003v) once it was approved—called for a moderate buildup of forces during Phase I, but retained a compressed timeline. To that end, many forces had already moved into theater and continued to do so for the next several months. In late November, Franks asked Secretary of Defense Donald Rumsfeld for permission to deploy forces to the Middle East in preparation for the possibility that the President decided to go to war against Iraq. The proposed deployment would send 128,000 troops to the Persian Gulf region by 15 February 2003. Franks also requested that the 101st Airborne Division (Air Assault) and various special operations forces be alerted and ready to deploy by 20 March 2003. Franks envisioned a total of 210,000 troops in theater by D-DAY, half the number required for Generated Start and considerably more than for Running Start.[1]

Operation Plan 1003V called for the 3rd Infantry Division to sweep northwest from Kuwait and enter Baghdad from the west. Meanwhile, the I Marine Expeditionary Force would sweep to the northeast along the Tigris River. The two divisions would meet up south of Baghdad before capturing the capital together. The speed of their advance would prevent Iraqi forces from falling back to defend Baghdad. The relatively small ground force would also convince the Iraqis that the main assault was still to come, either from the west or the north. This misconception would allow the ground forces to penetrate all the way to Baghdad. In the south, the British 1st Armoured Division would execute an isolating hook around Basra to protect the Rumaylah Oil Fields. The plan also called for the 4th ID to attack south from Turkey—pending cooperation from that country—and for special operations forces to secure the western desert. Coalition air assets would support the entire maneuver. The plan was ambitious, but Franks felt that with speed and decisive firepower, it would work, and began to prepare Coalition forces accordingly.[2]

As the military prepared for war, diplomatic options were also aggressively pursued. The United States moved one step closer to war with Iraq on 5 February 2003, when Secretary of State Colin Powell addressed the United Nations Security Council. In his presentation, Powell made the connection between Saddam Hussein and weapons of mass destruction. Citing intelligence reports and showing intelligence

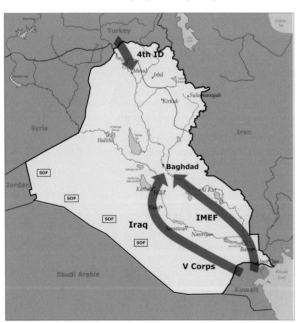

Figure 3.1 Map showing Hybrid 1003 plan of attack.

photographs, Powell made the case for enacting the penalties provided for in UN Security Council Resolution 1441. Powell also made the link between al-Qaeda and Iraq, which increased the likelihood of weapons of mass destruction being used by terrorists against the United States and its allies. With talk of force circulating in the halls of the United Nations, it became increasingly clear to the U.S. military that preparations and plans needed to be finalized as quickly as possible. War was on its way.[3]

ARSOF PREPARATIONS

With conventional preparations moving swiftly forward, Army special operations forces struggled to catch up. Not only were ARSOF elements already committed to missions around the world, but sufficient personnel and materiel for additional missions were also difficult to come by, and time was even scarcer. Time constraints forced preparations to begin even before plans were solidified, a situation that plagued ARSOF during the entire pre-war period.

Further complicating efforts to prepare for Operation IRAQI FREEDOM were ARSOF's ongoing commitments around the globe. Special Forces units were still required to support conventional operations in Afghanistan, and Civil Affairs and Psychological Operations units were heavily involved in rebuilding efforts there. Special Forces units were also committed to missions in the Philippines, Colombia, and Africa. The 160th Special Operations Aviation Regiment and Special Operations Support Command supported ARSOF operations wherever they were needed. Each mission required critical resources, which placed planners in the position of competing with their own commands for personnel, funding, and equipment in order to prepare the force for Operation IRAQI FREEDOM.

Preparations were complex and interdependent; each change in planning caused shifts in other plans. The various aspects of preparation also had to be carried out simultaneously, adding further strain to already overtaxed systems. While the four phases of ARSOF preparations efforts—organizing, mobilizing, equipping, and training the force—are discussed below as discrete stages, in reality, each complicated the next and each priority competed with the others for time and resources. Below are some of the most significant preparation issues—and solutions—that ARSOF confronted in the months, weeks, and days before IRAQI FREEDOM began.

Organizing the Force

Before serious war preparations could begin, ARSOF had to organize. Command relationships were many and complicated, making staffing vitally important. From U.S. Special Operations Command (USSOCOM) down to the ground units, the success of all planning and execution efforts depended on getting enough personnel trained to the level necessary for such a varied and important operation as IRAQI FREEDOM. All too often, key personnel were expected to quickly make decisions without even basic information. Nevertheless, Special Operations Command Central managed to compile a strong force and provide the coordination necessary to complete its mission.

Special Operations Command Central

Figure 3.2 SOC-CENT logo.

Figure 3.3 Brigadier General Gary Harrell.

Figure 3.4 SOCJF-COM shoulder patch.

At the end of September 2002, Brigadier General Gary Harrell felt it was time for Special Operations Command Center to begin "leaning forward" and increase its preparation efforts for IRAQI FREEDOM. To refine its planning, SOCCENT "asked the smart joint staff doctrine guys at SOCJFCOM [Special Operations Command, Joint Forces Command] in Norfolk [Virginia]—Colonel Mike Findlay, Lieutenant Colonel Wes Rehorn, Don Richardson, and others—to come down to assess our SOF campaign plan, to evaluate our staffing procedures, and to help our staff sections prepare specific joint mission-essential task lists," recalled Colonel Patrick Higgins, the SOCCENT operations officer. "After a week working with our staffs, Colonel Findlay and team conducted an executive session for the commanding general and principal staff. That's when he gave us specific recommendations to orient us towards success." SOCJFCOM staff mentoring during the refinement of 1003V and the joint mission–essential task list development was crucial to SOCCENT's joint staff training process.[4]

Besides training his staff in joint staff work, Harrell needed to build his force. Central Command was a relatively new combatant command and did not have any dedicated assets—no combat units, no support units, not even auxiliary staff. Thus, a large part of CENTCOM and SOCCENT's early preparation consisted of identifying and recruiting the people and units necessary to accomplish their missions.

To SOCCENT's advantage was that it already had troops in theater participating in scheduled training and exercises. Exercise Early Victor provided American and Jordanian special operations forces a yearly opportunity to train together. Beginning on 6 October 2002, the 1st Battalion, 5th Special Forces Group, trained with its Jordanian counterparts in the country's deserts, giving the Special Forces soldiers valuable environmental training. Support personnel and equipment also participated in Early Victor, which gave SOCCENT the ability to start building bases in the region as soon as December 2002.

Joint Communications Signal Element

As part of its organization efforts, SOCCENT had to consider its ability to communicate with the myriad commands and units involved in IRAQI FREEDOM—most of which were not SOF, many of which were not Army, and some of which were not even American. The 112th Special Operations Signal Battalion needed to be supplemented in order to provide SOCCENT with the joint communications capability it required. When Lieutenant Colonel Jay Santiago became the SOCCENT deputy signal officer in the summer of 2002, he inherited the dilemma. The solution came in the form of a Joint Communications Signal Element, which supported SOCCENT's forward element in Qatar during Operation ENDURING FREEDOM. The capability this element brought to SOCCENT was a much more powerful communications suite tailored for joint operations. Combined with the 112th's own powerful signal package, the Joint Communications Signal Element enabled SOCCENT to communicate in every way imaginable with anybody it needed to, all simultaneously.[5]

Figure 3.5 112th SOSB insignia.

Figure 3.6 JCSE shoulder patch.

Psychologists

One special addition to his staff that General Harrell made during Operation ENDURING FREEDOM was Colonel Morgan Banks, the U.S. Army Special Operations Command psychologist. Banks served in Harrell's tactical Red Cell during ENDURING FREEDOM. His psychological profiles of al-Qaeda, Taliban, and Northern Alliance leadership taught the general the value of having a tactically experienced psychologist on staff. This staff officer built personality profiles based on leaders' known behavior, which were extremely useful for tactical analysis and in negotiations. Harrell believed these skills to be so valuable that he asked USSOCOM to provide tactically experienced psychologists for each Combined Joint Special Operations Task Force (CJSOTF) during IRAQI FREEDOM.[6]

Alerted by General Harrell, Banks called two experienced colleagues to ascertain their availability: Lieutenant Colonel John Chin, who had been a SOF command psychologist for more than fifteen years, and Colonel Thomas Williams, who had done special projects for the Army Intelligence Command. Army clinical psychologists with tactical experience were rare commodities, so arranging temporary releases for the men while maintaining operational security was challenging, but well worth the effort.[7]

The benefits of having an experienced psychologist at each CJSOTF were varied. Each could act as a special advisor to the commander, provide psychological personality profiling of enemy leadership, observe and analyze enemy prisoner of war interrogations, and even assist with Psychological and Information Operations. The psychologists' analytical skills and tactical experience made them good "sounding boards" for commanders, as they assessed the validity of planning assumptions and intelligence estimates. The psychologists also knew how to conduct research from both open and classified sources, and make assessments based upon their findings. The psychologists were valuable as monitors of staff health; as trained, skilled observers they could detect early indications of combat stress, such as personality changes and panic attacks. Their psychological medicine skills expanded the capability of unit medical teams.

After matching tactical experience and backgrounds with the mission sets of each CJSOTF, Banks contacted Colonel John Mulholland of the 5th Special Forces Group and Colonel Charles Cleveland of the 10th SFG, the two commanders who would run the CJSOTFs in Iraq, to confirm his choices for each. Like Harrell, Mulholland had served in units with assigned psychologists, and as a JSOTF commander in Afghanistan, he had worked with ARSOF psychologist Major Gary Hazlet. For IRAQI FREEDOM, Mulholland was pleased to have Chin, whom he had known for years. He knew what an experienced psychologist could contribute to the preparation of the battlefield, and was especially anxious for such help in CJSOTF-west, which had an especially tough unconventional warfare mission involving the Shia community in Iraq. Chin's ability to increase cultural awareness well beyond a generic understanding of the Middle East would help the commanders and teams as they planned their missions.[8]

Chin joined the 5th SFG at Fort Campbell, Kentucky, in the midst the group's final preparations for Operation IRAQI FREEDOM. Chin accompanied Mulholland on a visit to the 1st Battalion in the Middle East, where it was participating in Exercise Early Victor. Once he had decided how he could best add value to the unconventional warfare mission, Chin began executing his plan: he constructed a personality profile of Saddam Hussein from a cultural perspective to help the 5th SFG "know its enemy," and compiled a profile of the Baath Party and the major Iraqi tribes in the south as background for the unconventional warfare mission.[9]

The personality profile of Saddam listed and explained the various factors that had influenced the development of the dictator's pathological personality, and explained how he had gained power and then retained it for more than twenty years. Saddam Hussein was the product of several significant influences: a dysfunctional family, family obligations and clan loyalties, Iraqi history, the Sunni-Shia conflict, and Baath Party ideology. Even a deconstruction of his full name, Saddam Hussein al-Majid al-Tikriti, contained a wealth of information. Saddam, his birth name, meant "Great Struggler" or "One Who Confronts." Hussein was his father's surname, and Majid was the family name; thus, the Hussein from the Majid family of the Tikrit region. Placing Saddam in context of his family and clan connections provided insight into his loyalties and power base.[10]

Chin also prepared a psychological perspective of the Iraqi tribes. This information covered the evolution of Iraqi tribes from early history to the present; tribal structures, myths, values, and functions; as well as Baath Party influence and the differences between Shia and Sunni Iraqis. A primer on the operational aspects of tribal culture—as in what to do and what to avoid—provided the Special Forces teams with rules by which to govern their actions with Iraqis. The guidelines included explanations of Iraqi perceptions of weakness and strength that were especially useful during negotiations. Chin also marked significant holy shrines and religious celebrations on maps and calendars to keep the team members mindful of the cultural context in which they were to operate. He indicated that Psychological Operations themes should stress cooperation. He also provided an educated prediction of which tribes would support a regime change, allowing the teams to focus their efforts. The psychologist's assessments were valuable and accurate. As Mulholland related afterward, "Doc Chin was right on about the Shia resistance."[11]

Based on the heavy unconventional warfare mission sets assigned to cjsotf-north, Banks recommended that Williams be assigned to that joint sof headquarters. He had had extensive experience performing behavior analysis personality profiling and additional experience with intelligence order of battle. Williams arrived in time to give Cleveland "a half-step advantage" in his negotiating role with the senior Turkish sof leadership. To ensure the psychologist did not "slip into an operator mentality," yet still receive total support from the staff, Cleveland introduced Williams as his "special advisor." While Cleveland was overseas in Stuttgart, Germany, and Ankara, Turkey, Williams became operationally focused. He started the research necessary to construct psychological profiles of the Iraqi military to correspond to order of battle architecture in northern Iraq, as well as the Kurdish leadership—which was actually a higher priority.[12]

The elements of the profiles were designed to enable Cleveland to prepare for meetings with leaders of the different cultures he worked with. Williams included in each profile information that would give Cleveland a credible context for his interactions with each man: personal information; how the subject interacted leader to leader; interpersonal style; interactions with U.S. subordinates; decision making style; trustworthiness; reactions during stress; attitudes about capitulation; and methods to influence, manage, and control the individual, or at least control a discussion with him.[13]

Besides compiling individual profiles, Williams gave the staff and team members of CJSOTF-North a more general profile of the Iraqis:

> *Having read the debriefs from the last Gulf War, the current [psychological operations] towards the Iraqi people seemed off target. I put together a 'typical Iraqi' personality profile to help our operations and intelligence staffs. In terms of personality traits, the Iraqis are a lot like Americans. They are very ingenious, ambitious, industrious, and individualistic. Though they are Arabs, they like to gain individual advantage, but they couch that predilection in the cultural expression, 'I have to do this to advance my family,' which advances them as well.*[14]

The CJSOTF-North psychologist contributed information to issues ranging from capitulation versus ceasefire versus co-option to creating protocols to conduct safe, legal, ethical, and effective interrogation and detainee operations. Williams more than proved the value of including a tactical psychologist in SOF headquarters.

Walk-ons

As a unit-poor command, SOCCENT was in no position to refuse volunteer unit participation, so even though the 75th Ranger Regiment, the 160th Special Operations Aviation Regiment, and the Special Operations Support Command were not force-listed in the original 1003 plan, they were welcome in Tampa. Each sent a small liaison cell to SOCCENT in July 2002 to volunteer for missions and coordinate participation. The Rangers and Aviators had been assigned lesser missions in Operation DESERT STORM, so they were all the more anxious to be "players" in the next desert war.[15]

Coalition Partners

International interest and world support for America's expanding Global War on Terrorism began to dwindle dramatically after the Taliban regime collapsed in Afghanistan; however, Australia and the United Kingdom remained staunch allies. Australia was especially proud of its long-time association with the United States; it was second to none as a reliable ally of the United States. Australia had sent troops to fight with U.S. forces in every major conflict of the 20th century—World War I and World War II, Korea, Vietnam, and the Gulf War—and was in Afghanistan as part of the Coalition. When planning began for Operation IRAQI FREEDOM, both the United Kingdom and Australia signed up for the duration.[16]

Figure 3.7 Australian flag.

The Australian government was committed to fighting terrorism in all its forms, and did not hesitate to support Operation IRAQI FREE-DOM. As Major General Duncan Lewis, commander of Special Operations Command Australia, recounted:

> *The Prime Minister, John Howard, felt personally committed to the American Global War on Terrorism because he was being driven to visit President George Bush at the White House when the terrorist-piloted airliner crashed into the Pentagon. The Australian [prime minister] and his staff were whisked off to an underground bunker in the Washington area. Since our ally had been attacked, the government invoked the [Australia, New Zealand, United States] regional defense treaty [of 1951]. Though the treaty was designed for a previous.era, it was dragged into the modern day. Under the provisions of that treaty, if any party were under attack, the others would consult closely and come to its assistance. The Australians felt an obligation to do just that.*[17]

Figure 3.8 Australian SASR badge.

Australian ground forces had just returned from a year in Afghanistan on 22 November 2002 to "refit and be reconstituted" when the possibility of a second Global War on Terrorism campaign arrived. The Howard government immediately anticipated involvement and authorized liaison teams to be assigned to U.S. commands.

The first issue that had to be resolved in Coalition planning was the matter of operational control. General Lewis attended major "what if" planning sessions in Tampa before making his decision. His assessment of SOCCENT was favorable: "The [Special Operations Commander], Gary Harrell, had taken charge and gotten the headquarters organized. The SOCCENT staff was involved in very deliberate planning. Commanders were talking to commanders at all levels all the way down. I was satisfied that it was all joined up. It was a textbook Coalition SOF operation all around." The British force did not as readily accept giving up operational independence, but when it came to either submitting to operational control by SOCCENT or exclusion from IRAQI FREEDOM, professionalism and reason prevailed over tradition. The Australian SOF elements were assigned directly to CJSOTF-west, while a colonel served as the Australian component commander to SOCCENT. "It was a very good relationship," stated Lewis. "And with a robust logistics element, we could provide proper support to our troops."[18]

Figure 3.9 Special Operations Command, Australia logo.

Unfortunately, many of the problems that plagued Coalition forces in Afghanistan were not as easily resolved before Operation IRAQI FREEDOM: top secret security clearances; access to secure compartmented intelligence facilities; access to the classified computer network routinely used by U.S. forces headquarters and staffs for opera-

Figure 3.10 British flag.

Figure 3.11 Major General Duncan Lewis, Commander, Special Operations Command, Australia.

Figure 3.12 Millennium Challenge 2002 logo.

tional command and control; and the Blue Force Tracker System for force protection. Access to all was controlled by the U.S. National Security Agency, and although America's "most trusted allies" were in the "intelligence onion layer" next to the center—U.S.-only access—clearances and access were still difficult to obtain. The Ministries of Defence of both the United Kingdom and Australia dedicated money and personnel to conduct the top secret–level background investigations necessary to gain even "supervised" intelligence access—an undertaking complicated by the fact that most of the British and Australian service branches had already reduced top secret access to minimize expenses. The United Kingdom incurred further expense when it leased the Blue Force Tracker System and other combat identification equipment from the United States.[19]

When top-down solutions to Coalition access problems were not forthcoming, commands and units developed their own fixes. Mulholland commented, "It fell straight down to colonel commanders in the field to take responsibility for the degree of access given to Coalition staff officers and Coalition force commanders. We developed work-arounds to function." For example, one practical solution developed at the tactical level was for the Australians to attach U.S. Air Force Special Tactics Squadron personnel, who carried Blue Force Trackers, to each Australian team. That way, security conflicts were avoided and situational awareness remained high.[20]

The Australians looked to recent experiences in Afghanistan to help them better prepare for Iraq. British ground forces had brought their own air assets to Afghanistan, giving them considerable flexibility and independence. This standard British practice was not lost on the Australians, and when they planned for Iraq, they made sure that their "force package included two C-130 Hercules transports and several CH-47 Chinook helicopters, as well as much more robust logistics package. We learned from Afghanistan. When you arrive with airplanes, you've brought the 'proper currency' to the fight," explained General Lewis.[21]

Australian and British preparations for IRAQI FREEDOM led them to participate in training exercises with the United States. Both countries sent contingents to participate in the U.S. Air Force Joint Forces Experiment 02, which was held concurrently with Exercise Millennium Challenge. Held at Nellis Air Force Base, Nevada, the JEFX included a small Australian group and a large British contingent of ground element fire support teams and Royal Air Force forward air control teams. Although fratricide had not been an issue for Australia in Afghanistan, coordination and deconfliction of fires had been ingrained in the Australian Army culture after Vietnam. "Working with the U.S. is very frightening for any minor ally. You never know what's going to happen. It is equally frightening for U.S.

ground troops to work under U.S. air. That's not a criticism; it's a fact," said Lewis. "I told the blokes before they left for Afghanistan that the single greatest threat to you is Coalition air. Then you guys can worry about the Taliban and al-Qaeda." The British were more circumspect, though no less cautious: "Working with the U.S. in a Coalition brings political, diplomatic, and military advantages—including the aggregation of capabilities, flexible war-fighting options, and the sharing of intelligence and risk. [British] forces need to be commanded, structured, equipped, and trained with this in mind." Developing joint fires protocols with U.S. elements at Nellis Air Force Base proved to be worthwhile for both allies. The Australian close air support procedures had been very closely aligned with the U.S. system, but the new grid system of "kill boxes" worked so well in Operation IRAQI FREEDOM that the Defence forces made the Nellis protocols standard.[22]

In December 2002, the United Kingdom and Australia National Command Element staffs participated in a long-planned CENTCOM exercise without troops—Internal Look 02. The exercise served as a mission rehearsal for the Coalition Iraq operation, which was, of course, the contingency uppermost in planners' minds at the time. It not only allowed Headquarters' staff to practice and prepare to conduct a Coalition operation led by the United States, but also enabled the United Kingdom to influence mission planning.[23]

Getting forces ready and deployed into theater proved to be a major challenge for both Coalition partners. A British description of their preparations and deployment into theater was quite reserved and typically understated: "Complications created by the uncertain diplomatic and political processes in the run-up to the start of the operation, and late changes to the campaign plan wherein [British] forces would operate in the south instead of the north, had significant effects on the smooth provision of forces ready for combat operations. Forces had to be generated in reduced timelines, using mechanisms and pragmatic solutions to bypass readiness and resourcing assumptions." The Australian description of troop deployment was a bit more direct and graphic: "The bizarre arrangement by which we got forces into theater for Iraq wouldn't have passed muster at the Staff College. The 'crossing over' was more akin to dodging the traffic about Times Square on Saturday morning," said General Lewis. Nevertheless, the plans did work and some 46,000 British and 2,000 Australian members of the Defence Forces joined the U.S.-led Coalition in military operations against Saddam Hussein's regime.[24]

U.S. ARMY SPECIAL OPERATIONS COMMAND

On 29 August 2002, Lieutenant General Philip R. Kensinger assumed command of U.S. Army Special Operations Command and ARSOF's

Figure 3.13 Lieutenant General Philip Kensinger.

Figure 3.14 USASOC shoulder patch.

Figure 3.15 USASOC insignia.

participation in the Global War on Terrorism. The war was a personal one to Kensinger—he had just left his office in the Pentagon minutes before the terrorist-piloted airliner crashed into the building on 11 September 2001. When Kensinger held his first USASOC staff briefing on 29 August, he presented his top two priorities for the command: first, to continue to field and manage ARSOF requirements in Afghanistan; and second, to prepare for the campaign in Iraq.[25]

The role of ARSOF in Afghanistan was changing by late summer 2002; ARSOF was now supporting a conventional force instead of leading the fight. Because the conventional Army was familiar with Joint Chiefs of Staff Publication 5, proper alignment according to joint doctrine would reduce confusion for all involved. Consequently, the USASOC staff concentrated on SOF "doctrinal sets" to fulfill CENTCOM requirements in Afghanistan. Preparing for Iraq also entailed a refocusing of staff efforts. The Special Forces training regimen needed a hard review—from initial accession to assessment all the way through the specialty training—to ensure that it was adequate and efficient. Furthermore, Kensinger addressed the possibility of the Army's stop-loss (moratorium on leaving the Army or changing jobs) on certain military occupational specialties being lifted, and what impact that might have on ARSOF.[26]

U.S. Army Civil Affairs & Psychological Operations Command

The U.S. Army Civil Affairs and Psychological Operations Command (USACAPOC) had the unenviable task of having to prepare for a plan that did not exist. Although planners had been sent forward to create a Civil Affairs campaign plan for IRAQI FREEDOM, the Civil Affairs Operational Annex to 1003V still had not been approved by late September 2002, when the Coalition Forces Land Component Command Civil Affairs section held a planning conference in Kuwait to address necessary force structure. Because the Civil Affairs concept of operations was still quite vague, the planners could only base Civil Affairs requirements and potential missions on CFLCC concerns and possible scenarios: Iraqi infiltrators and deserters might mix with dislocated civilians; Iraqi armed forces might use civilian movement to mask their withdrawals, causing Coalition forces to hesitate in engaging Iraqis with fire; and the Iraqi government might force a movement of civilians towards Coalition forces during combat phases to disrupt Coalition efforts along the main supply routes south of the Euphrates River. Planners also worried that the Iraqi Army might maneuver civilians to disrupt a build-up of Coalition forces inside Iraq, and even exploit civilians for propaganda purposes, perhaps claiming Coalition mistreatment of the innocent.[27]

Unfortunately, these general concerns and possible scenarios were based on generalized assumptions made in the absence of good intelligence. Planners assumed that decisive combat operations could generate as many as eighty thousand dislocated civilians in the V Corps' area of operations, and the number could double in the transition period between Phase III and Phase IV. Since the Office of U.S. Foreign Disaster Assistance was the government entity responsible for providing humanitarian aid overseas, a CFLCC Executive Steering Group had to be established to coordinate with the Office of U.S. Foreign Disaster Assistance and its Disaster Assistance Response Teams to provide emergency and sustainment aid to Iraqi civilians—water, food, medical care, shelter, and sanitation assistance.[28]

Figure 3.16 USACAPOC shoulder patch.

The CFLCC civil military operations focus was on displaced civilian operations and humanitarian assistance designed to minimize civilian interference with military combat operations, and to mitigate humanitarian crises resulting from the same. Civil military operations were also directed toward establishing an acceptable, stable, new Iraqi government, and helping in recovery and reconstruction efforts. Initial priorities were to restore essential life support civilian infrastructures in Iraq, such as hospitals, water systems, electricity, and sewage systems.[29]

Figure 3.17 USACAPOC insignia.

The Civil Affairs job in Iraq was not only projected to be much bigger than in Afghanistan, but would also require extensive coordination with nonmilitary organizations. Unfortunately, planning became bogged down in the approval process, leaving the Civil Affairs soldiers and their commanders without concrete guidance. In spite of the lack of a coherent Civil Affairs plan, USACAPOC was helpless to stop or change the deployment momentum dictated by the Time-Phased Force and Deployment List; Civil Affairs units already force-listed in 1003 would be mobilized and deployed—whether or not they had a job to do. Responsible for executing the Civil Affairs plan that did not exist, Major General Herbert Altshuler committed USACAPOC to send 150 Civil Affairs soldiers to Kuwait to facilitate the arrival of the Civil Affairs units arriving in theater. Somebody had to greet the units as they arrived, and help them coordinate with the conventional CFLCC units that they would support. This was the best USACAPOC could do for what became the largest call-up of Civil Affairs soldiers in American history.[30]

Figure 3.18 Major General Herbert Altshuler.

Mobilizing the Force

Although a considerable number of Reservists and National Guard soldiers were already serving tours of duty, many more were needed for Operation IRAQI FREEDOM. Getting those soldiers mobilized, equipped, and trained was a battle in and of itself.

SPECIAL OPERATIONS COMMAND CENTRAL

As the new commander of SOCCENT, General Harrell faced significant challenges—personnel issues being some of the most intractable. Most primary staff officers rotated in the summer of 2002, just as Harrell did. Because the previous commander of SOCCENT had been a Navy flag officer, by tradition the majority of his active duty key staff had been naval special operations officers. Now those positions would be filled by Army personnel, whom Harrell had to find and hire. "But, that wasn't all bad," recalled Harrell. "It gave me the opportunity to recruit a new team to fight the next war."[31]

Finding appropriate staff officers was complicated by the fact that, like most special operations headquarters in wartime, Reservists filled four-fifths of the SOCCENT staff billets. To make matters worse, most of the Reservists and Guardsmen who were available had already been mobilized for two years and were scheduled to demobilize before the Iraq campaign began. Time further affected mobilization as competition increased among the services for individual Reservists and Guardsmen, and SOCCENT had to compete with higher headquarters for quality staff officers. Because most of the forces listed in 1003V were conventional units, SOCCENT also had to fill liaison billets, requiring even more staff. Fortunately, the liaison assignments could be filled by USSOCOM special operations detachments. Staffing issues continued to plague SOCCENT and its subordinate commands well into the war.[32]

U.S. Army Special Operations Command

Because USASOC provided most of the warfighters and support units, it found itself bearing the brunt of SOCCENT's mobilization issues. In addition to filling out its own staff requirements, USASOC had to manage its subordinate command and unit requirements, which were many. The challenges would be met.

U.S. Army Special Forces Command

Balancing Special Forces requirements worldwide was the responsibility of Major General Geoffrey Lambert, commander of U.S. Army Special Forces Command at Fort Bragg, North Carolina. In order to "stand up" CJSOTF-Afghanistan by 1 April 2002 with its complement of Joint Manning Document augmentees, about three hundred officers and soldiers from the 20th Special Forces Group (Army National Guard) had been integrated into the 3rd SFG, which was acting as the joint SOF headquarters in Bagram, Afghanistan.

Figure 3.19 USASFC shoulder patch.

Serious consideration of the 20th SFG to assume some of Special Force's Command's obligations called for formal validation of the 20th SFG capability to serve as a Joint Special Operations Task Force. Since U.S. Joint Forces Command in Norfolk, Virginia, was conducting Joint Training Exercise Millennium Challenge 02 in September 2002, Special Forces Command initiated a request through USASOC and USSOCOM to have SOCJFCOM train and validate the 20th SFG headquarters during the exercise. The possibility of the 20th SFG supplementing the 3rd SFG as a JSOTF was raised—a solution that inadvertently locked the 3rd SFG headquarters into the Afghanistan rotation, and ultimately allowed for the participation of the 3rd Battalion in IRAQI FREEDOM.[33]

Figure 3.20 20th SFG beret flash.

U.S. Army Civil Affairs & Psychological Operations Command

By the spring of 2002, virtually all Civil Affairs and Psychological Operations requirements in Afghanistan and the Philippines were being filled by Army Reserve units, and Plan 1003V called for even more. General Altshuler had to figure out how to mobilize and train enough USACAPOC soldiers to fulfill the command's obligations.

Sustaining Civil Affairs and PSYOP unit rotations in Afghanistan had already begun to stretch the capacity and capabilities of the Army Reserve force structure. Authorized level of organization rates had been kept several levels below rates for active forces for more than thirty years. The post–World War II standards of readiness meant that the majority of Civil Affairs and PSYOP units could not be mobilized, equipped, and trained to go to war in less than four to six months. In addition, the percentage of military occupational specialty (MOS)-qualified soldiers in all Civil Affairs and PSYOP Guard and Reserve units was only 65 percent, and that was after ambitious training programs during Operation ENDURING FREEDOM.[34]

Department of Defense funding kept Reserve units understrength, underqualified, and minimally trained for decades. Having only small cadres of officers and noncommissioned officers qualified and trained for Civil Affairs and PSYOP, units could not be made operationally ready simply by rapidly infusing personnel. Units needed MOS-qualified personnel, equipment, and time to conduct collective training. "If [Civil Affairs] and PSYOP units could not be readily deployed in the 1990s to the Balkans, how could they be readied for a major conflict in less than six months? Some units were so poorly funded that they lacked equipment with which to train. The 'quick fix' solution—'gutting' a large unit, like a brigade, to fill a battalion with MOS-qualified soldiers in order to deploy—destroyed the cohesion of several units and simply compounded the problem in the future," stated Altshuler.

Better alternatives to this conundrum had to be found, and found quickly.[35]

The mobilization system itself was akin to a operating a rusty steam locomotive whose rivets were constantly popping as pressure built up. The system was designed for ponderous mobilization efforts leading to a prolonged single war, not for the "plan fast, deploy fast" pace of IRAQI FREEDOM. What made matters worse for Civil Affairs and PSYOP mobilization was the fact that USACAPOC did not have sufficient mobilization resources to handle all the units and soldiers it needed to accomplish the mission.

By default, Civil Affairs and PSYOP mobilizations had become USACAPOC's responsibility when the command was formed in 1992. Although more than 90 percent of USACAPOC's troops were Reservists, USACAPOC's home base—Fort Bragg—was not designated as a Force Projection Platform by Army Forces Command. The Army, therefore, would not provide mobilization funds to the command. Training ammunition, billets, mess halls, and transportation, were allocated at Fort Bragg based only on active units assigned to the base. Yet USACAPOC's mobilizing units were required to report to Fort Bragg, leaving USACAPOC scrambling to house, feed, transport, and train its units before they deployed.

Since Fort Bragg was not a designated Force Projection Platform, neither Fort Bragg nor USASOC had large mobilization staffs. Neither had mobilization plans. USASOC's Army Reserve advisor four-person cell was tasked to coordinate all mobilization support at Fort Bragg. The lack of personnel and resources led to innovative ideas about how to prepare the USACAPOC units for Iraq. Exceptions linked to the Global War on Terrorism gave USACAPOC authority to use an "involuntary" annual training cycle for individual training, allowing the normal thirty-day-or-less annual training period to be used for collective unit training, based on an Army alert order for mobilization. The resourceful combination of annual training cycles enabled composite units to work on team building before deploying, a vital step in getting them ready for Iraq. Gaps in time mandated for pre-overseas requirements training were filled with other tasks: new equipment training; combat survival skills; and development of tactics, techniques, and procedures based on recent lessons learned, such as tactical convoy procedures, immediate action drills, and the threat of improvised explosive devices. Despite the unorthodox training cycles and cobbled-together nature of the training schedules, the USACAPOC units somehow managed to get ready for IRAQI FREEDOM.[36]

Some training required cooperation from units outside of USASOC. A Memorandum of Agreement was drafted between USACAPOC and the five Army Reserve Training Divisions which included CAPO (Civil Affairs PSYOP) Training Battalions. These battalions were responsible for MOS reclassification of enlisted personnel, qualifying them in either MOS 38A (Civil Affairs) or 37F (Psychological Operations). USACAPOC agreed to provide Civil Affairs and PSYOP instructors to augment the five CAPO battalions, and the period of instruction was compressed into two two-week annual training periods. The "Two-Plus-Two" program gave the CAPO battalions the ability to produce groups of fifty Civil Affairs and fifty PSYOP MOS-qualified soldiers one right after another.

While this "through-put" training system raised levels of MOS-qualified soldiers in Army Reserve Civil Affairs and PSYOP units above 80 percent, Army funding levels negated overall progress. The units needed equipment and collective training to become fully functional, which were slow in coming. "It was a 'Catch-22' situation. At best, the Army Reserve force was designed to be a C-3 asset [delayed deployment]," Altshuler added.[37]

U.S. Army John F. Kennedy Special Warfare Center & School

During Operation ENDURING FREEDOM, the U.S. Army John F. Kennedy Special Warfare Center and School (SWCS) had "ramped-up" Civil Affairs and PSYOP training conducted by the 3rd Battalion of the 1st Special Warfare Training Group. The number of annual advanced individual training classes for Civil Affairs and PSYOP enlisted soldiers were increased to help fill the requirements of ENDURING FREEDOM. The wartime program of instruction for Reserve Civil Affairs and PSYOP advanced individual training was "compressed" to twenty-nine days. SWCS provided updated training materials to the five CAPO battalions to ensure that Reservists being reclassified as Civil Affairs and PSYOP soldiers received commensurate training. Between November 2001 and March 2002, SWCS conducted seven mobilization Civil Affairs courses, compressing the four-week course into two weeks, and trained over 500 soldiers.

Figure 3.21
USAJFKSWCS
shoulder patch.

At the same time as SWCS received the requirement to train more Civil Affairs and PSYOP soldiers, the school had to train an increasing number of new Special Forces soldiers. Sustained combat and a future of multiple overseas combat tours dictated more graduates in order to maintain Special Forces strength, and USASOC was having to supplement its Army-internal recruitment efforts with new Special Forces candidates who were not in the Army. Simultaneously SWCS became responsible for turning "regular" soldiers into Special Forces and turning civilians into soldiers before Special Forces training.[38]

Figure 3.22
USAJFKSWCS
insignia.

Figure 3.23 SOS-
COM insignia.

Figure 3.24 528th
SOSB insignia.

Figure 3.25 167th
Theater Support
Command insignia.

Special Operations Support Command

Colonel Kevin Leonard, commander of Special Operations Support
Command, faced personnel issues when he realized that with ARSOF
spread so thinly between two campaigns, SOSCOM needed to expand
the logistics and maintenance capability of the 528th Support Battalion. Subsequently, a third company for the 528th was approved, with
personnel provided from the Army National Guard and the Army
Reserve. Identification of combat service support units for mobilization that were operationally ready and not already force-listed for
1003 was a challenge, because any units not so obligated were only at
an authorized level of organization of two or higher. This meant that
they were not readily deployable. SOSCOM finally compiled an ad hoc
unit. The 1103rd Support Battalion (Corps) of the 167th Theater Support Command, from Eufaula, Alabama, furnished a headquarters,
and the balance of the company consisted of the 1157th Transportation Company from Oshkosh, Wisconsin; the 812th Quartermaster
Company, from Harlingen, Texas; the 777th Direct Support Maintenance Company from Nashville, Tennessee; and the 261st Ordnance
Detachment from Cross Lanes, West Virginia. C Battery, 3rd Battalion, 115th Field Artillery from Memphis, Tennessee, furnished a security element. The addition of Guardsmen (and women) and Reservists
to the 528th enabled the battalion to fulfill all of its support obligations around the world.[39]

Equipping the Force

One of the bigger challenges ARSOF had to face while preparing for
Operation IRAQI FREEDOM was the matter of equipment. Operation
ENDURING FREEDOM took its toll on active-duty units, as had decades
of underfunding for Army Reserve and Army National Guard units.
USSOCOM and USASOC had to carefully manage materiel resources
in order to keep the force protected and safe. Not only did damaged
and worn-out items need to be replaced, but updated equipment also
needed to be issued to Reserve and Guard units to bring them up to
operational standards. The harsh environments of Uzbekistan and
Afghanistan had been especially hard on communications and computer systems, whose components were degraded by sandstorms and
ever-present grit. Because Army National Guard Special Forces teams
and Army Reserve Civil Affairs and PSYOP elements were tasked with
active-Army SOF missions, they had to be equipped with compatible
radio suites, computers, reinforced vehicles, and heavy crew–served
weapons. And all that took money.

U.S. Special Operations Command

Lieutenant General Bryan Brown confronted budget difficulties when he transferred to USSOCOM after relinquishing command of USASOC. He recalled:

> *When I walked in as the new deputy on 12 September 2002, I was informed that USSOCOM had to brief a [Program Integration Decision Memorandum] the next day in Washington on future SOF growth and additional money needed to fight [the Global War on Terrorism]. Quite frankly, USSOCOM did not have a plan for either. Those big, strategic, operational documents take time to produce and the constantly moving [budget] process does not give you that time. Without those long-range operational plans, we had little to base our funding on. We had to make it up on the fly, and quite frankly, I wasn't sure at the time that we got it right. After that humbling experience in Washington, it was painful for the directors, but the USSOCOM staff got their act together, believe me.* [40]

So did its subordinate units and commands.

U.S. Army Special Operations Command

General Brown was the commander of USASOC until September 2002, and had personally worked to gain increased funding from USSOCOM in order to properly equip ARSOF troops. Brown also managed to convince the Army to adjust its equipment fielding priorities to support the large SOF role in 1003v. "Resourcing had always been the hardest nut for USASOC to crack," commented Brown. He continued,

> *The Army SOF component of USSOCOM had not been getting its fair share of the money from the several large Congressional GWOT [Global War on Terrorism] funding plus-ups. We received [only] $31 million dollars out of the first $323 million dollar 'slug' accorded USSOCOM, and we had the preponderance of the special ops force. With supporting data in hand, I flew to Tampa to meet with General Charles Holland, Lieutenant General William Tangney, Major General Eldon Bargewell, and Brigadier General Jim Parker. I told them, 'You guys have got to do better.' In the next 'slug' of money USASOC got $61 million. And that helped, but it was still not a fair share for the SOF component that had the largest number of people in combat and preparing to go again. We kept the Army informed. It was a struggle, but with the Army monitoring, USSOCOM began to*

Figure 3.26 General Bryan Brown.

support USASOC properly. After that episode, the command was well resourced.[41]

160TH SPECIAL OPERATIONS AVIATION REGIMENT

USASOC Deputy Commanding General Brigadier General Howard Yellen was charged with overseeing the 160th Special Operations Aviation Regiment, the 75th Ranger Regiment, and the Special Operations Support Command. This responsibility included oversight of the Title 50 funding used to support unconventional warfare missions. He had to intensely manage the existing ARSOF helicopter fleet, watch organizational growth, and find funding for aviation research and development. Yellen also had to find money for annual maintenance inspections that needed to be done ahead of schedule due to high combat flying hours.

Figure 3.27 Brigadier General Howard Yellen.

The highest unexpected expense was the replacement of helicopters lost or seriously damaged in combat or accidents. Operation ENDURING FREEDOM missions in Afghanistan and the Philippines took their toll on scarce helicopter assets. Both replacement and repair required valuable time and constant reprioritization—and some "appetite suppression," as SOAR commander Colonel Richard Polczynski commented.[42]

The two MH-47E Chinooks recovered after Operation ANACONDA in Afghanistan underwent detailed battle damage assessments, and the findings prompted modifications to MH-47G replacement aircraft on the Sikorsky assembly line. Fortunately, "the structural design strengths of the MH-47E enabled the Night Stalker maintenance teams at Fort Campbell [Kentucky] to rebuild one of the two helicopters shot down on Takur Ghar virtually from the ground up. Even this former 160th SOAR commander was truly amazed by that effort," said Yellen.[43]

Figure 3.28 160th SOAR insignia.

Polczynski was acutely aware of close air support fratricide incidents involving Air Force aircraft in Afghanistan. While no lives were lost, one of the ARSOF MH-47Es shot-down on Takur Ghar was destroyed by the Air Force in a coordinated action with USSOCOM. Although the Night Stalkers of the 160th SOAR already provided very close-in close air support with their attack helicopters, Polczynski proposed replacing some of the Air Force support with more specialized SOAR aircraft. General Brown, a former commander of the SOAR himself, authorized "test-configuring" several of the 3rd Battalion's MH-60L Black Hawks as Defensive Armed Penetrator helicopters. Polczynski was given permission to test four aircraft using "strap-on/strap-off" weapons systems from the operational 30mm chain gun and 2.75 inch rocket pod spares. The testing and training was accomplished with spare SOAR resources and personnel, without compromise to the regiment's ongoing mission requirements.[44]

5th Special Forces Group

When the 5th SFG turned responsibility for Afghanistan over to the 3rd SFG, it left most of its equipment behind for the new element, which meant the 5th SFG had to scramble to reequip itself before deploying for IRAQI FREEDOM. Colonel Patrick Higgins, the SOCCENT operations officer stated

> *5th Group had to be refitted. Almost all of their vehicles, communications, and heavy weapons had been left behind for CJSOTF-Afghanistan. Refit costs that amounted to almost $300 million dollars resulted in major fund reprioritizations at Fort Bragg and Tampa. Time became the 'enemy of preparedness.' Equipment—radios, computers, weapons, and vehicles—had to be procured and fielded in time to allow the 5th Group soldiers to train with it before going into combat again. Thus, the money flow—slow or fast—impacted operational readiness for combat.*[45]

Beyond team equipment, the 5th SFG needed additional headquarters equipment in order to function as CJSOTF-west. Mulholland remembered

> *One of the 'hard sells' to [Special Forces] Command and USASOC was the need to buy the tentage and equipment necessary to establish a JSOTF headquarters overseas in a bare base environment. What I learned from [ENDURING FREEDOM] was that there is a geometry component in how to set up a joint operations center. An asymmetrical layout to access key personnel quickly was critical. The linear layout at K2 [Karshi Kanabad, Uzbekistan] (that we euphemistically called 'the worm') proved to be a nightmare at times. The individual you needed to talk to at a critical moment always seemed to be at the extreme end of the worm. We basically needed what Colonel Mark Phelan, 3rd SFG commander, had available to establish CJSOTF-Afghanistan in Bagram. An SFOB [Special Forces Operating Base] simply does not have the equipment necessary to accommodate the exponential expansion of the staff necessary to operate as a CJSOTF.*[46]

In addition to being fielded with new Ground Mobility Vehicles, the vehicles had to be modified to the Special Forces model approved by USSOCOM. Anticipating that one of the 5th SFG battalions would be used to locate and counter the SCUD missile threat in the western desert of Iraq, the battalion needed to be fully mobile and organized into

Figure 3.29 Special Forces model GMV.

company-sized forces. Two companies in 1st Battalion were already so organized and had fought as mobile units before, so 1st Battalion received the mission. Mulholland's intent to organize the other battalions like the 1st Battalion was precluded by the unavailability of GMVs, and the time required to modify the vehicles they did have. Adjusting to these and other factors, Mulholland gave the 1st Battalion the priority for GMVs and internally reassigned personnel to give it three full-strength Special Forces mobility companies to fulfill the western desert requirement. Because unconventional warfare would be the principal mission of the other two battalions, they would use nonstandard tactical vehicles—Toyota pickup trucks carrying a variety of crew-served weapons that could be loaded into the 160th SOAR MH-47D Chinooks. Both vehicle types performed well in Iraq.

Training the Force

Once the force was organized, mobilized, and equipped, all that was left was to train it. This last stage of preparation, which actually took place concurrently with the other three, was vital to ARSOF's success in Operation IRAQI FREEDOM. Army SOF units participated in a number of training exercises in 2002 and early 2003, which enabled commanders and individuals to enhance the force's readiness beyond what could be achieved through routine training methods.

MILLENNIUM CHALLENGE

The biennial U.S. Joint Forces Command experiment Millennium Challenge was conducted from 24 July–15 August 2002, and included all military services and combatant commands. As intended, Millennium Challenge was a critical building block in the U.S. military's transformation to joint operations. Using a combination of computer simulations and live field exercises, the participating elements played out a scenario based on a hypothetical high-end, small-scale contingency that had the potential to escalate to a major theater war. In the course of Millennium Challenge, ARSOF staffs and units were able to achieve joint training goals and increase their probability of success.

Figure 3.30 Millennium Challenge 2002 logo.

A key part of Millennium Challenge was the concurrent Joint Expeditionary Force Exercise (JEFX) held at Nellis Air Force Base. U.S. and Allied air components provided aviation assets, and teams from the 5th SFG, the 75th Ranger Regiment Fires Support Element, as well as British and Australian ground teams provided ground assets. Working together over the course of three weeks, the JEFX participants worked out critical new protocols and systems for coordinating air and ground operations.[47]

Much to the ground forces' astonishment, the JEFX revolved around a complicated "spiral development" cycle involving sophisticated computer modeling and rapid decision cycles. Hundreds of simulations and several live-flying exercises tested newer technologies to improve battle management. Chief among the improvements was better connectivity among the services and the development of a common operating picture. "It was really much more about integrating systems to provide better command and control capability for operators who need to make real-time combat decisions," said Colonel Kevin Erikson of the U.S. Air Force Electronic Systems Center. "We worked hand-in-hand with operators to develop and refine systems and human procedures."[48]

Figure 3.31 Aircraft at Nellis Air Force Base during Millennium Challenge 2002..

As each iteration of the experiment was completed, the participants evaluated the results and developed solutions and improvements to any problems they encountered. In a feat of instant feedback, the next iteration incorporated the changes, which were then tested. Air Force Lieutenant Colonel Tracy Tynan, JEFX 02 program manager, said: "The uniqueness of the 'spiral' approach is that you have total involvement with the warfighters from the very first step in the process through to the experiment and live exercise. And, since no segment or system is tested in a vacuum, the JEFX team can see the effect one segment might have on another and look for any interoperability problems."[49]

Because Millennium Challenge could transform joint war fighting doctrine based on lessons from ENDURING FREEDOM, and promised to standardize and upgrade command and control communications suites with the latest advances in technology, the ARSOF community had great expectations for the exercise. In addition to addressing air coordination issues, SOCJFCOM would use Millennium Challenge to train and validate the capability of the 20th SFG headquarters to serve as the JSOTF in Afghanistan.

SPECIAL OPERATIONS COMMAND CENTRAL

While SOCCENT worked to develop a supporting SOF campaign for 1003V, every command involved tailored training according to specific mission requirements and operational needs. With almost a completely new staff, General Harrell thought that a "crawl, walk, run" methodology was the best approach to training. Soccent staff elements oriented and trained new personnel at the same time as they were writing their sections of the sof campaign plan. While difficult, the dual effort proved good for team building and acclimated soccent personnel to the staff effort necessary to sustain around-the-clock combat operations. The jsotf staff training conducted by soccent was augmented by training conducted by socjfcom.[50]

Special Operations Command Joint Forces Command

Figure 3.32 SOCJF-COM logo.

Colonel Higgins gave socjfcom's Colonel Mike Findlay the soccent staff augmentation priorities: the 5th sfg, then the 10th sfg, and no augmentees to the Naval Special Warfare Group 2. While socjfcom had provided experienced joint staff officers to augment Mulholland's jsotf staff in Afghanistan, most of those officers had moved on by the summer of 2002. With the 5th sfg slated to run cjsotf-west for iraqi freedom, Mulholland needed experienced personnel. socjfcom provided a number of senior joint staff officers to serve as core staff of cjsotf-west, and trained and mentored the rest. When it became evident that the 10th sfg was not going to get experienced joint staff augmentees from usasoc or ussocom, Findlay also sent five socjfcom staff officers to fill out Cleveland's cjsotf-north staff.[51]

Personnel rotations and new replacements with minimal joint staff experience meant considerable training as soccent prepared for war. "Trying to train-up the soccent, 5th sfg, 10th sfg, and Naval Special Warfare Group 2 staffs on joint warfare planning, coordination, and operations before all joint manning documents were filled was really tough," said Dave Stephenson, deputy director of the Joint Special Operations Forces Training Center at socjfcom. "Some Reserve augmentees initially felt like second-class citizens. Some had to become joint staff officers in the crucible of fire. It took several iterations to train most of the staffs. Our teams did not get to everyone because there was simply too much going on, considering that staff principals were regularly overseas or in Tampa and Fort Bragg for planning sessions."[52]

Rangers

Figure 3.33 75th Ranger Regiment scroll shoulder patch.

The Rangers focused the majority of their training on maintaining the skills responsible for their reputation as the best light infantry in the world. Battalion rotations to the Joint Readiness Training Center at Fort Polk, Louisiana, and the National Training Center at Fort Irwin, California, provided opportunities to rehearse appropriate tactics, techniques, and procedures developed during enduring

FREEDOM. "We practiced 'jumping' [moving forward] and splitting the regimental and battalion TOCs [tactical operations centers] and forming small, mobile command and control cells to direct multiple missions simultaneously," explained Colonel Joseph Votel, the 75th Ranger Regiment commander.

5th Special Forces Group

In addition to obtaining the proper equipment for its unconventional warfare missions, the 5th SFG concentrated on desert training. Colonel John Mulholland explained,

Figure 3.34 5th SFG beret flash.

> Desert training was no problem for the 1st Battalion, because it was scheduled for [Exercise] Early Victor in Jordan, a [joint combined training exercise] that SOCCENT had allocated to 5th Group for many years. This would enable them to deploy overseas competent in mobile desert operations and proficient with their new equipment and [tactics, techniques, and procedures]. It also supported the CENTCOM plan to use established regional exercises to get forces forward deployed in theater. The 2nd Battalion trained one company at a time at Fort Bliss, Texas, using an established 5th SFG desert site. The 3rd Battalion got the short end of the stick, with just small elements making it to Fort Bliss because time was eating us up.[53]

When Early Victor was extended, the CJSOTF-west commander pre-positioned more of the 5th SFG's equipment forward into the Middle East.

Mulholland sent staff observers to Millennium Challenge, but his principal interest was the JEFX at Nellis Air Force Base. Close air support to counter SCUDs was an integral part of the CFLCC joint fires plan for Iraq, and CJSOTF-west had the ground mission. On Mulholland's initiative, Lieutenant Colonel Robert Green of SOCJFCOM was fire support liaison between the 9th Air Force and CJSOTF-west, and arranged a series of joint close air support simulations followed by live exercises at Nellis to develop joint fire protocols acceptable to both the pilots delivering ordnance and the ground combatants calling it in. Colonel Cliff Franklin, the designated Coalition Forces Air Component Command "SCUD czar," had worked with Green to build and execute three "live fly" exercises based on the computer simulations ("chair flys") to validate the TTPs (tactics, techniques, and procedures). The TTPs would be used to open and shut close air support "kill boxes" throughout Iraq. The country had been divided into grid squares, which were then designated open or closed to air strikes. The TTPs had to be developed and validated "from the bottom up"—by the 5th SFG operational detachment alphas calling for tactical air strikes and

Figure 3.35 9th Air Force shoulder patch.

pilots conducting the close air support. The objective was to develop TTPs that both ground and air parties could live with on the battle-field. "We got the practical part down fast. The toughest part was cus-tomizing computer programs that opened and closed the 'kill boxes.' The technology kicked our butt," recalled Mulholland.[54]

10th Special Forces Group

Figure 3.36 10th SFG beret flash.

Colonel Charles Cleveland prepared somewhat differently than did Mulholland. While 1003V assumed forward basing in Turkey for CJSOTF-North and the 4th Infantry Division (Mechanized), the lack of a firm commitment left Cleveland "straddling the EUCOM and CENTCOM fence." Furthermore, in spite of the fact that the 10th SFG was slated to support the 4th Infantry Division in northern Iraq, III Corps did not send its tactical air control party to any of the exercises held at Nellis Air Force Base. Without teams with which to rehearse joint fire support procedures, Cleveland had his two U.S.-based bat-talion commanders exercise their forward operationing bases, refine operating procedures, and finalize their plans in the South Post area of Fort Carson, Colorado. He also sent observers to Nellis for the JEFX, but they could not directly participate.

Cleveland was initially an observer at Millennium Challenge, but after watching SOCJFCOM operate as a JSOTF for the 20th SFG for sev-eral days, he called Fort Carson to send the 10th SFG staff principals and/or deputies to Norfolk to "right seat" the JSOTF trainers. They needed to capitalize on the joint staff expertise, learn critical battle space management architecture and integration, effect technology transfers, and copy the joint operations center model communica-tions layout. It was "worlds different" from the hybrid joint operations center used for Exercise Flintlock Reborn in Stuttgart in April 2002. The group's timing was ideal, the training worked well, and afterward some of these SOCJFCOM staff officers filled key positions in CJSOTF-North.[55]

After Millennium Challenge, SOCJFCOM attached Air Force Lieu-tenant Colonel Paul Wida to CJSOTF-North. He explained the joint fires problem quite succinctly:

> *Task Force Viking, like the rest of SOF, had no organic assigned targeting capability like most conventional ground forces. In Afghanistan, Air Force strategic air assets had been routinely used by SOF for close air support. Only ABCCC [airborne command, control, and communications] aircraft possessed the authority to divert tactical air. That authority went away when the ABCCC departed the battle area. Most senior SOF commanders do not know the tacti-cal and strategic weapon capabilities. Thus, it was difficult*

to set priorities by munitions. Conventional forces had organic [Air Force] tactical air control parties to assist their commanders. While Army field artillerymen assigned to the [joint fires element] could help with deconfliction and coordination measures, ad hoc [tactical air control parties] had to be fielded to provide the necessary expertise."[56]

20th Special Forces Group

Colonel Michael Findlay served as the commander of the JSOTF that SOCJFCOM operated for Millennium Challenge. He provided this perspective:

I chose not to train the 20th SFG as a JSOTF during [Millennium Challenge] 02, but to exercise them as the [Army special operations task force] because it was a huge [Department of Defense] experiment . . . 20th SFG did not need the added pressure. As an [Army special operations task force], the headquarters would be faced with many of the same challenges that a JSOTF had to deal with—battle space geometry, command and control relationships, collaborative tools, information sharing, intelligence integration, etcetera.

Figure 3.37 Colonel Michael Findlay.

The SOCJFCOM motto for Millennium Challenge was, "Practice what we preach," stated Findlay. "We were going to practice information sharing, integration, collaboration, and supported-supporting relationships and see how they worked in the highest [operational tempo] environment that we could create."[57]

Set up less than half a mile away, the 20th SFG's Colonel James Champion and his staff had open access to the JSOTF. Findlay reported,

They organized their TOC [tactical operations center] for real—using all the collaborative tools, built their web page, incorporated Blue Force Tracking, and their ODAs [operational detachment alphas] used UAVs [unmanned aerial vehicles] at Tonopah Proving Grounds, Nevada. The 20th SFG's staff received a good process focus—command and control, and headquarters functions, like monitoring, assessing, planning, and directing—on how to run joint operations; the purpose for and the writing of staff [standing operating procedures]; and learned the mechanics through mentorship.

Figure 3.38 20th SFG beret flash.

SOCJFCOM did its best to replicate real-world circumstances, "However, having to work within a rapid decision cycle, and integrating with service partners in a computer simulation experiment did not induce risk nor real stress." commented Findlay.[58]

Figure 3.39 7th SFG beret flash.

After the conclusion of Millennium Challenge, USASOC and USASFC agreed that the 20th SFG was capable of operating as the CJSOTF-Afghanistan starting in September 2002. General Lambert explained, "Since two of the 20th SFG battalions were approaching the end of their federal mobilization, it was decided that the 2nd Battalion, 7th SFG, would 'balance' the [National Guard Special Forces] battalion. It would be the first time that an Army National Guard SFG would have operational control of an active duty [Special Forces] battalion while supporting an Army corps headquarters in combat."[59]

3rd Special Forces Group

Figure 3.40 3rd SFG beret flash.

When the 20th SFG assumed the CJSOTF-Afghanistan mission from the 3rd SFG shortly after the end of Millennium Challenge, this gave the 3rd SFG commander Colonel Joseph Celeski the opportunity to focus on preparing the 3rd Battalion for its mission with the 10th SFG in northern Iraq. Celeski assumed that because the 3rd Battalion mobile force would require a large portion of the 10th SFG airlift to get into theater, it would be among the last going; he made sure that the battalion made maximum use of the available training time. Celeski exercised Forward Operating Base 33 at Camp Pickett, Virginia, which was the same training site used by the 3rd SFG to prepare for Afghanistan. The battalion also rehearsed close air support coordination with Navy and Marine air wings at Tonopah Proving Grounds, Nevada.[60]

Army Civil Affairs & Psychological Operations Command

SOCOM, USASOC, and USACAPOC efforts to have Joint Forces Command include Phase IV post-conflict military scenarios in Millennium Challenge failed. "Our requests never got above the two-star level at JFCOM," said General Lambert. In a last effort to prompt some interest, General Altshuler loaded a cross-section of his staff in rented nine-passenger vans, and went to Norfolk. That ploy elicited less than a half-day of civil military exercise play, the normal amount of time dedicated at the National Training Center and the Joint Readiness Training Center.[61]

U.S. Army John F. Kennedy Special Warfare Center & School

SWCS attacked the problems with close air support in Afghanistan as a training need. Based on the Nellis Air Force Base JEFX, SWCS created a special operations tactical air control course at Yuma Proving Ground, Arizona, to provide Special Forces teams close air support training and regular interaction with Air Force tactical air control parties, enlisted tactical air controllers, and field artillery fire support teams. This enabled all elements involved to become familiar with each other's capabilities and limitations. The Special Forces teams worked with simulators first, then advanced to live close air support missions using the latest state-of-the-art optics and technology. Special Forces teams also learned to check Air Force proficiency just as they did one another on cross-trained skills.[62]

Figure 3.41 SOTAC. *The Special Operations Terminal Air Comtronller's Course was used early in the Global War on Terrorism. These Special Forces soldiers are conducting operations in Afghanistan.*

INTERNAL LOOK

Central Command conducted the second and final major joint exercise during the preparation phase of IRAQI FREEDOM in late 2002. Internal Look 2002 was a biennial Joint Chiefs of Staff–sponsored, computer-based command post exercise based on a contingency plan. It was focused on joint battle staff war fighting at the strategic and operational level, and was designed to exercise the CENTCOM battle staff abilities to command, control, and communicate from a forward-based location in the theater while maintaining seamless connectivity with main headquarters in Tampa. Joint staff battle procedures to be rehearsed included the latest command and control technology and operational concepts that had been validated during Millennium Challenge.[63]

Internal Look 2002 had several phases. Deployment of the CENTCOM portable operations center to As Sayliyah Military Base near Doha, Qatar, constituted phase one of the exercise, and was completed in November. Staff mentoring and joint mission essential task list development during the refinement of 1003V had been phase two of the joint staff training. The final phase would be accomplished in Qatar in late November–early December 2002 before and during Internal Look 02. Caught up in the scramble to get ready for the exercise, SOCJFCOM worked closely with SOC-CENT staff officers.

Since General Harrell intended to fight Operation IRAQI FREEDOM in theater—specifically in Qatar—the SOCCENT headquarters

Figure 3.42 Internal Look 2002. *Internal Look 02 validated the CENTCOM portable operations center in Qatar.*

needed time to build necessary infrastructure to accommodate the expanded joint operations center command and control nodes. The staff elements also needed time to physically set up and get organized. It was a scramble for everyone.

Numerous steps had to be accomplished before the multiple echelon staffs could begin exercising various planning options via computers. "While this might appear mundane, these parts were critical to headquarters preparing to fight a war. And these things had to done while newly activated individual Reservists from all services were arriving overseas to fill joint wartime staff positions in SOCCENT and the other headquarters," said Colonel Higgins. The physical set up and staff arrangement in multiple joint operations centers and establishing network connectivity and software installation to accommodate the improved command and control technology proved more demanding than anticipated by all echelons.[64]

While the numerous staffs scrambled to become operational, the CENTCOM component commanders had the opportunity for mentorship. General Franks invited numerous retired generals with considerable joint operations experience to spend "quality time" with his commanders as part of Internal Look. Seasoned commanders representing all services attended, and some remained through the coming war with Iraq. General Gary Luck, a former commander of USASOC, the commander of XVIII Airborne Corps during DESERT STORM, and the commander of the United Nations Command, Korea and Eighth Army, headed the mentor team. General Peter Schoomaker, another former USASOC and USSOCOM commander, and the current Chief of Staff of the Army accompanied General Luck. General Harrell later recalled, "Internal Look gave me some real quality time to discuss SOF tactics, techniques, and procedures, my 1003V campaign plan, the importance of setting conditions, mission-type orders, and risk levels with my personal mentor, General Pete Schoomaker. And I had the chance to talk through many of what I thought would be tough issues in the west, north, and south with both him and General Luck. That was great."[65]

Numerous lessons from Operation ENDURING FREEDOM and Millennium Challenge were incorporated in Internal Look 02. Command and control and the employment of SOF would follow joint doctrine in Operation IRAQI FREEDOM, and Coalition Forces Special Operations Component Command (SOCCENT became CFSOCC during IRAQI FREEDOM) would be responsible for conventional SOF in theater. Unfortunately, not all command and control inefficiencies were ironed out. After the exercises, CFSOCC had a better information management plan. CFSOCC's joint fires element was integrated in the joint air component element and a relationship established with the joint forces air component. Differences between joint operating areas and joint special operations areas in the battle area of operations had also been clarified and acknowledged by all parties. In spite of all that coordination, final decision authority for air missions requested by the SOF teams still rested with the joint special operations air component commander instead of the commander of CFSOCC. This arrangement cut CFSOCC out of the appeal loop and plagued the CJSOTF-west commander throughout the war.[66]

When CFSOCC built its ground operations plans, Coalition Forces Air Component Command graphics for close air support were used. Joint special operations areas conformed exactly to the "kill boxes" that CFACC had established, because the CFSOCC mission was to support CFACC and CFLCC—in the traditional SOF force multiplier role. The only exception was unconventional warfare because that spanned the entire area of operations and the CJSOTFs controlled those efforts. Since the JSOAS were in CFLCC maneuver space, "no fire zones" and other protective restrictions were placed around SOF elements, as coordinated during Millennium Challenge.[67]

Figure 3.43 CF-SOCC logo.

ARSOF commanders who attended Internal Look benefited from the staff coordination. Colonel Mulholland (CJSOTF-west), Colonel Votel (Rangers), Colonel Polczynski (160th SOAR), and Colonel Leonard (SOSCOM) all worked through the scenario and solidified plans. Absent from Internal Look was Colonel Cleveland, who had been called to participate in the negotiations with the Turks. CJSOTF-North critically needed an in-theater forward base to pre-position its forces, and a destination for the Air Force planners trying to finalize airflow arrangements.

In Colonel Findlay's words,

> *Internal Look proved to be a good workout for the component commands and established the war fighting roles of [c]FSOCC and the two JSOTF commanders. Collaboration worked among the senior commanders, but immaturity of the staffs caused problems. It seems that collaboration improves the higher one goes; the further down the echelons that one moves, the more that principals and staff officers resort to e-mail, liaison officers, printed orders, policies, etcetera.*[68]

Millennium Challenge and Internal Look contributed significantly to ARSOF preparations. SOCJFCOM joint staff training and validation of the 20th SFG headquarters was vital to aligning Special Forces requirements worldwide. The 10th SFG and 75th Ranger Regiment staffs received quality joint staff training and acquired the latest technology upgrades from SOCJFCOM while the latter functioned as the JSOTF for the 20th SFG. The joint fires simulations and live exercises of JEFX 02 enabled the 5th SFG, the Rangers, and the British and Australian contingents to solve the fratricide problems of Afghanistan, and

provided the joint fires protocols that promoted success during IRAQI
FREEDOM. Internal Look "shook down" the major command battle
staffs and established confidence in the command, control, and communications networks. Having seasoned general officers as mentors
available to service component commanders and senior staff officers
proved very insightful on the part of General Tommy Franks. The
major shortfalls of both joint exercises were the lack of strategic and
operational Civil Affairs guidance to make up for the absence of exercise scenarios beyond Phase III.

While the preparation phase of Operation IRAQI FREEDOM was one
of competing requirements and overlapping commitments, ARSOF
commanders and units worked through the challenges and produced
a strong, capable force. When it came time to deploy into theater and
stage for combat operations, ARSOF was not only willing, but was also
ready to go to war against Iraq. Only the execute order remained.

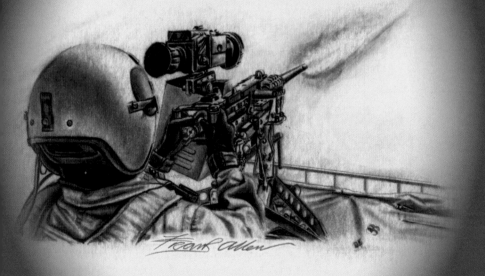

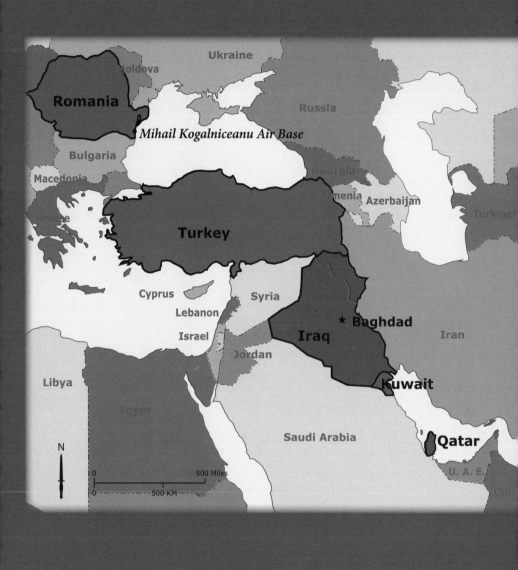

Chapter Four

Staging for War

*F*OR THE ARMY SPECIAL Operations Forces, the pending war with Iraq fell neatly into three distinct campaigns. In the north, the presence of well-armed and organized Kurdish militias promised to be the key to engaging the Iraqi Army units stationed along the Green Line. Forcing the Iraqi corps in the region to remain in place prevented them from reinforcing the regime forces arrayed around Baghdad. In the western desert region, the likely presence of SCUD missiles with the potential to carry weapons of mass destruction warheads as far as Israel required the presence of ARSOF to seek out and neutralize the weapons. In the south, the drive of the conventional ground forces toward Baghdad required ARSOF support in the form of special reconnaissance and liaison teams. These three primary missions and a host of others dictated the configuration of the ARSOF elements as they prepared for Operation IRAQI FREEDOM.

Green Line *The Green Line represents the ad hoc political boundary established between the traditional Kurdish strongholds and Saddam's Iraq in the northeastern part of the country. Since 1991, the Kurds patrolled the Green Line which corresponded to the boundaries of the provinces the Iraqi army had left at the end of the Gulf War.*

THE FORCE

When General Tommy Franks had his final prewar meeting with President George W. Bush and the National Security Council on 5 March 2003, over 200,000 troops were already in the Persian Gulf. That number grew to 292,000 Coalition forces by the third week

Figure 4.1 General Tommy Franks. *The CENTCOM commander orchestrated the campaign to topple the Hussein regime.*

of March—more than enough for Franks' Hybrid plan. The only part of Plan 1003V not yet in place was the invasion from the north. Turkey refused to allow the 4th Infantry Division to transit its country to invade Iraq, leaving more than 15,000 troops with no place to go.[1]

By March, Franks and the Central Command planners had worked for over a year on the timing of the Hybrid variant. Although forces flowed into theater at only half the rate required for Generated Start, CENTCOM planners and combatant commanders managed to plan an attack more akin to Running Start: air, ground, and special operations forces were to begin operations almost simultaneously, with just forty-eight hours of notice. That notice came on 17 March, when President Bush issued Saddam Hussein and his sons an ultimatum: leave Iraq within forty-eight hours, or Coalition forces would attack.[2]

The President's ultimatum was CENTCOM's cue to move from Phase I to Phase II and then rapidly into Phase III. Almost 300,000 Coalition soldiers, sailors, airmen, and Marines from twenty-three nations were poised to quickly and decisively dismantle Saddam Hussein's regime. Just as Franks and his team had conceived more than twelve months previously, the ground and air wars would begin within hours of each other. And as Franks envisioned in his five-fronts concept, SOF would play a key role in all phases.

CFLCC

The forces arrayed for Operation IRAQI FREEDOM were divided into three component commands. Coalition Forces Land Component Command was the single largest element of the Coalition force. U.S. Third Army's Lieutenant General David McKiernan was chosen to be the CFLCC commander, with responsibility for 170,000 ground forces. CFLCC's major subordinate elements were the V Corps and the I Marine Expeditionary Force. Lieutenant General William Wallace commanded the V Corps which was composed of the 3rd Infantry Division, the 101st Airborne Division (Air Assault), the 2nd Brigade of the 82nd Airborne Division, and eventually the 4th Infantry Division, which was still awaiting permission to land in Turkey. In turn,

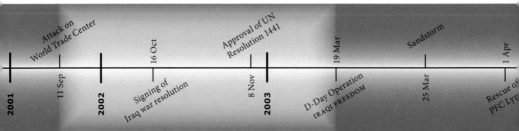

I MEF under Lieutenant General James Conway fielded the 1st Marine Division, the 3rd Marine Aircraft Wing, and the British 1st Armoured Division. Also under I MEF control was Task Force Tarawa, consisting of one Marine infantry regiment and two Marine Expeditionary Units, a total of five infantry battalions, and two companies of Abrams tanks. CFLCC was primarily responsible for the ground invasion from Kuwait and the main push northward to Baghdad.

CFACC

Lieutenant General T. Michael "Buzz" Moseley commanded the Coalition Forces Air Component Command. His available forces were based at friendly regional air bases and on aircraft carriers in the Persian Gulf and Mediterranean Sea: three Air Force Expeditionary Wings and five Naval Air Wings. CFACC was responsible for air operations throughout the country of Iraq, but time-distance factors initially limited most missions to the southern and western portions of the country, the latter being its official area of responsibility. CFACC provided critical air support to all ground forces in addition to maintaining an aggressive bombing campaign against key regime targets.

CFSOCC

Brigadier General Gary Harrell commanded Coalition Forces Special Operations Component Command. CFSOCC—essentially Special Operations Command Central after SOCCENT arrived in theater—established three regional task forces. Those units assigned to the western desert fell under Combined Joint Special Operations Task Force–West, also known as Task Force Dagger. Task Force Dagger was made up of the 5th Special Forces Group, Coalition SOF teams, and a company from the 19th SFG. The 75th Ranger Regiment, a quick reaction force from the 82nd Airborne Division, and one High Mobility Artillery Rocket System battery composed Task Force 20, another SOF task force assigned to the west and the south. The second SOF task force was the Naval Task Force, which included Polish commandos and U.S. Navy SEALS.

The third SOF task force was CJSOTF-North, or Task Force Viking, which consisted primarily of the 10th SFG. The original mission of Task Force Viking was to conduct unconventional warfare operations in support of the 4th Infantry Division invasion from Turkey. When it became clear that permission for the transit would be denied,

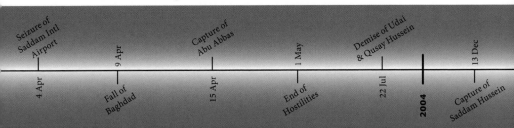

Figure 4.2 SCUD missile on launcher. *Intermediate range missiles such as this were the prime targets of Task Force Dagger in the western desert. The threat of a strike against Israel drove the mission.*

CJSOTF-North transitioned from being a supporting element to being the supported command. Without a strong infantry presence in the north, it fell to the 10th SFG to organize the Kurdish peshmerga and keep thirteen Iraqi infantry and armored divisions north of Baghdad busy. The 173rd Airborne Brigade (-), originally slated to support the 4th ID, was quickly offered to CJSOTF-North as an alternate infantry presence. The brigade (-) jumped into Bashur Airfield a week after D-DAY. The drop zone was guarded by 3,000 peshmerga under Brigadier General James Parker's direct control when the 173rd jumped in.

EVENTS

Army special operations forces units and headquarters faced a myriad of tasks in the weeks prior to the start of the campaign. Every conceivable contingency received the attention of the staffs, with issues such as the handling of embedded media and defining the rules of engagement occupying specialized staff elements. Issues of preparedness and troop positioning were handled at all levels—from Special Forces teams on up to the U.S. Army Special Operations Command. The stories and essays that follow highlight various aspects of ARSOF activities in the period immediately preceding Operation IRAQI FREEDOM. The account is not meant to be comprehensive; rather, the units and accomplishments represent those of the entire ARSOF community.

RULES OF THE GAME

As U.S. forces prepared for combat in Iraq, the discussion of the fundamental rules of the game—the Rules of Engagement—were widely debated from the highest levels of the government down to the soldiers on the ground. Ultimately, the ROE affected the conduct of combat in the theater and the decisions of the ARSOF troops out on the front lines. For Navy Lieutenant Commander Garth Benson*, the SOCCENT staff judge advocate, the ROE presented a host of legal issues and definitions needing resolution in order to provide the best guidance to the SOF units in the field.

*Pseudonyms have been used for all military personnel with a rank lower than lieutenant colonel.

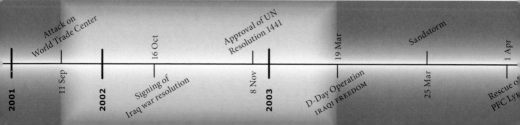

Attack on World Trade Center

11 Sep

2001

2002

Signing of Iraq war resolution

16 Oct

Approval of UN Resolution 1441

8 Nov

2003

D-Day Operation IRAQI FREEDOM

19 Mar

Sandstorm

25 Mar

1 Apr

Rescue o PFC Lyn

In an unconventional warfare scenario, the predominant legal issues generally involve questions pertaining to the funding, equipping, and training of indigenous forces by U.S. troops under Title 10 of the United States Code. While these issues took up a significant portion of Benson's time, the more immediate problems in the buildup to the invasion centered on developing the rules of engagement for the ARSOF units going into combat. From the perspective of a joint headquarters, Benson needed to be sensitive to the different requirements of each of the services in terms of the ROE. For the Army, the ROE generally governed actions at the tactical level—at whom and under what circumstances troops could fire—while the Air Force and the Navy looked at the ROE from a more strategic position, that of servicing deliberately planned targets.[3]

Figure 4.3 Ground forces. *For troops on the ground, the Rules of Engagement determined who was a legitimate target.*

SOCCENT's role in the strategic joint fires arena consisted of the nomination of targets and the calling in of close air support; SOCCENT operated between the strategic and tactical levels with requirements at both. Benson's involvement in the development and dispersion of ROE guidance to the ARSOF elements consisted of an intense scrutiny of the topic and a formulation of working definitions to clarify questions from the field. With fourteen subordinate staff judge advocates at the CJSOTFs and Special Forces forward operating bases, the distribution of information was problematic. Benson had to develop a framework that provided guidance for the units to use as situations arose. In Benson's words, "You can't have a little card covering every contingency. As Brigadier General Harrell said, 'Guys don't have time to read cards in combat.'" They needed a working definition of the ROE.

Benson's most simplistic definition of the ROE was that it "is nothing more than a delegation of authority—who can authorize what. Often, it is a question of whether something is ROE versus TTP [tactics, techniques, and procedures]. ROE is not designed to handle every individual case. What is called ROE is often a TTP; an example is self-defense."

For Benson, this concept crystallized when he attended a briefing given to General Franks on developing the CENTCOM Rules of Engagement guidance for approval by the Joint Staff. In Frank's opin-

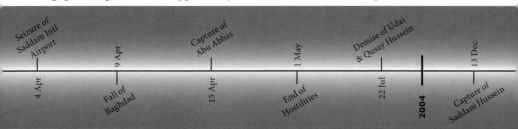

Seizure of
Saddam Intl
Airport

9 Apr

Capture of
Abu Abbas

1 May

Demise of Udai
& Qusay Hussein

13 Dec

4 Apr

Fall of
Baghdad

15 Apr

End of
Hostilities

22 Jul

2004

Capture of
Saddam Hussein

ion, the working ROE was: 1) Kill the enemy, 2) Protect your friends, 3) Do not kill civilians, 4) Avoid collateral damage, and 5) Obtain positive identification before you execute. In essence, this connected the ROE to the mission at every level, and served as the framework that gave ARSOF troops working guidance in their approach to their particular situations. As the campaign unfolded, this concept served the units well in most instances. In many cases, questions from the field were better served with more mission guidance as opposed to a more detailed ROE.

STANDING UP THE CJSOTFs

In the weeks and months preceding the start of Operation IRAQI FREEDOM, planners and commanders worked hard to pre-position SOF troops and equipment. "The 'good news story' for SOF was that the senior military leadership, based on the Afghanistan experience, understood the critical need to get SOF into Iraq early," recalled Colonel Patrick Higgins, the SOCCENT operations officer. While the 5th SFG, as CJSOTF-West, was fortunate in its ability to begin staging in the region as early as the fall of 2001, the 10th SFG, as CJSOTF-North, fell victim to politics and had to scramble to get forces and equipment into theater.[4]

CJSOTF-West

By late 2001, CJSOTF-West was receiving pressure from SOCCENT to finalize its SOF campaign plan. While the mission and commander's guidance from Brigadier General Gary Harrell were very broad. When Exercise Early Victor was extended, the 5th SFG took advantage of the opportunity to pre-position more equipment forward. This enabled the 5th SFG to get forces into position in a timely fashion.[5]

The 5th SFG began deploying advanced echelons of its battalions into forward bases in early January. These advance teams prepared to do bare base construction for three elements—CJSOTF-West and two 5th SFG battalions—major tasks to be performed before the main bodies of troops and equipment arrived in theater. CJSOTF-West also dispatched special operations command and control elements to work with CFLCC headquarters and I MEF.[6]

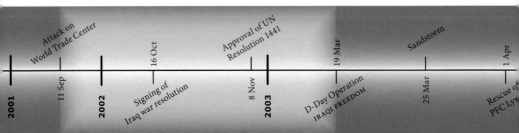

CJSOTF-NORTH

When Colonel Charles Cleveland and a small planning team from
10th SFG went to Europe in November 2002, they found themselves in
the middle of high-level international politics. The Turkish military
was against any large U.S. military presence in its country. Without
a deployment order, but with the concurrence of U.S. Army Special
Forces Command, SOCCENT, and Special Operations Command
Europe, Cleveland moved a planning cell to
Stuttgart, Germany, in the first week of January 2003 so the cell would be in the same time
zone as SOCEUR and closer to Qatar. A make-
shift CJOSTF-North was established before he
departed on a ten-day coordination trip to
Turkey. "When we arrived in Stuttgart, we
discovered that the EUCOM [European Com-
mand] staff was working hard to make [a U.S.
military presence in Turkey] politically pal-
atable. SOF needed forward basing in Turkey
and a line of communication to enter north-

Figure 4.4 Map of Turkey and surrounding area.

ern Iraq," stated Cleveland. But, the ongoing negotiations with the
Turks were shortening the time available to position and prepare
CJSOTF-North forces.[7]

During a second session with a Turkish special operations general
in December 2002, Cleveland roughed out a proposal. It was agreed
that 150-man Kurdish elements could be "security" for CJSOTF-North
forces. In return for Turkish cooperation, CJSOTF-North would not
permit any large Kurdish elements south of the Green Line. The Turks
were concerned about possible Kurdish occupations of Kirkuk and
Mosul, which would give the Kurds effective control of the northern
oil fields. "This simple operational protocol was worked out, one-on-
one, between the Turkish special ops general and me in an unheated
school classroom, in the middle of Turkey, in December," remembered Cleveland.[8]

The concept had already been briefed to the Turkish General Staff.
Cleveland recalled, "They knew up front 90 percent of what we planned
to do. When they demanded that Turkish special forces teams accompany the American [Special Forces teams], I challenged them: 'What
part in killing Iraqis do you, the Turks, want?' They wanted absolutely
no part and backed off immediately. The concession granted was to

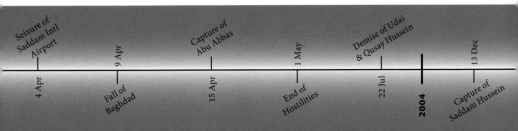

have a Turkish sof element set up outside the cjsotf-North facility, whether it was Diyarbakir or Batman."[9]

The original plan negotiated by Cleveland was for cjsotf-North to base out of Diyarbakir, Turkey. Shortly after the agreement was made, Air Force Colonel O.G. Mannon, the 352nd Special Operations Group commander who doubled as the cjsotf-North deputy commander, flew a small advanced echelon into Diyarbakir aboard two mc-130 aircraft. The Turkish Congress voted in late January 2003 against U.S. basing, and denied permission for military overflights. The eucom staff began to scramble for alternatives. Fortunately, soceur had

Figure 4.5 Joint Operations Center Constanta. *The Joint Operations Center at Task Force Viking was the hub of information flow and decision making for the task force prior to moving into Iraq.*

recently invested $300,000 in an extensive survey of Constanta, Romania, to support a regional sof training exercise. Brigadier General Mike Jones, soceur commander, contacted the Joint Chiefs of Staff to gain permission to approach his Romanian military contacts. When the Romanians responded positively, the eucom staff took over the negotiations. "[Romania] promised 250 percent support including force protection for U.S. forces. Constanta was a resort city on a large lake with plenty of empty hotels during the non-peak tourist season. The Romanian Air Force said that they would make an airfield available and arrange fuel," remembered Jones. Since it had no forward basing site until January 2003, the 10th sfg lost its original position in the airflow "queue." It was not until early February 2003 that the two Colorado-based battalions of the 10th sfg arrived in Constanta.[10]

To accomplish the forward basing mission and unconventional warfare missions involving the Kurds in northern Iraq, soccent and soceur had to get creative. Lieutenant General Colby Broadwater, the nato emissary and lead eucom military negotiator with the Turks, arranged conciliatory talks with the Kurdish elements in northern Iraq. His official negotiating party required a moderately sized personal security detail to provide force protection; soccent tasked the 10th sfg to provide that detail. Cleveland chose Major Paul Robertson*, a mature and experienced Special Forces company commander, to lead the mission. Each 10th sfg battalion commander was told to select his most experienced unconventional warfare personnel, preferably those who had dealt with the Kurds in earlier missions. With

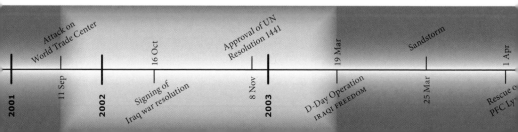

a little luck, this cadre might be left in northern Iraq after the Broadwater mission was completed.

Each vehicle in the negotiating party carried Blue Force Trackers, which enabled CJSOTF-North to track the team's movements. Cleveland said,

> The CJSOTF-North staff in Constanta was glued to the computer screen that monitored the Blue Force Trackers of the [Special Forces] teams with General Broadwater. Turkish border guards [had] required General Broadwater and his entire mission to disembark from their bus while they thoroughly inspected it before entering Iraq. As the party came back to the Habur Gate, Major Robertson's was the only [Special Forces] vehicle accompanying the bus. The rest of his team had been left in the last covered area and were prepared to join him if the Turkish border guards raised any objections. There were some very tense moments as we watched to see what would happen. When the Blue Force Tracker showed that the Broadwater bus was crossing back alone, we held our breaths until Major Robertson rejoined his men. Then, it was like we had won the Super Bowl as everyone cheered.[11]

The "Lost 37," as the Turks referred to them, headed to join the Kurdish units they were assigned to. Shortly afterward, Cleveland managed to get his two battalion commanders with their operations officers into northern Iraq. The night before the ground offensive started, Brigadier General James Parker arrived at Qatar to serve as the SOCCENT deputy commander. He was just in time for the 10th SFG insertion and played a key role in the execution of the insertion and subsequent operations.

173RD AIRBORNE BRIGADE (-)

Before Colonel Cleveland departed Ankara, Turkey, Lieutenant General McKiernan asked him how he would employ the 173rd Airborne Brigade (-) if CJSOTF-North received that asset. Given the nature of the battlefield and CJSOTF mission, Cleveland decided not to use the 173rd in a direct combat tactical role; it would occupy and guard the oil fields of northern Iraq instead.[12]

In late January, the CJSOTF-North operations officer, accompanied by the commanders and operations officers of the 2nd and 3rd Battalions of 10th SFG, went to a planning conference in Italy. "Neither [the

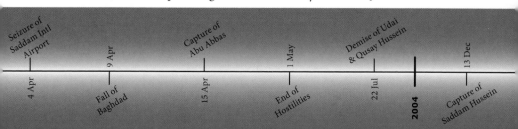

Figure 4.6 C-17s in Aviano, Italy. *The C-17s to carry the 173rd Airborne Brigade (-) into* IRAQI FREEDOM *on the runway in Aviano. The aircraft required to bring them into the battle severely restricted the airflow to support Task Force Viking.*

U.S. Army Southern European Task Force] nor the 173rd Airborne Brigade (-) staff had any idea how large a CJSOTF headquarters was, what its capabilities were, and the joint SOF assets it controlled. The use of a [tactical local area network], web page operations management, and satellite communications were foreign concepts. They envisioned an infantry brigade tactical operations center. Neither understood how the CJSOTF could command and control a conventional force." Interestingly, despite not being force-listed for Plan 1003, the 173rd was included in the time-phased force deployment list. "They knew their airflow and had been planning aircraft loads," recalled Cleveland.[13]

OUT OF TURKEY

Part of the original plan for the invasion of Iraq was for the 10th SFG to stage from Diyarbakir, and drive across the border into northern Iraq ahead of the 4th Infantry Division. Among various other forward elements located in Turkey preparing to execute the plan was a small team from U.S. Army Special Operations Command and Special Operations Support Command. SOSCOM's Lieutenant Colonel Mark Edwards served as the logistics officer for CJSOTF-NORTH, and supervised the support actions in Turkey as part of his duties. However, it was the USASOC contracting officer, Captain Tad Woodcock*, who turned out to be the key man in what became the CJSOTF's saga of nonstandard vehicles.

Even before CJSOTF-NORTH troops deployed to Europe, USASOC support planners had authorized the 10th SFG a fleet of 236 nonstandard vehicles—commercial trucks modified for military use. Beginning in October 2002, Woodcock and Chief Warrant Officer 4 Jose Molinaro* from SOSCOM's 528th Special Operations Support Battalion worked through SOCEUR's logistics officer to draw up the specifications of the fleet. Woodcock was given a preliminary budget of over $5 million to purchase, modify, and transport the vehicles to the 10th SFG at Diyarbakir.[14]

After evaluating various commercial vehicles, Woodcock and Molinaro concluded that Land Rover Defenders best suited the 10th

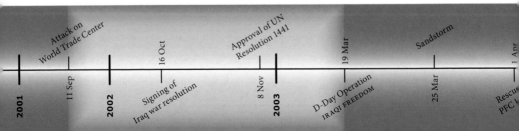

2001   11 Sep — Attack on World Trade Center   2002 — 16 Oct — Signing of Iraq war resolution   Approval of UN Resolution 1441 — 8 Nov   2003 — 19 Mar — D-Day Operation IRAQI FREEDOM — Sandstorm — 25 Mar — 1 Apr Rescu PFC

SFG's needs in northern Iraq. Land Rovers were legendary off-road vehicles common to the area, were already used by special operations forces around the world, and had a solid reputation for reliability. Land Rover also had an assembly plant in Turkey, and Woodcock reasoned that the vehicles would not only be cheaper in Turkey, but also by purchasing them locally, they would avoid having to arrange and pay for shipping.[15]

When Woodcock negotiated with Land Rover Turkey management, the best price Woodcock could get was $36,000 for each vehicle—before modifications. Woodcock had allotted $30,000 per vehicle in order to stay within budget and still have the funds to make the required combat modifications. Wisely declining Land Rover Turkey's offer, Woodcock went in person to the Land Rover factory in Solihull, England, to see if he could negotiate a better deal. Telling the Land Rover salespeople that he was there to purchase replacement vehicles for an operation, Woodcock detailed that the vehicles were to be shipped to a warehouse in Izmir, Turkey, where they would be stored until needed. The prospect of a large order satisfied management, and Woodcock negotiated a factory-direct price of less than $25,000 per Land Rover Defender—including almost all modifications and delivery costs.[16]

Figure 4.7 Land Rover Defender. *The Defender by Land Rover was the nonstandard vehicle of choice for the teams of Task Force Viking working with the Kurdish forces in northern Iraq.*

The purchase deal with Land Rover left Woodcock with enough funds to purchase thirty Toyota Tacoma pickup trucks in Germany and another twenty-five vehicles in Turkey to use around the projected CJSOTF-North headquarters at Diyarbakir. By mid-March, Woodcock had over two hundred vehicles stored in the warehouse he had leased in Izmir. This warehouse became Woodcock's duty station for several weeks, as he and a team of mechanics outfitted the trucks with satellite tracking devices and radio platforms, added bumper numbers to each, and permanently attached extra keys to the dashboards.[17]

As war neared, it became clear that the Turkish government would not allow U.S. forces to use Turkey as a staging area for an attack on Iraq. The Turkish authorities placed Woodcock's warehouse under armed guard and scrutinized everything and everybody going in or coming out. According to Edwards, "The Turkish government had twenty-four hour guards on us. Anything we did with regards to get-

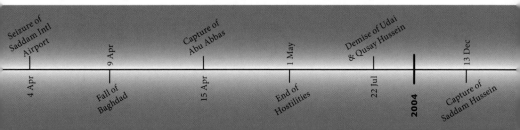

ting mechanics in and out of there was under close scrutiny. In general, anything you wanted to bring into country or wanted to take out of country, you had to account for down to serial number detail. They didn't want to know how many containers you had; they wanted to know what was in each container."[18]

Around the first of March, Woodcock was ordered to make arrangements to get the vehicles out of Turkey as soon as possible. The customs impound restriction was rescinded, but the Turks would not allow the logistics team to drive the vehicles across the border into Kurdish-controlled northern Iraq. Woodcock then set about arranging to ship the vehicles by barge from the port of Marmaris, some three hundred kilometers southeast of Izmir, to a Greek island where they could be transferred to a Greek ferry, taken to the Greek side of the island of Cyprus, and from there flown into Iraq on U.S. aircraft. The plan was solid, as far as transportation logistics went. Unfortunately, this particular plan did not take into account the politics of the situation.[19]

As soon as arrangements were finalized, Woodcock led the first convoy of twenty-five vehicles on the long drive to Marmaris. No longer under customs restriction, the convoy made the trip during daylight hours with no attempts to disguise the vehicles. Turkey was abuzz with news and controversy over the expected U.S. attack on Iraq and what part Turkey might play in it. Woodcock and his convoy of white Land Rovers sporting gun mounts and military markings was a media magnet and news crews filmed the convoy the entire way. When the convoy finally arrived in Marmaris, it was greeted by police officers and threats of arrest. While Woodcock successfully reminded the police that the Status of Forces Agreement prohibited them from arresting him or any of the American soldiers under his command, he could not protect his Kurdish drivers. Later

Figure 4.8 Kurdish truck driver. *The reliability and industry of the Kurdish truck drivers were instrumental in hauling the vehicles of Task Force Viking from Turkey into northern Iraq.*

Woodcock found out that in fact there was no Status of Forces Agreement between the United States and Turkey.[20]

Woodcock watched in dismay and frustration as the police rounded up his drivers: "I knew if I just let them take the drivers, they would beat them up, run them off, and I'd be stuck with all these vehicles." Woodcock finally told the police that if they took his drivers into cus-

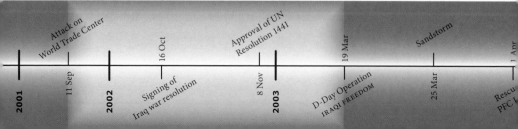

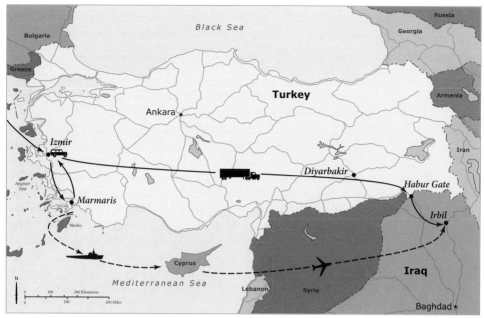

Figure 4.9 Map showing NSV infiltration of the 10th SFG.

tody, they would also have to take him since they were in his employ. Woodcock "accompanied" his drivers to the police station, where the drivers were held and interrogated for twelve hours before everyone was finally released and allowed to return to the hotel. While the team was technically free, the police put armed guards on the vehicles and refused to let Woodcock or the others near them. The police also followed Woodcock and his party whenever they left the hotel. By this time, Woodcock suspected that in addition to the issue of the military vehicles, the Turks seemed insulted that he had hired all Kurdish drivers.[21]

The senior Turkish military representative in Marmaris was a high-ranking naval officer who soon made a point of involving himself in the conflict. He made no pretense at hiding his negative feelings regarding the convoy, and informed Woodcock in no uncertain terms that if he could, he would arrest them all—Americans included—and confiscate the vehicles. He actually did attempt to bully Woodcock into moving the vehicles onto his naval installation, but Woodcock declined, knowing that if he gave in, he would never see the vehicles again. Woodcock's resistance was rewarded when the U.S. Embassy made it clear to the Turkish authorities that the vehicles were con-

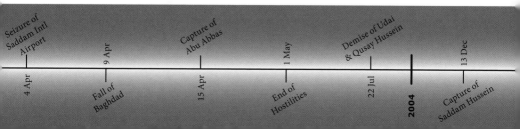

sidered to be U.S. military equipment, and demanded that the Turks release the trucks and all the U.S. personnel and contracted drivers immediately. The Turks complied with the embassy's request, but they scuttled Woodcock's plan to ferry the vehicles out of the country by intimidating the contracted ferry owner into reneging on the plan. Foiled at the coast, Woodcock had no choice but to return the vehicles to the warehouse in Izmir.[22]

About this time, Colonel Cleveland sent Lieutenant Colonel Keith Anderson to negotiate with the Turkish government for the release of the vehicles. After some very hard and intense negotiations, Anderson obtained the necessary release, though with conditions. Due to the politically sensitive nature of Turkey's involvement with the American military, the Turks insisted that the vehicles be transported on enclosed trucks and that all travel be conducted at night. Major protests were already occurring all along the route to the Iraqi border, exacerbated by the fact that the hundreds of supply trucks from the 24th Theater Support Group out of U.S. Army Europe had effectively blocked traffic on the main highway between Izmir and Diyarbakir.[23]

Woodcock contracted with a Turkish transport company for thirty-five cargo trucks. Edwards explained, "When we finally did get permission to leave, the way we did it was by three convoys: 210 vehicles broken into three convoys, two vehicles per truck. They were really small trucks with tarps over [them], so you couldn't tell what was in the back." Feeling a distinct sense of personal responsibility for the success of the mission, Woodcock took it upon himself to accompany each convoy to the delivery point in Irbil, Iraq. While he led the first convoy from Izmir to its final destination, thereafter the lead driver was given the bill of lading and other documents for getting through the border checkpoint. Woodcock then met each new convoy a few miles inside Turkey and accompanied it across the border into Iraq and the rest of the way to Irbil.[24]

The first convoy departed the warehouse in Izmir on the night of 25 March 2003. Woodcock rode in the cab of the lead truck. As the convoy headed for Habur Gate, the only border crossing point between Turkey and Iraq, Woodcock found that the biggest challenge was not the long, dusty journey or the horde of civilian traffic, but the Turkish government: "Every time we came up on a Turkish police vehicle, they stopped us and checked all our documentation."[25]

While security was a constant concern for this convoy representing a country newly at war, once the trucks crossed into Iraq, para-

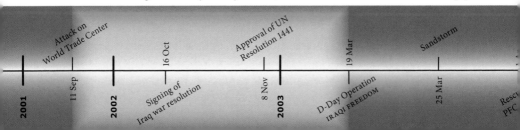

doxically Woodcock and the drivers felt a sense of relief. Most of the route through Iraq was actually in Kurdish territory, which made the Kurdish drivers feel much more at home than they had felt in western Turkey. Even so, the only hostile activity against any of the convoys occurred in Mosul. An Iraqi taxi raced around one of the trucks and halted suddenly, causing the vehicle to make an emergency stop. While they were stopped, a crowd of Iraqis gathered and began to throw rocks at the trucks, breaking a windshield. While the incident was stressful, it was not lethal, and they were soon able to maneuver around the taxi and continue on to Irbil.[26]

In Woodcock's mind, the more realistic threat was that one or more of the contracted drivers might simply disappear with his truck and sell the nonstandard vehicles on the black market. Since he always rode in the lead vehicle with no way of communicating with the other trucks, Woodcock could not keep track of every truck every minute of the journey. At each rest break, he routinely checked each vehicle before they resumed traveling, both for safety and for inventory purposes. During one such rest break, Woodcock counted trucks and came up one short. His first thought was that the driver had absconded with the valuable cargo and Woodcock was out two nonstandard vehicles. By this time, the drivers knew the route to Irbil, so Woodcock told the lead driver to take the convoy on to Irbil while he took the last truck in line back toward Tur-

Figure 4.10 Unloading in Irbil. *Unloading a Land Rover in the northern Iraqi town of Irbil, at the end of the long convoy from Turkey.*

key to look for the missing truck. Woodcock backtracked all the way back to the border with no luck. Convinced that the truck and driver had vanished, Woodcock turned his truck around in resignation and headed toward Irbil. Along the way, however, he met up with his now-empty trucks returning to Turkey. Upon talking to the lead driver, Woodcock learned that the missing truck suffered a flat tire and left the convoy to get it repaired at a truck stop. Once the tire was fixed, the missing driver caught up with the rest of the convoy and delivered his cargo in Irbil. Woodcock and his driver simply missed seeing him in the mass of vehicles at the truck stop. Woodcock reported that he was pleasantly surprised and impressed with the honesty and work ethic of his drivers.[27]

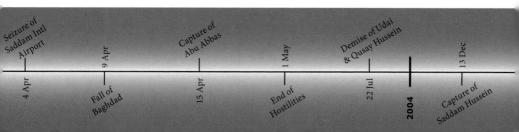

The successful delivery of all the nonstandard vehicles had perhaps as much to do with Woodcock's efforts to encourage loyalty among his drivers as their inherent honesty. He went out of his way to treat the contractors more like coworkers than hired hands, making gestures that cost him little but meant quite a bit to the drivers. Woodcock paid for the drivers' meals at the roadside rest stops, and when they arrived in Irbil, they were fed at the American mess. Woodcock also allowed the drivers to take advantage of the drastically lower fuel prices in Iraq to increase their profit margins. Fuel in Turkey was between two and three dollars per gallon, but only fifty cents per gallon in Iraq; the drivers put just enough fuel in their trucks to get them out of Turkey and to the first truck stop in Iraq, where they then refueled for much less. Although the chosen fuel point only had one hose and, therefore, refueling stops took an extraordinarily long time, the strategy kept the drivers happy and Woodcock's nonstandard vehicles safe.[28]

The last thirty-six nonstandard vehicles arrived in Irbil on 7 April. After nearly two weeks of nonstop convoy travel, all 236 vehicles finally found their way to the 10th SFG. As the Special Forces teams exchanged their locally procured vehicles for their custom-built Land Rovers or Toyota trucks, a tired and road-weary Captain Woodcock looked on with pride. After six long months of effort, his mission was finally completed.[29]

SUPPORT IN ROMANIA

In late 2002, the Bravo Forward Support Company, 528th Special Operations Support Battalion, drew one of the biggest jobs it had ever confronted—support the 10th SFG and CJSOTF-North in the war with Iraq. By the time Operation IRAQI FREEDOM actually began on 19 March, Bravo Company personnel were already deployed to two continents, providing vital logistics expertise and support in diverse conditions.

Bravo Company spent the last months of 2002 preparing for its upcoming deployment. Master Sergeant Caleb Ballard*, the company first sergeant, played a key role in ensuring that the numerous predeployment tasks were accomplished:

> *In preparation for [deployment], we went through a lot of pre-planning with regards to ordering fuel bags and nozzles and [other] equipment that we thought would better facilitate our ability to support the mission. Requirements were changing daily, and we were trying to adjust to those*

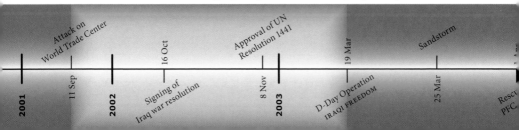

changes. Our focus was preventive checks and inspections of equipment . . . to ensure we as soldiers had what we needed on the battlefield. We ensured that every soldier had [desert camouflage uniforms] and tent gear and all the equipment that they needed. The last couple of weeks prior to the actual deployment was spent lining vehicles up, and getting vehicles loaded and [joint airlift inspected] for the purpose of being able to ship them on aircraft into theater. Again, the dates kept changing, but we remained flexible.[30]

In early February, company commander Major Richard Geery* dispatched a two-man movement control team to Fort Carson, Colorado, to assist the 10th SFG with its air movement to its intermediate staging base in Stuttgart. In the past, the 10th SFG had deployed only a relatively small number of people at any one time and had depended upon the installation movement control team for assistance. The deployment of the entire 10th SFG plus other units at Fort Carson exceeded the installation's capabilities. First Lieutenant Carl Hancock*, a veteran of operations in Afghanistan, headed up the forward support team sent to help the 10th SFG deploy.[31]

Figure 4.11 Movement Control Team. *The Movement Control Team of the 528th Support Battalion assist with the loading of the Task Force Viking equipment in Stuttgart.*

The two-man team from Bravo Company brought with them subject matter expertise and practical experience working with Air Force load teams. Hancock worked with each company to prepare its equipment for deployment: "That involved creating load plans, keeping track of equipment, weighing and marking [equipment], calculating the center of balance, and making sure they were abiding by the proper safety guidelines." Thinking ahead, the movement control team also installed customized software on the 10th SFG's computers to help with load plans and hazardous material certification for future deployments.[32]

Once the airflow was underway, Geery dispatched another team to Germany to assist with the reception of the unit personnel and equipment. Stuttgart was only intended to be a temporary staging base until the political issues with Turkey were settled. Then everything would flow into the planned intermediate staging base at Diyarbakir Air Force Base, Turkey.[33]

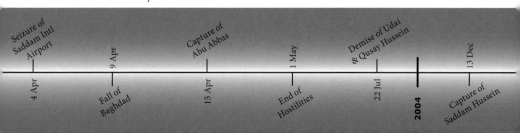

As troops and equipment began building up in Germany, Colonel Cleveland opted to move the intermediate staging base to Constanta, Romania, to get as close as possible to the operational area. Mihail Kogalniceanu Air Base could accommodate the large C-5, C-141, and C-17 Air Force transports, and had enough ramp space to park a number of these aircraft on the ground for unloading, loading, and overnight stops. Nearby Constanta contained enough hotels to billet the force and everything else needed could be contracted locally. At the time, it seemed likely that even if Turkey did not allow basing or ground transit of U.S. forces, they would allow aircraft overflight. That assumption initially proved to be false.[34]

Figure 4.12 Air Force MH-53s. *Air Force MH-53s in Constanta prior to deployment. In December, Constanta is a far cry from the sunny beach resort of the summer months.*

After three weeks of around-the-clock effort, Bravo Company finished deploying personnel and equipment from Fort Bragg, North Carolina, to Romania. Constanta may be a resort area during the summer, but in late February and early March of 2003 it was an empty, cold, bleak, and windy place.[35]

The first troops on the ground lived and worked in unheated tents on the windswept airfield for approximately two weeks. Once the local supply and service contracts were in place, conditions improved dramatically. The troops were supplied, fueled, transported, billeted, and fed by contracted sources coordinated and supervised by Bravo Company. While CJSOTF-North remained in Constanta, all tactical operations were coordinated and planned from Mihail Kogalniceanu Air Base. Bravo Company personnel helped set up the CJSOTF-North Joint Operations Center at the airfield and established the power to run the lights, computers, and other electronic devices. The company's mechanics worked long and hard ensuring all deploying vehicles were modified to carry the increased amounts of equipment, fuel, and weapons needed to operate independently in northern Iraq. As was typical for Bravo Company, the support soldiers performed any job necessary. Power generation expert Specialist Cameron Owens* ended up helping to prepare equipment pallets, set up heaters, and pitch tents. Owens noted, "I even helped some Croatian contract technicians set up the Titan system (radio frequency tagging system) used to track our pallets and containers of equipment."[36]

When the planned ground assault through Turkey was scrapped, CENTCOM planners looked to the 10th SFG and the 173rd Airborne

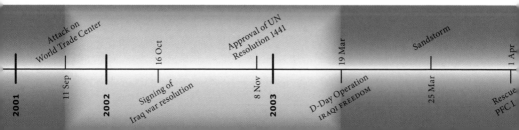

Brigade (-) as a way to put as many U.S. troops on the ground in northern Iraq as quickly as possible. The 10th SFG had already changed its planning to incorporate the seemingly inevitable air infiltration, but the decision to send in the 173rd caused a shift in airlift priority—especially for the C-17s originally tasked with transporting the 10th SFG's support package. With the C-17s diverted in anticipation of the 173rd's infiltration, the 10th SFG was forced to reconfigure its loads for transport by MC-130s.[37]

As the infiltration phase of the operation began, nearly everyone available in Bravo Company helped prepare the Special Forces teams' vehicles and equipment. The company's four-man movement control team formed the nucleus of a larger ad hoc team to support the entire CJSOTF-North as it prepared to deploy its forward elements. The rest of the support team was manned by drafting unit truck drivers, mechanics, and anyone else who was available. The team loaded and unloaded aircraft, certified loads, prepared load plans, and adjusted to the airflow.[38]

Staff Sergeant Mitchell Davis*, usually in charge of maintaining an ammunition supply point, remembered that the airflow and the type of aircraft were constantly changing: "We would build a pallet for a C-17, and two hours later we would be told we were getting a C-130 and we'd have to tear down the pallet and rebuild it [to fit the new aircraft]. You didn't know what bird [the equipment] was leaving on until it showed up."[39]

Supporting the 10th SFG and CJSOTF-North as they prepared for infiltration into northern Iraq was a job ideally suited to the 528th Special Operations Support Battalion. Bravo Forward Support Company solidified the battalion's reputation for flexibility, ingenuity, and plain hard work as it ensured that the soldiers and equipment headed for war were taken care of no matter where they were—Colorado, Germany, or Romania.

BUILDING CJSOTF-WEST

As Colonel Mulholland's 5th SFG completed its training and preparations in the United States, it was faced with its next set of challenges—deploy to the Middle East and set up operating bases. CFSOCC tasked CJSOTF-West with two missions: deter the launch of SCUDs from western Iraq, and support conventional forces in their attack in southern Iraq. This meant setting up and resourcing several operating bases in two countries separated by over seven hundred miles.[40]

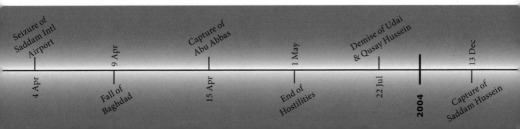

Exercise Early Victor alleviated part of the deployment problem when Forward Operating Base 51 deployed to the Middle East in September 2002. Headquarters Company First Sergeant Darryl Vaught* supervised the loading of over thirty containers packed with everything the battalion needed for a prolonged stay in the Middle East. Vaught and his team were all experienced in deployments in the Middle East and had recently completed seven months in Afghanistan.[41]

On 11 September 2002, a small predeployment site survey element from the 5th SFG Group Support Company deployed to another airfield, staked out the requirements for the CJSOTF-west headquarters, and was followed by the main body of the company on 26 September. The detachment found an austere setting at the airfield, but immediately began building joint operations, support, and signal centers. Using an old gymnasium, the soldiers built secure planning and meeting rooms to be used as the joint operations center, but they had to build two full-sized buildings from the ground up in order to house support and signal centers.[42]

Instead of redeploying back to Fort Campbell, Kentucky, after the conclusion of Early Victor, the 5th SFG's 1st Battalion remained in the region and continued training. The additional month extended the mission into early November and allowed for a rigorous desert training program. During this time, the battalion relocated from the training area to H-5 Airfield. Once the battalion relocated and FOB 51 established its operations center, the majority of the battalion's soldiers returned to Fort Campbell at the beginning of December for the holidays. A skeleton crew secured and maintained FOB 51's equipment and facilities. In early January 2003, the battalion began slowly filtering back to H-5, and by the end of the month, the entire battalion was back on station.[43]

While 1st Battalion and the group headquarters built up their bases, the 2nd and 3rd Battalions prepared to deploy to Kuwait. Because Plan 1003v required such a large conventional force, real estate for a staging area was a scarce commodity in Kuwait. The SOF planners knew the base camps already established at Camp Arifjan and Camp Doha would be extremely crowded, so their plans called for hastily constructed camps in the Kuwaiti desert. Advanced parties from both forward operating bases staked out their areas to make a special operations area at Ali As-Salim Air Base, soon called "Camp Chariot" by the Army headquarters in Kuwait.[44]

The special operations soldiers arrived in early January to find a new, empty building and camp area. Everything necessary for thou-

sands of soldiers to live and work had to be built or bought quickly. Hangar 17, soon known as "SOF LAND," became the center of special operations activity at Ali As-Salim Air Base. For the next few weeks, the base was a flurry of activity—putting in communications lines, building bomb shelters, erecting tents and mess halls, and bringing in latrine and shower facilities. Each forward operating base built in its respective areas an operations center and planning, isolation, living, and logistics areas. As January turned into February and then into March, the special operations forces at Camp Chariot refined their plans.[45]

Late attachments to CJSOTF-west, or Task Force Dagger, were two National Guard and one Regular Army infantry companies. The three infantry companies provided security and a quick reaction force for each of the forward operating bases. C Company, 1st Battalion, 124th Infantry Regiment, Florida Army National Guard, was attached to FOB 51 at H-5. C Company, 2nd Battalion, 14th Infantry Regiment, from the 10th Mountain Division, supported FOB 52, while the remainder of the battalion went to support CJSOTF-north. FOB 53 received B Company, 1st Battalion, 152nd Infantry Regiment, Indiana Army National Guard. Immediately upon arrival in Kuwait, FOB 53 assigned Operational Detachment Alpha 915, from the 19th SFG, to conduct additional quick reaction force and direct action training with the Indiana Guardsmen as support for its ODAs in the field. On 11 March 2003, B Company's 3rd Platoon, with the company executive officer and first sergeant as a command element, deployed as a security force for CJSOTF-west headquarters.[46]

By February 2002, Task Force Dagger's preparations neared a conclusion. The unit successfully managed the movement of over 2,100 personnel and 1,500 short tons of equipment by ground, sea, and air to the Middle East. The three widely separated forward operating bases and the task force headquarters were ready for war.[47]

PSYOP SUPPORT FOR CJSOTF-WEST

CJSOTF-west's psychological operations support came from B Company, 9th Psychological Operations Battalion. B Company faced a daunting task. Organized to support one task force, Major Chris Parker* found himself with the mission to support two, each with a different focus and located hundreds of miles apart. To add to the situation, Parker's company was understrength.[48]

Figure 4.13 124th Infantry Regiment insignia.

Figure 4.14 14th Infantry Regiment insignia.

Figure 4.15 152nd Infantry Regiment insignia.

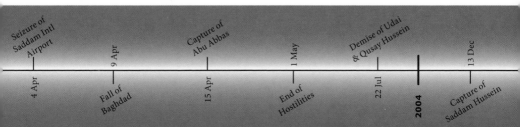

Figure 4.16 9th POB insignia.

To support Task Force Dagger, B Company became a multi-component unit (active and Reserve troops together) with a Coalition element attached. B Company was at about 70 percent strength in the fall of 2002. "There was no way I was going to become 100 percent strength without having Reservists to fall in on," said Parker. The additional soldiers came from the 301st Psyop Company based in San Diego, California, which mobilized in January 2003 and joined B Company at Fort Bragg in February. The 301st Psyop Company trained with 9th POB, integrated well with B Company, and became full members of Parker's team. Tactical Psyop Detachment 960, a sub-element of B Company made up almost entirely of soldiers from San Diego, supported FOB 53. Parker later stated, "Reservists were key to our being successful in this mission."[49]

While the 301st PSYOP soldiers integrated into B Company, Parker and a small advance party deployed from Fort Bragg and joined CJSOTF-west headquarters in mid-January 2003. The soldiers spent their first two weeks helping construct the CJSOTF-west joint operations center. The remainder of the company, primarily the tactical PSYOP teams, deployed in late January and joined FOBs 52 and 53 in Kuwait.[50]

To support the southern mission, the company's product development center deployed to Kuwait. With only one such center in the company, additional support came from an Australian Army product development team. Although psychological operations was still a new field for the Australians, the four-man team's more advanced printing equipment could produce leaflets faster than the Americans' equipment could.[51]

The PSYOP soldiers attached to Task Force Dagger were in position and ready for war. When the CJSOTF-west headquarters main body arrived in mid-February, Brigadier General Parker and his team intensified planning. In a few short weeks, all their hard work would pay off.[52]

160TH SOAR Deploys to H-5

Due to its large requirement for transport aircraft, the 160th Special Operations Aviation Regiment was one of the last SOF elements to arrive in theater. While the 3rd Battalion, 160th SOAR, deployed from Hunter Army Airfield, Georgia, directly to the H-5 Airfield to support Task Force Dagger, the other two Night Stalker battalions deployed to Ali As-Salim Air Base, Kuwait. Predeployment site survey teams

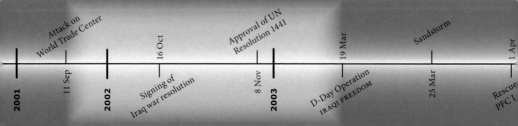

went ahead of the main bodies, but the 160th SOAR ironically fell victim to a scarcity of air assets and the rest of the regiment was severely delayed.[53]

The 3rd Battalion's predeployment site survey team arrived at H-5 Airfield on 7 January 2003. Its mission was simple, though extensive in scope: find a home for the battalion. The team needed to find a location that would provide space for aircraft parking, equipment storage, a repair shop, motor pools, living areas, a tactical operations center, and an aviation logistics operations center. In short, room enough for everything necessary to plan and maintain operations for eight MH-47D Chinooks, six MH-60L Black Hawks, and all of the paraphernalia associated with the fourteen helicopters.[54]

The four-man team had only a few weeks to make the planning a reality. Looking for a suitable area on the already crowded Air Base was difficult. The team finally managed to obtain an open field to the east of the main airstrip for its use. The sole accommodations were a few hardened aircraft hangers. By March, however, part of the field had been leveled and covered in asphalt to make a parking area for the aircraft. The paving made

Figure 4.17 Pad at H-5. *With the pad in place, the helicopters of the 3rd Battalion, 160th SOAR, were able to rapidly prepare for missions.*

site maintenance easier, and prevented severe dust storms every time helicopters took off or landed. With the necessary improvements made, the 3rd Battalion began operations as Joint Special Operations Air Detachment-West (forward) shortly before the beginning of the war.[55]

Deploying a special operations aviation unit halfway across the world was not an easy task. At Hunter Army Airfield, maintenance personnel began dismantling the helicopters for deployment in January. After checking and rechecking the equipment, support personnel loaded the helicopters onto Air Force transport aircraft. The first C-17 arrived at H-5 with two Black Hawks on 21 January 2003. Airplanes carrying helicopters and equipment followed for the next two weeks. Once the main body of troops arrived at H-5 on 10 February, the battalion was once again whole.

After a welcome briefing that included an orientation of the base rules and procedures, the soldiers began a rest cycle, followed by a work cycle that began at dusk. Working at night not only allowed

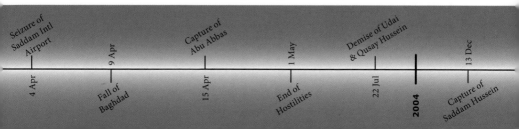

Figure 4.18 MH-60L DAP. *The Defensive Armed Penetrator configured for transport in a C-17. The DAPs were a critical component of the 160th SOAR in IRAQI FREEDOM.*

the support soldiers to work in the cooler temperatures of the desert night, but also prepared them to match the mission cycle, which called for night operations and day rest. As soon as the entire battalion arrived, each section unpacked its equipment and set up its shop. Then they began to reassemble the helicopters.

The buildup procedure for the MH-60L Black Hawks took four to six soldiers approximately one hour to complete. The larger MH-47D Chinooks required a more intensive buildup, requiring ten to fourteen soldiers. Because of the troop's extensive deployment experience, the SOAR Chinooks were usually rebuilt in a single day, instead of the week it takes many conventional aviation units.[56]

Even as the 3rd Battalion finished setting up its base and readying its aircraft, the soldiers continued training for combat. All personnel, mechanics included, participated in nuclear, biological, and chemical training. Meeting the exacting maintenance standards for the SOAR Black Hawks and Chinooks was one thing, but having to perform the work while wearing nuclear/biological/chemical protective suits was a new challenge. The Downed Aircraft Recovery Team even rehearsed mission scenarios in full gear—just in case.[57]

While the maintenance personnel and crew chiefs worked to ready the aircraft, the staff and pilots refined plans with the staff of CJSOTF-west. The 3rd Battalion aviators and maintenance personnel prepared to provide CJSOTF-west with rapid, flexible, and lethal special operations helicopter support. Their mettle would be tested in the following weeks, with exceptionally long infiltrations supporting special operations soldiers from several countries, and the first combat test for the newly created Defensive Armed Penetrators.[58]

AOB 910: FROM DESERT SPRING TO IRAQI FREEDOM

When the 5th SFG arrived in Kuwait, it was met by A Company, 1st Battalion, 19th SFG—Advanced Operating Base 910. AOB 910, which consisted of 110 soldiers, was already in Kuwait supporting Operation DESERT SPRING—a UN-approved ongoing contingency deployment

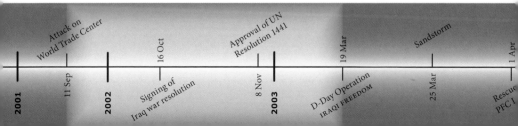

in support of Operation SOUTHERN WATCH, the enforcement of the no-fly zone in southern Iraq.[59]

The Special Forces commitment for DESERT SPRING was a reinforced company of between five and nine Special Forces teams, operating as Coalition support teams training and working with the Kuwaiti Army. In the event of aggression by Iraqi forces, the Special Forces teams would provide support to the Kuwaitis, deconflict any problems between Coalition units, and provide terminal guidance for close air support in defending the Kuwait-Iraq border.[60]

Between 26 and 28 September 2002, AOB 910 arrived in Kuwait and immediately set to work. Its primary mission was training and conducting liaison duties with elements of the Kuwaiti Armed Forces. Some of AOB 910's ODAs trained with the Kuwaiti 35th Mechanized Brigade and other conventional units, while other ODAs trained with the Kuwaiti Naval Commandos and a military police battalion. One of the most important tasks accomplished was extensive close air support training, including an urban scenario on the Faylakah Island range complex. The reinforced company also conducted extensive demolitions and live fire training with Ground Mobility Vehicles—High-Mobility Multipurpose Wheeled Vehicles modified for desert operations.[61]

Figure 4.19 19th SFG beret flash.

By November 2002, the staff of AOB 910 began planning and training to support the 5th SFG in the event of combat operations against Iraq under Plan 1003v. According to the plan, two Special Forces forward operating bases—FOBs 52 and 53—would operate in southern Iraq supporting CFLCC's move north to Baghdad. To aid in planning with CFLCC, five of the company's noncommissioned officers were tasked to form a special operations integration detachment during the planning and buildup of forces in Kuwait. The detachment, consisting of special operations soldiers from the 5th SFG, AOB 910, and other special operations forces, was located at Camp Doha in the CFLCC-Main headquarters.[62]

Under Major Gabe Alexander*, AOB 910 also began training for a Special Forces liaison element mission with Coalition forces. The Special Forces planners' major concern was avoiding fratricide of ODAs conducting special reconnaissance and unconventional warfare missions beyond the forward edge of the battle area. In January, even as planning progressed, ODA 912 was given a special mission tasking it to CFSOCC headquarters. With ODA 912 at CFSOCC and a number of men with the 3rd SFG in Afghanistan, the rest of A Company were

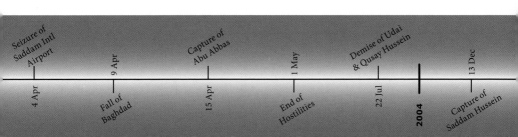

Seizure of Saddam Intl Airport

4 Apr

9 Apr

Fall of Baghdad

Capture of Abu Abbas

15 Apr

1 May

End of Hostilities

Demise of Udai & Qusay Hussein

22 Jul

2004

13 Dec

Capture of Saddam Hussein

assigned as Special Forces liaison elements to both U.S. and Coalition conventional ground forces.[63]

As war neared, the remaining five ODAS of A Company began their liaison missions. ODAS 911 and 913 were assigned to I MEF, primarily supporting the 1st Marine Division. ODA 915 became the liaison element for the 101st Airborne Division. ODA 914 operated as a split team to support both the British 1st Armoured Division and the U.S. 3rd Infantry Division. The ODA commander and the team sergeant led the "A" split and supported the British. The "B" split joined ODA 916 in support of the 3rd Infantry Division, whose mission comprised the main effort of Operation IRAQI FREEDOM: the assault on Baghdad.[64]

SOSCOM DEPLOYS

By the time Exercise Early Victor was extended twice, Special Operations Support Command knew that it would soon be at war with Iraq. Although the 528th Special Operations Support Battalion returned to Fort Bragg in December, it left its equipment in Jordan; the soldiers knew they would be coming back.

Figure 4.20 SOS-COM insignia.

CFLCC was responsible for all Coalition ground forces in IRAQI FREEDOM and provided them with logistics support. Major General Claude Christiansen was the CFLCC logistics officer, and in the fall of 2002, began planning for what might easily have become a logistics nightmare. Strategists and planners were focusing significant attention on the SCUD hunt in the western desert of Iraq during the early part of the war. With SOF playing such a large role in that portion of IRAQI FREEDOM, Christiansen turned to SOSCOM for help. SOSCOM commander Colonel Kevin Leonard recalled, "General Christiansen said, 'I want the SOSCOM to come in and work all logistics in the West,' which is where SOF was heavily committed. 'If I have questions on SOF logistics, you're the guy.'" In other words, SOSCOM got the opportunity to do what it was designed to do: support SOF at war.[65]

General Christiansen originally wanted SOSCOM to support all SOF in theater, including the joint task force. Once it became clear that the joint task force might need more support assets than SOSCOM had available, Lieutenant General Philip Kensinger, commander of U.S. Army Special Operations Command, relieved SOSCOM of the joint task force requirement. General Christiansen agreed to the change in mission, and indicated that CFLCC would form a logistics task force with SOSCOM at its core—Logistics Task Force–West. CFSOCC's Brigadier General Gary Harrell also approved the arrangement, effectively

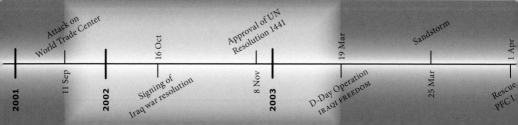

placing a special operations asset under conventional control, while also giving SOF access to conventional logistics.[66]

SOSCOM received the alert order for deployment to the Middle East on 26 December 2002. Most of the command's equipment was already in theater, left over from Exercise Early Victor in Jordan. The remaining equipment had been prepared and palletized in anticipation of deployment. Beginning in January, elements of both the 112th Special Operations Signal Battalion and the 528th Special Operations Support Battalion deployed. Twenty-five soldiers from SOSCOM headquarters followed in late February 2003. Although it was the SOSCOM headquarters' first time ever deploying as a unit, the headquarters was set up and operational within forty-eight hours of arriving in the Middle East.[67]

When Colonel Leonard arrived at CFLCC headquarters, he assumed command of Logistics Task Force–West, which included all SOF and Regular Army logistics assets in the CJSOTF-west area of operations. LTF-west's primary mission was, in Leonard's words, to provide "General Christiansen, the Coalition logistics officer, with visibility of all logistics efforts in that region." SOSCOM staff officer Major Wes Wickham* explained further: "Our charter was to go in and make sure that any logistics issues in the western [area of responsibility] were taken care of. We tried to anticipate problems and solve them. That way the operator didn't have to worry about [logistics], and the commanders of the JSOTF and the [special operations commander] didn't have to worry about anything logistically."[68]

LTF-west included more than SOSCOM's assets: "We took control of elements of the 155th Corps Support Battalion and the 30th Corps Support Group," explained Leonard. "We helped deploy them from home station, because when the [Time-Phased Force Deployment Lists] were filled, these guys got lost in the shuffle. These were Reserve [and National Guard] units due to come and support all Army units in the west. We received, staged, integrated, and trained a Reserve corps support battalion and a [National Guard] corps support group."[69]

The logistics task force was also tasked with creating a contingency plan for flowing supplies to Baghdad from the west. Although the planning was completed and the assets placed, the need to use the contingency plan never arose. Instead, LTF-west concentrated its efforts on supporting the activities of the soldiers and airmen in the western desert. The task force took charge of the base at H-5, relieving the Alpha Forward Support Company, 528th SOSB, of the responsibility of running a base rapidly filling with troops. Under the guidance

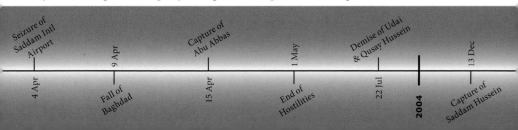

of LTF-west, the 30th Corps Support Group of the North Carolina Army National Guard took over base operations. The support soldiers were soon augmented by hundreds of Kellogg, Brown and Root contractors.[70]

Due to the nature of operations being conducted by CJSOTF-west, LTF-west had the opportunity to execute a number of different support missions. The task force provided forward logistics elements where needed, and conducted over one hundred successful air delivery missions in support of the 5th SFG teams in the Iraqi desert. One

of the most unusual tasks that LTF-west performed was stevedore service to the U.S. Navy. When the USNS *Pomeroy* arrived in theater, it docked at a port where the local longshoremen were on strike. Leonard recounted, "This boat shows up with all this equipment on it and we're the only ones there. Christiansen says, 'Hey, you guys have got to unload it,' so we did."[71]

Being comprised primarily of SOSCOM assets, LTF-west often turned to the 528th SOSB to carry out support missions, especially for SOF units. However, when a need arose that the 528th was not equipped to fill,

Figure 4.21 USNS *Pomeroy. When the USNS Pomeroy docked during a longshoreman's strike, SOSCOM personnel stepped in and unloaded the cargo.*

LTF-west acted as liaison and coordination element. Wickham: "We would coordinate through the [special operations commander] and through the CFLCC headquarters, through their [logistics officer] to task a conventional Army unit that was in the area or at that location to do the mission. For example, at [a location nearby], the Air Force ran all the base operating support, so the CJSOTF headquarters there was pretty much covered by the Air Force."[72]

Although the successful mission in the west and the rapid liberation of Baghdad resulted in a logistics mission of less intensity and length than planners had anticipated, SOSCOM found ample work to do. As the core of LTF-west, SOSCOM headquarters needed to coordinate logistics and support operations in as far-flung locations as Kuwait, H-5, and the barren deserts of western Iraq. While LTF-west could not affect the challenging logistics situations that plagued CJSOTF-North, the task force monitored the situation as closely as it could from so far away, and offered help when possible. SOSCOM headquarters worked for CFLCC in a "conventional" job, but drew on its special operations

origins by acting as the logistics interface between conventional and special operations units.

PSYCHOLOGICAL OPERATIONS TAKE TO THE AIR

Psychological Operations is potentially one of the most powerful tools the military possesses. Conveyed to foreign audiences in a variety of ways, PSYOP messages support U.S. goals and objectives—offensive, defensive, or peaceful in nature. Properly applied, PSYOP can wear down an enemy's resolve to fight, diffuse a tense standoff between would-be attackers and U.S. troops, and ensure fair distribution of humanitarian aid. Psyop activities leading up to and during Operation IRAQI FREEDOM used a number of means to deliver Coalition messages to the Iraqi military and the civilian population. Two of the more notable methods of distribution were radio and television broadcasts of Coalition programming.

A large part of the PSYOP activities in IRAQI FREEDOM consisted of media broadcasts directed at the Iraqi military and civilian populations. The Special Operations Media System–Broadcast and the EC-130E Commando Solo both proved to be capable and valuable broadcast platforms. Working independently and in concert, the SOMS-B and Commando Solo teams successfully delivered their crucial messages to audiences throughout Iraq.

The SOMS-B consisted of two primary subsystems: the Mobile Radio Broadcast System and the Mobile Television Broadcast System. Between the two subsystems, the SOMS-B could broadcast via AM, FM, and short wave radio, as well as television. The Joint Psyop Task Force made up of elements of the 4th Psyop Group

Figure 4.22 SOMS-B. *The ability to establish broadcast capability anywhere on the battlefield is the hallmark of the SOMS-B.*

initially set up a SOMS-B in Kuwait in mid-December 2002. This task force immediately began to broadcast messages throughout southern Iraq. In the beginning, the SOMS-B unit broadcast radio messages for five hours a day, but by February, transmission times extended to eighteen hours daily. When combat operations began on 19 March, the SOMS-B broadcasts provided PSYOP support twenty-four hours a day.[73]

Captain Roger Campbell*, commander of the SOMS-B element, requested additional SOMS-B equipment be brought into theater to

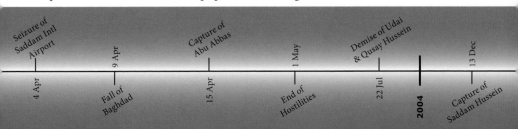

supplement his unit's capability. The new unit, a SOMS-B "light" consisting of just the radio subsystem, accompanied the 3rd Infantry Division north to Baghdad. A third SOMS-B arrived from Romania and began broadcasting from Baghdad International Airport once that location had been secured. With three systems established between Kuwait and Baghdad, together with daily Commando Solo broadcasts, almost all of Iraq had access to Coalition messages via AM, FM, and short wave radio.[74]

Figure 4.23 193rd Special Operations Wing insignia.

The EC-130E Commando Solo aircraft played a significant role in broadcasting PSYOP messages in Iraq. Based in Harrisburg, Pennsylvania, the Air Force National Guard's 193rd Special Operations Wing was home to the Commando Solo aircraft and was tasked with providing aerial transmission of PSYOP messages. The Commando Solo platform broadcast on the commercial AM/FM and short wave radio bands, VHF/UHF television bands, and military VHF/HF/FM frequencies. Having such comprehensive broadcast capabilities in an aircraft enabled the 193rd SOW to support military operations worldwide. Since the 193rd was the only unit in the Air Force dedicated to this mission, the Commando Solo crews truly supported global operations.[75]

A Detachment of the 193rd SOW, commanded by Lieutenant Colonel Geral Otterbein, arrived in the region on 24 March. The detachment consisted of one EC-130E Commando Solo aircraft, two full EC-130E crews of eleven members each, two support C-130s, and the associated staff and support personnel. The Commando Solo detachment brought aerial television transmission, AM/FM/HF radio broadcast, and "net intrusion" (military radio net interruption) capability into theater, allowing wider distribution of PSYOP messages.[76]

The 193rd SOW detachment was fully operational within forty-eight hours of arriving in theater. Under the tactical control of the Joint Psychological Operations Task Force in Qatar, the detachment was given areas to target with the television and radio broadcast tapes that the Commando Solo crews received from the 4th PSYOP Group at Fort Bragg. The Army PSYOP liaison attached to the 193rd SOW, Sergeant Daniel Romer*, reviewed the taskings and planned and coordinated all broadcast plans with the detachment's operations officer, Lieutenant Colonel Kevin Satow.[77]

Flight planning proved to be a delicate undertaking. The 193rd SOW initially flew missions outside Iraqi airspace, yet still close enough to allow transmission into the majority of western Iraq. The JPOTF urged Otterbein to broadcast to cities north of the Euphrates River, requiring flights over western Iraq, thus making the aircraft vulner-

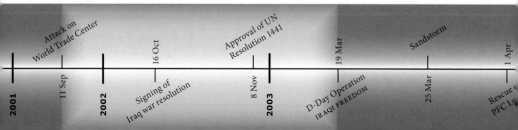

able to attack. The EC-130E mission called for it to orbit in "tracks" for long periods of time. The EC-130E was also an extraordinarily heavy aircraft, lacking the maneuverability necessary to react quickly to threats. While transmitting, the aircraft normally trailed a four hundred-foot long wire antenna, further reducing maneuverability. Major Dick Riemer*, an aircraft commander in the 193rd, explained that with the antenna deployed, the aircraft "can make one reaction from a threat. If there's a follow-on, a second one, you're going to guillotine the aircraft or cut the wire and then our AM broadcasts are done." Further risk lay in the fact that the aircraft's APR-47 missile warning system was inoperative. In short, the 193rd SOW did not conduct flights over hostile areas until the Joint Special Operations Air Detachment and 193rd SOW detachment intelligence officers decided the threat was at an acceptable level.[78]

With clearance from the JSOAD, the detachment advanced operations to an area north of the Euphrates River in the first week in April. The JPOTF added television broadcasts to the unit's mission the following week, giving the EC-130E crews more responsibility than usual. One of the first broadcasts from the new Coalition television service, called "Towards Freedom TV," included an interview with opposition group members, information on humanitarian aid deliveries, and a feature on Iraqi culture and arts. Another broadcast contained a joint message to the Iraqi people from President George W. Bush and British Prime Minister Tony Blair. The programming was outsourced to World Television, a production company in Iraq, which transmitted the programming by satellite daily to the

Figure 4.24 Commando Solo. *The EC-130E Commando Solo can provide nearly continuous broadcast capability with its sophisticated electronic systems. It is a key component of the PSYOP campaign.*

4th PSYOP Group at Fort Bragg for approval and distribution. Once approved, the 4th PSYOP Group transmitted the program by satellite to Qatar, where it was transferred to videotape for broadcast by the EC-130E Commando Solo and SOMS-B units.

Of the increase in the EC-130E's workload, Riemer observed, "I've never run this many frequencies and missions out of the back end as an aircraft commander...Usually it's two tasks, and a third one if you get around to it." Despite the pressure of extended missions over Iraq, the members of the 193rd SOW detachment remained focused. Colonel Otterbein stated, "We're aware of the impact we have on the theater

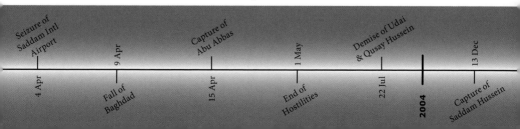

Seizure of Saddam Intl Airport

4 Apr

Fall of Baghdad

9 Apr

15 Apr

Capture of Abu Abbas

End of Hostilities

1 May

22 Jul

Demise of Udai & Qusay Hussein

2004

Capture of Saddam Hussein

13 Dec

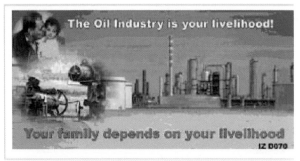

Figure 4.25 Oil leaflets. *Oil leaflets such as these helped prevent the destruction of the petroleum systems by the Iraqis.*

battle…If we get one person to put his gun down and surrender, think about how many Americans that might have saved."[79]

The 4th PSYOP Group turned to the air for more than electronic broadcasts; it also made liberal use of airdropped leaflets to spread important PSYOP messages. Between 12 December 2002 and 18 March 2003, U.S. forces dropped over twenty million PSYOP leaflets into Iraq. By mid-April the total exceeded forty million. The 4th PSYOP Group, who orchestrated the entire PSYOP effort of the war, designed the leaflets and delivered them to U.S. Navy aircraft carriers by computer, where they were printed and packed in canisters typically holding sixty thousand leaflets each. Naval F-18 jets stationed aboard the aircraft carriers, including the USS *Harry S. Truman*, the USS *Theodore Roosevelt*, and the USS *Constellation,* then dropped the leaflet bombs in targeted areas throughout Iraq.[80]

One of the more successful leaflet efforts addressed the need to protect Iraq's petroleum production and processing facilities. Leaflets urged Iraqi citizens and soldiers to remember that oil was a vital part of the nation's economy, and the destruction of the oil infrastructure would negatively impact their families. The combination of the PSYOP leaflet program and the advancement of combat operations is credited with preventing Iraqi forces from perpetrating the kind of environmental devastation that was committed in 1991, when they set oil fields ablaze in Kuwait.[81]

Major General Victor Renuart, Central Command director of operations, discussed the PSYOP impact in his 10 April 2003 Operation IRAQI FREEDOM briefing:

> We mentioned the forty-some-odd million leaflets. And the people have said, 'Well, so what do they really do for you?' Well, let me give you an example. As we were going back into the oil fields with the [British] engineers, U.S.

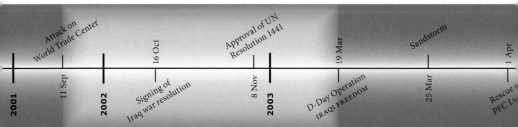

engineers, Kuwaiti engineers, and returning the Iraqi oil workers back to the sites, we were interviewing the staff of the Iraqi oil industry. We noticed that many of these wells had, in fact, been wired to be destroyed. And we also noticed that many of them, even though there were explosives set in place, had the valves turned off, so that, even if you had an explosion, it wouldn't necessarily damage the oil well. And we said, 'You all were here. You watched this happen. How did they do this?' And they said, 'We read your leaflets. We heard your broadcasts. We understand that keeping the oil infrastructure was important to our future. And so while we complied for our own protection with the regime, we ensured that true damage to the oil fields would not occur.'[82]

The 4th PSYOP Group seldom used only one method of disseminating PSYOP messages. Radio and television broadcasts were coordinated with leaflet drops as often as possible, in order to reach the maximum number of people and reinforce the messages. The PSYOP efforts surrounding the Coalition's "Information Radio" program were a prime example of broadcast-leaflet coordination. While the radio programs were obviously a broadcast media distributed by SOMS-B and from the EC-130E Commando Solo broadcast platform, leaflet drops were used to advertise the programming and encourage Iraqis to tune into Information Radio for accurate and pertinent news.[83]

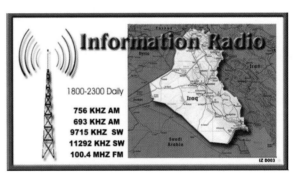

Figure 4.26 Information Radio. *The 4th POG leaflet alerting the Iraqi's of the presence of continuous information radio.*

Under the direction of the 4th PSYOP Group at Fort Bragg, PSYOP efforts in Operation IRAQI FREEDOM took many forms and met many needs in the early days of the war. Whether urging cooperation with Coalition forces or providing much needed information about the new government, PSYOP messages advanced the Coalition's cause and saved lives. The close cooperation of all branches of the U.S. military allowed for the widest possible distribution of PSYOP messages. Coordination of diverse media—from radio and television to printed leaflets—reinforced important messages and helped the messages reach diverse segments

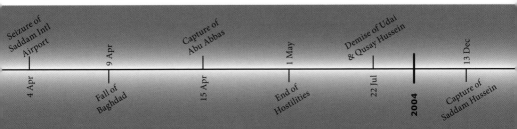

of the population. Psychological Operations still play an important part in the stabilization and rebuilding efforts going on in Iraq today and will continue to be a vital component of U.S. military strategy in the years to come.

SUMMARY

By 18 March, Army special operations forces were poised to execute their assigned missions. Those with CJSOTF-West deployed along the Iraqi border, ready to cross and disperse into the western desert to wrest control of the terrain from the regime. The Night Stalkers of the 160th SOAR were ready to execute an orchestrated plan to destroy the visual observation posts along the border and blind the Iraqis to the U.S. movements. In the face of seemingly insurmountable obstacles, CJSOTF-North succeeded in infiltrating teams and individuals into northern Iraq to link up with their Kurdish counterparts, though the bulk of CJSOTF-North forces waited in Romania. The time for planning and preparing had passed; war was at hand.

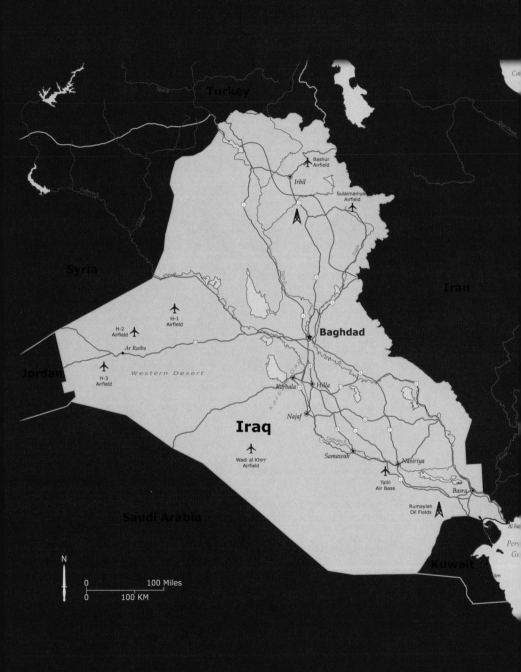

Chapter Five

War Begins

D-Day through D+4
19–23 March

O N 19 MARCH 2003, two days after delivering an ultimatum to Saddam Hussein and his sons, President George W. Bush once again addressed the nation: "My fellow citizens, at this hour, American and Coalition forces are in the early stages of military operations to disarm Iraq, to free its people and to defend the world from grave danger. On my orders, Coalition forces have begun striking selected targets of military importance to undermine Saddam Hussein's ability to wage war. These are the opening stages of what will be a broad and concerted campaign."[1]

True to the President's statement and General Tommy Franks' plan, the campaign against Iraq was, indeed, broad and concerted. Special operations forces participated in every aspect of the campaign, and were given the privilege of striking the first blow against Saddam Hussein's regime when aircraft from the 160th Special Operations Aviation Regiment destroyed visual observation posts along the Iraqi border. From that moment forward, Army special operations forces led the fight. In northern Iraq, Combined Joint Special Operations Task Force–North allied with Kurdish forces to tie up the Iraqi Army divisions arrayed along the Green Line, preventing them from reinforcing units defending Baghdad. In the western desert, ARSOF teams secured strategic airfields and hunted SCUD missile sites to prevent potentially provocative strikes on Israel and deployment of weapons of mass destruction. ARSOF elements also preceded and accompanied the main thrust toward Baghdad, providing targeting information and acting as liaisons with the local populations. At the beginning of Operation IRAQI FREEDOM, ARSOF played a prominent role in the first strikes into Iraq.

CONVENTIONAL OPERATIONS
D-DAY

D-DAY was 19 March, and H-HOUR was 2100 hours Iraqi time. Helicopters from the 160th SOAR attacked and destroyed visual observation posts on the border of Iraq. At 2000 hours on 20 March, air and ground reconnaissance began. Two hours later, Coalition special operations forces—including Polish commandos—began securing offshore oil and gas platforms and the tanker terminal at Al Faw to prevent sabotage. That same night, SOF teams infiltrated the desert in the west and southwest, and began moving on SCUD sites and securing strategic airfields.[2]

G-DAY

When intelligence reports indicated that Saddam was, indeed, moving to sabotage the Rumaylah Oil Fields on the Iraq-Kuwait border, General Franks and Lieutenant General David McKiernan pushed the ground war up almost twenty-four hours from its original start time. G-DAY had been scheduled for 21 March at 0600 hours, just fifteen hours before the air assault began, but the ground assault actually began at 2130 hours on 20 March. A-DAY could not be pushed up, due to the complicated nature of the air operations, and began at 2100 hours on 21 March, as planned. By the time major air operations began, ground forces were well within Iraq and moving fast.[3]

The ground war officially began the evening of 20 March at 2100 hours, when reconnaissance forces from the I Marine Expeditionary Force and V Corps crossed the berm separating Kuwait from Iraq. The rest of I MEF and V Corps forces followed within hours, crossing in the early morning hours of 21 March. Although G-DAY came earlier than scheduled, the change simply allowed Franks to further build on the element

Timeline		
VISOBs	19 March	2100
SOF	20 March	0200
Recon	20 March	2100
GOPLATS	20 March	2200
G-Day	21 March	0300
A-Day	21 March	2100

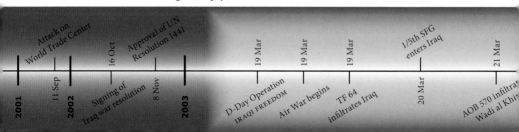

of surprise. The Iraqis never expected the ground war to precede the air war, and the ground forces were intent on moving fast and hard to penetrate Iraqi defenses and reach the critical oil fields and Baghdad before the enemy could regroup and retrench.[4]

By first light on 21 March, the 3rd Infantry Division brigade combat teams (BCTS) and Marine regimental combat teams (RCTS) were closing in on their first objectives and pushing toward Baghdad. Each combat team included approximately five thousand troops with armor, mechanized infantry, and artil-

Figure 5.1 M2 Bradley Fighting Vehicle. *The 3rd Infantry Division spearheaded the Army component of the Coalition ground forces that drove across the Kuwaiti border.*

lery. Though the teams advanced along separate routes, they could meet up and combine firepower on strategic targets. Each team was also supported by close air support.[5]

The 3rd Infantry Division BCTS headed directly for Tallil Air Base, southwest of Nasiriya. Special operations forces teams scouted the bridge across the Euphrates River at the juncture of Highways 1 and 8. The 3rd BCT's third objective was just south-west of Nasiriya itself. By daylight on 22 March, Tallil Air Base and the Highway 1 bridge were secure. Blocking positions between Highway 1 and Nasiriya were in place, establishing a safe route north for the ground forces that followed. As planned, the 3rd BCT handed off the bridge to Task Force Tarawa, part of I MEF, early on 23 March. The 3rd ID continued rolling north along Highway 8 to Samawah.[6]

While the 3rd ID spent 21 March pushing north to Nasiriya, I MEF and the attached British 1st Armoured Division initially followed a different route out of Kuwait and into Iraq. Their objective was Basra and the Rumaylah Oil Fields. I MEF turned northwest at Basra and followed Highway 8 toward Nasiriya, securing the oil fields on its way. Task Force

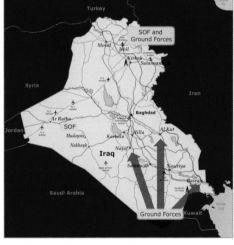

Figure 5.2 Map of conventional operations.

Tarawa took possession of the bridge on Highway 1 from the 3rd BCT on 23 March, allowing that team to move on to its next objective. The British took charge of clearing out Iraqi opposition in the south and eventually attacked Basra itself.

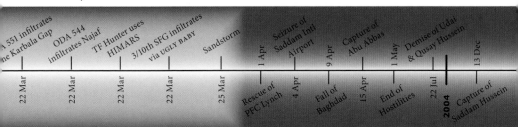

Figure 5.3 TLAM. *The Tomahawk Land Attack Missile was a major component of the Coalition's initial assault—the "shock and awe" campaign.*

Saddam Fedayeen
Paramilitary force established in 1995 by Saddam Hussein's eldest son Uday. Translates to "Saddam's Men of Sacrifice." Acted as an internal police force for Saddam's regular army units, killing soldiers who attempted to surrender. The more generic term fedayeen refers to irregular guerrillas. The term was first used in the 1950s and applied to Arab commandos conducting cross-border raids against the fledgling state of Israel.

A-DAY

A-DAY came at 2100 hours on 21 March. Fighter planes, bombers, cruise missiles, and tactical land-air missiles descended on Baghdad. Carefully selected targets disintegrated before the eyes of the world, filmed by news teams holed up in the Palestine Hotel. The "shock and awe" campaign was designed to decapitate the regime, yet it was carefully controlled to leave enough infrastructure in place to allow the country to rebuild.[7]

The 3rd ID's lead combat elements spent 22 March moving northwest toward Samawah and Najaf. The 1st and 2nd BCTs bypassed the 3rd BCT at Nasiriya and drove north along Highway 28 toward Najaf. The 2nd BCT reached Objective Rams, a few kilometers southwest of Najaf, the afternoon of 22 March. The team's objective was to secure a logistics support area for V Corps, which would enable the fight to continue to the north. After more than twelve hours of fighting irregular forces, the 2nd BCT secured the objective at 1000 hours on 23 March. The team then defended the objective for two days against waves of paramilitary forces coming out of Najaf.

Once the 2nd BCT had secured Objective Rams, the 1st BCT passed through the 2nd BCT's lines and moved north along Highway 28 to Objective Raiders. The pipeline road was clear of opposition until the 2nd BCT reached the Najaf escarpment—a 250-foot-high wall of earth. The only way up the natural obstacle was via a steep, single-lane causeway running between a marsh and a lake. The Iraqis had not overlooked the defensible nature of the escarpment and bombarded the team with artillery and mortars. The 2nd BCT responded with artillery of its own and called in close air support. The planes made the difference, and the 1st BCT reached its objective and established a blocking position north of Najaf on 23 March.

Once the 3rd BCT was relieved at Nasiriya, it moved north to its next objective. When the first element of the 3rd BCT reached Samawah, however, it encountered a nasty surprise—the fedayeen. Intelligence sources had not picked up on the fact that Saddam had deployed these fierce, irregular forces at key locations throughout south-

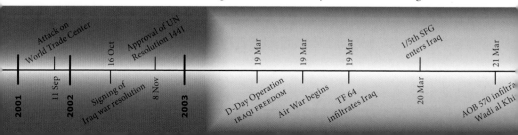

2001 · 11 Sep Attack on World Trade Center · 2002 · 16 Oct Signing of Iraq war resolution · Approval of UN Resolution 1441 · 8 Nov · 2003 · 19 Mar D-Day Operation IRAQI FREEDOM · 19 Mar Air War begins · 19 Mar TF 64 infiltrates Iraq · 20 Mar · 1/5th SFG enters Iraq · 21 Mar AOB 570 infiltra Wadi al Khi

ern and central Iraq. Iraq's regular military forces—the Iraqi Army and the elite Republican Guard—were capitulating fairly quickly, but the fedayeen would prove a thorn in the Coalition's side for months to come.[8]

The fight at Samawah began on 23 March when 3rd Squadron, 7th Cavalry Regiment, encountered fedayeen on the approach to the city. While the fedayeen's AK-47s and rocket-propelled grenades had no effect on the American M1 Abrams tanks, their Bradley Fighting Vehicles were more vulnerable and troops were forced to engage the fedayeen.

Figure 5.4 Marine Corps artillery. *The Marines of I MEF advanced toward Basra and the crucial southern oil fields in the early days of the war.*

The cavalry held its own until the 3rd BCT caught up and took control at 1430 hours, sending the cavalry north toward Najaf. Once the 3rd BCT assumed the fight at Samawah, it coordinated closely with Special Forces teams in the area, who provided timely and accurate intelligence on the situation. The 3rd BCT kept the lines of communication open by holding off fedayeen attackers until 29 March, when the 82nd Airborne Division's 2nd BCT relieved it.[9]

ARSOF OPERATIONS

ARSOF participated in almost every aspect of the first five days of the war. At H-HOUR, 160th SOAR aircraft destroyed visual observation posts along the Iraqi border, allowing SOF teams to cross undetected into Iraq just hours later. ARSOF teams spread out through the western desert in search of SCUD launchers and other strategic sites. Other teams preceded the V Corps and I MEF advance north, providing targeting information and other intelligence. In the north, the advance teams of Combined Joint Special Operations Task Force–North continued to work with Kurdish leaders while anticipating the arrival of the rest of the task force. Colonel Charles Cleveland and the rest of the CJSOTF-North finally got into northern Iraq once the "UGLY BABY" air infiltration route was established. Below are accounts representing ARSOF's participation in the first days of Operation IRAQI FREEDOM.

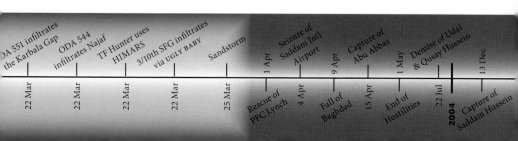

CJSOTF-North

When the war began on 19 March, CJSOTF-North was still desperately seeking a way to get its forces into theater. Turkey refused to allow overflight for the invasion, forcing air planners to devise a new infiltration route. The final flight path stretched over one thousand miles and flew over numerous Iraqi antiaircraft batteries. Once the Coalition proved to Turkey that it would place troops in northern Iraq no matter what, Turkey acquiesced, and the rest of CJSOTF-North began to flow in.

OPERATION UGLY BABY

The Turkish refusal to allow U.S. forces to pass through its territory was a near disaster to the soldiers of the 10th Special Forces Group. Months of contingency planning had been conducted, and equipment had been painstakingly pre-positioned at an intermediate support base in Turkey. The soldiers of the 10th SFG truly showed their mettle by adjusting plans and executing operations in an extremely austere and flexible environment.

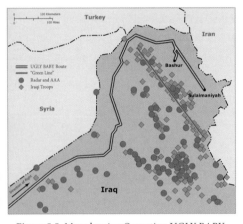

Figure 5.5 Map showing Operation UGLY BABY route.

A key to the operations in the north was to get soldiers on the ground in order to show U.S. commitment to the Kurds. Based on their experiences during the Gulf War, the Kurds were initially reluctant to commit to a U.S. effort to oust Saddam. A primary responsibility of Special Forces was to show the Kurds that the United States was seriously committed to combat. The only way to show U.S. resolve was to get Special Forces soldiers on the ground and involved in conducting combat operations with the Kurdish peshmerga units. This meant getting as many operational detachments alphas (ODAs), the basic combat unit of the Special Forces, into northern Iraq as quickly as possible. To that end, a Special Forces company organized as an advanced operating base successfully infiltrated from its pre-position location into the northern sector and made initial coordination with the Kurdish resistance organizations.[10]

Turkey's initial refusal to allow overflight to Coalition aircraft also prevented the rest of the 10th SFG from infiltrating across the Turk-

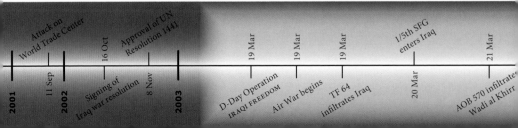

ish–Iraqi border as planned. When driving across the border was no longer an option, the 10th SFG and the 352nd Special Operations Wing (serving as Joint Special Operations Air Detachment–North) began planning an air infiltration. Time was quickly running out on the carefully developed unconventional warfare plan. As the 10th SFG staff adjusted the overall plan, logistics soldiers worked with the ODAS and aircrews to load MC-130s for infiltration flights only to see those flights cancelled because of the overflight denial. A swift decisive move was required or the United States ran the risk of losing Kurdish support on the northern front, which would then free up the Iraqi divisions arrayed along the Green Line to reinforce Baghdad against the Coalition offensive.[11]

Green Line *The Green Line represents the ad hoc political boundary established between the traditional Kurdish strongholds and Saddam's Iraq in the northeastern part of the country. Since 1991, the Kurds patrolled the Green Line which corresponded to the boundaries of the provinces the Iraqi army had left at the end of the Gulf War.*

After days of frantic effort, the planners finally figured out a way to get forces in theater via a long, indirect air route. The first leg of the bold two-day air-land infiltration was conducted by six MC-130H Combat Talon aircraft from the 7th Special Operations Squadron, JSOAD-North, flying from Constanta, Romania, to another staging base in theater. The second leg began at 1730 hours (Zulu Time) on 22 March, when three MC-130s carrying soldiers from the 2nd Battalion, 10th SFG, took off for Bashur Airfield, and another three MC-130s carrying the 10 SFG's 3rd Battalion soldiers, headed for the airfield at Sulaimaniyah. The circuitous infiltration route covered 590 miles at altitudes less than 500 feet and required the use of night vision goggles for nocturnal navigation. The Air Force later called this the longest low-level infiltration since World War II. The soldiers knew it as Operation "UGLY BABY"—only a mother could love it.[12]

In planning the high-risk movement, the commanders and staff were forced to make many tough decisions. Load plans for all ODAS were altered due to weight limitations on the aircraft. Personnel were cross-loaded and all ODAS were task organized for split team operations: in the event of an aircraft loss, the mission could continue. ODA 062 almost experienced that grim possibility.

Figure 5.6 MC-130 launching chaff. *The Combat Talons possessed a sophisticated system to avoid antiaircraft fires. Chaff and flares were fired from the aircraft to deceive incoming missiles.*

For most of the soldiers, the beginning of the flight into Iraq was uneventful. The commander of ODA 062, Captain David McDougal*, commented that during the first hour they experienced some turbulence, but it was minor enough that it felt like flying on a training

*Pseudonyms have been used for all military personnel with a rank lower than lieutenant colonel.

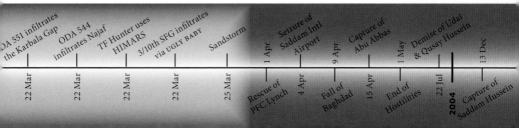

ODA 551 infiltrates the Karbala Gap — 22 Mar

ODA 544 infiltrates Najaf — 22 Mar

TF Hunter uses HIMARS — 22 Mar

3/10th SFG infiltrates via UGLY BABY — 22 Mar

Sandstorm — 25 Mar

Rescue of PFC Lynch

Seizure of Saddam Intl Airport — 1 Apr

4 Apr

Fall of Baghdad

Capture of Abu Abbas — 9 Apr

15 Apr

1 May

End of Hostilities

Demise of Udai & Qusay Hussein — 22 Jul

2004

Capture of Saddam Hussein — 13 Dec

mission from Fort Carson, Colorado, to Fort Polk, Louisiana. The first indication that the flight was not routine came when the MC-130 suddenly dropped in altitude. People and equipment floated in the simulated weightlessness, the cargo load visibly lifting and straining the ratchet straps that held it in place. Soldiers were barely held in place by straps hooked into the plane's deck. As the aircraft's descent slowed, weight returned with a vengeance, and the soldiers and payload slammed back down onto the deck. The inside of the aircraft was filled with the unmistakable sound of chaff firing as the aircraft rolled and jumped to avoid antiaircraft artillery. Blinded by the darkness, McDougal focused on the sound of shrapnel hitting the aircraft and anxiously "waited for the side of the plane to open up." Then, almost as suddenly as it had dropped, the plane leveled out and flew straight to Bashur Airfield.[13]

Figure 5.7 Passengers on UGLY BABY infiltration. *Despite restraining straps, the troops were thoroughly shaken during the violent evasive actions on the UGLY BABY infiltration.*

The aircraft crew performed a good landing, and the 2nd Battalion soldiers executed a combat off-load. All were grateful to have land under their feet again. As arranged, the infiltration team met members of its battalion and peshmerga fighters of the Kurdistan Democratic Party. McDougal and his half of ODA 062 quickly set to work training a KDP peshmerga quick reaction force company, but found they had to do so without the rest of their team. Assistant detachment commander Warrant Officer 1 Thomas Zolitck* and his half of ODA 062 had landed in Turkey.[14]

Zolitck and the "B" split of ODA 062 experienced a much different flight than McDougal's half of the team. Zolitck remembered hearing the pinging and popping of antiaircraft artillery rounds hitting the sides of the aircraft, and then watching as the padded insulation covering the inside of the aircraft suddenly began to shred as shrapnel cut through the skin and bounced around the interior. Once out of the heavy fire, the pilot continued evasive maneuvers and the soldiers quickly checked for casualties. Miraculously, the only casualty inside the aircraft was a box of rations. To the soldiers' surprise, the crew chief then passed the word that they were diverting to Incirlik Air Base, Turkey.

Though the anxiety was high for the rest of the journey, no one inside the aircraft actually knew the full extent of the damage. The

Attack on World Trade Center

16 Oct — Approval of UN Resolution 1441

19 Mar

19 Mar

19 Mar

1/5th SFG enters Iraq

21 Mar

2001

11 Sep

2002 — Signing of Iraq war resolution

8 Nov

2003

D-Day Operation IRAQI FREEDOM

Air War begins

TF 64 infiltrates Iraq

20 Mar

AOB 570 infiltrate Wadi al Khirr

MC-130 landed without problem, and as it taxied, the ramp lowered, and the crew chief stepped out onto the ramp to conduct his visual checks. He quickly returned and yelled, "Run!" Responding to the alarm, the soldiers conducted an emergency exit and assembled one hundred meters to the left rear of the aircraft. Only then did they see the extent of the damage—the left number one engine was blackened from fire and fuel was gushing out of both wings. The next morning the soldiers discovered that the pilot's windshield had been blown out from shrapnel, forcing the pilot to fly using instruments alone. They all felt very lucky to be alive.[15]

Figure 5.8 Windshield of MC-130. *Antiaircraft fire shattered the windshield of the MC-130. Miraculously the crew landed the aircraft safely.*

After landing, the soldiers were led by Air Force personnel to an American reception area, and stayed at Incirlik for a day. They loaded into a C-17 on the afternoon of 24 March, and after a quick stopover at Ramstein Air Force Base, Germany, flew back to their starting point—Constanta. Finally, on 27 March, ODA 062 "B" landed at Sulaimaniyah Airfield and met up with the 3rd Battalion. The forty-nine 2nd Battalion soldiers then moved north by ground convoy to rejoin their parent unit.[16]

The 2nd Battalion, 10th SFG, soldiers in a lead aircraft had had an excellent view of the Iraqi air defenses that had given their colleagues such trouble. To pass time on their flight, a few soldiers of the 2nd Battalion decided to look out the windows wearing their night vision goggles. Because the night was cold, they could easily observe Iraqi soldiers huddled around burn barrels for warmth while manning a cluster of four antiaircraft artillery guns. As the aircraft passed overhead, the Iraqis looked up in surprise. They scrambled to man their guns, but were too slow to fire at the first aircraft. The trailing aircraft were not as fortunate.[17]

Sergeant First Class Curtis Yates* of ODA 085 was sleeping in one of the trailing aircraft, only to be woken by men moving around the cargo hold. He recalled, "The next thing that I know a buddy of mine on my team had his goggles on looking out the window. So I crawled over to look out the window, and I could see tracer fire all over the place." Even as the Special Forces soldiers observed the antiaircraft artillery, their pilot took evasive action and chaff soon accompanied the light show.[18]

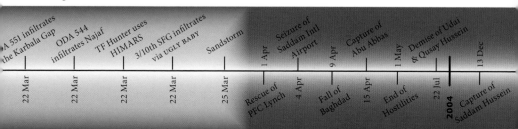

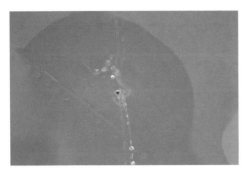

Figure 5.9 Fuel pouring out of MC-130 tank. *A direct hit punctured one of the fuel tanks of this Combat Talon during* UGLY BABY.

The flight for ODA 094 also began normally. Many of the soldiers fell asleep, only to be awoken thirty minutes into the flight when "all hell broke loose." The aircraft initially received small arms fire, but heavier fire soon began to crackle in the air outside the aircraft, with shrapnel "splashing" on the metal skin. Dust blanketed the soldiers as they were thrown around the cargo hold by the pilots' evasive maneuvers. Sergeant First Class Carson Jones*, the senior weapons sergeant on ODA 094, described being thrown three body lengths forward and then, just as suddenly, up in the air, only to be slammed back onto the aircraft deck by the next maneuver. Soon one of the crew chiefs began to yell for the soldiers to "check for holes," a task they performed with alacrity.[19]

The aircraft continued to maneuver radically for the next fifty minutes, prompting one veteran Special Forces trooper to remark to his teammate, "I don't know if we are going to make it, man. I don't feel good about this ride." Through a combination of skill and luck, however, the aircraft did make it to Sulaimaniyah Airfield and ODA 094 joined the rest of the 3rd Battalion and met up with the Patriotic Union of Kurdistan peshmerga without further incident.[20]

The high-risk gamble of infiltrating by air via a circuitous and low-altitude air route paid off. In a single movement, nineteen ODAs and four operational detachment bravos from the 10th SFG deployed to northern Iraq and linked up with the Kurdish peshmerga units. This bold move also caused the Turkish government to reconsider the ban on overflight of its territory. Turkey finally granted overflight clearance to a flight of three MC-130s on 23 March, enabling more soldiers and much needed supplies to be brought into the fight.

The UGLY BABY flight quickly faded into memory as the soldiers focused on their mission. The Special Forces teams moved via buses, dump trucks, and civilian cars directly to the Green Line almost immediately after arriving. There they arrayed against opposing Iraqi forces and tied up valuable Iraqi military resources. In the southern part of the CJSOTF-North's area of operations, the command groups at Forward Operating Base 103 and Advanced Operating Base 090 prepared for the attack on the Ansar al-Islam near the town of Halabja, an operation that proved crucial to Coalition success in the north. Perhaps most importantly, the UGLY BABY flight allowed the United

States to keep its promise to the Kurds by placing Special Forces teams on the ground in force. In that respect, getting there was the entire battle.

Signal in the North

Although special operations signal support is designed to be powerful yet portable, the 112th Special Operations Signal Battalion seldom gets the opportunity to push the limits of its equipment or its soldiers. Bravo Company's support of CJSOTF-North provided a rare opportunity to do both.

Staff Sergeant Daniel Travieso and the rest of his four-man SCAMPI team deployed in early January 2003 to Stuttgart, Germany, where they supported ODB 080, 10th SFG. The SCAMPI system provided secure and nonsecure communications via a high-capacity T1 carrier with variable bandwidth ("bandwidth-on-demand") capability. The powerful "pipe" and sophisticated signal equipment combined to provide multiple means of communication: secure and nonsecure internet (SIPR and NIPR), video teleconference, secure and nonsecure telephone, "Red" phone (direct line from field commander to next higher echelon commander), and access to proprietary defense communications networks. All that connectivity was packed into transit cases designed to safely and easily transport the equipment to and from the field.[21]

Figure 5.10 SCAMPI rig. *The 112th Signal Battalion deployed a bare bones operation to support Task Force Viking.*

After it became clear that Turkey would not allow a full staging base inside its borders, Travieso and his team deployed ahead of the main force to Constanta, arriving in late January. Along with the rest of the personnel assigned to CJSOTF-North, the team suffered from the cold. As Travieso put it, it was so cold that "the crows froze on the power lines at night and fell onto the team tents." Once the rest of the CJSOTF began arriving in February, the communications squadron from the Air Force 352nd Special Operations Wing took over primary support duties and the SCAMPI team focused on keeping the Sensitive Compartmentalized Information Facility connected. Meanwhile, the rest of Bravo Company, 112th Signal Battalion caught up with Travieso and the others in Romania.[22]

When Colonel Charles Cleveland began preparing to move his command post forward into Iraq, he informed Travieso that his

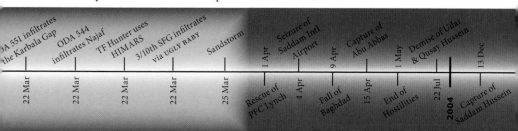

SCAMPI team would go as well. The impending 173rd Airborne Brigade (-) parachute jump led to a shortage of C-17 air transport and the entire CJSOTF had to downsize its equipment package in order to deploy on the available MC-130s. Already a portable communications package, the SCAMPI system was pared down even further. The team assessed system vulnerabilities and calculated what equipment absolutely had to be backed up due to its environmental sensitivity, and then left the rest behind. In full sympathy with their equipment, the signal soldiers also left behind their "snivel gear"—extra clothes and any personal items not strictly necessary to complete the mission.[23]

On 23 March, Travieso and four other soldiers from the 112th found themselves on an MC-130 with five members of Cleveland's staff headed for northern Iraq. After a long, low flight, the aircraft touched down at Bashur Airfield—and kept on going. The combat off-load took less than a minute; pallets rolled off the ramp and the soldiers followed, gathering themselves just in time to see their ride disappear into the night. Greeted by darkness and rain, the small group looked around in puzzlement, hoping they would not be left alone on the seemingly deserted airstrip. The dark was soon broken by a score of lights on the horizon, a sight that was initially less comforting than alarming: "It scared the crap out of everybody," recalled Travieso. Fortunately, the headlights belonged to trucks driven by friendly Kurds who were to escort them.[24]

Figure 5.11 112th SOSB insignia.

After a bumpy ninety-minute ride, the staff and signal element arrived at the location where Cleveland had temporarily based CJSOTF-North. Brigadier General James Parker, Coalition Forces Special Operations Component Command deputy commander, was already on site; he had a six-man cell with satellite phones and a tactical satellite radio package with him. It then fell to the 112th's SCAMPI team to put the commanders in contact with the rest of the world. The signal soldiers worked quickly and efficiently, and the CJSOTF had communications capability in a matter of minutes. For the next four days, Travieso supervised the small signal team as it supported CJSOTF-North through vast and complicated combat operations.[25]

Once Coalition troops liberated Irbil on 1 April, Cleveland moved the CJSOTF to an abandoned airstrip just outside the city, where the SCAMPI team's fellow Special Operations Support Command soldiers from Bravo Forward Support Company, 528th Special Operations Support Battalion, were building Camp Loki. Travieso and the other signalmen had communications up again within thirty minutes of arriving at their new location. This unusually quick connection time

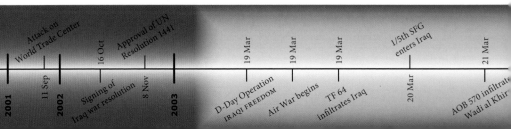

was due in part to the cooperation of the Air Force STEP (standard tactical entry point) sites, through which the SCAMPI system gained access to the Defense Information Services Network, and through DISN to the NIPR and SIPR computer networks. The STEP sites waived the usual administrative justification requirements, which allowed CJSOTF-North full connectivity in record time.[26]

Once a C-17 became available, the rest of Bravo Company joined the SCAMPI team in Irbil, bringing with them the TSC-85 satellite package. Conditions at Irbil were slightly better than at the temporary site, but still not ideal for sensitive communications equipment. In spite of the potential for failures in the complicated electronics, the generators gave them the most trouble. Contaminated fuel sold by local Kurdish entrepreneurs led to clogged fuel filters and engines requiring more maintenance than usual. Sand was not a problem in that lush northern clime, but water damage did need to be avoided. All the equipment was elevated above probable waterlines in the event of flash floods.[27]

The SCAMPI team and the rest of Bravo Company, 112th Special Operations Signal Battalion, left Irbil in May when CJSOTF-North gave way to CJSOTF–Arabian Peninsula in Baghdad. Looking back on the eventful series of deployments—from Fort Bragg, North Carolina; to Stuttgart; to Constanta; and ultimately to Irbil—Travieso concluded that the highlight of the tour was being able to push the SCAMPI system to its limits. The team validated the system's portability in a way never done before and was gratified to see that the small package was just as capable as a regular communications van package. The team also validated its own ability to perform well under pressure and in adverse conditions. Travieso's final comment on the deployment demonstrates the attitude that makes the soldiers of the 112th such a valuable asset to the special operations community: "We were used and abused, but we loved it!"[28]

CJSOTF-West

CJSOTF-west was responsible for the counter-theater ballistic missile hunt and area denial mission in the western desert, as well as for providing intelligence for the Coalition Forces Land Component Command main advance. As Special Forces teams combed the desert for SCUD sites, they also secured other strategic locations, including the isolated Wadi al Khirr Airfield. Far in front of the CFLCC advance was another Special Forces team, which was tasked with infiltrating the

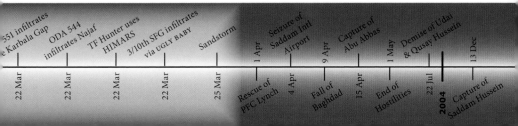

Karbala Gap in preparation for V Corps. Whatever its location, ARSOF overcame infiltration challenges and mission snafus to accomplish CJSOTF-west objectives.

Key to all aspects of the CJSOTF-west mission was the ability to coordinate air support with the joint fires element. Available air assets included a dedicated air wing of A-10s and F-16s based at H-5 and another base nearby. When SOF teams began to make more contacts and encounter higher resistance than predicted, Colonel John Mulholland and the joint fires element found themselves in a predicament. The Air Force was already flying ninety to one hundred counter-SCUD sorties a day, yet had to provide more and more close air support for ODAS in contact with hostile forces. Fearing that the aircraft would expend all their ordnance on contact missions and not be able to engage a SCUD on short notice, Mulholland directed the SOF units to focus on the counter-SCUD mission and avoid contact if at all possible until all the identified launch sites were cleared. As this issue of air coordination illustrates, CJSOTF-west's mission became very complicated, very quickly.[29]

Figure 5.12 Task Force Dagger logo.

HELICOPTER TROUBLE

In the southern area of operations, Forward Operating Base 52 commander Lieutenant Colonel Christopher Conner struggled with a worrisome problem in the days running up to Operation IRAQI FREEDOM. Three of his ODAS were selected for special reconnaissance missions supporting the conventional forces once they had crossed the Kuwait-Iraq border. These ODAS—551, 553, and 555—all needed to be infiltrated into Iraq three days before D-DAY in order to be in place and able to provide intelligence for the CFLCC advance. Conner's staff worked with Joint Special Operations Air Detachment–South staff to plan the infiltration; the major problem was the scarcity of aircraft, specifically the MH-53J Pave Low helicopters designated to support SOF infiltrations in southern Iraq—only ten were available.[30]

Each Special Forces team was given a special reconnaissance target in western Iraq, and needed to reach those targets before conventional troops did. Captain Mark Donaldson's* team, ODA 555, would observe and if necessary, secure two critical bridges south of Samawah on the Euphrates River. Captain Jamie McMaster's* team, ODA 553, would do the same at Nasiriya. Both cities were key locations along V Corps' line of advance. Time and resources dictated an aggressive infiltration

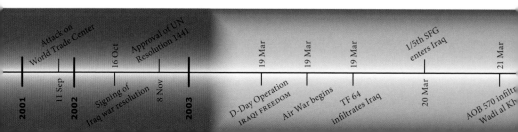

schedule and, after intensive planning, Conner decided that ODAS 553 and 555 would infiltrate the same night, one team after the other.[31]

ODA 553 was first, and once the six Pave Lows delivered the team to its infiltration location, the helicopters would return for ODA 555. At least, that was the plan. When the six MH-53JS began to set down to off-load ODA 553, five made it safely. The sixth helicopter's left front tire hit a sand dune, causing the aircraft to pivot abruptly and then roll over. Inside the aircraft's cargo area, the three Special Forces soldiers riding in the cab of their truck were tossed to and fro, but were not seriously hurt. The rear gunner, however, was only secured to the truck bed with a cargo strap and was injured. Fortunately, the heavy cargo straps held the truck in place, which prevented a true tragedy. ODA 553 salvaged what it could from the wreckage, taking special care to secure sensitive equipment, but the truck and the helicopter were total losses. The combat search and rescue helicopter accompanying the infiltration then landed, prepared the wrecked plane for demolition, and carried the MH-53J crew back to Kuwait.[32]

Figure 5.13 MH-53 Pave Low. *The Air Force's MH-53 was a critical component in the infiltration and resupply of SOF teams in the western desert.*

In spite of what could have been a serious setback, ODA 553 continued the mission it had trained for. The loss of the Pave Low also affected the rest of the insertions. ODA 555 quickly reallocated gear and people to a five-truck configuration, instead of one using six trucks. Once the team made a successful infiltration, it moved out to Samawah. Availability of air assets, especially SOF helicopters, continued to be an issue throughout the war.[33]

CROSSING THE LINE

For Major Jack Gray*, commander of Operational Detachment Bravo 520, 1st Battalion, 5th SFG, it seemed as if the planning conferences never ended. The 1st Battalion's mission to prevent Saddam Hussein from a repeat performance of Operation DESERT STORM—launching SCUD missiles at Israel and Saudi Arabia—was a SOF mission of clear strategic importance, but these planning meetings were like flogging the proverbial dead horse. Gray and his ODAS concentrated on little else after he took command in July 2002. Exercise Early Victor kept the battalion training in the deserts of Jordan for almost six months,

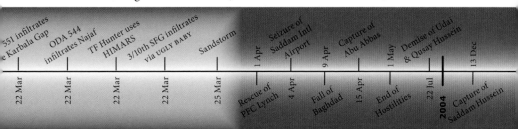

Figure 5.14 ODAs refueling. *The great distances the teams covered in their search for* SCUDs *made refueling a regular event.*

and everybody knew that the fight was coming soon. As he sipped a cup of lukewarm, ancient coffee, Gray reconciled himself to another day of "what ifs." Just as he pulled his notes and folders from his bag and took a seat at the large conference table, a sergeant tapped him on the shoulder and said he had an urgent call on the secure phone. Gray recognized the familiar voice of the battalion operations officer; the message was short—return to H-5 as soon as possible.[34]

On the helicopter flight from CJSOTF-west to Forward Operating Base 51 at H-5, Gray contemplated his company's preparations for the upcoming operation. Since taking command of ODB 520 nearly nine months earlier, this mission had consumed his days and nights. It had been a long road that required a fundamental change in how his company and ODAs operated. The first challenge was to transform a company with an unconventional warfare focus into one capable of mounted special reconnaissance and direct action. Simultaneously, he had to retrain and reequip his ODB to be a real fighting headquarters instead of just an administrative unit.[35]

Accomplishing a major transformation of the company was a tall order under any circumstances, but severe time and material constraints further complicated things. The vehicles needed to be acquired, modified, and ready for loading on ships bound for Exercise Early Victor by 19 August 2002. Now, as Gray watched the desert streak by the window of the low flying Chinook helicopter, he was still amazed that the modifications to their GMVs and Light Medium Tactical Vehicles (LMTVs)—new springs, tires, gun mounts, racks, radio mounts, and a hundred other things—were completed in time. Considering the condition of some of the vehicles they had received from other units, it was nothing short of a miracle. It was a true team effort.[36]

Training the men and developing solid mounted tactics, techniques, and procedures took longer. Gray knew that the vehicles were their "legs," so he sent people to Army Material Command schools to obtain better maintenance training. The teams spent hours and hours, both day and night, bumping through the desert learning how to drive cross-country. The ODB used situational training exercises to develop standing operating procedures for likely scenarios. Call-

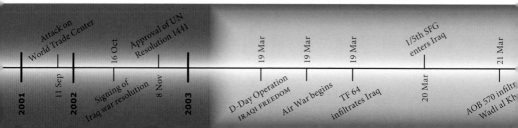

ing in close air support was not only a mission-essential task for the counter-SCUD mission, but if the ODAs made contact with larger Iraqis units, it could also mean the difference between living and dying.[37]

During these operations, the ODB functioned as a mobile advanced operating base, designated as AOB 520—both the command and control node and the primary means of resupply for the ODAs—functions normally preformed by the forward operating base with many more assets. The ODB troops worked to develop new skill sets and procedures for battle tracking and logistics operations. Standard LMTVs were converted into rolling supply bases, dubbed "motherships," capable of resupply and self-protection, mounting a combination of M240B machine guns, .50 caliber machine guns, and MK19 grenade launchers. A thousand details were addressed in preparation for this mission, and while they could probably do more, Gray was confident that the preparations they had made were sufficient.[38]

The CJSOTF-west plan called for infiltrating FOB 51's two advanced operating bases—each with six ODAS—by ground at designated border crossing sites. AOB 520's sister unit, AOB 530, moved by MC-130s to a remote airfield where the unit staged for infiltration. The distance to AOB 530's infiltration point required it be airlifted to the vicinity of its crossing point. It reached its destination in time and began

Figure 5.15 LMTV of 5th SFG. *The "Motherships" from the advanced operating bases kept the teams supplied in both Task Force Dagger and Task Force Viking.*

preparation for its crossing. Coalition forces were also scheduled to use these border crossing sites to enter their operational areas.[39]

The western Iraqi desert was divided into four joint special operations areas. The western and the southern JSOAs were parceled out to the United States—1st Battalion, 5th SFG—while the northern and central JSOAs were the responsibility of other Coalition special operations units. Within each of those JSOAs were a number of designated areas representing the intelligence community's best guess of potential SCUD launch sites. The analysis was based on historical data from the first Gulf War: the range of the missiles, likely targets, road networks, concealment, known air defense sites, and communications facilities. Once across the Iraqi border, the SOF teams would move as quickly as possible to their respective areas and search for evidence of SCUDs or other weapons of mass destruction. Any SCUD launchers or support equipment the teams located would be destroyed using

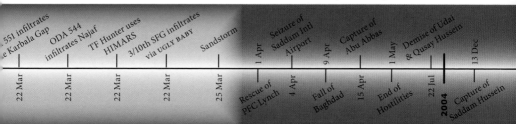

dedicated close air support aircraft, or direct action by the teams if necessary.[40]

Once Gray was back on the ground at H-5, he found that the SOF base was a picture of measured and deliberate activity as the ODAs and mission support units made final preparations for the infiltration. Operational security concerns and the political sensitivity to the U.S. presence in the region was cause for discretion. The presence of U.S. combat forces in the host country was an extremely sensitive political issue and movement of American forces off the base was closely monitored and controlled. Consequently, the movement to the assembly area was planned for the hours of darkness and the guards were told that the Americans were going to a range firing exercise. The movement plan for B Company from H-5 called for a series of small convoys to leave intermittently. The guards, however, became suspicious after the first group had left and refused to let subsequent convoys off the base until their commander gave the okay. Once the authorization was given, the infiltration force assembled at the range/rally point before departing in one large convoy for the assembly area. At approximately 1600 hours, the convoy arrived at the assembly area, a slight depression three miles from the Iraqi border.[41]

The actual breach of the berms along the Iraqi border was made in the early morning hours of 19 March. The border area was delineated by two parallel antitank berms approximately one hundred meters apart, with occupied guard towers on both sides. A large enough corridor had to be cut through the berms to allow the ODAs to pass through in their GMVs. Using bulldozers to cut the corridor was considered during planning, but for operational security reasons, it was decided to do the digging by hand. The FOB force protection unit—C Company, 2nd Battalion, 124th Infantry Regiment, Florida Army National Guard—accepted the mission to dig through the berms using shovels and picks. Staff Sergeant Jesse Dundee*, a squad leader in C Company recalled, "There was some joking about it being a great mission for the Guard since we had so much practice filling sand bags and all," due to disaster relief efforts during hurricane season in Florida. The Guardsmen got to the business at hand and organized their digging party into two ten-man squads. They conducted numerous rehearsals of the operation and practiced digging in full combat gear. The plan was a simple one: the Guardsmen would do the digging and two ODAs, plus an AC-130 Spectre gunship overhead, would provide security. Captain Wayne Pelham*, platoon leader for the operation, said they were told, "If there's any shooting going on, just keep digging. We'll end it!"[42]

Figure 5.16 124th Infantry Regiment insignia.

The night was clear, windy, and cold as the Guardsmen loaded up at the assembly area for the short ride to the border. The bright light from the full moon allowed them to see the berms and guard towers clearly as they approached the breach site. Approximately three hundred meters from the border they dismounted their vehicles, continuing on foot. The host country border guards briefly protested the American presence, then, duty fulfilled, stayed out of the way. Once the security forces were in place, the Guardsmen began digging through the nearside berm. They had been told that the berm would mostly be loose sand, two to three meters high; it turned out

Figure 5.17 Guardsmen digging through the berm. *The men of C Company, 2nd Battalion, 124th Infantry, cut a passageway through the two berms to assist the movement of the Coalition special operators.*

to be five or six meters high, one meter across at the pinnacle, and mostly rock and concrete rubble baked and compacted over fifteen years. They quickly determined that picks were the tool of choice rather than shovels. In the dark, the powerful blows of the picks sent showers of sparks and rock splinters flying. Private Noel Platz* commented, "It was more like chiseling than digging!" Instead of rotating squads, Pelham put both squads into action digging simultaneously on opposite sides of the berm. It took just twenty-three minutes for the squads to lower the berm enough for ODA 522 to roll through into the no-man's-land between the berms.[43]

The B Company infiltration force considered a preemptive strike on the single Iraqi guard tower, but decided not to engage unless the Iraqis showed hostile intent. The tower remained dark and silent. On the signal from the security force on the far side of no-man's-land, Pelham sent sixteen diggers forward to begin on the larger Iraqi berm. He also posted two squad automatic weapons teams atop the breached berm to provide additional covering fire if it proved necessary. The berm on the Iraqi side was a much more formidable obstacle. Once again the two squads, this time with eight men each, attacked the berm from two sides at once with their picks and shovels. The Guardsmen's faces were streaked with dirt and their desert camouflage uniforms were patterned with large spreading sweat stains as they feverishly worked with their shovels and picks. After forty-five exhausting minutes, a lane through the Iraqi berm was cut and the SOF vehicles were signaled through. The Guardsmen proudly produced the American and State of Florida flags and planted them atop the berm. The pla-

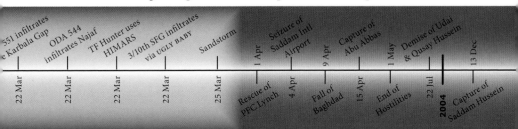

Figure 5.18 American Flag at the breach of the berm. *The U.S. and Florida flags fly at the berm as the soldiers of the Seminole Battalion opened the infiltration route.*

Specialist Jeffrey M. Wershow

Specialist Jeffrey M. Wershow of Gainesville, Florida, was one of the Florida National Guard soldiers digging through the berm on the night of 19 March. Once the digging was completed, Wershow placed a pole with both the American and Florida State flags on top of the berm and saluted the first vehicles as they crossed. C Company continued missions with CJSOTF-west for the next month and then moved to Baghdad at the end of May. On 6 July 2003, Wershow was part of the security detail for a Civil Affairs mission at Baghdad University when he was shot and killed by a lone gunman. Specialist Wershow was awarded the Bronze Star and the Purple Heart before being buried on his family's farm near Gainesville.

toon stood beside the breach watching as each vehicle passed into Iraq, proudly returning the "thumbs up" they received from the infiltrating soldiers. The first units through the breach were the Coalition forces. The American teams were the last through the gap, and as the rumble of their engines faded away, the Guardsmen climbed back in their vehicles for the journey back to H-5. Theirs had not been a glorious nor glamorous mission, but it was an important one that was clearly appreciated by the SOF units. That was all the thanks they needed.[44]

Finally in Iraq, the ODAs fanned out and headed for their initial target areas. Their guidance was to drive hard and reach the target areas as soon as possible. Each ODA developed a list of objectives consisting of hide sites, roads, and facilities to check in its sector based on a mission analysis. FOB 51 instructed the teams to continue moving during the daylight hours if necessary, and let the Iraqis know they were in the area. The FOB felt that the mere presence of the heavily armed and mobile ODAs would deter the Iraqis from setting up and launching their missiles. In addition to the impressive array of firepower on the vehicles, the teams could quickly call on the overwhelming armada of aircraft flying overhead.[45]

In the western JSOA of CJSOTF-west's area of operations, two of AOB 520's key target areas were the airfields that made up the H-3 base cluster and the town of Ar Rutba. The H-3 base cluster consisted of a primary airfield and two smaller supporting airfields, with a number of hardened aircraft shelters, bunkers, revetments, and ammunition storage areas that had to be cleared. During the 1991 Gulf War, H-3 was suspected of being a storage facility for chemical munitions, and

in the months leading up to Operation IRAQI FREEDOM, Coalition aircraft enforcing the Southern No-Fly Zone repeatedly bombed the airfields. With a population of fifteen thousand and sitting astride the major road network leading to Baghdad, Ar Rutba was of obvious strategic importance.[46]

ODAS 523 and 524, commanded by Captain John Sluthey* and Captain Mark Pointer* respectively, were teamed to search the mines southwest of Ar Rutba for missiles or weapons of mass destruction. After a grueling 130-kilometer cross-country drive to the target, they arrived at the mines only to discover that they were just that—mines. The teams found no indication of military activities at the site, and after a thorough search, concluded that it was a legitimate gypsum and quartz mining operation. They made favorable contact with the locals and decided to use the quarry as a base for their reconnaissance operations along Highway 10. The teams were surprised at the volume of civilian traffic on the highways on 20 March, but the people they encountered seemed friendly and favorably disposed toward the Americans, so the teams were not overly concerned.[47]

Further to the west, the mission of ODAS 522 and 581 was to clear the H-3 base cluster. By daylight on 20 March, the teams reached H-3 Southwest, one of the smaller airfields. With no evidence of military activity on the abandoned airfield, the two detachments prepared to move on to H-3 Main. An intelligence report cautioned them that there were indications a force of two to three hundred Iraqis were occupying H-3. A fragmentary order instructed them to keep H-3 under observation, but not to engage in any clearing operations. In addition to being at a disadvantage should they encounter a large Iraqi force, firefights could interfere with the teams' counter-theater ballistic missile mission.[48]

While ODA 581 was keeping H-3 under observation, ODA 522 cleared potential hide sites along Highway 1. Early on the morning of 21 March, Iraqis ambushed the team at a highway overpass. The Iraqis—firing rocket-propelled grenades, AK-47s, and PKM machine guns—were well concealed and caught the ODA by surprise. Riding in a Mercedes cargo truck and a tan sport utility vehicle, the Iraqi troops were difficult to distinguish from the civilian traffic on the road until they opened fire. The ODA's Air Force enlisted terminal air controller (ETAC) requested immediate close air support, and in a matter of minutes three F-16 Falcons delivered, with terminal guidance from the ETAC, three 1,000-pound bombs on top of the Iraqis. The ODA then captured six of the survivors and secured the cargo truck that was filled

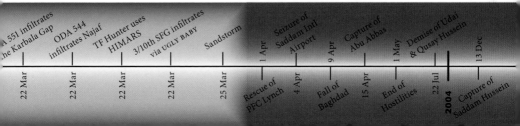

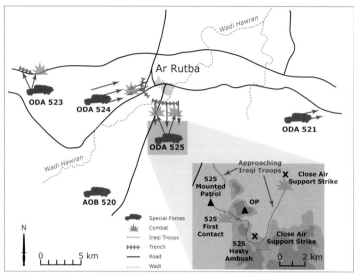

Figure 5.19 Map of Ar Rutba battle.

with mortars and ammunition.[49]

That same morning, ODA 525 moved into an area southsouthwest of Ar Rutba. A few hours before daylight, Staff Sergeant Fred Sawolski* and Chief Warrant Officer 2 Jared Krenolski* established an observation post on a small hill to watch a building suspected of housing enemy troops. After a short time, an Iraqi patrol in five pickup trucks maneuvered between the observation post and the rest of the ODA, threatening to cut off Sawolski and Krenolski. As the men on the hill watched, men in black uniforms—fedayeen—drove along the team's vehicle tracks directly toward the observation post. The team members quickly relocated in their GMVs, setting up a hasty ambush for the Iraqis. Soon, .50 caliber bullets and 40mm grenade rounds pelted the Iraqi trucks, which fled the area in confusion. The ODA relocated its vehicles just as trucks began streaming out of Ar Rutba, heading directly for the base of the hill. Coming to a halt, Iraqi soldiers jumped out of the trucks and took cover in a concealed trench line. The soldiers at the observation post counted over one hundred Iraqis, supported by several pickup trucks, each with a DSHK heavy machine gun mounted in the bed of the vehicle. The situation did not look good for the lone ODA.[50]

Sergeant First Class Alex Bingham*, ODA 525's intelligence sergeant, was monitoring the radio net from the team's hide site. After hearing the situation at the observation post, Bingham immediately transmitted the brevity code word "SPRINT" across the satellite radio "SCUD" net, alerting everyone listening that ODA 525 was in danger of being overrun. The constant flurry of activity at FOB 51's tactical operations center suddenly stopped and the area became quiet as the news registered. The brevity word they had practiced in numerous exercises now had an ominous meaning. Within seconds, the silence

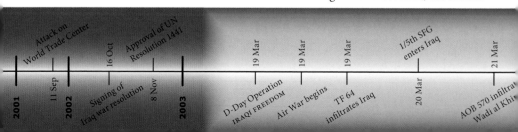

was replaced by frantic activity to support the team. ODA 525's ETAC
called in for close air support to help the team break contact, and Gray
called for ODA 524, which was operating to the south of ODA 525, to
move in and engage the enemy. As ODA 524 drew close to the sound
of the guns, it took fire from two Iraqi 23mm antiaircraft guns. ODA
524's ETAC sent close air support to take care of the new contact, freeing the team to proceed. ODA 521, located to the east of the fight, also
moved to join in the fray, and soon three ODAs were involved in the
escalating conflict.[51]

The battle now took on an aura of controlled chaos, with Bingham
receiving reports from the observation post and the rest of the ODA,
the ETACs requesting air support, and the FOB fire support cell and
the Airborne Warning and Control System flying above routing the
aircraft. The Air Force passed multiple aircraft sorties to the team—
everything from F-16s to A-10s—and British Tornado fighter-bomb-
ers dropped 500 and 2,000 pound bombs on the Iraqi attackers. The
ODAs continued to engage the enemy, dealing with repeated enemy
assaults. At the same time, Sawolski and Krenolski continued firing
while directing close air support on the enemy trench system at the
base of the hill. ODA 524's ETAC commented, "By this time the enemy
that had advanced, we pushed back. They advanced again, and we
pushed them back once more."[52]

At about 1400 hours, the firing dropped off and the observation
post reported that the enemy forces were withdrawing back into the
city. Gray saw this as an opportunity to get Sawolski and Krenolski
off the hill. Gray quickly coordinated a linkup with the observation
post using ODA 521 to provide security for the exfiltration at the same
time four aircraft provided additional cover. The eight GMVs quickly
moved to the hill as Sawolski and Krenolski pulled out, with ODAs
523 and 524 providing flank security. The ODAs coordinated a linkup
with AOB 520 about ten kilometers southwest of the battle to replenish
ammunition and prepare for the next fight.[53]

The fight south of Ar Rutba along Highway 10 was one of the first
battles for Special Forces during Operation IRAQI FREEDOM. After
nearly seven hours of intense fighting, over one hundred Iraqis lay
dead and fifteen vehicles were destroyed. The triumphant AOB 520
teams, on the other hand, had suffered no casualties or equipment
loss. The aggressive maneuver and direct fire from the ODAs, combined with well-coordinated close air support, proved to be a deadly
combination for the Iraqi forces.[54]

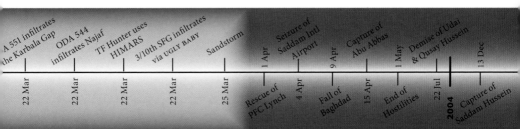

Wadi al Khirr

In the battle area of the western desert of Iraq, the 5th SFG looked for ways to help shape the battlefield for conventional forces attacking toward Baghdad. Once the ground war began, Central Command's plan was to keep the Iraqis off balance by hitting them hard and fast with armored and mechanized ground forces. Ahead of the conventional forces juggernaut, the Special Forces operators planned to support the maneuver forces with ODAs conducting deep reconnaissance of strategically important areas and making contact with anti-Saddam resistance groups. The challenge for SOF planners was how to insert the ODAs rapidly and efficiently deep into Iraq using a limited number of aircraft in order to support Central Command's plan.[55]

The SOF planners knew that Air Force MC-130 aircraft were required for any deep infiltration mission. The immediate problem was locating a suitable desert landing strip that met both the Air Force landing criteria and the Army's mission requirements. MC-130 Combat Talons were capable of landing on unimproved runways, but they needed a stretch of reasonably flat, firm, and open ground at least 3,500 feet long and 60 feet wide. The Air Force also insisted that runway conditions be validated on the ground by trained and qualified Air Force controllers. The Army's mission required that the infiltration be accomplished well before the conventional forces began their attack, that the landing strip be near the Karbala-Najaf area, and that the infiltration site be away from known enemy concentrations.[56]

The mission to find such a place was given to Major Boyd Sinclair* and ODB 570. He was told to develop a primary and an alternate plan to establish an advanced operating base at a desert landing strip deep within Iraq. The desert landing strip would be used to infiltrate ODAs and other SOF teams for missions in support of conventional forces. His detachment needed to be prepared to receive the first ODAs within twenty-four hours of verification, and continue to operate the landing strip for up to forty-eight hours. When the last teams were on the ground, Sinclair's base would exfiltrate on the last aircraft. The forces available for the operation included Sinclair's ODB 570 under its operational designation of AOB 570, ODA 574, and four Air Force combat controllers from the 23rd Special Tactics Squadron. The detachment was on a tight time schedule—all mission preparations had to be completed in anticipation of launching as early as the night of 17 March.[57]

AOB 570 was fortunate to have a highly qualified and experienced Air Force combat control team from the 23rd STS assisting in the planning for the operation. Three members of the team were veterans of Afghanistan with first-hand experience operating desert landing strips. The savvy controllers cautioned that simple dirt landing strips tend to become badly rutted after only a few landings, and the mission profile for this operation called for multiple aircraft and multiple sorties.[58]

The experienced judgment of the Air Force controllers caused the team to look for existing hard surface landing strips that might be useable. Unfortunately, the intensive bombing campaigns of Operation DESERT STORM and the post-Gulf War enforcement measures

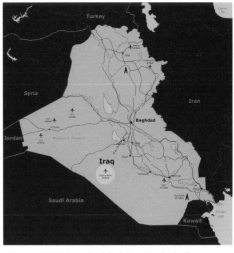

Figure 5.20 Map highlighting Wadi al Khirr.

in the Southern No-Fly Zone left most of the existing flight strips in Iraq severely cratered or otherwise damaged. However, after a careful analysis of existing imagery and some additional low-level, high-quality photos provided by British Tornado reconnaissance aircraft, the team felt that the abandoned Iraqi fighter base at Wadi al Khirr might meet the mission needs.[59]

Wadi al Khirr Airfield, located 240 kilometers southwest of Baghdad, was built in the 1980s by Yugoslav contractors and had a single 9,700-foot long runway. At one time, the air base had twelve hardened aircraft shelters, but bombings during DESERT STORM had reduced them to piles of rubble.[60]

The 23rd STS reasoned that between the main runway and a parallel taxiway, a suitable landing strip could be pieced together. For the Special Forces, Wadi al Khirr was reasonably close to the key Karbala-Najaf area, and the only known enemy facilities in the vicinity of the airfield were Iraqi border posts nine miles away.[61]

Once it had selected a primary site for the desert landing strip, the AOB had to plan and coordinate the myriad of details that make all the pieces of a joint operation fit together. Deep penetration SOF aircraft were limited—in the opening days of the war, competition for air assets was keen. Thus, getting the AOB to Wadi al Khirr was one of the first issues to be addressed. Both ODA 574 and the 23rd STS team were high altitude–low opening qualified, which made parachute entry an option offering a degree of economy in air assets. However,

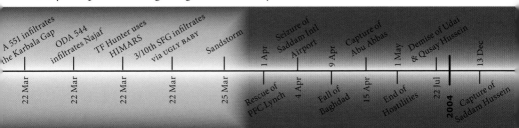

Figure 5.21 ATV of 5th SFG. *The all-terrain vehicle proved to be a versatile addition in Task Force Dagger.*

Figure 5.22 NSV loaded for combat. *The nonstandard tactical vehicles were widely used by the SOF forces throughout the campaign.*

lessons learned from DESERT STORM made a convincing case that in a desert environment, dismounted Special Forces teams were at a distinct disadvantage if compromised. The planners decided to use Air Force MH-53J helicopters to infiltrate the twenty-six AOB 570 soldiers and airmen, as well as five nonstandard vehicles (NSVs) and four all-terrain vehicles (ATVs).[62]

The days before AOB 570's infiltration were long and filled with critical tasks as the soldiers prepared themselves and their equipment for action. The soldiers checked and packed equipment, configured load plans, planned air and ground routes, coordinated fire support, scheduled aircrew briefings, and finalized communications plans. Each soldier and airman was involved in the planning, and through a series of informal brief-backs, each man knew the plan well enough to meet any contingency. Finally, the soldiers and airmen conducted detailed rehearsals for key parts of the plan to validate the concept of operations. On 17 March, AOB 570 was standing by, ready to go.[63]

No mission is conducted in a vacuum, and this mission was no different. In large campaigns such as IRAQI FREEDOM, multiple operations planned for the same time periods often competed for the same assets. In such cases, the commander must decide which of the competing missions is the most critical to the overall success of the campaign. In IRAQI FREEDOM, it was recognized that the "lynch pin" for SOF deep infiltrations was the availability of aircraft. During the same time period that AOB 570 planned to fly into Wadi al Khirr, U.S. Navy SEALs planned to conduct an air assault onto the Al Faw peninsula to seize and protect the strategically important oil infrastructure there. Both the AOB 570 and the SEAL operations planned to use U.S. Air Force MH-53s; however, there were only enough aircraft to support one mission. The Al Faw mission got the resources and the Wadi al Khirr mission was put on hold.

Decisions in war often have a ripple effect. The delay in air assets caused FOB 52 (2nd Battalion, 5th SFG) to scramble for another means to infiltrate ODA 551, which had a time-sensitive, special reconnaissance mission in the Karbala area critical to the 3rd Infantry Division's scheme of maneuver. The 3rd Infantry Division had imagery and signal intercept data, but the division commander wanted eyes on the target to provide him with ground-truth intelligence. ODA 551 flew to H-5 Airfield to link up with 3rd Battalion, 160th SOAR, for infiltration into Iraq on its MH-47DS. As ODA 551 flew to H-5, AOB 570 waited for a ride into Iraq.[64]

After two nights of waiting at the forward operating base, AOB 570 finally received the order to execute on 19 March. The mission used five Air Force MH-53JS, with a sixth for Combat Search and Rescue support. The AOB loaded five NSVS and four ATVS into the Pave Lows, and then distributed the personnel among the aircraft, paying particular attention to make sure that the four air controllers were on different aircraft. The controllers were critical to operating the landing strip; without at least one of them on the ground, the whole mission would have to be aborted. As always, the AOB had a "bump plan" establishing priorities for every person and major item of equipment in case one or more aircraft became inoperable. In the event of the failure of one of the aircraft, the most important people and equipment could quickly be shifted to the remaining aircraft and the mission could continue. After the AOB was loaded, one of the helicopters did indeed develop an electronics problem that could not be resolved. The load on that aircraft was transferred to the empty Combat Search and Rescue helicopter with minimal disruption and time delay. Captain Doug Hoffman*, ODA 574 commander and the man tasked to provide security for the operation, recalled, "The scariest part of the whole operation

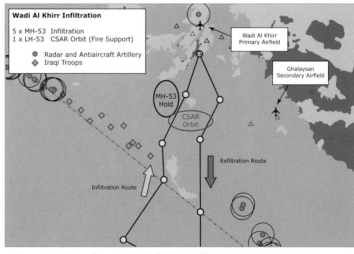

Figure 5.23 Map showing Wadi al Khirr infiltration route.

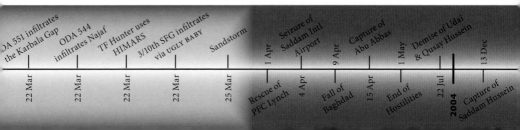

for me was flying in those MH-53s." Drawing on his past experiences, he added, "They are so old that you usually need twenty to get five." But he gave credit where it was due by allowing that, "This time it only took six!" Even First Lieutenant Chris Hill*, one of the 23rd STS air controllers, breathed easier as the flight of five helicopters headed west from Ali As-Salim Air Base, Kuwait. He said, "We had problems with three [MH-53s] on the rehearsal; only one had a problem on the mission."[65]

The flight route into Iraq had the SOF soldiers skirting the Iraqi border for hundreds of kilometers until they dashed north to Wadi al Khirr. The helicopters rendezvoused with Air Force tankers twice to refuel in-flight. The night of AOB 570's flight into Wadi al Khirr was the same night the Air Force began its "shock and awe" campaign. First Lieutenant Wayne West*, commander of the 23rd STS team, was listening in on the chatter of the helicopter pilots through a headset in the cargo compartment: "It was a little disquieting to hear the pilots talking about the [Tomahawk Land Attack Missiles] flying by above and below the helicopters."[66]

Aside from transiting a somewhat crowded night sky, the flight into the objective area was uneventful. The plan called for the AOB to be flown into a helicopter landing zone approximately ten miles from the airfield. About twenty minutes out from the landing zone, the crew alerted the soldiers and airmen to get ready. As the helicopters hovered to land, the rotor wash kicked up so much dust that the pilots decided to land two at a time instead of all at once in order to avoid colliding with one another in the "brown out" conditions.[67]

Once the group assembled on the ground and the helicopters lifted off, the soldiers moved a short distance and conducted a security halt to make sure the landing had not been detected. Hearing or seeing nothing to cause alarm, they moved to an objective rally point near the landing strip. The moon had not yet risen, so the night was clear, dark, and cold. The special operations forces put the nonstandard vehicles and their bed-mounted M240 machine guns in the lead, followed by the four ATVs. Travel was slow and difficult across terrain littered with large, sharp rocks.[68]

Intelligence reports stated that the area was infrequently traveled, but the AOB crossed numerous fresh vehicle tracks and several scraped, well-maintained, and recently used roads. The threat of discovery was uppermost in everyone's minds. Master Sergeant James Robins* from the 23rd STS was concerned that the loud whining noise of the ATVs carried too far in the cold, desert night air. In addition,

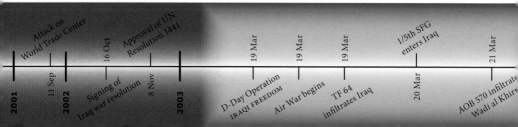

each ATV had an engine light pinpointing its position. Nevertheless, after two hours of deliberate and careful travel, the AOB reached its objective rally point, approximately five kilometers from Wadi al Khirr.[69]

After arriving, Sinclair sent an NSV-mounted security team from ODA 574 to lead the Air Force ATV-mounted survey team to the airfield. Sergeant Major Thad Berino* of AOB 570 provided rear security with his NSV. By this time, the moon was up and the improved visibility made the movement to the airfield easier; the bright moonlight also

Figure 5.24 Hide site. *A 5th SFG hide site in the western desert.*

revealed how open the terrain was and how vulnerable the soldiers were to enemy observation. Once the small convoy reached the airfield, the security team established an overwatch position at the west end to provide surveillance and covering fire with its M240 machine guns. Robins and Master Sergeant Bill Dayton* traded their ATVs for Berino's quieter, more heavily armed NSV and took a quick look at the main runway and taxiway.[70]

The combat control team was working against a tight deadline for completing the survey. If Wadi al Khirr were unusable, the contingency plan called for a small security and survey element to be air-lifted to the alternate site at Ghalaysan Airfield seventy kilometers to the southeast. The rest of the AOB would then move cross-country to Ghalaysan. The two MH-53s for the contingency were orbiting in a holding pattern, but could only stay on station for three hours, so the decision needed to be made quickly. The movement to the objective rally point and then to the airfield had used up most of that time. Robins said that based on their pre-mission study, he and Dayton were, "about ninety percent sure we could use either the main runway or the taxiway." They made a quick sweep east along the main runway. They found that while most of the runway was intact, near hits had thrown huge slabs of concrete and massive amounts of dirt onto the surface. At the end of the runway, they cut over to the parallel taxiway and drove back to the west. They soon decided that while the secondary strip would have to be cleared of debris, it would be much less work than the primary runway and it was well suited for the MC-130s.[71]

Dayton and Robins passed the message to Sinclair that the airfield was usable. Sinclair released the orbiting MH-53s and led the rest of the AOB to Wadi al Khirr. Upon arrival, the remaining ODA 574 security

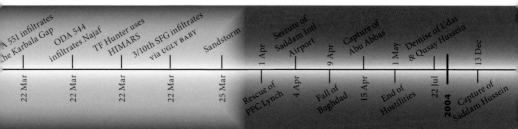

teams quickly moved to their positions on the high ground surrounding the airfield. Meanwhile, Sinclair established the AOB command post near the center of the runway and made his initial reports to FOB 53. The primary mission for the remainder of the night was removing all the debris from the taxiway and that portion of the runway to be used as a turnaround to prevent any dangerous objects getting sucked into the engines or damaging tires. In the words of AOB 570 medic, Sergeant First Class Bruce Kroll*, "What it amounted to was one very long, tedious, boring police call."[72]

Figure 5.25 Modified NSV Tacoma pickup truck. *The Toyota Tacoma was one of the most popular models of nonstandard vehicles in use by the Special Forces teams.*

Although the AOB had procured four wide-blade shovels to hasten the job, much of the shrapnel and chunks of concrete had to be picked up by hand. Working in shifts, the men moved on line to clear a swath 4,500 feet long and 66 feet wide. Despite the bitingly cold desert night, the men were soon dripping with sweat as they shoveled and picked up hundreds of pounds of debris. As daylight approached, the entire AOB moved under cover for "stand-to"—armed and alert, the AOB stood ready for action from enemy attack. After stand-to, a lot of runway still needed clearing. Although the plan was to stay out of sight during the day, everyone agreed that the flight strip needed clearing even if it meant taking the risk of being seen. However, at Berino's recommendation, the soldiers rested before resuming the backbreaking work.[73]

The rejuvenated soldiers finished picking up the debris by noon, but they still had to deal with several large mounds of dirt that bombs had dumped on the flight strip. It was impossible to shovel all the dirt off the flight strip, but the soldiers came up with an innovative way to knock off the humps and smooth the surface. Berino scavenged around the old base and found a large piece of metal siding, which he rigged to the winch on his NSV, creating a slide similar to those used to smooth a baseball diamond infield. Two of the larger SOF soldiers stood on the siding to weigh it down as Berino pulled the metal across the uneven piles of dirt. By 1400 hours, Dayton and Robins were satisfied with the team's work and reported to the command post that the flight strip was ready to receive aircraft.[74]

For the rest of the daylight hours of 22 March, the AOB remained under cover to minimize chances of compromise. The troops hardly had time to hunker down when, at 1500 hours, the western security

team reported two civilian vehicles coming toward the airfield from the southwest. The AOB had contingencies for chance contacts with civilians and decided that unless the civilians displayed hostile intent or their presence jeopardized the mission, the teams would let them pass unmolested. Hoffman and his teams kept the vehicles under observation and determined that they were water trucks driven by Bedouin shepherds. The vehicles stopped and the drivers conversed briefly before driving off in the direction of one of the Iraqi border posts destroyed by air strikes the night before. It appeared to the security team that the Bedouins were intent on salvaging anything of value from the ruins. When the Bedouins left the destroyed outpost, they returned along the same route, but made a wide circle around the airfield. Throughout the afternoon, the team spotted dust clouds from vehicle traffic in the distance, but had no other close encounters.[75]

During the afternoon and into the evening, the air controllers provided the aircrews with the flight landing strip layout, updated weather conditions, and digital imagery via e-mail. After dark, Dayton and Robins ventured back out onto the flight strip to place the runway lights—marking the runway and key points on the flight strip with infrared strobe lights visible only to incoming pilots.[76]

Hill, as primary air controller for the night's operation, was responsible for talking with the aircraft pilots, advising them of current conditions on the flight strip and clearing them for landing and takeoff. West positioned himself with Sinclair, where he kept him advised on the status of the aircraft operations. On their ATVs, Dayton and Robins operated as a kind of tag team once the aircraft were on the ground. Dayton played the role of the "follow-me" truck and guided taxiing aircraft to the turnoff point, where he handed the aircraft off to Robins, who then guided the aircraft to the off-load area.[77]

Once the troops and vehicles were off-loaded, Berino led the teams to the release point away from the landing operations. There the AOB passed on pertinent information to the team leaders. After receiving confirmation that all team personnel and equipment were present, they launched on missions throughout southern Iraq.[78]

The first aircraft arrived at 2210 hours, followed by a second aircraft two minutes later. The first aircraft stirred up a huge dust cloud and literally disappeared into the cloud. The SOF teams quickly unloaded their vehicles in the flying sand and in less than fifteen minutes, both aircraft thundered down the runway to take off again. The arrival and departure of the first two aircraft blew any remaining debris off the flight strip, making future landings easier. The first two aircraft

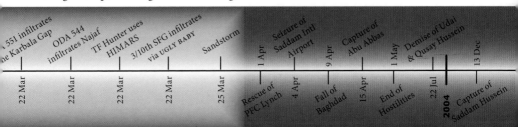

were followed by two more flights of two at twenty-minute intervals. The first six aircraft brought in ODA 544, an intelligence team, and a CBS television crew. ODA 544 and the intelligence team quickly left to complete their missions in the Najaf area, but the CBS crew recorded a story on the flight operations at Wadi al Khirr which was then broadcast on the news a few days later.[79]

The next group of six aircraft landed at Wadi al Khirr at 0100 hours. The first set of two airplanes brought in ODA 572 to relieve ODA 574 of the airfield security mission so the team could exfiltrate on the second set of aircraft. By the time the next two MC-130s arrived with more SOF teams, ODA 574 was ready to exfiltrate. When the last aircraft arrived with ODA 583 onboard, Sinclair transferred responsibility for the airfield to ODA 572 and loaded the AOB command and control node and the Air Force control team on the last two aircraft for the flight back to Kuwait.[80]

Figure 5.26 5th SFG resupply site. *The teams employed camouflage nets and other techniques to reduce their signature in the western desert.*

The operation was an unqualified success and a testament to the planning and operational expertise of special operators from both the Army Special Forces and the Air Force. It was a bold move to establish a clandestine airfield deep in enemy controlled territory. With few exceptions, the actual operation followed the scenarios anticipated in the plan. West simply said it was a "seamless operation." Sinclair summed it up: "I wouldn't call it Desert One [referring to the desert landing strip established in Iran during Operation EAGLE CLAW in 1980], but it got five teams on the ground ahead of the conventional force and put eyes on the target."[81]

Najaf

"Oh, great! One of the most experienced HALO [high altitude low opening] teams in the Group and we're going to drive to the war!" said Sergeant First Class Tim Kreiler*, the intelligence and special weapons sergeant for ODA 544. ODA 544 was equipped and trained to parachute deep into enemy territory and clandestinely conduct a range of special operations missions. Under his breath, Kreiler muttered, "What's the point of all the training and all the night jumps into God-knows-where if we're never going to be used?" ODA 544,

from 2nd Battalion, 5th SFG, had just learned that it would participate in the invasion of Iraq as a mounted unit—a far cry from the extreme airborne infiltrations it was trained for. Kreiler was an old, no-nonsense Ranger with over fifteen years of Special Forces experience and a reputation for telling it like he saw it. He was not in the least bit thrilled at the prospect of becoming "motorized."[82]

Captain Roy Clinger*, the detachment commander, received word of the mission in August 2002. ODA 544 would conduct unconventional warfare—the primary mission of Special Forces—to organize and train anti-Saddam resistance forces around Najaf in support of the U.S. ground maneuver forces. In addition to that primary mission, the team was assigned a number of "be prepared" missions, including locating counter-theater ballistic missiles, conducting special reconnaissance, and performing security assistance–stability operations. In other words, Clinger said, "The intent was to [do] anything and everything to support CFLCC."[83]

ODA 544 was chosen to be one of the first teams into Iraq because it was one of the most experienced teams in 2nd Battalion, with four members of the team possessing more than fifteen years of Special Forces experience. Most of the others had at least ten years of experience; the most junior member had four.[84]

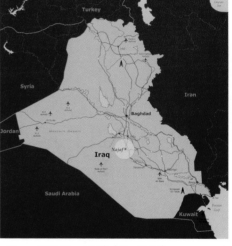

The plan was straightforward: infiltrate into a remote desert site by MC-130 aircraft, then, under the cover of darkness, drive to Najaf and establish a clandestine patrol base. Arriving at least forty-eight hours ahead of the conventional forces, ODA 544, with the help of accompanying Iraqi expatriates, would establish contact with resistance forces in the city. Through the resistance forces, the ODA would warn Iraqi noncombatants to stay

Figure 5.27 Map highlighting Najaf.

in their houses, and try to persuade hostile Iraqis to surrender. ODA 544 conducted a number of similar exercises in preparation for the mission, so the team's confidence was high.[85]

When the mission warning order was received in late November, ODA 544 went into a practice isolation phase at Fort Campbell, Kentucky, and began to conduct an area study and do background research. Using FalconView mapping software for terrain analysis, the team pored over maps of the city and surrounding area, choos-

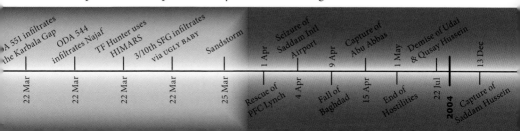

ing its travel routes and likely hide sites. By the time they had finished their area studies, team members could navigate the area by
memory. The men were also well versed on religious factors, political
factions, and ethnic and tribal affiliations in
and around Najaf.[86]

Figure 5.28 GMVs in a desert sandstorm. *Severe sandstorms halted operations on several occasions.*

The late arrival of ODA 544's vehicles added
to the tension felt by soldiers more accus-
tomed to free falling than driving into battle.
The team had just enough time to pick up the
GMVs, do an inventory, load them on a train,
and send them to the port for shipment before
deploying by air themselves. ODA 544 finished
its stateside preparations, said its goodbyes,
and deployed to FOB 52 at Ali As-Salim Air
Base. The last of the team arrived in Kuwait
the first week in February, but it was two more
weeks before the vehicles arrived—without
gun mounts and other essential equipment.[87]

With all its men and vehicles in theater, ODA 544 conducted the
vehicle training it needed and increased its weapons training. Even
Kreiler began to feel more comfortable with the "mounted" aspect of
the mission after more training—especially driving cross-country at
night. Planning changes left the team with two of its original GMVs
and two modified Toyota Tacoma pickup trucks. The mix of vehicles
provided a greater degree of flexibility for moving by air; both vehicle
types fit inside MC-130 and MH-47 cargo compartments, but only the
nonstandard vehicles could fit inside the Air Force MH-53s.[88]

The team's initial plan was to go in without any additional personnel attached, but the "team" grew and included, according to Kreiler,
"just about every agency known to man." In addition to the Air Force
tactical control party, it included some intelligence officers, several
former Iraqi Army officers, and other ARSOF elements. The senior
Iraqi Army officer, a colonel from Najaf who had been living in exile,
and his four lieutenants were supposed to help the team establish contact with resistance forces in Najaf. The other attached personnel had
their own missions to complete, but needed assistance in getting to
Najaf.[89]

In the seventy-two hours before ODA 544 was scheduled to enter
Iraq, the higher headquarters reviewed the infiltration plan. The original plan was to fly everyone into Wadi al Khirr on MC-130s. With
twenty-four hours to go, FOB 52 informed the group that the aircraft

had been changed to MH-53s. For ODA 544, that meant the GMVs would be left behind and all accompanying equipment transferred to the two NSVs, which could not hold everything. Consequently, everyone scrambled to select the most important equipment and adjust the load plans to meet the load profiles for the helicopters. As the team sweated to adjust to the loads, the infiltration plan was changed once again: now they were to conduct a tactical road march behind the 3rd Infantry Division instead of flying. Mercifully, before the ODA could react to the latest change, word came that the original plan was back on. Of the constantly changing plan, ODA 544's senior medic, Sergeant First Class Mark Combs*, generously remarked, "I can only hope the leadership was doing the best they could with what they had."[90]

At long last the waiting was over and ODA 544 prepared to infiltrate Iraq. The team flew on the night of 21 March on two MC-130s traveling in complete blackout conditions from Ali As-Salim Air Base to a newly secured airstrip at Wadi al Khirr. Carefully loaded into each of the two MC-130s was one GMV, one NSV, and half the ODA. The various attached personnel and their equipment took later flights. After a quiet flight, the MC-130s touched down and the team and its vehicles rolled down the aircraft ramps onto the airstrip. Sergeant Major Thad Berino* of AOB 570 met the team and led them to a holding area just off the active runway.[91]

The first minutes of the insertion did not go according to plan. The GMV driven by Combs quickly rolled off the ramp. A stubborn ratchet strap used to secure the NSV during flight delayed the plane's departure. After a few frustrating minutes the crew chief released the strap; however, the GMV was already out of sight and in the holding area, so the NSV driver had to hurry to catch up. In his haste to link up, he took the most direct route to the holding area and drove into a huge bomb crater. After twenty minutes of arduous effort, the NSV was pulled from the crater; fortunately, neither the vehicle nor anyone riding inside was seriously hurt or damaged.[92]

After the delay, Clinger organized the group and led his column into the desert. A total of twelve vehicles moved in formation—four belonging to the Special Forces team and the rest carrying the attached personnel. The column drove in single-file to reduce the chances of hitting a landmine and to lessen the ground signature of the vehicles, as well as to maximize the column's speed. The first planned hide site was only twenty-four kilometers from the airfield but since the column made such good time on the first leg of the route, Clinger decided to continue on while darkness lasted. He knew it was criti-

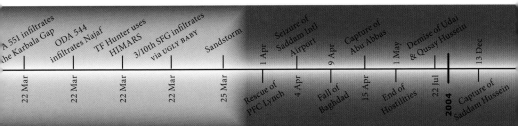

Figure 5.29 ODA 544 watch the 3rd ID's tanks as they enter Najaf. *ODA 544 followed the tanks of the 3rd Infantry Division into the city of Najaf.*

cal to get to Najaf ahead of the 3rd Infantry Division and this was an opportunity to gain some time.[93]

As the heavily loaded convoy journeyed through the night, the terrain became increasingly more challenging. Kreiler remembered that they drove hard until an hour before dawn through "some of the ugliest stuff I've ever seen." As dawn broke, the column found a wadi, or dry streambed, in which to hide the trucks, camouflaged the vehicles with netting, set a security perimeter, and settled down for some well-earned rest.[94]

When ODA 544 made that day's scheduled communications contact with FOB 52, it learned that the 3rd Infantry Division was moving faster than expected. The team was ordered to move to Najaf as quickly as possible. Having rested only a few hours, the column loaded up and drove the remaining seventy-five kilometers across the desert, not stopping until they arrived outside Najaf that night. As they raced across the desert, Senior Airman Sergio Manchini*, ODA 544's enlisted terminal air controller, kept in constant communication with CJSOTF-west's joint fires element. He turned "on" and "off" the pre-established No Fire Areas along the route to Najaf, protecting the column from attack by friendly aircraft.[95]

The column arrived at Najaf without mishap and linked up with ODA 556. The two teams moved to an abandoned cement factory and set up a temporary security position. As ODA 544 settled in at the cement factory, the intelligence representative and the Iraqis were eager to begin operations. They wanted to move to the outskirts of town in an attempt to link up with their contacts. Clinger and Chief Warrant Officer 3 Sidney Schwarz* recommended that they hold off until they had a better idea of the situation in Najaf, but the intelligence representative and the Iraqi colonel were adamant. Over Clinger and Schwarz's objections, two of the Iraqi colonel's lieutenants were sent into Najaf.[96]

While most of the ODA remained at the cement factory to rest, Combs and a few other team members accompanied the intelligence representative and the Iraqi lieutenants to the drop-off point on the outskirts of the city. When Combs noticed two American M1 Abrams tanks nearby, straddling the road leading into Najaf, he coordinated with the section leader and lay down on the tank deck to try and

nap. He was exhausted from the drive from Wadi al Khirr to Najaf, and realized that his last real sleep had been on the plane to the airfield.[97]

Explosive ordnance demolition units had been busy blowing captured ammunition and explosives caches all day, so the muffled explosions Combs heard in the distance did not cause him any particular concern. Gradually, through his exhausted dozing, it dawned on the medic that the explosions were getting closer. Suddenly, two big explosions rattled him back to full consciousness; the explosions were impacting artillery rounds, one of which had just hit the far tank. With his hand on the hatch handle, the tank commander told Combs that they were going to button up (seal up in the tank) and asked if he would like to join them inside. Combs made a quick assessment of the situation and replied, "No thanks! You're the target!" He scrambled off the tank, sprinted to his vehicle, and sped out of the kill zone. He had hardly cleared the area when another salvo crashed down, scoring a direct hit on the tank he had just left. While the artillery rounds did little damage to the heavily armored tanks, anyone on the outside of the tank would have been shredded. Combs breathed a sigh of relief; he knew he had just dodged a big bullet.[98]

Figure 5.30 5th SFG GMV. *Fully loaded, the GMV was the workhorse of the 5th SFG teams in the west.*

The two Iraqi lieutenants were not so lucky in their introduction to Najaf. Enemy security forces quickly captured them, and the next time the team saw them alive was as prisoners on a broadcast on Iraqi state television. The intelligence representative in charge of making contact with resistance groups decided not to send anyone else in their place; he did not want to risk the colonel or the two remaining lieutenants. With no liaison to resistance organizations in Najaf, ODA 544 was left without a way to accomplish its primary unconventional warfare mission.[99]

Sergeant First Class Tad Holley* commented, "The situation in the city wasn't exactly the way we had hoped. It didn't fall apart like we were hoping: that they'd just run away or give up. It made it hard to get [into Najaf]." ODA 544 spent the ensuing week gathering intelligence for the 3rd Infantry Division's bombing campaign of the city. In addition to working with information gathered by the intelligence representative and his contacts, the team interviewed civilians to develop information on potential targets. Using the information gathered

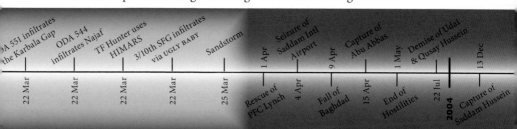

ODA 551 infiltrates the Karbala Gap — 22 Mar

ODA 544 infiltrates Najaf — 22 Mar

TF Hunter uses HIMARS — 22 Mar

3/10th SFG infiltrates via UGLY BABY — 22 Mar

Sandstorm — 25 Mar

Rescue of PFC Lynch

Seizure of Saddam Intl Airport — 1 Apr

Fall of Baghdad — 4 Apr

Capture of Abu Abbas — 9 Apr

End of Hostilities — 15 Apr

Demise of Udai & Qusay Hussein — 1 May

22 Jul

Capture of Saddam Hussein — 13 Dec

2004

from all these sources, the ODA worked up target nominations for attack with precision-guided munitions (smart bombs). Najaf was heavily urbanized, which made it difficult to actually see the targets when engaging them. The Special Forces team's intelligence made it possible to target Baath or fedayeen headquarters, artillery positions, and military compounds.[100]

On 28 March, 101st Airborne Division relieved the 3rd Infantry Division and began a deliberate campaign to clear the city block-by-block and ODA 544 moved on to other missions.

Karbala Gap

The Night Stalker pilot slowly throttled the aircraft down, raised the nose, and reached for the ground with the rear landing gear. The passengers felt the reassuring thump as the wheels made contact and the pilot brought the MH-47D helicopter to the ground. The crew chief lowered the ramp and swirling dust filled the back of the chopper. As sand hit the soldiers inside, so did the realization that their mission had finally begun.

The journey for ODA 551 began in September 2002 when, fresh from Afghanistan, Captain Don Raintree* and his veteran Special Forces team were told to prepare to do "SF stuff" around Karbala. Even by Special Forces standards, the mission was a bit broad. But, having faith that the mission would be narrowed for them eventually, the team went to work compiling its area studies on the Karbala region.[101]

Karbala is situated on the edge of the desert, some twenty miles southwest of Baghdad, with a population of more than half a million. The city is revered in the Shia community as the site of Husain's martyrdom, which is at the root of Shia Islam. In Karbala there are shrines to Husain and his half-brother Abbas, and the city is second only to Najaf in religious significance to the Shia. While Karbala's religious significance is important, its geographic location was what concerned military planners. Karbala sits astride a western approach to Baghdad, between the Euphrates River to the east and Lake Razzaza (sometimes called Lake Karbala) to the west. The relatively narrow area of land between the river and the lake, called the Karbala Gap, was a natural choke point for U.S. forces, especially if heavily defended by the Iraqis. The 3rd ID wanted to punch through the Karbala Gap on its attack to Baghdad. A more easterly route would be more restrictive, slower, and require extensive bridging assets. Considering the signifi-

Husain *Following the death of Mohammad, the Muslims split into two groups. Husain was a leader of the Shia party. He and Ali, another leader, were slain, enabling the Sunni party to become the dominant sect of Islam.*

2001
Attack on World Trade Center

11 Sep
2002

16 Oct

Approval of UN Resolution 1441

Signing of Iraq war resolution

8 Nov

2003

19 Mar
D-Day Operation IRAQI FREEDOM

19 Mar
Air War begins

19 Mar
TF 64 infiltrates Iraq

20 Mar

1/5th SFG enters Iraq

21 Mar
AOB 570 infiltrates Wadi al Khir

cance of the route choice, the 3rd Infantry Division commander did not want to rely solely on satellite imagery for intelligence. The solution was to get eyes on the target; this meant a Special Forces reconnaissance mission, which was assigned to ODA 551.[102]

ODA 551 was a direct action team, which meant it had no vehicles and no mounted training as a team. Luckily, some of the soldiers had mobility team experience, which shortened the learning curve. In the short time allowed before the deployment to the Middle East, ODA 551 conducted a three-week desert mobility training exercise at Fort Bliss, Texas, using the new Ground Mobility Vehicle. The exercise at Fort Bliss

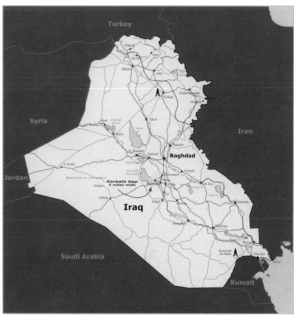

Figure 5.31 Map highlighting the Karbala Gap.

was valuable, and ODA 551 used its time there to develop and practice mounted tactics, techniques, and procedures. The soldiers mastered reacting to ambushes, breaking contact, convoy security, and many other situations that they thought they might confront in Iraq. They also worked to improve their desert driving techniques in both day and night conditions, practiced mounted land navigation, learned GMV maintenance, and worked out vehicle recovery techniques. Each vehicle mounted a crew-served weapon—either a .50 caliber M2 machine gun or MK19 40mm grenade launcher—which would give the team enough firepower to defeat or disengage from an enemy if it were detected or compromised. The team did as much training with the .50 caliber machine guns and the grenade launcher as possible, since as a direct action team it was already very proficient with its M4 carbines, M9 pistols, and M240B machine guns.[103]

ODA 551 deployed from Fort Campbell to Ali As-Salim Air Base in late January 2003. Once in Kuwait, ODA 551 received NSVs in addition to their GMVs. While ideally the mission should dictate the equipment used, in this case the availability of infiltration aircraft heavily impacted on mission planning. The first choice for the infiltration was Air Force MC-130 Combat Talons, since the GMVs could be loaded

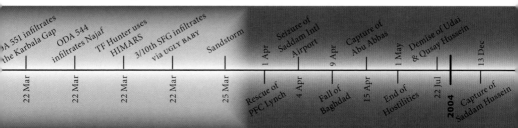

Figure 5.32 MH-53 Pave Low helicopter. *The Air Forces' special operations helicopter, the MH-53 Pave Low, was an integral part of the infiltration of Special Forces teams in the west.*

without removing the gun mounts, weight would be less of a factor, and perhaps most importantly, they would not have to be modified for flight. When the GMVs rolled off the ramp they would be ready for action. Knowing that first choices do not always work out, the team made contingency plans for helicopter insertion by either Army MH-47D Chinook or Air Force MH-53 Pave Low helicopters. Although weight was a factor for both helicopters, the MH-47D carried a greater payload and accommodated the GMVs, albeit with only three inches of clearance on either side. Loading and unloading a GMV onto a helicopter is a tedious, stressful, and potentially hazardous task under the best of circumstances. Doing it at night with no lights, under combat conditions, gives "tedious, stressful, and hazardous" new meaning. Needless to say, the team did a lot of practice loading and unloading of its GMVs on MH-47 mock-ups. If MH-53s became the infiltration platform, then only NSVs could be used. While the NSVs fit in MH-53s, they carried significantly less equipment than the GMVs, making the Pave Low the less desirable option.[104]

ODA 551 continued to train in Kuwait. Major adjustments had to be made on the team's Toyota Tacoma trucks in order to make them combat ready. Specifically, the team welded gun mounts to the truck beds and then tested them to ensure they would not fail under combat conditions. The team continued refining mounted combat techniques, concentrating on driving at night wearing night vision goggles. "We did a lot—I mean a lot—of driving at night when we got to Kuwait," said Sergeant First Class John Spencer*, the senior engineer sergeant. Team personnel also cross-trained on communications, medical, and heavy weapons duties. Weapons training was more difficult to arrange with the Special Forces competing with "Big Army" units like the 3rd Infantry Division for the same types of ammunition and ranges.[105]

Avoiding fratricide was a major concern for Special Forces planners and ODAs conducting special reconnaissance and unconventional warfare missions well forward of the conventional forces. Once the special reconnaissance mission was complete, ODA 551 was to evacuate the area and link up with the 3rd Infantry Division—without being fired upon. To facilitate the linkup, ODA 551 trained in Kuwait with the

3rd ID Special Forces liaison element, composed of two ODAS (ODAS 916 and part of 914) from A Company, 1st Battalion, 19th SFG. ODA 551 and the liaison element conducted face-to-face coordination with designated 3rd ID units, and then rehearsed the linkup procedures. During the coordination with the 3rd ID staff, battalion commanders identified the likely companies, and then platoons, in each battalion tasked with the on-order mission to conduct the linkup. ODA 916 developed a training plan and practiced the drill with all of the designated platoons.[106]

While the team sharpened its skills, mission planning continued. Raintree reviewed after action reports from Operation DESERT STORM special reconnaissance missions. From those, he concluded that the best way to avoid compromise was to stay mobile and avoid digging in if at all possible. If the team stayed too long in one place or left a big hole behind, the desert-dwelling Bedouins or Iraqi patrols would either pick up signs of its presence or simply stumble upon it. Raintree planned to move daily and to select hide positions that took advantage of natural features that would make digging unnecessary. Terrain analysis and route selection were absolutely critical to the success of the mission.[107]

Figure 5.33 19th SFG beret flash.

For its terrain analysis, the team used the FalconView software program, which provided a variety of maps and overlays with much greater detail and accuracy than standard paper maps. Using FalconView, the team selected potential reconnaissance and surveillance positions and then produced visibility profiles for each. This allowed them to quickly select those sites with the best potential to see the target area.

Since the 3rd Infantry Division planned to push through the Karbala Gap on its way to Baghdad, it needed timely, accurate information about any obstacles, enemy units, and mine fields that might affect its progress. ODA 551 needed to get into position as soon as possible in order to provide that information without being compromised. Intelligence reports indicated that the elite Medina Republican Guard Division was positioned to the north and east of Karbala. Of more immediate concern to the team were reports of a battalion-sized fedayeen unit in Karbala proper, and a fedayeen training camp located north of Karbala.[108]

As the team had feared, it was not able to infiltrate into the Iraqi airfield at Wadi al Khirr on the roomy MC-130s. The team quickly changed gears and prepared to infiltrate by MH-47Ds; however, there were no MH-47s at Ali As-Salim. The team had completed its isolation

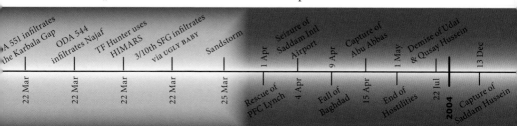

planning and training and was just waiting for the word to go: "Sitting on G, waiting on O!" as Staff Sergeant Charles Godfrey* put it.[109]

Rather than wait, Colonel Mulholland decided to move ODA 551 to CJSOTF-WEST's location and infiltrate using MH-47DS from the 3rd Battalion, 160th Special Operations Aviation Regiment. As Raintree hurriedly completed coordination at the FOB 52 headquarters, a sergeant called to him: "Hey sir, your mission is on CNN!" To his shock, Raintree watched as retired U.S. Army Major General David Grange told the world that in order to get the intelligence picture it wanted, the Army would put a Special Forces team in the Karbala Gap. Adrenaline quickly replaced Raintree's shock when he was told to be ready to leave for H-5 in four hours. ODA 551 finally loaded onto MC-130s and landed at H-5 very early in the morning (0200–0300 local time) on 20 March. Once on the ground, the team linked up with the assigned SOAR crews and began transferring its vehicles and equipment into the MH-47DS. The team resolved the issue of one GMV being too heavy by quickly shifting equipment to other vehicles to balance the loads and bring all vehicles within the weight tolerance. Eventually everything was loaded and the team left the tarmac in search of a place to get a few hours of rest before its mission.[110]

Figure 5.34 MH-47 Chinook. *The medium lift MH-47 in its various configurations was one of the primary aircraft for the insertion of special operations teams.*

While the rest of the ODA dealt with the helicopters, Raintree coordinated with the 3rd Battalion, 160th SOAR, battalion commander, Lieutenant Colonel Robert Welch, and his staff. As an experienced officer, Raintree contemplated what he described as the "helicopter factor." Typically, when helicopters are involved, either command or mechanical issues cause delays. This mission was no exception. The first change to the plan was scrubbing the planned in-flight refueling because of air corridor problems. The night of the infiltration, the Air Force began its "shock and awe campaign." The Tomahawk Land Attack Missile air corridor—established between 350 and 3,500 feet—crossed the flight route, which made the planned refueling too hazardous. The plan was modified to allow for a refueling stop and then a straight flight going as fast as possible. Timing was critical— the infiltration had to be made early enough for ODA 551 to drive to the first hide site and for the helicopters to leave Iraqi airspace before daylight.[111]

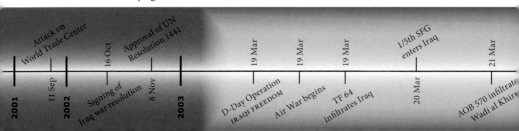

Attack on World Trade Center

11 Sep

16 Oct

Signing of Iraq war resolution

Approval of UN Resolution 1441

8 Nov

19 Mar
D-Day Operation IRAQI FREEDOM

19 Mar
Air War begins

19 Mar
TF 64 infiltrates Iraq

1/5th SFG enters Iraq

20 Mar

21 Mar
AOB 570 infiltrate Wadi al Khirr

2001
2002
2003

The infiltration began in earnest after dark on 21 March, when ODA 551 assembled at the ramps of its assigned aircraft. The mission called for three MH-47DS, escorted by two defensive armed penetrators MH-6OLS. The MH-6OL is a standard MH-60 Black Hawk helicopter extensively upgraded in terms of armament, with a weapons configuration of a nineteen-shot 2.75 inch rocket pod, a 30mm Gatling gun, and two 7.62mm miniguns. With ODA 551 loaded and the planes rolling for takeoff, the "helicopter factor" struck. One of the MH-47DS broke its landing gear while taxiing, and another reported a hydraulic leak. The 160th SOAR routinely kept one backup aircraft for missions, but not two. Fortunately, the hydraulic leak was quickly fixed and once the equipment on the broken helicopter was transferred to the backup aircraft, the rest of the infiltration proceeded without further incident.[112]

After the scheduled refueling stop, the Night Stalker Chinooks streaked north through the Iraqi desert just above the dunes. As they crossed the border, some startled border guards managed to shoot off a few rounds but caused no damage. As the helicopters approached the landing zone, ODA 551 geared up and prepared its vehicles for a rapid exit. Even before the aircraft fully stopped, the crew chief lowered the ramp and the team members removed the tie downs from their vehicles. The noise of the engines was deafening as the rotor wash whipped the landing zone into a choking dust storm. On the crew chief's signal, the team rolled slowly off the helicopter. Chief Warrant Officer 2 Clyde Hawks*, assistant detachment commander, commented that the tight fit of the GMVs inside the Chinooks made loading and unloading a delicate operation: "It is the longest three minutes of your life, trying to get those things out of the helicopter without [causing any damage]."[113]

Everybody on the infiltration team worked quickly to get the Special Forces team unloaded and on its way. As Hawks described it, "They were in a hurry to get away and we were in a hurry to get the noise and dust gone!" As ODA 551 off-loaded the vehicles, a crew chief grabbed Hawks and told him, "Everything looks good in the local area, but you've got vehicles about ten miles away and they're headed this way!" With that warning, the helicopters took off and disappeared into the darkness. ODA 551 quickly mounted the machine guns and grenade launcher onto its vehicles, moved a short distance away from the landing zone, and conducted a "stop-look-listen;" the team members shut off the vehicles, manned their weapons, and listened to determine if they were being pursued. After several minutes

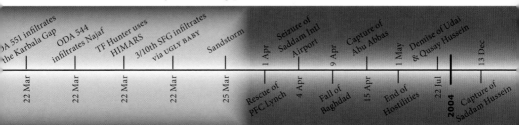

and no sign of approaching vehicles, the team set off to its selected hide site some seventy kilometers distant. There was no time to lose; daylight was just hours away. The clock was running, and every ODA 551 soldier knew the team had to get to the Karbala Gap as rapidly as possible.[114]

CHANGE OF MISSION

Mission changes are nothing new to special operations forces, however the men of ODB 560, 2nd Battalion, 5th SFG, took flexibility to a new level. Assuming that its assigned mission would be the one it conducted in Iraq, ODB 560 conducted extensive planning to that end in the fall of 2002. By the end of the January 2003, the majority of Major Jerry Baxter's* unit had arrived in Kuwait, and the Special Forces soldiers dove into mission preparation activities, conducting multiple live-fire range exercises, mission rehearsals, and outfitting newly assigned vehicles. In spite of such extensive planning and preparation, ODB 560's mission did, indeed, change soon after the team arrived in Kuwait.[115]

The team's original mission was to infiltrate Iraq ahead of any conventional forces. Once in Iraq, it was to establish an advanced operating base near Amarah and exercise command and control of its ODAs conducting unconventional warfare operations in the area. The ODAs would provide intelligence, target information, and direct action, assisting conventional forces as they advanced north to Baghdad. However, the mission planning process showed that there was scant evidence of a credible resistance force in the area of operations—a necessity for unconventional warfare operations. So ODB 560's mission changed. Instead of stealthily infiltrating, it would cross the border with the I Marine Expeditionary Force and the British 1st Armoured Division and assist in the capture of Basra.[116]

The tactical plan called for I MEF to lead the way into Iraq with the British close on its heels. After seizing the Rumaylah Oil Fields and other key areas on the approaches to Basra, the Marines would hand those areas off to the British. AOB 560 (ODB 560's designation in combat) would follow the British 7th Armoured Brigade, while the ODAs would be out front with the Marines in an effort to get to the operational area as soon as possible.[117]

During the mission preparation phase, ODB 560 was assigned a wide variety of units: one Civil Affairs Team–Bravo and two Civil Affairs Teams–Alpha from C Company, 96th Civil Affairs Battalion;

Tactical Psychological Operations Team 952, from the 4th Psychological Operations Group; Special Operations Team–Alpha 502; and two Defense Human Intelligence Service personnel. The attachments, plus the ODB's ten-man headquarters, a mechanic, and three ODAS, gave Baxter a forty-man special operations task force with a variety of capabilities.[118]

Figure 5.35 Lined up in the tactical assembly area of AOB 560. *The vehicles of AOB 560 loaded up and ready to go.*

On the night of 21 March, the thundering artillery and roaring engines of hundreds of tank and armored personnel carrier shattered the quiet of the Kuwaiti desert—the Coalition ground forces rolled across the border. Tucked securely behind the heavily armored Marines, Captain Jeff Davis'* ODA 554 was not just hitching a ride; his team was a key player in the plan to seize and protect the Rumaylah Oil Fields. ODA 554's original mission was to conduct unconventional warfare in Basra, but like many other ODAS, the team's mission changed shortly after it arrived in Kuwait. The new mission was to infiltrate the Iraqi border to link up with Iraqi resistance fighters in the Rumaylah Oil Fields. An intelligence contingent was attached to coordinate with the resistance fighters. Together ODA 554 and the resistance fighters would secure the oil fields, preventing their destruction until the Marines arrived.[119]

Just days before the planned start of Operation IRAQI FREEDOM, Iraqi forces moved into the oil fields, changing the plan yet again. The Rumaylah Oil Fields were the responsibility of the 51st Iraqi Division, and with Coalition forces massing on the Kuwaiti border, the division commander moved his troops into the oil fields. The arrival of conventional forces chased away the resistance forces the Special Forces team was supposed to link up with. The infiltration plan for ODA 554 was quickly revised; ODA 554 split into two elements, with Davis leading one team and his assistant detachment commander, Chief Warrant Officer 2 Jason Nichols*, leading the other. Each team would clandestinely rendezvous in Az Zubayr, a large suburb of Basra, with four friendly Iraqi oil production technicians whose skills and knowledge were

Figure 5.36 Crossing the tank ditch into Iraq. *An engineer bridge provided the way across the tank ditch during AOB 560's infiltration into Iraq.*

3/351 infiltrates the Karbala Gap — 22 Mar

ODA 544 infiltrates Najaf — 22 Mar

TF Hunter uses HIMARS — 22 Mar

3/10th SFG infiltrates via UGLY BABY — 22 Mar

Sandstorm — 25 Mar

Rescue of PFC Lynch

Seizure of Saddam Intl Airport — 1 Apr

4 Apr

Fall of Baghdad

Capture of Abu Abbas — 9 Apr

15 Apr

End of Hostilities — 1 May

Demise of Udai & Qusay Hussein — 22 Jul

2004

Capture of Saddam Hussein — 13 Dec

Figure 5.37 On the road to Basra. *The effect of the Coalition bombing is evident on the road to Basra.*

needed to operate the Rumaylah Oil Fields. Once each team contacted the technicians, it was to protect and escort them to the outskirts of Az Zubayr, where the Marine units charged with the oil field security would take custody of them.[120]

Time was of the essence as ODA 554's split teams followed on the heels of the 7th Marine Regimental Combat Team as it punched across the border at Safwan. As the two teams cautiously infiltrated into Az Zubayr, they could hear and see fighting all around. Az Zubayr had large numbers of Baath Party militia and fedayeen, and was also the home of the loyalist Al Sadun tribe. ODA 554B carefully passed undetected through Az Zubayr, as tank battles and fierce infantry gunfights between the Marines and fedayeen illuminated the night sky. With some difficulty, but within four hours after crossing the border, ODA 554B had the technicians and was on the way to the linkup with the Marines outside of Az Zubayr.[121]

ODA 554B was making its way toward the linkup point, when it came under fire. "They picked the wrong people to engage. It was a bad day for them," said Master Sergeant Mitch Semmes*, ODA 554B's team sergeant. A squad-sized group of fedayeen dressed in black uniforms fired at the group of vehicles with AK-47s and rocket-propelled grenades. ODA 554B returned fire with its .50 caliber and M240B machine guns as Semmes and Nichols climbed to the top of the overpass for a better view of the enemy. The fedayeen were only about 150 meters away, but made no attempt to flank or break contact. However, approximately 600 meters to the rear of the fedayeen was a group of buildings with civilians, well within the .50 caliber machine guns' range. Rather than risk hitting the civilians, Semmes made the .50 caliber machine gunner stop firing, and the rest of the team continued to engage with their M4 and M240B machine guns. The gun battle continued for an hour, until the Marines came up from the rear, evened the odds, and quickly finished the battle. When the smoke cleared, four fedayeen were dead and the survivors beat a hasty retreat. ODA 554B handed the Iraqi oil technicians over to the Marines, completing the first phase of the team's mission.[122]

Farther to the west, more fighting between the Marines and the fedayeen held up ODA 554A's mission. Although only a kilometer from the linkup point, the fighting was too intense to allow the team to

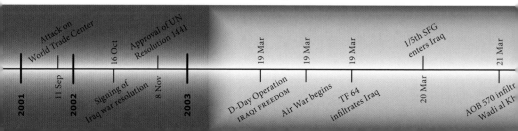

pass. The heavy fighting continued through the night. Not until the next morning did Davis's team finally link up with its technicians and get them to the Marines.[123]

With their missions completed, ODA 554's split teams reunited and established a safe house on the outskirts of Az Zubayr as a base for further operations in the area. Based on its Afghanistan experience, ODA 554 planned to use the same techniques successfully used in Afghanistan against the fedayeen and Baath Party militia. The ODA piled into its nonstandard vehicles on its first day in Az Zubayr and traveled through town to a Baath Party checkpoint in order to make its presence known. The plan was simple: approach to within three or four hundred meters, then send a civilian to tell the men at the checkpoint that the Americans wanted to talk with them. The idea was that the show of force would convince the fedayeen that resistance was useless, and the best thing for all concerned was for them to go home.[124]

The Special Forces soldiers quickly adjusted, as the first mission did not go as planned. The location information was wrong and before it realized the error, the ODA drove to within twenty-five meters of the checkpoint. At least ten Baath Party militia soldiers were visible in prepared fighting positions, armed with AK-47s, rocket-propelled grenades, and light machines guns, while the ODA was out in the open. "They had the drop on us," said Semmes. To make matters worse, the checkpoint was surrounded by a large crowd of civilians directly in the line of fire. Luckily, the Iraqis must have been surprised and intimidated by the SOF vehicles and weapons, because they held their fire long enough for the Americans to put their vehicles in reverse and quickly move away. The soldiers were glad to let this confrontation end in a draw.[125]

ODA 554 returned to the safe house and concluded that it was not in Afghanistan anymore and needed a new plan. While the checkpoint foray would undoubtedly provide some good bar stories, more importantly it gave the ODA a "ground truth" intelligence assessment of the Baath Party militia and fedayeen. Az Zubayr was supposed to be a semi-permissive area, but, as Semmes put it, "The Baathists and fedayeen were in there like ticks on a hound." All intelligence assessments were woefully wrong—the Baath Party militia and fedayeen neither ran away nor surrendered; they were well armed, had prepared defensive positions, and were ready and willing to fight. Az Zubayr was their power base in Basra, and from their perspective, they had nothing to lose and everything to gain by staying and fight-

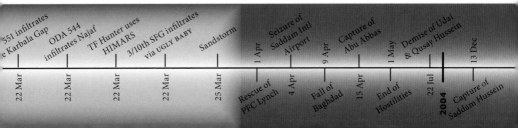

ing. Davis estimated that there were between 500 and 1,000 Baath militia and fedayeen in Az Zubayr, which would pose a problem for the British.[126]

Meanwhile, Baxter and the three-vehicle GMV advance party for AOB 560 left the tactical assembly area Barnsley, the temporary home of the British 7th Armoured Brigade, and crossed the berm into Iraq behind the Marines. As the column slowly moved out, Baxter reviewed the attack plan. The Marines had to simultaneously seize the Rumaylah Oil Fields and clear Az Zubayr, thereby seizing the nearside bridge crossings to Basra. The 7th Armoured Brigade would conduct a relief in place allowing the Marines to continue their advance to Baghdad. The old Army saying, "no plan survives the first contact," certainly held true in this case. The resistance in Az Zubayr was greater than expected, and the time required to clear the town would keep them from more important objectives. Therefore, the Marine commanders decided to contain and bypass Az Zubayr and continue north. The British forces, which planned to pass through a pacified Az Zubayr, found themselves in a hornet's nest of Baathists and fedayeen. It took over a week of street fighting and house-to-house searches before Az Zubayr was secured.[127]

The first several days in the area around Basra were chaotic and confusing as the British forces tried to gain control of the situation on the ground. No definite demarcation between enemy and friendly forces existed; on one block the civilians would be smiling and waving to the Coalition forces, then a few blocks down the street, they would be firing at those same soldiers. Swarms of civilians filled the streets, adding to the confusion to the identification of the enemy. The SOF soldiers saw evidence that Iraqi Army forces shed their uniforms and just went home, taking their weapons with them. By day there were throngs of military-age men walking about unarmed and mostly smiling, but at night those same men recovered their weapons to ambush the British.[128]

Figure 5.38 British Challenger main battle tank.

The Baath Party leadership orchestrated the resistance—the Saddam Fedayeen provided the fighting manpower. The Baathists used a combination of terror and disinformation to control the townspeople. Baath Party-controlled television and radio broadcasts, along with the presence of so many fedayeen among the people, discour-

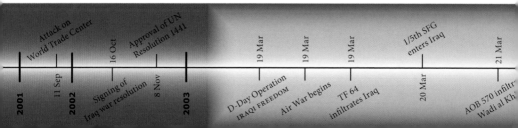

aged cooperation with British and American forces. The Coalition had flooded the area with leaflets before the invasion, but conducted no follow-on information program to counter the very active Iraqi disinformation campaign.[129]

In its mission planning, the AOB 560 staff selected a tentative base of operations near one of the bridge crossings into Basra. However, while attempting a reconnaissance of the buildings, the AOB found the area embroiled in a fierce firefight, which ended when British Challenger tanks blew apart the team's selected buildings, along with the fedayeen fighters inside. Basra International Airport was the AOB's alternate selection, but there was also heavy fighting around that area, so for the first several days AOB 560 operated from its vehicles. In an attempt to develop a more complete intelligence picture, the ARSOF soldiers interviewed civilians in the area. [130]

Figure 5.39 Destroyed Iraqi tank T-72. *Iraqi armor proved to be no match for Coalition air power.*

Even before the fighting subsided, Iraqi civilians started looting all the abandoned government buildings and installations. With the battle still in progress, the British forces could have done little without detracting from the primary mission. The SOF soldiers were concerned that once the government buildings were cleared out, the looting would spread to private homes and businesses. Captain Paul Hampton* observed an amusing scene while accompanying a British patrol as it attempted to disperse a large crowd looting a government facility. The crew of a British tank stopped an Iraqi male, telling him to drop his loot and go home. Despite the fact that he was staring down a Challenger tank's 120mm gun barrel, the man protested loudly and emphatically about being singled out while so many others were getting away. "This is an injustice!" he shouted and then moved away in a sulk.[131]

On 23 March, AOB 560 was finally able to secure a small piece of Basra International Airport as its operational base. Several mechanic bays were used for the GMVs, and there was ample space for the AOB. One of the Civil Affairs sergeants hotwired a bulldozer, then used it to build a two-meter-high berm around the AOB area for force protection. The remainder of the AOB—the Civil Affairs Team–B, a mechanic, and three trucks loaded with extra equipment and supplies—joined the advance party at the airport.[132]

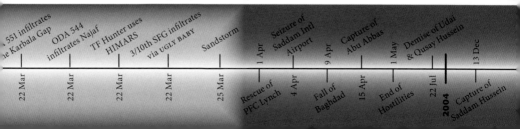

Figure 5.40 AOB 560 clearing buildings at Basra International Airport.

Even as it was occupied setting up a base of operations, the AOB continued intelligence missions. Over the next two days, the attached interpreters helped the British with the interrogation of captured Baathists. Bits and pieces of information gathered during interrogations, combined with civilian street interviews, produced a mosaic of the Baath Party and fedayeen resistance. The AOB even discovered a notebook listing the names, addresses, and phone numbers of key Baath party members in Basra and surrounding towns.[133]

As soon as AOB 560 was operational at the airport, Baxter sent out patrols to gather intelligence. Hampton led one patrol to the bridges over the canal leading into Basra. The British held the near (western) side of the bridges and the fedayeen held the far side. Neither side closed the bridges to civilian traffic and the ebb and flow of humanity and vehicles back and forth gave the scene a surreal quality—almost as if there were no war at all. Women walked around carrying baskets on their heads and men impatiently urged on the donkeys pulling their heavily laden carts. The interpreters with Hampton joined British units at traffic control points to query Iraqis at random about conditions in Basra. In time they found the best sources of information were often the taxi cab drivers. These drivers traveled more of the countryside and had more exposure to different people than the average civilian. Over the course of a day, their simple questions and conversations would paint a revealing picture of enemy positions and capabilities.[134]

Special Operations Team–A 502 became another invaluable source of information. Capable of intercepting a wide variety of signals from radios and telephones, Sergeant First Class Sam Magruder* and his two intercept operators listened in on radios transmissions and phone conversations by Baathists and Iraqi military officers. The information provided by these intercepts allowed the command to gauge the effectiveness of Coalition operations, conditions of the enemy, morale among the resistance, and potential targets. Magruder developed a signal intercept and direction-finding system with the British and Marines that allowed them to triangulate the location of select transmissions. Then, at the discretion of the commanders, the identified

target could be attacked with artillery or ground forces as appropriate.[135]

After the close call at the Baath checkpoint, ODA 554 modified its tactics and recruited local agents to gather information. The Baath Party militia appeared as normal civilians during the day, but established checkpoints to threaten the civilians and attack the British at night. Unlike the Americans, the local agents could move freely pinpointing the Baath Party hideouts and checkpoints. Using cell phones and special global positioning system locators, the friendly agents identified enemy locations. ODA 554 then passed the information to a British armoured unit, which raided the locations. After a week of highly effective raids, enough fedayeen and Baath militia had been killed and captured that the remainder slipped off to safer environs.[136]

With Az Zubayr finally secured, the British forces turned their full attention to Basra. While the British surrounded Basra they made no attempt to enter the city. Baxter and his ODAs were eager to get into Basra to assess and exploit the unconventional warfare potential in the city. However, it soon became painfully obvious that the British did not intend to allow the Special Forces teams to enter Basra under any conditions. The British strategy was to contain Basra until the conditions were right to capture the city.[137]

Figure 5.41 Captured Iraqi flag. *Troops of AOB 560 with an Iraqi flag taken in Basra.*

The American SOF soldiers looked to influence the battle with close air support. By tapping into the SOF aviation assets and developing high-value targets, Baxter felt he and the ODAs could make a significant contribution. However, planning and coordinating air strikes through the division and brigade staffs proved a frustrating effort on many levels. First, there was an exaggerated concern for collateral damage and civilian casualties from air strikes. Ironically, the British units had no reservations about firing field artillery or tank cannons at targets, both of which caused much more collateral damage than an air strike. Second, the British command and control systems did not mesh with the U.S. air support planning cycle. While the U.S.-preplanned air support worked on a nomination cycle running twenty-four-hours-out, the British 1st Armoured Division headquarters did not know the plans of its battle groups until twelve hours beforehand. It was a frus-

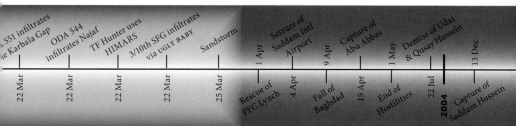

trating, lockstep process for the Special Forces troops, who were used to a more dynamic, flexible approach to operations. The situation was made worse by the impression that the British were not overly interested in making it work. Finally, targets identified and nominated through indigenous agents, even when corroborated by unmanned aerial vehicle flights or signals intercepts, were cancelled for "lack of positive identification."[138]

Prohibited from entering Basra, Baxter looked for other ways for his battalion to contribute to the fight. He sent the Civil Affairs teams forward to conduct assessments of key public facilities and began coordinating for the delivery of basic food and water supplies to needy areas. The Tactical Psychological Operations Team conducted numerous missions supporting the British forces. The ODAS continued to gather intelligence.[139]

Figure 5.42 British 1st Armoured Division logo.

As time went on, coordination problems continued to hamper AOB 560's operations with the British. Even though FOB 52 placed a four-man Special Forces liaison element from A Company, 1st Battalion, 19th SFG, at the division level, and a British 7th Armoured Brigade liaison officer was located at AOB 560, deconfliction of SOF operations was a problem that persisted throughout the campaign. Davis cited an incident when a British Marine Commando unit relieved the British armoured battalion operating in Az Zubayr. ODA 554 started a basic combat skills training program for a volunteer indigenous force to infiltrate and fight pro-regime forces inside Basra. The soldiers armed and equipped the Iraqis, and allowed the would-be guerrillas to conduct live fire practice with their weapons. However, during the hand-off, the British armoured unit never informed the Commando unit about either ODA 554 or the Iraqi volunteers. Davis just happened to make a coordination visit to the new unit and discovered that the Commandos thought the volunteers were a fedayeen cell and were planning to raid it that evening.[140]

Frustrated with the fluid situation and constrained by the British, Major Baxter and AOB 560 provided the best support possible for the battle for Basra. In the process, the Special Forces battalion proved its ability to change missions on short notice and still conduct them with professionalism. In a matter of days, ODB 560 learned it would not infiltrate Iraq as planned, discovered it would conduct a different infiltration, contacted and transported key oil field technicians, established a presence in Az Zubayr, conducted intelligence missions, and supported Marine and British armoured operations successfully

in and around Basra. The soldiers of AOB 560 had no idea what would come next, but they knew they could handle it, whatever it was.

SUPPORT IN THE WESTERN DESERT

U.S. Army Special Operations Command quietly began deploying units to the Middle East in preparation for possible war, even as the debate over action in Iraq raged in the United Nations. After participating in Exercise Early Victor in Fall 2002, Alpha Forward Support Company (AFSC), 528th Special Operations Support Battalion, redeployed within the Middle East to H-5, where it established a forward operating base for the 5th SFG. The move was accomplished at night over the course of two weeks in late November/early December, with 5th SFG vehicles traveling on the back of other trucks and soldiers traveling by bus in order to protect the clandestine nature of the deployment and to hide the military vehicles.[141]

When the AFSC arrived at H-5, the support soldiers did what they do best: they quickly created a base where days before there had only been open ground. The company's movement control team ran the airfield until the Air Force arrived to take over, and AFSC fuelers were able to hot-fuel (refuel while the engines are still running) C-130s, C-17s, and A-10s—a job also usually reserved for the Air Force. The soldiers in charge of clean water almost outstripped the fuelers in

the handling of large amounts of liquids by producing over 600,000 gallons of potable water in a matter of weeks. The ammunition supply point soldiers controlled all ammunition on the base, including that belonging to the Air Force. The AFSC continued to support all Coalition troops at H-5 until the contract company Kellogg, Brown and Root took over most base operations in February 2003.[142]

After the base at H-5 was completed and 5th SFG was established in its new home in the desert, most of the AFSC traveled home to the United States for the holidays. In mid-February, the entire company returned from leave and the unit, along with the rest of the base,

Figure 5.43 Fuel bladder at the FARP. *Fuel bladders are a main component of the forward arming and refueling point operations.*

began preparing in earnest for war. By that time, forces were flooding into H-5 in preparation for combat operations, and equipment and support personnel followed. Staff officers from the 528th deployed

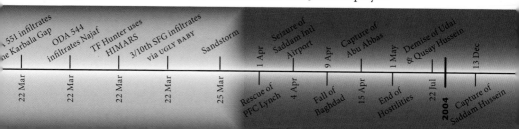

to H-5 in February, expecting to help with base operations, only to find that CFLCC had already arrived and that the logistics officer had assumed those responsibilities before delegating them to Lieutenant Colonel Edward Parrish and the small staff of the Special Operations Theater Support Element. Lieutenant Colonel Michael Saulnier and the 528th Special Operations Support Battalion staff worked in support of SOTSE until the 30th Corps Support Group of the North Carolina Army National Guard took over base operations along with Kellogg, Brown and Root—using 900 people to accomplish what the AFSC had done with 130.[143]

In addition to planning how their own unit would move into Iraq, the AFSC soldiers supported 1st and 2nd Battalions, 5th SFG, in preparation for their infiltration. In the course of the planning, it was discovered that the 5th SFG had a serious equipment problem—its tires were too big. The group had put rugged 38-inch Super Swamper tires on its GMVs during Exercise Early Victor. At the same time, the 160th SOAR acted on lessons it had learned in Afghanistan and had reinforced their MH-47 helicopters with bullet-resistant Kevlar sheeting on the sides and floor of the cargo compartment. The two modifications resulted in GMVs inches too tall to fit inside the MH-47s, precluding the 5th SFG deploying its vehicles internally.[144]

The usual solution to over-height vehicles would be deflating the tires, thereby subtracting vital inches if the fit were tight. In this case, however, the infiltration was supposed to be "hot," with the GMVs rolling off the still-running helicopters, ready to move out. Having to take time to inflate the GMVs' tires would leave the soldiers open to enemy discovery and vulnerable to attack. The AFSC's mechanics and the 5th SFG soldiers tried damping down the shocks, or compressing the springs, as far as possible, but it was not enough. In the end, the 5th SFG ordered 36-inch tires to replace the 38-inch tires. When the new tires finally arrived in mid-March, every AFSC mechanic—and anybody not otherwise occupied—engaged in an all-out tire-changing effort. Nobody knew when the order to move out would come, so the work had to be done immediately. With amazing stamina and efficiency, the AFSC replaced over 700 tires (five per vehicle, four wheels plus a mounted spare) in less than eighteen hours.[145]

In mid-February, the AFSC received word that it needed to provide a forward logistics element (FLE) to support 1st Battalion, 5th SFG's infiltration in case the battalion went by ground, not by air. First Lieutenant Robert Winston* led the FLE, which was made up of ten AFSC soldiers (including Winston) and five vehicles: Winston as the

officer-in-charge, Sergeant First Class Lowell* as the noncommissioned officer-in-charge, four mechanics, a medic, two fuel tankers, and one truck driver; one Heavy Expanded Mobility Tactical Truck, two HMMWVs (High-Mobility Multipurpose Wheeled Vehicle, one of which was a "contact truck" dedicated to maintenance), and two 5-ton Medium Tactical Vehicles—one with a trailer.[146]

Figure 5.44 Convoy in the desert. *The 528th SOSB supplied fuel and supplies to keep Task Force Dagger operating.*

As it happened, it was decided to send B Company, 1st Battalion, 5th SFG, into Iraq by ground, instead of air. Knowing that the FLE was definitely going to be needed, Winston and the rest of the element stepped up their preparations. As Winston described it, "Everybody on the FLE had special classes off to the side; everybody got commo classes, everybody got first aid. We did a round robin of everything so anybody could do anything. Then it was just squat, hold, and wait."[147]

On 17 March, the FLE was notified to get ready to move out in forty-five minutes. "Everybody ran and scrambled to grab their [personal gear], then we ran over to the trucks and we sat there for about two hours." After a rousing "hooah, hooah speech" by Colonel Mulholland, the FLE and Special Forces teams loaded back into their vehicles, and at 2200 hours, commenced the deception designed to get them past the host-country guards at H-5's outermost gates. In keeping with the ruse that the troops were going to a range for additional training, the convoy of FLE and Special Forces teams left the base in small groups. The FLE was in the first group that made it off the base after a small confrontation between the host-country guards and the group's interpreters—who, incidentally, believed the group really was going on a training exercise.[148]

The FLE and the rest of the group reached the designated range and settled in to await the arrival of the rest of the convoy. "We sat there, and we sat, and we sat, and we sat. At about six o'clock in the morning, everybody else started to show up. Come to find out later on, they wouldn't let them out the gate," Winston said. Once the rest of the groups arrived at the range and linked up, the convoy moved out toward its assembly area. Beginning at approximately 0700 hours on the 18th, the convoy drove the 150 miles to the location chosen by the 5th SFG reconnaissance as its assembly area, arriving around 1600 hours. The shallow valley was located two or three miles from the

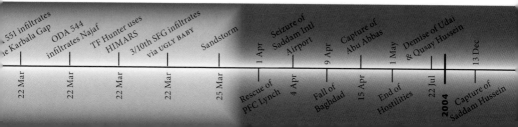

551 infiltrates | the Karbala Gap | ODA 544 infiltrates Najaf | TF Hunter uses HIMARS | 3/10th SFG infiltrates via UGLY BABY | Sandstorm | Seizure of Saddam Intl Airport | 1 Apr | Capture of Abu Abbas | 9 Apr | Demise of Udai & Qusay Hussein | 1 May | 13 Dec

22 Mar | 22 Mar | 22 Mar | 22 Mar | 25 Mar | Rescue of PFC Lynch | 4 Apr | Fall of Baghdad | 15 Apr | End of Hostilities | 22 Jul | 2004 | Capture of Saddam Hussein

border with Iraq, and provided the group with adequate cover from border guards.[149]

With its customary efficiency, the FLE set up its support site in forty-five minutes. All vehicles and gear were covered with camouflage netting and the FLE was ready to receive vehicles for maintenance by evening. In accordance with the mission commander's orders, the ODAS and ODB waited until the next morning (19 March) to send their vehicles through final maintenance checks. The FLE refueled trucks, supplied water, and provided the teams with rations from the FLE's stocks so that the teams' combat loads would not be depleted. The FLE personnel kept busy throughout the day with maintenance and repairs, including support given to units who passed through the site. Some Coalition troops, however, declined the American rations.[150]

At approximately 2000 hours, the combat elements moved forward to the first berm at the Iraqi border, while the FLE remained at the assembly area and monitored the action by radio. After the host-country border guards were calmed and convinced not to interfere, Florida Army National Guardsmen from C Company, 2nd Battalion, 124th Infantry Regiment, set to work with picks and shovels. Beginning at midnight, the soldiers cut a pass over the first berm, which took about twenty minutes. The assault group moved across the open land to the second berm and waited while the Guardsmen cut a pass through the rubble. At approximately 0200 hours the morning of 20 March, seven ODAS in their GMVs and one ODB in trucks crossed the berm and continued into Iraq.[151]

Once the Special Forces soldiers moved into Iraq, the FLE was no longer needed. A convoy of the FLE, a mortar platoon, the Florida Guardsmen, and an interpreter—who did not want to cross the border—drove about two hours away from the border and camped in a small valley. After setting a perimeter, the soldiers finally got a chance to rest and slept until mid-morning. The small convoy then traveled with minimal delay back to H-5. Along the way, the FLE did get to change a few tires and mend a trailer mount, but for the most part, the element's mission was completed uneventfully. Upon returning to H-5, the FLE soldiers were reabsorbed into the AFSC and continued their primary mission as before—providing SOF-specific support whenever and wherever it was needed.[152]

"ALARM RED!"

The sound of the warning siren became almost commonplace to the 112th Signal Battalion soldiers stationed at Ali As-Salim Air Base in the first few months of 2003. It was always followed by an announcement indicating that the following alarm was only an exercise, and then the alarm itself. Though soldiers dutifully donned their MOPP (mission oriented protective posture) gear each time the alarm sounded, familiarity was definitely breeding contempt, and enthusiasm for the drills was waning fast.

The air base had four levels of alarm status, ranging from green to black, each indicating the magnitude of the threat. The alarm levels also dictated whether or not personnel had to dress in MOPP suits or merely keep the gear close by. The highest level of pre-attack alert was Alarm Red, indicating that a missile attack was imminent or in progress and all personnel were to assume MOPP IV status—wear all protective gear. Alarm Yellow indicated that an attack was probable in less than thirty minutes and put everybody at MOPP II, where some gear was worn and the rest carried. The primary status of the air base was Alarm Green, normal wartime conditions, which only required that people keep their MOPP gear on-hand at all times. In order to keep everybody in practice, Alarm Red exercises were conducted with numbing regularity.

MOPP Alarm Levels	
MOPP Level	**Alarm Color**
MOPP I	Green
MOPP II	Yellow
MOPP III	Orange
MOPP IV	Red
MOPP V	Black

Thus was the situation and mindset of the 112th Signal soldiers when they once again heard the Alarm Red siren in the early days of Operation IRAQI FREEDOM. At first, Private First Class Brenda Meter* thought it was another drill and waited for the inevitable "Exercise" announcement. Instead, she only heard the words "ALARM RED! ALARM RED!" echo across the base, and realized this was no drill— the base was under attack.[153]

In true Army fashion, Staff Sergeant Melvin Pelham* had just remarked facetiously, "Ain't war hell?" while enjoying an ice cream cone, when the alarm was sounded. The ironic timing of the comment was not lost on First Lieutenant Kyle Ruger* as he raced out of the dining hall and headed for his assigned bunker. Pelham's remark took on new significance just moments later, when Ruger realized that he had neglected to keep his MOPP gear with him and had to run back to his tent to retrieve it. Catching a whiff of an odor he did not recognize, Ruger found himself thinking as he donned his protective mask,

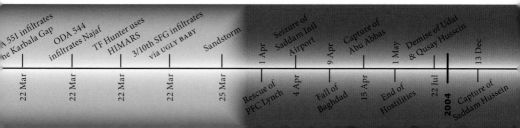

Figure 5.45 Soldier in MOPP IV. *Constant alarms were a way of life at the fixed installations, forcing the soldiers into MOPP IV.*

"I've been gassed! I never expected to die this way!" As his training kicked in, however, Ruger calmed down and realized, with great relief, that nobody around him was exhibiting symptoms of a gas attack.[154]

Meter stepped outside her tent to assess the situation and found "people going everywhere. There [was] no organization to it." Some were racing to take shelter in bunkers, while others were scrambling back to their tents for their MOPP suits. Meter even witnessed people colliding at intersections. The confusion was heightened by the fact that some personnel on the base had taken to ignoring the drills and were therefore all the more excited by the actual alarm. In the melee, a frantic airman initially picked up Staff Sergeant Dale Durham's* mask; fortunately, it was returned by the time Durham ushered his people out of the communications room and was ready to head to a bunker. In contrast, Meter noticed that the Special Forces soldiers were calmly doing what they needed to do, seemingly unfazed by the chaos around them.[155]

Taking cover was almost as strenuous as the attack itself. Meter and her supervisor crowded into an upstairs room surrounded by three-foot thick concrete walls, their designated bunker. To everybody's discomfort, the bunker was full of people—"It was packed." To make matters worse, the day was hot. With everybody wearing unventilated MOPP suits in such heat and proximity, the floor became "literally wet" with sweat. Each Alarm Red kept people at MOPP IV and in bunkers for at least thirty minutes.

Reinforcing the knowledge that the war had come to Ali as-Salim, the alarms continued off and on for the next two days, even rising from Alarm Red to Alarm Black at one point, indicating a missile had struck close by. To drive the point home, the soldiers could hear Patriot missiles launch to intercept incoming missiles. The alarm was often closely followed by the "boom, boom!" that indicated a battery had fired.[156]

Figure 5.46 Patriot Missile System battery in position. *Patriot Missile Systems protected the air bases and fixed installations against the threat of incoming missiles.*

Eventually the danger passed and the alarms subsided, bringing Ali As-Salim Air Base back to Alarm Green and "normal" wartime conditions. The soldiers of C Company, 112th

Signal Battalion, continued to fulfill their communications mission in Kuwait until they were redeployed to Baghdad in May 2003. The job they did in Kuwait was a familiar one, but the sound of "ALARM RED! ALARM RED!" made the mission memorable for the 112th.

OTHER ARSOF

VISUAL OBSERVATION POINTS

On the night of 19 March 2003, the Night Stalkers of the 160th Special Operations Aviation Regiment fired the first rounds of Operation IRAQI FREEDOM at visual observation posts (VISOBS) on the southern and western borders of Iraq. Two serials of helicopter gunships conducted armed reconnaissance and direct action missions against numerous targets along the border. The serials consisted of a flight of two MH-60L Defensive Armed Penetrator (DAP) gunships and a flight of four Black Swarm teams. The Black Swarm teams were composed of a pair of AH-6 Little Bird gunships and one MH-6 Little Bird lift helicopter. The Night Stalkers destroyed over seventy VISOBS during the moonless night, mostly buildings and watchtowers. This opened the way for the cross-border infiltrations by U.S. and Coalition SOF teams, which penetrated deep into Iraq using ground vehicles and helicopter insertions. The successful elimination of the VISOBs allowed unhindered access to western Iraq, and made a bold statement at the beginning of combat operations. At the same time, it blinded the regime and nullified Iraq's early warning capability.

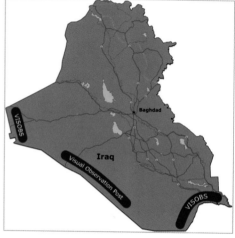

Figure 5.47 Map of VISOBs locations.

Chief Warrant Officer 3 Travis Walter*, the DAP flight leader, departed the forward support base with his flight of DAPs and flew toward the western tri-border area of Iraq. It was a very dark night, and the suspended dust in the air reduced visibility to less than three miles. H-HOUR (the mission execution time) came at 2100 local time, and Walter anticipated sending rounds down range exactly as his digital timer displayed 1800 Zulu (2100 local time). Walter's confidence in his crewmembers stemmed from their service together in Afghanistan. A veteran, cohesive team, they knew each other well.

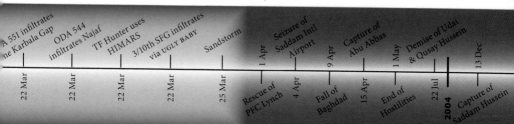

Figure 5.48 AH-6 Little Bird. *The swift and agile AH-6 Little Bird uses both rockets and cannon as part of its armament.*

As the flight headed for the target area, Walter checked in with the ground forces preparing to breach the berm on the border in Restricted Operations Zone Honolulu. All was well and the special operations troops anxiously awaited H-HOUR.[157]

The MH-60L DAP features an integrated fire control system utilizing the Airborne Electro-Optical Special Operations Payload Forward Looking Infrared (FLIR) sensor. This system integrates a laser range finder and target acquisition for laser-guided weapons, with a pilot's heads-up display for rapid processing of information. The DAP is armed with two M134 7.62mm miniguns (a six-barreled, electrically-driven Gatling gun with a rate of fire of up to 4,000 rounds per minute), two 30mm chain guns (a cannon capable of firing 625 rounds per minute out to 4,000 meters), two 2.75 inch rocket pods (a nineteen-tube rocket system firing a variety of special purpose warheads), and Hellfire missiles (a laser guided missile, capable of defeating any armored vehicle). The weapons systems can be configured in any combination of each. Fully loaded, the DAPs possess devastating firepower.

As Walter and his team approached his first target, a small building resembling a guardhouse, he readied the weapons systems and launched the first Hellfire missile precisely at H-HOUR from nearly two miles away. The first missile was a near miss but the pilots quickly followed with 30mm cannon fire, and destroyed the ten-by-ten single-story building. Operation IRAQI FREEDOM had begun. Walter quickly processed the effects of the suspended dust on his weapons systems and made a mental note to make adjustments for the next engagement.[158]

The FLIR, coupled with the helicopter's computer-based mission management system, provided the SOAR pilots with excellent situational awareness. The FLIR immediately tracks to the next target location based on the waypoints previously entered into the mission management program software. Once an active target is selected, the FLIR can "look out" more than five miles. Coupled with the laser designator, it is very effective at fixing the target. The next target was a big building complex three or four miles away. For this engagement, both Walter and Chief Warrant Officer 3 John Curry*, his "–2" or "dash two" wingman, "lased" the intended impact point of the Hellfire. The

DAPs launched two missiles from over three miles away that impacted directly on target. To the crews, the missiles' twenty-six second flight seemed to take forever. The missiles effectively destroyed the building complex. For good measure, the DAPs leveled the structures with additional 30mm cannon fire.[159]

The Night Stalkers continued engaging targets along the length of the western border. At a few outposts, soldiers milled about outside, but most of the buildings appeared empty. That is, until rockets or missiles impacted, then the survivors hiding inside ran for cover. If they carried a weapon, they became a viable target and were killed; if not, then they were allowed to live. (Few saw the sun rise the next day.) "The DAP crews," Walter said, "continued taking care of business until it was time to refuel."[160]

Walter checked in with the special operations forces now rapidly moving north into western Iraq. The ground forces encountered little resistance. Walter led his flight to the aerial refueling checkpoint and joined up with a MC-130P Combat Shadow tanker south of the Iraqi border. The aerial refueling was uneventful, and Walter headed toward the next set of targets.

While en route, they noticed a vehicle with four Iraqis approaching the SOF ground forces. The driver attempted to deceive the helicopter crews by flashing his lights on and off, indicating a "friendly" vehicle. Unfortunately for him, it was not the correct authentication, and the SOAR pilots destroyed the vehicle with cannon fire. As Walter approached another building complex, he

Figure 5.49 Aerial refuel. *The capability to conduct aerial refuel gives the 160th SOAR the ability to conduct operations deep into enemy territory.*

could not discern if it was an active site or already rubble. Not taking any chances, Walter rolled in with 30mm rounds and Curry followed with rockets—it was definitely rubble afterward. Thus went the night, and the DAP crews finished flying after five hours of initial combat. The next day, when Walter watched his FLIR video being broadcast to the American public on the television in the operations center, he could not help but feel pleased with the night's work.[161]

Unlike the heavily armed DAPs who fought in pairs, the Little Bird pilots used a proven three-aircraft technique: the Black Swarm team. Not used since Operation PRIME CHANCE—the 1987 mission to protect oil tankers from Iranian gunboat attacks while passing through the Persian Gulf—the Black Swarm worked in a fashion similar to

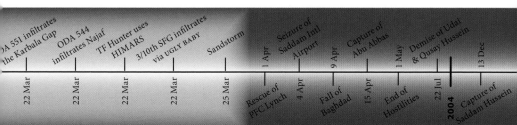

the scout-gun team concept of conventional Army aviation. The lead MH-6 pilot located or "spotted" planned targets and directed a team of two AH-6 gunships to the target with a laser designator. The AH-6 flight leader controlled the engagement. A pair of Air Force A-10 Thunderbolt attack aircraft augmented each Black Swarm team for extra firepower against hardened targets. The AH-6 flight leader coordinated with the A-10, affectionately known as the Warthog, to deliver either 30mm cannon fire or Maverick missiles, based on the target. In another unique aspect of this mission, the AH-6 helicopters stripped off their FLIR sensors in order to carry more munitions. The MH-6 now mounted the FLIR system to spot targets and film engagements. Up to this point, the MH-6 pilots possessed minimal experience in effectively utilizing the FLIR, but their proficiency increased rapidly by the end of the first night of VISOBs missions.[162]

Two flights of Little Birds simultaneously departed the forward support base and headed north into the dark, featureless desert. The

Figure 5.50 VISOBs building. *Most of the Iraqi visual observation posts were destroyed in the first night of operations, effectively blinding the Iraqi higher command.*

formations split prior to the border with one pair of AH-6 Little Birds entering a holding pattern, while the Black Swarm team flew to the targets. Once the first pair of gunships expended its munitions, the second pair conducted a relief in place while the MH-6 remained "on station." The lighter, unarmed MH-6 Little Birds were able to remain over the target area twice as long as the heavier AH-6s. The Black Swarm teams operated in Restricted Operations Zone Knoxville, which was divided in half by a hard surface road that delineated two sectors—one for each Black Swarm team. The road represented the "line of death"—the deconfliction line between the two flights. Each team worked from east to west in its given sector, engaging targets along the way.[163]

Chief Warrant Officer 4 (CW4) Daniel Clement* departed the forward support base in the lead MH-6 with CW4 Timothy Parkens'* team of gunships following. CW4 Doug Carter's* team flew in trail; they covered the eastern sector. Similarly, CW4 Smalley's MH-6 led CW4 James Melvin's* and CW4 Mark Willington's* AH-6 teams toward the western sector—flying several minutes behind the first flight. Upon entering Restricted Operations Zone Knoxville, Parkens and Melvin checked in with their respective A-10 pilots who let them know it was "game on." On this night, a total of ten A-10 attack aircraft covered the

mission, and were "stacked" miles high, ready to cycle into the target area. The two flights separated on reaching the highway and both Carter and Willington entered holding patterns at their respective waypoints.[164]

Pleased with the performance of the FLIR in his first combat experience with the system, Clement noted, "The FLIR did a terrific job of identifying the targets three to five miles out." As he arrived in the vicinity of the first target, Clement used the FLIR to positively identify the VISOB. He held an Infrared Zoom Laser Illuminator/Designator pointer out the aircraft door, "walking it into the target by looking through the FLIR."[165]

Figure 5.51 DAP firing. *The Defensive Armed Penetrator was a lethal addition to the capabilities of the 160th SOAR.*

Precisely at 2100 Iraqi time, Parkens flew "blind" toward the target with his team following Clement's designator. With the target illuminated by the laser beam, the gunships rolled in firing .50 caliber rounds and 2.75 inch rockets at the adobe building. At the same time, across the highway in the western sector, Melvin engaged an outpost flying an Iraqi flag. The two teams methodically cleared the sector.[166]

ARSOF elements breached the southern Iraqi border in Restricted Operations Zone Knoxville in the same manner as they did on the western border. However, Knoxville was much busier this first night because of the scheduled arrival of Coalition special operations aviation helicopters thirty minutes after the clearing of the VISOBs. Deconflicting the flight corridors was a major concern for all elements. Commanders at every level and their aviation liaison officers worked feverishly in the various tactical operations centers to prevent any fratricide. The number of SOF troops crossing the border and flights of Coalition helicopters transiting the restricted operations zone presented a real challenge, especially with all the changes in movement plans occurring right up to the time of execution. Taking out the VISOBs in a timely fashion proved crucial.[167]

Each Black Swarm team systematically destroyed outposts along its route until the gunships ran low on fuel or munitions. Parkens radioed Carter, calling for relief. As Carter's team arrived, Clement, the spotter, headed to the next building. Smoothly entering the rhythm of the action, Carter engaged a small set of buildings with .50 caliber rounds and his "–2" pounded it with rockets. Willington soon relieved Melvin's team in the western half of the sector and headed

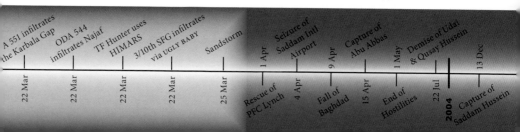

A 551 infiltrates the Karbala Gap — 22 Mar

ODA 544 infiltrates Najaf — 22 Mar

TF Hunter uses HIMARS — 22 Mar

3/10th SFG infiltrates via UGLY BABY — 22 Mar

Sandstorm — 25 Mar

Rescue of PFC Lynch — 1 Apr

Seizure of Saddam Int'l Airport — 4 Apr

Fall of Baghdad — 9 Apr

Capture of Abu Abbas — 15 Apr

End of Hostilities — 1 May

Demise of Uday & Qusay Hussein — 22 Jul

2004

Capture of Saddam Hussein — 13 Dec

for a complex of hardened bunkers. For this target, Willington contacted the A-10 pilots and coordinated for the Warthog to cover the team's gun run with a Maverick missile. The MH-6 captured the attack sequence on FLIR video. In rapid succession, the first AH-6 engaged with its Gatling gun; the second Little Bird fired rockets; and finally, a missile streaked down from the A-10 overhead, and the compound exploded in a cloud of dust, a testament to the precise timing between the elements.[168]

During the seven-hour mission, the Black Swarm teams repeatedly delivered an unstoppable attack. In total, over seventy VISOBS were destroyed during the night. One key to the Night Stalkers' success was the flawless forward arming and refueling operations at the forward supply base. Once the second pair of AHS ran low on fuel, the MH-6 and AH-6 team returned to the base and rapidly rearmed and refueled. The resupply went like clockwork despite the support teams having to move the fuel points and ammunition off and on the taxiway between iterations to accommodate landing Air Force planes. The refueling teams never missed a beat during the long night.[169]

Figure 5.52 FARP operation. *The rapid turn-around in refueling and rearming the Little Birds at the forward arming and refueling point was a key component of the success of the operations against the VISOBS.*

The Night Stalkers launched the first rounds of IRAQI FREEDOM, and destroyed the screen of enemy observation positions on the night of 19 March. Their success enabled over fifty Coalition SOF teams to enter Iraq without incident. Cut off from its outposts on the western and southern borders, the regime increased the level of radio and cell phone transmissions, greatly aiding the collection of signals intelligence. Both the DAPs and the Little Birds, working in close concert with the Air Force A-10s, opened the borders for the initial assault on the Hussein regime.

CROSS-BORDER INSERTIONS

The Night Stalkers of the 3rd Battalion, 160th SOAR, provided CJSOTF-west with rapid, flexible, and lethal special operations aviation helicopter support for the entire SOF campaign plan in western Iraq. The eight MH-47D Chinooks, four MH-60L DAPs, and two MH-60L Black Hawks were the aviation workhorses of Task Force Dagger. The Night Stalkers infiltrated vehicle-mounted teams many miles into Iraq;

resupplied those teams with fuel, water, and ammunition; destroyed visual observation posts along the Iraqi border; conducted casualty evacuations; and delivered a quick reaction force within hours of notification. The entire battalion deployed to meet this demand, except for three MH-60s attached to the regiment's 2nd Battalion, which was supporting Operation ENDURING FREEDOM in Afghanistan.

Figure 5.53 MH-60L Black Hawk. *The MH-60L Black Hawk provides the lift capability for many of the 160th SOAR's special missions.*

The members of 3rd Battalion maintained a habitual working relationship with SOF, specifically with Special Forces, through biannual and combined exercises at the national training centers in the United States. The pilots and crewmembers were very familiar with the environmental conditions of the Middle East, were experts in the long-range infiltration of GMVs, and were proficient in helicopter aerial refueling during low or zero illumination night conditions. In 2003, the 3rd Battalion conducted similar missions for over six months in Afghanistan. The battalion's most recent mission involved the modification of five MH-60Ls into the heavily armored DAP configuration. In fact, the crews' final gunnery training was only completed in the weeks leading up to 19 March. According to Lieutenant Colonel Robert Welch, the battalion commander, "the result of going to Afghanistan was that the 160th's reputation preceded our arrival, and we have established incredible credibility with our Coalition Special Operations Forces."[170]

The SOF infiltration plan changed several times in the weeks prior to 19 March, but one fact remained constant: the special operations troops needed to be air lifted from across the border into their joint operations areas. It would be impossible to move so great a distance by ground in one night. The task of flying the insertion fell to the Night Stalkers of 3rd Battalion. Having worked with a similar force in Afghanistan, the SOAR crews understood the mission, equipment, and vehicles involved. Chief Warrant Officer 3 Donald Harley*, the 3rd Battalion Chinook flight leader, was responsible for getting the SOF elements to the designated landing zones. He fully understood the necessity of having the complete "package" inserted at the same time; security and firepower resulting from numbers on the ground was the key to survival in hostile territory.[171]

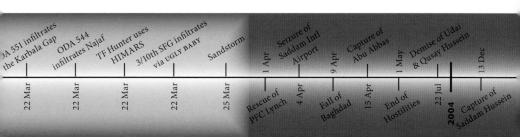

With an experienced and cohesive team around him, Harley integrated a new capability—armed reconnaissance by the DAPS—into the mission plan. During the month before the start of the war, the crews

Figure 5.54 MH-47D Chinook. *The strong and versatile MH-47 Chinook lined up awaiting its next mission.*

and Coalition ground "customers" rehearsed loading and unloading the large desert vehicles on and off the D-model Chinook. Each Chinook carried one 13,000-pound GMV. The fit was tight, and there was little room for error; during loading and unloading, the last thing anyone needed was for a hydraulic line to be damaged. The crew chiefs worked closely with the SOF units to get the loads packed and balanced just right. Before nightfall on the evening of 19 March, the six GMVs were loaded onto the Chinooks without incident. The accompanying DAPs were loaded with a full complement of missiles, rockets, and 30mm rounds, and their crews were anxious to get started.

At 1900 hours Iraqi time, the two DAPs departed H-5 Airfield with Chief Warrant Officer 4 Tim Frailly* in the lead and his wingman Chief Warrant Officer 3 Tommy Starling* close behind. Harley departed with his flight of six Chinooks twenty-five minutes later, and proceeded along the same route as the DAPs to a helicopter aerial refueling track. The DAPs were receiving fuel from the MC-130P Combat Shadow tanker when Harley and the Chinook flight arrived. The first aircraft refueled successfully, but when the fourth aircraft attempted to hook into the hose, the refueling probe tip broke. The Chinook's pilot, Chief Warrant Officer 4 Mark Rogan*, diverted to a forward support base where 1st Battalion, 160th SOAR, was located and ground refueling was available. The two DAPs provided escort for the Chinook. Shortly after Rogan's aircraft left the formation, Chief Warrant Officer 3 Mitch Larkin* noticed that his Chinook was siphoning fuel from its probe, and announced to Harley that he needed to land and fix it. Once on the ground at the support base, the crew chiefs worked their magic and the helicopter was flying again in less than fifteen minutes. The rest of the flight stayed with the tanker receiving fuel.[172]

As Rogan refueled at the forward support base, Frailly departed with his DAP flight to a location just short of the border and checked in with the 1st Battalion AH-6 Little Bird teams busily destroying the Iraqi border outposts in prelude to the infiltration. Once he received fuel, Rogan and the DAPs rejoined the Chinook flight and headed

to the border. It was now 2225 hours, and they were almost an hour behind schedule. The DAPs crossed first, with the Chinooks fifteen minutes behind. The border penetration was uneventful; the Little Birds having cleared the way. As the flight raced across the desert at less than one hundred feet above the ground, the crews saw tracer fire in the distance. It was far enough away to pose no threat, but could easily be seen through their night vision goggles.

The DAPs reconnoitered the landing zone and determined it was clear. The Chinook crew chiefs gave their passengers the ten-minute warning to get ready to off-load. Each Chinook landed with little problem. The troops unloaded their vehicles in record time, as the DAPs scouted the surrounding area and finally signaled "all clear" to the mounted SOF teams as they began rolling north to their first checkpoint. When Harley received the "all ready" call from the teams, the flight departed, leaving a huge dust cloud lingering in the area.

Harley altered the original return route and sent the two DAPs with Rogan and his Chinook back to the forward support base for fuel. The remaining five Chinooks flew at maximum speed to get clear of the area. Once the Night Stalkers crossed the border out of Iraq, Harley and his flight flew back to the aerial refueling track. The tanker was precisely where it was supposed to be, and right on time. By now, many of the Chinooks were below the reserve fuel limit of twenty minutes flying time. Larkin had only 700 pounds of fuel left, enough for only twelve minutes of flight time, and he plugged into the refueling tanker first. Once everyone had refueled, Harley led the flight back to H-5 without further problems. Rogan and the DAPs refueled at the forward support base and returned forty-five minutes later.[173]

Despite potentially serious refueling problems during the mission, the Night Stalkers persevered and transported the Coalition SOF team deep into Iraq. The 3rd Battalion crews penetrated deeper into Iraq than any Coalition element that first night of the war, with only the protection of the DAPs and the Chinook 7.62mm miniguns. The successful insertion of the teams set the tone for future Night Stalker missions.

Under the Big Umbrella

Firepower is always a concern for military forces. This is true for both conventional and special operations forces. In 1943, Lieutenant Colonel William Darby, the 1st Ranger Battalion commander, requested additional firepower for his lightly armed Rangers after they fought

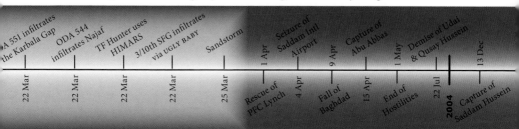

against tanks with captured antitank guns. Darby's solution was four half-tracks mounting 75mm antitank guns that could also be used in the indirect fire mode. For additional firepower, Darby later received the 83rd Chemical Mortar Battalion with its 4.2 inch mortars for the 6615th Ranger Force during the Italian campaign. Jumping ahead sixty years, the 75th Ranger Regiment—the descendants of Darby's Rangers—looked for additional firepower during Operation IRAQI FREEDOM. They found it at Fort Bragg.[174]

The 75th Ranger Regiment made its foray into the domain of the King of Battle (Artillery) beginning on 21 March, with the first tactical employment of the High Mobility Artillery Rocket System

Figure 5.55 HIMARS before and after firing.

(HIMARS). During its ten-day raid into southwestern Iraq—not a typical location for a corps-level artillery element—Task Force Hunter provided indirect general- and direct-support fires for the Rangers and attacked the antiaircraft artillery sites in the CJSOTF-west area of operations. Task Force Hunter demonstrated the ability of the Rangers to incorporate a combined arms team on the modern battlefield, especially for those teams willing to accept a certain amount of combat risk.

The HIMARS is a multiple rocket system launcher mounted on a truck rather than a heavy tracked vehicle. A HIMARS shoots six rockets at a time, or one long-range Army Tactical Missile System–guided missile. The missile is one of two types: either the Block I or Block IA—the first delivering 950 baseball-sized antipersonnel/antimateriel M74 grenades to targets over 160 kilometers away, and the second delivering 300 M74 grenades over 300 kilometers away. Because the HIMARS is mounted on a truck and can be transported in a C-130 aircraft, it can be rapidly deployed into areas previously inaccessible to artillery. The system is powerful enough to engage and defeat enemy artillery, air defense weapons, and light armor. Because it can launch its weapons and move away at high speed, the HIMARS provides a lethal and highly mobile artillery option.[175]

Figure 5.56 18th Field Artillery Brigade shoulder patch.

The HIMARS is also unique in that it is a prototype system—there are only four in the Army, with three assigned to C Battery, 3rd Battalion, 27th Field Artillery, at Fort Bragg. C Battery's parent unit, the 18th Field Artillery Brigade, received the first HIMARS in 1998 as an experi-

ment in field artillery equipment. The brigade retained the system in 2002, with some input from special operations commanders.[176]

General Bryan Brown, commander of U.S. Special Operations Command, first heard about HIMARS in 1999 when a colonel from the 18th Field Artillery Brigade offered him a briefing on the system. The firepower and mobility of the HIMARS impressed Brown, who agreed that an all-weather fire support system provided much needed support for special operations units. The HIMARS neutralized the indirect fire and armor threat to the mobile but unprotected Rangers. General Brown immediately instructed his staff to prepare a letter in support of a HIMARS capability, and 18th Field Artillery Brigade found a new mission.[177]

Colonel Joseph Votel, 75th Ranger Regiment Commander, also recognized the benefit of having the HIMARS support his command. After convincing his superiors that the force of choice to employ and to protect the system were the Rangers, Votel assigned the security mission to 3rd Ranger Battalion in January 2003. Task Force Hunter commander Major Ted Hall* immediately organized a team to prepare a training program and develop tactics, techniques, and procedures for securing the HIMARS. Hall worked closely with Major Ralph Morgenstern*, an operations officer for the 18th Field Artillery Brigade, and established the command and control relationships, resupply procedures, and fire control procedures at a January joint planning conference. The two biggest challenges the planners needed to solve were the issues of communications equipment compatibility—the HIMARS lacked satellite communication radios—and the large logistics train required to maintain and resupply the system.[178]

Figure 5.57 27th Field Artillery insignia.

The Rangers worked with Captain Stan Knell*, given command of the HIMARS battery in January, as he developed a training plan for his troops. Task Force Hunter also received the bulk of an antitank company—D Company, 2nd Battalion, 325th Airborne Infantry Regiment—for additional force protection. Together, since the artillery and infantry were both located at Fort Bragg, the combined arms team established communication procedures and tactics, technique, and procedures for immediate action drills.[179]

Figure 5.58 D/2/325 security force. *D Company, 2nd Battalion, 325th Airborne Infantry Regiment provided some of the security force protecting the HIMARS.*

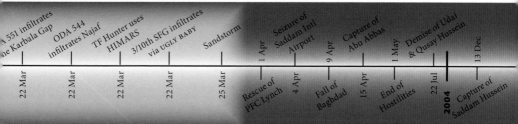

A 551 infiltrates the Karbala Gap — 22 Mar

ODA 544 infiltrates Najaf — 22 Mar

TF Hunter uses HIMARS — 22 Mar

3/10th SFG infiltrates via UGLY BABY — 22 Mar

Sandstorm — 25 Mar

Rescue of PFC Lynch

Seizure of Saddam Int'l Airport — 1 Apr

4 Apr

Fall of Baghdad

Capture of Abu Abbas — 9 Apr

15 Apr

End of Hostilities — 1 May

Demise of Uday & Qusay Hussein — 22 Jul

13 Dec

2004

Capture of Saddam Hussein

Figure 5.59 Rangers on security. *Rangers provided the perimeter security for the HIMARS operations. The combination of Rangers and conventional troops proved effective.*

The training pace was fast and furious, and launcher drivers and the support personnel received only a limited amount of night driving training. Unfortunately, Knell could only simulate the desert terrain on the drop zones at Fort Bragg. The lack of desert night driving training became a major problem in Iraq, one made worse by the fact that while the Rangers were experienced in the use of night vision goggles, the other troops were not. To compound the problem, the artillerymen only owned a limited number of goggles, and those were older PVS-7 models, not the most modern equipment.[180]

During the first days of March, Hall, Knell, and the task force's senior noncommissioned officer, Master Sergeant James Bradley*, scrambled to organize and prepare their force at their forward support base in the Middle East. A logjam of Air Force C-17 and C-5 transport aircraft, carrying troops and equipment into the Central Command area of responsibility, caused much of the task force's logistics assets to arrive late. Some vehicles and personnel arrived mere hours before Task Force Hunter started its trek north to the Iraqi border, forcing Knell to depart with only two of the three HIMARS launchers. Once the vehicles and soldiers regrouped at the forward support base, the third launcher took the same route north and caught up with the main force the next day. Hall's command eventually included over 200 soldiers: one platoon of 3rd Ranger Battalion, a Ranger 120mm mortar section, two Ranger reconnaissance detachment teams, the HIMARS platoon with its various support vehicles and soldiers, the infantry antitank company, and a squad of engineers from B Company, 27th Engineer Battalion. Back at the forward support base, an infantry platoon from the 101st Airborne Division waited as a quick reaction force.[181]

Figure 5.60 27th Engineer Battalion insignia.

The evening of 21 March, Task Force Hunter departed the base. The long convoy used a nearby system of wadis to bypass the civilian road system, because the presence of Americans in that area was a sensitive issue. Sergeant First Class Christopher Marrow* described the movement as "a slow and painful process." The fifty-nine-vehicle task force stretched for miles, and moved at twenty miles an hour in the moonless night—an extremely challenging command and control operation. Divided into five separate serials of vehicles, it took several

2001 | Attack on World Trade Center | 11 Sep | 2002 | 16 Oct | Signing of Iraq war resolution | Approval of UN Resolution 1441 | 8 Nov | 2003 | D-Day Operation IRAQI FREEDOM 19 Mar | Air War begins 19 Mar | TF 64 infiltrates Iraq 19 Mar | 20 Mar | 1/5th SFG enters Iraq | AOB 570 infiltrat Wadi al Khi 21 Mar

hours to reach the Iraqi border. The antitank company breached the border berm with little difficulty, and the reconnaissance detachment pushed ahead to reconnoiter the route to the first HIMARS positioning area.[182]

Once the task force crossed the border, Marrow worked with the CFACC command net to coordinate the convoy's journey through the desert with aircraft patrolling above. Everybody in the task force feared that Air Force planes might mistake the odd caravan deep inside Iraq for the enemy. In a prearranged plan, all of Iraq was divided into "touchpads" (gridded zones), which provided positive fire control deconfliction between ground operations and air operations.[183]

Using a combination of hard roads and dirt trails, the task force continued its slow progress into Iraq. Having traveled seventy kilometers and encountering no enemy forces, Task Force Hunter reached its first firing position at 0600 Iraqi time on 22 March. Hall and Knell moved the force off the road, positioned the three launchers, readied the firing positions, and prepared to fire on their preplanned targets. Bradley orchestrated setting up the perimeter, which covered over six kilometers. At first light, Marrow confirmed the team's touchpad location with his higher command and oriented the mortar section. Registration of the mortars was not possible because of the possibility of compromising the location of the task force.[184]

Figure 5.61 530th Service and Supply Battalion insignia.

By 1500, Task Force Hunter was ready to execute its first mission. Knell fired six missions the first day on several preplanned targets and several targets relayed from Morgenstern, located at the joint operations center at the forward support base. Morgenstern and Knell were "writing doctrine" on a daily basis, and kept copious notes on what worked and what did not. One precaution they validated was that the Rangers needed to stay clear of the 400-meter surface danger zone around the HIMARS launcher, which could ignite debris when the battery was fired. The artillerymen simply closed the cab of the launcher and remained unaffected. During the first several engagements, location coordinates were slightly off due to a discrepancy between the aviation grids used by CFACC and the military grid reference system used by the artillery. The confusion was quickly corrected and, since HIMARS is fully automated, the conver-

Figure 5.62 Convoy operations conducted by the 530th Supply and Services Battalion. *Keeping the teams supplied in the western desert involved convoy operations by the advanced operating bases.*

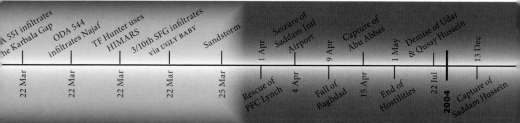

A 551 infiltrates the Karbala Gap — 22 Mar

ODA 544 infiltrates Najaf — 22 Mar

TF Hunter uses HIMARS — 22 Mar

3/10th SFG infiltrates via UGLY BABY — 22 Mar

Sandstorm — 25 Mar

Rescue of PFC Lynch

1 Apr · Seizure of Saddam Intl Airport — 4 Apr

Fall of Baghdad

9 Apr · Capture of Abu Abbas — 15 Apr

End of Hostilities

1 May · Demise of Uday & Qusay Hussein — 22 Jul

13 Dec · 2004 · Capture of Saddam Hussein

sion was simple to make. The officers noted that the HIMARS-fired Block 1A missiles produced good "effects on target."[185]

Task Force Hunter used its mobility for protection. As each launcher fired its missiles, the battery quickly relocated to a new position. Hall had a well-planned movement and firing agenda, and with help of his subordinate commanders and noncommissioned officers, negotiated the desert terrain. The task force traveled mostly at night, which challenged the artillerymen and support personnel. The Rangers were conditioned to operate with little sleep for extended operations and were at ease with night operations. Therefore, Hall emphasized to Bradley that it was the Rangers' responsibility to monitor the conventional force. Knell's support element experienced difficulties moving off-road with its tactical vehicles, but the challenges were overcome with determination and Ranger ingenuity. Captain James Estrich*, the Task Force Hunter operations officer, managed the security force, which chased off several Iraqi vehicles that approached the firing positions. The curious men quickly departed in the face of the tremendous firepower marshaled by the antitank company and the Rangers.[186]

Figure 5.63 Headquarters' vehicle for communicating with CFACC.

The Rangers were not used to having to support the HIMARS long logistics tail; speed and economy of force are two of SOF's strengths. In order to meet the logistics and maintenance requirements for the task force, B Company, 2nd Ranger Battalion, was ordered to escort large vehicle convoys north into Iraq and then back to the forward support base. Designated Team Spear, B Company found that moving twenty to thirty vehicles through the Iraqi desert at night—with support drivers inexperienced at driving with night vision goggles—was a difficult proposition. To make the job even harder, the sandstorm that hit on 24 March wreaked havoc with operations, reducing visibility to less than thirty meters and causing several accidents. Needless to say, Team Spear experienced many challenges, yet in typical Ranger fashion, continued the mission with determination.

Amidst the more prosaic incidents was one accident resulting in more than its fair share of drama. A heavy truck loaded with the HIMARS ammunition swerved off the road, breaking the axle. When the truck slammed into a ditch, the force of the collision caused one of the missiles it was carrying to break out of the carrying pod. For-

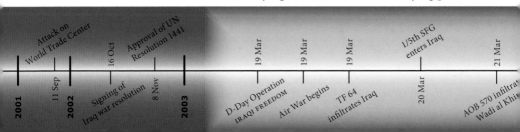

tunately, the missile did not explode. After a tense radio discussion with the forward support base, several explosives experts were brought in to deactivate the warhead—which was then loaded on a truck, moved to another location, and eventually destroyed.[187]

Task Force Hunter moved constantly during its ten-day raid, conducting a series of fire missions. Estrich and Marrow kept the joint operations center informed and the launch areas deconflicted with CFACC. "We let the CFACC know where we went using the touchpad system," said Marrow, "which was driven by terrain and positioning of fires." Task Force Hunter moved as far north as Najaf, and pro-

Figure 5.64 M977 HEMTT and loose HIMARS missile. *During a night convoy, one of the HEMTTS hauling HIMARS missiles ran off the road. A missile broke out of the container causing some problems.*

vided support for the Rangers' raid on Objectives Sidewinder South and North on 27 and 29 March. The task force prevented the massing of combat power against the 3rd Infantry Division, and effectively destroyed several air defense artillery positions in support of aviation missions. The task force worked its way south and returned to the forward support base on 31 March with a strong record of successful fire missions.[188]

Upon return, Task Force Hunter disbanded and the various elements hurriedly refitted and were sent on to other missions. The war, however, was not over for the artillerymen. The next day, Knell loaded his HIMARS battery on C-17s and deployed to H-1, the airfield that the 3rd Ranger Battalion had secured several days earlier. From H-1, the HIMARS could cover the entire area of operations, from the Syrian border to eastern Baghdad to northern Iraq. Indeed, the HIMARS fired twelve missions from H-1 in support of the Rangers at Haditha Dam.[189]

Task Force Hunter was a notable success. Operationally, the Rangers, artillerymen, and support units fully demonstrated the capability of a combined arms team. The participants overcame many obstacles—from terrain to sandstorms to logistics challenges—and prevailed. The task force delivered precise direct- and general-fire support to the special

Figure 5.65 Missile being reloaded. *The troops of the battery rapidly secured the missile and the operation continued.*

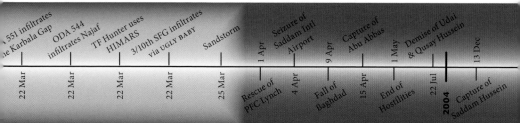

operations and conventional commanders. Key leaders also developed new doctrine for the tactical employment of the HIMARS behind enemy lines and validated the HIMARS/SOF relationship. In less than a month, HIMARS proved itself on the battlefield, greatly increasing SOF's leverage and ability to meet the operational needs of combatant commanders.

SUMMARY

From D-DAY on 19 March until D+4 on 23 March, ARSOF led the Coalition assault on Saddam Hussein's regime. The decision to bypass Turkey with the "UGLY BABY" infiltration unlocked a critical situation and opened the way for CJSOTF-North to execute its mission. In the west, the 160th SOAR destroyed the visual observation points, blinding the regime and paving the way for the cross-border infiltration of SOF teams. CJSOTF-west dispersed ARSOF units throughout the western desert in search of SCUDS and other strategic targets. Likewise, Task Force Hunter attacked a number of key targets as the Rangers executed their missions under the protective umbrella of the HIMARS.

All branches of ARSOF worked together to support the Coalition as it launched Operation IRAQI FREEDOM. This cooperation continued in the weeks that followed, as ARSOF units supported conventional operations in central and southern Iraq, and executed operations of their own in the west and the north.[190]

6

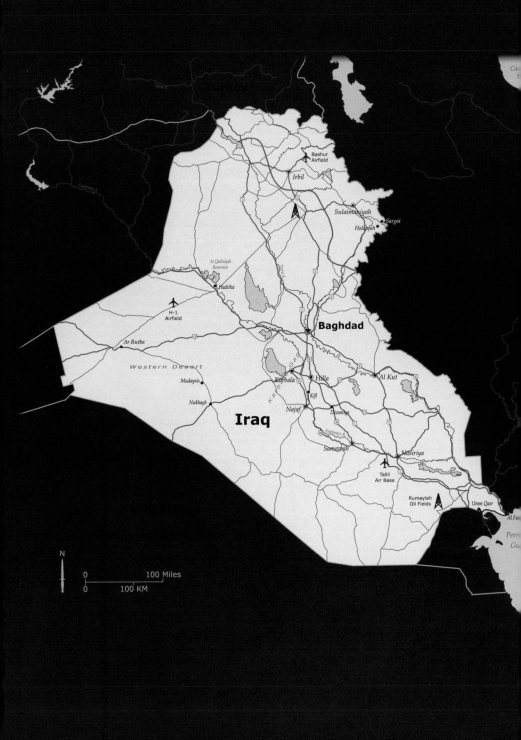

War Pauses

D+5 through D+12
24–31 March

AS OFFENSIVE OPERATIONS CONTINUED deeper into Iraq, it became evident that Central Command's plan was working. Special operations forces dominated two of the three main battlefronts—the north and the west—and SOF elements were thoroughly integrated into all of the conventional force operations in the south. Coalition forces had successfully accomplished their missions during the first four days of Operation IRAQI FREEDOM; however, as the week progressed, a series of "hiccups" delayed the campaign.[1]

CONVENTIONAL OPERATIONS

When Task Force Tarawa took control of the Highway 1 bridge north of Nasiriya on 23 March, the I Marine Expeditionary Force was able to surround Nasiriya. After fierce fighting with Republican Guard units in Nasiriya, I MEF crossed the Euphrates on 24 March and continued its assault through the fertile land between the Euphrates and Tigris Rivers. The Marine 1st Regimental Combat Team followed Highway 7 north toward Al Kut, while the 5th and 7th RCTs followed Highway 1 north toward Diwaniya, where they turned right and met the 1st RCT. Part of the 1st RCT also split off and confronted Iraqi divisions positioned near Amarah on Highway 6.

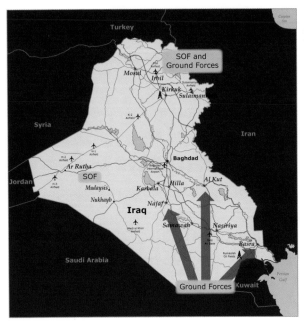

Figure 6.1 Map of conventional operations. *The disposition of forces in the war on Iraq. Note that SOF controls two of three fronts (west and north).*

The "mother of all sandstorms" hit Iraq on 25 March. As elemental interference with military operations goes, the timing was not that bad. The 3rd Infantry Division and I MEF were both halted in their positions to refuel and regroup before the next phase of the attack. The 3rd ID had troops within one hundred miles of Baghdad. Environmental catastrophe was averted when SOF prevented sabotage of the Rumaylah Oil Fields, the Al Faw manifold, and the oil and gas platforms in the Persian Gulf. Marines and British commandos secured Umm Qasr and soon opened it for the reception of humanitarian aid. If Coalition ground forces had to stop in their tracks for two days, they could do so without losing ground—the Iraqis were stuck, too.

General Tommy Franks and Lieutenant General Buzz Moseley used the lull in the ground war to fracture the Republican Guard units arrayed between the Coalition forces and Baghdad. From the night of 25 March through the morning of the 27th, aircraft flew above the sandstorm to deliver precision-guided bombs and missiles on the unsuspecting enemy. The enemy quickly figured out what was going on, yet could do nothing about it, so the media concluded that the campaign had stalled. The media was wrong.[2]

Najaf lay between the 3rd ID and the Karbala Gap—the route to Baghdad. As the 2nd Brigade Combat Team had learned at Objective Rams, the fedayeen in Najaf were numerous and willing to die fighting. Unlike Samawah and Nasiriya, which the division simply isolated and bypassed, Najaf needed clearing so that the fedayeen would not be able to attack the logistics area at Rams—an area vital to the assault on Baghdad.

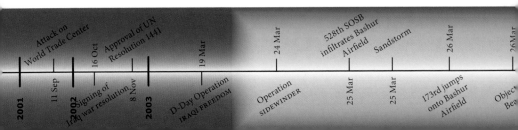

Late on 24 March, the 1st BCT received the order to seize the bridge over the Euphrates River at Kifl north of Najaf. The highway from Hilla was used to bring enemy fighters into the Najaf area. Although the 1st BCT was strung out between Najaf and Nasiriya, it took the mission. At 0200 hours on 25 March, the brigade's air defense artillery battery assaulted the bridge and ran into deeply entrenched opposition. The brigade's quick reaction force came to its aid, and by 1030 hours, the west bank was cleared of Iraqi defenders. By the end of 26 March, the brigade had seized the east bridgehead using M1A1 Abrams tanks and Bradley Fighting Vehicles, and had even engaged in hand-to-hand combat. By securing the bridge at Kifl, the 1st BCT prevented reinforcements from joining the fedayeen and Iraqi troops in Najaf.[3]

The cordon around Najaf closed from the south on 25 March, when the 3rd Squadron, 7th Cavalry Regiment, moved to take the Highway 8/80 bridge across the Euphrates south of the city. In spite of the sandstorm, the battalion secured the bridge by 1000 hours. Elements of the battalion then attacked north from the east side of the bridge toward Najaf, relying on precision munitions from aircraft high above the swirling sand for support throughout the night. In an attempt to retake control of the bridges, Iraqis attacked all American elements east of the river on 26 March. Meanwhile, the 2nd BCT at Objective Rams worked to clear the routes south and east of Najaf, completing the cordon and relieving some of the pressure on the cavalry. The battalion finally withdrew at noon on 27 March, when fedayeen from Najaf stopped flowing south and attacking the 3rd ID's supply lines.[4]

Figure 6.2 Three-day sandstorm. *Army SOF "hunker down" at a mechanized infantry laager during the advance to Baghdad during the March three-day sandstorm. Many soldiers commented on the orange tint during the day as a result of the sand obscuring the sun.*

On 26 March, the 2nd Brigade of the 82nd Airborne Division was placed under operational control of V Corps. Reinforced by units from the 1st Armored Division (specifically 2nd Battalion, 70th Armor Regiment, and 1st Battalion, 41st Infantry Regiment, both based at Fort Riley, Kansas) and the 101st Airborne Division (Air Assault), the 82nd derigged the equipment it had prepared to air drop and drove from Kuwait to Tallil Air Base, meeting the troops as they debarked C-130s. The airlift and three convoys took twenty-four hours, begin-

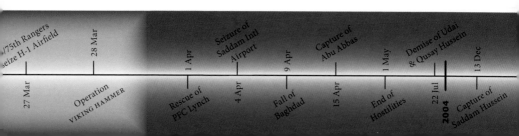

Figure 6.3 173rd Airborne Brigade (-). *C-17's loaded with part of the 173rd Airborne Brigade (-) await orders to load and launch in support of Operation IRAQI FREEDOM.*

ning on 27 March. On 28 March, the 82nd moved to Samawah, and on 29 March, the paratroopers relieved the 3rd ID's 3rd BCT. The 3rd BCT then moved north to Objective Rams, where it regrouped for the push through the Karbala Gap. The 82nd coordinated with SOF teams in and around Samawah, and prepared to clear the city on 31 March.[5]

On 28 March, the 1st and 2nd BCTs of the 101st Airborne Division finished moving to Forward Arming and Refueling Point Shell, putting the division in place to support V Corps through the Karbala Gap. However, the division's first task was to clear Najaf. Lead elements of the 101st entered Najaf on 28 March, and the division began communicating with the 3rd ID's 1st and 2nd BCTs. By 30 March, the 1st BCT cleared Kifl and completely secured that portion of the line of communication south from Hilla.[6]

Conventional infantry finally entered the picture in northern Iraq on 26 March, when the 173rd Airborne Brigade (-) jumped onto Bashur Airfield. In an unusual turn of events, while the 173rd was a conventional asset, it was under special operations control. The airborne brigade (-) was originally meant to provide security for the 4th ID moving south from Turkey, but when Turkey refused permission to move U.S. troops through it's country, the 173rd's parent command—European Command—put the brigade (-) under the operational control of Coalition Forces Special Operations Component Command, and in turn Combined Joint Special Operations Task Force–North.

Peshmerga
Kurdish for "those who face death." The term used by the Kurds to refer to freedom fighters. These trained armed retainers are generally affiliated with the political parties or prominent personalities in the Kurdish independence movement. They often wear traditional Kurdish garb, the baggy sharwall trousers, plain jacket and a colorful sash.

The 173rd executed its combat jump (into a secure environment) the night of 26 March, beginning at 2000 hours. The ten heavy-drop platforms were dropped first, followed by 963 paratroopers—only thirty-two troopers did not make it out the door before the aircraft cleared the drop zone. The paratroopers plunged through the darkness and scattered widely around the muddy airfield. SOF teams, support personnel, and Kurdish peshmerga met the "little groups of pissed-off paratroopers" on the ground. Later on the 27th, an additional twelve C-17s landed bringing in the brigade's vehicles and another 1,200 soldiers.[7]

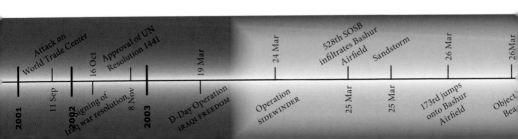

While SOF teams had previously linked up with Kurdish peshmerga forces and quite capably tied up Iraqi units along the Green Line, the Coalition lacked a robust presence in northern Iraq. Dropping the infantry brigade (-) in the middle of the country proved to Saddam that the Coalition could put troops anywhere it wanted whenever it wanted, and also signaled to the Kurds that the Coalition was serious about defeating the regime. The two-battalion infantry brigade gave the CJSOTF-North commander, Colonel Charles Cleveland, the ability to deploy troops that could take and hold ground, including the northern oil fields. Unfortunately, that capability came with a price—air assets. Positioning the 173rd to jump into northern Iraq, and then flying in support and enough equipment and supplies to maintain the brigade (-), tied up valuable C-17 aircraft. Over the course of ninety-six hours, the Air Force flew eighty-nine C-17 sorties (round trips) to deliver and support the 173rd. On 7 April, Task Force 1-63rd Armor, the European Command's Heavy Ready Company/Medium Ready Company of M1A1 Abrams tanks, Bradley Fighting Vehicles, and M113 armored personnel carriers, required another thirty C-17 sorties to bring them in, raising the brigade support requirements.[8]

ARSOF OPERATIONS

Combined Joint Special Operations Task Force–West continued its operations according to plan. In the southern area between the Kuwaiti border and Baghdad—primarily centered on the reinforced Forward Operating Base 52—Special Forces fulfilled liaison and coordination, unconventional warfare, and special reconnaissance missions. After being successfully inserted by the 3rd Battalion, 160th Special Operations Aviation Regiment, Chinooks escorted by Defensive Armed Penetrators, Operational Detachment Alpha (ODA) 551 made its way to the Karbala Gap, where it furiously transmitted intelligence reports ahead of the 3rd ID advance. Far to the south, other Special Forces teams supported the advance itself.[9]

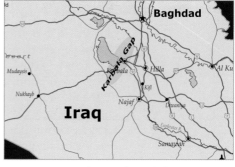

Figure 6.4 Map showing the Karbala Gap. *A successful and speedy passage of the Karbala Gap was key to the Coalition strategy.*

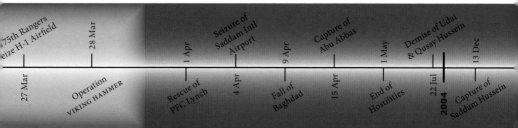

A critical component of the special operations forces' missions in Operation IRAQI FREEDOM was to support V Corps during its drive into Iraq. Besides directly supporting the conventional ground forces, SOF was tasked to capture a variety of critical, strategic objectives, such as the southern oil fields and offshore production platforms. Made up mostly of members of the 5th Special Forces Group (SFG), the southern offensive also included air support from Air Force Special Operations Command, Naval Special Warfare elements, and SOF units from various Coalition allies.[10]

Figure 6.5 422nd CAB insignia.

Figure 6.6 9th POB insignia.

In the southern area of operations, Civil Affairs and Psychological Operations units supported both special operations and conventional units on the drive to Baghdad. The 422nd Civil Affairs Battalion and C Company, 9th PSYOP Battalion, moved north with the 3rd ID, while the 431st CAB and the 318th PSYOP Company supported the 101st Airborne Division. With I MEF to the east, the 305th and 307th PSYOP Companies supported the Marines and British, respectively.[11]

In northern Iraq, CJSOTF-North was almost in place. Because of the successful completion of the high-risk Operation UGLY BABY, Colonel Cleveland now had two complete 10th SFG battalions, plus one company of the 3rd Battalion, 3rd SFG, on the ground and mounted in Ground Mobility Vehicles. With Turkey allowing overflight of its airspace, the rest of the 3rd Battalion was en route with the remainder of CJSOTF-North's ad hoc task force support, and its attached signal, support, Civil Affairs, and PSYOP units. CJSOTF-North's primary mission was to support combat operations by teaming up with Kurdish peshmerga forces against Iraqi forces and fixing the Iraqi divisions on the Green Line, thereby preventing the Iraqis from affecting the approaching battle for Baghdad. On the Green Line, CJSOTF-North ODAS called in numerous Coalition aircraft to bomb the Iraqi forces. Special Forces teams also took on the strategically critical job of capturing the oil fields of Kirkuk, thereby guaranteeing that there would be a source of national income for Iraq following the war.[12]

The adventures and accomplishments related in the accounts below are indicative of the challenges and conditions ARSOF units encountered as the war progressed. While not comprehensive nor exhaustive, the details provided are representative of the ARSOF experience. The presentation will go from north to west before concerning other ARSOF.

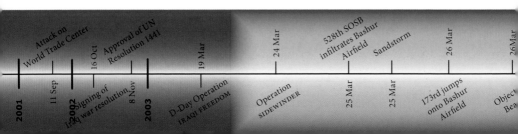

CJSOTF-North

Task Force Viking's build-up at the onset of hostilities ultimately reached fifty-one ODAS working with upward of sixty thousand Kurdish fighters. Two distinct missions confronted the task force: reinforcing the Kurdish peshmerga facing three Iraqi Corps along the Green Line to fix those forces in place preventing the reinforcement of the regime in Baghdad, and eliminating the terrorist Ansar al-Islam stronghold on the northeastern border with Iran, thereby reducing the threat the terrorists posed to the Kurdish rear area.

> ### Kurdish Political Parties
>
> *Kurdistan Democratic Party*
>
> **KDP.** Kurdish secessionist party led by Massoud Barzani. Tribal-based, with a large militia (peshmerga).
>
> *Patriotic Union of Kurdistan*
>
> **PUK.** Leftist splinter party of KDP led by Jalal Talabani and urban intelligentsia.

Forward Operating Base 102 (2nd Battalion, 10th SFG) covered 180 kilometers of the Green Line front, centered on the city of Mosul. In this early period of the campaign, the teams of FOB 102 worked with their Kurdistan Democratic Party counterparts, planning and training for operations in their sector. The initial posture of the Task Force Viking elements along the Green Line remained defensive in nature. With the clearing of the Ansar al-Islam stronghold and the arrival on 29 March of the task force's tactical command post at Bashur Airfield, the unit began the switch to offensive operations.

The fight against the Ansar al-Islam fell to the 3rd Battalion, 10th SFG, in its doctrinal role as FOB 103. Operation VIKING HAMMER, initiated on 28 March, followed several days of preparatory air strikes against the Ansar al-Islam stronghold. In thirty hours, the Special Forces troops and their peshmerga allies of the Patriotic Union of Kurdistan routed the Ansar al-Islam from its mountain redoubt. This action eliminated the threat to the Kurdish rear and refocused the entirety of Task Force Viking's efforts against the Iraqi Army along the Green Line. With Task Force Viking firmly established in sector, the full attention of the two forward operating bases turned to the preparation of the Kurdish fighters for the action to come.

Figure 6.7 Task Force Viking logo.

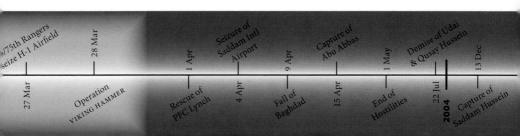

OPERATION *VIKING HAMMER*

In preparing his campaign plan for operations in northern Iraq, Colonel Cleveland faced a two-pronged dilemma. His primary opposition in the region came from three Iraqi corps—more than 150,000 troops massed along the 140-kilometer political demarcation boundary known as the Green Line. To confront this force, Cleveland's three hundred Special Forces soldiers joined with more than fifty thousand Kurdish fighters arrayed against Iraqi forces. Before engaging the Iraqi frontline forces, Cleveland determined he needed to eliminate the threat to the Kurdish rear area posed by the Ansar al-Islam terrorist organization.[13]

The Ansar al-Islam routinely skirmished with the Kurdish troops from its stronghold above the town of Halabja in the mountainous Khurma region near the Iranian border. With well-developed defensive positions on the high ground above the valley, the seven hundred–strong Ansar al-Islam was a formidable threat to any Kurdish operations against the Green Line. A contingent of Iranian-supported Kurds—the Islamic Group of Kurdistan—also occupied a sector in the northern portion of the area and needed to be dealt with along with the Ansar al-Islam. One final threat, a suspected weapons of mass destruction site, was located in the village of Sargat at the foot of the Shandahari Ridge.

Figure 6.8 Map highlighting Operation VIKING HAMMER. *The destruction of the Ansar al-Islam was the focus of Operation* VIKING HAMMER. *This operation eliminated the threat to the Kurdish rear area.*

The 10th SFG developed Operation VIKING HAMMER to deal with the Ansar al-Islam. Cleveland assigned the mission of reducing the Ansar al-Islam threat to the 3rd Battalion, which was already fighting Iraqi forces along the Green Line. A reinforced C Company, 3rd Battalion, would counter the Ansar al-Islam threat in the east, then rejoin the remainder of the 3rd Battalion on the Green Line, where it was currently fighting alongside the 2nd Battalion, 10th SFG; the 3rd Battalion, 3rd SFG; and Kurdish forces. Pushing the Iraqi divisions off the Green Line would open the way for the capture of Kirkuk and Mosul, clearing the northern approaches to Baghdad.[14]

The principal allies in the fight against Ansar al-Islam were the 6,500 peshmerga fighters of the Patriotic Union of Kurdistan, under the ground force command of Kak Mustafa. Mustafa looked to the Special Forces to provide the firepower and close air support he desired for an attack against the Ansar al-Islam. Mustafa also realized that having U.S. forces by his side deterred Iran from openly backing the Ansar al-Islam in battle. Lieutenant Colonel Kenneth Tovo, commander of the 3rd Battalion, and Mustafa formulated a six-pronged attack to drive the Ansar al-Islam out of the valley and seize the suspected weapons of mass destruction site at Sargat. Before the

Figure 6.9 Lieutenant Colonel Kenneth Tovo and PUK leadership planning the attack against Ansar al-Islam.

attack commenced, however, a demonstration of U.S. firepower and resolve was in order.[15]

In position for the operation, ODA 081 occupied a small house in Halabja, looking down the flat valley toward the Ansar al-Islam stronghold in the hills above. On the evening of 21 March, Tovo and Mustafa stood on the roof of the house looking up the alley in anticipation of

the first missile attack on the Ansar al-Islam forces. An anxious twenty-five minutes after the scheduled strike time, the first Tomahawk Land Attack Missile droned overhead and impacted the Ansar al-Islam positions. Every few minutes for the next three hours, another Tomahawk struck the target. By the end of the bombardment, sixty-four Tomahawks had impacted in the region of the Ansar al-Islam base of operations, though with minimum effectiveness, since after the first missile, the enemy took shelter in its caves. Missiles detonated around the weapons' facility at Sargat and throughout the targeted sector, but did not significantly degrade the Ansar al-Islam's defensive positions. However, the Tomahawk strikes did drive the Islamic Group of Kurd-

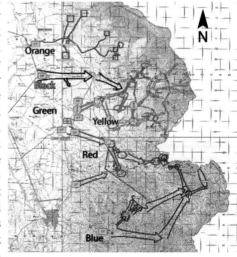

Figure 6.10 Map of VIKING HAMMER. *Six-prong attack of the operation against the Ansar al-Islam.*

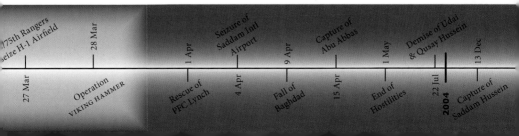

istan from its positions, and eliminated that organization as a factor in the battle.[16]

Though the Tomahawks prepared the battlefield on the 21st, the ground attack was delayed until the 3rd Battalion could get more troops on the ground and air support lined up. Operation VIKING HAMMER was built around a six-pronged attack up the valley: from north to south, the assault routes were designated Orange, Black, Green, Yellow, Red, and Blue. Each prong consisted of 900–1,500 peshmerga fighters, each accompanied by members of a Special Forces team. In order to command the fight, Tovo colocated FOB 103 with Major Greg Tsouris'* Advanced Operating Base 090 on Hill 654, where it could almost see the entire valley. Members of AOB 090 also manned mortars in support of the Green and Red routes, with supplemental targets on the Blue route.[17]

*Pseudonyms have been used for all military personnel with a rank lower than lieutenant colonel.

At 0600 on 28 March, the attack commenced. The Yellow Prong aimed for the devastated weapons' site at Sargat, and the flanking prongs targeted the Ansar al-Islam on the succession of hills and ridges around the site. The speed of the peshmerga attack resulted in a rapid advance on all the routes. "The pesh[merga] generally looked for a weak point, attacked it with all their weapons, then bum rushed the target," described Sergeant First Class Mitch Greenlaw*, who was in charge of the three-gun mortar section supporting the Yellow Prong. The Kurdish fighters' pace made it difficult for the mortar section to follow the frontline trace. Coupled with the reluctance of the peshmerga to allow supporting fires close to its own troops, the speed frequently required Greenlaw and his crew to halt in order to pinpoint the targets.

Figure 6.11 Mortar support. *A mortar section supports the Blue Prong during the attack on Ansar al-Islam. Accurate mortar support proved critical to the assault.*

Due to the onrush of the peshmerga up the valley, the Ansar al-Islam fighters were unable to deliberately retrograde and take advantage of their prepared positions and caches of weapons and equipment.[18]

The combined force made considerable progress along all the assault routes that first day. Troops advancing along the Red and Blue Prongs secured several of the small villages in the valley. The Blue Prong advanced up the valley and halted for the night at the village

of Biyara. As they swept through the valley, the Special Forces and peshmerga soldiers observed the Ansar al-Islam fighters fleeing higher up the valley from the Biyara area to more heavily fortified positions on the slopes of Shram Mountain. The swift capture of Hill 868 allowed the troops on the Green route to overwatch the Yellow Prong advance toward Sargat. The Yellow Prong forces seized the Ansar al-Islam checkpoint, cleared a series of caves along the route, and split to send one element against the town of Bahka Kon. The northern element headed to Sargat, which was secured at approximately 1000 hours.[19]

Figure 6.12 Sargat facility. *View of the Sargat facility after the battle as seen from the north.*

Troops assigned to the Black Prong served as the reserve force. On the northernmost route, the forces on the Orange Prong attacked east from Shilamar to Hill 1351, where they were stopped for the day. The hill supported a communications tower and bunker with approximately twenty Ansar al-Islam troops, who withstood three air strikes and kept the peshmerga from advancing closer than two hundred meters from the bunker. Once darkness fell, the Kurdish troops regrouped and consolidated their positions. Four AC-130 gunships maintained pressure on the scattered Ansar al-Islam fighters, and prevented them from regrouping. By morning, the peshmerga were ready to resume the offensive.[20]

The attack continued on 29 March with the forces on the Green Prong advancing northeast and seizing the high ground on Hill 1365. The Yellow Prong forces pushed out from Sargat and expanded their perimeter to include the villages of Hanidind and Daramar. The Red Prong consolidated its gains in the vicinity of Biyara. The Black Prong, held in reserve the previous day, joined with the Orange Prong to conduct a coordinated attack up the Zalm Valley and the northern approaches, where they secured Hill 1351.

Throughout the rest of the day and into the next, the peshmerga chased the Ansar al-Islam toward the Iranian border—where many crossed without difficulty, while others were met with fire from the Iranians and forced back toward the peshmerga. By 30 March, the Patriotic Union of Kurdistan was in control of the formerly Ansar al-Islam–dominated valley and held the high ground overwatching

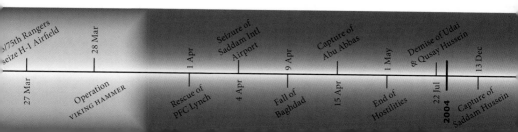

the area running toward the Iranian border. Operation VIKING HAM-
MER had eliminated the Ansar al-Islam as an effective fighting force,
and removed the threat to the Kurdish rear area. With this accomplished, the mission transitioned to supporting the Kurdish forces on
the Green Line.[21]

The presence of the Special Forces teams helped the peshmerga in
numerous ways, from providing close air support and indirect fire, to
assisting with command and control and combined planning before
the attack. Their presence was important in less quantifiable ways
as well. As Tovo remarked, "the morale boost for the PUK [Patriotic
Union of Kurdistan] forces of seeing U.S. Special Forces in their ranks
cannot be understated. The ODA members attacking with them were
tangible proof that the U.S. was committed to providing them assistance."[22]

In the weeks that followed the assault, chemical and biological
inspection survey teams and document exploitation teams examined the secured Sargat site. The Patriotic Union of Kurdistan spent
its time consolidating its hold over the region and planning for the
next stage of its long-awaited fight against Saddam's regime. With the
Ansar al-Islam threat gone, the 3rd Battalion and the peshmerga were
free to join the rest of the Kurdish forces attacking the Iraqis on the
Green Line and open the way for Coalition control of the north.

FUEL SYSTEM SUPPLY POINTS IN NORTHERN IRAQ

Deep penetration into enemy territory and a high operations tempo
required CJSOTF-North to establish fuel system supply points in
northern Iraq. The Bravo Forward Support Company, 528th Special
Operations Support Battalion, supported CJSOTF-North in Constanta,
Romania, so its fuel teams drew the mission to set up the points.

Two six-man fuel teams deployed from Romania, one to Bashur
Airfield and the other to Sulaimaniyah Airfield. Their missions were
to provide forward refueling for combat search and rescue and SOF
aircraft operating in the area. The first fuel team, led by Staff Sergeant
Juan Uleses*, infiltrated into Bashur Airfield in support of FOB 102.
After a four-day layover in Greece, on the night of 25 March 2003, the
team accomplished a combat off-load (without the plane stopping)
from a C-130 in full blackout conditions. As fuel handler Specialist
Randy Brown* described the scene, "It was pitch black out. It was

Figure 6.13 528th
SOSB insignia.

raining and miserable out there. And here we are, full battle rattle, with just our Gator [utility vehicle] and a pile of our stuff. We couldn't even see or hear anybody coming toward us to help us carry this stuff off."[23]

A group of Special Forces soldiers and Air Force personnel finally met the fuel team and helped them move off the runway. After showing the fuel team where to stow its gear, the welcoming committee informed the team that it had to spend the rest of the night standing guard. Those fuel handlers not pulling guard duty tried to grab some rest anywhere they could, though the cold rain made sleep difficult. The night, however, was not without further surprises. Brown recalled that, "A couple of hours later, we kind of saw something because the moon was finally starting to show. We started seeing little things dropping. It was the 173rd [Airborne Brigade (-)] jumping in."[24]

Uleses described the scene in even greater detail: "It was pure mayhem. We didn't know that they were coming…In the past ten days, that was the worst rain [Bashur] had gotten in over a hundred years. So these guys were jumping in, and instead of pulling guard, now we were helping these guys out of the mud." The team was able to use its ever-handy Gator to good effect as wet and muddy paratroopers slogged their way through the drop zone. When the sun rose, Brown was surprised to find himself in the middle of a vividly green landscape, a far cry from his notion of desert Iraq. He felt very conspicuous in his desert camouflage uniform. Then again, he matched the mud-covered paratroopers: "Just then, 173rd's people start coming up just covered in mud. I mean, head to toe. Vehicles are going around getting stuck because they're trying to gather everyone's equipment, and people are trying to push the vehicles out of mud holes. It was a mess."[25]

Now that daylight had come, the fuel teams began to set up their fuel points. Unfortunately, the site survey team had not properly prepared the site ahead of time. "They had nothing prepared for us," recalled Brown. "They were supposed to build berms, lay out liners for us. Nothing. It was just a flat area. A flat mud hole." Doing the best it could under the conditions, the team went to work. The senior Air Force controller on the ground indicated that he needed the fuel point set up as soon as possible, so the team had no choice but to make do with inadequate site preparation. In spite of the challenges, the team

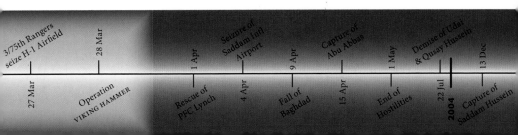

set up the point in four hours, ready to receive fuel from a C-17 that night.[26]

Late that night, the fuel team was summoned to fill its fuel bag from the C-17. However, when the fuelers reached the point, they found that the fuel bag had been blown out of its location by an airplane, and had landed upside down in a puddle fifteen meters away. The team had no choice but to let the C-17 go, fuel and all. Uleses decided that in light of the team's exhausted condition and the work required to reposition the fuel bag, the fuelers could leave the job until daylight. Brown's morning assessment of the situation was that "it was a mess." That evening Sergeant Wayne Allred* arrived from Romania with a replacement fuel filter for one that had been mangled by propeller wash. After the team had set up the fuel bag once again, they had engineers from the 173rd build a low berm around it to prevent a repeat incident. That night, the team received fuel from another C-17 and it was back in business.[27]

Figure 6.14 FSSP with onion skin. *The* BFSC, *528th Support Battalion, established fuel system supply points in northern Iraq in order to provide fuel support to aviation elements, such as the* CH-47 *helicopter shown here. Fuel pods, or "onion skins," are surrounded by earthen berms for protection and containment.*

Three days after the Bashur Airfield fuel team landed in Iraq, Sergeant Don Travis* and his team of self-described "Fuel Dawgs" deployed to Sulaimaniyah in support of FOB 103. The team of eight fuelers loaded the pumping unit, two collapsible fuel bags, and fifty 10-foot sections of 4-inch fuel hose on the floor of the aircraft. Due to weight restrictions on the long flight from Romania, the team had to leave its High-Mobility Multipurpose Wheeled Vehicles (HMMWVs) behind; instead, it loaded Gators to move the equipment off the aircraft and position the fuel pods. Travis' team strapped its only pallet, loaded with the pumping unit, onto the ramp of the aircraft.[28]

When the fuel team arrived at Sulaimaniyah, they found that the mud near the airfield was so deep that it was impossible to set up the fuel bags without some site preparation. The team contracted Kurdish locals to dig pits and line them with gravel to prevent the fuel bags from disappearing in the mud when filled. Once the fuel point was up and running, it serviced the special operations MH-47s and MH-53s that comprised the majority of its clients. On one memorable occasion, however, the fuel team serviced an MC-130 that landed at the airfield critically low on fuel. The fuel point received its fuel resupply

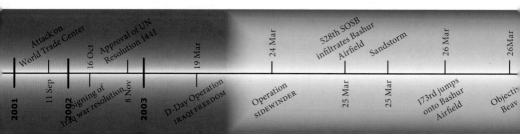

via c-130s using the "wet-wing technique," where an incoming plane emptied all the fuel from its tanks into the fuel bags except for what it needed to return to the rear area.[29]

Unexpected customers occasionally interrupted the daily routine of refueling aircraft. Once it became known that the Bashur Airfield fuel point was operational, Coalition aircraft from all over the area of operations began making pit stops. On one noteworthy event, thirty-two U.S. Marine Corps helicopters beset the fuel point, which was at half strength. Uleses had taken half of the team to prepare a fuel point near Camp Loki, leaving only three soldiers to deal with the thirsty fleet of helicopters. "Thirty-two of them in one day. I don't even know what mission they were running, but they weren't technically supposed to come to us," recalled Brown.[30]

True to their reputation, the Bravo Forward Support Company fuel handlers managed to refuel all thirty-two helicopters by working throughout the night. Also true to their reputation for ingenuity, the bfsc soldiers made do with what they had on hand, which in this case included the 173rd Airborne Brigade (-) fuel. Allred remembered that they "pumped all the fuel in the whole camp. Just two or three thousand [gallons] left." Brown explained further: "The funny thing with that was that we had two bags and the 173rd had three. We drained ours and then we kind of borrowed 173rd's, because these choppers needed it!" On the occasions when bfsc "borrowed" fuel from the 173rd's 20,000-gallon fuel bags, the team served some of the 173rd vehicle-borne customers from the company's fuel truck. The arrangement worked well because bfsc generally refueled aircraft at night, while the 173rd fuel point only refueled vehicles during the day.[31]

While the various Coalition partners and American service components got along fairly well and shared equipment and support in Iraq as needed, once in a while an incident occurred that caused a commander to place stricter control on his assets. One such incident involved an Army fuel bag and a Marine helicopter. The Bashur fuel point moved to Camp Loki near Irbil in mid-April, and the fuel handlers were forced to temporarily colocate with some Marines waiting for orders to move elsewhere in northern Iraq. In preparation for a pending move, the Marines gathered their rucksacks and other baggage and placed it all underneath a large piece of plywood. A Marine ch-53 landed, the Marines loaded their baggage and themselves onto the helicopter, but left the sheet of plywood on the ground. When

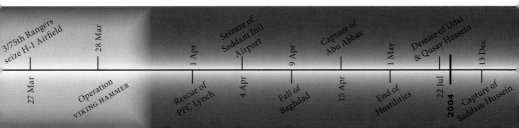

Figure 6.15 528th SOSB soldiers conduct a hot refuel of an MH-53.

the helicopter took off, the propeller wash sent the plywood flying past the BFSC soldiers (almost decapitating one) and into a 10,000-gallon fuel bag. "It looked like a fountain," remarked Allred. Brown added, "It was just shooting out."[32]

The fuelers tried to pump fuel from the punctured bag into other fuel bags, but those were already full. In the end, the fuel emptied itself into the berm enclosure: "It was like a swimming pool," according to Allred. "The [c]H-53 wasted 10,000 gallons," as Allred put it. Brown continued the story: "The next day we get up to drain it out, and there's no fuel in the berm. Somehow it had all leaked into the ground." They contracted for local Kurdish workers to remove the contaminated soil, but could not help but laugh at the futility of the gesture when the team discovered that the soil had simply been spread over a SOF parking lot down the road. The fuel handlers placed a new 50,000-gallon fuel bag on the site. And what happened afterward? Colonel Cleveland banned Marine helicopters from landing near or using the fuel point after the incident.[33]

404TH CIVIL AFFAIRS BATTALION

Figure 6.16 404th CAB (Special Operations) insignia.

One of only four special operations Civil Affairs battalions in the Army Reserve, the 404th Civil Affairs Battalion, from Fort Dix, New Jersey, found itself tasked with a daunting mission—support CJSOTF-North. That mission grew, not only to provide direct support to CJSOTF-North, but also to provide the 101st Airborne Division (Air Assault) later. In addition to directing and performing civil military operations, the 404th CAB executed a multitude of missions—including running airports, overseeing currency exchange, distributing food and water, reestablishing local schools, managing transportation systems, and assisting in the formation of the Iraqi Civil Defense Corps. However, the magnitude of the actual mission was almost eclipsed by the effort to get to northern Iraq.[34]

With hints of a possible mobilization by the summer of 2002, the battalion staff began the planning process. By September 2002, the mobilization and subsequent deployment to Iraq became a certainty.

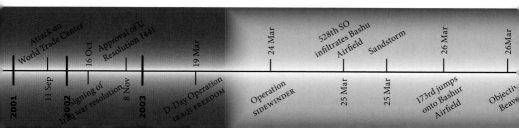

Planning team members went to Fort Carson, Colorado, to coordinate with the 10th SFG. Coordination also began with Major Derek Storino*, the commander of D Company, 96th CAB—which would initially support CJSOTF-North until the 404th CAB arrived. Based on guidance from Colonel Cleveland, the battalion staff designed and executed a rigorous training plan, including the integration of more than sixty soldiers from the 443rd CAB from Rhode Island, the 304th Civil Affairs Brigade from Philadelphia, Pennsylvania, and the 353rd Civil Affairs Command from New York City.[35]

The mobilization process for the 404th CAB began on 3 February 2003 at Fort Dix. After six days of training there, the battalion moved to Fort Bragg instead of its requested mobilization station of Fort Carson. What should have taken ten days stretched into a five-week-long mobilization process at Fort Bragg. Then came the wait for aircraft availability, until the battalion finally deployed from Pope Air Force Base, North Carolina, on 17 March. It took seventeen C-17 aircraft over five days to relay the 404th CAB's fifty-five vehicles, sundry equipment, and 194 soldiers—not to Iraq, rather to Constanta, the interim staging base for CJSOTF-North. Bottlenecked in Romania due to the Turkish refusal to allow U.S. forces to fly over its airspace, CJSOTF-North continued planning for the upcoming operation.[36]

In Constanta, the 404th CAB staff began coordinating and integrating with the CJSOTF-North staff. At the same time, the CJSOTF-North staff was preparing for the 22 March Operation UGLY BABY infiltration into northern Iraq. It was not until 25 March that a small Civil Affairs element from D Company, 96th CAB, flew into Irbil with elements of the 10th SFG. The majority of the 404th CAB went to Bashur Airfield, but not until the first weeks of April, due to aircraft availability. The battalion immediately established its headquarters with the CJSOTF-North headquarters at Irbil and began operations.[37]

CJSOTF-West

As Operation IRAQI FREEDOM progressed, two distinct missions split CJSOTF-west's mission focus. In the west, FOB 51's units continued searching for SCUDs and hitting the enemy forces wherever the Special Forces teams found them. The Iraqis attempted counter-reconnaissance operations against the special operations units; however, they were looking for twelve guys with big rucksacks, the Special

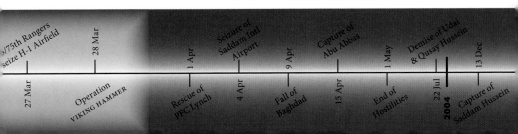

75th Rangers seize H-1 Airfield · 27 Mar · 28 Mar · Operation VIKING HAMMER · 1 Apr · Seizure of Saddam Intl Airport · Rescue of PFC Lynch · 4 Apr · 9 Apr · Fall of Baghdad · Capture of Abu Abbas · 15 Apr · 1 May · End of Hostilities · Demise of Udal & Qusay Hussein · 22 Jul · 2004 · Capture of Saddam Hussein · 13 Dec

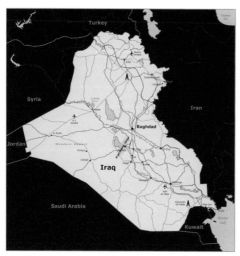

Figure 6.17 Map highlighting the Karbala Gap. *The Karbala Gap is a strategic choke point for the ground battle for Iraq.*

Forces model from Operation DESERT STORM, not three or four Ground Mobility Vehicles bristling with weapons.[38]

CJSOTF-west's largest mission was to support the conventional forces in the drive to Baghdad. In the south, FOB 52 continued its support to V Corps and I MEF. In less than a week, FOB 52's presence in Iraq rose from two advanced operating bases controlling fifteen ODAS to five AOBs controlling over twenty ODAS—all supporting Coalition Forces Land Component Command units or missions as the conventional forces rolled north. AOB 560 stayed with the British around Basra, and FOB 53 remained in reserve.

ODA 551's special reconnaissance in the Karbala Gap continued as V Corps steadily advanced north. The team was so far north of CFLCC conventional forces that its Blue Force Tracker signal became the highlight of the Pentagon daily update. ODA 551 was nearing mission completion as the 3rd ID rolled northward, and ODA 916 soon executed the linkup plan and safely returned the exhausted team to U.S. lines.[39]

In the midst of these vital, time-sensitive missions, the three-day sandstorm—called a *shamal* in the Middle East—hit. While it slowed CFLCC's advance, it did not fully stop operations and the ARSOF units of CJSOTF-west stayed on the job, whether that job consisted of direct action or stability operations. Some of their stories follow.

EYES ON THE TARGET

The first objective for ODA 551 was to get to the remain-over-day site as quickly as possible. The helicopter landing zone was 292 kilometers further north than Assembly Area Nasiriya, where the lead elements of the 3rd ID were located, and it was absolutely necessary to get into the Karbala Gap as soon as possible. The movement to the site went without incident, but it had taken longer to cover the seventy kilometers from the landing zone than expected. Moving in a loose "V" formation kept the trail vehicles from eating the lead vehicles' dust

and provided for more firepower to the front in case of contact. As the morning sky of 22 March was turning from black to gray, the team found a wadi (dry streambed) large enough for the vehicles and quickly parked and camouflaged them. Captain Don Raintree* put the team on 30 percent security, and ODA 551 spent the remainder of the day resting and waiting for darkness. As the sun quickly rose, they spotted what appeared to be a Bedouin camp about fifteen hundred meters from the team's location. Throughout the day, everyone kept a close watch on the Bedouins, looking for signs the team had been compromised. The team's apprehension was confirmed when Raintree later learned that the Bedouin camp was actually an Iraqi outpost.[40]

Once darkness fell, the team quietly slipped out of its hiding place. After backtracking south for some distance, ODA 551 circled wide to the east around the Bedouin encampment. Movement was not as easy as the previous night; the team quickly ran into a wadi system that caused considerable problems. The soft sand in the wadi bottoms caused the heaviest vehicle to become stuck twice, requiring the other two to pull it free. While the team was pulling out the vehicle the second time, the security team reported seeing headlights and hearing engine noises. It appeared that they were being followed. They decided to find a way out of the wadi so they could make better time. Once they were out of the wadi, the pursuing vehicles fell off. As they moved through the desert, the enlisted terminal air controller coordinated with the Air Force in case they

Figure 6.18 Special Forces supporting conventional forces near Najaf. *The Special Forces soldiers scan the horizon for potential threats near Najaf.*

needed close air support and to ensure that friendly units did not mistake them for an Iraqi unit. The ODA had to move fast; it had more than sixty kilometers to travel to reach its proposed hide site for the special reconnaissance. Its destination was soon in sight: "Not long after we got out of the wadi system, we started picking up the lights from Karbala; mostly the lights from the brick factory," reported Master Sergeant Albert Bones*, the operations sergeant. "The lights were so bright that they were 'whiting out' our NODs [night observation devices]."[41]

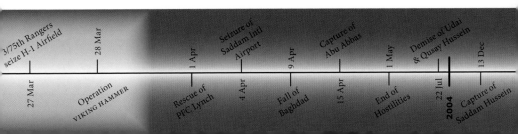

3/75th Rangers seize H-1 Airfield
27 Mar
Operation VIKING HAMMER
28 Mar
1 Apr
Rescue of PFC Lynch
Seizure of Saddam Intl Airport
4 Apr
9 Apr
Fall of Baghdad
Capture of Abu Abbas
15 Apr
1 May
End of Hostilities
Demise of Udai & Qusay Hussein
22 Jul
2004
13 Dec
Capture of Saddam Hussein

Figure 6.19 Karbala Gap hide site. *Hundreds of miles behind enemy lines, ODA 551's special reconnaissance mission was critical to the 3rd ID's mission. Photo taken 23 March.*

The team moved into its planned hide site and sent a contact report to FOB 52. Using satellite imagery, Raintree planned to use an abandoned Iraqi air defense school about ten kilometers south of the Karbala Gap as a mission support site. The imagery showed a series of berms constructed to protect air defense batteries, but once it arrived the team discovered that the berms were less than a meter high. Raintree decided to continue north into the gap to find a better mission support site.[42]

One item of equipment was constantly slowing down the progress—the bulky chemical suits everyone wore. During intelligence updates before infiltration, the anticipated use of chemical weapons in the Karbala Gap was discussed not as a possibility, but as a fact. Therefore, Raintree had the team in mission-oriented protective posture II (chemical suit and protective overboots) as it infiltrated the objective area. He planned to go to MOPP IV (chemical suit, mask, and protective overboots and gloves) when they got closer to Karbala. As they moved into the objective area, he made the decision to defer going to MOPP IV, since doing so would significantly reduce the soldiers' ability to detect an enemy presence and increased chances of compromise. Besides, the volume of civilian traffic along the roads and the number of barking dogs were evidence enough that there were no chemical agents present. As a precaution, however, the team taped chemical detection papers to its vehicles and turned on the chemical alarms.[43]

Mission-Oriented Protective Postures

MOPP Level	Protective Gear Worn	
MOPP I	Overgarment Field Gear	Mask Carrier
MOPP II	Overgarment Field Gear	Mask Carrier Footwear Covers
MOPP III	Overgarment Field Gear	Mask/Hood Footwear Covers
MOPP IV	Overgarment Field Gear Gloves	Mask/Hood Footwear Covers

The three Ground Mobility Vehicles continued north parallel to a dirt pipeline road until they reached a blacktop road south of Lake Razzaza. Carefully timing their crossing with traffic on the highway, they crossed the road in a serious version of "headlight tag." Quickly find-

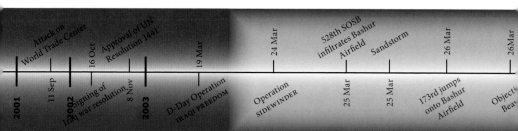

ing a deeply eroded wadi, thirty feet deep with numerous branches to hide the GMVs, the team settled in. However, as Chief Warrant Officer 2 Clyde Hawks* observed the site, he thought to himself, "This is great for hiding but it's going to be difficult to get out in a hurry." The team covered sixty-four difficult kilometers that night, and in the predawn darkness of 24 March, it worked quietly and quickly to camouflage the GMVs. Then two soldiers established a listening and observation post that allowed them to watch the roads and beyond. The hide site was only six hundred meters from the road, but the wadi's depth made it impossible to see the team from anywhere around. From the post, any vehicles which could not be observed directly, could be heard. The team was in place and ready to carry out its mission.[44]

Evidence of ODA 551's successful infiltration into the Karbala Gap appeared in the command center in Kuwait—and throughout the world—on computer screens, tracking Operation IRAQI FREEDOM through the Blue Force Tracker System. Computer generated maps showed small blue rectangles designating units on the battlefield. Near Nasiriya was a large cluster of units representing the 3rd ID, then red diamonds representing Iraqi units, but over two hundred kilometers in front of the nearest Coalition unit was a small rectangle with crossed arrows and the designation "551."[45]

During ODA 551's first night in position, one of the outlying reconnaissance and surveillance sites picked up something moving slowly and deliberately toward them. The ODA went to alert status. The soldiers checked their weapons and scanned the area in the direction of the noise for the intruder. Much to the sol-

Figure 6.20 Brick factory. *View from ODA 551's Karbala Gap hide site to the brick factory on 23 March.*

diers' relief, instead of the Iraqi soldier or lost Bedouin they expected to see, the culprit was a one hundred–pound female hyena. The team had established a reconnaissance and surveillance position close to a shallow cave that apparently served as the hyena's den. The hyena came by every evening until the team left, wondering, no doubt, if she would ever be able to move back into her den. The presence of the hyena den also eased Raintree's concerns about the site selection—if

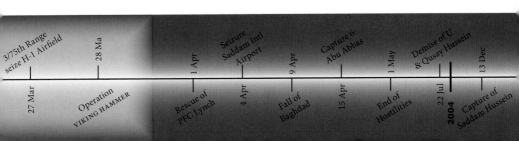

3/75th Range seize H-1 Airfield   28 Ma   1 Apr   Seizure Saddam Intl Airport   9 Apr   Capture o Abu Abbas   1 May   Demise of U & Qusay Hussein   13 Dec

27 Mar   Operation VIKING HAMMER   Rescue of PFC Lynch   4 Apr   Fall of Baghdad   15 Apr   End of Hostilities   22 Jul   2004   Capture of Saddam Hussein

the hyena was there, then that should mean that little human presence was in the area.[46]

Over the next couple of days, the team established additional reconnaissance and surveillance positions away from the hide site to increase its coverage of the target area. From their hidden positions, the team members used a variety of optical aids to view the surrounding area. In addition to regular binoculars, they used M122 spotting scopes and another high-powered scope someone had nicknamed the

Figure 6.21 Hide site in sandstorm. *Photo of the hide site and the eastern observation post during the three-day sandstorm. Note the visibility—these photos were taken at about 1400 hours on 25 March.*

"Hubble." The great expectations for the Hubble were largely unrealized, though, because of the mirage effect—once the air warmed up, the heat rising off the sand created so much distortion that it was impossible to see the targets clearly through the scope.[47]

Surveillance revealed very little military traffic and no evidence of armored or mechanized units. The few military vehicles the team saw were mostly stake-bed cargo trucks. However, the soldiers observed a great deal of civilian traffic, taxis, and white trucks on the roads in and out of Karbala. From the markings on the vehicles and the occupants, the team assumed they were fedayeen. In those first days, the team also observed several vehicles and fedayeen in black uniforms around the brick factory.[48]

While the team members believed their own eyes, the higher command did not. Hawks recalled that "when the team sent its reports back [to Kuwait], there was some disbelief concerning the accuracy of our information." The intelligence analysts and commanders expected a significant defensive buildup and numerous enemy units in the area. However, as ODA 551's observations proved, the intelligence was faulty. One example of the misinterpretation of intelligence sources was the report that the large numbers of excavations in the Karbala Gap indicated defensive preparations. The ODA soon discovered that the excavations were, indeed, legitimate quarries or open pit mines.[49]

For the next three days, the ODA successfully conducted its mission. The team spotted an Iraqi Roland antiaircraft launcher, and the attached air controller directed aircraft onto the target to destroy the site. On another occasion, the airborne Joint Surveillance and Target

Attack Radar System moving target indicator radar picked up what was thought to be tanks in the Karbala area. Although the "tanks" turned out to be military fuel tankers, the Air Force ran the mission anyway and the team's air controller talked the aircraft in on the target. As gratifying as it was to see the Iraqi vehicles disappear in a ball of flame and smoke, the team's priority was to identify and neutralize only high-value targets. Raintree reasoned that if they attacked too many targets, eventually the Iraqis would figure out that they were in the area, and come looking for them.[50]

The mission took a detour when the "mother of all sandstorms" hit the area on 25 March. The storm heavily affected all Coalition operations, but for the isolated ODA, it was especially dangerous. The team shifted into survival mode, as the wind at times gusted to over fifty miles per hour, carrying with it tons of fine sand. "For three days, you couldn't see your hand in front of your face," Hawks remembered. "It was so bad that your pockets filled up with sand. During this time we were vulnerable to someone just stumbling upon us, so we had to maintain good security all the time." The team spent much of its time during the storm keeping the guns clean and operable in case of compromise. Sergeant First Class John Spencer* explained, "It was important to have the guns operational in case the Iraqis stumbled on us. It was a tense time. [We] couldn't see and couldn't hear anything." Even the team's Kuwaiti interpreter commented that it was the worst sandstorm he had ever experienced.[51]

The day after the storm subsided, FOB 52 ordered the team to link-up with lead elements of the 3rd ID. The three–five-day special reconnaissance mission had already stretched to nine, so the ODA was ready to move. The team was running low on food and water; it had already reduced rations to one meal per day, and only had about ten gallons of water remaining per vehicle. After dark on 29 March, ODA 551 left its hide site and headed south. Visibility was so poor that night that the lead vehicle almost drove into a 20 foot-deep ravine. The team ended up ground-guiding the vehicles until they made it to level ground.[52]

As ODA 551 left its position, the Special Forces liaison element briefed the 3rd ID linkup force. The four Special Forces soldiers of ODA 916B reviewed the procedure with the leadership. A short time later, the linkup force—consisting of the Special Forces GMV, two tanks, and a scout platoon with Bradley Fighting Vehicles—moved into the darkness. Linkup is normally a tense operation, conducted in contested

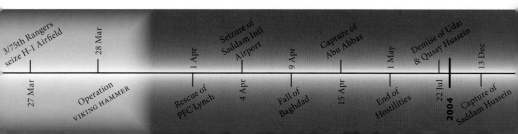

territory where the threat could just as easily come from a friendly unit as the enemy. Following the procedure previously rehearsed in Kuwait, ODA 916B made radio contact with ODA 551. With the successful radio contact, ODA 551 moved to a designated place and ODA 916B looked for the near recognition signal: ODA 551's vehicle thermal panels. The tanks, however, had trouble making a positive identification using thermal sights. So ODA 551's air controller used his Vislet—a powerful infrared pointer to identify targets to attacking aircraft—to signal the linkup force. ODA 916B then moved to ODA 551 and brought them back to the rest of the force. The effort expended during the training proved worthwhile; the linkup was successfully completed and the team returned to the 3rd ID task force.[53]

Once it was safely behind the 3rd ID lines, the team began briefing the various command levels in succession all the way up to the division on the true intelligence picture on the Karbala Gap. The team's eyes-on-target information disproved or corrected much of the faulty intelligence on which the 3rd ID had based its planning. In many cases, imagery had been misinterpreted; e.g., an oil-filled trench was in reality a new asphalt road and the dug-in tanks were fuel tanks with berms around them. Some of the intelligence reports contained ambiguous language, and others were either blatantly false or, worse, fabricated. The intelligence report that had the team in MOPP II indicated that blue barrels full of chemicals were stored in the basement of the Hussein Mosque in Karbala; the barrels were traffic control barrels used to cordon off the mosque during recent renovations. One piece of intelligence proved interesting to ODA 551: its hide site had been an artillery firing range for the Iraqi Army, which is probably why no one ventured into the area.[54]

With a clear intelligence picture formed from ODA 551's reports, the 3rd ID attacked through the Karbala Gap on 1 April. The intelligence ODA 551 passed to the 3rd ID was key in providing situational awareness to the task forces, brigades, and division. The 3rd ID's primary mission was to isolate and seize Baghdad, so the division decided to contain and bypass the fedayeen in Karbala. The strategy was successful, and Baghdad was liberated in record time.

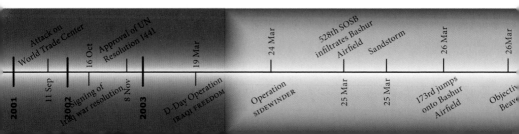

OTHER ARSOF

While the Special Forces units comprising the bulk of the two CJSOTFs executed their missions in the early days of the campaign, two other ARSOF components—160th Special Operations Aviation Regiment and the 75th Ranger Regiment—brought their considerable skills to bear in a number of vital operations. The 3rd Battalion, 75th Ranger Regiment, successfully executed a combat parachute jump to seize the airfield designated H-1 and provide a forward base of operations for further actions. A and C Companies of 1st Battalion, 75th Rangers, used a lengthy ground convoy movement to assault and seize the towns of Nukhayb and Mudaysis, codenamed Sidewinder South and North. The destruction of the Iraqi forces in the vicinity of these towns opened the way for use of the nearby airfields, confirmed the destruction of the visual observation posts in the area, and started the process of winning over the Iraqi people through distribution of humanitarian aid. The Rangers further collaborated with the Night Stalkers of the 160th SOAR on the seizure of a suspected biological weapons facility.

In an operation requiring superior flying skill, split-second timing, and violence of action, the Al Qadisiyah Research Center received a nighttime visit from the Rangers. The Rangers rode in on MH-47E Chinooks and MH-60K Black Hawks accompanied by MH-60L Defensive Armed Penetrators, and AH-6 and MH-6 Little Birds—the full complement of Night Stalker aircraft. In a swift and decisive raid, the Rangers overran the lakeside palace that constituted the research center, although not without a fight from its occupants. These missions served to demonstrate the range and abilities of the Rangers and 160th SOAR, capabilities employed to great effectiveness as the campaign progressed.

Figure 6.22 160th SOAR insignia.

OBJECTIVE BEAVER

On 26 March, 160th SOAR aircraft and Rangers from B Company, 2nd Ranger Battalion, raided a suspected chemical and biological weapons testing facility in central Iraq. The Al Qadisiyah Research Center was a suspected chemical and biological weapons research complex along the southern shore of Al Qadisiyah Reservoir, approximately twenty-five miles northwest of the town of Haditha. The United Nations Spe-

Figure 6.23 2nd Ranger Battalion scroll shoulder patch.

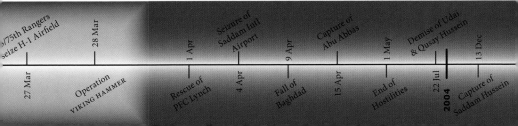

cial Commission on Iraq failed to inspect the facility during its tenure; however, an intelligence assessment indicated that it warranted
an investigation. Though the results of the collected samples were not
disclosed, the special operations task force duly demonstrated the
"fight like you train" principle in the search for the elusive smoking
gun—evidence that would demonstrate Iraq's mass effect weapons
program. The complicated mission was an illustration of precise planning, excellent training, and synchronized execution. Every element
of the task force performed its functions, especially contingency procedures, in a manner that prevented a disastrous ending, and saved
the lives of two soldiers.

Chief Warrant Officer 3 Richard Hoyt*, an MH-60K Black Hawk
pilot and overall flight leader, received the assignment to plan the
mission. It was a multifaceted mission requiring helicopter aerial-
refueling, en route linkups, precise preparatory fires, and sequenced
landings—all performed in zero illumination conditions over an austere desert. Intelligence analysts predicted little organized resistance
from the local populace, which led to conjecture that the target was
probably a "dry hole," containing no evidence of weapons testing.
Military history, however, is replete with examples of the effects of
complacency on the battlefield, and the environmental conditions
can kill just as swiftly as a well-aimed round. Therefore, the SOF planners assumed they would encounter resistance and were confident
that they would, in fact, find proof of an illegal weapons program.[55]

The plan emerged as follows: four MH-60K Black Hawks would
insert the Rangers into four blocking positions around the objective; two MH-47E Chinooks would infiltrate the main assault force
near the designated target building; two MH-60L DAP gunships, two
AH-6 Little Bird gunships, and two MH-6 Little Bird sniper platforms
would provide close air support around the target; and two additional
MH-47E's would wait nearby, ready to insert an immediate reaction
force or provide search and rescue if needed. The special operations
task force was ready to execute within two days.[56]

On the night of 26 March 2003, Chief Warrant Officer 4 Travis
Buras* led the flight of MH-6 lift and AH-6 gunship helicopters to a
desert landing strip named Roadrunner. The landing strip, secured by
the 3rd Battalion, 75th Ranger Regiment, a few days earlier, functioned
as a forward arming and refueling position and an emergency medical evacuation transfer site for this mission, since it was only thirty-

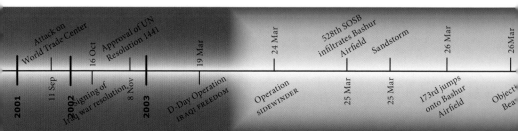

five miles from the objective. Upon landing, Buras and his "dash two," Chief Warrant Officer 4 Bradley Elliot*, refueled, picked up four special operations snipers for the mission, and waited until their designated departure time. Two hours after the Little Bird flight departed, Hoyt took off from the forward support base with his armada of aircraft to rendezvous with an MC-130P Combat Shadow tanker. Riding in the lead Chinook, Lieutenant Colonel Jeffrey Colt, the air mission commander and senior ranking Night Stalker, busily monitored the sequence of events with an execution checklist, which linked events with specific code words. He was the final onsite decision maker. The conditions for the assault on Objective Beaver were on schedule.

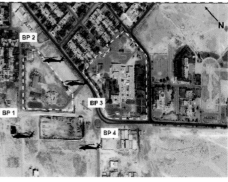

Figure 6.24 Blocking positions at Objective Beaver. *Four MH-60K Black Hawk helicopters delivered Rangers at designated blocking positions around Objective Beaver. In spite of enemy fire, all of the "Kilos" completed their infiltrations successfully.*

However, the initial rendezvous with the tanker foreshadowed the events of the night. The first tanker flew past Chief Warrant Officer 4 Thomas Brady* in the lead DAP. This was not a good sign, because the mission was helicopter aerial-refueling dependent—it would be aborted if the helicopters were unable to aerial refuel. Fortunately, a second tanker moved into position, and Brady maneuvered his flight into position for refueling. During the refueling operation, Brady received a call from his colleague, Chief Warrant Officer 4 Randall Ramsey*, in a joint command and control aircraft. Ramsey informed him that a pair of A-10 Thunderbolts were delayed on another aerial-refueling track, and were unable to prosecute a target on the objective. Therefore, Brady's new task was not only to cut the electricity from the power station on the city's outskirts, but also to limit any collateral damage—an unusual request. Once his wingman had refueled, Brady departed the tanker and raced with only fifteen minutes left before H-HOUR: 2300 Iraq local time.[57]

Meanwhile, shortly after departing the refuel track, Hoyt spotted the flight of Little Birds on the horizon. The Little Birds proceeded along a different route to Objective Beaver. The two separate flights conducted an often rehearsed aerial linkup without a hitch. As the Night Stalkers approached the release point—the point at which pilots cease following a designated route and freely maneuver in order to

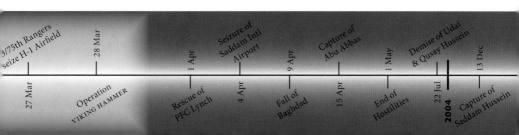

avoid potential threats—the Little Birds sped up to arrive at the target several minutes before H-HOUR to identify potential hazards or enemies. As the lights of the city partially illuminated the arriving gunships, various small groups of people rushed about on the ground or peered out windows, searching for the source of whining helicopters. In the lead AH-6, Chief Warrant Officer 4 James Melvin* and his copilot feverishly looked for anyone who exhibited hostile intent, the prerequisite for launching an attack. Sixty seconds later, the pair of MH-6s arrived east of the objective, looking for belligerents but primarily focusing on the targeted building. The element of surprise was gone, and the next ten minutes on the objective became the most intense for all involved.[58]

Observing from an MH-6, Elliot saw sparks from small arms fire directed toward the lead Black Hawk as it landed at Blocking Position 1, but he could not identify the source. Then a vehicle drove up and parked in front of Hoyt's helicopter. Luckily, the driver simply watched the events unfold as Army Rangers jumped from the helicopter and took up defensive positions. Melvin soon pinpointed the source of the gunfire. He immediately rolled in and fired a rocket right through the front door of the government building across the street from the landing zone. It was a spectacular close range shot and instantly eliminated the threat. As Hoyt departed, Chief Warrant Officer 3 Harry Bibeau* flew the second MH-60K through a barrage of bullets half a mile from the landing zone. Sergeant Owings*, stationed at the left-side window, automatically countered with his M134 minigun, sending a hail of 7.62mm rounds back toward the enemy. Once they landed at Blocking Position 2, Captain Theodore Shaffer* noticed a large explosion in the distance to the south. Four kilometers southwest of the objective, Brady shot the first power transformer with his 30mm M230 chain gun, and right behind him, Chief Warrant Officer 4 Fred Hamilton* shot the second. Their attempts to limit collateral damage backfired, igniting the oil in the transformers instead and illuminating the previously dark sky from horizon to horizon. "It looked like a nuclear bomb went off," according to Chief Warrant Officer 3 Walter Moeschet*, who was hovering over the objective in the lead MH-6.[59]

The resulting fire had another unintended consequence; it silhouetted the remaining inbound aircraft. The Iraqis could now visually engage the decelerating helicopters. In spite of enemy gunfire, Chief

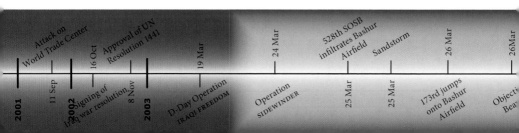

Warrant Officer 3 Peter Striker* managed to land the third MH-60K at Blocking Position 3 unscathed, narrowly missing a light pole with a timely rotation of the tail of the helicopter. The Rangers dismounted and raced into position as the last Black Hawk landed at Blocking Position 4. Iraqi gunmen fired at the stationary helicopter. A round entered through the cabin door, struck a Ranger in the back, exited through his chest, and then lodged in his body armor. As the other Rangers leapt out the door, an accompanying Navy SEAL's gear got hung up, so he stayed behind. Sergeant First Class John Pulley* and the SEAL grabbed the wounded Ranger and began first aid. Wasting no time, Chief Warrant Officer 3 Andrew Schupp* pulled pitch, rapidly departing the area while radioing Hoyt that he had a wounded Ranger aboard.[60]

The MH-60Ks quickly formed a flight en route and proceeded directly to Restricted Operations Zone Roadrunner, bypassing the planned checkpoints on the egress route. In the back of a blacked-out, bouncing helicopter, Pulley and Sergeant Jeremy Witts*, both combat lifesaver–qualified, applied a pressure dressing on the Ranger's sucking chest wound, started an intravenous line of saline solution, and treated him for shock. Schupp landed the helicopter near a surgery-equipped C-130, and the crewmembers carried the Ranger to the airplane.[61]

The situation intensified as radio chatter about a casualty made its way up the chain of command. With the flight of Chinooks minutes away, Elliot restricted the flight path of his MH-6 to a few hundred meters above a nearby hospital building. All of a sudden, a sniper aboard his aircraft calmly announced a target and dropped a gunman running toward the objective. The Little Bird was like a fifty-foot mobile deer stand.[62]

The inbound Chinooks carried the main assault force. Flying in the lead Chinook, Chief Warrant Officer 3 John Foul* had been in this situation before, in the mountains of Afghanistan. Luck was on his side again as he flew through a salvo of gunfire to the landing zone near Blocking Position 3; even so, an enemy bullet struck a utility hydraulics line, hindering aircraft control. The assault force rushed off the helicopter as soon as the ramp fell. Foul wrestled the helicopter into the air and began his egress.[63]

Responding to announcements of intermittent gunfire, Chief Warrant Officer 3 Charles Adkins* automatically adjusted his Chinook's

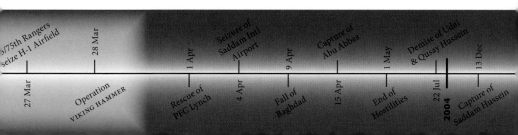

flight path wide to the east and landed in the same place Foul had used. Staff Sergeant Marty Milner*, stationed at the right ramp area, turned and shouted the one-minute time warning to the assaulters over the din of roaring engines. He watched in amazement as rounds passed through the Chinook, miraculously missing everybody inside. More gunfire erupted from the buildings adjacent to the landing zone, and a round struck Sergeant Greg Eisner* in the head, knocking him backward. Milner immediately dropped the ramp, and the assaulters exited in seconds. When all personnel were clear of the ramp, aircraft commander Chief Warrant Officer 3 Casey Johansson* grabbed the controls, lifted off, and immediately joined the lead Chinook in its flight to Roadrunner.[64]

The flight back to Roadrunner was fraught with tension, as Chief Warrant Officer 2 Barry Littleton* and another soldier worked to save Eisner's life. The unconscious flight engineer was still breathing, but had foamy blood coming out of his mouth. Working in the dark with a red lens flashlight, Littleton located the entrance wound above Eisner's right upper jaw and delicately applied a pressure bandage to the area. At the halfway point of the egress, Eisner suddenly stopped breathing. Yelling above the roar of the helicopter, Littleton and the other soldier began cardiopulmonary resuscitation, kneeling on the blood-covered floor. After five exhausting minutes, Eisner opened his eyes, spat a bit of blood, and began to breathe on his own. Landing in a dust cloud at Roadrunner, Johansson parked as close as he could to the specially configured c-130 medical transport. Littleton and two other crewmembers carried a blood-soaked Eisner to the Ranger security force guarding the airplane. The soldiers transferred Eisner to a litter and the Rangers took over from there, carrying him into the c-130. In short order, the airplane departed with both Eisner and the wounded Ranger aboard.[65]

With the infiltration phase completed, the ground assault force methodically searched Objective Beaver for evidence of a chemical weapons program. For protection, two concentric rings of close air support surrounded the objective area, and the Ranger blocking positions secured the main avenues of approach to the site. The AH-6 gunship pilots combed the area at a slightly higher altitude than the MH-6s, responding to Ranger calls for fire and engaging observed combatants. The gunships destroyed most of the initial resistance, which consisted of small armed groups that quickly formed across

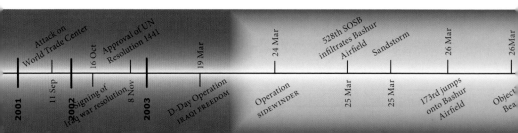

the street from the landing zones. After the main force infiltrated, the MH-6 pilots were free to maneuver over the target and engage enemy combatants. Moeschet spotted two Iraqi gunmen running from a driveway, each closely dragging a woman for protection. As Buras positioned his sniper closer and lower, one gunman lost his grip on the woman, and the sniper immediately killed him. The second gunman backed into a concrete building and held the woman tightly. Buras decided that it was more prudent to return to the target and reluctantly disengaged. In the other MH-6, Elliot spotted a vehicle racing toward a Ranger blocking position. The Rangers unleashed a storm of heavy weapons fire, but the driver kept going. As the vehicle approached the second Ranger position, machine gunfire stopped the vehicle and two armed men ran for cover. The Rangers killed one instantly. The second gunman ran down an alley out of their sight, but well within range of a sniper's bullet from Elliot's aircraft; the man was shot dead within seconds.[66]

Patrolling an outer ring, the DAP pilots focused on preventing any reinforcement of the target, primarily looking for vehicular movement toward the research facility along the main north–south road through the town. The rules of engagement required that a warning shot be given to stop vehicles. If the vehicle proceeded, then it presented a hostile intent and could be attacked. During Brady's initial circuit around the objective area, a Toyota Hilux truck approached the intersection leading to the objective. Brady fired a short burst from his chain gun, but the vehicle continued. On the second pass, the driver stopped and shut off his lights as the DAPs approached. Once the flight turned outbound, the driver started moving again. On the next turn, both Brady and Hamilton fired 30mm rounds into the vehicle, destroying it. The occupants ran for cover in a nearby building, and were never seen again. A short time later, another vehicle rapidly approached the same intersection. The two occupants stopped when given a warning shot, and dove into a ditch, only to fire at the helicopter on the next pass. Flying with Brady in the lead DAP, Chief Warrant Officer 3 Walter Florenson* watched tracer fire blaze past his chin bubble. Brady swiftly banked the DAP into a firing position and released a barrage of bullets at the source. One gunman died, and the other retreated into a building, safe for another day. So it went until the call for exfiltration came.[67]

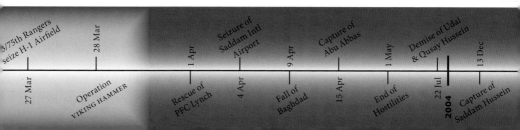

After nearly forty-five minutes on the objective, the assault team called for exfiltration. Chief Warrant Officer 3 James Nattier*, the second Chinook flight leader, in a holding pattern at the release point, anticipated implementing the contingency exfiltration plan. His flight of two helicopters carried the immediate reaction force and the search

and rescue element. By pushing the helicopter to its physical and operational limits, Nattier calculated that two Chinooks could transport the assault force. Wasting little time, the Chinooks cycled in and out of the objective with all the assaulters. The Black Hawks, having departed Roadrunner earlier, extracted the Rangers from their respective landing zones. Coming into their landing zones, the Black Hawk pilots took note of the carnage the Rangers and their fellow Night Stalkers had wrought; dead Iraqis appeared to be every-

Figure 6.25 MH-47 aerial refueling from an MC-130P.

where. Some pilots repositioned so they would not land on the dead bodies. The Rangers boarded, and Hoyt led his flight to Roadrunner, with the Little Birds and DAPs following in trail. The objective was behind them, but the operation still held surprises for the fatigued Night Stalkers.[68]

As the helicopter fleet landed at Roadrunner, dust clouds churned up by the rotor wash obscured the entire area. Crewmembers and pilots could not see past the probes of the helicopters and most stayed where they had landed. Low on fuel, Nattier led a flight of Chinooks and DAPs to the aerial-refueling track, rendezvousing en route to avoid a collision during takeoff. The tanker met Nattier's flight and all went well until the DAPs moved into position for refueling. While maneuvering into refueling position, Brady noticed that his fuel burn rate was higher than normal. Spotlighting the helicopter's probe, he saw fuel leaking. He decided to refuel anyway and connected with the hose of the tanker. The alternative was to end up as a search and rescue mission. Luckily, the gamble paid off—once Brady disconnected the leaking stopped as suddenly as it had begun. Back at Roadrunner, the MH-60K crews waited for the tanker to land so they could refuel with help from the refueling crew. That turned out to be a prudent decision; a crewmember noticed that his own refueling probe had been struck by a bullet and was leaking. He affixed a temporary patch and refu-

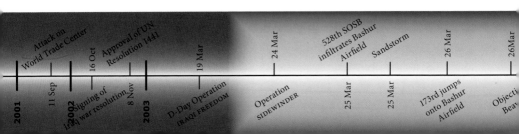

eled. The entire helicopter fleet finally reached the forward support base two and one-half hours later.[69]

The raid on the Al Qadisiyah Research Center proved to be a greater risk to man and machine than expected. Two Chinooks and three Black Hawks sustained damage from armor piercing rounds—not the type of munitions one would expect at a research center. In spite of the stiff resistance, the special operations forces' realistic training in peacetime enabled them to complete the mission. The Night Stalkers executed several contingency plans without a disruption of the mission; Rangers and attack pilots kept the enemy from reinforcing the objective; and two men's lives were saved by combat lifesaver–qualified crewmembers. Once again, SOF proved its worth by completing an important mission ideally suited to its unique capabilities.[70]

OBJECTIVE SIDEWINDER

The events of the first days of the war caused plans to change and missions to shift. With the Ranger assault on Saddam International Airport on hold or canceled, the 1st Battalion, 75th Ranger Regiment, received a new mission: seize Objective Sidewinder in western Iraq. The twofold operation required the Rangers to destroy the Iraqi forces garrisoned at the small airfield outside the village of Nukhayb—Sidewinder South—and to seize the more heavily defended airfield at Mudaysis—Sidewinder North. The Rangers were also tasked to conduct civil military operations in Nukhayb, in order to promote goodwill among the villagers. The mission would not only provide the opportunity to verify the destruction of the visual observation posts attacked on 19 March by the helicopter gunships of the 160th SOAR, but also allow the Rangers to reconnoiter and evaluate the Nukhayb and Mudaysis airfields for future operations.[71]

Figure 6.26 Map highlighting Objective Sidewinder. *Other operations were launched in the western desert from Sidewinder.*

On the evening of 23 March, A Company drove its newly issued Ground Mobility Vehicles to the first staging area: a desert landing strip designated Objective Coyote. Although

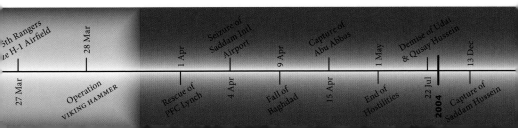

no air cover was available, the GMVs allowed the Rangers to move quickly enough to offset their lack of protection. The ground convoy movement took close to twelve hours to complete, and the Rangers arrived after first light on the 24th. The daylight arrival was fortunate, since unexploded ordnance littered the landing strip. Encountering no resistance, A Company set up blocking positions for security, positioned the Headquarters Company mortar section in a strategic defensive location, and began preparing for its portion of the mission: the attack on Objective Sidewinder South. Once the area was secure, explosive ordnance disposal personnel cleared the munitions off the airstrip. Objective Coyote was to serve as the mobile support site for the Sidewinder mission, which meant the airstrip needed to support landing aircraft.[72]

Figure 6.27 Rangers at Objective Coyote. *Rangers from A Company, 1st Battalion, "hunker down" at Objective Coyote during the three-day sandstorm. Note the Ranger in the turret trying to protect the M2 .50 caliber machine gun from the sand with a poncho.*

The 1st Battalion commander, command sergeant major, and a Tactical Operations Center I element accompanied A Company on its journey to Coyote, and set up a command post on the east side of the airstrip. The key leaders at both the battalion- and company-level planned their respective parts of the Sidewinder mission by drawing in the sand and writing on butcher paper. They established the phase lines and target numbers for the buildings indicated on imagery of the objective, and distributed the limited number of maps on hand. Planning for the mission was well underway when the 24 March sandstorm hit, forcing the Rangers to simply "hunker down" for two days until it passed.[73]

The weather finally cleared after sunset on 26 March. As the Rangers dug themselves out, they received their execution order. After using water to get the sand out of its MK19s and .50 caliber machine guns, A Company moved the thirty-five miles to the vicinity of Objective Sidewinder South. Sidewinder South consisted of the village of Nukhayb, a small military garrison, and an airfield with a border guard security post. Intelligence estimated 150–200 enemy troops to be on the objective. They were expected to defend from their established defensive

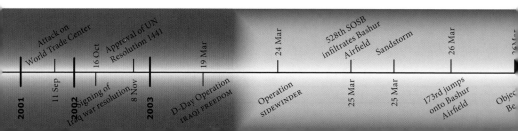

positions while under direct fire, and then break contact and flee the area or attempt to surrender.[74]

At 0300 Iraq time on 27 March, the Rangers quickly established blocking positions to isolate the garrison, and initiated pre-assault mortar fires on the breach point and on a large three-story structure believed to be a command and control node north of the town. The 120mm mortars pounded the breach point, but did not destroy the building. In concert with the mortars, the Rangers manning the support position opened up from the road on the western side of the objective. The 3rd Platoon assault force moved across the objective in a southeast direction.

During the ensuing twelve hours, the Rangers cleared over seventy-five buildings in the town, remaining ever vigilant while attempting to garner support from the villagers. Amidst ineffective resistance, the Rangers located several weapons caches—which they destroyed in the afternoon—and processed ninety-three individuals, of whom eleven were military. With Sidewinder South secured, an element of A Company remained at Nukhayb and prepared for the assault on Sidewinder North, while the rest of A Company returned to Objective Coyote.[75]

On the night of 27 March, a C-17 airplane landed at Coyote, bringing additional personnel and supplies. The 1st Battalion's C Company was accompanied by D Company, 2nd Battalion, 325th Airborne Infantry Regiment, which came to provide added security at the airstrip. The remainder of the Tactical Operations Center I element also came in on the C-17 to reinforce the command post, and Major Charles Vasek*, the 1st Ranger Battalion operations officer, took control of the tactical operations center. As A Company planned for its next raid, another SOF detachment operating in the area for several days supplied additional intelligence information on Sidewinder North. The Ranger reconnaissance detachment from Task Force Hunter added its assessment of the area as well.[76]

C Company, commanded by Captain Jeffery Roche*, was tasked to relieve A Company and conduct civil military operations at Nukhayb. Leaving the 2nd Platoon at Objective Coyote to provide security, C Company headed for Sidewinder South. Left behind at a bleak landing strip in the middle of a barren desert, Sergeant First Class Christopher Barron* discovered that the hardest part of the security mission was keeping his Rangers motivated and alert. To keep them

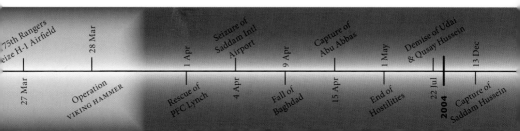

Figure 6.28 Civil military operations in Nukhayb. *C Company, 1st Battalion Rangers and 96th Civil Affairs Battalion soldiers conduct civil military operations handing out the rations to the villagers in Nukhayb.*

awake and ready, Barron talked to his troops, keeping them informed, and moved Rangers around positions to provide at least some variety. Conditions eased that night when MC-130 Combat Talons delivered a six-wheeled Gator utility vehicle and several quad runners (all-terrain vehicles), which improved the Rangers ability to move around the area.[77]

Taking possession of A Company's GMVs, Roche and the majority of C Company drove to Nukhayb and relieved the A Company element still in the village. Later that day, Roche sent his Civil Affairs team leader to meet with the locals and find out their reaction to A Company's assault through the village. After a few hours work, the Civil Affairs team and the Rangers made progress befriending the villagers, and identified key buildings with diagrams and numbers. The locals proved helpful and escorted the Rangers around the village, directing them to a school holding ammunition and chemical protective gear. The villagers even showed Roche ambush positions with mortar rounds and rocket-propelled grenades still in place, which the Rangers subsequently destroyed.[78]

On 30 March, early on C Company's arrival in Nukhayb, three Iraqi soldiers surrendered to the Rangers manning blocking positions on the outskirts of the village. One told of his brother captured during the Gulf War and how the Americans had treated him fairly, which was why he chose to surrender. According to Roche, "at first [the prisoners] were comfortable with us because we fed them, but then they started complaining that we were not treating them well." This was strange because, of course, Roche provided the Iraqis the same spartan standard of food and amenities as his Rangers.[79]

Figure 6.29 1st Ranger Battalion scroll shoulder patch.

As part of their humanitarian assistance effort in Nukhayb, the Rangers broke open over a hundred cases of rations, and in deference to the Iraqi culture, extracted all the pork products. Seeking to be as nonthreatening as possible, Roche decided to allow the Iraqis to take the food and water directly from the GMVs instead of having to wait for the Rangers to hand them out. Embedded media recorded and broadcast the 1st Battalion's "Kodak moment:" when it was time to

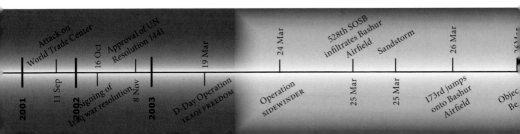

depart, an old man began crying, begging the Rangers not to leave because he feared the return of the Iraqi military.[80]

While dealing with the locals at Nukhayb, the stay-behind element of A Company busily planned the assault on Objective Sidewinder North. Located thirty-six miles from Sidewinder South, Sidewinder North was a large airfield with a main runway, taxiway, and parking aprons, several aircraft hangars, multiple buildings, and several visible antiaircraft artillery sites. Nearby was the large town of Mudaysis. A special operations forces detachment reported 100–150 enemy personnel on the airfield, and believed that the antiaircraft artillery positions were also occupied. Sidewinder North presented a formidable target for the assault element. By late afternoon on 29 March, the plan was ready to execute.[81]

The mission to capture Objective Sidewinder North was a combined arms operation involving integrated fire support and close air support. Captain Daniel Gutierrez*, A Company's fire support officer, arranged for a full package: 120mm mortars, AH-6 Little Bird helicopter gunships, and A-10 Thunderbolts. The tactical operations center kept busy coordinating with the various elements up until the time of mission execution.[82]

On the night of the 29th, A Company traversed the relatively short distance north from Nukhayb to Mudaysis, where it paused outside the town. The fire support element then went to work on the target: the mortar section fired at the breach point of the fence surrounding the airfield, the A-10s hit the larger buildings on the east side of the objective with Maverick missiles, and the AH-6 Little Bird attack pilots conducted armed reconnaissance, while the MH-6 Little Bird pilots used their Forward Looking Infrared Radar to identify targets. The Little Birds also destroyed several S60 antiaircraft artillery pieces and reacted to Ranger calls for close air support.[83]

The Rangers assaulted the airfield from south to north, meeting little resistance along the way. The Little Bird pilots destroyed multiple antiaircraft pieces, and reconnoitered the objective as the Rangers assaulted. As one Ranger platoon moved to the north, the AH-6 pilots rounded a building and saw the gun barrel of a Soviet T-55 tank pointing at them. For Chief Warrant Officer 3 George Caper*, "it was an emotional experience, especially, since there was not supposed to be any armor on the airfield." On the next pass, the team of gunships destroyed the tank with rockets and .50 caliber rounds. The Rangers

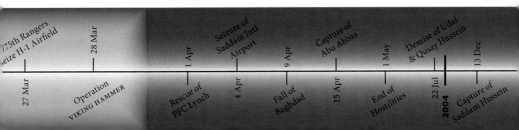

approved of the action and reported that the tank was well shot. As daylight approached, the Night Stalkers departed. The Rangers controlled the objective, though it took over ten hours to clear it.[84]

At daylight on the 30th, the Rangers destroyed the weapons and ammunition caches they had discovered during the night. Once the objective was cleared, the Rangers received orders to withdraw to Coyote and prepare to redeploy back to their forward support base. Exhausted from three days of desert driving and assault operations, A Company nevertheless executed another ten-hour convoy move, returning to the forward support base as ordered. C Company remained for another day, departing on 31 March. In roughly seventy-two hours, the 1st Ranger Battalion conducted two raids on potential lodgment airfields, demonstrating the Rangers' stamina, flexibility, and ability to integrate into combined arms operations—qualities that make the Rangers the U.S. Army's premier light infantry force.[85]

OBJECTIVE SERPENT

Figure 6.30 3rd Ranger Battalion scroll shoulder patch. *The jump on Objective Serpent was the A Company, 3rd Ranger Battalion's second combat jump since Objective Rhino during Operation* ENDURING FREEDOM *on 19 October 2001.*

Perhaps one of the most fearful experiences a soldier can have is to jump into enemy territory at night. The 3rd Battalion, 75th Ranger Regiment, conducted two night combat parachute assaults during Operation IRAQI FREEDOM in order to seize two critical airfields in the western part of Iraq. While less publicized than the later parachute assault of the 173rd Airborne Brigade (-) at Bashur Airfield, the Ranger combat jump to seize the H-1 Airfield (known as Objective Serpent) provided one of the first forward operating bases deep within Iraqi territory.

For the Rangers, airfield seizure is a primary mission. Their actions on the ground were the result of months of preparation. The training focus in the United States centered on a regimental-sized jump to seize Saddam International Airport, later renamed Baghdad International Airport. The 75th Ranger Regiment conducted two airfield seizure rehearsals: the first on Dekkar Airstrip at Fort Benning, Georgia, and the second, Exercise Savage Strike, at Fort Bragg, in February 2003. The Fort Bragg rehearsal included practice clearing heavy equipment from a runway, a task taught and facilitated by B Company, 27th Engineer Battalion.

In the first week of March, the Rangers deployed to the Middle East. Two weeks later, A Company, 3rd Battalion, 75th Ranger Regi-

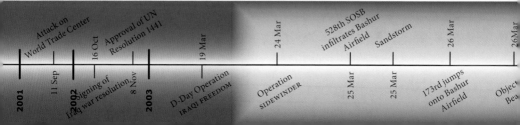

ment, received a warning order to seize Objective Serpent by parachute assault. The order arrived the same day that the 3rd Battalion was busy supporting C Company's parachute assault on Objective Roadrunner, a smaller desert landing strip. A Company took responsibility for the mission to take Objective Serpent and immediately went into planning mode. Over the next few days, Rangers at all levels conducted rehearsals and made preparations for the assault.

Three c-17s full of Rangers took off in the darkness of 27 March, headed for the deserts of western Iraq. The first part of the four and one-half–hour flight was uneventful, but approximately two hours out from the objective, the aircraft took some enemy antiaircraft fire. During the remainder of the flight, the c-17s took evasive maneuvers, "jinking" to avoid fire. Stoically enduring the bumpy ride, the Rangers began jump preparations when they felt the plane suddenly descend from 30,000 to 500 feet. The descent coincided with the ten-minute warning to get ready to jump, which caused some problems as the Rangers attempted to stand up while struggling against the effects of gravity. Anticipation increased when the jump doors opened and filled the interior of the aircraft with cold, dry, desert air.

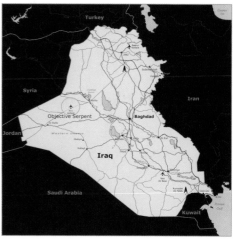

Figure 6.31 Map highlighting Objective Serpent. *Objective Serpent became a major SOF staging base in western Iraq.*

In the crowded troop compartment of one c-17, Staff Sergeant Jack Barker* felt that the aircraft hardly slowed down at all as the aircraft continued to jostle. As if to confirm his observation, the Ranger standing next to Barker fell down and yelled in pain as he seriously injured his knee. The grounded Ranger was moved out of the stick for the return trip to get medical care. The effect of the rapid descent and evasive maneuvers on the Rangers was exacerbated by the unusual weight of their rucksacks and jump gear. In order to prepare for multiple combat contingencies, each Ranger carried more than 250 pounds of equipment—parachute, ammunition, food, and extra radio batteries—mostly crammed in his rucksack. Exiting the aircraft would be a relief to many. As one squad leader shuffled to the door, he observed that the anchor line cable was only two feet from the deck because of the jumpers' weight on it.[86]

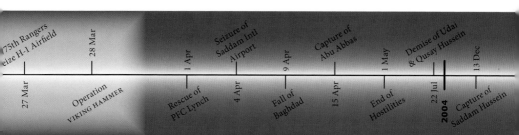

Jumpmaster Sergeant First Class Ronald Redmond*, the 3rd Platoon sergeant of A Company, led the Rangers in his plane through the jump commands and then the Ranger Creed—a 3rd Battalion tradition carried on from its combat jumps into Panama during Operation JUST CAUSE, and later at Objective Rhino in Afghanistan during Operation ENDURING FREEDOM. Jump commands given and creed recited, the Rangers were ready to jump.[87]

The jump light flashed green and the Rangers exited the aircraft without incident. As each man stepped into the uncertainty of the cold, dark, Iraqi desert night, his fate depended on the wind, gravity, and, in some cases, luck. Barker had just lowered his rucksack before executing a parachute landing fall. Almost immediately, he heard the telltale noise of someone landing to his right, and knew from the sound that the newcomer was hurt. After securing his gear, Barker moved toward the noise. He quickly discovered that the unlucky Ranger had blown out his knee on a patch of hard sand filled with large, jagged rocks. After verifying that the Ranger was stable and did not have any other injuries, Barker called in the injury to the medics and then continued with his mission.

Barker's platoon leader, First Lieutenant David Hess*, exited the aircraft without a problem, but hit the ground with a numbing jolt. He felt somewhat disoriented, yet began to secure his equipment in what he thought was just a few minutes after landing. However, when Hess came up on the platoon's radio net, his radio operator told him it had been about twenty minutes since they had jumped. Shaken, but not out of action, Hess rejoined his platoon.[88]

Recovering as quickly as possible from the jump, the Rangers moved rapidly to their designated assembly areas. Although prepared for an enemy force on the drop zone, they noted no tracer fire or enemy activity. Even the Rangers' night vision goggles revealed little in the dense darkness. Barker could make out dark spots throughout the area, but no detail. Later, he discovered that these were rocks, piles of sand, or the rusted hulks of armored vehicles used to block the runway. As Barker moved up the runway toward his platoon's assembly area, he noticed equipment the Iraqis had used to block the runway.

Accompanying the Rangers was a heavy drop of engineer equipment and the same engineers from B Company, 27th Engineer Battalion, who had participated in the rehearsal at Fort Bragg. The engineer equipment landed badly—all three vehicles were on their sides. The

first task for the engineers was to get their equipment into operation and clear the runway for the follow-on forces. Once finished, the engineers began trying to make up for lost time and cleared the runway in record time.

Although there was no enemy gunfire, the radio net was filled with status reports—mostly injuries, including several from Barker's squad. One of the squad automatic weapon gunners, a former Marine named Davidson*, came on the radio and very calmly stated that he may have broken his ankle upon landing in a patch of jagged rocks. "Broken" was an understatement. Using the infrared light on his night vision goggles, Barker saw that Davidson had suffered an open compound fracture just above the ankle, so severe the bones had punctured through his boot, pants, and chemical protective suit. Barker called in the casualty report to the platoon sergeant, and requested one of the four-wheeled all-terrain vehicles that had been heavy-dropped specifically for casualty evacuation. The ATV soon arrived and took Ranger Davidson to the casualty control point.

Figure 6.32 27th Engineer Battalion insignia. *The engineers proved their worth by quickly clearing the runway despite having equipment problems during the jump.*

Once gathered in their platoon assembly areas, the Rangers moved to their assigned objectives. In the case of the 3rd Platoon, its objective was a series of bunkers that turned out to be several cement slabs once used as taxiways for fighter jets. With no visible enemy threat, the platoon moved to its final security points on the perimeter of the battle position. From there, the Rangers watched as the engineers worked feverishly to clear the runway. Their perseverance and hard work paid off, and within five hours, the airstrip at H-1 was operational.

The first plane to land at H-1 was a MC-130 for casualty evacuation. Besides Specialist Davidson, A Company had sustained ten other casualties, including several broken legs, feet, and a badly sprained back. As the casualties were evacuated, their sensitive items and duties were consolidated and redistributed. In the case of one squad, a team leader and the squad automatic weapon gunner—the squad's two senior Rangers—were evacuated. The next ranking Ranger was a private first class nicknamed "Ozzy," a nineteen-year-old from Chino, California, who had been in the Army less than a year. He was one of the newest soldiers in the squad, with five months as a Ranger, but with previous deployment experience to Afghanistan. He remained the team leader for the remainder of the tour in Iraq.[89]

Months of training and days of Ranger planning at home and in theater came to fruition in the early morning hours of 27 March. The

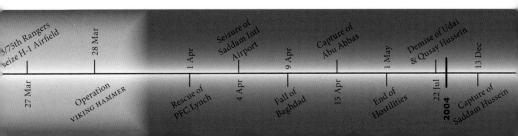

jump onto Objective Serpent was a relatively small operation in the scope of the war in Iraq; however, it was a critical part of the overall campaign in the western desert of Iraq. H-1 Airfield became a mission support site (staging area) for other operations across the western half of Iraq, including the B Company, 3rd Ranger Battalion, assault on Haditha Dam.

305TH PSYOP COMPANY

Figure 6.33 I MEF insignia. *The 305th Psyop Company supported the I MEF from Kuwait to north of Baghdad.*

The 305th Psyop Company (Army Reserve) spent nearly two months at Fort Bragg going through the mobilization process and conducting military occupation specialty–specific training in preparation for its deployment to Iraq. The Upper Marlboro, Maryland-based company understood it would support either the 3rd Infantry Division or the I Marine Expeditionary Force, and prepared to accompany either unit.[90]

Upon arriving in Kuwait, the 305th learned its mission was in support of the Marines. The company linked up with elements of I MEF at Camp Matilda, Kuwait, during the first week of March, and focused on making last minute preparations for combat operations. When war commenced on 19 March, the 3rd ID and I MEF led the initial devastating ground attacks into Iraq.[91]

In order to support the various elements of I MEF, the 305th divided into tactical PSYOP teams and distributed the units throughout the task force. These teams used loudspeakers mounted on their HMMWVs

to broadcast a myriad of sounds and messages to their target audience. So popular were these teams with the Marines that each TPT rotated between units within the I MEF, in some cases moving every two or three days. It seemed there were never enough PSYOP teams to meet the demands of the Marines.[92]

In actions representative of the entire company, TPT 41 distinguished itself while in support of the 2nd Battalion, 8th Marines. The three-man team consisted of team leader Sergeant Doug Voil*, Sergeant Kaper*, and Private First Class Vargas*. On 23 March, TPT 41 found itself in support of Task Force

Figure 6.34 Task Force Tarawa vehicles. *Light Armored Vehicles of the Marines Task Force Tarawa on the move north near Nasiriya.*

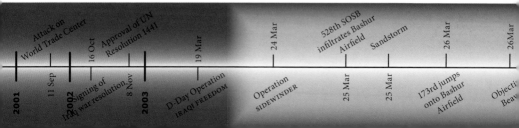
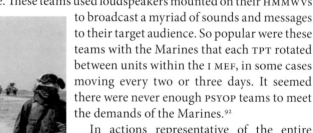

Tarawa, just outside of the ancient desert city of Nasiriya, which had been key in the Shiite Muslim rebellion that followed Operation DESERT STORM. Calculating that Saddam Hussein would not risk another uprising and would place Republican Guard units and loyalists in the city, Task Force Tarawa approached cautiously. Unbeknownst to TPT 41, Task Force Tarawa was about to engage in one of the bloodiest battles of IRAQI FREEDOM.[93]

Figure 6.35 Loudspeaker mounted on a HMMWV. *The* PSYOP *soldiers were used for crowd control duties on many occasions.*

As the Marines maneuvered to secure the eastern bridges over the Euphrates River, they encountered stiff resistance from enemy troops occupying a military hospital on the eastern side of the southernmost bridge. Enemy mortar and machine gun elements used the hospital to fire on the Marines when they crossed over the bridges. The enemy could not be displaced. After three days, TPT 41 approached the building and broadcast surrender appeals and a warning about the inevitability of defeat. The team also informed the fighters that if they did not surrender immediately the hospital would be bombed. Ten minutes into the broadcast, enemy personnel started emerging, doing exactly what the PSYOP team told them to do. The Marines confiscated AK-47s and rocket-propelled grenade launchers, searched the men, and sent them to enemy prisoner of war camps in the rear. Upon further investigation of the hospital, the Marines discovered a cache of two hundred weapons, Iraqi military uniforms, three thousand chemical protective suits, and nerve agent antidote injectors—quite a haul, considering words were TPT 41's only weapon in the battle of wills.[94]

PSYOP SUPPORT TO I MEF

Three 305th PSYOP teams provided exceptional psychological operations support to I MEF in its drive on Baghdad. TPTs 41, 42, and 43 each contributed its PSYOP expertise and soldier skills to the Marines' mission in a variety of ways. In at least one case, the soldier skills proved more valuable than the training in psychological operations. The following episodes highlight the diversity of the tactical PSYOP teams' experiences as they supported I MEF.

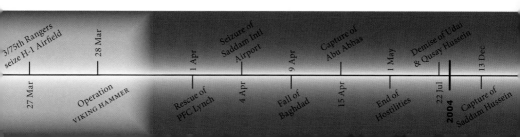

TPT 43 consisted of team leader Staff Sergeant Jason Graham* and team members Corporal Tyson* and Private First Class Folson*. It was attached to the Light Armored Vehicle Company of the 3rd Battalion, 2nd Marines. The LAV Company occupied a former Republican Guard headquarters in Nasiriya, and used this position to attack the strongholds of irregular forces across the Euphrates River. At 0900 on 30 March, a white pickup truck screeched to a halt in the middle of the western Nasiriya Bridge and its fedayeen passengers fired on the Marines manning the bridge checkpoint. Driven from their vehicle by the Marines' small arms fire, the fedayeen ran back and forth from the truck to the bridge abutments, firing weapons along the road to the west of the LAV Company. Reacting instinctively to the action unfolding in front of him, Graham and his team moved on foot approximately two hundred meters, positioning themselves perpendicular to the bridge on an underlying road and within small arms range of the enemy. Graham placed his squad automatic weapon gunner in a protected building with a good field of fire, and gave the third team member spotter and security duties. With his men in place, Graham moved forward to communicate with the Marines engaged with the enemy. After speaking to the senior man, Graham knew the location and number of Marines on the bridge. He then directed his team to engage the fedayeen; Graham directed the gunner to lay down suppressive fire while he himself took single shots. With effective fire coming from an unexpected angle, the fedayeen broke off their engagement with the Marines and attempted to engage the new target—TPT 43. With the enemy distracted, the Marines at the checkpoint broke contact and withdrew from the bridge. The PSYOP team kept up the suppressive fire until the fedayeen retreated into the city and the Marines were safe on the south side of the bridge.[95]

TPT 42, led by Sergeant Joel Hobbs*, was a little perplexed when a Marine commander ordered the team to the Iraqi town of Ash Shatrah to play some "helicopter music." Not until Hobbs was told that snipers were harassing Coalition forces in Ash Shatrah did the situation became clearer: the commander wanted the PSYOP team to fool the snipers into thinking they were being attacked by helicopters. Using the low frequency speaker module on their HMMWV to broadcast a recording of a helicopter in flight, the three-man team toured the streets of Ash Shatrah. The recording did, indeed, convince the snipers that an attack by approaching helicopters was imminent, and

they quickly left their positions and disappeared. Without firing a shot, the PSYOP team forced the evacuation of the enemy from the battlefield.[96]

As the I MEF units resumed their drive on Baghdad, TPT 42 traveled with the fast-moving 3rd Battalion, 1st Marines. To keep pace, the PSYOP team was forced to discard much of its equipment. Most of the computers and office supplies the team had brought for the PSYOP dissemination mission—its original mission—was left behind. Personal gear, too, was severely limited. "Initially each soldier was told he could bring a rucksack and a duffel bag, and that's it," Hobbs said. "Then it got down to 'just bring a rucksack.'" The team then spent time ferreting out a global positioning system unit, a radio, and other necessary tactical gear for the trek north.[97]

What personal gear the team did carry was often turned to tactical uses. Private First Class Matt Ortega* used his digital camera to document the detachment's move north, and Hobbs used his portable MP3 player instead of the team's assigned minidisc player for PSYOP

Figure 6.36 Nasiriya ambush site. *Elements of Task Force Tarawa at the 507th Maintenance Company ambush site in Nasiriya, where Private First Class Jessica Lynch was taken prisoner.*

messages. The MP3 player cued up recordings faster than the minidisc player, and the lack of moving parts made it more reliable in the dusty environment of Iraq.[98]

TPT 42's frontline mission provided the team with the unique opportunity to deliver the products it had developed firsthand. "We would protect the local populace from what was going to roll through their area by warning civilians to stay clear of vehicles and troops," Corporal Andrew Urvina* explained. In addition to prerecorded messages, the team relied on Ali, a volunteer translator from Kuwait, to tailor messages for specific incidents. Ali proved to be an alert and responsible translator whose ability allowed the PSYOP soldiers to issue more detailed instructions to the civilians during crowd control missions and building raids. "We would use Ali a little more often than the prerecorded scripts," Urvina said.[99]

In one unfortunate situation, the PSYOP warnings could not prevent the harming of innocent civilians. While the team was assisting the Marines at a checkpoint, Ortega was manning the loudspeaker

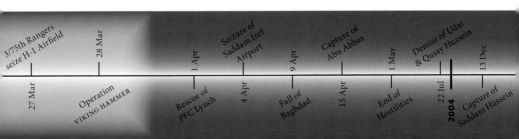

27 Mar

3/75th Rangers seize H-1 Airfield

28 Mar

Operation VIKING HAMMER

1 Apr

Rescue of PFC Lynch

Seizure of Saddam Intl Airport

4 Apr

9 Apr

Fall of Baghdad

Capture of Abu Abbas

15 Apr

1 May

End of Hostilities

22 Jul

Demise of Uday & Qusay Hussein

2004

13 Dec

Capture of Saddam Hussein

with Ali when two men with AK-47 rifles jumped out of a blue dump truck following a car carrying an Iraqi family. Ali instinctively gave instructions for the family to move out of the way and for the men to drop their weapons, but the Marines were already poised to return fire. Shortly after the last word rang through the air, Ortega heard a shot. In response, the Marines "lit up" the gunmen and TPT 42 member Urvina returned fire with his squad automatic weapon. Despite the pandemonium, Ortega insisted on reissuing a warning to the gunmen during a lull in the shooting. When the dust settled, the mother of the Iraqi family was dead and her husband and young daughter were badly wounded. Only the two-year-old boy was uninjured. During a post-firefight sweep, the Marines uncovered a cache of weapons in the back of the dump truck.[100]

Figure 6.37 305th POC loudspeaker vehicle at a rest stop.

As a newly minted PSYOP soldier, Ortega admitted his apprehension on being placed on a tactical team. He had originally trained to be a graphic illustrator on the product development detachment. When word came of his assignment to a TPT working with the Marines, "I was reassured, 'you'll be on the reserve team; you probably won't see any action.'" His fear of combat vanished that day at the checkpoint, for he remained with the vehicle and continued to broadcast during the exchange of fire. "I had to do that," he says modestly; "it's PSYOP protocol."[101]

The Marines came to depend on the TPTs for more than their broadcasting capabilities. In the months before deployment, Hobbs' team had studied Iraqi customs and religion extensively in order to develop accurate PSYOP products. This knowledge was not wasted as the team began its support of the Marines—the PSYOP soldiers quickly became the subject matter experts on Iraq in the eyes of the Marines. Ortega remembers explaining to edgy Marines that the ubiquitous black flags outside Iraqi villages were not anti-American displays, but merely religious markers. He also explained that in Iraq, hand holding between two men was perfectly normal.[102]

In a hard push north with a logistics train from L Company, 3rd Battalion, 1st Regiment—an operation known by the team as "Operation Run the Gauntlet"—Hobbs and his soldiers reached Saddam City outside Baghdad. Here they were reassigned to the 1st Battalion,

4th Marines, working with a Navy SEAL sniper team. The SEALS told the team members that their new mission was to be "sniper bait." Ortega listened incredulously as the Navy SEALS explained how they planned to use the team's HMMWV to draw out enemy snipers, who tended to converge on broadcasting vehicles. His teammates conveniently neglected to tell him that the parked vehicle would be empty and the messages would be broadcast remotely from a nearby rooftop. After successfully employing this ruse, the team affixed a plaque to its HMMWV reading "Sniper Bait."[103]

Following the end of combat operations, the tempo of the team's frontline mission slowed and it returned to its primary duty of creating PSYOP products. In reflecting on their time as a tactical PSYOP team in combat, the PSYOP soldiers recognized the unusual nature of some of their experiences. They applied every aspect of their soldier and PSYOP training, and still needed to develop new skills to cope with the situations around them. In the end, Ortega admitted, "There was so much that the [twelve-week PSYOP] course didn't train me for."[104]

A Day in the Life of a PSYOP TPT

After enduring two days of sandstorms, Task Force Tarawa resumed its advance north. On 26 March, the commander of Task Force Tarawa's 2nd Battalion, 8th Marines, ordered TPT 41 to conduct civilian noninterference operations along Route 7. The team would ensure that noncombatants moved out of Nasiriya toward the town of Albu Azim so they would not block the advance. Initially encountering a large group of Iraqi civilians congregating at the intersection of Routes 7 and 8, the PSYOP team used its loudspeaker to direct the civilians to move east along Route 7.[105]

Moving along the crowd, TPT 41 met a group of men who wanted to surrender to U.S. forces. The group included a Republican Guard colonel, a lower-ranking enlisted soldier, and one very well-dressed civilian who kept waving to members of the TPT. The team's interpreter agreed that these three individuals definitely needed to be questioned. The

Figure 6.38 305th POC HMMWVs at a stop during the three-day sandstorm. *A family of camels penetrated the security perimeter. They simply wandered through.*

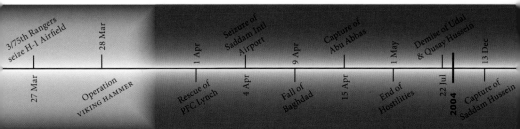

3/75th Rangers seize H-1 Airfield

27 Mar

28 Mar

Operation VIKING HAMMER

1 Apr

Rescue of PFC Lynch

Seizure of Saddam Intl Airport

4 Apr

9 Apr

Fall of Baghdad

Capture of Abu Abbas

15 Apr

1 May

End of Hostilities

Demise of Uday & Qusay Hussein

22 Jul

2004

Capture of Saddam Hussein

13 Dec

two military prisoners were kept under guard in a separate building while the team searched the well-dressed individual: he carried a cell phone and American, Kuwaiti, and Iraqi currency. The cell phone was suspicious, but their Kuwaiti interpreter was able to determine that the man was a Kuwaiti operative working undercover in Iraq.[106]

Further questioning of the Kuwaiti man revealed that he had seen several U.S. prisoners of war at the Saddam Hussein General Hospital not far from the team's location. The man stated that some of the prisoners had been dragged out from the backs of cars with chains, and others had been executed; however, there was a live, white, female soldier being kept there. TPT 41 kept the man—handcuffed and masked at his own request—until a military intelligence team finally arrived to interview him. The man's information contributed to the rescue of Private First Class Jessica Lynch.[107]

That same evening, TPT 41 was again asked to conduct crowd control. The combat engineers needed to blow up all the shops and buildings being used for cover near an intersection, and to destroy a large cache of confiscated materiel. They planned to create vehicle obstacles by detonating cratering charges in the road at points eight hundred and two hundred meters east of the intersection. The PSYOP team drove north along Route 7 until it reached a group of twenty civilians roughly four hundred meters from the intersection. The team instructed them to stay in place until the charges were detonated. Roughly ten more people joined the group, bringing the total to thirty individuals.[108]

As the sun went down, the team spotted movement along the west side of the road, north of the team's position. Voil moved forward with the interpreter to instruct the civilians to come in and join the others. Instead of approaching, the suspicious group moved further into the woods and began firing at the PSYOP team from the wood line. Voil directed his team to open fire, activated the infrared beacon on his rifle, and began returning fire with 5.56mm bullets and 40mm grenade rounds.[109]

While Voil and the soldiers placed effective fire on the enemy, Voil kept moving between his team and the civilians to calm and control the frightened bystanders. Once the enemy fire dissipated, the TPT moved the civilians two hundred meters further north and again set up security. Voil ordered Vargas to position the vehicle at an angle providing a better field of fire for the gunner and to shield

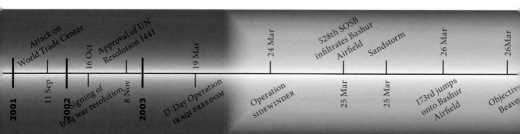

the civilians. Although the team was in a vulnerable position, alone and without backup, the civilians were less secure. The team stayed put. The team once again began receiving enemy small arms fire, this time from both sides of the road. The team returned fire, Voil engaging targets in buildings approximately 250 meters east of the team. He continuously checked on the civilians in his care. After several minutes of sustained fire, enemy fire once again subsided.

With the enemy fire finally eliminated, TPT 41 drove slowly up the road toward TPT 43's position, shielding the civilians with the team's HMMWV the entire way. Once the group reached a Coalition-controlled area, the team instructed the civilians to continue walking east into the local village to find shelter. In unusual recognition of the PSYOP team's actions protecting the civilians, Voil was awarded the Bronze Star for valor.[110]

SUMMARY

During the last week of March, Coalition forces were fully engaged in executing Central Command's plan to remove Saddam Hussein from power. V Corps and I MEF continued their advance north, bypassing pockets of fedayeen and loyalist resistance in order to reach Baghdad as soon as possible. ARSOF units in western Iraq continued to hunt SCUDs and secure strategic airfields. In northern Iraq, CJSOTF-North completed its infiltration and linkup with Kurdish peshmerga forces. The combined strength of Patriotic Union of Kurdistan peshmerga troops and Special Forces firepower routed Ansar al-Islam terrorists from their stronghold near Halabja. ARSOF support and signal elements worked in both theaters to ensure mission success, and PSYOP and Civil Affairs units supported both conventional and special operations forces, sometimes in unexpected ways.

On 30 March, the eleventh day of combat operations, General Franks provided an operational update briefing. After reviewing major accomplishments by Coalition forces in Iraq, Franks concluded his briefing by stating, "This campaign…has made remarkable progress. Lots remains to be done. The days ahead will see ups and downs—the ups and downs of war. We don't need to remind ourselves that the outcome has not been, is not, and will not be in question."[111]

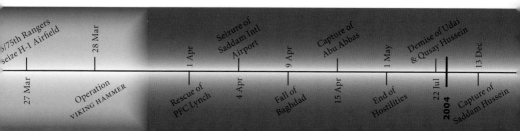

ARSOF personnel certainly experienced their fair share of both the ups and downs of war in the days and weeks to come. CJSOTF-North participated in several battles with its Kurdish allies while securing northern Iraq. CJSOTF-west teams in western and central Iraq performed a variety of challenging missions ahead of and in support of CFLCC's march toward Baghdad. ARSOF aviation and Ranger elements continued to seize objectives of military and environmental importance. The fight for Iraq became fierce in April, but the response of ARSOF was stronger.

Chapter Seven

War Accelerates

D+12 through D+21
31 March–9 April

O PERATION IRAQI FREEDOM BEGAN to accelerate in early April. Coalition Forces Land Component Command's V Corps and I Marine Expeditionary Force were rapidly closing in on Baghdad, and follow-on units were cleaning out pockets of resistance behind the main thrust. The slight pause in operations during and after the 24–26 March sandstorm had allowed Central Command to wage a heightened air campaign against unsuspecting Iraqi Army and regime targets. The ground forces used the time to regroup and resupply, readying themselves for the next big push. Special operations forces, on the other hand, worked right through the storm and kept the pressure on Iraqi units and fedayeen in all regions of the country. The unconventional warfare campaigns that Army SOF units began at the end of March gained momentum in April. By 9 April, Baghdad was in Coalition hands, as were the major northern cities of Mosul, Kirkuk, and Irbil. The pace was brutal, but the ten days beginning on 31 March brought the Coalition closer to its ultimate goal—a stable, free Iraq.

CONVENTIONAL FORCES

After pausing to regroup and resupply, Coalition Forces Land Component Command's ground force commenced the next phase of its advance on Baghdad on 31 March. The I Marine Expeditionary Force continued to fight its way north via Highways 1 and 7, and the British spent more than a week containing Basra in the south. The main focus of the conventional effort, however, was V Corps' push for Baghdad. After conducting a feint and positioning operation with five simultaneous attacks, V Corps sped through the Karbala Gap. After heavy fighting, the 3rd Infantry Division secured objectives cordoning Baghdad from the west. Once I MEF crossed the Tigris River and secured the eastern side of the capital, Baghdad was cut off from further reinforcement, and it was only a matter of time before Coalition forces took control.

FIVE SIMULTANEOUS ATTACKS

After a short period to rest, consolidate, and plan, V Corps commenced five simultaneous attacks designed to confuse the Iraqis and to position forces for the final move on Baghdad. The first of the attacks was on Objective Murray, near Hindiya on the Euphrates River southeast of Karbala. The objective of the 2nd Brigade Combat Team, 3rd ID, was to convince the enemy that the Coalition's main thrust for Baghdad would take place south of Karbala, not through the Karbala Gap. After clearing enemy forces northeast of Objective Rams on 30 March, the 2nd BCT was ready to move in Objective Murray.

At 0600 hours 31 March, the 2nd BCT attacked east to Objective Murray along three routes converging on Hindiya. The element assigned to take the bridge across the Euphrates met resistance, but quickly secured the west bridgehead. The 2nd BCT did not cross, and eventually withdrew from Hindiya, but the brigade presented enough of a threat to force units on the east side of the bridge to remain in place, preventing them from moving north to reinforce the Karbala Gap. The 2nd BCT also maintained control of Highway 9 southwest of Hindiya, which would allow the 1st BCT to move up and attack through the Karbala Gap.[1]

The second of V Corps' five attacks ultimately took much longer than the assault on Objective Murray. V Corps was reluctant to

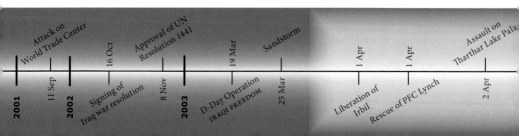

attack one of Shia Islam's holiest cities, but continued fedayeen activity from Najaf eventually drew the 101st Airborne Division (Air Assault) into a situation where clearing operations in the city were unavoidable. On 31 March, the 101st Airborne's 1st BCT attacked from the southwest. After conducting a feint toward Hilla, the 2nd BCT of the 3rd ID joined the fight from the north, and the two brigades systematically cleared Najaf of fedayeen. Key to the brigades' success was well-coordinated joint fires. The BCTs used tanks, infantry, close air support, precision guided mis-

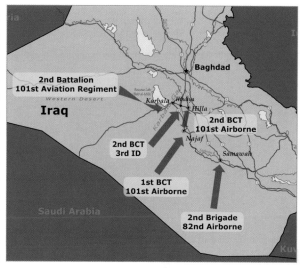

Figure 7.1 Map showing V Corps simultaneous attacks.

siles and bombs, air cavalry, attack helicopters, and artillery to ensure the division's domination of the city. The mission was accomplished by 4 April.[2]

The third V Corps attack was designed simply and solely to deceive the Iraqis: the 101st Airborne's 2nd BCT thrust twenty-five kilometers north, as if to attack Hilla. The feint commenced at 0600 hours 31 March, and continued through the morning against heavy resistance. The brigade halted two kilometers south of Hilla, as planned, and remained there engaging the enemy until 1830 hours. The 2nd BCT then turned around and joined the 1st BCT's attack on Najaf. The feint was convincing; the Iraqis retained units at Hilla to defend against another thrust along Highway 9.[3]

The fourth of V Corps' simultaneous attacks was an aerial reconnaissance by the 2nd Battalion, 101st Aviation Regiment. The AH-64 helicopters scouted the area southwest of Bahr al-Milh Lake, checking for enemy resistance on the 3rd ID's flank. The pilots met only token ground resistance, but did locate a large ammunition supply point, which helicopters returned and destroyed on 1 April. The 3rd ID's western flank was protected for the attack on the Karbala Gap.[4]

The 2nd Brigade, 82nd Airborne Division, conducted the fifth and final of V Corps' attacks on 31 March—the clearing of the town of

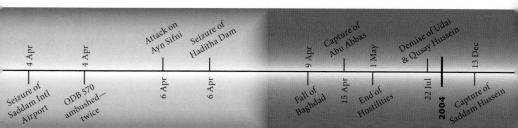

Samawah. The 2nd Brigade relieved the 3rd Battalion, 7th Cavalry Regiment, outside Samawah on 28 March. After probing the fedayeen's defenses to gain intelligence on resistance within the city, the 2nd Brigade attacked on 31 March. Of the V Corps assaults that began that day, the 2nd Brigade's lasted the longest. Not until 6 April did the last of the resistance in Samawah collapse. After seven long days of fighting, the brigade finally declared the city cleared.[5]

Figure 7.2 Troops of the 101st Airborne Division battle in the streets of Najaf.

In spite of Iraqi assumptions to the contrary, CFLCC did indeed intend to attack through the Karbala Gap. The flat geography between the city of Karbala and Bahr al-Milh Lake provided the best opportunity for high speed movement on the way to Baghdad, and would serve as part of the V Corps supply route supporting the assault on the capital and afterward. The five simultaneous attacks fixed Iraqi divisions south of the gap, and positioned the 3rd ID units for the assault.

At midnight on 1 April, the 3rd ID's 3rd BCT passed through the 2nd BCT at Objective Murray and attacked the east side of Karbala. Two hours later, at 0200 hours on 2 April, the 3rd ID's 1st BCT attacked the west side of Karbala toward Objective Muscogee. By 0600, the 1st BCT secured the bridge across the Euphrates northwest of Karbala, seized the dam, and cleared Highway 8. The Karbala Gap was secure.[6]

With the gap secure, the 1st BCT moved north to attack Objective Peach, the bridge across the Euphrates designated to serve as the division's primary crossing site. Meeting an infantry battalion and elements of a reconnaissance battalion, the 1st BCT spent the afternoon of 2 April securing the western approach to the bridge. Although the Iraqis managed to blow the north span of the bridge, the brigade's engineers prevented the Iraqis from destroying the southern span. The 1st BCT infantry crossed the bridge and secured the eastern bridgehead. The 3rd ID was through the gap.[7]

While the 1st BCT secured Objective Peach, the 2nd BCT maneuvered behind (with one part of the brigade taking a slow detour through the wetlands east of Karbala), finally reaching the bridge at 0800 on 3 April. The 2nd BCT arrived just in time—the 1st BCT had spent the night defending Objective Peach against the counterattack by the Medina

Division of the Iraqi Republican Guard. Although the 2nd BCT was supposed to cross the bridge and proceed east to secure Objective Saints, it instead relieved the 1st BCT at Objective Peach, enabling the 1st BCT to move northeast and attack Objective Lions.[8]

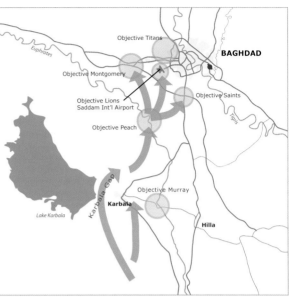

Figure 7.3 Map showing the assault thru the Karbala Gap.

Lead elements of the 2nd BCT passed through Objective Peach on 3 April, moving northeast to attack Objective Saints. This intersection of Highways 1 and 8 lay south of Baghdad; control of the intersection would block enemy forces in the capital from reinforcing or being reinforced by units in the south. The 2nd BCT met irregular forces, infantry, tanks, and other combat vehicles on the objective. By 1930 hours, Objective Saints was under the 3rd ID's control, giving V Corps domination over the southern approach to Baghdad. The brigade spent the next several days clearing the area of enemy units trapped between Saints and Hilla. But only the southern edge of the cordon was in place.[9]

While the 2nd BCT secured Objective Saints, the 1st BCT moved north to Objective Lions—Saddam International Airport. Capturing the airport would do three things for V Corps: deprive the regime of a significant strategic location, provide Coalition forces with a powerful staging point for operations in Baghdad itself, and put further pressure on regime forces already reeling from CFLCC's rapid advance. The 3rd ID kept up the pressure.

The 1st BCT engaged Objective Lions with artillery fire at 1719 hours on 3 April. Two infantry columns approached the airport

Figure 7.4 Artillery of the 1 BCT of the 3rd ID directing fire on Objective Lions. *The artillery fires supported the attack on Saddam International Airport that fell to the troops of the 3rd ID.*

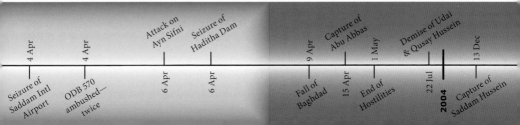

Figure 7.5 3rd ID in Baghdad. *Despite "Baghdad Bob's" claims to the contrary, the 3rd ID vehicles were in Baghdad on 4 April.*

from the south, breaching the wall at 2300 hours. The entire western column was inside by 0100 hours 4 April, and secured the eastern end of the main runway. The brigade's sector of the airfield was secure by 0430 hours. The Americans were, indeed, in Baghdad, in spite of the Iraqi information minister's declarations to the contrary.[10]

Although the 1st BCT gained a foothold on the edge of Baghdad on 4 April, the cordon was not closed. The Four Corners area outside the airport's east gate gave the brigade trouble for several days, Republican Guard units had to be cleared from nearby training facilities.

Beyond Objective Saints, the 3rd Squadron, 7th Cavalry Regiment, moved north to secure Objective Montgomery on 3 April. After destroying twenty enemy T-72 tanks, the cavalry regiment controlled the western approach to Baghdad, the intersection of Highways 1 and 10.[11]

The third objective in V Corps' area of responsibility in the Baghdad cordon was the northwestern approach. On 6 April, the 3rd BCT swung north out of Objective Peach, past Objective Saints, and through Objective Montgomery. Once past the cavalry, the 3rd BCT fought through enemy resistance, moving as quickly as possible to secure the quadrant. The first fight at Objective Smith lasted several hours, as each element of the brigade fought through the objective without stopping to clear it. Similar resistance was encountered at Objective Custer, but the brigade pressed on using the close air support on hand. At 1530 hours, the 3rd BCT seized Objective Patton, where Highway 1 crossed a canal running east–west. With Patton secure, an armored element moved south and seized Objective Monty—the main highway bridge over the Tigris River. The tanks and Bradleys fought off a strong counterattack, and stabilized the situation by 1900 hours. By sunset on 6 April, Objective Titans, that encompassed all intermediate objectives, belonged to the 3rd BCT, and V Corps controlled its half of the cordon around the city.[12]

Far to the south, British Royal Marine Commandos commenced a second attack to clear Basra on 30 March. The British had encountered stiff opposition in Basra a week earlier, and after wearing the enemy

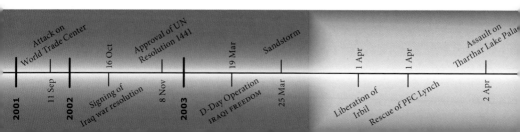

down with artillery and close air support, were ready to take the city. British armor, infantry, and Marines defeated Iraqi artillery, armor, and heavy pockets of Baathist and fedayeen enemy in the course of the weeklong battle. On 6 April, the ancient gateway to the city was in British hands, and a few days later, Basra was completely secure.[13]

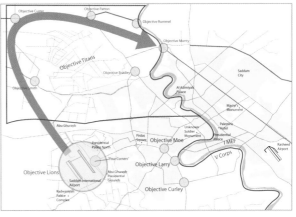

Figure 7.6 Map of the cordon around Baghdad including the sweep through Objective Titans.

After crossing the Euphrates River at Nasiriya, the I Marine Expeditionary Force main body split into two columns. Regimental Combat Teams 5 and 7 followed Highway 1 northwest toward Diwaniya, while RCT 1 took Highway 7 north toward Al Kut. Halfway to Al Kut, the Marines swung east to confront enemy units near Amarah on the north–south Highway 6 between Basra and Al Kut. RCT 1, 1st Marine Division, hooked right at Diwaniya, feinted an attack on Al Kut, then proceeded northwest on the Tigris. En route they defeated an Iraqi tank battalion at Aziziyah, and arrived at the outskirts of Baghdad on 3 April. After battling through Al Kut, RCTs 7 and 5 turned northwest along the Tigris River and met up with RCT 1 outside Baghdad. As the 3rd ID cordoned off the western side of Baghdad, the Marines pushed into the southeastern suburbs to seal off their half of the capital city.[14]

Figure 7.7 I MEF in Baghdad. *Marines of the I MEF pushed into Baghdad and sealed off the southern approaches to the city.*

By 6 April, with CFLCC's two main columns controlling the approaches to Baghdad, the Coalition began to squeeze the city into submission. The 3rd ID's 2nd BCT began "thunder runs" on 5 April, carving paths through Baghdad's defenders. The 3rd BCT defended against a strong counterattack in Objective Titans in the northwest quadrant of the city from 6 to 8 April. On 7 April, the 2nd BCT captured three strategic cloverleaf intersections—dubbed Curly, Larry, and Moe—and spent the night in Saddam Hus-

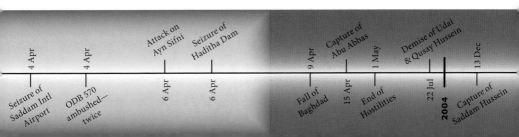

Seizure of Saddam Intl Airport — 4 Apr

ODB 570 ambushed twice — 4 Apr

Attack on Ayn Sifni — 6 Apr

Seizure of Haditha Dam — 6 Apr

Fall of Baghdad — 9 Apr

Capture of Abu Abbas — 15 Apr

End of Hostilities — 1 May

Demise of Udai & Qusay Hussein — 22 Jul

2004

Capture of Saddam Hussein — 13 Dec

sein's main Baghdad palace. That same day, the Marines attacked at Diyalah Bridge in eastern Baghdad. By 9 April, I MEF forces captured Rasheed Air Base as well. On 9 April, the 4th Marine Regiment helped the Iraqis topple the giant statue of Saddam Hussein in Firdos Square, an act that symbolized to the city and the world that Saddam's regime had fallen.[15]

ARSOF OPERATIONS

In the days between 31 March and 9 April, ARSOF units and individuals demonstrated an unparalleled level of competence and flexibility. Their ability to plan, adjust, adapt, and execute gave the Iraqis no respite. In the north, the 3rd Battalion, 3rd Special Forces Group, had arrived to bring its swift and lethal mobility to Combined Special Operations Task Force–North. In the west, Task Force Dagger found itself stretched to the breaking point. Coalition Forces Special Operations Component Command created Task Force Seminole using a special operations detachment and infantrymen of the Florida National Guard to help alleviate the problem of enemy prisoners of war. The Rangers and the 160th Special Operations Aviation Regiment worked together on several successful operations including the rescue of Private First Class Jessica Lynch from captivity in Nasiriya, and securing the vital Haditha Dam complex. The pace of ARSOF operations accelerated, moving the decisive operations phase of the war toward a swift conclusion.

CJSOTF-North

During the first week of April, Task Force Viking reached its full strength. The task force support battalion arrived and built up the support base at Irbil. The base stood only thirty kilometers from the Iraqi front lines, exposed to long-range artillery fires if the Iraqis felt so inclined. Forward Operating Base 33 was committed to the battle and encountered a tough fight at Debecka Crossroads. An equally difficult battle concluded on 6 April, when the town of Ayn Sifni fell to the troops of FOB 102 and Kurdish peshmerga. As the conventional forces pushed toward Baghdad, CJSOTF-North had to expend almost as much effort controlling the eager advance of the Kurdish forces on

the cities of Kirkuk and Mosul as it took to defeat the retreating Iraqi Army.

AYN SIFNI

The small village of Ayn Sifni occupies a strategic location on the main road north of Mosul, close to the Green Line indicating the political boundary between greater Iraq and Kurdish territory to the north. In order to confront the Kurdish forces, the Iraqi 108th Regiment, 8th Infantry Division, maintained two battalions in the traditionally Kurdish village. The liberation of Ayn Sifni by U.S. and Kurdish forces opened the route to Mosul and helped protect the Kurdish lines of communication.[16]

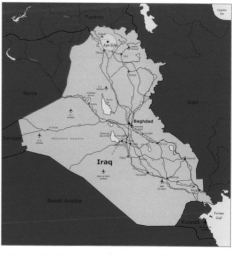

Figure 7.8 Map highlighting Ayn Sifni.

Since arriving in Bashur on 23 March, Captain Grant Carthage* and his Special Forces team linked up with other 10th Special Forces Group personnel and Kurdish forces in the vicinity of Ayn Sifni. The well-organized Kurdish *supays* (battalions) occupied positions on the ridgelines north of the village and maintained constant surveillance of the occupying troops. The supays rotated personnel from the ridgelines in thirty-day increments, as they had done for a number of years.

*Pseudonyms have been used for all military personnel with a rank lower than lieutenant colonel.

From these positions the Kurdish forces could muster 200 fighters in thirty minutes, and 600 in two hours. As events in Iraq unfolded and the strategic value of the village was revealed, the 10th SFG commanders and their Kurdish counterparts developed a plan to attack and seize Ayn Sifni.[17]

Two weeks on a steady diet of potato soup, rice, bread, and tea did little to dampen the ardor of the Special Forces operational detachment alphas (ODAs) working with the Kurdish forces. Originally deployed to the area as hunter–killer teams against Iraqi armor, the American troops easily transitioned to their new mission. In an effort to drive the Iraqis

Figure 7.9 Special Forces troops call for close air support. *The ability to quickly bring in U.S. air power was a decisive factor in many of the battles including Ayn Sifni.*

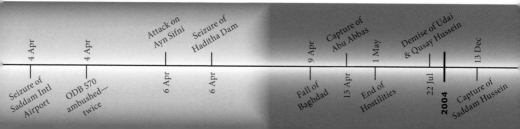

4 Apr — Seizure of Saddam Intl Airport
4 Apr — ODB 570 ambushed—twice
Attack on Ayn Sifni — 6 Apr
Seizure of Haditha Dam — 6 Apr
9 Apr — Fall of Baghdad
Capture of Abu Abbas — 15 Apr
1 May — End of Hostilities
Demise of Udai & Qusay Hussein — 22 Jul
2004
13 Dec — Capture of Saddam Hussein

Figure 7.10 Hill 003. *Hill 003 provided observation of Ayn Sifni from the northwest. The dead space immediately west of the village was unobservable, a factor that favored the Iraqi defenders in the town.*

out of Ayn Sifni at minimal cost, the ODAS initiated an orchestrated bombing campaign against the Iraqi units occupying the village.[18]

Unfortunately, lack of dedicated close air support aircraft hindered the effectiveness of the bombing campaign, and in one instance allowed an entire Iraqi battalion to board buses and trucks in broad daylight and pull out of the area unscathed. After that, intelligence estimates put the remaining Iraqi strength in Ayn Sifni at two platoons. In order to open the road to Mosul, Ayn Sifni would have to be neutralized.[19]

Special Forces Advanced Operating Base 050—composed of ODAS 051, 055, and 056— focused on the liberation of Ayn Sifni. AOB 050 established a program of reconnaissance that concentrated on the areas north and west of the village, and provided, with one exception, good observation of the objective. On the southeast side of the village, low ground pre-

Figure 7.11 Observing Ayn Sifni. *Special Forces personnel observe the village of Ayn Sifni from the high ground north of town.*

vented direct observation by the teams, and they were unable to maneuver to a position to see into the dead space. South of Ayn Sifni, the main southerly road out was under observation all the way to its intersection with the main highway. The groundwork had been laid for an offensive against the village.

On 5 April, word came that the Kurds were advancing along the Green Line and that Ayn Sifni needed to be taken to facilitate the movement on Mosul. The deployment of forces against Ayn Sifni on 6 April required that the Special Forces teams split and link up with the various elements of the supay. ODA 051 commander Captain Monty Dennings* colocated his team with the commander of the 12th Supay and three hundred peshmerga warriors on the east side of the village. Dennings considered the upcoming operation to be the culmination of a mission that had begun more than a month earlier with a tension-filled land infiltration and a stressful, personal security detail. After

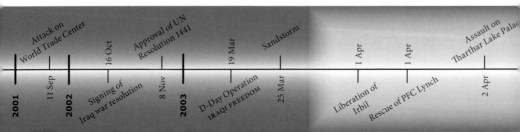

three weeks of intensive training with his Kurdish allies, Dennings was finally in a position to see the fruits of the team's labor.[20]

In the area north of the village, four members of ODA 056, part of ODA 051, and a peshmerga 82mm mortar platoon established an observation post. Further to the west, a peshmerga section of heavy weapons teamed with ODA 055. The two weapons elements would begin firing on Ayn Sifni thirty minutes before the commencement of the ground attack, allowing the eastern element to infiltrate into the village.

Behind the high ground on the west side of town, ODA 056 (minus those on the north side observation post) accompanied three hundred peshmerga as they began moving toward the top of the hill. The significance of the unobservable dead space soon became evident; a fusillade of fire erupted as the force crested the hill.[21]

Figure 7.12 Ayn Sifni street. *The streets of Ayn Sifni reflect the damage sustained as Coalition forces swept through the village during the battle.*

Pinned down on the hill, Carthage and the peshmerga took to the ground to avoid the intense fire. The ODA 056 soldiers on the northern observation post worked to bring in close air support to relieve the pressure on the men pinned down on the hill, while ODA 051 and the three hundred peshmerga of the 12th Supay began to attack Ayn Sifni from the east. Heavy fighting continued for more than four hours as the estimated two platoons of Iraqis turned out to be more than three hundred troops. The original plan for an assault from the east, supported by fires from multiple locations, dissolved into a multi-pronged attack from three separate directions.[22]

On the western side of the hill northeast of town, Sergeant Major Sean Roark* led 150 peshmerga off the hill and into a ravine running toward the low ground on the edge of the village. Roark and his men, aided by close air support from F-14s and F-18s, calmly advanced through the hail of fire to scatter the Iraqi forces pinning the bulk of the troops down on the hill. This action opened up the west side of the village to the assault.[23]

Once the Iraqi position had been reduced, the peshmerga forces swept into the village. The supay commander wanted to halt and plan the next stage of the assault. After considerable discussion, Den-

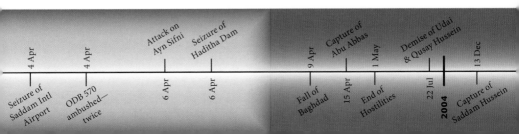

4 Apr
Seizure of Saddam Intl Airport

4 Apr
ODB 570 ambushed twice

Attack on Ayn Sifni
6 Apr

Seizure of Haditha Dam
6 Apr

9 Apr
Fall of Baghdad

Capture of Abu Abbas
15 Apr

1 May
End of Hostilities

Demise of Udai & Qusay Hussein
22 Jul

2004

13 Dec
Capture of Saddam Hussein

nings managed to convince him that the forces needed to sweep to the southern edge of the village, and consolidate their position before stopping to plan further. The assault force soon reached the southern edge of Ayn Sifni and began to consolidate. At this point, the Iraqi forces launched a counterattack.[24]

The Iraqi forces south of the town approached in trucks, dismounted from their vehicles, and began to advance across an open field toward the village. The counterattack force employed 82mm mortars to support its assault. From the protection of the buildings on the edge of village, the peshmerga forces reacted quickly and met the attack with mortar and machine gunfire. The Special Forces troops added their .50 caliber sniper rifle to the fight. After eliminating the leaders, the counterattack failed, and the Iraqi force retreated.[25]

Figure 7.13 Peshmerga. *The rough and ready peshmerga forces proved to be reliable allies for the Coalition.*

In the village itself, the peshmerga conducted a house-to-house search for stay-behinds and abandoned military equipment. Carthage noticed that the Kurds were very selective about which houses they entered. Houses with unlocked doors were not touched during the sweep, while any locked doors were kicked in and the house subjected to an intensive search. When he inquired about the selection procedure, Carthage was told that the Kurdish residents of the village had been told in advance to leave their doors unlocked when the peshmerga entered the village. By default, any locked doors belonged to the occupying Iraqi forces. Carthage noted with interest the ability of the Kurds to pass information in and out of the occupied village without compromising the mission.[26]

The liberation of Ayn Sifni opened the way for the Coalition move on Mosul. In the course of the battle, 33 Iraqis were killed, 54 wounded, and 230 taken prisoner. The only friendly loss was a single peshmerga fighter. The Iraqi weapons captured explained the enemy's ability to bring heavy fire on the attacking troops on the northeast hilltop: five 82mm mortars, one D20 artillery piece, two 37mm and one 57mm air defense artillery weapon, and one 73mm recoilless rifle, in addition to numerous machine guns ranging in caliber from 7.62mm to 23mm. In the end, the Kurds regained control of a traditionally Kurd-

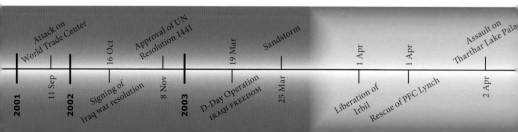

ish village, allowing their reintegration into the Kurdish population. For the soldiers of the 10th SFG, the battle of Ayn Sifni was another example of Special Forces' ability to live, train, and fight with indigenous populations—exactly what Dennings and his teammates had signed up for.[27]

Debecka Crossroads

On 24 March, the 2nd Battalion, 10th SFG (FOB 102), occupied the western half of CJSOTF-North's area of responsibility. Situated along the Green Line, the 2nd Battalion faced four dug-in and well-equipped divisions of the Iraqi 5th Corps. Covering a 200-kilometer front with little more than light antitank weapons, limited close air support, and assistance from their peshmerga allies, FOB 102's dual mission was to defend the north, and to tie down as many Iraqi troops as possible to prevent their return to Baghdad.[28]

The 2nd Battalion accomplished the mission by dividing the front into three company sectors: AOB 050 to the west in Dahuk, AOB 370 in Aqrah, and AOB 040 to the east in Irbil. Within these sectors, the companies observed seven targeted areas of interest covering the main avenues to the south. During an initial defensive phase, which lasted approximately a week, FOB 102 watched the Iraqi positions from its observation posts and called in close air support to degrade the enemy threat.[29]

During the first few days of April 2003, FOB 102 and its peshmerga counterparts took the offensive. While advancing south, they liberated numerous villages and steadily drove the enemy toward the urban centers of Kirkuk and Mosul. In some cases, progress was unopposed and rapid, the enemy having abandoned positions following the devastation wrought by successive air attacks. In others, they encountered a determined enemy who not only fought to hold terrain, but also launched multiple counterattacks to reclaim

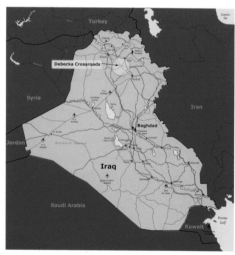

Figure 7.14 Map highlighting the Debecka Crossroads.

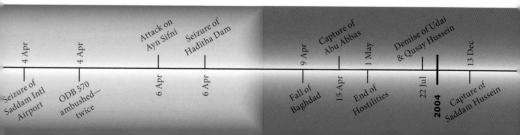

what had been lost. Perhaps the most intense resistance faced by FOB 102 was in Debecka, on 6 April.[30]

The town of Debecka, located forty kilometers south-southwest of Irbil sits to the southeast of a four-way intersection where the northeast–southwest road from Irbil to Al Qayyarah meets the northwest–southeast road from Kirkuk to Mosul. Approximately three kilometers northeast of the main intersection, a bypass road leads off the Irbil–Qayyarah road back into the northwestern section of the town, which sits on the Kirkuk–Mosul road. Still further to the northeast, approximately five kilometers from the crossroads, is Zurqah Ziraw Dagh Ridge. Referred to by Americans as "Dog Ridge," it is over one hundred kilometers long and four hundred meters high, and is bisected by the Irbil–Qayyarah road. On the northeast side of the ridge, twenty kilometers from the crossroads, is a small village named Pir Da'ud, where ODA 044 established an observation post during the initial stages of Operation IRAQI FREEDOM.[31]

According to intelligence reports, Iraqi forces occupied positions along the northern base of Dog Ridge as recently as two days before ODA 044's arrival, when the enemy displaced to the crest of the hill. During the days preceding the attack on Debecka Crossroads, ODA 044 observed Iraqi soldiers manning mortar, heavy machine gun, and antiaircraft artillery positions. Although the team's exposed position was subject to enemy artillery and rocket fire, ODA 044 retaliated by calling in close air support and drove the Iraqis back to the southwestern face of the ridge.[32]

On 5 April, as the threat lessened and the likelihood of a successful assault increased, the local peshmerga commander announced that he was going to attack the ridge and sent engineers to clear the road of mines. Shortly thereafter, the Special Forces soldiers heard the sound of small arms fire and exploding artillery rounds near the ridge. The peshmerga were compelled to abandon their assault, and for the next three hours, the Iraqis shelled several local villages in retaliation. Later that evening, Major Earl Hoffman*, AOB 040's commanding officer, met with General Mustafa, the Kurdistan Democratic Party commander of the Western Military District. They discussed the necessity of seizing the ridge and agreed that a coordinated Coalition attack would commence the next day.[33]

The assault force assembled in Pir Da'ud that night to prepare for the attack. In addition to ODAS 043 and 044, four ODAS from FOB 33

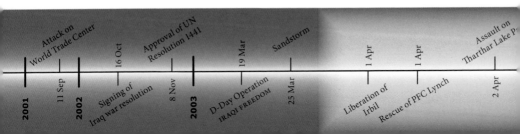

had also arrived to support the attack with gun-mounted Ground Mobility Vehicles. The plan was to soften the ridgeline with close air support that evening, cross the line of departure at sunrise, and launch four simultaneous assaults against the ridgeline. To the southeast, Sergeant First Class Thad Shelton's* half of ODA 044 (044B) and 150 peshmerga would attack the "T" intersection formed by the bypass to Debecka and the Irbil–Qayyarah road north of Debecka—Objective Rock. ODA 391, led by Captain Ed Wood*, and ODA 392,

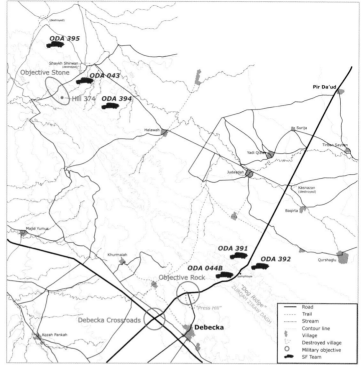

Figure 7.15 Map detailing the Battle of Debecka Crossroads. *The Battle of Debecka Crossroads was a three-pronged assault against Iraqi forces over Zurqah Ziraw Dagh ("Dog") Ridge. Objective Stone was the westernmost objective and required considerable close air support before it could be secured.*

led by Captain Marcus Sommers*, would support the dismounted infantry with heavy machine gunfire. In the center, near Hills 419 and 429, a pair of 250-man peshmerga columns would attack independently. To the northwest, Captain Drake Fowler's* ODA 043 and 150 peshmerga would attack Hill 374—Objective Stone. To the north, ODA 394, led by Captain Justin Spindler*, and ODA 395, led by Captain Ethan Stanwick*, would support the northwest assault by fire. Although aerial reconnaissance suggested that the ridge was lightly defended, prior contact with brigades from the Iraqi 1st Mechanized Infantry Division made the outcome of the attack far from certain. After the meeting, several ODA splits rolled south to watch for enemy activity, but only the sound of friendly close air support missions against the objective disturbed the evening.[34]

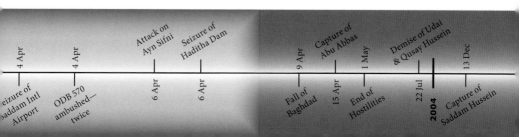

Figure 7.16 Close air support. *Close air support provided by U.S. Air Force and U.S. Navy planes was invaluable to the advance and engagements in the Battle for Debecka Crossroads. Here an Air Force F-15E Strike Eagle provides close air support.*

On 6 April, the Coalition marshaled their forces in the assembly area at 0600 local time. Although they did not cross the line of departure until 0700, an hour later than planned, progress was swift and the assault forces quickly reached their attack positions at the base of the ridge. The two independent peshmerga columns met only limited opposition, and reaching their objective first, swarmed across the central portion of the ridgeline. However, the two flank columns faced much greater resistance and the assault became a battle.[35]

To the northwest, ODAS 394 and 395 waited in their vehicles for the close air support to do its job before moving into their designated support-by-fire positions. When the close air support arrived, only one of four bombs dropped hit the target. The teams then closed to within seventeen hundred meters and began to engage the enemy with MK19 40mm automatic grenade launchers and M2 .50 caliber machine guns. Before long, the Iraqis responded with their own heavy machine guns and mortars. Although the ODAS suppressed the objective for more than thirty minutes, expending approximately half of their ammunition, the peshmerga refused to assault without additional close air support.[36]

Now in contact with the enemy, ODA 043 was able to get support from both U.S. Air Force B-52s and U.S. Navy F-18s. While ODA 043 coordinated the close air support missions, ODAS 394 and 395 used the distraction to disengage and withdraw four kilometers to the rear. Because they continued to receive 120mm mortar fire, they withdrew a second time and used the opportunity to refresh their ammunition supply. The teams then returned to the wadi (streambed) where Fowler and the peshmerga prepared to assault the ridge.

Although ODAS 394 and 395 moved to resume their support-by-fire positions, rough terrain precluded swift vehicular movement and the assault force crested Hill 374 before the teams could bring their guns to bear. The peshmerga quickly disposed of the Iraqi defenders, capturing several prisoners, mortars, and heavy machine guns.[37]

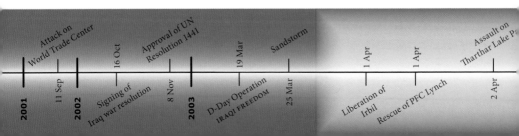

The teams led by Shelton, who served as the ground force commander for the southernmost objective, rolled together to the attack position at Kasnazan. This abandoned village was located midway between Pir Da'ud and a pump house at the base of Dog Ridge. As they continued on, using the road as a control feature, ODA 391 traveled along the northwestern flank, ODA 392 took the southeastern parallel, and ODA 044B and the peshmerga took the middle. The mounted heavy gun teams operated in two vehicle sections, each armed with MK19s and M2 .50 caliber heavy machine guns. Each of the maneuver elements possessed its own forward air controller and, because he expected ODA 044B to meet the stiffest resistance, Hoffman granted it priority of fires.[38]

Although the original plan called for returning to the paved road once they had reached the base of the hill, the Iraqis had blocked the road with a large mound of earth and numerous land mines. After waiting fifteen minutes while the peshmerga attempted to clear the obstacle, the ODAs decided to continue the advance cross-country. The teams forged ahead on goat trails that wound toward the top of the ridge, with ODAs 044 and 392 to the east, and ODA 391 to the west of the road.[39]

Figure 7.17 Objective Rock. *ODAs 391, 392, and 044B accompanied peshmerga soldiers as they advanced over Dog Ridge toward Objective Rock. The peshmerga cleared a minefield and insisted that the Americans follow the road over the ridge. When the attack force encountered a large dirt roadblock just below the ridge that could not be breached quickly, the teams bypassed the obstacle by abandoning the road and crossing the ridge elsewhere.*

The assault force initially met only limited Iraqi resistance, but once it reached the reverse slope on the southeast side of the road, it encountered dug-in troops supported by heavy weapons. During a brief skirmish, Special Forces and peshmerga soldiers captured approximately thirty enemy prisoners, including several officers and two Republican Guardsmen. One Iraqi lieutenant colonel confirmed

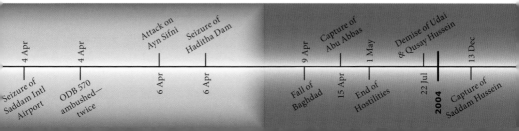

that the aerial bombardments demoralized his soldiers, although not as much as being abandoned by their own armor and artillery units the previous day. In the end, the Iraqis on the ridge welcomed the opportunity to surrender.[40]

After the ridge was secure, the peshmerga force continued toward the crossroads. Unable to overcome the Iraqis independently, the peshmerga requested support from ODA 044B. Although directed to halt at the objective, Shelton realized that Coalition forces were in direct contact. Thick fog impaired his ability to control the battle from Objective Rock. The level ground was essentially indefensible. Blocked by the ridgeline from communicating with Hoffman and the company's B team for further guidance, Shelton decided to press the attack and directed all but a few Special Forces teams to proceed to the crossroads.[41]

Figure 7.18 Javelin antitank missiles. *Special Forces troops firing Javelin antitank missiles destroyed five T-55 tanks in the engagement around the Debecka Crossroads.*

Upon reaching the crossroads, the Special Forces teams quickly gained the upper hand and established control over the area. Split teams from ODA 391 took up positions to the northwest and southeast, to cover the flanks, while another split from ODA 392 overwatched the intersection from three hundred meters to the north. Then, having spotted two enemy mortar tubes between the town and the crossroads, ODA 392 regrouped and moved off in pursuit. Meanwhile, ODA 391 engaged several enemy trucks and nontactical vehicles (identified by the peshmerga) near Debecka with Javelin missiles and heavy machine guns. The teams dominated the fight for approximately forty-five minutes before the battle turned again.[42]

The Special Forces teams found the situation quickly deteriorating. First, ODA 391 spotted a suspicious vehicle parked two kilometers south of the intersection. Special Forces soldiers destroyed another vehicle that attempted to skirt the blocking position and refused to heed warning shots. Then the group began to receive mortar and artillery fire. After the Special Forces element leaders conferred, they spotted another vehicle followed by several troop carriers 400 meters away moving toward them. The Special Forces teams paused to determine the convoy's intent; the lead vehicle was flashing its lights (a

prearranged surrender signal), but the Special Forces soldiers thought they saw muzzle flashes.[43]

Hostile intent became clear when several tanks suddenly materialized on either side of the road behind the vehicle, and another tank and several armored personnel carriers appeared west of their position. The ODAs began to receive direct fire from the tanks and quickly withdrew to an intermediate ridgeline halfway between the crossroads and Objective Rock. Before departing the crossroads, ODAS 391 and 392 each attempted to engage an armored personnel carrier with Javelin antitank missiles, but the weapon trackers took too long to activate and they pulled back without firing.[44]

ODAS 391, 392, and 044B established a hasty linear defense at the intermittent ridge, with the mounted heavy gun teams situated on the eastern and western sides of the road. As they continued to receive tank, mortar, and heavy machine gunfire, at least five Iraqi tanks, four armored personnel carriers, two troop trucks, several command vehicles, and a company of infantry assaulted the intersection. The ODAS quickly returned fire with Javelin missiles and heavy machine guns, forcing the enemy tanks to halt behind an embankment parallel to the south side of the east–west road. Dismounted infantry from the armored personnel carriers took cover in an abandoned hamlet. Their success caused the Special Forces teams to choose to defend the ridge, rather than delay the counterattack.[45]

As the battle continued, Hoffman and the B team from AOB 040 pushed forward to Objective Rock to better control the situation. Also gathering at this location were numerous peshmerga fighters, Kurdish officials, and members of the media. Unfortunately, an incoming F-14 mistook the cluster of Coalition forces at Objective Rock for the enemy at Debecka Crossroads and dropped a 2,000-pound bomb in their midst. The blast killed or wounded ten to fifteen peshmerga, including Kurdistan Democratic Party leader Massoud Barzani's son, and destroyed five vehicles. Ignoring his shrapnel wound, Hoffman stayed at his post.[46]

Wood's half of ODA 391 arrived at the site of the blast within minutes. Sergeant Micah Rasband*, the only Special Forces medic on the scene, took control of the situation and began coordinating the treatment and evacuation of the casualties. Although Wood immediately called the other 391 split for assistance, they were in heavy contact with the enemy and could not disengage. Ten minutes later, after call-

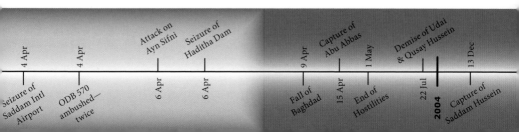

ing several close air support missions against the crossroads, the soldiers at Objective Rock called for all available medics.[47]

As the Iraqis began to hit the intermediate ridge with smoke, the ODAs realized that the enemy had ranged its positions and the teams decided to pull back to the second ridge, which was quickly dubbed "Press Ridge" in reference to the gathering media. The team medics, who until then were firing Javelins, immediately began to assist with the casualty evacuation. Shortly thereafter, Captain Ryan Barge's* split of ODA 044 arrived from Objective Stone, and Major Houston's* B team from AOB 390 arrived with more ammunition.[48]

Reeling from the combined air-ground onslaught, the second Iraqi counterattack faltered badly. Several enemy soldiers actually appeared to be walking north toward the Special Forces troops with their hands clasped behind their heads, presumably to surrender, when an Iraqi sport utility vehicle came up behind them and started shooting the

men. Although the incident took place at maximum effective range, the atrocity committed against fellow soldiers outraged the ODAS, who immediately engaged the apparent Saddam Fedayeen vehicle.[49]

When more Iraqi trucks appeared and began to dismount troops a kilometer south of the crossroads for a third counterattack, the ODAS disrupted that attempt with heavy machine gunfire. Although the teams discussed capturing the crossroads that evening, more close air support was on its way to hit the intersection and they did not want to risk

Figure 7.19 Destroyed Iraqi vehicle.

another errant bomb in the falling darkness. Houston assumed tactical control of the FOB 33 detachments and directed them to establish a defensive perimeter near Objective Rock. ODA 391 set up on a hilltop to the west, ODA 392 bracketed the road with its vehicles, and the recently arrived ODA 374 established a blocking position along the bypass to Debecka.[50]

At the end of the first day, 6 April, Shelton's force had driven the enemy from Zurqah Ziraw Dagh Ridge, repelled three successive armored counterattacks, and broken the critical line of communication at Debecka. The intense battle for the crossroads had itself lasted for two and one-half hours, and when it was over, the small force of

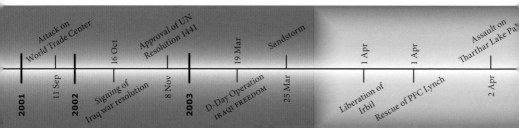

Special Forces and peshmerga fighters had destroyed five T-55 tanks, three armored personnel carriers, eight cargo vehicles, and neutralized ninety enemy troops.[51]

The teams moved closer to the crossroads the next day, and remained on guard against continued counterattacks for another seventy-two hours. Although the Special Forces teams observed Iraqi forces near the intersection and engaged them from their positions, they were not given an opportunity to physically clear the area. Throughout the period, the ODAS received sporadic mortar fire, and in one memorable incident, Sergeant Major Jack Watkins* responded to the fires by eliminating an Iraqi forward observer's position with his own 60mm mortars.[52]

In itself a triumph of courage and determination, the battle for Debecka Crossroads also served a larger strategic purpose. Besides safeguarding the city of Irbil and dealing a significant blow to conventional Iraqi forces, the victory facilitated future Special Forces and peshmerga advances toward Mahkmur and Al Qayyarah. Special Forces once again provided leadership and supported the peshmerga, but it was the combined effort that succeeded.

CAMP LOKI

The hydraulics of the MC-130 whined in protest as it twisted and turned, climbed and dropped through the dark Iraqi sky. Hours earlier in Romania, the troopers of Bravo Forward Support Company, 528th Special Operations Support Battalion, loaded and strapped their equipment to the floor of the aircraft and buckled themselves into the jump seats. The battle for northern Iraq was raging and CJSOTF-North needed a command post closer to the fight. For weeks BFSC worked in Romania safe and secure, far from the battle; now it was about to set down in the middle of "Indian" country to build a base for the 10th Special Forces command group. Its destina-

Figure 7.20 Camp Loki sign. *Once an empty landing strip, Camp Loki became a vital cog in the special operations support to the 10th SFG in its fight along the Green Line.*

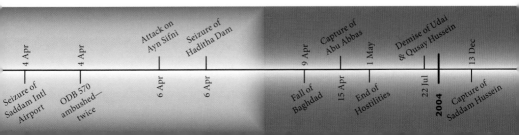

Seizure of Saddam Intl Airport — 4 Apr

ODB 570 ambushed—twice — 4 Apr

Attack on Ayn Sifni — 6 Apr

Seizure of Haditha Dam — 6 Apr

Fall of Baghdad — 9 Apr

Capture of Abu Abbas — 15 Apr

End of Hostilities — 1 May

Demise of Udai & Qusay Hussein — 22 Jul

2004

Capture of Saddam Hussein — 13 Dec

Figure 7.21 Future Camp Loki. *The abandoned Iraqi airstrip in the early stages of the construction of Camp Loki. Every aspect of the camp was built from scratch.*

tion was an abandoned Iraqi airstrip outside the city of Irbil in northern Iraq.[53]

During their preflight briefings, the loadmaster informed the BFSC soldiers that the aircraft would be doing a combat off-load. He explained that the area around the airfield was considered hostile and the combat landing was necessary to minimize the aircraft's time on the ground. Although several of the BFSC soldiers had been in combat in Afghanistan, none had ever done a combat landing in an MC-130. Inside the bucking aircraft jammed with soldiers and equipment, there was not a lot of talking going on; each soldier was lost in thought. Some went through a mental checklist of what they had to do on the ground. Others thought of loved ones back home and remembered more pleasant times. Still others nervously checked their weapons and ammo one last time—again. And some, the more fortunate ones, drifted off to sleep.

When the loadmaster gave the twenty-minute warning, the interior lights were switched from white to red to help the soldiers' eyes to adjust to the dark. Wherever their minds had been before, the soldiers were focused now. There was a flurry of activity as the troopers checked the quick release on the ramp pallet and geared up. To minimize exposure to enemy ground fire, the aircraft would not come to a complete stop, but continue rolling while the pallet slid off the ramp, followed by the soldiers. The loadmaster gave the one-minute warning. The soft red light revealed everyone was ready. The aircraft banked sharply, the hydraulics screamed, and the landing gear thumped as it locked in place. Then, for what felt like hours although it was only a few seconds, the plane seemed suspended in the air while the wheels reached in the dark for the ground. Every trooper silently breathed a sigh of relief as the wheels made contact.

The MC-130 taxied quickly to the end of the flight strip and made a 180-degree turn. As it turned, the loadmaster opened the tailgate and lowered the ramp. The cavernous space where the ramp had been reminded the troopers of a black hole in space. The equipment pallet was released and was sucked into the black hole. With the plane still moving, the loadmaster turned to the section leader and yelled, "Go,

go, go!" The bfsc troopers hurriedly followed the pallet into the darkness and took up security positions on the edge of the runway. Even as the last soldier was leaving the aircraft, the loadmaster was raising the ramp and the pilot was gunning the engines for takeoff. In mere seconds, the mc-130 was airborne and vanished into the darkness.[54]

At the end of March, cjsotf-North deployed forward from Romania to an abandoned Iraqi airfield near Irbil, where it could better direct and support operations. Once the airfield was secure, the bfsc personnel deployed from Romania to establish a more permanent forward operating base. On the night of 30 March, Sergeant Ethan Gibson's* team loaded aboard an mc-130 for a fully blacked-out infiltration into Irbil. "The first priority that night," said Gibson of their actions once they off-loaded from the plane, "was to dig a fighting position and hunker down."[55]

Sergeant Chad Martin's* team flew in the next night along the same route as the infamous "Ugly Baby" infiltration. Of the experience, Martin exclaimed, "It was pretty crazy; the night was pitch black. You couldn't see anything!" When morning came, Martin received perhaps an even bigger surprise; instead of the desert he had expected to see, he discovered the airfield was surrounded by lush green vegetation.[56]

When daylight came, the bfsc and 10th sfg troops secured the base camp location and began to work to establish a forward base for cjsotf-North. That first group of support personnel included engineers and the other specialists needed to provide the headquarters' most basic needs, such as a water sup-

ply. Over the next twelve days, personnel and equipment continued to flow into the base, this time from Bashur Airfield (which could handle c-17s)—a thirteen-hour drive to the forward operating base.

The bfsc personnel worked steadily for twelve days to set up Camp Loki (named by Task Force Viking for the Norse god Loki). In short order, they had facilities and services in place, ranging from air-conditioned tents and a tactical operations center to a laundry room and maintenance operations. The responsibility for feeding the 1,700 troops the base would

Figure 7.22 Construction skills. *The construction of facilities at the camp tested the skills and ingenuity of everyone involved in the establishment of the camp.*

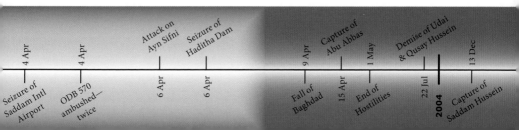

4 Apr
Seizure of Saddam Intl Airport

4 Apr
ODB 570 ambushed twice

Attack on Ayn Sifni
6 Apr

Seizure of Haditha Dam
6 Apr

9 Apr
Fall of Baghdad

Capture of Abu Abbas
15 Apr

1 May
End of Hostilities

Demise of Udai & Qusay Hussein
22 Jul

2004

13 Dec
Capture of Saddam Hussein

eventually support first fell on the BFSC, then local contractors, and back again to the BFSC—certainly a compliment to its cooks. No detail was too small, and the BFSC personnel even installed lights to shine on the American Flag so it could be flown twenty-four hours a day.[57]

While the BFSC personnel excelled at improvising, having the right equipment to do the job was key to their efficiency and success. Two of their smaller vehicles turned out to be their most valuable tools: the John Deere Gator utility vehicle and the Bobcat. The Bobcats were used to clear land, to dig trenches for communication and power cables, to excavate latrines, and even to prepare fighting positions. The Gators were small, but sturdy, all-around utility vehicles used to haul small amounts of any kind of supply; as one soldier put it, "the Gator could be considered a motorized wheelbarrow."[58]

Figure 7.23 528th SOSB's Bobcat. *Troops of the 528th Support Battalion used the Bobcat loader to great advantage in the construction of Camp Loki.*

As part of base operations, the BFSC established supply points for all classes of supply, including ammunition. Using Kurdish contractors, the BFSC built an ammunition supply point approximately three kilometers outside the base camp. Staff Sergeant Mitchell Davis* and his team served all special operations forces in northern Iraq, so the ammunition supply point was quite large. The supply point's outer perimeter was a twenty-foot high, mile-long dirt berm. Inside were six interior berms to separate ammunition by type. The local Kurdish peshmerga provided an outer ring of security for the Americans, and Davis recalled, "the Kurds were extremely hospitable, friendly people" and brought his team hot tea every morning.[59]

Possibly the hardest working and most indispensable soldiers of the BFSC were the truckers. These drivers and their trucks (half of which had been left in Romania) were critical to the movement of supplies from Bashur Airfield, Sulaimaniyah, Irbil, Mosul, and Kirkuk, to the SOF units. The BFSC truck squads moved urgently needed food, water, ammunition, and supplies both day and night over rough and hazardous roads. The platoon also provided convoy escort for local contract vehicles, as well as providing its own convoy security. The truck pla-

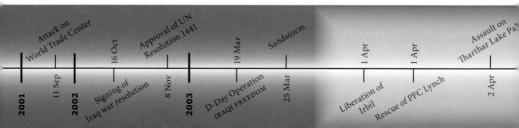

Attack on World Trade Center

11 Sep

2001

2002

Signing of Iraq war resolution

16 Oct

Approval of UN Resolution 1441

8 Nov

2003

D-Day Operation IRAQI FREEDOM

19 Mar

25 Mar

Sandstorm

Liberation of Irbil

1 Apr

Rescue of PFC Lynch

1 Apr

2 Apr

Assault on Tharthar Lake Pa'

toon logged over ten thousand miles without losing a single vehicle or soldier to accident or hostile action.[60]

The impact of the BFSC far exceeded the number of soldiers deployed. Small teams worked largely unseen at critical nodes to ensure that the supplies and equipment needed by SOF operators were delivered on time and in the correct quantities. The normal ratio of support troops to combat soldiers

Figure 7.24 Aerial view of Camp Loki.

is on the order of at least six to one, but the BFSC's ninety deployed soldiers supported approximately three thousand SOF personnel in those first days of the war, a ratio of about one support soldier for every thirty combat soldiers. When asked how the unit was able to accomplish so much with so few, Chief Warrant Officer 3 Fern Roads* replied, "In our shop at Bragg, we have a sign that says 'We are MOS gender-benders,' which means that we cross-train everybody. When you are a small unit you have to pitch in and help wherever you're needed." It was just such an attitude that enabled the men and women of BFSC, 528th Special Operations Support Battalion, to provide the critical support required in northern Iraq.[61]

HIGH-VALUE TARGET HOLDING AREA

In the planning prior to deployment, ODA 041 of A Company, 2nd Battalion, 10th SFG, concentrated on preparing to conduct a classic unconventional warfare mission working with the Kurdish peshmerga. However, when the team landed in Irbil, it received a new mission that tested the team's ingenuity and flexibility. Rather than help ready the peshmerga to attack the Iraqi Army along the Green Line, ODA 041 found itself tasked with establishing the high-value target holding area in Irbil.

ODA 041 experienced some personnel turbulence prior to deployment. It was a depleted team led by Sergeant First Class Malcolm Gaston* that took on the mission of establishing a prisoner-of-war holding area in northern Iraq. By negotiating with the Kurdish leadership, Gaston obtained the use of an abandoned building in downtown Irbil to use as the detention facility. After quickly constructing rudimentary holding cells, ODA 041 opened for business. The team's first and,

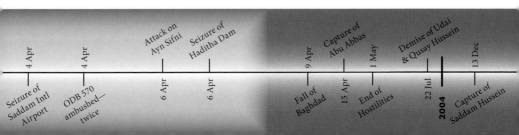

Figure 7.25 Holding facility. *The holding facility constructed by ODA 041 never filled to capacity in the short time the team ran it.*

as it turned out, sole "customer" for the first week was an older Baath Party member who proved to be a minor functionary. "This guy was basically a fifty-two-year-old [sergeant]" Gaston recalled. "He stayed with us for the ten days we ran the facility. We eventually got about five more."[62]

A significant reason for the lack of business at the detention center stemmed from the basic cultural difference between the Americans and the Kurds in how they handled detainees. The Americans followed their standing protocols involving an initial search and interrogation of everyone who came into their custody. The Kurds viewed this treatment as unnecessarily harsh. "The Kurdish way was more like, 'hey, how are you, sit down, have some tea' with no real interrogation or search involved," noted Gaston. It was "more like, we are all brothers, with no real animosity between the Kurds and Iraqis." They hardly turned anyone over to us.[63]

After eleven days of running the facility, for a population of prisoners that reached the half-dozen mark, ODA 041 turned the facility over to the 10th Mountain Division troops in Task Force Viking, and began preparing for more challenging missions. While not the mission it had originally planned for, ODA 041 reacted with typical Special Forces ingenuity and drive, and got the facility up and running. "Our only complaint," said Gaston, "came from our one long-term [prisoner]. He said we fed him too much."[64]

CJSOTF-WEST

ARSOF units in CJSOTF-west continued to secure locations throughout western and central Iraq in support of the CFLCC drive to Baghdad. Tactical Psychological Operations teams supported both conventional and special operations forces. Unstructured unconventional warfare missions in Najaf, Shia Islam's holiest city, were a challenge to the ARSOF teams.

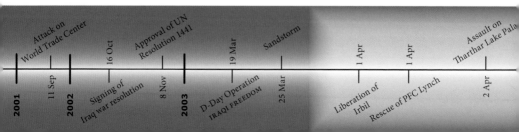

TACTICAL PSYCHOLOGICAL OPERATIONS

On the night of 4 April 2003, two MH-47 Chinook helicopters inserted Tactical PSYOP Team B-961 into H-3 Airfield in western Iraq, where it linked up with Operational Detachment Bravo 520. The small convoy of ODB 520 and TPT B-961 vehicles wound its way through darkened, often hostile, Iraqi villages, to their camp outside Ar Rutba. Sergeant Alan Dover*, TPT B-961 team leader, remembered the tension his team felt that night: "We didn't know what we were going to see, or know what kind of fire [we would encounter]. And if we did, [we didn't know] what we were going to do." Fortunately, the PSYOP team's only engagements in western Iraq were those involving the spoken word.[65]

TPT B-961's first mission was a "tactical deception" to simulate a larger force. Dover and his team set up their loudspeakers northeast of Ar Rutba and broadcast recordings of armored vehicles to create the impression that an armor brigade was approaching the city. Unfortunately, the loudspeakers were located too far away from the population center to be heard, so that mission was abandoned.

On 6 April, the commander of AOB 520, Major Jack Gray*, assembled several ODAs on a ridge outside Ar Rutba as a show of force. Seizing the town was well within AOB 520's capabilities, but the use of direct-fire weapons in the town itself would likely have caused significant harm to noncombatants. Instead, Gray planned to use his company's standoff capabilities and Information Operations to draw the enemy out of the city. As he explained: "So we wouldn't have to root them out in street fighting."[66]

The interpreter from the western Iraqi liaison element used the PSYOP loudspeaker system to taunt the leaders of the Baath Party and members of the fedayeen in Arabic:

> *To the cowards of Saddam—we know that you are cowards, hiding behind the noble women, children, and elders! Surrender yourselves now and leave the city of Ar Rutba to the noble Iraqi people! We will give you three choices. One: leave Ar Rutba now. Two: stop hiding in the homes of the noble Iraqi people, show yourselves and fight us on the battlefield. You say you want to be a martyr. Come out and we will make it easy for you to leave this life! Three: surrender to us and we promise humane treatment and safety.[67]*

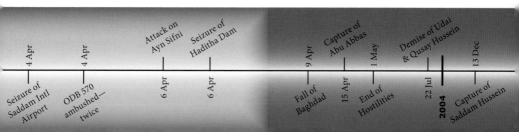

4 Apr | 4 Apr | Attack on Ayn Sifni | Seizure of Haditha Dam | 9 Apr | Capture of Abu Abbas | 1 May | Demise of Udai & Qusay Hussein | 13 Dec

Seizure of Saddam Intl Airport | ODB 570 ambushed—twice | 6 Apr | 6 Apr | Fall of Baghdad | 15 Apr | End of Hostilities | 22 Jul | 2004 | Capture of Saddam Hussein

Dover's team broadcast a second message declaring that the Coalition had no intent to hurt civilians, and played western music between messages. Townspeople came out to listen throughout the day, which gave TPT B-961 the opportunity to give out handbills instructing the civilians not to carry weapons and assuring them that the Coalition intended to rebuild the town. So many people came out to visit the team that it had trouble keeping the civilians away from its vehicles. TPT B-961 repeated the mission the next day on the southern edge of

town, and an estimated 2,500 people visited the team throughout the day. ODA 523 capitalized on the peaceful interaction to mingle with the Iraqi civilians before they returned to the town, building familiarity and good will between the civilians and soldiers. Dover reported that ODA members were "ecstatic" about the success of the mission.[68]

Collecting intelligence, the Special Forces soldiers in Gray's company easily identified hostile positions in Ar Rutba. They then called in highly accurate close air support strikes on the known Baath Party and fedayeen locations. On 9 April, B Company learned that all the hostile enemy forces had abandoned the

Figure 7.26 HMMWV-mounted loudspeaker. *TPT 961 used its HMMWV-mounted loudspeaker to great advantage in its support to AOB 520. The versatility and mobility of the system was a valuable combat multiplier for the AOB.*

city—AOB 520 had effectively used PSYOP as a force multiplier. Gray recalled, "With the surgical strikes and with the PSYOP, we were able to . . . effect a decisive engagement."[69]

Gray moved his company into Ar Rutba on 10 April, arranging for U.S. Air Force fighters to fly low over the city at the same time as a further show of force. Again, AOB 520 used TPT B-961 as a force multiplier. The PSYOP team drove at the head of the convoy, broadcasting a message declaring the soldiers' intent to help the civilians and force out the Baath Party and fedayeen. Gray recalled, "We had the PSYOP vehicle right out in front, keeping the crowd back, letting everyone know what was going on." No doubt to the team's relief, Dover recalled, "Not one round was fired at our convoy on the way in there."[70]

Once the convoy reached the police station, the traditional seat of power, the AOB used the PSYOP loudspeaker to call for all the town leaders to emerge from hiding and work with the Americans.

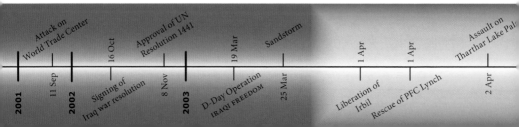

Many officials complied, including the directors of public works and local sheiks. Though the police chief declined to emerge, his father responded to the PSYOP message and came to meet the U.S. soldiers. Gray later stated that the capability of the PSYOP team to broadcast the AOB's intent was key to building rapport with the population. His opinion was, in short, "Those guys are great." Ar Rutba fell with minimal collateral damage and no friendly casualties due to the combined efforts of Special Forces and Psychological Operations.[71]

TASK FORCE SEMINOLE

As SOF units assigned to CJSOTF-west searched the western deserts of Iraq for SCUD launchers, they collected a substantial number of enemy prisoners of war. CJSOTF-west soon realized that the growing burden of processing and caring for enemy prisoners distracted from the critical SCUD hunting mission and other crucial tasks, and the task force lacked the resources to address the growing number of prisoners and their support requirements. As a result, at the request of 5th SFG commander Colonel John Mulholland, CFSOCC established a task force in western Iraq specifically to deal with the prisoners—Task Force Seminole. The new task force, under the command of Florida Army National Guard Special Forces officer Colonel Jerry Vaughn, also inherited the mission to coordinate, plan, and execute emergency humanitarian assistance operations.[72]

Figure 7.27 96th CAB insignia.

Task Force Seminole grew with its mission, eventually consisting of an infantry platoon from the 2nd Battalion, 124th Infantry Regiment, Florida Army National Guard, a platoon of the 463rd Military Police Company from Fort Leonard Wood, Missouri, the majority of the battalion staff of the 96th Civil Affairs Battalion, a command element from Special Operations Command Central (special operations detachment augmentees), a Defense Human Intelligence Service cell from the Defense Intelligence Agency, and a U.S. Air Force Tactical Air Control Party.[73]

While it was fairly easy to establish Task Force Seminole, no unit in either CFSOCC or CJSOTF-west had sufficient assets to support the task force. The task force possessed minimal personnel and equipment, but the 96th CAB brought much to the organization in terms of critical personnel assets: the battalion commander assumed the position of task force deputy commander, the battalion staff judge advocate

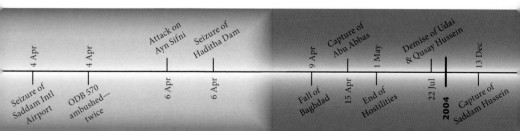

4 Apr — Seizure of Saddam Intl Airport

4 Apr — ODB 570 ambushed— twice

Attack on Ayn Sifni — 6 Apr

Seizure of Haditha Dam — 6 Apr

9 Apr — Fall of Baghdad

Capture of Abu Abbas — 15 Apr

1 May — End of Hostilities

22 Jul — 2004

Demise of Udai & Qusay Hussein

13 Dec — Capture of Saddam Hussein

became the task force Judge Advocate General, the battalion surgeon was the task force surgeon, and the rest of the 96th staff filled the majority of the task force operations and logistics staff positions.[74]

Equipment was scarce, and most of the vehicles, weapons, and medical equipment came from the 96th CAB and the 2nd Battalion, 124th Infantry. The rest of the supplies were procured from Logistics Task Force–West and consisted primarily of host nation rations, blankets, cots, and additional medical equipment. The task force procured much of the lift-support equipment, latrines, and showers locally before moving into Iraq.[75]

While the task force organized and equipped itself, the big question was how and where to insert Task Force Seminole into Joint Special Operations Area–West. Because of the austere organization of the task force, it was seriously limited in its capability to support itself. After reviewing the available options, the decision was made that the task force be colocated with some other unit or organization. Therefore, Task Force Seminole would set up at H-1 Airfield in western Iraq, where other SOF elements were already established. H-1 was also where the majority of the prisoners were being brought. This decision coincided with the Logistics Task Force–West decision to push considerably more medical assets forward into the Joint Special Operations Area, so Task Force Seminole moved into the H-1 compound with a portion of a combat support hospital. Additional support in the form of Civil Affairs teams to support the humanitarian assistance mission soon followed, including Civil Affairs Team–Bravo personnel to round out the task force staff and two Civil Affairs Teams–Alpha. As soon as the task force was established on the airfield, it began its primary mission of enemy prisoner-of-war handling.[76]

Figure 7.28 124th Infantry Regiment insignia.

The task force established the prisoner holding area in an old, bombed-out prison near the H-1 Airfield. The structure had a roof, but no walls, and the camp was essentially a transient holding facility. Task Force Seminole processed as many as sixty-five prisoners at one time, but usually averaged fifteen per day. To no one's surprise, the task force handled more than Iraqis. According to First Lieutenant Michael Aaron* of C Company, 2nd Battalion, 124th Infantry, whose platoon administered the prisoner camp, "terrorists from Hezbollah, Hamas, and Islamic Jihad were in custody at H-1, as well as fighters from Syria and Iran, and arms smugglers from across the region. In

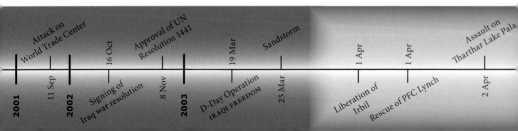

fact, the number of regular Iraqi soldiers processed at the facility was relatively low."[77]

A major feature of the prisoner operation was the capability of the task force to interrogate and evaluate intelligence on-site with the Defense Human Intelligence Service element. This capability permitted selected targeting by SOF elements based on intelligence gathered from prisoners shortly after their capture. Vaughn observed that the blending of human intelligence personnel with the rest of the task force was "a good marriage."[78]

The task force continued enemy prisoner-of-war operations until the end of April when the 3rd Armored Cavalry Regiment began relieving the CJSOTF elements in JSOA-west, and H-1 was abandoned. Task Force Seminole moved to Al Asad Airfield, where it built a new detainee compound and trained the 3rd Army Cavalry Regiment soldiers to conduct proper enemy prisoner-of-war operations. On 2 May, Task Force Seminole was ordered to stand down and all elements redeployed to fulfill other missions.[79]

The combination of assets in Task Force Seminole—military police, infantry, Civil Affairs, and strategic intelligence—provided a distinctive capability to CJSOTF-west. Task Force Seminole served to handle and sustain enemy prisoners, supported the early interrogation of prisoners, and could evaluate the tactical value of collected intelligence on the spot. This capability was undoubtedly a combat multiplier to CJSOTF-west, and provided a foundation upon which future CJSOTFs can plan for prisoner and intelligence exploitation operations.[80]

THE DOUBLE AMBUSH

Major Boyd Sinclair*, Advanced Operating Base 570 commander, made notes and studied the map as the battalion operations officer and the battalion commander briefed him on his upcoming mission. He was in the operations center of the 3rd Battalion, 5th SFG, at Ali As-Salim Air Base, receiving orders to join the 101st Airborne Division near Najaf. This would be the second mission into Iraq for Sinclair and his detachment in less than a week. Five days earlier they had established a critical desert landing strip at Wadi al Khirr, which was used by follow-on ODAs to infiltrate deep into Iraq. Now he would take his team back into Iraq; this time as the Special Operations Com-

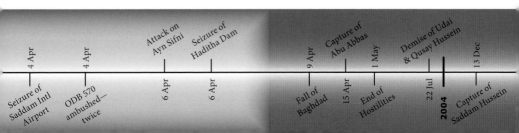

4 Apr — Seizure of Saddam Intl Airport

4 Apr — ODB 570 ambushed—twice

Attack on Ayn Sifni — 6 Apr

Seizure of Haditha Dam — 6 Apr

Fall of Baghdad — 9 Apr

Capture of Abu Abbas

15 Apr — End of Hostilities

1 May

22 Jul — Demise of Udai & Qusay Hussein

2004

13 Dec — Capture of Saddam Hussein

mand and Control Element to plan and coordinate SOF in support of the 101st Airborne Division.[81]

The ground tactical picture that emerged during the initial days of the war had the British grappling with stiff resistance in the critically important port city of Basra, while the American Marines and the Army's 3rd Infantry Division were attacking north on opposite sides of the Euphrates River. Both punched through the first line of Iraqi defenses in the south, and all attention was focused on continuing the attack north to capture Baghdad and crush Saddam Hussein's regime.

Figure 7.29 Date palm plantation. *All of Iraq is not a desert as exemplified by this date palm plantation on the road to Najaf.*

The 101st Airborne Division was following closely behind the advance of the 3rd ID, waiting for the opportunity to use its vast fleet of helicopters to leapfrog ahead and encircle Baghdad from the north. Sinclair's parent unit, 3rd Battalion, 5th SFG, was the SOCCENT reserve for the initial combat phase of the campaign, but as the fight reached Baghdad, the 3rd Battalion prepared to enter the capital to organize and assist Iraqi resistance groups within the city. As the conventional forces tightened the noose on Baghdad, Lieutenant Colonel Timothy Williams, the 3rd Battalion commander, wanted to position as many of his ODAs as he could with the resistance forces to best exploit any opportunities they might have to enter Baghdad. That was the principal reason Sinclair and AOB 570 were going back into Iraq.[82]

On the evening of 28 March, Sinclair and a small advance party loaded their Toyota pickup nonstandard vehicles and other equipment onto Air Force MH-53 helicopters for the flight from Ali As-Salim to the 101st Airborne Division forward command post southwest of Najaf. The rest of the advanced operating base traveled as part of a dusty two-day convoy with the 101st Division Support Command trains from Kuwait to Najaf. Before Sinclair and his team could settle in and begin work, a change in the ground tactical situation in turn caused the mission of the 101st Airborne Division to change. The basic assumption before the war was that the enemy would fold quickly and there would only be limited resistance. That assumption proved false as the attacking American forces neared cities and towns along the

Tigris and Euphrates Rivers. It became clear that the Iraqi strategy was to give up territory in the south, then withdraw the security forces into the cities and towns where they could both control the population and use these urban bases to attack the long U.S. supply lines stretching from the Kuwaiti border. The Central Command counter to this strategy was to have the heavy armored and mechanized units bypass the urban areas on their way north, then use light infantry units like the 101st and 82nd Airborne Divisions to root out Iraqi fighters in the cities and secure the main supply routes. Securing Najaf became the 101st Airborne Division's new mission.[83]

Figure 7.30 AOB 570. *The troops of AOB 570 and one of the Toyota NSVs, modified for use by SOF. The capability of the vehicle would be sorely tested in the move to Baghdad.*

When the 101st mission changed, so did the mission for AOB 570. Special Forces units from the 2nd Battalion, 5th SFG, were already operating in the Najaf area and they would assist the 101st. However, Williams still wanted to get as much of his battalion as close as possible to Baghdad. With that in mind, he directed Sinclair to link up with ODA 572, commanded by Captain Al Pollard*, which was operating just north of Najaf. Pollard's ODA 572 was one of the advance teams flown into Wadi al Khirr on 22 March. Since then, the team had provided valuable reconnaissance and intelligence on enemy forces and terrain in the Karbala Gap. Pollard intended to follow the division as it continued north to Baghdad.[84]

Sinclair and AOB 570 linked up with ODA 572 on 30 March. They spent the next several days assisting where they could and waiting for the 3rd ID to continue its attack north. On 2 April, the 3rd ID unleashed its battalions of M1 Abrams tanks and M2 Bradley Fighting Vehicles through the Karbala Gap, crushing the Medina and Nebuchadnezzar Republican Guard divisions. The momentum of the attack carried the Americans all the way to Saddam International Airport just outside of Baghdad.

Figure 7.31 ODA 572 prepare to move into Wadi al Khirr.

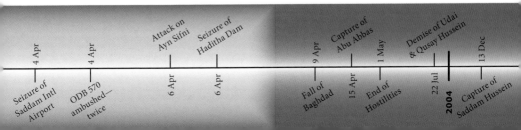

On 3 April, Forward Operating Base 53 of the 3rd Battalion, 5th SFG, learned that the 3rd ID had seized what was now called Baghdad International Airport, and ordered AOB 570 and ODA 572 to move there as quickly as possible to position themselves for a move into Baghdad city. The forward operating base also told the detachment commanders that the 3rd ID units had opened several routes to the airport area. Sinclair and Pollard looked at the open routes on a map and chose what appeared to be the most direct one, across the Euphrates at al-Musayyib and up Highway 9. Sinclair sent ODA 572 ahead to wait at Objective Rams, an area just a few kilometers west of al-Musayyib, while the advanced operating base replenished the supplies on its Light Medium Tactical Vehicle. The LMTV, dubbed "the Mothership" by the soldiers, carried resupply items for the company, including ammunition, rations, water, and five hundred gallons of fuel.[87]

As the sun was fading, Pollard and ODA 572 found an abandoned Iraqi tank training facility at Objective Rams and set up there for the night. While the team waited for the others to arrive, Staff Sergeant Juan Nahuel*, the attached Air Force combat controller, contacted the Air Support Operations Center and began the deconfliction process for the detachment's route to the airport. The purpose of the coordination was to inform the air support controllers that there would be a friendly convoy moving through the area, reducing the chances that the team would be mistaken for the enemy. Nahuel also worked the same process with the Army's artillery fire support coordinators. Well after midnight, Sinclair and the advanced operating base finally joined ODA 572 and grabbed a few hours sleep before the sun signaled the start of another day.[86]

At the first hint of daylight, an impatient Sinclair roused his soldiers. Sergeant First Class Louis Kowalski*, ODA 572's operations and intelligence sergeant, recalled feeling an ominous foreboding as he and the other soldiers prepared for the convoy. Kowalski, whose job was to stay abreast of the enemy situation, had not been able to study the planned route to Baghdad, but remembered that the area on the far side of the river was the home ground of the Republican Guard's Medina Division. The situation did not give Kowalski a "warm and fuzzy" feeling.[87]

In the early morning light, Sinclair put the convoy's nine vehicles and twenty-six soldiers into march order. ODA 572's four Ground Mobility Vehicles would lead, followed by two nonstandard vehicles,

the Civil Affairs team's High-Mobility Multipurpose Wheeled Vehicle and trailer, the Mothership, and a third NSV bringing up the rear. Three of the GMVs sported .50 caliber machine guns and one had an MK19 40mm grenade launcher for heavier firepower. The HMMWV and the LMTV had no external weapons systems, and while the NSVs all had bed-mounted M240B machine guns, there were only enough men to place a gunner on the last vehicle. By 0600 hours, everyone was lined up and ready to go.[88]

As the convoy left the compound, Staff Sergeant Joel Percy*, driving the second GMV, noticed something strange: all the 3rd ID vehicles were taking a different route than the Special Forces convoy. Percy called Kowalski on the radio and asked, "Are you sure this is the right way?" Fresh in his mind was an incident the week before when ODA 572 earned the dubious distinction of being the first Americans to enter Najaf, after it was given an incorrect grid coordinate for a Military Police enemy prisoner-of-war camp.

Figure 7.32 Map check. *Sergeant Major Thad Berino* checks the map on the convoy movement prior to the ambush.*

The ODA had hastily withdrawn as the Iraqis celebrated the arrival of the Americans by mortaring them. In spite of Percy's misgivings and Kowalski's foreboding, the Special Forces convoy continued along its chosen route.[89]

Just outside the tank-training compound where they spent the previous night, Warrant Officer 1 Bill Brande* noticed two of the 3rd ID's M2 Bradleys covering the road the convoy was traveling down. Brande raised his hand and waved as he passed the Bradleys, but got no reaction from the crews—only stares. A little further down the road, Percy yelled back to Sergeant First Class Samuel Lester* and Staff Sergeant Glen Broderick* in the rear seats of his GMV, "I don't see no more friendly forces, do you?" Nobody in the convoy realized that the two Bradleys marked the last friendly position between them and the Euphrates River.[90]

The planned route was not complicated, but something did not seem right as the convoy progressed. It was four kilometers to al-Musayyib and the bridge across the Euphrates River, and then another forty kilometers north up Highway 9 to Baghdad International Airport. Beyond the two Bradleys, the convoy passed through a picturesque

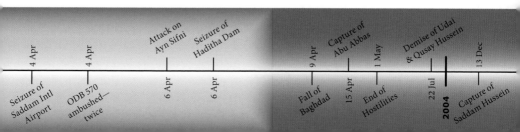

belt of neatly laid-out, lush green date palm plantations. Scattered here and there were several battle-damaged Iraqi military vehicles, evidence of the 3rd ID's presence in the area.[91]

As the convoy progressed it began to get strung out, but the route was supposed to be a cleared, secure route so nobody worried about the tactical laxity. The closer they came to al-Musayyib, the more civilians they encountered along the road. Further to the south, Iraqi civilians had lined the roads waving and were giving the Americans a "thumbs up;" however they seemed nervous and surprised to see the Americans. Another group of civilians, startled by the American vehicles, had scattered, and run back to their houses, prompting Staff Sergeant Garth Madison* in the lead vehicle to announce over the radio, "Yes, there's a new sheriff in town!" Thirty seconds later, Kowalski reported that a white pickup, with several men in the back, suddenly did a "U-turn" in the road and raced away from the convoy toward town.[92]

Kowalski's report got everybody's attention; they knew that Baath Party loyalists were using white pickups to ferry around fedayeen fighters. The hair on the back of Kowalski's tingled: "Something was not right." The closer the convoy came to al-Musayyib, the more white vehicles it saw. The convoy traveled on down the hill where it intersected with the four-lane divided highway that would take it to the bridge across the Euphrates River. As the convoy approached the intersection where it would turn left toward the river, there was a big blue sign that said "Baghdad" to the left. When his driver asked, "Which way?" Kowalski sarcastically replied, "Just follow the big blue sign!" The simple statement had enormous consequences.[93]

The lead vehicle made the left turn into a bad situation. Out of the corner of his eye Kowalski saw a man with an AK-47 standing in the alley to his right. He had just enough time to say "Oh, s——!" before he heard his gunner yell, "Game on!" followed by the bark of the .50 caliber machine gun. Looking to the front, he saw a large number of equally surprised uniformed Iraqis grabbing for their AK-47s and scrambling to find cover. Scores of the fleeing enemy crumpled as the powerful .50 caliber bullets tore into them. Kowalski radioed, "Action left, dismounted troops left!" to alert the rest of the convoy. ODA 572's standing operating procedure for an ambush was to return fire and break contact. But to turn around under fire in the crowded street would be suicide. Kowalski quickly determined the only alternative

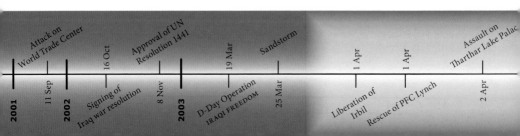

was to go forward, so he yelled at the driver, "Floor it!" The turbo-charged GMV leaped toward the bridge through a hail of gunfire to escape the kill zone with the number two GMV right on its bumper with guns blazing.[94]

Kowalski's contact report and the roar of gunfire ahead brought the situation into sharp focus for the rest of the convoy. Team Sergeant Jacob Vasili*, whose number three GMV was short of the kill zone, returned fire and started maneuvering to break contact. But, when he saw the lead GMVs break for the bridge, he yelled for his driver to follow them. Behind Vasili's vehicle, Brande's GMV with the MK19 grenade launcher held fast to lay down suppressive fire. The weapon jammed after firing only a few rounds.[95]

Driving the Mothership, Sergeant First Class Wilson Wynn* had just reached the intersection when the shooting broke out. Behind him was the Civil Affairs team with its HMMWV and trailer, and Sergeant Major Thad Berino* in an NSV bringing up the rear. Wynn was trying to turn the lumbering Mothership around when Sinclair told him that they were going to blow through the contact. Sinclair had seen the first three GMVs break for the bridge and feared a split in the convoy.[96]

At the rear of the convoy, Berino had driver Sergeant First Class Bruce Kroll* stop the Toyota pickup while he dismounted to provide close-in security and Staff Sergeant John Toller* on the M240B laid down suppressive fire from the back for the vehicles turning in front of them. The Iraqis had recovered from their initial surprise and the volume of fire increased, especially from the left side. An Iraqi in a black uniform emerged from the tall grass along the road with a rocket propelled grenade (RPG) launcher on his shoulder. He approached the road and knelt to fire at the NSVs. Berino fired a quick burst from his M4 carbine that spun the fedayeen around; his next burst put him on the ground for good. After the Iraqi fell by the roadside, Toller continued to hammer away with the machine gun. Berino yelled for him to cease fire, thinking that all the threats were gone, but Toller—standing in the elevated bed of the truck—could see that the grassy area was still full of Iraqis and responded, "Bull s——! I still got targets!" The sergeant major yelled back "Good call, keep shooting!"[97]

Once Wynn finally got the Mothership straightened out, he aimed it down the road toward the bridge and punched the accelerator. The shooting was just a blur as he concentrated on driving.

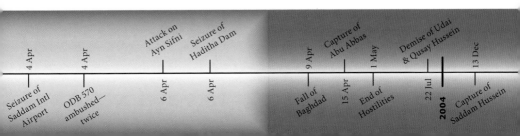

The Civil Affairs HMMWV with its trailer was harder to turn, but the driver managed to turn it around and charged after Wynn. Once the HMMWV and the LMTV had cleared the ambush, the remaining three pickups raced out of the kill zone and over the bridge. Brande's GMV with its troublesome MK19 grenade launcher stayed behind, laying down suppressive fire until the soft-skinned vehicles were clear of the ambush and across the bridge. As the American vehicles were turning around to speed out of the ambush, Brande watched in disbelief as a man on a donkey cart passed right through the middle of the melee, oblivious to the firefight. As one of the vehicles swerved to avoid the cart, he thought to himself, "Don't hit the d—— donkey!"[98]

While Sinclair was getting the AOB turned around and across the bridge, Kowalski's GMV made it across and halted in the median of the four-lane highway after crossing the bridge. He wanted to make a quick assessment of their situation. Kowalski was very familiar with the area from his pre-mission study of the terrain and suspected enemy positions.[99]

At the sound of the first shot, Nahuel furiously tried to call for air support on his radio. He started switching frequencies in an effort to get a response from anybody. Frustrated he finally made a blind emergency call on the Guard Net and got Bipod 05 lead aircraft for a flight of A-10s to answer. (The Guard Net is a common, nonsecure, open frequency used by aviators and others to send emergency messages.) Nahuel explained the situation to the A-10 pilot and let him know that he was talking with a "Tango," a certified air controller. Once he had positive contact established, Nahuel gave the pilot his radio frequency and cleared the Guard Net.[100]

The trail vehicles in Sinclair's convoy took fire from buildings on the right as they crossed the bridge. Across the bridge, Sergeant First Class Lee Forrest's* vehicle passed a gas station surrounded with defensive positions. When Forrest checked his rearview mirror he saw truckloads of black uniformed fedayeen dismount and take up positions in and around the gas station.[101]

Once the entire convoy had reassembled on the highway median, Sinclair radioed a situation report to FOB 53 and asked where the closest friendly unit was located. Nahuel had contact with Bipod 05 who was starting to direct aircraft to the team's location. The highway median proved not to be the best place to stop. The SOF soldiers were able to keep approaching civilian traffic at bay with warning shots,

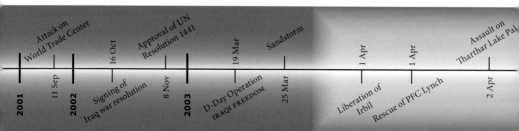

but fedayeen were maneuvering their white cars and vans to surround the beleaguered convoy. The long-shooting, .50 caliber machine guns kept most of the enemy vehicles at a distance, but nearby tall, grassy fields and buildings limited vision and fields of fire. After a quick map reconnaissance, the convoy moved away from the highway into one of the nearby farm fields, where the gunners had better fields of fire and observation.[102]

The first field proved troublesome; scattered groups of grazing sheep, goats, and cattle momentarily lifted their heads to check out the intruders and then indifferently went back to nibbling grass. Once the local herders moved the animals out of harm's way, the convoy "circled the wagons" and the leaders gathered at Sinclair's vehicle for a council of war. Unfortunately, the "wagon train" had circled under a set of high voltage power lines that interfered with its communications gear. "Ain't that the way it always is?" remarked Berino, shaking his head. "When the s——'s on, Murphy's right with you and nothing works." Fortunately, two A-10s arrived overhead and helped direct the convoy to another field clear of the power lines. Everyone felt a lot better about things with the A-10 Thunderbolts looking out for them as they relocated.[103]

Once again the convoy circled and its leaders gathered to review the options. The team established communications with FOB 53 and learned that Blue Force Trackers indicated that the nearest friendly unit was thirty kilometers to the north. With a bird's-eye view of the area, the A-10 pilots reported that to the north there was possibly a battalion of Iraqi tanks, and to the south, large numbers of dismounted troops were moving in and around al-Musayyib. Having been in the field for over half an hour, the Iraqis were once again attempting to box in the isolated Americans.

Figure 7.33 A-10 Thunderbolt. *The A-10 Thunderbolt proved its worth as a close air support aircraft when it assisted the ODA in its run through the city. The deadly suppressive fires from the A-10 wreaked havoc among the enemy.*

Sinclair knew they had to do something soon. Even with the A-10s overhead, the thin-skinned vehicles were no match for tanks. However, Sinclair judged that with close air support, the convoy could handle what it had seen on the way in. He told the men that going back

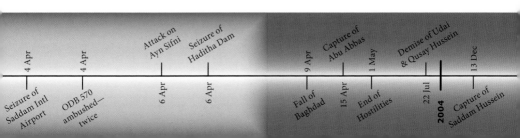

4 Apr — Seizure of Saddam Intl Airport

4 Apr — ODB 570 ambushed—twice

Attack on Ayn Sifni — 6 Apr

Seizure of Haditha Dam — 6 Apr

9 Apr — Fall of Baghdad

Capture of Abu Abbas — 15 Apr

1 May — End of Hostilities

Demise of Udai & Qusay Hussein — 22 Jul

2004

13 Dec — Capture of Saddam Hussein

through the ambush a second time violated most basic tactical rules, but it was the best option available.[104]

Berino and Vasili reorganized the convoy to sandwich the unarmed LMTV and HMMWV between the armed vehicles. ODA 572 would lead with two .50 caliber machine gun–armed GMVs, followed by two NSVs with M240B machine guns. The third NSV and the two remaining GMVs, with the MK19 grenade launcher and a .50 caliber M2 machine gun, would bring up the rear. They also rearranged personnel to man every mounted weapon, and double-checked that everyone was geared up—not that anybody really needed to be told to wear his body armor and Kevlar helmet.[105]

Without wasted effort or panic, the men prepared to enter battle once again. Percy felt good about their chances and reassured his buddies, "We'll be all right with the A-10s; they come in low." When Nahuel asked the sergeant major what their route out would be so he could pass the information to the A-10s, Berino smiled and responded, "Nachos, it's real simple. The exfil route is the infil route."[106]

When the troops completed their preparations, Sinclair gave the order to move out. The tactics were simple; get back on the highway, turn right, and go hard and fast back to the start point. Once again, Kowalski's GMV was out front. Not far from the bridge, a civilian semi-truck pulled out in front of the convoy. Kowalski had no way to tell if the truck was a civilian in the wrong place at the wrong time, or part of a fedayeen plan to block the bridge. He could not afford to guess wrong. Just as he was about to tell his .50 caliber gunner to disable the truck, it turned off the highway.[107]

Figure 7.34 Ambushed GMV. *The rugged GMV of ODA 572 survived many hits during the ambush.*

Approximately two kilometers from the bridge, the convoy approached the bunkered gas station. Suddenly the building lit up with muzzle flashes from every window and door; a fedayeen platoon had occupied the gas station after the Americans had passed. Now the convoy was closed up tight and speeding down the highway at fifty to sixty miles an hour. The SOF soldiers fired broadsides at the gas station as they roared by. Berino thought that the bright flashes he saw in the windows of the building were rockets being fired at the convoy until

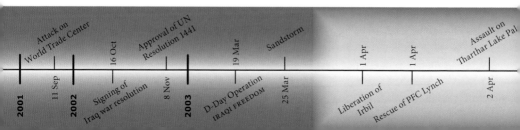

he realized they were exploding grenades being fired by Sergeant First Class Wade Stockard*, the MK19 gunner on the trail GMV. "He was thumping the hell out of it!" admired Berino.[108]

Nahuel, in the second GMV, told the A-10 pilots they were receiving heavy fire from the gas station and requested a west to east run as the last convoy vehicle passed. As Brande passed the gas station, he heard a large weapon fire. Brande thought the Iraqis had fired an antiaircraft gun at them, but the sound was the A-10's 30mm canons firing as they screamed past, 250 feet above the target. The A-10 pilots timed it perfectly, and the masonry building disintegrated. As the A-10s climbed and turned for another pass, the station's gas tanks exploded, making martyrs of the few fedayeen who had survived the Special Forces machine guns and the Thunderbolt's 30mm cannons.[109]

The convoy enjoyed a brief respite from hostile fire after clearing the gas station, but the shooting intensified with a vengeance as it reached the bridge. It only got worse as the convoy drove deeper into al-Musayyib. "When we crossed the bridge and made the right turn back through town," Wynn recalled, "all hell broke loose." The convoy went through a gauntlet of fire reminiscent of a violent war movie scene: RPGs crisscrossed in flashes across from the right and left, there was the distinctive "thump-thump-thump" sound of the Soviet-made DSHK 12.7mm heavy machine guns resonating among the buildings, and the green tracers flashed menacingly close.[112]

Ahead of Wynn's Mothership, Master Sergeant Don Cuomo* blasted away at targets with an M240B machine gun. The vehicles hurtled through the inferno, weaving and turning to avoid obstacles the Iraqis had placed in the road. Suddenly, Wynn saw Cuomo spill out of the truck, clinging to his gun while his legs dangled over the road. Wynn was certain Cuomo had been hit in the hail of bullets; luckily, he had only lost his balance when the truck had turned unexpectedly. Tethered to the gun mount by a safety strap, Cuomo managed to pull himself back into the truck bed. Wynn could not believe his eyes as he watched Cuomo claw his way back into the truck and then, without missing a beat, start shooting again. Later, Cuomo, in his typically self-effacing fashion, attributed his superhuman feat to adrenalin.[113]

Behind the lead GMVs, Forrest tried to concentrate on driving his Toyota pickup truck. He drove with his right hand and used his left hand to shoot his M9 Beretta pistol out the window at targets on his side of the road. Driving was made difficult because the Iraqis had lit-

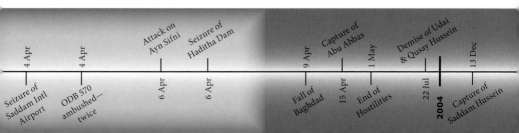

Figure 7.35 Wrecked Iraqi vehicles. *Wrecked Iraqi vehicles such as this were obstacles to the ODA during its frantic dash through the city.*

tered the road with wrecked vehicles, burning tires, cinder blocks, and other debris to slow the convoy. Then, without warning, Kowalski in the lead vehicle started dropping out white Heavy Cloud smoke grenades to provide cover for the convoy. Normally this would have been a good tactic, but on this day there was no wind and the thick smoke from the grenades filled the roadway. The smoke was as much a hindrance as it was an aid as the convoy drivers negotiated the obstacles littering the road.[112]

From his position behind the lead GMVs, Forrest witnessed a masterful and lethal display of marksmanship by the ODA 572 machine gunners. It was suicide for any Iraqi who stepped into the open to fire at the convoy, as the .50 caliber machine gunners literally tore the enemy soldiers apart. Some of the fedayeen sought safety from the deadly fire behind low stucco walls along the road, holding their AK-47s above the wall with one hand and firing wildly. The ODA 572 gunners took them out by punching huge holes right through the walls with their powerful machine guns.[113]

Finally, Kowalski's GMV approached the last turn out of town. As he entered the intersection, Kowalski's driver glanced to his left and saw an Iraqi aiming an AK-47. Somehow as Madison turned the corner, he drew his pistol out and shot the Iraqi.[114]

In the middle of the convoy, the Mothership was a bullet magnet. Larger than the other vehicles and unarmed, it was an appealing target to the Iraqis. Inside the cab, Wynn heard the "plink-plink" of rounds smacking the vehicle and the sound of shattering glass as the windows were shot out. All around him, there was a steady crescendo of explosions from the Iraqi RPGs and the A-10 strafing runs. Riding shotgun for Wynn, Captain Scott Watson fired 40mm rounds from an M79 grenade launcher out the right side window of the truck, and spotted obstacles for Wynn as they raced through the smoke. Wynn kept thinking about the five hundred gallons of fuel in the back of his truck and prayed.[115]

Kroll, Berino, and Toller followed the Mothership and Civil Affairs' HMMWV in another unarmored NSV. Everything the Iraqis aimed at

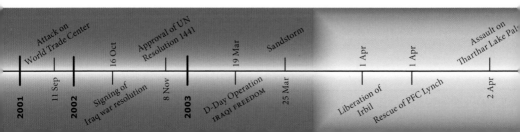

the two larger vehicles that missed them seemed to be hitting their NSV. The air was thick with bullets. Kroll heard them buzzing by the cab of the truck like angry hornets. As a bullet whizzed through the cab and took out the side window, Berino fired at fedayeen with his M4 from the right window. In the truck bed, Toller alternated fire from side-to-side with his M240B machine gun. From one side came a flash and an RPG round skipped across the windshield of the Toyota without exploding. Right after that, Kroll heard a loud explosion and the back of his truck filled with sulfurous-smelling smoke. Both Kroll and Berino thought an RPG had tagged them. An RPG had indeed hit the truck, but as it glanced off without exploding, its trail of flames had ignited an AT-4 antitank rocket stowed in the back of the truck. Fortunately, the AT-4 launched without damaging the truck or seriously injuring Toller. "I thought Toller was dead," said Berino, "but it just knocked him goofy for a while!"[116]

Figure 7.36 LMTV Mothership. *The unwieldy "Mothership" took a number of hits in the dash to safety.*

In the rear of the convoy, Stockard, the MK19 grenade machine gunner on the trail GMV, was having problems with his temperamental weapon. It had jammed during the first contact and then again after the action at the gas station. While it was difficult to clear a malfunctioning MK19 while traveling at high speed and being shot at, Stone managed. By the time they had crossed the bridge, he was back in action, arching 40mm grenades ahead of the convoy to lay down a tunnel of fire for the trail vehicles to pass through. In front of Stone, the .50 caliber machine gun in Vasili's GMV was blasting away when an RPG exploded against a nearby concrete telephone pole. The explosive force lifted the GMV up on two wheels. Brande thought they were going to flip. The two GMVs were so close together that Vasili thought that the RPG which had missed his vehicle had hit Brande's. Vasili's gunner yelled down that he could not see Brande's vehicle. After a long two seconds, the trailing GMV burst through the smoke, causing Vasili to breath a sigh of relief, and a realization that "it would have been ugly if we had to police up wounded."[117]

Up ahead, billowing clouds of smoke obscured the road. As Vasili's and then Brande's GMVs broke through on the other side of the smoke,

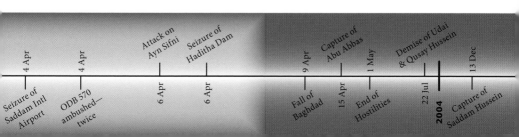

a white van filled with Iraqi troops suddenly appeared on the right. Brande fired at them with his M4 as they were dismounting; two or three soldiers twisted and fell to the ground as the van sped away to safety, leaving men behind.[118]

After clearing the last turn leading out of town, the firing fell off rapidly. Though the convoy had finally cleared the town and were headed back to friendly territory, two trucks filled with die-hard fedayeen continued to give chase and fired erratically at the trail GMVs. The guardian A-10s overhead terminated the pursuit effort abruptly.[119]

As the convoy limped back toward friendly lines, it met ODA 583, which was about to follow the same route to Baghdad. Following close behind ODA 583 was a 3rd ID maintenance convoy headed the same way. A quick "ground truth" intelligence update got them turned around. Sinclair checked his watch and calculated that the whole ordeal had taken less than three hours from start to finish, though it had seemed like days. Miraculously, no one had been hit by hostile fire and no vehicles had been lost. As the convoy passed the two Bradley Fighting Vehicles still sitting in their blocking position, Vasili stopped to ask the crews: "Why in the hell did [you] let this convoy pass two hours ago if the route wasn't clear?" The answer was inadequate.[120]

Figure 7.37 LMTV tire. *The front tire of the LMTV was destroyed in the escape from the ambush.*

When the convoy pulled back into its original staging area and stopped, everyone rejoiced in relief. When the celebrations were over and the soldiers had calmed down, they assessed the damage to their vehicles and discovered that every one of them had been hit multiple times. Wynn's Mothership, now dubbed the War Wagon, had taken the most hits; the front tire—hit twice—was flat, the hydraulic lines for the brakes had been cut, the water pump was hit, and several rounds that had passed through the cab had taken out the ignition wiring and the rear windows. The LMTV was on its "last legs" by the time Wynn drove it into the staging area, but it had gotten home.[121]

Reflecting on how they were able to come through what was essentially a 2,000 meter–long ambush unscathed, the team members

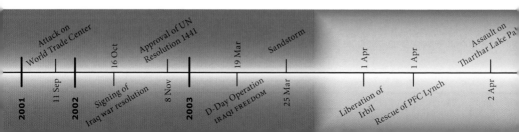

offered different opinions. Sinclair believed that the detachment's speed and heavy firepower surprised the Iraqis and caused their counter fire to be ineffective. Berino credited the A-10s with a tremendous job of support and offered, "The convoy had two angels on that run through town; the one upstairs and the A-10 pilots." He added a twist to Sinclair's speed and shock theory when he added, "I believe those guys thought we were insane for coming back a second time." Wynn thought that it was their aggressive nature that brought them through the ambush: "We knew we had to fight our way out." Then he added that desperation might have also played a part: "We knew what would happen to us if we were captured."[122]

BASRA

As time went on, the relations between AOB 560 and the British 1st Division and 7th Armoured Brigade continued to deteriorate. It became clear to the Special Forces soldiers that the British command had no intention of forcing its way into Basra. The British logic was that as soon as Baghdad fell, the resistance in Basra would collapse. Until then, the British kept Basra surrounded and contented themselves with minor raids and incursions across the bridges, seizing small sections of the city, holding them for a short time just to prove they could, then withdrawing back across the canal. AOB 560's commander, Major Jerry Baxter*, grew increasingly irritated at the British units' lack of aggression, but he and his staff continued to develop targets, interview civilians, question prisoners, go on patrols and raids, and generally help as they could.[123]

The situation came to a head on the night of 2 April 2003, when British tanks received fire from unidentified assailants and reports of an uncoordinated JDAM (Joint Direct Attack Munition) strike came to the British commander's attention. It was alleged that the tank assailants wore civilian clothing, but drove an American HMMWV. The British command suspected that Special Forces soldiers were to blame for both incidents and that Baxter was stonewalling when he denied knowledge of the reports.[124]

Figure 7.38 Entering Basra. *AOB 570 entering the city of Basra. The unit's relationship with its Coalition allies was a test for both parties.*

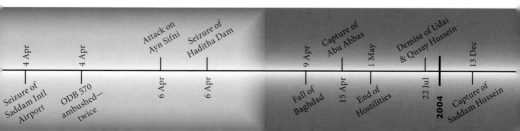

4 Apr — Seizure of Saddam Intl Airport

4 Apr — ODB 570 ambushed twice

Attack on Ayn Sifni — 6 Apr

Seizure of Haditha Dam — 6 Apr

9 Apr — Fall of Baghdad

Capture of Abu Abbas — 15 Apr

1 May — End of Hostilities

Demise of Udai & Qusay Hussein — 22 Jul

2004

13 Dec — Capture of Saddam Hussein

Figure 7.39 Intelligence update. *Members of ODA 544 provide an intelligence update to Major General David Petraeus, commander of the 101st Airborne Division. Accurate, real-time intelligence, often passed across the hood of a vehicle was one of the primary missions for the ODA. ODA 544 briefed Petraeus on potential targets in Najaf.*

For their part, the Special Forces soldiers were quite frustrated by the British stonewalling time-sensitive targeting. Baxter considered this to be a classic example of British timeliness. Shortly before AOB 560 left Basra on Saturday 5 April, the British approved a JDAM strike request twelve hours late. Intelligence indicated that Ali Hassan al-Majid, better known by his nickname "Chemical Ali," would be at his residence in Basra at 1100 hours—the target was not hit until 0100 hours the next morning. Not surprisingly, Chemical Ali was not there.[125]

Between accusations and claims of innocence, relations between the two elements went from strained to impossible. The British placed severe constraints on the American ODAS' movements and operations. The AOB had to provide twelve hours notice for all movements, give detailed briefings of operation plans, and have British liaison officers. Considering that Special Forces teams are designed for mobility and speed, the new parameters effectively stifled AOB 560's operations capability. It was apparent to Baxter that his AOB and ODAS were not welcome in the British sector, so he requested that Forward Operating Base 52 relieve them of their mission around Basra and employ them elsewhere.[126]

Lieutenant Colonel Christopher Conner, commander of the 2nd Battalion, 5th SFG, traveled to AOB 560 to evaluate the situation in person. He found that the teams under AOB 560 were appropriately engaged in their missions: two ODAS were working closely with British battle groups around Basra; ODA 546 had literally flown the wings off an unmanned aerial vehicle used for locating targets, and ODA 565 was conducting the same sort of targeting mission on the north side of Basra. ODA 554 was working to ferret out the remaining Baathists in Az Zubayr, southwest of Basra. While Conner was satisfied that AOB 560 had the correct battle focus and was exercising effective command and control over its assigned ODAS, he discerned that little information was passed to the British 1st Division headquarters from the battle groups with whom the Special Forces teams were working.[127]

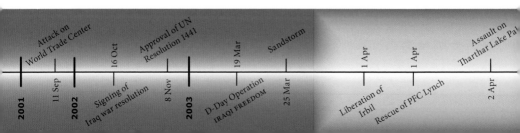

When British SOF transferred from the Western Desert to the control of the 7th Armoured Brigade, Conner observed that the British conventional forces worked better with their own SOF than they had with the Americans. A personal visit with the British brigadier confirmed his opinion that the ODAS could be better used in another area. After conferring with Colonel Mulholland, 5th SFG commander, Conner ordered AOB 560 and its subordinate ODAS withdrawn in order to address an emerging mission to train the Free Iraqi Forces in Central Iraq.[128]

NAJAF

The 101st Airborne Division relieved the 3rd Infantry Division in Najaf on 28 March and began a street-by-street clearing operation to secure the city. ODA 544 remained in Najaf to support operations by locating targets and either calling in air strikes or passing the information to the 101st for ground action. On 3 April, the team finally had the chance to conduct the unconventional warfare it had trained for, but had not carried out in the preceding weeks. ODA 544 made contact with Abdul Munim Abud, a resistance leader with a deep hatred of Saddam Hussein. Locally known as Abu Haydar, the former colonel led the National Unity Coalition, an ill-equipped resistance group of approximately twenty-five followers. This was the connection the team needed.[129]

Mere hours after ODA 544 had made contact with Abud, he and his resistance fighters participated in a worldwide news media event. The Special Forces team learned that a group of 101st Airborne Division combat engineers were rigging a nearby statue of Saddam Hussein for demolition. With so much press in the area, the engineers thought it would look better if an Iraqi actually set off the charges that toppled the statue, so Captain Roy Clinger* asked Abud if he would like the honor of setting off the explosives. Despite Clinger and Chief Warrant Officer 3 Sidney Schwarz's* warning that the publicity of such a dramatic event could place him at risk, Abud chose to

Figure 7.40 Abdul Munim Abud in Najaf. *ODA 544 made contact with former Iraqi colonel Abdul Munim Abud (in black cap), also known as Abu Haydar, in Najaf on 3 April 2003. Abud and his resistance group were invaluable in helping U.S. forces root out important enemy personnel and weapons caches.*

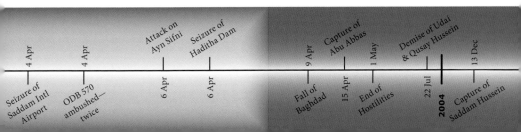

Seizure of Saddam Intl Airport — 4 Apr

ODB 570 ambushed— twice — 4 Apr

Attack on Ayn Sifni — 6 Apr

Seizure of Haditha Dam — 6 Apr

Fall of Baghdad — 9 Apr

Capture of Abu Abbas — 15 Apr

End of Hostilities — 1 May

Demise of Udai & Qusay Hussein — 22 Jul

2004

Capture of Saddam Hussein — 13 Dec

participate. Amid great fanfare, Abud activated the detonator switch and the statue of the dictator he hated so much disappeared in the resulting flash and smoke. News crews with microphones and cameras surrounded the resistance leader, eagerly vying to transmit his words and image to the world. Freed from the lifesaving anonymity required by the violently oppressive atmosphere of Hussein's regime, Abud welcomed the publicity and sought to use it to his advantage as he maneuvered for power in Najaf.[130]

Figure 7.41 Abdul Munim Abud. *Abdul Munim Abud courageously called for an* intifada *(uprising) against Saddam Hussein, clearly allying himself with Coalition forces determined to dismantle Hussein's regime. Abud capitalized on his early alliance with Coalition forces in Najaf to build his following and maneuver himself into positions of power within the city.*

While the men of ODA 544 avoided the press, the media attention energized Abud. Ready to throw caution to the wind, he wanted to clear Najaf's mosques of Baathists and other troublemakers. It seemed to Clinger that most people in Najaf were waiting for the Americans to "take care of the Baathists," who were hiding in mosques to stay beyond the Americans' reach, so he decided to allow Abud and his men to attempt a clearing action.[131]

The ODA escorted Abud and his small band of resistance fighters into the area of Husain Mosque (one of Islam's holiest shrines, the site of the tomb of the martyr Husain—Muhammed's grandson), where he could talk with the crowds. At the first place he stopped, Abud gathered a crowd of about 2,500 people around him as he spoke of the need to rid the mosques and Najaf of the Baathists and other criminals. This first group of Iraqis seemed to be generally in agreement with Abud, and approximately five hundred men joined him as he ventured closer to Husain Mosque. However, even as Abud drew support, more radical or loyalist men circulated in the crowd, inciting violence against Abud and the American soldiers. The nearer Abud and his followers came Husain Mosque, the larger and more menacing the crowds grew. Sergeant First Class Mark Combs*, feigning good humor as he manned his .50 caliber machine gun, could tell that, "The place was full of bad guys. You could see the old regime people moving through the crowd, getting them worked up." In the face of the growing hostility, Abud's newly won supporters melted away and he quickly found himself alone and talking to a decidedly unsympathetic audience. As Schwarz observed, "It was

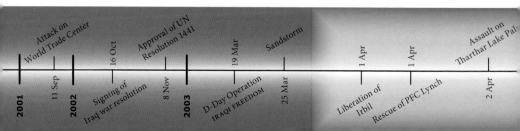

definitely tense." Once it was clear that the crowd was not going to join Abud in his mission, the ODA and Abud withdrew to safer environs.[132]

In the days that followed, ODA 554 armed and equipped Abud's men with captured Iraqi uniforms and weapons. Though less than ideal, the equipment was all that was available and operational. Abud and his growing group of followers provided the team with information on Baath and loyalist hideouts. In the course of a number of successful raids based on intelligence provided by Abud, the team captured several important suspects and secured strategic weapons caches. Abud's honesty and tenacity impressed the ODA to the point that it affectionately nicknamed him and his men "Bulldog and the Regulators." Meanwhile, Abud continued to garner support in Najaf, building a power base for his political aspirations.[133]

In early April, Abud's contacts discovered that an Iraqi general was hiding in Najaf and was planning to escape soon in a red Volvo sedan. Acting on the intelligence, ODA 544 located the house where the general was hiding and, together with Abud and about twenty-five of his men, planned a raid to capture the officer. The plan called for the Special Forces team to establish an outer ring of security around the general's hiding place while Abud and his men initiated the raid. Abud's men would do the initial breach for several reasons, not the

least of which was safety. Abud's men had had little training, and none with the ODA, so the Special Forces soldiers were concerned about fire discipline—the resistance fighters had none. When attacked, the Iraqis tended to fire wildly and were as much a danger to themselves and their allies as their intended targets.[134]

The morning of 6 April, ODA 544 and Abud's group executed the plan—mercifully without gunfire. Abud and his men searched the house and questioned the family members, but found nothing unusual. Once the house was secure, Clinger and Schwarz entered and conducted a second search. When they opened the door to the unlit pantry, they noticed toes sticking out from under a low table—some-

Figure 7.42 Captured Iraqi arms and uniforms. *ODA 544 supplied Abud's followers with captured Iraqi arms and uniforms. Though none of the resistance fighters enjoyed wearing the uniforms of a regime they detested, and the guns were old, the men realized that both served their purpose.*

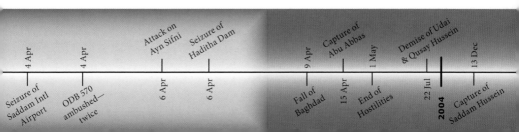

4 Apr — Seizure of Saddam Intl Airport

4 Apr — ODB 570 ambushed twice

Attack on Ayn Sifni — 6 Apr

Seizure of Haditha Dam — 6 Apr

9 Apr — Fall of Baghdad

Capture of Abu Abbas — 15 Apr

1 May — End of Hostilities

Demise of Udai & Qusay Hussein — 22 Jul

13 Dec — 2004 — Capture of Saddam Hussein

Figure 7.43 Cache of Iraqi dinars. ODA 544 usually found more than people in its raids on hide sites in and around Najaf. This photograph shows the AK-47 and large cache of Iraqi dinars seized by the team in late April.

how the 6-foot 4-inch Iraqi had managed to squeeze himself into the incredibly small hiding place. The Special Forces soldiers pulled the general out from under the table, put flex cuffs on him, and took him back to Abud's headquarters for questioning. Under interrogation, the general revealed two other hide sites. Searches of those locations produced a book with potential suicide bombers—complete with identification pictures, addresses, and phone numbers—which were turned over to military intelligence. The ODA also found a large amount of money in the general's house, and various maps, one of which depicted the U.S. airfield at Wadi al Khirr—the same airstrip ODA 544 had used for its infiltration just weeks earlier.[135]

Information gleaned from the general's interrogation led to a raid the next day in Abbas, northeast of Najaf, to capture another general and two senior Baath Party officials. The ODA planned to follow the same technique for this operation as the day before. Abud's men would make the initial breach while the Americans would secure the perimeter and provide fire support if required. Once the Iraqis had secured the building, an ODA search team would go in to do a detailed clearing. With the plan in place, a split team, led by Schwarz and Master Sergeant Scott Ryder*, and Abud's men loaded up on trucks and headed for Abbas on 7 April.[136]

As the raiding party approached the hide site, it spotted one of the targeted Baath Party officials about to get into his car. Seeing the soldiers, he turned and ran back into the house, with Abud hot on his heels. After he was in custody and Abud's men signaled that the house was clear, Schwarz, Ryder, and Sergeant First Class Tim Kreiler* entered the building to conduct a detailed search. The men found documents and a great deal of money, but none of the other individuals they were seeking.[137]

As the Special Forces soldiers and Abud's men emerged from the house with their single captive, they received AK-47 fire from a group of buildings about seventy meters away. The ODA returned fire but as the soldiers scrambled for cover, they realized that Abud's men had carelessly boxed in the GMVs with their own vehicles. Meanwhile,

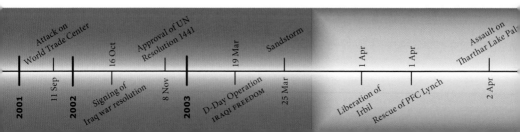

Abud's men reacted by firing in every direction, making the situation all the more dangerous for everybody. "As we saw in the next couple of weeks," commented Schwarz, "every time gunfire started, our 'Gs' [guerrillas] would just shoot in every direction. It makes it a little more chaotic, because they're running and you're worried about getting shot by one of them." After sorting out the wild fire coming from his own allies, Schwarz finally identified muzzle flashes coming from windows across the street and estimated four or five enemy shooters.[138]

Over the cacophony of gunfire, Ryder and the interpreter yelled for everybody to get back, meaning that they should get out of the kill zone. Abud's men interpreted it as a command to run for their lives. When the team members looked around they saw that the Iraqis were gone and had abandoned their vehicles. Under intense fire, Kreiler moved to the last Iraqi truck, jumped in the cab, and backed the truck out of the narrow alley, unblocking the team's GMVs. ODA 544 proceeded to use its vehicle-mounted heavy weapons—.50 caliber and M240B machine guns, MK19 40mm grenade machine gun, and M203 grenade launcher—to break contact, and withdrew in stages.[139]

The team caught up with Abud's men about two kilometers down the road. The split team called for a quick reaction force platoon from the 101st Airborne to accompany them back to the area of the attack. After a short situation report, the ODA, Abud's men, and the quick reaction force returned, only to find the area quiet. Although they found blood trails, they found no bodies and were not fired upon again. In fact, all the expended shell casings had been picked up, removing almost all evidence that the firefight had even taken place.[140]

When Schwarz's split team reunited with the rest of ODA 544 at Police Headquarters (now controlled by Abud, who had approximately two hundred policemen working for him), Abud learned that an enemy group had kidnapped one of his female relatives and was holding her hostage. The girl's hysterical mother begged Abud to save her daughter. In response, Abud organized a rescue party and immediately left to rescue the hostage. ODA 544 volunteered to provide backup and additional security.[141]

After a short drive, the rescue party arrived at the house where the kidnappers were holding the girl, located on a narrow street within a walled and gated compound. Abud, who was not short of courage, strode up to the door, pounded, and in a loud voice demanded the

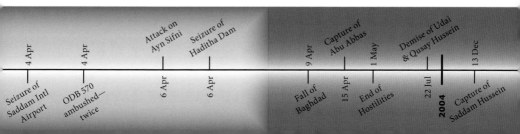

girl's release. The answer came in a hail of bullets through the door. Miraculously, no one was hit. As Clinger described it, "As soon as they started shooting, all hell just broke loose. There were bullets zinging everywhere." In seconds, one of Abud's men fired a rocket-propelled grenade from a distance of about twenty feet. Where the door had stood there was suddenly smoke, flames, and debris. Clinger watched in disbelief as he noticed that not only had the door disappeared, but so had the RPG gunner. When the smoke cleared, the gunner was seen running away as fast as he could.[142]

The battle continued, with bullets flying in all directions. It was a classic gunfight between the men in the building and Abud's forces in the street. Unfortunately, the ODA was in the middle. With the telltale puffs of dust from impacting rounds rising around their feet, windshields being shattered, and chips of stone from walls flying through the air, Schwarz, ever cool and prudent, suggested that they might want to "get the hell out of there" until the shooting died down. Crouching down below the wall, the Americans began to move quickly to the corner. As they headed away Schwarz noticed Clinger stumble, recover, and then continue moving. Once they reached relative safety, the team discovered that Clinger had been hit in the back and leg by bullet fragments. Sergeant First Class Tudor*, the team medic, bandaged the commander's wounds and transported him out of the area when the firefight was over.[143]

Finally suppressing the hostile fire, Abud's men breached the house, rescued the unharmed girl, and dragged out four men. Two had been killed, and two were badly wounded, one of whom died soon after. The Special Forces medic treated the surviving enemy fighter, initially believing that he was one of Abud's men out of uniform. Combs laid him out on the hood of his GMV and started to get a chest tube in, administer morphine, and connect a pulse oximeter to take vital signs. The man had been hit several times in the neck and had a severe chest wound from which Combs drained twelve ounces of dark red blood. Part of the man's left hand had also been blown away.[144]

ODA 544 then faced a situation right out of the Robin Sage Exercise in the Special Forces qualification course: some of the Iraqis were unhappy that the enemy fighter was being treated. Clinger commented:

> *The mayor [Abud] walks up to [Combs] and says 'What are*
> *you doing?' And [Combs] said, 'Well, I'm working on this*

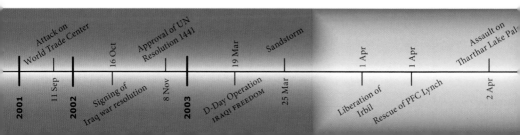

guy.' [Abud says] 'Well, he's the enemy. Why don't you just let him die?' We gave him the standard American answer: 'We don't do that.' I [Clinger] had been shot during the fight, so they were also trying to evacuate me. [Combs] finished patching him up and left him in the care of the locals. The last thing [Combs] said is, 'you guys need to take him to the hospital. I'll be back to check on him, but you take him to the hospital. We thought we would never see this guy again. We thought they were either going to let him die, or they were going to kill him.

To the team's mild surprise, when they did check on the man's status two days later, he was in the hospital. "Sure enough, the guy was still alive. After we left [after the battle], Abud and his lieutenants got together and they decided they didn't want to be known like the last regime, killing prisoners or anything like that."[145]

As is often the case in unconventional warfare, ODA 544 was forced to walk the fine line between working with willing resistance guerrilla fighters to achieve its goals and not encouraging unsavory practices by those same allies of convenience. In the case of Abdul Munim Abud (Abu Haydar), the soldiers of ODA 544 found an enthusiastic ally and a true leader who could help them accomplish their objectives in Najaf. They supported him as well as they could, while also trying to instill in him the higher principles that U.S. forces revere and live by. Abud's short career as a political leader in Najaf illustrated the influence and the power a single Special Forces team can have on such a man.

On 11 April, U.S. forces gathered an ad hoc city council, which selected Abud to be interim police chief and mayor of Najaf, formalizing his position as city leader. ODA 544 continued to work with Abud, to the point of ensuring that he received credit for as many improvements to the city as possible. The appointment was ratified by U.S. leadership in May, in spite of local objections—Abud was not only a Sunni in a city dominated and revered by Shiites, but was widely accused of being a Baathist. When the Marines took over security duties in Najaf, they worked less with Abud than ODA 544 and the 101st had, reducing some of Abud's influence and authority, though not his aspirations for power. Without the constant restraint of a Special Forces team, the real Abud emerged. On 30 June, the Coalition

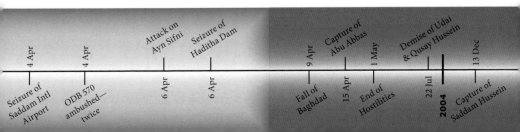

Provisional Authority arrested Abud and sixty-two of his aides on numerous charges of corruption and violence.[146]

OTHER ARSOF

Both the 160th Special Operations Aviation Regiment and the Rangers engaged in a constant sequence of missions during the first nine days of April. In all cases, they supported and complemented each other, as in the rescue of Private First Class Jessica Lynch and while securing the Haditha Dam. The virtually nonstop pace of operations involved dangerous daylight flights for the Night Stalkers and the unusual pairing of Rangers with conventional armored forces. Each mission brought new challenges and dangers, but the ARSOF soldiers persevered and successfully accomplished each objective.

HADITHA DAM

On 1 April, B Company, 3rd Battalion, 75th Ranger Regiment, stormed the Al Qadisiyah (Haditha) Dam complex northwest of Baghdad. Its mission was to prevent Saddam Hussein and his forces from destroying the dam. If the dam were breached, the resulting flood would not only impede the 3rd Infantry Division's advance through the Karbala Gap en route to Baghdad, but also devastate the population and agricultural centers in the floodplain and cut a vital source of national electricity. However, the Rangers proved their effectiveness as a strike force by fighting and winning a fierce weeklong battle to prevent any strategic delay, or humanitarian and environmental disaster.[147]

B Company arrived at H-1, a dusty airfield in west-central Iraq, on 29 March 2003. There, they linked up with the bulk of the 3rd Ranger Battalion, which had parachuted in five days earlier. The new arrivals had little time for reunions, however, as they were almost immediately ordered to move out to a clandestine site to the northeast, and conduct operations with Coalition forces already in the area. The 3rd Battalion's mission was to draw the Iraqi Army's attention way from Objective Lynx—Haditha Dam—so that other special operations forces could cross and secure the facility. At least, that was the plan.[148]

Since B Company had arrived dismounted, the first order of business was to obtain vehicles. B Company drew GMVs from the other

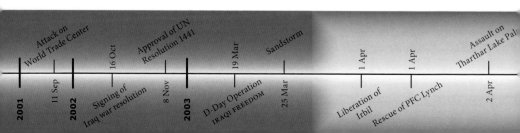

3rd Battalion assets at H-1, with two platoons receiving five GMVs. The company also
received a section of two 120mm heavy mortars and three mechanics from the battalion
headquarters company. Due to a shortage of
vehicles, the 3rd Platoon remained at H-1 as a
security force.[149]

On 30 March, Captain Dirk Dillard* led B
Company and the attached section of 120mm
heavy mortars from H-1 to a remote desert
landing strip—Objective Roadrunner—for
refueling on the way to a remain-over-day
site. Dillard soon figured out that his mission
was expanding by the minute, because at the
desert landing strip his company was supplemented by a third platoon from C Company
and the 3rd Battalion's seven-man Tactical
Operations Center II. Once everybody was
refueled and positioned, the ground assault
convoy of seventeen vehicles and 140 Rangers
drove into the moonless night.[150]

Figure 7.44 Map highlighting Haditha Dam.
*Haditha Dam, one of the largest earthen dams in
the Middle East, was the scene of a weeklong battle.
The primary focus of the fighting took place in the
administrative buildings in the center.*

The company arrived at the remain-over-day site just as the sun
welcomed a new day. While gathering intelligence about enemy loca-
tions and troop strengths, Dillard received a message from Major
Albert Kilburn*, the battalion executive officer; at 1400, B Company
received a digitally transmitted fragmentation order to seize Haditha
Dam and prevent its destruction. Returning to the site, Dillard and
Kilburn assembled the first sergeant and Sergeant First Class Stan
Morgan*, the fire support noncommissioned officer, to develop a plan.
Opening his well-worn Ranger handbook on the hood of his vehicle,
Dillard constructed an operations order in about twenty minutes.
Platoon leaders furiously took notes as Dillard laid out the plan on
his map, and the group surveyed the scant imagery available. Morgan
and Kilburn coordinated close air support and scheduled bombing
targets with the regimental headquarters. The time: 1730 hours.

The Rangers anticipated that the dam would be very well defended,
with at least a platoon on Objective Lynx, and a mechanized company
to the south, near Haditha Village. Dillard outlined the plan: the 2nd
Platoon would lead the main effort, seizing a foothold on the dam and

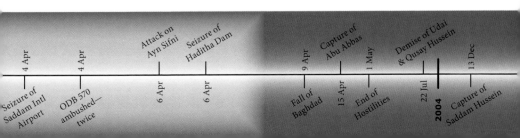

Seizure of
Saddam Intl
Airport
4 Apr

ODB 570
ambushed—
twice
4 Apr

Attack on
Ayn Sifni
6 Apr

Seizure of
Haditha Dam
6 Apr

Fall of
Baghdad
9 Apr

Capture of
Abu Abbas
15 Apr

End of
Hostilities
1 May

Demise of Udai
& Qusay Hussein
22 Jul

2004

Capture of
Saddam Hussein
13 Dec

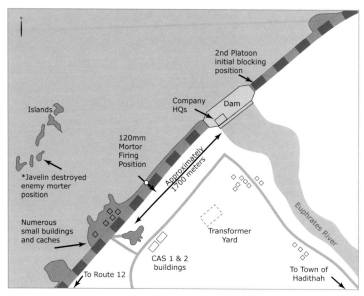

Figure 7.45 Sketch of Haditha Dam.

clearing the inside of the dam complex; the 1st Platoon would be the supporting effort, seizing the dominating high ground to the west of the dam with two to four buildings on it; and in the center, the 3rd Platoon, C Company, would clear Objective Cobalt, an area south of the dam structure comprising power station buildings and a transformer yard. The plan called for quick action, and Dillard projected the operation to last less than twenty-four hours, but prepared to stay on-site for forty-eight.[151]

Believing they only had two hours to prepare, platoon and squad leaders further defined their units' missions and disseminated the plan of the operation to the soldiers. While Rangers scrambled to finalize operational details, a pair of AH-6 Little Bird attack helicopters arrived at the assembly site to provide aerial escort and close air support to the assault force. Dillard briefed his plan to the 160th SOAR pilots, and tweaked the fire support plan.

After several coordination delays, the Rangers ultimately moved out at 2240, two hours later than planned. With First Lieutenant Gary Whittle* on point, the convoy headed northeast into the night, following a route designed to avoid enemy troop concentrations. The terrain grew more treacherous as they neared the dam, with barren desert giving way to scrub-covered hills and dry wadis. Only two kilometers from the objective, the convoy lost its aerial escort when a GMV broke down, delaying progress to the point where the Little Birds had to divert to their support base for fuel. The 1st Platoon's GMV had broken all four bolts from its steering gearbox, normally a catastrophic mechanical failure; but the resourceful mechanic took

one bolt from each of the three other the GMVs and fixed the problem in thirty minutes, all the time working in night vision goggles.[152]

Although the Little Bird pilots had diverted to a concealed forward arming and refueling point for gas, a replacement flight was soon on its way. As the first flight of Little Birds provided aerial reconnaissance to the Rangers traveling toward Haditha, another AH-6 attack team conducted a hot helicopter offload from a C-17 Globemaster at H-1 Airfield. Chief Warrant Officer 4 Mark Willington* quickly departed with his flight of two AH-6 gunships. Racing toward the dam, Willington coordinated by radio a rendezvous en route at the clandestine forward arming and refueling point, approximately twelve kilometers west of the dam. Willington received a quick battle handover that included the map that depicted the Rangers' graphics and the pertinent details of the assault.[153]

The two flights swiftly departed in opposite directions. Once airborne, Chief Warrant Officer 3 George Caper*, seated next to Willington, contacted the Ranger fire support element for a situation report. Morgan recognized the familiar voice on the radio since he had worked closely with Caper on several operations. Morgan relayed the Rangers' current position. The Night Stalker flight quickly closed on the convoy just as it reached the outer perimeter of the dam.[154]

With the flight of Little Birds providing reconnaissance, the Rangers breached the final barrier, a chain-link fence, and raced to reach the dam before daylight broke. Whittle and his driver, Sergeant Thomas Corley*, guided the formation through the narrow breach in the fence and up onto a gravel road, which dropped precipitously thirty feet down on each side. Whittle desperately searched in the dark for the gravel road that would lead them to the dam. Then, as if in a movie, it was there in front of them, he hit it dead on: the gravel road, and the asphalt causeway road was two hundred meters further on. This was the cue to steel for the assault.

The Rangers rapidly closed the distance between vehicles, and headed toward the objective at sixty kilometers per hour. As they approached the six-mile-long dam in the growing moonlight, the Rangers recognized the spillway, the dam crane, and the tall entrance towers on either side of the spillway, under the eerie green light of their night vision goggles. The dam itself was an enormous concrete structure rising more than fifteen stories from the river level up to the roadway on top, and boasted six major spillways. The convoy sepa-

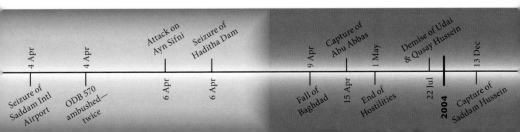

rated as the Ranger platoons followed the assault plan, each focusing on its assigned objective.[155]

OBJECTIVE LYNX

Dividing the 2nd Platoon into two elements, Whittle led one section toward the western administrative tower, and his platoon sergeant, Sergeant First Class Jerry Dunbar*, led the other section eastward across the causeway. The lead Rangers in Dunbar's element dismounted their vehicles near the western entrance of the dam and paused to get their bearings. Spotting two armed Iraqi guards through his night vision goggles, lead vehicle gunner Specialist Walters* aimed his M2 .50 caliber machine gun at them. Holding fire and calling out commands in Arabic, Staff Sergeant James Narrow* and several other Rangers flex cuffed the surprised guards to a handrail alongside the road. As the section moved into blocking positions, they suddenly heard gunfire.[156]

Figure 7.46 Eastern side of the Haditha Dam complex. *The fifteen-story eastern half of the dam complex took two Ranger squads two hours to search. Once the buildings were cleared, the 3rd Platoon used its roof as a temporary camp.*

While Whittle was searching for an entrance to the western administrative buildings, he heard a Ranger shout, "He's got a gun!" Staff Sergeant Smothers* had observed someone dive under a piece of sheet metal, and then spotted the barrel of a weapon. Smothers aimed and registered the first enemy kill of the operation. Soon after that, two other Rangers discovered three armed and dazed guards in an apparently unmanned shack. The ensuing firefight eliminated that threat. Having made enemy contact, the Rangers were on alert and ready for further combat. Surprisingly, nobody exited the eastern side of the dam.[157]

Finally locating a door into the administrative building, Whittle called up two squads to clear the facility and search for emplaced demolitions. Using a Hooligan Tool—a combination axe and crowbar used by emergency rescue personnel—the Rangers pried open the heavy metal door. Whittle soon realized that clearing the administrative building would take at least three hours. The onerous task of working their way down, clearing nine floors of ten offices each, a control room, locked bathrooms, and balconies, rested solely on Whittle's

section of approximately twenty Rangers. In true Ranger fashion, the section methodically cleared the building by kicking down doors, blowing off locks, and placing items with potential intelligence value into the hallways. To complicate matters, as they descended into the dam, they lost radio communication with the commander. To solve the problem, Whittle put his radioman at the top of the stairs and shouted instructions up to him. The Ranger then stepped out into the doorway to relay the message. The Rangers were beginning to flag from the grueling work when they got a real adrenaline boost.[158]

On the sixth floor, the Rangers found twenty-five startled civilian dam workers. Energized by the encounter, the Rangers separated the dam workers into cells, photographed each man, and temporarily restrained them. The senior employee of the group expedited the search for demolitions by guiding a squad to key locations within the facility. After four hours, Whittle radioed Dillard and reported that the building was clear. Leaving a small guard detail for the workers, the rest of the Rangers moved topside and observed that outside the building "all hell had broken loose."[159]

After this initial encounter, Dunbar's element saw little action until after daybreak. As the sun illuminated the surrounding terrain, sniper Staff Sergeant Ronald Jones* spotted Iraqis shooting RPGs from the west side of the river, nine hundred meters away. One man stood in front of an apparent propane tank with an RPG, and the two others were standing behind the tank. Narrow cleared Jones to engage, and in seconds the silent round from Jones' rifle struck the first Iraqi, passed through his body, and hit the propane tank, which exploded and killed the other two men.[160]

Soon after the three Iraqis were eliminated, Dillard directed Dunbar to move his element to secure the eastern side of the dam. A quarter of the way across, a truck came barreling down on the Rangers. Walters fired several hundred .50 caliber rounds into the vehicle, stopping it cold. Five of the armed Iraqi guards died instantly, and another nine piled out of the truck, taking cover behind the concrete railings along the dam. In the course

Figure 7.47 Iraqi guards charge the Rangers. *A single vehicle carrying fourteen Iraqi guards charged a 2nd Platoon squad as it crossed the dam. Several hundred .50 caliber rounds stopped the truck cold, but left nine of its occupants alive to challenge the Rangers in an hour-long firefight.*

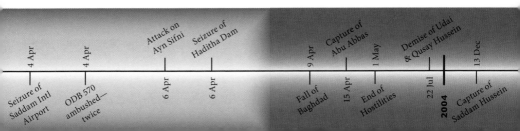

4 Apr

4 Apr

Attack on Ayn Sifni

Seizure of Haditha Dam

9 Apr

Capture of Abu Abbas

1 May

Demise of Udai & Qusay Hussein

13 Dec

Seizure of Saddam Intl Airport

ODB 570 ambushed— twice

6 Apr

6 Apr

Fall of Baghdad

15 Apr

End of Hostilities

22 Jul

2004

Capture of Saddam Hussein

of the ensuing hour-long firefight, the Rangers killed or wounded several guards and forced five to surrender.[161]

During the clash, two of the wounded Iraqis jumped the concrete barrier and tried to escape down the steep embankment. Command Sergeant Major Alan Beech* and Dunbar decided that they could not leave the wounded men to die. Dunbar radioed Dillard, relayed the situation, and requested permission to recover the wounded Iraqis. With permission granted, Beech and Dunbar sprinted under 23mm antiaircraft artillery fire (firing in a direct-fire mode) from the south one hundred meters down the hill. The two Rangers located the guards, rendered first aid, and carried them back up to the top of the dam, while being fired on from the south. Beech and Dunbar earned Silver Star commendations for their bravery.[162]

OBJECTIVE COBALT

When the 2nd Platoon began its assault, the 3rd Platoon, C Company, was focused on seizing Objective Cobalt—an entry control point to the power station, the power station itself, and the transformer yard south of the earthen dam. Unable to access the area from the top of the dam, First Lieutenant Josh Thomas* directed his men to reverse course and head back through the 1st Platoon's blocking position. With the 1st Squad leader Staff Sergeant Justin Regal* in the lead, three vehicles and twenty-seven Rangers maneuvered down the steep embankment toward Objective Cobalt.[163]

In the predawn darkness, the Rangers spotted three armed individuals standing in front of a small building, seemingly just curiously looking around. Based on their recent Afghanistan experience, the Rangers knew that a guy with a weapon did not actually indicate combatant status; everyone carried weapons, both militia and civilians. However, when the Iraqis shot at the lead vehicle and then dove into a bunker, the Rangers knew that these armed individuals were, indeed, enemy combatants. As Thomas was moving forward to the lead vehicle, team leader Staff Sergeant Peter Corrigan* tossed a grenade and yelled, "Frag out!" The fragmentation grenade exploded, illuminating the objective and enough Iraqis to cause the platoon to pull back to regroup.

Thomas quickly adjusted his attack. He directed the 1st Squad to suppress the guards while the 3rd Squad flanked from the left and

entered close to the gatehouse. Platoon sergeant Sergeant First Class Roger Sherry* spotted an Iraqi peeking out from behind the gatehouse, but he was quickly captured. Meanwhile, the Rangers pulling rear security had located a bunker with five armed Iraqis and several RPG launchers. Seemingly resigned to their fate, the men simply sat there and looked at their captors impassively. The

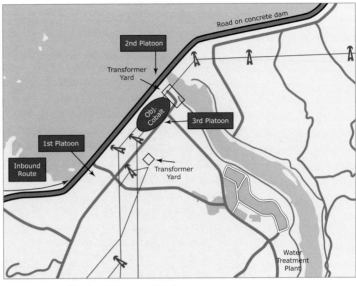

Figure 7.48 Sketch of Objective Cobalt.

Rangers accepted the Iraqi's surrender, but left them in the bunker, disarmed and flex cuffed; the platoon did not have the manpower or time to guard them.[164]

Having penetrated the objective, Thomas called for a vehicle that he had left on top of the dam with the Tactical Operations Center II element. Unfortunately, Specialist James Allen* had made a wrong turn on the way down, and ended up in front of the 1st Platoon's position. Almost immediately, RPG and small arms fire crisscrossed over the hood of the vehicle. One round struck Alan's right foot and then penetrated the truck's oil filter. As the vehicle retreated, leaving a trail of oil behind it, another round hit MK19 gunner Corporal Jon Gale* in his body armor, slamming him backward, but he recovered quickly and returned fire. In the back of the GMV, Corporal Steve Pierce* fired his M240B machine gun at the enemy as Alan floored the gas pedal and drove out of the kill zone on three flat tires. The bullet-riddled and oil-leaking vehicle finally died just short of the 1st Platoon position. The Rangers pushed it the final fifty meters to safety. Amazingly, Alan escaped with only a gunshot wound to his toe, and Gale was unhurt.[165]

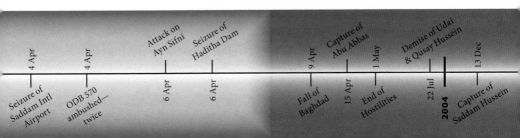

BLOCKING POSITIONS

Last in the movement order, the 1st Platoon established two blocking positions across the road leading to the dam complex. The first
three Iraqis the Rangers encountered in the guard shack were secured
and flex cuffed within thirty seconds. A few minutes later, two Iraqis
appeared out of the brush firing wildly. Five Rangers fired simultaneously at the threat, dispatching it quickly.[166]

The second part of the 1st Platoon's mission began as the platoon
sergeant, Staff Sergeant James Lauder*, led the 3rd Squad to the south
side of the road to clear buildings. Anticipating two to four buildings
as they topped the small hill, Lauder and his men were surprised to
discover twelve more buildings not drawn on their maps. Searching
the additional structures, the Rangers found that the complex was a
training base for Iraqi antiaircraft artillery units in the Haditha area.
The buildings contained sand tables of western Iraq, posters detailing
Iraqi weapon systems, photographs of artillery pieces, and scores of
AK-47s and other weapons stacked in the arms room. It appeared to
Lauder that the Iraqis fled when they heard gunfire, since he found
half-fried eggs on the stove.[167]

Soon mortar fire began hitting around the hilltop, and Lauder
called his platoon leader, First Lieutenant Jared Husky*, for reinforcements. Armed Iraqis were streaming out of Haditha Village toward
prepared positions at the bottom of the hill
and firing at the Rangers. Husky sent the 2nd
Squad to neutralize the threat. The squad
moved two GMVs from the north side of the
road and turned its MK19 grenade launchers
and heavy weapons on the Iraqi attackers.
Lauder called in Little Bird attack helicopters
for additional support. After thirty minutes of
intense fighting, the Night Stalkers destroyed
the mortar positions, and the Rangers broke
the enemy counterattack.[168]

Suddenly mortar fire erupted again, hitting the hilltop. Lauder, Husky, and dozens of
Rangers scanned southward for the source of
the new threat and were surprised when the
1st Squad leader pointed behind them, toward

Figure 7.49 Blocking position at Haditha Dam.
*The 1st Platoon, B Company, 3rd Ranger Battalion
established and maintained a blocking position
south of the dam. While clearing the area, the 1st
Platoon Rangers discovered training materials for
the antiaircraft artillery school.*

a small island in the lake. Unable to spot the mortar, they could see the puff of smoke when it fired. Lauder had Private First Class Jim Rich* fire a Javelin missile at the position. The missile launched, reaching the island in seconds, then exploded right on target, ending the mortar fire. The hit prompted a cheer from the Rangers. Later, A-10 Thunderbolts dropped bombs on the island to ensure the threat was totally eliminated.[169]

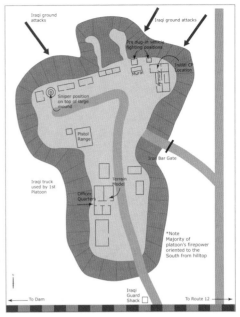

HARD FIGHT WON

With the 1st Platoon still engaged in its firefight, Dillard repositioned his troops and prepared for the next phase of the mission: to prevent the destruction of the dam. Dillard pulled the 3rd Platoon back to the dam and positioned it between the 1st and 2nd Platoons. Knowing that the Night Stalkers had stayed long past the point where they benefited from the protection of darkness, he

Figure 7.50 Sketch of blocking position. *Illustration of blocking position based on 1st Platoon, B Company, 3rd Ranger Battalion's sketch.*

released them with gratitude. By midday of April 1st, Dillard felt that the Rangers effectively controlled the dam. Taking advantage of the bright daylight, he directed his platoons to concentrate on clearing areas skipped during the frenzy of the initial assault. The 2nd Platoon took the time to fortify its positions on the east side of the dam. The 3rd Platoon spent the morning consolidating enemy prisoners and improving its own fighting positions.[170]

For the next five days, receiving almost continuous enemy fire, the 1st Platoon held the hill. Nearly every hour for the first three days, groups of between two and twelve black-uniformed Iraqis sallied from the village, firing in the direction of the Rangers. Mortar and 152mm artillery hit the hill in one-to-four-round salvos. To the immediate south of the 1st Platoon's position were two buildings, soon dubbed CAS1 and CAS2, from which the bulk of the enemy force had rallied and attacked.[171]

In the afternoon, Dillard ordered Thomas to clear the eastern half of the dam complex. Thomas took twenty men from the 3rd Platoon

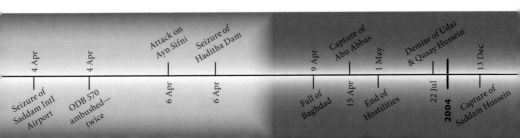

and began the arduous task of clearing nine stories and over one hundred offices. The Rangers followed the same procedure as in the western building: breaking and blowing down doors, and collecting all items of potential intelligence value. Two hours later, the building was clear. Mission complete, Thomas consolidated his platoon atop the dam and hunkered down for the night.[172]

Dawn brought further counterattacks on the dam. As darkness dissipated, the Iraqis attacked both flanks of the dam with squad-sized elements of ten to twelve men. The Rangers quickly repelled the initial assault, but as the morning passed, the volume of indirect fire increased. A combination of mortar and 152mm artillery shells rained down on the concrete surface near the Ranger positions. Fortunately, the Rangers had ample close air support and passed the fire mission to the A-10 Thunderbolt pilots. Throughout the day, the A-10s relentlessly pounded the enemy.

During the second day at the dam, some of the Rangers caught sight of an Iraqi in a kayak paddling in and out between the small islands in the lake. He darted in and out of view and appeared to have binoculars and a radio. An MK19 gunner fired a warning shot, and the kayaker hurriedly paddled out of view behind one of the islands. He reemerged four hours later, paddling furtively toward the shore, intent on escape. After several .50 caliber shots, the kayak was hit, sinking beneath the lake. A Ranger fire team secured the hapless kayaker/forward observer once he reached shore, wet and shaken but not wounded. A search of the man turned up sketches of the Ranger positions.[173]

During that same day, Whittle pushed his squads east, out past the dam buildings. But in the night, the enemy closed to within two hundred meters of the 2nd Platoon's positions, pinning down the Rangers with RPGs. Iraqis hidden in a dead space prevented the Rangers from returning effective fire, so they called in air support. Within minutes, an A-10 rolled in and dropped two 1,000-pound bombs just 300 meters from the 2nd Platoon's location. The bombs obliterated the attackers and shattered every window in the dam complex.

By 3 April, the enemy mortar fire had declined to one round every two hours. Unfortunately, 152mm heavy artillery from the southwest replaced it. While most rounds went into the lake, every platoon had a few shells land within a kilometer of its position. One round hit on the top concrete dam rail only seventy-five meters from Dillard's

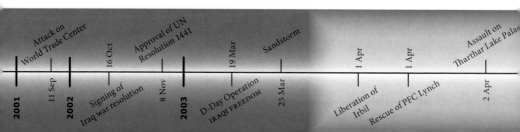

command post; luckily, it did not explode. Not everyone was so lucky. Another artillery round did explode next to the Ranger mortar position.[174]

Closest to the location of the explosion, Lauder—a former Ranger medic—raced to the impact area with medics and his driver, stopping short because the position was an artillery target. The Rangers left their vehicle behind a three-foot concrete wall and ran the final hundred meters on foot. An explosion had put artillery shell fragments into Specialist Jay Fielding's* face, penetrating the right orbital lobe. When Lauder and his team arrived, Fielding had stopped breathing and his face was turning blue. The medics removed Fielding's blood-covered helmet and suctioned his airway, hoping to avoid a tracheotomy. Fielding did, indeed, resume breathing on his own, and the color returned to his face, giving everybody new hope for his survival. In the midst of incoming artillery fire, the medics bandaged Fielding's face, checked him all over for other injuries, and then carried him to the truck. Lauder and his team loaded him in their truck and raced to the center of the dam. There Fielding was safe until medical evacuation arrived.[175]

The H-1 operations center reacted quickly to news of casualties on the dam, scrambling the 160th SOAR crews from their beds. In less than forty minutes, a flight of three helicopters departed H-1 for the dam: an MH-47E Chinook with a surgical team aboard and two MH-60L Defensive Armed Penetrators. Flying in broad daylight, the flight arrived at the dam less than an hour after Fielding went down. The Chinook evacuated Fielding during a break in the artillery fire. Doctors began working on him as soon as he was aboard. At H-1, medical personnel transferred Fielding to a forward surgical team for emergency care. Fielding received a Purple Heart for his injuries and a Bronze Star for valor.[176]

The artillery attack seemed to be a turning point in the battle for Haditha Dam. Over the course of the next few days, mortar and artillery fire steadily decreased. Tanks from C Company, 2nd Battalion, 70th Armor Regiment, arrived on 6 April, and local clerics intervened with enemy forces. The combination of heavy armor and political support ensured Ranger control of the dam and surrounding area. They secured the CAS1 and CAS2 buildings to the south and cleared out the cache of munitions. With all enemy combatants under either Coalition control or having fled, by the end of the week the Rangers turned

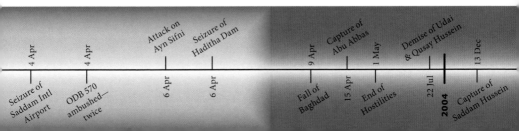

Figure 7.51 Happy Motoring sign. *B Company, 3rd Battalion, 75th Ranger Regiment, secured Haditha Dam after a weeklong battle with Iraqi guards. The Rangers' triumph guaranteed that the dam would not be destroyed and release a flood onto the plains to the southeast, and assured friendly forces and local inhabitants a safe place to cross the Euphrates River.*

their attention to help the newly arrived Civil Affairs team charged with rehabilitating the dam.[177]

The Rangers' seizure of Haditha Dam was crucial in the early stages of Operation IRAQI FREEDOM. It prevented a potential humanitarian and environmental disaster along the Euphrates River, and mitigated the risk to Coalition forces rapidly advancing toward Baghdad. The dam's capture also prevented any further use of the facility as a river crossing site by foreign terrorists, while ensuring its availability to Coalition forces. The Rangers demonstrated the value a flexible, cohesive, and highly-trained assault force can bring to the modern battlefield.

SOAR over Haditha

The aviators of B Company, 1st Battalion, 160th Special Operations Aviation Regiment, had established a reputation for being able to deliver close air support in even the most challenging conditions. The Night Stalkers lived up to and exceeded all expectations while supporting the 75th Ranger Regiment's assault on Haditha Dam the morning of 1 April. Using well-established operating procedures, the SOAR attack pilots demonstrated their value and flexibility on the battlefield.

Chief Warrant Officer 4 Doug Carter* and his team of two AH-6 Little Bird attack helicopters were marking time at a dusty airfield in west-central Iraq when they received word of the mission. Having arrived at H-1 five days earlier on an ostensibly overnight mission, the team looked and felt scruffy. Carter and the rest of the team were awaiting their replacements when they received the mission to support the Rangers' occupation of Haditha Dam. Only knowing part of the Rangers' attack plan, the SOAR crews loaded their helicopters with munitions appropriate for ground support and took off.[178]

Carter's team arrived at the Rangers' assembly site on the afternoon of 31 March. Captain Dirk Dillard* greeted Carter and briefed him on the Rangers' tactical plan. The two commanders had known

each other for years, and worked together during training exercises and deployments. Together, they devised a fire support plan based on their collective experiences and standing operating procedures. With the Rangers' graphic control measures—route, checkpoints, phase lines, and assault positions—annotated on a map, Carter went back to the landing site to brief his air team.

Fully expecting to execute the plan he had developed with Dillard, Carter was dismayed when events orchestrated a change. After several delays, the Rangers ultimately launched at 2240 hours, two hours later than planned. Darkness soon enveloped the Ranger formation, and the terrain slowed the ground advance. The attack was further delayed when the steering gearbox failed on one of the Ground Mobility Vehicles. Resourceful mechanics had the gearbox repaired within thirty minutes, but the delay forced the Little Bird pilots to divert to a concealed forward arming and refueling point for gas.

As Carter's AH-6 team provided aerial reconnaissance to the Rangers traveling toward Haditha, another AH-6 attack team arrived at H-1 Airfield. Having conducted a hot off-load of AH-6s from a C-17 Globemaster (meaning that the helicopters and pilots were headed directly into combat), Chief Warrant Officer 4 Mark Willington* and his flight of two AH-6 gunships quickly departed from H-1. Racing toward the dam, Willington contacted Carter with his satellite communication radio and coordinated a rendezvous en route. The team met at a clandestine forward arming and refueling point, approximately twelve kilometers west of the dam. Carter hastily conducted a battle handover to Willington, handing him the map with the Rangers' graphics, and providing him with the pertinent details of the assault.[179]

After the handover was completed, each flight quickly lifted off in opposite directions. Chief Warrant Officer 3 George Caper* contacted the Ranger Fire Support noncommissioned officer, Sergeant First Class Stan Morgan*, for a situational report. Morgan relayed the Rangers' current position, and within minutes, the Night Stalker flight closed on the convoy as it reached the outer perimeter of the dam.[180]

From the SOAR pilots' perspective, the Rangers seemed to be taking the dam without resistance. The Night Stalkers flew south and reconnoitered the surrounding area as enemy forces fired sporadically at the nearly invisible helicopters. Chief Warrant Officer 3 Dave Setter*, in the trail Little Bird, spotted a vehicle rapidly approaching

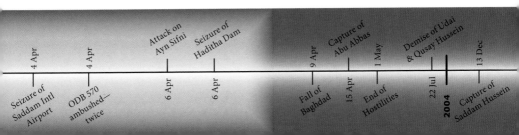

from the south with its lights shining. He relayed the information to Willington in the lead aircraft, and Willington swung his flight around for a closer look. Unsure of the intent of the occupants, the pilots waited until the combatants exited their vehicle with RPGs and rifles. In response to this obvious display of hostile intent, Willington launched a salvo of .50 caliber bullets into the party. Setter followed immediately with another barrage, eliminating the threat.[181]

On the return flight north to the dam, the SOAR pilots noticed an equally deadly enemy: a massive spider web of wires and power poles emanating from the dam. As dangerous as any enemy fire, the nearly invisible high-tension wires could easily snare and destroy a helicopter. The wires were a constant reminder to maintain gun run discipline, to check altitude, and not to fixate on a target.

As the Iraqis moved through the bottomland up the west side of the river, fifteen- to twenty-foot dunes covered their movement. The enemy moved into the defilade and shot at the Rangers, but the Rangers could not see the Iraqis to return fire accurately. However, the Little Bird pilots could easily survey the area, and killed several fighters with 7.62mm minigun rounds and 2.75 inch rockets. After six fire missions, Caper notified Morgan that they needed to return to H-1 for fuel. As the flight departed the area, the pilots listened to the reports of increased enemy activity. During the nineteen-minute flight to the airfield at H-1, mortar attacks from the south intensified.[182]

While refueling, Caper tuned the radio to monitor the Ranger command net and heard an agitated, familiar voice. Morgan was contacting the Ranger tactical operations center and requesting the status of the Little Birds. Caper could tell by the tone of his voice that something was wrong. As the Night Stalkers repositioned for departure, Morgan called the center again, requesting the time inbound for the Little Birds. Caper alerted Willington, who selected the radio on his communication console, and the flight departed. Willington radioed Morgan when the flight was six minutes away. Gunfire echoed during the radio transmission.[183]

Approximately a mile away from the objective, the Night Stalkers saw gunfire crisscrossing the western side of the dam. The 1st Platoon was fiercely engaged with the same enemy fighters that the aviators had seen maneuvering through the rolling dunes along the Rangers' western flank. The pilots saw tracers and flashes from the Rangers' heavy weapons: MK19 40mm grenade machine guns and M2 .50 caliber

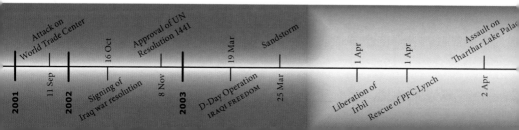

machine guns. As Caper looked southward, two mortar tubes flashed 200 meters away. He radioed Morgan and gave a situation report. Morgan passed him over to the Ranger controlling fires in the 1st Platoon's sector.[184]

Suddenly, two more flashes were spotted in the same location, as well as a massing enemy force. Willington contacted the forward observer and requested clearance to shoot. The forward observer began a full call-for-fire request, which is thoroughly drilled into even the greenest Rangers. Radio chatter filled the communication channels, forcing both Caper and Willington to broadcast on all radio nets that they "had the Rangers' positions and needed clearance to shoot." Finally, Morgan

Figure 7.52 Power lines at Haditha Dam. *The multilevel Haditha Dam complex houses six large generators and six turbines, which provide electricity to the surrounding region. Only one was fully operational when the Rangers seized the objective.*

yelled into the radio, "D—— it, cleared hot! CLEARED HOT! CLEARED HOT!" The Little Bird pilots got the message.[185]

The Night Stalkers separated laterally from the Rangers and quickly rolled in on the first mortar position, delivering .50 caliber rounds and rockets into the mortar position. As Setter's gunship discharged its rockets, the pilots in each helicopter saw muzzle flashes everywhere they looked. "Quite a sight to behold," commented Caper, "I've never seen so many muzzle flashes in my life." Five Iraqis ran into a nearby building, so the Little Birds came around for a second run and leveled the building. As the dust rose from the attack, the adept pilots divided their attention between their human and environmental adversaries, ever cognizant of the wire-ridden death trap above the mortar positions. At the second mortar position, an adjacent natural gas main erupted from the rocket effects, and burned for nearly a week afterward. At night it could be seen from seventy miles away and served as a beacon for incoming flights.[186]

A sizeable enemy force began to attack the Rangers from the south. Caper identified an element maneuvering along the shoreline. Within minutes, the pair of attack helicopters fired on at least two platoons of dismounted troops. As one pilot flew each helicopter, the other pilots got into the fight by leaning out the side door and engaging militia forces with their personal M4 rifles. The smell of cordite filled the air.

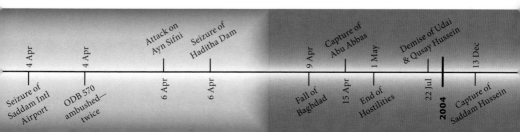

4 Apr — Seizure of Saddam Intl Airport

4 Apr — ODB 570 ambushed— twice

Attack on Ayn Sifni — 6 Apr

Seizure of Haditha Dam — 6 Apr

9 Apr — Fall of Baghdad

Capture of Abu Abbas — 15 Apr

1 May — End of Hostilities

Demise of Udai & Qusay Hussein — 22 Jul

2004

13 Dec — Capture of Saddam Hussein

As the Night Stalkers flew low during their attack runs, they could hear the bolt actions of the enemy's AK-47s.

The enemy force was finally suppressed just as dawn broke. With daylight comes increased probability of small arms fire hitting a helicopter, so Dillard soon ordered the Little Birds to leave. As the flight departed, Morgan radioed the AH-6 pilots, and with appreciation evident in his voice, declared, "The beer's on us!"[187]

The 160th SOAR pilots supported the Rangers with the ferocity that the ground fighters had come to expect. The expertise garnered through joint exercises and proven procedures enabled one team of Night Stalkers to flawlessly complete the mission begun by another team. When the battle intensified, the Night Stalkers were there to deliver the precise close air support that the Rangers needed, staying on station even as the morning sun stripped away the protection afforded by the night. Years of bilateral training forged a mutual respect between these elite units, and produced a generous return on investment with the successful seizure of Haditha Dam.

CIVIL AFFAIRS AT HADITHA

On 2 April, Brigadier General Vincent Brooks, CENTCOM spokesman, announced that special operations forces had seized Haditha Dam, "a very important dam that could potentially flood the Euphrates River leading down toward Baghdad, and particularly in the area of Karbala." That short statement belied the significance of the dam, and barely hinted at the problems encountered within the structure itself. Though the operation that led to the dam's capture was dramatic, the struggle to keep the dam operational was just as intense and at least as dangerous.[188]

In the early morning hours of 1 April, elements of the 3rd Battalion, 75th Ranger Regiment, assaulted and captured Al Qadisiyah (Haditha) Dam. Measuring eight kilometers at its widest point, Haditha Dam is the one of the largest such earthen structures in the Middle East. The resulting Qadisiyah Reservoir has a capacity of 8.2 billion cubic meters, about two-thirds the volume of water of Lake Roosevelt behind the Grand Cooley Dam, and is a critical source of water for irrigation and electrical power in western Iraq. By capturing the dam, Coalition forces ensured that Iraqi forces could neither use the facility as a stronghold nor destroy it and flood the valley. Seizing

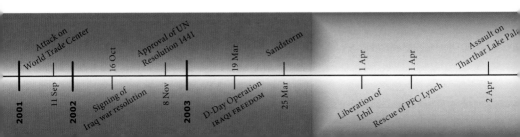

the Haditha complex also protected the water supply and ability to provide electricity, both of which became critical resources during the approaching summer months.[189]

While Rangers excel at capturing objectives, the assault force was not well suited to actually operating the dam. The Rangers quickly called for assistance from E Company, 96th Civil Affairs Battalion, which had been attached to the regiment for just such an eventuality. Regimental commander Colonel Joseph Votel ordered Sergeant First Class Karl Compton*, a member of Civil Affairs Team–Alpha 52, to deploy to the dam on 2 April. Compton had twelve years of Special Forces experience as an engineer, and was better qualified to emplace demolitions on a dam than to manage one, but his three months work on a dam in Virginia following his high school graduation made him the most qualified person available. Compton's mission was to con- duct a rapid assessment of the dam structure, take photographs of parts in need of repair, and return to base at H-1 within twenty-four hours.[190]

Figure 7.53 96th CAB insignia.

Intense Iraqi artillery barrages targeting the Rangers on the dam delayed Compton's mission for two days. On 4 April, Compton finally found a seat on an MH-47 Chinook loaded to capacity with personnel and supplies. The helicopter arrived at the dam late that evening, dur- ing a break in the mortar and artillery attacks. Compton wasted no time in starting his assessment, and immediately began making his way through the honeycomb-like levels of the dam, identifying sig- nificant electrical and structural problems within the facility. In the course of his assessment, Compton discovered that the dam's situa- tion was more critical than he had originally been told. A transformer had been hit by enemy mortar or artillery fire, causing it to backfeed into the dam and shut down power. By the morning of the fifth, only one of the six generators had been repaired, and five of the six turbines were down for maintenance or lack of spare parts. It was obvious that the dam had been operating at less than 50 percent efficiency for some time.[191]

Figure 7.54 75th Ranger Regiment scroll shoulder patch.

When Compton conducted his first meeting with the Iraqi dam manager to get his appraisal of the condition of the facility and the status of the dam workers, Compton found that the manager was reluctant to share information:

> *Keep in mind, the manager and all the dam workers had been held in a secure section of the dam for nearly one week.*

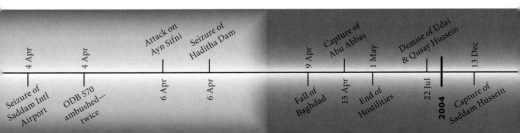

4 Apr   4 Apr   Attack on Ayn Sifni   Seizure of Haditha Dam   9 Apr   Capture of Abu Abbas   1 May   Demise of Udai & Qusay Hussein   13 Dec

Seizure of Saddam Intl Airport   ODB 570 ambushed— twice   6 Apr   6 Apr   Fall of Baghdad   15 Apr   End of Hostilities   22 Jul   2004   Capture of Saddam Hussein

The dam workers—at that time approximately twenty-five personnel broken into two shifts—were escorted by guards whenever they moved about the complex and were then returned to one of the two worker rooms where they were kept.[192]

Following his initial discussions with the dam manager and his assistant, Compton determined his top priorities were to organize the dam employees in order to ensure the continuous operation of the facility and to repair critically damaged components. Though Compton was scheduled to return to H-1 the next day, the Ranger company commander on-site informed him that no aircraft were scheduled to arrive in the next twenty-four hours. Stranded at the dam, Compton used the time to develop a more detailed appraisal of the problems found throughout the dam facility, including those involving the dam personnel.

In the course of working with the dam manager and his deputy, Compton concluded that many of the dam workers believed that the U.S. forces would destroy the dam, not preserve it. Compton worked to improve his relationship with the manager and to help him understand that they were there to help repair the hydroelectric facility and return it to normal operations. Compton also permitted the dam manager and eight higher-level workers to listen to the radio on a regular basis. "This worked in our favor in getting the dam workers to completely understand the Americans were in charge." Through the radio broadcasts, the employees learned that U.S. forces had captured Baghdad, and began to believe that the Coalition forces were there to stay. As word spread beyond the facility, most enemy soldiers in the town of Haditha and the surrounding villages put aside their weapons, removed their uniforms, and departed the area. With their departure came increased cooperation from the civilians who remained behind.[193]

Figure 7.55 Haditha Dam manager.

After nearly a week of managing one of the largest dams in the Middle East by himself, Compton was joined by two Civil Affairs teams on 11 April: CAT-A 51, composed of Captain Ken Brown*, Ser-

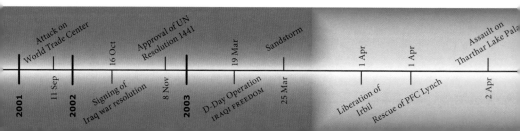

geant First Class Earl Hampton*, SFC Tom Everest*, and medic SFC Samuel Jeeter*; and the rest of Compton's own CAT-A 52, composed of Major Walter Hillbottom*, SFC Charles Atlas*, and medic SFC Kevin Goodin*. Compton, the team engineer on CAT-A 52, was exhausted and relieved that the two teams had finally arrived. The two Civil Affairs teams began by immediately identifying team tasks and individual responsibilities. CAT-A 52 took charge of managing the dam workers and facility operations, while CAT-A 51 took responsibility for organizing and supervising shift changes and coordinating for the return of Iraqi remains to local villages. The rest of CAT-A 52 soon became familiar with the challenges Compton had been facing alone.[194]

Compton's assessments revealed that maintenance on the facility had been neglected for years. Designed by the Soviets and built by the Iraqis during the 1970s, it had been expanded in the late 1980s. The facility was then placed in "cold storage" shortly before the Gulf War in 1991. Throughout its life, the dam seemed to suffer from a consistent lack of attention. After the Gulf War, the dam was brought online and began producing electricity, though efficiency was hampered by neglect and lack of resources. The Iraqis blamed UN sanctions for the lack of desperately needed spare parts, but the dam's problems ran deeper than that. Compton discovered that most of the door seals in the lower levels of the complex were rotted, which would allow the entire facility to flood if water rose to the level of the deep well pumps. If flooding did occur, it could cause an imbalance within the facility structure itself, resulting in a catastrophic failure capable of rupturing the dam. The local workers were all too aware of the extent of the electrical and structural problems of the dam, and the majority of them wanted to return home rather than risk the dam's collapse with them inside.

While the battle outside the facility waned, the difficulties inside the dam escalated. By 10 April, the situation was critical. The generators continually broke down, hampering efforts to bring the main turbines back online. However, the generators were only half the problem; each time a turbine was started, the turbine would blow out the electrical panels and immediately stop again, cutting power to the pumps that kept the facility from flooding. In addition, the shaft of the only "working" turbine was warped. Under normal circumstances, the warped shaft would have rendered the turbine useless, but rising levels of water forced the dam crew to use it anyway. As

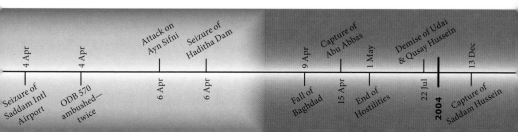

soon as the turbine was engaged, the warped shaft caused a vibration that reverberated throughout the entire structure. Compton and Hillbottom were in the lowest level of the dam assessing the condition of the deep well pumps and checking on the level of the rising water when the vibrations began. Alarmed by the violent shaking, Hillbottom thought the dam might be collapsing and began running toward the stairs to get up and out of the lower levels of the facility. Compton, knowing the volume and intensity of the water that would rush in if the dam actually collapsed, calmly called to the departing major: "No sense in running; you can die tired or just die."[195]

Workers managed to shut down the broken turbine before the dam collapsed, and they immediately began checking for significant structural damage. The water continued to rise, and with it, the workers' fears. Several times, Compton had to literally force the dam employees to work on the facility, even as they insisted that nothing could be done to fix the dam. Their fear of the rising water was justified; if the water had risen approximately six more inches than it had, it would have reached the electrical components in the deep well pumps, requiring all personnel to be evacuated. In spite of the danger and the resistance, Compton and the Iraqi dam employees eventually repaired one of the turbines, and brought a second turbine online soon after that. Only one deep well pump was running by noon on 11 April, and to continue running that pump alone would eventually burn it out. The dam workers eventually got two deep well pumps to function, though that still left them short of the three required to prevent the water from rising. Problems continued with the generators and other electrical components; however, the crew's increasing experience in resolving a multitude of problems—and Compton's effective management of the dam workers—helped everyone respond better to challenges whenever they occurred.

Approximately one week after the dam was captured, an Army Corps of Engineers assessment team consisting of one officer and two noncommissioned officers arrived to assist in the operation of the dam. None of the personnel had the training or experience to evaluate or operate the dam, so the assessment team chief conducted daily, real-time video teleconferences with the Army Corps of Engineers technical experts in Mobile, Alabama, and other dam specialists in North Carolina. Realizing that the dam manager was more knowledgeable about the facility than anybody else could be, the Corps of

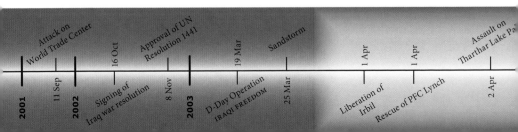

Engineers representatives in North Carolina asked to have the dam manager present during the video teleconferences. Including him in the conferences also accorded him the proper respect necessary to restore the dam to full operation. With the arrival of the Corps of Engineers team, Compton was relieved from his temporary and unexpected duty as the noncommissioned officer in charge of the fifth-largest dam in the Middle East.[196]

None of the CAT-A personnel had anticipated managing a hydro-electric complex when they initially deployed for Operation IRAQI FREEDOM. Compton certainly did not plan to take charge of Haditha Dam when he set out to conduct his initial assessment. Yet, managing a dam is exactly what Compton and his fellow Civil Affairs soldiers found themselves doing in April 2003. Through sheer persistence and creative thinking, Compton prevented environmental, logistical, and strategic disaster by keeping the dam operational. Compton summed up his tour at Haditha in this way:

> *I knew that if the dam had busted, even due to structural failure, most Iraqis would have blamed the Coalition forces. I told workers when they wanted to leave the dam that they were required to remain at the facility and continue operations; we were going to get it working, whatever it took. If we had lost the dam, it would have had an enormous impact on the war. It could have turned the people against us. Not only would the U.S. be seen as destroying the dam, there would have been a lot of bridges washed out downriver and floods all the way to Karbala, not to mention the deaths of civilians and potentially U.S. military personnel.[197]*

As is often the case in Civil Affairs, Compton and the other members of CAT-A 51 and CAT-A 52 successfully performed a seemingly isolated mission that, in reality, had a significant and far-reaching impact on U.S. interests abroad.

FREEDOM FROM CAPTIVITY

On 23 March, two serials of the 507th Maintenance Company became lost outside the town of Nasiriya as the unit attempted to regain contact with the 3rd Infantry Division's 600-vehicle convoy moving north and west ahead of them. After almost sixty hours of continuous movement, beset with vehicle breakdowns and wrong turns, the exhausted

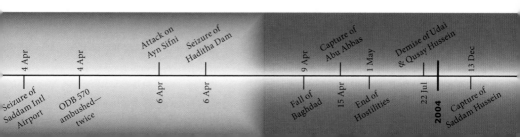

troops of the 507th were ambushed as they attempted to find the correct route through the city. In the ensuing chaos, eleven soldiers were killed, seven captured, and nine wounded (including some of those captured). First Sergeant Rick Dawson's* HMMWV crashed into the rear of one of the unit's five-ton wreckers, killing the first sergeant and severely injuring the other four occupants of the HMMWV. Iraqis took Private First Class Jessica Lynch from the vehicle, alive but unconscious. Her capture set in motion the U.S. military's first successful prisoner-of-war recovery operation since World War II.[198]

Lynch's captors initially took her to an Iraqi military hospital near the site of the ambush, but soon moved her across the city to Saddam Hussein General Hospital, the town's primary civilian medical facility. The basement of the seven-story hospital was used as a Baath Party headquarters. (Under the Geneva Convention, hospitals are protected from attack *unless* they are used to commit acts harmful to the enemy. By locating its headquarters within the hospital, the Baath Party forfeited the hospital's protected status.) One of the adjacent buildings housed forty of the Saddam Fedayeen. On 27 March, 32-year-old lawyer Mohammed Odeh Rehaief learned of Lynch's presence in the hospital while visiting his wife, who worked there as a nurse. Rehaief took it upon himself to cross the war-torn streets of Nasiriya to deliver news of the American's presence in the hospital to Coalition troops. He was able to contact the U.S. Marines and made several trips back and forth to the hospital to ascertain the woman's exact whereabouts and the layout of the facility.

The soldiers of ODA 553 were working in the city and when they learned of Rehaief, they collected and sent the information up the chain. They were persistent in pushing for a rescue attempt. At FOB 52, the consensus was that further proof of Lynch's presence was needed and steps were taken to secure the necessary information from the hospital. Marine Gunnery Sergeant Lance Hartman*, attached to the FOB from the Defense Human Services Agency, flew to Nasiriya and linked up with the team. A man of considerable talent when it came to developing innovative solutions to complex problems, "Gunny Gadget" put together a remotely controlled camera hidden in a shoulder bag for Rehaief to carry into the hospital.[199]

Working with ODA 553, Rehaief made several trips into the hospital and took a series of pictures that accurately portrayed the situation there. The team processed the crucial intelligence gathered by

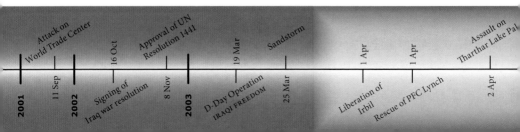

Rehaief's forays and passed it up through the chain of command. Once this intelligence passed up the chain, a task force of special operations and conventional troops was rapidly assembled to mount a rescue operation.[200]

Elements of the 1st Battalion, 160th SOAR, participated in the rescue. Chief Warrant Officer 4 Randall Ramsey* arrived at Tallil Air Base on 30 March to prepare to receive the rest of the regiment's contribution to the task force. In the twenty minutes he had, Ramsey scrambled to prepare for the first flights of MC-130s that brought in the MH-6 and AH-6 Little Bird helicopters which played key roles in the rescue. The helicopter crews parked the helicopters along the edge of the flight line and spent the first night camped on the tarmac next to their helicopters.[201]

The MH-60K Black Hawks of the 1st Battalion, 160th SOAR, flew to the airfield. After all the SOAR aircraft had arrived, the Army aviation element was comprised of four MH-6 and AH-6 Little Birds, four MH-60K lift helicopters, and two MH-60L Defensive Armed Penetrators armed with rockets and cannon. Eventually the headquarters established itself in an abandoned bunker. This became the staging area for the operation. Ramsey was deeply involved in the planning, going forty-eight hours with little sleep as he and the flight lead pilots worked feverishly to integrate their elements into the larger rescue plan.[202]

ARSOF elements continued to arrive at Tallil Air Base, including the 2nd Battalion, 75th Ranger

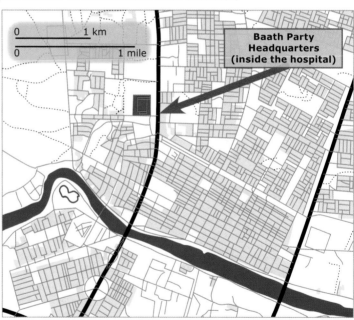

Figure 7.56 Map of Nasiriya. *The Baath Party located its headquarters in the basement of the Saddam Hussein General Hospital, thereby forfeiting the hospital's protected status under the Geneva Convention.*

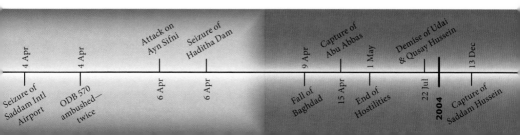

Figure 7.57 Marine Corps CH-46.

Figure 7.58 Marine Corps CH-53. *The Marine CH-46 and CH-53 were used to insert the Rangers and other SOF elements outside the hospital.*

Regiment, augmented by B Company, 1st Battalion, and liaisons from the Marines of Task Force Charlie. As the elements arrived, the planning intensified at a couple of small card tables in the bunker. The plan which evolved was essentially simple, but fraught with potential disaster if the enemy chose to prevent the rescue.[203]

The rescue plan concentrated overwhelming force on the hospital and immediate vicinity. A ground team would rapidly breach the hospital's main entrance, extract Lynch, and then withdraw, covered by the assault forces. Marine CH-46 and CH-53 helicopters would be used to insert the Rangers who would establish blocking positions outside the hospital to prevent any reinforcements coming into the area. The plan called for the Rangers to move on foot to their positions along a major road network, known during the operation as the "Mogadishu Mile," a tribute to the closing scene of the Rangers' dramatic battle in the Somali capital in October 1993. A ground assault force of Rangers, reinforced with Marine tanks and armored vehicles, would simultaneously move into the area from the north.[204]

The MH-6s would insert snipers into the hospital compound. The MH-60K lift helicopters had a variety of missions: one helicopter would land troops on the hospital roof, one would carry in the primary breaching element with assault personnel, and a third would transport a medical team. This third MH-60K would remain on the ground near the hospital entrance to fly Lynch and the assault team out of the area. The AH-6s would provide close-in overhead fire support. Additional fire support was available from an on-station AC-130 gunship. The mission would commence when the Marines of Task Force Charlie initiated a diversionary attack to seize the Euphrates River bridges near the hospital. The Marines, bloodied by fierce fighting in the city, relished the opportunity to use the joint operation to secure a bridgehead.[205]

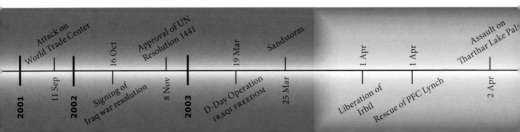

The intense planning went on throughout the night of 31 March. At one point, Ramsey noticed that the insertion point for the Marine helicopters carrying the Rangers would probably be "browned-out" by the other aircraft bringing in the assault force. He brought this up and the Rangers were placed in a better location. The absence of the Marine pilots during the planning phase concerned Ramsey, but when they ultimately arrived, he briefed them and they handled their end of the mission competently and professionally. A large, detailed sand table built with ration boxes was constructed, and all the participants went through a timed "rock drill" to rehearse specific tasks and missions and to clear up any questions. The sand table drill worked well until a Marine helicopter decided to reposition and blew away the model buildings with its rotor wash. Fortunately, by this time the briefing was winding down and no further use of the sand table was required.[206]

Figure 7.59 Black Hawks over the Euphrates River. *MH-60K Black Hawks, such as these flying over the Euphrates River, were one of the primary lift helicopters used in the rescue of Private First Class Jessica Lynch. One remained on the ground outside the hospital entrance to evacuate the rescued prisoner of war.*

The operation commenced at 0100 hours on 1 April when the Marines began their diversionary assault on the designated bridges from the south side of the Euphrates River. As planned, the Marines cut the power to the city five minutes before the assault on the hospital was scheduled. Within moments, the hospital's generators came online, providing a splash of color in a sea of black.[207]

Chief Warrant Officer 4 James Melvin* and Major Mark Mohan* led the AH-6s onto the target area and immediately encountered fire from heavy weapons. It turned out to be rounds from the Marines' enthusiastic assault south of the river. The pilots had no recourse but to hold their pattern around the hospital for several minutes. Melvin did reverse the course of the orbit at one point to, as he said, "put the commissioned man toward the fire." Eventually they got through on the radio to the Marines and asked them to adjust their fires.[208]

Figure 7.60 2nd Ranger Battalion scroll shoulder patch.

The MH-60Ks followed the Little Birds, with one MH-60K executing a one-wheeled landing and letting the snipers out onto the roof. The second MH-60K put its assault force down in front of the hospital entrance. The rescuers quickly disappeared into the massive building, leaving Chief Warrant Officer 4 Harry Bibeau* and Captain Theo-

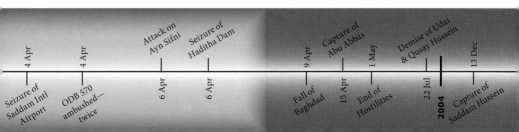

4 Apr
Seizure of Saddam Intl Airport

4 Apr
ODB 570 ambushed— twice

Attack on Ayn Sifni
6 Apr

Seizure of Haditha Dam
6 Apr

9 Apr
Fall of Baghdad

Capture of Abu Abbas
15 Apr

1 May
End of Hostilities

Demise of Udai & Qusay Hussein
22 Jul

2004

13 Dec
Capture of Saddam Hussein

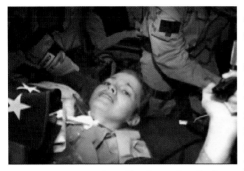

Figure 7.61 Private First Class Jessica Lynch after her rescue by a combined SOF team.

dore Shaffer* sitting alone in their helicopter, awaiting the rescuers' return.

The Rangers in the ground assault force arrived as planned and immediately swarmed over the area. "It was a relief to see them. They were like ants on that compound," said Shaffer, who watched anxiously from his position in the helicopter on the ground. During the insertion of the Rangers into their blocking positions, the Marine CH-46 carrying the Ranger battalion commander clipped a wire on its approach, nearly causing the bird to nosedive to the ground. Fortunately, the pilot recovered in time to narrowly avert a disaster.[209]

After a thirteen-minute eternity, the assault force sent out a call that it had secured Private Lynch and she was being extracted out of the target area. As the code word was relayed to the various rescue elements, the joint operations center at Tallil Air Base erupted into cheers. Bibeau and Shaffer flew Lynch and the medical team back to Tallil, where they transferred Lynch to a fixed-wing aircraft and flew her to Kuwait for further medical attention and an eventual reunion with her family.[210]

Lynch was safe, but the forces on the objective were not quite finished with their mission. Iraqis within the hospital directed the troops to the morgue, where they found two American bodies. U.S. forces also learned that the soccer field adjacent to the hospital grounds allegedly held more bodies. The Rangers immediately secured the area and began to excavate the freshly dug graves. Having no tools, the Rangers worked steadily with their hands and eventually retrieved the remains of nine more bodies. The recovered bodies were placed in GMVs and returned to Tallil with the ground assault force. The recovery took the Rangers and the AH-6s flying overhead into the daylight hours. Ultimately, all forces returned to Tallil Air Base intact, with no loss of life among the 488 participants.[211]

The rescue of Private First Class Jessica Lynch caused a media frenzy. Initial reports sensationalized the event in virtually every particular, and the military was criticized for ostensibly hyping her rescue. As the facts became clear, what stood out was the exceptional

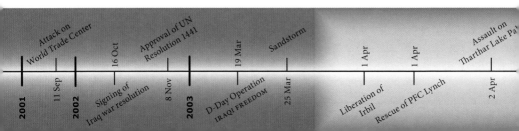

competence and professionalism of the participants, and their over-riding dedication to leaving no soldier behind.

2 APRIL MISSION

In what became known as the "2 April Mission" the men of C Company, 1st Battalion, 160th SOAR, responded to a request for an emergency casualty evacuation and close air support. A special operations force was in a gunfight with Iraqi forces north of Haditha Dam. With little rest from a long flight the night before, a flight of two MH-60K Black Hawks and two MH-60L Defensive Armed Penetrators departed in daylight from a forward support base and flew through hostile territory to execute the mission. Their daring rescue and devastating application of close air support saved the life of one soldier and wrenched victory out of the hands of a fanatic enemy.

For several days an Iraqi force of roughly a hundred Saddam Fedayeen trailed a much smaller group of U.S. special operations soldiers. The Saddam Fedayeen were an irregular force of "volunteers" dedicated to the protection of the Baath Party regime and Saddam Hussein. They ambushed the Americans on the morning of 2 April, and the special operations force called its tactical operations center for help, requesting emergency casualty evacuation and close air support. Chief Warrant Officer 4 Fred Hamilton* and Chief Warrant Officer 3 Richard Hoyt*, the flight leads for the DAP and Black Hawk flights respectively, had only slept for three hours before the mission alert came. Groggily they headed to the center for a briefing. The details were limited: an ambushed special operations element needed immediate evacuation of its casualties and fire support in order to break contact with the enemy. Hamilton and Hoyt fully understood the increased risks of a daytime flight in enemy territory; nevertheless, they prepared their crews without hesitation.[212]

Chief Warrant Officer 4 Thomas Brady*, designated the air mission commander with overall responsibility, energized his crews for the mission. The increased activity roused other Night Stalkers still recovering from the previous evening, and with a solid group effort, four helicopters departed the forward staging base within forty-five minutes of notification. With two MH-60K lift helicopters in the lead and the two DAPs on the flanks, the flight raced at maximum speed fifty feet above the desert floor to a spot in central Iraq, using coor-

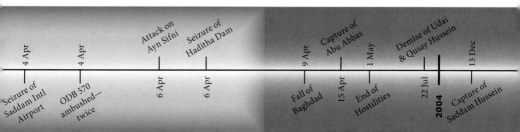

dinates hastily scribbled on a scrap of paper. Hamilton remained in contact with the tactical operations center, which relayed intelligence updates, suspected weapons systems, and the enemy situation. The center also informed him that two sorties of Air Force A-10 Thunderbolt II attack aircraft were en route, but would not arrive until after the helicopters reached the objective. Ninety minutes later, the Night Stalkers neared the engagement area.[213]

Hamilton's first job was to check in with an E3 Sentry, Airborne Warning and Control System, in order to alert U.S. Air Force jet aircraft flying high above the Iraqi desert, and to deconflict airspace along their route north with conventional aviation and conventional ground forces. Without a preplanned flight route, the risk of fratricide increased exponentially for an already dangerous mission. The complex air coordination order, a system designed to deconflict flights of jet aircraft with all other flying objects, unmanned aerial vehicles, artillery, HIMARS, and Patriot weapon system required at least seventy-two hours notice in order to electronically distribute flight information throughout the theater of operations. Hamilton contacted the Airborne Warning and Control System controller and requested clearance, informing him that they were on an emergency evacuation mission. The controller acknowledged and tracked the flight's progress.[214]

By late morning, Iraqi reinforcements had arrived and the opposing forces were in an intensive firefight. Both sides had sustained casualties. When the helicopters arrived at the objective, Hamilton checked in with the ground force, which immediately cleared the DAPs "hot"—the code word that grants permission to engage the enemy at will—and requested that the MH-60Ks hold on the periphery. The DAP, an armed version of the Black Hawk, can be configured with a combination of 2.75 inch rocket pods, 30 millimeter chain guns, and two fixed 7.62mm miniguns. As Hamilton's aircraft accelerated forward searching for potential targets, Brady in the trail DAP thought, "What's the big deal? I don't see anything." Then he spotted the American forces hunkered down on a ridgeline to his front, which he thought odd because they usually took the fight to the enemy.[215]

Deviating from the flight course of the DAPs, Hoyt radioed his flight's position to the ground commander, and received the enemy situation and landing zone coordinates. The MH-60K pilots quickly located their comrades on the ridgeline, and landed close by to facili-

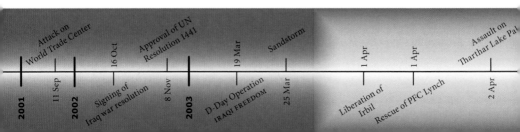

tate the loading of the casualties. The ground commander immediately requested that the pilots reposition the helicopters to the designated coordinates, which he deemed a more secure area. As Hoyt repositioned his flight, he saw the DAPs in a "bump" (attack posture) and smoke billowing from the chain guns. He thought, "Now that's an impressive sight."[216]

Moments earlier, the DAP flight circled the objective twice before Sergeant Jeffery Landis* spotted the Iraqi combatants lying prone on the ground; they looked dead but were actually playing possum. It was very difficult to pick out the enemy because their clothing blended in so well with the terrain. In the trail DAP Landis noticed that one Iraqi slightly turned his head as the helicopters flew away from him. Grabbing his M4 carbine, Landis aimed his rifle and shot near the Iraqi on the next pass. Instantly the fighter jumped to his feet with his weapon, and started running and jumping away from the rounds. "It looked like a scene in a Western gunslinger movie where the guy is made to dance," recalled Landis later.[217]

The movement quickly caught the attention of Hamilton in the lead helicopter. He reflexively banked his DAP hard to the right and fired the chain gun, instantly killing the Iraqi. Within moments the scene changed. Now the DAP crewmembers could easily identify the threat, and proceeded to give the enemy, in the words of Brady, "a whooping and a whopping." The pair of gunships conducted a deadly aerial ballet over the desert for the next fifteen minutes, never making a complete circle without shooting and killing enemy fighters. It was a testament to finely honed crew coordination skills and adroit shooting. The added fire support enabled the special operations element to move its casualties to the landing zone south of the ridgeline.[218]

Figure 7.62 DAP. *The heavily armed Defensive Armed Penetrators were instrumental in relieving the enemy pressure on the beleaguered special operations forces.*

While the DAP pilots systematically destroyed Iraqis in their firing positions, Hoyt directed his flight to the specified landing zone, and waited for the ground force to arrive. Within moments, several vehicles rapidly approached the helicopters from the side. Several of the helicopter crewmembers scanned the horizon for the enemy, and cov-

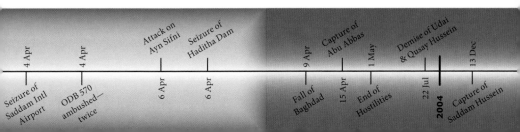

Seizure of Saddam Intl Airport — 4 Apr

ODB 570 ambushed twice — 4 Apr

Attack on Ayn Sifni — 6 Apr

Seizure of Haditha Dam — 6 Apr

Fall of Baghdad — 9 Apr

Capture of Abu Abbas — 15 Apr

End of Hostilities — 1 May

Demise of Udai & Qusay Hussein — 22 Jul

Capture of Saddam Hussein — 13 Dec

2004

ered the casualty transfer with their 7.62mm six-barreled miniguns, while others helped with the casualties. A wounded team member boarded the first Black Hawk, and, regretfully, a body draped in the U.S. flag was loaded on the second. Without delay the flight departed to H-1 Airfield. At about the same time, the first pair of A-10s arrived on station and Hamilton released the two Air Force aircraft to cover Hoyt's flight to H-1.[219]

Once Hoyt departed, the two DAPs continued combing the area. Chief Warrant Officer 3 Walter Florenson*, seated next to Hamilton in the lead DAP, spotted a truck with mortar tubes in the bed and several armed Iraqis standing nearby. He announced the target to Hamilton, who swiftly maneuvered his flight for a gun run. Thirty seconds later, the vehicle was destroyed and the fighters were dead. After several engagements, the militants began kneeling and firing shots at the helicopters flying away from them. The special operations snipers observed what was happening and effectively covered the helicopters' break with .50 caliber shots at the unsuspecting Iraqis.[220]

The second pair of A-10s arrived ten minutes later, and the lead pilot excitedly announced that his flight was fully armed; each aircraft had six 500-pound bombs, two cluster bombs, and four high-explosive bombs. The Night Stalkers pinpointed a large group in a ravine two hundred meters north of the U.S. ground force's position and Hamilton directed the A-10 pilot to drop a 500-pound bomb on the location of the DAP's last engagement. The pilot dove in and dropped the bomb, which was programmed to airburst in the center of the enemy position. The explosion sent shrapnel within twenty meters of the special operations soldiers, but destroyed the enemy in the ravine. Brady's crew felt the heat of the explosion as the helicopter raced to clear the area. The DAP pilots turned back around and eradicated any surviving enemy fighters as the ground force prepared to move through the ravine to secure the next ridgeline to the north.[221]

Confident that the A-10s could effectively cover the ground force's maneuver, the DAP pilots broke off from the objective and flew northeast to see what they could find. The original mission plan only allotted them fifteen minutes of station time, so the Night Stalkers furiously searched for enemy positions. They located several mortar positions that had initially trapped the Americans on the ridgeline. Hamilton rolled in first, with Brady a few seconds behind him, and the two DAPs destroyed the mortar positions with 30mm rounds. Five uniformed

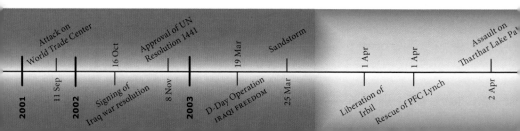

individuals firing back toward the battle area became the next target. Seemingly oblivious to the bombs just dropped on their comrades, these fighters soon perished under several short bursts of minigunfire. The pair of DAPs continued to ruthlessly search and destroy targets. Calculating their fuel burn rates in excruciating detail, the Night Stalkers stayed forty minutes beyond their allotted station time before lack of fuel forced them to finally break off their hunt.[222]

Fifty minutes after the arrival of the helicopters, all the Iraqis were dead. The MH-60Ks successfully evacuated the wounded Americans in the midst of the fight. The team of DAPs and the pair of A-10s delivered a devastating attack, turning the tide of battle. Hamilton notified the special operations commander that they had to depart, having reached the limit of their fuel. The commander released them with heartfelt appreciation. Reluctantly, the Night Stalkers headed to H-1 for fuel. They avoided enemy concentrations along the Euphrates, and landed on fumes—their fuel tanks virtually dry. The biggest surprise were the orders to shut down once refueled, and stay at H-1 for the night. The unplanned stop caused some discomfort for the crews because they didn't have the opportunity to pack extra gear when they had initially launched on the mission and they were forced to bunk in their aircraft.[223]

This mission epitomized the inimitable bond between elite ground and air warriors of the U.S. Army special operations. The SOF community consists of members who are willing to respond to a comrade in harms way, despite the danger involved. Without hesitation or reservation, the Night Stalkers departed in daylight on short rest to evacuate wounded soldiers, and quell an attack that had threatened to overrun a U.S. force.

TEAM TANK

Although Army special operations forces are not usually associated with armored units, they have been known to work together when the situation has warranted heavy support. During World War II, the legendary Colonel William Darby formed the provisional "Cannon Company" of four M3 half-tracks

Figure 7.63 75th Ranger Cannon Company half-track during World War II.

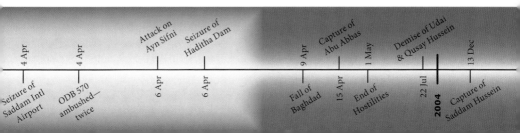

mounted with 75mm guns to give additional firepower to the Rangers during the Italian campaign. However, not until Operation IRAQI FREEDOM did ARSOF again work with armor forces to any appreciable degree, and even then, the association was weak.[224]

Early in the campaign, armored Task Force 1-63 airlifted into Bashur Airfield in support of Combined Joint Special Operations Task Force–North. After taking three days to arrive, however, the armor force was not able to effectively leave the airfield perimeter to provide an immediate impact on the combat situation in northern Iraq. In fact, three days after Task Force 1-63's arrival, the major Iraqi elements in the north surrendered, and Kurdish peshmerga and Task Force Viking seized Kirkuk and Mosul. Task Force 1-63 entered operations in the north as an occupying force in the cities controlled by Task Force Viking. The mix of armor and ARSOF in the north accomplished little; the Rangers, however, had an opportunity to demonstrate the value of armor in special operations.[225]

Figure 7.64 1st Ranger Battalion scroll shoulder patch.

Figure 7.65 70th Armor Regiment insignia.

In a situation reminiscent of that faced by Darby and the Rangers in World War II, the 75th Ranger Regiment found itself in need of armor support in Iraq. The Regiment discussed attaching an armor force during mission planning, but no formal arrangements were made. In the course of their operations in the western and northern deserts, however, the Rangers concluded that they required an armor force to confront Iraqi tanks, and to send the message that tanks were operating almost unopposed along Highway 1 north of Baghdad. The request for forces worked its way to Coalition Forces Land Component Command, down to V Corps' headquarters, and ultimately to C Company, 2nd Battalion, 70th Armor Regiment.[226]

While it is not clear whether C Company was specifically selected for the mission or if it was simply luck, the Rangers were getting a very experienced armor unit. The company had previously spent six months in Kuwait during Operation DESERT SPRING (May–October 2002), returning to Fort Riley, Kansas, in November 2002. After deployment to Kuwait in February 2003, C Company fought from the Kuwaiti border to Objective Rams, just south of Baghdad, attached to the 3rd Brigade, 3rd Infantry Division, before moving back south and being attached to Task Force 1-41 fighting near Samawah.[227]

On 31 March, C Company was fighting as part of Task Force 1-41 Infantry attached to the 82nd Airborne Division near Samawah. The next day Captain Sean Carlson*, the commander of C Company,

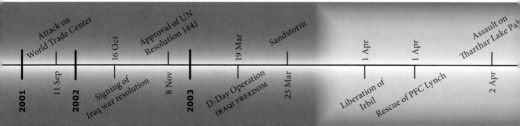

received what some may have considered an early April Fool's Day message after the hard fight north: move almost one hundred kilometers south to Tallil Air Base, located twenty kilometers southwest of Nasiriya, and then conduct an air movement back north to support CJSOTF-west. Carlson was ordered to leave one tank platoon with Task Force 1-41, and wait for heavy equipment transporters to move his tanks south. After waiting several hours for the promised transporters, Carlson ordered his company to move out under its own power. At 0100 hours on 2 April, C Company headed south.[228]

Arriving at the air base approximately five hours later, Carlson met with a liaison officer from the 75th Ranger Regiment. Carlson and his Headquarters' platoon leader then flew in and reported to the Ranger tactical operations center, where they discovered that their armor company, newly dubbed "Team Tank," would fall under the operational control of the 1st Battalion, 75th Ranger Regiment. While the Ranger Regiment included some commanders with mechanized experience, most had not operated with armor for many years. One of Carlson's first tasks, therefore, was to brief the capabilities and logistics requirements of the M1A1 Abrams tank. Planners focused on fuel consumption as a key concern, since a single M1A1 used almost as much fuel as an entire Ranger company in GMVs.

While Carlson worked with the Ranger staff, the rest of Team Tank prepared for air movement. The air movement of tanks by C-17 was new to both the tankers and the Air Force loadmasters. In fact, most of the armor soldiers had never even flown in a C-17 during peacetime, much less in a combat zone. The tank crews worked through the process of draining three-fourths of the fuel and securing the tanks by chain to the aircraft. Due to weight limitations, only one tank and its crew could be transported per C-17 sortie. First Sergeant Matt Unger* flew on the first sortie with the company commander's tank and crew to set up for the rest of the company while the executive officer "pushed" the tanks from Tallil Air Base. One tanker recalled that the burdened aircraft performed "a long, slow takeoff that felt like it was doing a wheelie."[229]

The air movement of Team Tank required three days to complete. The company's ten M1A1 tanks, three M113 armored personnel carriers, one fire support vehicle, three cargo trucks, two fuel trucks, and a HMMWV required a total of fifteen C-17 sorties between Tallil Air Base and H-1 Airfield, located five hundred kilometers to the northwest.

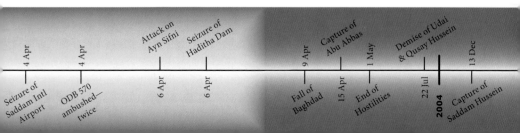

Figure 7.66 Tanks and special operations vehicles refuel at H-1 Airfield.

As each lift arrived, the tankers consolidated in a *laager* site, conducted maintenance, and prepared for their next mission. The last two tanks and crews arrived only two hours before the ground armored convoy departed H-1 for Mission Support Site Grizzly, a desert landing strip located between the Haditha Dam and Tikrit.[230]

On the surface, Team Tank's mission seemed simple enough: support the Rangers in a series of raids, and interdict main avenues of escape for regime loyalists and high-value targets attempting to flee to Syria. Once Coalition forces had blocked Highways 2 and 4 through the western desert, Highway 1 became the primary avenue of escape. High-value targets would follow Highway 1 north as far as they could, then cut west toward Syria on any number of lesser roads running through the desert. In order to carry out its mission, Team Tank would be participating in raids that included between fifty and one hundred kilometers of movement each way. While the tanks had no problem maneuvering once on the objectives, they were not built to travel long distances. Through hard work and perseverance, the tank crews and the company's small maintenance section made up for the lack of direct support maintenance and kept the tanks running in spite of the intrinsic stresses of multiple operations.

The first operation out of Mission Support Site Grizzly earned the soldiers of Team Tank the Rangers' respect as they proved that armor soldiers were as hard as their tanks. On 9 April, C Company, 2nd Battalion, 70th Armor Regiment, and 1st Battalion, 75th Ranger Regiment, conducted a night attack to secure Objective Camel—K2 Airfield—under conditions of zero illumination and little visibility after the initiation of mortar fire. As the tanks began the attack, Carlson suddenly dropped off the command net. The Ranger operations officer commanding the attack tried to raise Carlson, but his efforts proved fruitless. The armor commander seemed to be out of action.

Carlson was, indeed, out of action, but it was not enemy fire that had disabled his tank; rather, the commander's tank had driven into a forty-foot deep hole in the middle of what appeared to be a wheat field. Traveling at between five and ten miles per hour with zero illumina-

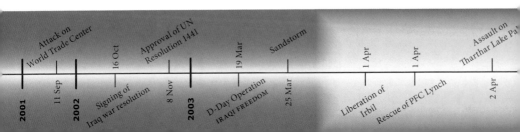

tion, the tank had unwittingly driven over the edge of a large hole and then rolled over until it rested upside down, directly on top of the turret. Luckily for Carlson and his crew, the captain had stressed rollover drills during predeployment training, so everybody in the company knew exactly what to do in this unfortunate situation. As soon as the company's executive officer, First Lieutenant Daniel Davis*, realized what had happened, he moved his tank forward and began recovery operations while protecting the crew of the overturned tank from enemy fire.

Meanwhile, Carlson and the rest of the crew were trapped inside a living nightmare. Over the next hour—though it seemed like an eternity—the men quickly assessed their situation and began their own recovery. In addition to the basic conditions that had trapped the crew, its self-rescue was hampered by fuel leaks, requiring the tank's power to be turned off. Using flashlights, Carlson and his gunner, Sergeant Abe Thomas*, performed first aid on the loader, Specialist Mark Czerniki*, whose left hand had been almost severed during the rollover. While Carlson and Thomas worked on Czerniki, driver Private First Class Curtis Book* wriggled his way through the narrow driver's hatch and began digging through the sand using his hands, eventually tunneling

Figure 7.67 Overturned M1A1 Abrams tank. *Captain Sean Carlson's* tank accidentally drove into a large hole and overturned as it traveled at high speed with zero illumination during the assault on Objective Camel.*

his way to freedom. Staff Sergeant Patrick* and his crew, who had stopped to guard the commander's tank and help in the rescue, met Book emerging from the sand. Patrick squeezed back through the driver's tunnel and entered the tank. Inside he dismantled the turret screens to make a pathway out. Carlson and Thomas pushed while Patrick pulled Czerniki through the tunnel to fresh air and medical attention. The tunnel was so narrow that Carlson had to strip off his chemical suit, emerging into the desert night clad only in his underwear and boots, and coated in a combination of fuel, hydraulic fluid, and Czerniki's blood.[231]

After Carlson verified that his crew had received proper care, he transferred to Davis' tank and continued the attack. Team Tank still needed to block Highway 1. With recovery assets over forty kilometers away, the company declared the overturned tank a total loss. Since the

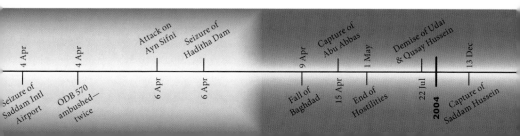

4 Apr — Seizure of Saddam Intl Airport

4 Apr — ODB 570 ambushed—twice

Attack on Ayn Sifni — 6 Apr

Seizure of Haditha Dam — 6 Apr

9 Apr — Fall of Baghdad

Capture of Abu Abbas — 15 Apr

1 May — End of Hostilities

Demise of Udai & Qusay Hussein — 22 Jul

2004

13 Dec — Capture of Saddam Hussein

Figure 7.68 M1A1 Abrams tank close up. *After hitting the deep well from the steep side, the tank flipped over and landed with its turret buried in the soft sand.*

wreck was located in hostile territory, filled with sensitive gear, loaded with ammunition, and soaked in fuel, they concluded that they had to destroy the tank. Two tank rounds provided an inglorious end to the tank. The crew members lost almost all their personal gear with that decision, and had to make do for the rest of their tour in Iraq. As for the respect generated during this episode, the Rangers recommended Davis for the Bronze Star for valor.[232]

The attack on Objective Camel ensured the continued association of C Company with the 75th Ranger Regiment. On 11 April, Team Tank and A Company of 1st Battalion, 75th Ranger Regiment, combined their strengths and conducted an attack on Objective Badger: Al Sarha Airfield and site of the Iraqi Air Force Academy. The mission was to attack and seize key terrain, and to interdict Highway 1 in order to prevent the escape of high-value targets. An on-order mission was to move to the site of a downed F-15E (designated Objective Falcon), search for survivors, and recover any remains of crewmembers. The combined Ranger and ground armored convoy, consisting of thirty-eight vehicles of nine different types, moved sixty kilometers cross-country under cover of darkness to Objective Badger.

After a short stop to refuel the tanks, the task force attack on Objective Badger began with mortar fire and 160th SOAR close air support. Satellite imagery indicated a fence line at the objective, but when the tanks assaulted the line, they found it to be an agricultural sprinkler system easily bypassed. Moving quickly through the first objective, the tanks and Rangers–mounted in GMVs—assaulted through several Iraqi vehicles destroyed by the helicopter gunships.[233]

The Rangers and the tankers coordinated closely as they dismounted to meet Iraqi resistance. Near one set of buildings, a few Iraqi defenders stymied one Ranger squad by ducking behind a brick wall and spraying automatic weapon fire over the wall. Every time the squad attempted to move forward, it was met with a renewed barrage of fire. The solution was simple for the tankers: fire two high-explosive antitank rounds through the wall. The Rangers then assaulted through the hole and killed the remaining stunned Iraqi infantry.

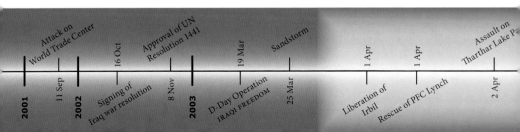

2001 · Attack on World Trade Center · 11 Sep · 2002 · Signing of Iraq war resolution · 16 Oct · Approval of UN Resolution 1441 · 8 Nov · 2003 · 19 Mar · D-Day Operation IRAQI FREEDOM · Sandstorm · 25 Mar · 1 Apr · Liberation of Irbil · 1 Apr · Rescue of PFC Lynch · Assault on Tharthar Lake Pa · 2 Apr

Once Objective Badger was secure, part of the force moved to Objective Falcon, where the remains of the F-15E crew were successfully recovered. The Rangers and tankers performed both missions without casualty. The Iraqis did not fare as well: their losses included several armored vehicles, including two T-55 tanks, twelve antiaircraft guns, and approximately seventy-five Iraqi soldiers. The tankers once again acquitted themselves with courage and skill, as exemplified by Carlson, who was later awarded the Bronze Star for valor for his actions at Objective Badger.[234]

Figure 7.69 Highway 1 blocking position. *Soldiers from C Company, 1st Ranger Battalion and soldiers from C Company, 2nd Battalion, 70th Armor Regiment established a blocking position on Highway 1 north of Tikrit. The units proved that Armor and ARSOF could work together successfully.*

The assaults on Objectives Camel and Badger proved that armor and ARSOF could work together effectively. The Rangers discovered that they had overestimated the tanks' ability to travel long distances quickly, but admired their ability to "burst" past the Rangers' vehicles and apply the advantage of speed and firepower against the Iraqi opposition. The operations also revealed that future night operation coordination had to reconcile the Rangers reliance on infrared sights versus the thermal sights the tankers use. In spite of these slight differences in operational capability, C Company, 2nd Battalion, 70th Armor Regiment, and the 75th Ranger Regiment validated Colonel Darby's Cannon Company experiment. In mid-April, Team Tank returned to Task Force 1-41 and the Rangers went about their usual operations, but their success working together opened the door wide for possible future cooperation.[235]

BAGHDAD INTERNATIONAL AIRPORT

Beginning the night of 5 April 2003, the 160th SOAR received the assignment to transport a contingent of Special Operations Forces staff and troops into Saddam International Airport. As conventional forces converged on Baghdad, it became apparent to many commanders that Saddam International Airport, renamed Baghdad International Airport, was the major lodgment center for Iraq. With its extensive runway network and large terminal areas, it was vital to lay claim to the airport as soon as possible. The capture of the airport

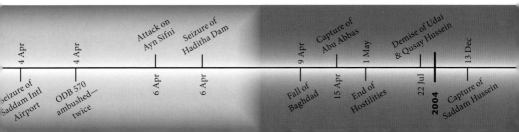

4 Apr — Seizure of Saddam Intl Airport

4 Apr — ODB 570—ambushed twice

6 Apr — Attack on Ayn Sifni

6 Apr — Seizure of Haditha Dam

9 Apr — Fall of Baghdad

Capture of Abu Abbas — 15 Apr — End of Hostilities

1 May

Demise of Udai & Qusay Hussein — 22 Jul

13 Dec — 2004 — Capture of Saddam Hussein

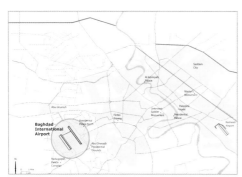

Figure 7.70 Map highlighting Baghdad International Airport.

was a significant psychological victory and marked the practical defeat of the Hussein regime, because it provided a central location from which to launch operations—a place that could accommodate large shipments of important supplies, equipment, and personnel—and was the center of gravity for transportation in and out of the country.

As Coalition forces approached Baghdad, Baghdad International Airport became prime real estate and military units began to stake out territory in anticipation of the arrival of rearguard forces. Unlike the conventional forces surrounding the city, the task force that the SOAR aviators worked for was dispersed between its forward supply base and H-1 Airfield in western Iraq and could not easily claim space at Baghdad International Airport for its headquarters. Chief Warrant Officer 3 James Nattier*, the SOAR's Chinook flight leader, developed a plan to use SOAR aircraft to collect the far-flung elements of the task force headquarters and deploy them to Baghdad International Airport. The plan called for using almost all the available SOAR aircraft.[236]

After deconflicting the routes with conventional aviation, artillery, and air defenses, a flight of three MH-47E Chinooks, two MH-60L Black Hawk Defensive Armed Penetrators, and four MH-60K Black Hawks departed their forward supply base with the task force's forward element on the night of 5 April, flying into the desert night. The dark sky was obscured with suspended sand and illumination was nearly zero. As the Night Stalkers approached the Iraqi border, the DAP pilots called Nattier and informed him that the conditions were beyond the capability of their aircraft to fly safely. The DAPs lacked the multimode radar systems of the Chinooks and MH-60K. These radar systems provided situational awareness beyond the capabilities of night vision goggles, and revealed obstacles to the front and sides of the flight path. Nattier advised Lieutenant Colonel Jeffrey Colt, the air mission commander, to abort the mission. He agreed, and Nattier turned the flight around and returned to the forward supply base.[237]

The weather failed to improve over the next several days, and urgency increased in the task force's tactical operations center to get people to Baghdad International Airport. On the evening of 7 April,

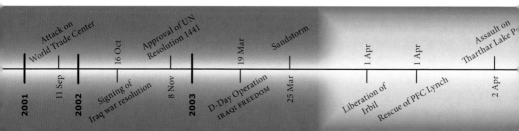

the weathermen forecast marginal weather conditions; the Night Stalkers would try again. However, the weather turned out to be worse than on the previous attempt and Colt and Nattier wasted no time in making the decision to abort the mission. To them the mission seemed to be more administrative, and the pilots decided it was not worth risking lives because of poor weather. Before they could even shut down their engines, both Colt and Nattier were called to the tactical operations center.[238]

When queried about available options, Nattier reported that the MH-60KS and MH-60ES could climb to a safe altitude, conduct an instrumented systems flight to the vicinity of Baghdad, then do a multimode radar "let down," since the air defense threat was negligible at this point in the war. However, he recommended that only the multimode radar–equipped aircraft go, for at some point the flight would have to descend through the dust and clouds before, hopefully, breaking out into clear skies. The DAPS were not equipped for such navigation. The task force commander agreed to the plan and assumed the mission risk. It was essential to get an advanced echelon on the ground and lay claim to part of the airport facility in order to receive the Rangers soon to arrive on MC-130s.[239]

Figure 7.71 Baghdad International Airport.

After Nattier briefed the pilots, the three Chinooks and four MH-60K Black Hawks departed the forward supply base. As planned, the flight leads relayed position and time at each waypoint along the route. In this manner, the pilots confirmed their location and point in space by comparing what the mission management software and navigational aids indicated with the flight lead reports. About forty-five minutes from Baghdad, the clouds began to break up and the pilots could spot the helicopters flying in front of them. Thirty miles from the airport, the pilots could see the ground and used their multimode radar simply as a backup to avoid obstacles.[240]

Nattier landed on what was designated "M" or "Mike" taxiway and taxied out of the way of the next Chinook. Chief Warrant Officer 2 Barry Littleton* landed next, followed by Chief Warrant Officer 2 Steve Bozeman*. The passengers deplaned and moved into the terminal area, eager to stake out sufficient space for task force operations.

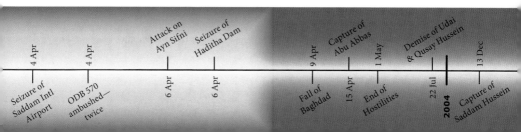

The Chinooks then repositioned near the middle of the airfield to receive fuel from an Apache helicopter refueling point already located at Baghdad International Airport.[241]

While Nattier and Littleton received fuel, the Black Hawks landed, dropped off their passengers, and joined the queue awaiting fuel. It was then that the significance of their location began to sink in. Chief Warrant Officer 3 Stanley Branson* allowed himself to admit: "Wow, we are actually in Baghdad."[242]

After his tanks were topped off, Nattier moved from the refuel point back to the taxiway. Then he heard a strange radio call to an MC-130 pilot by the Air Force combat controller on the ground: "Cleared to land at the box and one." Nattier looked down, and beneath the Chinook's chin bubble was an outlined and illuminated box with a one. He immediately repositioned, calling Littleton to do the same. After scrambling out of the way, the two helicopters videotaped the first landing of an MC-130 at Baghdad International Airport using their forward looking infrared radar sensors. Nattier instructed Littleton to shut down to conserve fuel while Bozeman refueled. Things had gone reasonably well, but the situation quickly changed for the worse.[243]

Enemy mortar fire soon began falling on the airfield and the Chinook pilots wasted no time in restarting their engines, and activating as many avionic and mission systems as possible. Chief Warrant Officer 3 Casey Johansson*, the helicopter commander flying with Littleton told Nattier that they were leaving. Since the concussion of the incoming rounds was reaching his aircraft, Nattier said that it was a good idea, and departed first, quickly followed by Johansson. Meanwhile, Chief Warrant Officer 5 Randall Grant* and Bozeman were still at the refueling point, wondering if they had missed a call to depart. They quickly figured out what was going on, and once they had received enough fuel, they took off along the planned egress route. The Black Hawk pilots, however, were stuck waiting to be refueled.[244]

In the air, the already bad situation immediately began to deteriorate. As Littleton raced to catch him, Nattier was struggling to get all of his systems online. Then the weather became even worse. Twenty miles into the flight, the two aircraft ran into severe turbulence. The huge Chinooks gyrated and bounced up and down through the air like out-of-control toys. Littleton recalled, "It felt like someone

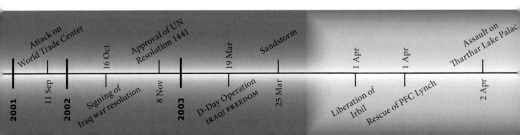

grabbed the aft landing gear and just shook the whole aircraft." The pilots in each helicopter struggled to keep the aircraft upright. With huge rates of descent and ascent—at times over three thousand feet per minute in both directions—the pilots found it nearly impossible to maintain control of the aircraft. They fought hard to keep a tenuous balance between being thrown to the ground and flung into the atmosphere.[245]

Nattier called over the radio that he was turning due south to fly away from an apparent squall line of thunderstorms. This course put the flight over some hostile sections of Iraq, but he had little choice. Bozeman was still several miles behind the first two Chinooks, and just as the call came to turn south, he and Grant hit the turbulence. All three Chinooks were caught in the violent winds. At one point, Nattier and Littleton sailed within a few feet of a towering construction crane, narrowly missing impalement on its arm. The Chinook pilots had escaped the mortar attacks on Baghdad International Airport only to confront an equally formidable enemy—weather![246]

The Night Stalkers continued along the a southerly course until they finally flew around the squall line, a full eighty miles off course in hostile territory and conflicted Coalition air defense corridors. Throughout the whole wild and crazy flight, Colt worked feverishly to shut down other traffic in the airspace and to get updated weather reports from the tactical operations center via the satellite radio. Once the turbulence subsided enough to regain full control, Nattier turned the flight west, and headed back to the forward supply base. Ninety minutes later, the three Chinooks finally arrived at the base—pilots and crews quite shaken, but alive.[247]

SUMMARY

With Baghdad International Airport in the hands of Coalition forces and the Iraqi capital surrounded, the already dim prospects for the Hussein regime were extinguished. As the word of the imminent fall of Baghdad reverberated throughout the country, the role of ARSOF began to shift. In the north, the Kurds began to press closer to the cities of Mosul and Kirkuk, their traditional strongholds. In the west, the threat posed by the SCUDs vanished, and the Special Forces teams began the process of securing key terrain and developing relations

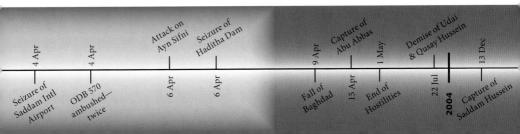

with the local populations. The Rangers and 160th SOAR shifted their focus from the destruction of Iraqi forces to the surgical removal or capture of high-value targets. The accelerating pace of early April slowed by mid-month, allowing the Coalition to stabilize conditions on the ground.

8

Baghdad and Beyond

D+10 through D+42
10 April–30 April

*T*HE END OF SADDAM Hussein's dictatorship effectively occurred as Baghdad fell on 10 April 2003. However, the fighting was far from over, especially north of Baghdad. The fall of the capital and the equally quick regime collapse made the Coalition rapidly move to stability and support operations while still conducting combat operations between Baghdad and the Green Line. Almost half of the conventional combat power was centered on the Baghdad area with its special operations forces supporting the overall Central Command mission.[1]

Army special operations forces contributed significantly to the rapid advancement of conventional forces. Combined Joint Special Operations Task Force–North successfully fixed the Iraqi forces along the Green Line and within days of the fall of Baghdad, and liberated the cities of Kirkuk and Mosul. CJSOTF-west continued operations in western Iraq while increasing units to accommodate expanding missions in the Baghdad area.

CFSOCC JUMPS TO BAGHDAD

Brigadier General Gary Harrell prepared his staff to move from Qatar to Baghdad. The 3rd Infantry Division set the conditions with the capture of Baghdad International Airport. After being "stuck" in Qatar for three weeks while the rest of its company waged war, Operational Detachment Alpha 912, Harrell's personal security team, finally made it to Iraq.

On 10 April 2003, Coalition Forces Special Operations Component Command Sergeant Major Jake Lincoln* and four members of ODA

Pseudonyms have been used for all military personnel with a rank lower than lieutenant colonel.

912 loaded a Ground Mobility Vehicle on an MC-130 from the Pennsylvania Air National Guard and flew to Baghdad International Airport in blackout conditions. The flight began uneventfully, but once it hit the Karbala Gap, the plane received heavy antiaircraft and ground fire, including rockets. The soldiers later learned that their plane was only the second one to land at Baghdad International Airport since the war had begun.[2]

A firefight between the 3rd Infantry Division soldiers and Iraqi defenders blocked the Special Forces soldiers and the sergeant major from moving directly from their plane to their final destination in the airport complex. While the 3rd ID troops were fighting in and around the airport, the newly arrived group found and secured a maintenance building on the west side of the airfield. The men joined several of the 3rd ID soldiers watching the red and green tracers flashing against the night sky, and soon saw their first "Baghdad sunrise"—a red sun rising through the dust and smoke of combat, outlining the landscape of the city.[3]

Figure 8.1 Saddam International Airport at sunrise on 11 April. *The sight that greeted the* CFSOCC *Early Entry Command Post.*

A few days later, General Harrell and the staff elements arrived in Baghdad by MC-130. The advance party secured one of Saddam's small palaces, about one kilometer south of the airport. The palace, which became CFSOCC forward headquarters, was three stories tall with thirty rooms, including several large ballrooms (perfect for the operations center), and a large pool within the compound. Once settled into its new team house (the pool cabana), ODA 912 added local patrols to its mission profile when not escorting the general. CFSOCC operated from the palace until redeployment in May.[4]

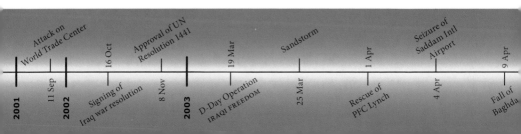

SOF and the Media

Some of the most exciting news reported during Operation IRAQI FREEDOM resulted from the Department of Defense's program to embed media with frontline troops, including special operations forces. Embedding allowed reporters and camera crews to record operations and events, as well as to experience the action themselves. Such intimacy gave both the media and the public new insight into the lives and trials of SOF personnel. The close cooperation also provided leaders and troops with the opportunity to learn how best to work with the media and turn the attention to their advantage.

In January and February 2003, the Department of Defense issued Public Affairs Guidance for activities in the Central Command area of responsibility, which became the basis for all other Public Affairs Guidance in Operation IRAQI FREEDOM. In contrast to the fairly restrictive policies initially followed in Operation ENDURING FREEDOM, the guidance for IRAQI FREEDOM went to great lengths to accommodate media interest: "The Department of Defense policy on media coverage of future military operations is that media will have long-term, minimally restrictive access to U.S. air, ground and naval forces through embedding."[5]

The same Public Affairs Guidance spelled out the rationale behind the Department of Defense's new openness and newfound realization that publicity was an effective tool of national security: "Media coverage of any future operation will, to a large extent, shape public perception of the national security environment now and in the years ahead. This holds true for the U.S. public; the public in allied countries whose opinion can affect the durability of our Coalition; and publics in countries where we conduct operations, whose perceptions of us can affect the cost and duration of our involvement." The Public Affairs Guidance also revealed an attitude that bordered on "if you can't beat 'em, join 'em." "We need to tell the factual story—good or bad—before others seed the media with disinformation and distortions, as they most certainly will continue to do."[6]

While special operations forces were included in the Department of Defense policy, the special circumstances of their missions did allow for variations in application of the embedding plan. As the public affairs officer for Special Operations Command Central, Lieutenant Commander Kyle Andersen* prepared the Public Affairs Guid-

Liberation of Kirkuk

11 Apr

Capture of Abu Abbas

1 May

Demise of Udai & Qusay Hussein

13 Dec

10 Apr

Liberation of Mosul

15 Apr

End of Hostilities

22 Jul

2004

Capture of Saddam Hussein

ance. He negotiated with the office of Assistant Secretary of Defense Victoria Clarke to ensure that reasonable compromises between SOF concerns and the embedding directive could be reached. The most important concession allowed the media to be assigned on a mission-by-mission basis instead of embedding them with SOF units for an indefinite length of time. This policy still provided for media access during pivotal operations, yet allowed SOF commanders to maintain crucial control over operations and security.[7]

In keeping with SOF's special status, and the high-profile nature of SOF participation in recent operations, SOCCENT requested and received specific reporters from the media pool, even though the embedding plan assigned slots to media organizations and not to individuals. SOF embeds were chosen with such factors in mind as seniority, past work with SOF, physical fitness, and readiness to travel. Among those reporters chosen to embed with SOCCENT were Kelly O'Donnell from MSNBC, Jonathan Ewing from the Associated Press, James Dao from the New York Times, and Jim Sciutto and Drew Millhon from ABC News. At the height of the war, the SOCCENT public affairs officer was responsible for coordinating eighteen embedded reporters or news teams.[8]

While the process for selecting media embeds went relatively smoothly, Andersen ran into problems filling out the public affairs officer requirements for the various SOCCENT component commands. By mid-December, only two of the four component commands—the Joint Special Operations Air Component and the Naval Task Force—had public affairs officers assigned to them. Both CJSOTF-North and CJSOTF-west lacked them, and every time an appropriate officer was identified, the request for assignment was denied. After Major Timothy spent months processing a number of such personnel actions at the U.S. Special Operations Command public affairs office, CJSOTF-west finally received a public affairs officer.[9]

Nye joined the 10th Special Forces Group at the intermediate staging base in Stuttgart, Germany, in early February 2003. Task Force Viking had originally planned to move to a staging base in Turkey, but those plans changed when Turkey objected to the United States using its bases in preparation for the invasion into Iraq. Romania was chosen as the alternative launch point, and the 10th SFG and the group's attached personnel arrived in Constanta on 3 March. While the selected media teams embedded with the 10th SFG in Constanta,

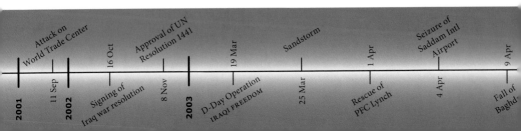

Nye and Major Rick Gaul* opened a joint information bureau in downtown Constanta in order to keep the nonembedded media away from the actual staging base, which needed to keep a low profile. As part of the effort to deflect attention away from the Special Forces presence, the staging base was passed off as an area for equipment and personnel in transit. To satisfy media curiosity and redirect interest, the information bureau even conducted a press conference at the "transit" base, complete with guided tour. The tour turned out to be one of the largest press events in Romania in over a decade.[10]

Back in Qatar, Andersen continued to coordinate the various component public affairs officers and associated embedded media in preparation for the war. Because SOF embeds generally did not remain with a unit for an extended period, they found themselves waiting in Qatar for mission assignments. Andersen and his staff went to great lengths to maintain operational security, and generally the media cooperated with the procedures. Many continued to question the public affairs officer, trying to ferret out details about their prospective assignments, but they also entered the spirit of the "game"

Figure 8.2 Photo of the GOPLATS. *Embedded media and combat camera crews documented SOF liberation of Iraqi offshore gas and oil platforms in the early days of IRAQI FREEDOM. Night vision goggles enabled Coalition soldiers to approach their objectives in the dead of night surprising the Iraqis.*

created by security requirements. Reporters and media crews enjoyed receiving mission instructions that seemed to be taken from a spy novel. Such directions as, "You will be met by a man in the lobby of your hotel . . . ," and, "Fly to Bucharest . . . ," were met with amusement and occasionally astonishment: "That's in Romania!"[11]

The first opportunity for Andersen's team to prove how well media embeds could work for SOF came on 21 March, when representatives from Fox News and The New York Times arrived on location just hours after special operations personnel liberated several gas and oil platforms off the Iraqi coast. The reporters and camera teams captured the military and environmental significance of the operation, and were prepared to release the story immediately. While the approval process was streamlined after Operation ENDURING FREEDOM and all footage and copy were cleared for release, General Tommy Franks wanted to wait until all platforms were secured before

Liberation of Kirkuk

11 Apr

Capture of Abu Abbas

1 May

Demise of Udai & Qusay Hussein

13 Dec

10 Apr

Liberation of Mosul

15 Apr

End of Hostilities

22 Jul

2004

Capture of Saddam Hussein

Figure 8.3 Navy SEALs. *The Naval Task Force secured offshore drilling facilities in the predawn hours of 21 March 2003. Positive media coverage of the GOPLATS mission proved the value of the embed program and provided a model for SOF-media cooperation throughout IRAQI FREEDOM.*

releasing details. The delay came to the attention of General Richard Myers, Chairman of the Joint Chiefs of Staff, and in the Defense Department briefing on 21 March, he settled the issue by announcing in reference to the platform operations that "there were embedded media with the SEALs, and their reports should be out shortly." With that statement, the SOCCENT public affairs officer received permission from CENTCOM to release the stories, along with Joint Combat Camera images recorded during the operation.[12]

With the infiltration of 10th SFG into northern Iraq, the CJSOTF-North public affairs officer found himself on the frontlines of military-media relations. Nye escorted an ABC News television crew as it accompanied 10th SFG on a joint offensive with Kurdish peshmergas against Ansar al-Islam forces in and around the city of Halabja. The news crew remained on the hilltops surrounding the valley of Halabja, interviewing soldiers at their observation posts in the Special Forces teams' few quiet moments between receiving hostile fire and calling in air strikes on the enemy below. As the soldiers saw that the media obeyed the Public Affairs Guidance and were not breaking security by filming them from the front or revealing their full names, soldiers accepted the news crew and even began to volunteer their own stories.[13]

At the conclusion of the battle, a Kurdish commander scheduled a press conference in Halabja. In order to maintain control of the situation, Nye organized the event and Lieutenant Colonel Kenneth Tovo, 3rd Battalion, 10th SFG commander, presided. While it was unusual for Special Forces ground commanders to participate in press events, the Halabja conference provided Tovo with the opportunity to officially state what had occurred during the battle. With public affairs officer coaching, Tovo carefully explained that Task Force Viking was only in the area to support Kurdish forces, and that while the troops had secured a suspected chemical weapons facility, the scientists were still evaluating the site and no conclusions had been reached regarding the presence of weapons of mass destruction. By cooperating with

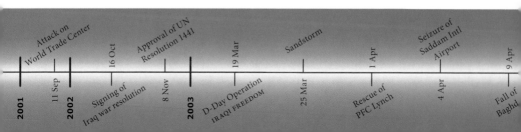

the press instead of stonewalling them, Tovo mitigated the possibly negative effects of the inevitable publicity given the operation.

An unexpected side effect of the success of the embed program was that nonembedded media sometimes became unofficially embedded with SOF units. One reporter embedded himself with the Kurds, which by default embedded him with the Special Forces troops fighting in Halabja. Nye directed the soldiers to continue to follow the guidance for media interaction, and in the end the reporter produced such Special Forces–favorable articles that the troops treated him as an official embed and allowed him the same access as the public affairs officer–assigned news crews.

Safety issues also created relationships where previously there had been none, as happened in Mosul. Soon after the Halabja operation, Nye joined with the staff of the 2nd Battalion, 10th SFG, in linking up with their commander, Lieutenant Colonel Robert Waltemeyer, at the airfield on the edge of Mosul. As Nye entered the terminal building to meet with the commander, he was shocked to see large numbers of reporters intermingled with the troops. Waltemeyer had offered the media shelter from the bombardment, effectively embedding them all with his battalion in the process.

Waltemeyer's actions that day, and for the rest of the week, gave further evidence of the more congenial relationship developed between SOF and the media. Nye arrived in Mosul to find that Waltemeyer and Colonel Charles Cleveland, 10th SFG

Figure 8.4 Local press conference. *Colonel Charles Cleveland and Lieutenant Colonel Robert Waltemeyer met with local leaders and press shortly after soldiers from 2nd Battalion, 10th SFG entered Mosul. SOF officers not only cooperated with the media during* IRAQI FREEDOM, *but also learned to capitalize on its presence.*

commander, had already scheduled a press conference for that day (and Nye was expected to run it). In an effort to stop violence between the Kurds and the Arabs, the Special Forces commanders used the high profile conference to announce that the 2nd Battalion was in control of Mosul and all warring factions would ultimately answer to them. Waltemeyer continued to hold daily press conferences and personal interviews, indicating that he was not only at peace with the media, but welcomed it as a vital aspect of governance.

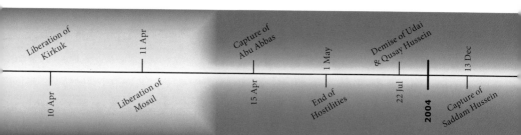

Less than a month after the war had begun, SOF had proved that they were not only willing to cooperate with the media, but also welcomed the presence of embedded news teams on selected missions. The Department of Defense's directive on the military acceptance of media embeds was carried out both by military leaders and individuals at the troop level, making the embed program a success within the SOF community. From Nye's perspective as a public affairs officer responsible for making the embed program work, the SOF soldiers accommodated the media "in a very professional manner. They understood the importance of it, they understood the mission, and they never tried to impede it." This resulted in better media coverage and greater public understanding of SOF's role in military operations—a situation that benefited all involved.[14]

CONVENTIONAL OPERATIONS

With Baghdad under Coalition control, the I Marine Expeditionary Force moved out on Highway 1 north toward Tikrit on 12 April. V Corps and I MEF had punched through enemy resistance south of Baghdad, and SOF with Kurdish forces had fixed numerous Iraqi divisions along the Green Line; I MEF was then tasked to close the gap between the north and Baghdad. When I MEF armor and infantry reached the outskirts of Tikrit—supposedly the regime's last stronghold—they defeated an Iraqi infantry unit and then rolled into the city on 13 April. After securing Saddam's palace, the Marines began rooting out the hard-core regime elements.[15]

Figure 8.5 3rd ID M1A1 Abrams tank in Baghdad.

Conventional forces spent the rest of April confronting pockets of fedayeen resistance and beginning stability operations. While the regime had collapsed, Saddam loyalists and other groups vying for power continued to attack Coalition forces.

The Marines, the 3rd ID, and the 101st Airborne Division (Air Assault) soldiers continued to work their way through Baghdad, isolating loyalists and wearing them down. The 4th ID finally arrived—in

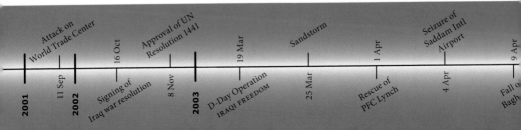

Attack on World Trade Center

11 Sep

16 Oct

Signing of Iraq war resolution

Approval of UN Resolution 1441

8 Nov

19 Mar

D-Day Operation IRAQI FREEDOM

25 Mar

Sandstorm

1 Apr

Rescue of PFC Lynch

Seizure of Saddam Intl Airport

4 Apr

9 Apr

Fall of Bagh

2001   2002   2003

Kuwait—and moved north, taking responsibility for the northern part of Iraq in conjunction with the 101st Airborne Division starting on 17 April. The newly arrived 3rd Armored Cavalry Regiment began moving into western Iraq, slowly taking responsibility from CJSOTF-west.[16]

422ND CAB: FROM THE BORDER TO BAGHDAD

The U.S. Army Reserve 422nd Civil Affairs Battalion crossed the berm into Iraq with the 3rd ID on 21 March 2003. Its assignment to the main invasion force placed the 422nd CAB at the forefront of ground combat operations, a place few Civil Affairs teams are ever found. Once the 3rd ID reached Baghdad, the battalion successfully made the difficult transition from the military side of civil military operations to the civil side, and was instrumental in helping the capital city move forward and begin to rebuild. The experiences of the Civil Affairs soldiers on the march north and in Baghdad itself epitomize the juncture between civil and military operations.

Six-man direct support teams from the 422nd CAB accompanied the 3rd ID's brigade combat teams during the rapid advance towards the capital. The 422nd CAB direct support teams were tasked with minimizing civilian interference with combat operations, which preserved both civilian life and combat momentum. Major Dustin Hilburn* described the battalion's planning process:

Figure 8.6 422nd CAB insignia.

> We focused on the ethnic makeup of the population, and whether they were pro-regime or not, agricultural or industrial, normal means of transportation, and what type of ethnic strife was going on in the city. We looked at the possibility for relocation of civilians and what direction they might move. We tried to plan how we would react to different sizes of groups. We had to differentiate between [displaced civilians] and civilians on the battlefield. We ended up surprising lots of Iraqis just coming home from their fields. During the combat operation, the [displaced civilians] were not a problem.[17]

While the 3rd ID did not confront significant civilian resistance to the advance, the direct support teams did have to deal with nonaggressive interference. One soldier in Direct Support Team 3, attached to the 3rd ID's 2nd Brigade, commented, "There were civilians who

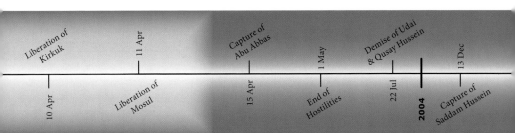

Liberation of Kirkuk

11 Apr

Capture of Abu Abbas

1 May

Demise of Udai & Qusay Hussein

13 Dec

10 Apr

Liberation of Mosul

15 Apr

End of Hostilities

22 Jul

2004

Capture of Saddam Hussein

Figure 8.7 422nd CAB soldier with 3rd ID in Baghdad.

would try to pass our convoy in cars and we would get on the bullhorn and pull them over and tell them [to] stay off the road for their own protection. They were scared at first, and then they were very happy." As the brigade entered villages, the Civil Affairs soldiers "would go find civilians and tell them to stay away from U.S. forces."[18]

Loudspeakers—"bullet magnets"—helped the teams broadcast their instructions quickly and effectively. On at least one occasion, DST 3 "cruised through the town broadcasting the message that [they] weren't there to harm them." The terrorized populace received the news cautiously: "We could see joy from the people, but it was restrained as there were still Baath Party personnel around," commented one Civil Affairs soldier. "In retrospect, I understood the ambivalence toward Americans, as the Iraqis were getting barraged by the Iraqi information minister saying how the Americans were getting the crap kicked out of them. They didn't know what to believe."[19]

Many of the civilians the direct support teams encountered were not aggressive toward the U.S. troops, but actually helpful. One DST 3 soldier recounted an incident that occurred near Najaf, which aptly illustrates the benefits of allowing Civil Affairs soldiers to do their job:

> On the outskirts of Najaf, there were a bunch of civilians at this bridge, and the infantry guys were wanting to light them up [because] they had been hit by a bus the day before. There were people working in their gardens about five hundred meters away, and I asked the company commander, 'If I could go over and talk to them, would you provide a squad for security?' We walked over there without [an] interpreter and these guys were just farmers, and they told us not to go that way because the Iraqi Army is there. And they told us where the Baath Party headquarters was. We brought that information back and farther down the road, there were fifty to a hundred people in the road, [so] I drove down there with two tanks as protection. The people were out in the road because it was their village and they were

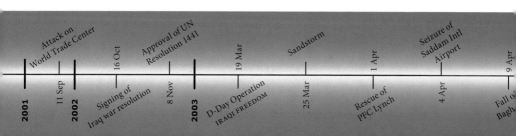

2001   11 Sep   2002   Signing of Iraq war resolution   8 Nov   2003   D-Day Operation IRAQI FREEDOM   25 Mar   Rescue of PFC Lynch   4 Apr   Fall of Baghdad

Attack on World Trade Center   16 Oct   Approval of UN Resolution 1441   19 Mar   Sandstorm   1 Apr   Seizure of Saddam Intl Airport   9 Apr

*wondering what was going on. We started talking to them
and they started telling us that the Iraqi Army pulled out
the night before.*[20]

As the direct support teams made sure civilians did not interfere
with the advance, the soldiers also took the opportunity to assess villagers' needs and tried to address them. Another DST 3 soldier related,
"the Bedouins would say they used to get water trucked to them, so
we would call back and get them some water from the [division] rear.
If a tank [ran] over water lines, we would also call back to the [divi-
sion] rear to handle it when they came forward." In another case, the
native Iraqis led the brigade to water: "We came across these Bedouins
and asked them where the water was, and one jumped in the HMMWV
[High-Mobility Multipurpose Wheeled Vehicle] to go show us. We set
a ROPU [reverse osmosis purification unit] up right there."[21]

The speed of the advance usually prevented the direct support
teams from providing immediate humanitarian assistance. As a DST
3 officer put it, "Our intent for humanitarian aid was like [dealing
with] a stray cat. If you put a bowl of milk out, you will get every stray
cat in the neighborhood. So we just didn't put a bowl out." Captain
Merino* of DST 4 corroborated the truth of that strategy: "The longer
we stayed outside Karbala, the more civilians came out asking for
water and food. We knew if we kept handing out food, it would bring
more civilians." Hilburn, the 3rd ID plans officer, recalled one incident
where the lack of humanitarian assistance was met with agreeable resignation by the civilians involved: "At Karbala, we had approximately
110 people come out to a checkpoint and request food and water. We
told them we didn't have any to give them at that time and to turn
around and return to their homes, and they did."[22]

The direct support teams and their assigned brigades did give as
much help as they could without compromising their own security
and missions. DST 3 encountered one such situation near the Karbala
Gap: "There was a fight that day—a lot of fighting. There was this one
Iraqi woman who came out and said, 'Please help me, please help.' We
stopped and got out to look, and the medic truck stopped and went
over to find that her husband had been shot in the butt. They treated
him and put him on a stretcher by the road, and we moved on. The
guy was waving at us as we all drove by him."[23]

At times, the direct support teams found themselves in the position
of taking instead of giving, ironically much to the civilian population's

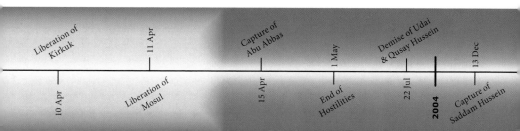

relief. The team led by Captain Ted Morgan* found itself in just such a situation on 31 March. Residents of the town of Khairat informed the team that a local school harbored a large Saddam Fedayeen weapons cache. The Civil Affairs soldiers passed the information on to the infantry and engineers, who investigated and discovered more than nine hundred mortars, twenty-six thousand AK-47 rounds, dynamite, and chemical protective gear. After removing and inventorying the cache, an explosive ordnance disposal unit dug a hole and detonated the weapons that could not be moved very far. The rest were disposed of in a field outside the village—after clearing it of sheep.[24]

Their positions with the forward brigade combat teams placed the direct support teams in live-fire situations much more often than they found weapons caches. A member of DST 3 described one of the team's more stressful moments as they neared Baghdad:

> As we pulled into this little town, there was this car sitting in the middle of the road. There was a dead man in the street, and the woman in the front seat was dead, and in the back seat was a teenage boy, shot but still alive. And in the lap of the dead mother was this baby who was untouched; [she] had these wide eyes and was just crying. The city was to our left and the canal to our right. The infantry guys were freaking out, as there were bullets flying everywhere. I went over to the girl and there was this fedayeen truck coming directly at us. I said, 'There's a truck!' and the .50 [calibers] just opened up, and this truck explodes. And then we started receiving all sorts of bullets [from] the guys [who] had jumped out of the back of the truck we hit. Then we heard this whoosh and a huge explosion up in the air, and I said, 'Holy s——!' The Bradleys and us went further into the city, and we dismounted and went inside a building to establish a fighting position. They called up a tank platoon, and it came forward and everything calmed down.[26]

Although the teams' primary mission was to clear civilians from the battlefield, occasionally events deteriorated forcing the soldiers to concentrate on fighting. DST 3 experienced one such incident near Najaf:

> We went to this bridge where a PSYOP [Psychological Operations] team was checking people walking across the bridge. There were fedayeen fighting positions underneath

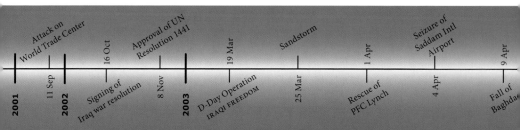

the bridge. We put up a PSYOP message on loudspeaker: 'Put your weapon down if you wish to surrender.' We had a couple of civilians who had already crossed the bridge and given us information on where the fedayeen fighting positions were located. The enemy then pushed about two hundred civilians across the bridge and we were totally overwhelmed. We then had to stop the people, as the company commander was scared. We told the people the bridge was closed, and this one Iraqi guy took charge of all the civilians and moved them back across the bridge. In hindsight, we should have detained him. He became very offended when we told him to leave. [Then] we were hit by mortars and RPGs [rocket-propelled grenades]. The CA [Civil Affairs] mission was pretty much over at that time.[26]

Beginning on 7 April, teams from the 422nd CAB moved into Baghdad. The battalion focused on controlling civilians on the battlefield during the advance with the 3rd ID, but now that Baghdad had been taken, the Civil Affairs soldiers shifted to civil military operations. Unfortunately, the battalion was not provided with a clear Civil Affairs plan from higher and was left to its own judgment in prioritizing missions. Hilburn explained, "A plan for Phase IV was never passed from CFLCC [Coalition Forces Land Component Command] to V Corps and on to 3rd ID. There was no guidance on which targets we needed to protect once we got into Baghdad. We weren't told to protect museums or banks, and we didn't expect the scale of the looting [that occurred]." Merino concurred: "There wasn't a plan for Phase IV, and there wasn't a plan to deal with all the civilians [flooding out of Baghdad]."[27]

The first challenge facing the 422nd CAB was the outflow of civilians from Baghdad. The battalion had met relatively few displaced civilians during the advance north, but was confronted with hundreds of scared people fleeing the battle in the capital city. Unfortunately, adequate plans for dealing with those civilians were not in place, in spite of the fact that they were considerably fewer than had been expected. Merino reported, "We had pages and pages of schools that were to be used as collection points, but they weren't outside the cities. We would look for areas that could be set up as collection sites. The schools inside the cities were not viable, as the Iraqis held the

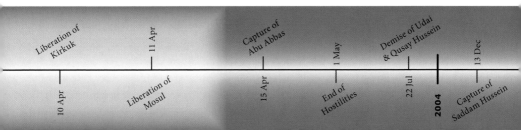

cities." In spite of the lack of a plan, the battalion managed to direct civilians to safe locations and provide them with basic necessities.[28]

Once in the city, the 422nd CAB turned its attention to infrastructure. Hilburn recalled, "We started looking at what we could do with a [civil military operations] focus that could have the most impact on the civilian population." In short order, the battalion concluded that power was the most important issue, since it controlled the water and sewage systems. On 10 April, battalion commander Lieutenant Colonel R. Alan King led a mission to locate and assess power transformers in the Firdos district of Baghdad. Local residents advised King's team that there were fedayeen forces operating in the local area, and that they had rocket-propelled grenades and other weapons. As King's team neared the transformers, it came under small arms fire. The team turned around, but was then ambushed with rocket-propelled grenades and more small arms fire. Several of the team's vehicles were struck by rounds, but functioned well enough to get the team back through the ambush—a tactic of last resort chosen because the route forward was blocked. King and the other Civil Affairs soldiers returned suppressive fire during their exit, killing several enemy personnel.[29]

The next morning, King's team set out once again on a mission to return power to Baghdad. This time, the team planned to meet the transformer engineer. Once again, the team ran into an ambush, this time involving a parked diesel tanker truck. Unable to retreat, the team proceeded down the middle of the fuel-soaked roadway, ducking small arms fire from two separate locations. The team called in Bradley Fighting Vehicles, which laid down suppressive fire. The team escaped unscathed and was able to return later in the day—accompanied by fifteen Bradleys—to secure the transformer site. The next day, the team located Baghdad's senior power plant engineers, who were instrumental in restoring power to the city thirteen days later.[30]

Figure 8.8 Baghdad fire truck. *Civil Affairs soldiers made a visit to the fire station along with Baghdad's new interim fire chief, Dr. Ali Saeed Sadoon.*

While Civil Affairs efforts were directed toward getting the Iraqis to rebuild their own infrastructure, U.S. soldiers had to step in and help at all levels. The 422nd CAB and the city

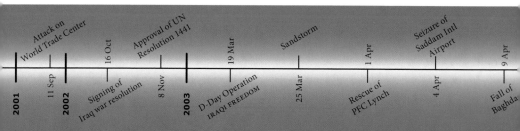

of Baghdad were fortunate to have Major Bob Glass*, whose civilian career was as a fire captain with the Greensboro, North Carolina, Fire Department. In late April, Glass met with Dr. Ali Saeed Saldoon of Civil Defense, who was able to report that twelve of the city's twenty-five fire stations were operable. Approximately four hundred fire fighters were still working as well. "The good thing about it is that they, like fire fighters around the world, are dedicated to their job," remarked Glass. "The majority

Figure 8.9 Dr. Ali Saeed Sadoon.

of them stayed on throughout the hostilities, and more were coming back each day. Within a matter of days we went from 400 to 892 fire fighters back on duty." Just weeks later, the number had risen to 1,100 out of the prewar force of 1,400 fire department personnel.[31]

The first priority after identifying available resources was to make sure that the operable equipment was distributed to those fire stations that were manned and operating. In rehabilitating the fire defense system, Glass focused on using the native resources as much as possible: "I wanted to utilize [Dr. Saldoon] to do this, because our job is not to stay here and do it for them, but to get them to do it and become self-sufficient. So I gave him the orders to do that, and then he went out and talked to his officers in turn." Getting as many fire stations operational as possible was vital, since by American standards Baghdad was woefully lacking in stations anyway. Other shortfalls in the fire system included the lack of a nine-one-one phone system and inadequate personal protection equipment. One advantage Baghdad did have, however, was the fact that most buildings were built of concrete and did not contain large amounts of "fire-load" to catch fire. The majority of fires historically occurred at power plants and refineries.[32]

Revitalizing the Baghdad police force was another high priority for the 422nd CAB. King appointed former Texas public safety officer Major Vaughn Christian* to be Baghdad's interim police commissioner, or the "Sheriff of Baghdad," as some called him. In turn, Christian looked to Baghdad's former police administration and officers to return to service. Christian and his team prioritized aspects of law enforcement, concentrating on the most immediate needs first. "Obviously I can't come in and start setting up an arson division, an

investigation division—that takes time. I tried to prioritize. The city had just come out of a war, so my priority was getting security back on the streets, for one." The department focused on traffic, facility security (hospitals, utility plants, and such), and patrols.[33]

Christian also concentrated on teaching the police department how to function in an ethical manner. He quickly put an end to such practices as transporting suspects in car trunks, openly carrying AK-47s, challenging U.S. Army soldiers at checkpoints, and various other abuses that were customary in the former regime. On at least one occasion, Christian turned a routine evidence check-in into a lesson in proper police procedure. Addressing the evidence room officer, Christian instructed, "You are the only person who belongs in this room. You count the money, and write down the amount and names of the officers who brought it in." Such basics needed to be explained and repeated as the 422nd CAB trained officers to represent and run what would be an entirely new kind of police force in Iraq.[34]

Figure 8.10 Policing Baghdad. *Major Vaughn Christian*, right, and Captain Ted Pendergrass*, of the 422nd CAB join a crowd of Iraqis working in the new Baghdad Police Department around a map of the city.*

In addition to the expected challenges of rebuilding a large city just emerging from tyranny and war, the 422nd CAB faced the unexpected chaos of rampant looting. With no concrete plan indicating which buildings and sites needed protection, the battalion and other Coalition forces in the city found themselves reacting to problems as they arose. Hilburn described the situation:

We would watch some TV broadcast live from Baghdad with the reporter saying this museum is being looted, and a few hours later we would get an e-mail [fragmentary order] down from higher to protect this museum. The same thing happened with banks and other locations. In a lot of ways it was planning by CNN. We were reacting to problems being identified [by the media]. One of the problems we ran into was museum names; we would be told one name and it did not exist. We got some wrong grid coordinates, which caused some confusion about where to protect. I would still receive e-mails a week after we had secured a museum that the

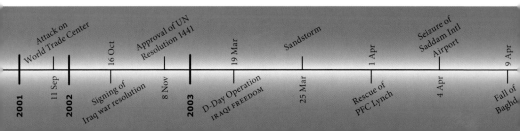

2001 — 11 Sep / Attack on World Trade Center

2002 — 16 Oct / Signing of Iraq war resolution — Approval of UN Resolution 1441 — 8 Nov

2003 — 19 Mar / D-Day Operation IRAQI FREEDOM — Sandstorm — 25 Mar — 1 Apr / Rescue of PFC Lynch — Seizure of Saddam Intl Airport — 4 Apr — 9 Apr / Fall of Baghd

museum was being looted and needed to be protected.[35]

U.S. forces were also surprised at some of the looters' targets. Hilburn remarked, "We were not prepared for the hospitals being looted. We did not plan for it and did not receive any information [that] we would have problems in these areas." While looting initially concentrated on buildings representing the former regime, the thievery quickly spread to all types of public buildings, including museums, hospitals, and schools. By the time schools were targeted, the looters were seeking basic building materials, such as electrical switches and wires, desks, blackboards, and plumbing fixtures. The thefts left the 422nd CAB scrambling for basic school items—like blackboards and desks—as they attempted to restore educational services to the city.[36]

Figure 8.11 Demonstrating police procedures.

One group of 422nd CAB soldiers ran into bigger crime than looting when they witnessed and foiled a bank robbery. Sergeant Chris Mercer* recounted the story: "We were driving . . . and we got stopped by [an officer] of the 3rd ID. He said, 'Hey, there's a bank robbery going on. You all want in on it?' 'Of course!'" The team proceeded to the bank and found that the would-be robbers had been at the bank

> *. . . for a while. Because you could see on the doors that they had beaten them with pickaxes, sledgehammers, mauls, whatever they had. Eventually they got some dynamite and were able to blow a small hole in the top of the safe, through about two feet of concrete and rebar, then the steel. It was just big enough to get a small child in there. So they had lowered a child in there, and he was coming and giving them money. We think they probably got away with about $2 million. We secured seven people inside the bank without incident. We went ahead and blew the other safe and pulled out $6.3 million in U.S. $100 bills. We took the money back to the airport and turned it over to the 3rd ID. While we were there [at the airport] we actually got called to another bank robbery, and went in and apprehended*

*two [people]. They hadn't blown the safes yet. It was just
another day in Civil Affairs.*[37]

The roles of Civil Affairs units in Operation IRAQI FREEDOM were
diverse and constantly changing. The 422nd CAB's experiences are
representative of the challenges met and the successes enjoyed by all
Civil Affairs units during the first months of the war. From managing
and protecting displaced civilians to protecting museums and catching bank robbers, the Civil Affairs soldiers stepped in wherever they
were needed. The lack of a comprehensive Civil Affairs plan often
left these units in positions of determining their own priorities and
reacting to situations as they arose. The units' ability to excel can be
attributed to a combination of training and serendipity. More often
than not, the individuals' own skills and talents created order from
the chaos of war-torn Iraq.

"AN AIMED SHOT WINS THE FIGHT"

It was a warm Sunday morning, about 0830 on 27 April, and the sun
was already beginning to bake downtown Baghdad. Colonel Warner
Anderson was preparing to depart for a meeting at the newly formed
Iraqi Ministry of Health. Anderson was attached to the 352nd Civil
Affairs Command out of Riverdale, Maryland, and was serving on a
public health team. Before deploying to Iraq, Anderson instructed
candidates training to become Special Forces medics at the John F.
Kennedy Special Warfare Center and School at Fort Bragg, North
Carolina. Before being mobilized to active duty and assigned to the
Joint Special Operations Medical Training Facility, Anderson served
as an emergency physician with the Indian Health Service, which is
part of the U.S. Public Health Service.

Figure 8.12 352 Civil
Affairs Command
insignia.

The Iraqi Ministry of Health had recently been organized and the
public health team was going to participate in the Ministry's first
official meeting, which was scheduled to begin at 1000 in the ministry medical complex, commonly referred to as Medical City. The
team was told the trip to the Ministry would have a Military Police
escort that would link up with the public health team at the Civil
Military Operations Center. Since the team did not have an interpreter, the operations center provided one of the contract interpreters, Ali Habib, a physician who went by Dr. Ali and spoke English
well. The Military Police support was scheduled to arrive at the center

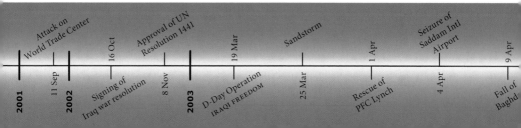

between 0845 and 0900. However, at 0930, they had not arrived and Colonel Robert Frame, the team leader, was unable to locate them. At that time, Frame picked up the team's other HMMWV and decided the team would conduct a two-vehicle convoy to the ministry. The team was given authorization to conduct the convoy without the Military Police escort. After everything was in order, the team departed the compound. Major Rendell Davis* drove the lead vehicle with Frame in the passenger seat as convoy commander. The trail vehicle was driven by Specialist Jim Lawson*, with Anderson in the passenger seat along with Dr. Ali in the right rear seat. Anderson recalled:

> We left the compound through its north entrance. We turned onto the avenue that had the first bridge, south to north. We crossed east over that bridge, came to a traffic circle, and proceeded northwest on a divided boulevard. The traffic northbound became congested pretty quickly, and with half an hour to get to the Ministry of Health we were in traffic that was moving about the speed of a slow walk. There were a lot of different vehicles, including buses and commercial vehicles, on the road with us. I had called the lead vehicle to tell them that we were about one click [kilometer] out, according to my GPS, and we had about three minutes to go until the meeting. Ten minutes after that, we came to a particularly congested area where traffic slowed down to virtually a standstill. We heard some shots, which is very common—we've been shot at several times before . . . but nothing has ever hit us before. This time, however, immediately upon hearing the shots, the front windshield broke out and I was hit by flying glass.[38]

Rounds hit both vehicles of the team. Lawson threw on the emergency brake and both he and Anderson piled out of the vehicle, searching for the location of the their assailants. Anderson was trying to pinpoint the source of the fire when he was hit. "I was looking for a target and I couldn't find a target. I remember being hit three times . . . in two areas. Once was in my right side, right at the level of my last rib. And the other time was in my arm. I didn't know the extent of the damage there. I assumed that the round that hit my rib had broken my rib because the pain was intense, and I assumed that it had entered my abdominal cavity and probably hit my liver. I seemed to be able to have good grip strength and could function. I didn't feel

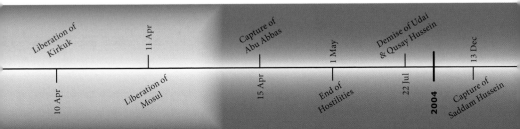

particularly weak, but I remember having the sense that I might be getting ready to go into shock."[39]

At this point Frame was hit and exited the vehicle with his left arm hanging uselessly, a large stain spreading over the sleeve of his uniform. Anderson yelled at him to get back in the vehicle. The vehicles were halted close together and Anderson retrieved his aid bag with a tourniquet from the HMMWV. There was a lull in the firing and Anderson was about to make his way forward to attend to Frame when a single shot rang out.

Figure 8.13 Crosswalk vantage point. *This elevated crosswalk is where the Iraqi gunman ambushed the Civil Affairs public health team convoy.*

As I was standing up, I still had the M16 in my hand and, as I recall, there was another shot and I took a round through my protective mask carrier, which was on my left thigh. I turned around and looked up. There was an elevated crosswalk that was about probably three meters, or maybe four meters, above the road. The Iraqis had scattered out—that reduced the number of potential assailants—and I looked up when this round came through my protective mask carrier, because I had that sense that it was coming from up above. I saw a figure that was dressed in . . . a black, traditional headdress and a black shirt. He was firing directly at me and I could see the muzzle flashes being directed at me. I was able to see his eyes, and he was intently concentrating on me, directing his fire at me. The bullets were kicking up in the pavement around me.[40]

Anderson was torn between the necessity of attending to the wounded Frame and the need to take care of the shooter on the crosswalk. Having located the gunman, he brought his M16 into action.

I raised the M16 with the first round . . . going wild, being fired as quickly as possible. My intent there was to throw off his mental balance. My second round, I was trying to get close to hitting him, but I was doing it by swinging the rifle up. But I planned for the third round to be an aimed shot, because I've always been told that an aimed shot wins the fight. When I fired the second shot, I must have been really close to him or maybe caused a grazing injury or

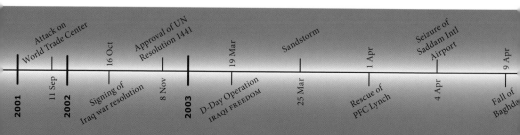

something, because he took off running. He presented his right side to me as he turned to his left and took off running across the elevated crosswalk, and I took an aimed shot. When I hit him, I had good follow-through on the shot, with the sights remaining on him, getting ready to fire yet a fourth shot. But he went down on my third shot and dropped basically like a bag of rocks.[41]

Anderson moved quickly up to attend to his wounded teammate. He applied a tourniquet above the wound on Frame's left arm, staunching the bleeding. He realized that the priority was to get out of the kill zone and get Frame to medical treatment. Leaving Frame in the lead vehicle, he told Davis—who was sitting somewhat dazed in the driver's seat—to get the vehicle out of the area. Then he ran back to the second HMMWV, and with Lawson driving, sped after the lead vehicle. An Iraqi jumped immediately out in front of them and pointed to the lead HMMWV, where Frame had jumped or fallen from the vehicle. Anderson, Lawson, and the Iraqi picked Frame up and placed him in the left rear of their vehicle beside Dr. Ali. Ali was moaning, "I'm hit! I'm hit! I'm dying! I'm dying! I'm an only son, I can't die." Anderson took this as a sign the Iraqi was mentally alert enough to recognize his situation. In a true case of "Physician, heal thyself," Anderson directed Ali to put a pressure bandage on his own wound as Lawson headed for Medical City. Davis drove off alone ahead of the second vehicle.[42]

The streets had cleared from the area around the ambush and the convoy quickly reached the Medical City complex. At one point Lawson was forced to bump a vehicle out of the way as the HMMWV's steering was freezing up from loss of hydraulic fluid. When they pulled into the facility, Anderson sent Lawson to get a litter, and when he returned they transported Frame to some U.S. medics, who turned out to be part of a forward surgical hospital that was set up on the porch of one of the buildings. The medics got an IV started and Anderson began to address the need to get Frame medically evacuated. "The medics wanted to evacuate Frame and I told them I wanted a helo medevac because the determining factor is time to the operating room for survival. So I wanted to get him to an operating room as quickly as possible. I didn't know there was a forward surgical team nearby. They said, 'we can't land a [helicopter] here, but we can land it on top of the building.' So I looked over and it looked [to be] about

a twelve-story building. I said, "Does the elevator work?" They said, "yes," so we picked up the litter and ran the litter into the hospital."[43]

As it turned out, the elevators were not functioning and the team returned to the ground floor where Frame was loaded into an ambulance. Lawson had suffered a gunshot wound to his thigh in the ambush and Anderson loaded him onto the ambulance also. At this point, a physician from the forward surgical hospital appeared and assured Anderson that the unit could provide the level of care Frame needed. With Frame under proper medical care, Anderson and Lawson were treated for their wounds; in Anderson's case dressing and bandaging his wounded elbow and the point where a bullet glanced off his rib cage. Lawson later developed an extensive infection that required surgery to repair. Davis, left behind at the ambush site, drove through the city until he came to a checkpoint manned by U.S. infantry. He received medical treatment for a collapsed lung, the result of a bullet entering his shoulder, and was medically evacuated. Dr. Ali was treated at the Medical City facility by both the Iraqis and Americans and later discharged. After extensive surgery, including grafting a vein from his leg to his arm, Frame began the process of rehabilitation to recover the use of his left arm.

Anderson later reflected on the confusion of the ambush scene and one of the major causes for his own personal "fog of war." He remembered:

> I said I had a sense of confusion. And part of that confusion came from the fact that when the glass was flying, I suddenly went—not quite legally blind, but close to it—in my left eye. And I couldn't figure out what was going on, what the injury was to my eye because there was no pain. I thought maybe that was because of the adrenaline rush or whatever, but I couldn't explain it. At about three minutes into this thing, I realized that it was because something had hit my left glasses lens and knocked it out. And so my vision in my left eye was uncorrected about 20/200. So my dominant eye was seeing 20/200 and my nondominant eye was its usual 20/15 corrected. And that made it hellish for me to locate the assailant and understand what was going on. At any rate, I had a spare pair of glasses with me, which I put on at the forward surgical team.[44]

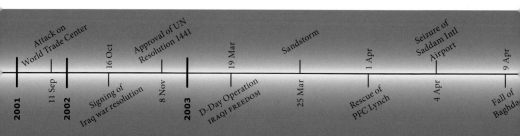

Anderson was awarded a Bronze Star for valor for his clear thinking and quick action not to mention a well-deserved Purple Heart. The incident emphasized the fact that while Civil Affairs operations in Iraq were peaceful by nature, they were carried out in a war zone and at times required Civil Affairs teams to be soldiers first and foremost.

CAMP BUCCA

While Psychological Operations missions are by their very nature diverse, the 13th Psyop Battalion has the unique mission of supporting Enemy Prisoner of War and Civilian Internee missions. The only unit of its type within the U.S. Army, the Arden Hills, Minnesota-based 13th POB is wartraced to the Army Reserve 800th Military Police Brigade (EPW) located in Uniondale, New York. Once the 800th MP Brigade began preparing in November 2002 to deploy to the Middle East, the 13th POB realized that it was probably going to be called up as well.[45]

The battalion received its first alert order on 2 January 2003. After a long and disorganized mobilization, 108 members of 13th POB arrived in Kuwait on 22 March. By 27 March, the battalion had orders to link up with the 800th MP Brigade at British Holding Area Freddy, near

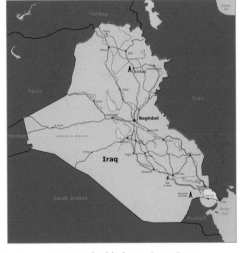

Umm Qasr, Iraq. The camp was turned over to the 800th and renamed Camp Bucca on 7 April, in honor of New York Fire Department Fire Marshal Ronald Bucca. Bucca was a member of the Army Reserve 3413th Military Intelligence Detachment, a subordinate unit of the 800th MP Brigade. He died trying to rescue survivors of the 11 September terrorist attacks on the World Trade Center in New York City.[46]

Being war-traced to the 800th MP Brigade (EPW), the 13th POB is specifically trained to provide Psychological Operations support to the brigade's enemy prisoner of war operations. While the MPs ran Camp Bucca, the 13th POB circulated among the prisoners and gathered information that would help the MPs

Figure 8.14 Map highlighting Camp Bucca.

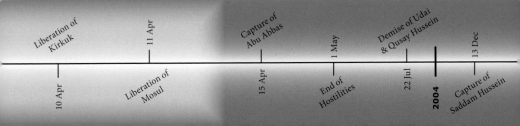

Liberation of Kirkuk

11 Apr

Capture of Abu Abbas

1 May

Demise of Udai & Qusay Hussein

13 Dec

10 Apr

Liberation of Mosul

15 Apr

End of Hostilities

22 Jul

2004

Capture of Saddam Hussein

control and aid the population. As Sergeant Ben Moore* described their job, "We kind of play the good cop. We try to win their trust and that helps us get information."[47]

One of the company's primary techniques was interviewing prisoners—not for military intelligence, rather for personal information and to monitor the camp's temperature, so to speak. Because one of its goals was to keep the peace, the interviews were conducted in as friendly a manner as possible. B Company commander, Major Jim Downing*, described the approach: "We [gave] them tea or something to drink and let them sit down. We put them at ease and that help[ed] everyone."[48]

A large part of the company's information gathering was related to morale issues within the camp. Downing recounted that "most of our work [was] simply getting into the enclosures and compounds day-to-day and providing the products and identifying issues among the prisoners that we [could] bring back to the MPs. We might go in and find that morale is high, or we might find that it is low and the prisoners [were] bored, so we suggest[ed] to the MPs that if they just provide[d] a soccer ball, the prisoners [would] have something to do and that [would] relieve the situation."[49]

Figure 8.15 800th MP Brigade insignia.

The 13th POB was also enlisted to prevent or quiet unrest within the compound. Specialist Bill Whatley* put his college disc jockey experience to good use by broadcasting basic camp rules and instructions in Arabic designed to relieve the stress of being relocated to the enemy prisoner of war camp. Similarly, the battalion broadcast orders for calm and order when the prisoners would begin fighting one another with rocks, tent stakes, and other improvised weapons. The broadcast instructions supported the MPs as they physically quelled incipient riots. As a 13th POB Information Paper recorded, tactical PSYOP techniques could be very effective:

> Camp teams responded to emergency situations on numerous occasions, defusing or minimizing potential danger. One such incident occurred after a storm leveled the infirmary, dining facility, and much of the shelter at the MARCENT corps collection facility. Some 2,000 rioting Iraqi prisoners stormed and tore down the wire, causing the Marine guards to fire over their heads. Two camp team PSYOP soldiers, accompanied by their Kuwaiti interpreter, and armed only with their loudspeaker system, entered the

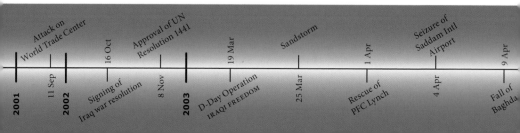

compound. They immediately restored order by explaining the procedures for distributing food and blankets and obtaining medical aid.[50]

In typical PSYOP manner, the same broadcast tools used to quell uprisings were also used to play Islamic call-to-prayer messages and readings from the Koran. The MSQ-85B mobile audio-visual systems enabled the battalion to produce instructional messages for broadcast throughout the camps. The MSQ-85B was also put to use as a movie projector, both for Coalition troop morale and as an incentive to encourage the prisoners to behave. Jean-Claude Van Damme movies were especially popular among the prisoners until the PSYOP soldiers realized the Iraqis considered the movies to be martial arts "training films."[51]

Figure 8.16 Flag of B Company, 13th POB, in Iraq.

An important aspect of keeping the enemy prisoners of war under control was identifying key leaders within the prisoner population. Specialist Tom Wilson* succinctly described that aspect of his mission: "We [tried] to find out who [was] in charge." In order to make reliable character judgments, he continued, "You have to look for the way someone holds themselves. Look at their body language. Their eyes. Things like that." Opportunities to make such assessments came as the battalion conducted morale-boosting activities within the camp, such as teaching English language classes, holding sporting events, and art contests.[52]

Interviews with the prisoners themselves also uncovered important information about individuals and groups. An interview with one young Iraqi corporal revealed that he spoke enough English to serve as a translator, and that he "led friends and other soldiers from his company to surrender (45 in all)." Another Sunni man was quite open with his low opinion of Shias and Kurds—"Beats Shia and Kurds just because he thinks they deserve it and it's fun"—and his disregard for others' opinions—"Knows that all prisoners hate and distrust him." That same man declared that he would "become an informant if it [would] guarantee his protection from retribution by other prisoners." Yet another interviewee was discovered to have "a large amount of peer influence among Shia but not Sunni prisoners. Enjoys lead-

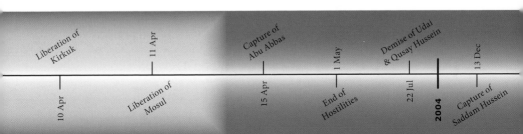

Figure 8.17 JPOTF logo.

ing troops." This potentially useful man was also "very arrogant" and "[would] not talk to females."[53]

With the PSYOP products' potential to have significant and wide-spread effect, the opportunity to gather information on what did and did not work was invaluable. One surrender appeal was instrumental in persuading an entire battalion from the Iraqi 48th Infantry Division to lay down arms—post-test data improved PSYOP efforts by explaining Iraqi reactions to PSYOP products. For example, post-test interviews revealed that red-bordered leaflets were ineffective because Iraqi soldiers were told that the red markings meant the papers were dangerous and should be left alone.[54]

Although the 13th POB was willing and able to conduct the product test mission, the JPOTF made the battalion's job slightly more difficult than it needed to be. Downing explained,

> One problem that we did run into was that when we [were] given a product for testing, we [were] supposed to be given that product in the native language—Arabic. We would find that we would get them in English only, and then we would have to translate them. That would create a different issue because we couldn't quite convince the JPOTF that they needed to send us these products in the native language. It's one thing to hand an [Iraqi] a printed medium in his own language and gauge his reaction to it. It's another thing altogether to hand him an English copy of that product, which he cannot read at all, or a copy that we translated here that may or may not be the best translation.[55]

Perhaps the best measure of the 13th POB's success at Camp Bucca was the lack of major rioting, which enabled the 800th MP Brigade to focus its efforts on providing the prisoners with sufficient shelter, security, and medical care. In late April, the camp began to release large numbers of prisoners. Throughout the month, the camp population had held steady at approximately six thousand prisoners, but the population decreased drastically as large releases outstripped new captures. To the credit of both the 13th POB and the 800th MP Brigade, released prisoners reported that conditions in the camp had been good. The Associated Press reported on 28 April 2003 that freed prisoners were generally complimentary of the Americans and happy that Saddam Hussein was no longer in power. Twenty-five-year-old Atheer Abdul-Karim stated his new allegiance most clearly: "They

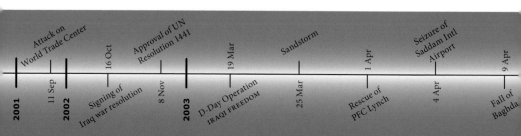

paid us 17,000 Iraqi dinars (U.S. $5.72) a month to fight Americans. I would have killed Saddam for one dollar."[56]

ARSOF OPERATIONS

CJSOTF-North

As Iraqi morale in the north eroded under the onslaught of the aerial bombardment orchestrated by Task Force Viking, the opportunity to move on the cities of Kirkuk and Mosul presented itself. On 10 April, Forward Operating Base 103 began a concentrated assault on Kirkuk, moving on the city from the north, east, and south. Concurrently, FOB 102 advanced alongside Kurdish forces on Mosul, entering that city on 11 April. The task force deployed forces to secure the critical northern oil fields near Kirkuk. At this point in the campaign, the task force's major concern revolved around establishing a visible American presence in the newly liberated cities.

With the collapse of the Iraqi forces imminent, Colonel Cleveland wrestled with the competing interests of those who sought to lay claim to northern Iraq. The two leaders within the Kurdish Autonomous Zone— Massoud Barzani, the leader of the Kurdistan Democratic Party and Jalal Talabani, leader of the Patriotic Union of Kurdistan—desired to expand their control in the cities of Tikrit and Mosul, respectively, and both possessed an intense desire to reclaim the formerly Kurdish-dominated areas subjected to Saddam's "Arabization" process. As the cities fell, many Kurds raced to see family members long isolated by Hussein's regime and the Baath Party. The substantial Turkoman population also vied for territory, and influence in the post-Saddam make-up of the region. The Special Forces and 173rd Airborne Brigade (-) soldiers quickly policed the insurgents with little resistance.[57]

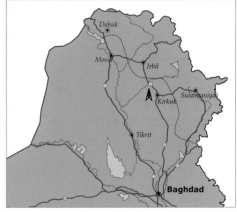

Figure 8.18 Map of CJSOTF-North area of operations. *FOB 102 led the assault on Mosul while FOB 103 joined the peshmerga in the capture of Kirkuk.*

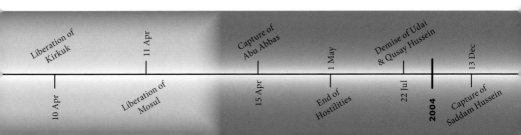

While united in their desire to oust the Iraqi Army and reclaim their hereditary control over the cities of Mosul and Kirkuk, the Kurds were far from a united people. The two major political factions, the Kurdistan Democratic Party and the Patriotic Union of Kurdistan, vied continuously for preeminence and territorial advantage. The presence of large numbers of Kurdish forces south of the Green Line was an issue of great political sensitivity, to the Turks in particular. The city of Kirkuk was very symbolic to the Kurds and its fall needed the closest attention from the Coalition.

After liberating Mosul, Kirkuk, and the oil fields near Kirkuk, Task Force Viking rapidly transitioned to stability operations. Cleveland's first priority was to restore law and order. With the fading of the Iraqi military into the civilian populace, bands of looters ransacked many locations, forcing inhabitants to secure their own neighborhoods. The 173rd (-) moved into Kirkuk and the oil fields in order to secure northern Iraq's lifeline of prosperity. After a night infiltration, a brigade-sized element from the 26th Marine Expeditionary Unit landed at Irbil, and without hesitation or rest, moved to reinforce the city of Mosul. Cleveland instantly recognized the benefit that the Marines brought to the fight. Along with the 2nd Battalion, 14th Infantry, 10th Mountain Division, the Marines provided a more visible American presence in the cities. The CJSOTF pinpointed PSYOP and Civil Affairs teams for use in the cities to help reestablish civil services and restore the infrastructure of the towns.

On 19 April, after eight days in Mosul, FOB 102 began the process of handing the city over to the 101st Airborne Division. On 23 April, the CJSOTF relinquished control of Mosul to the 101st and began the process of preparing to redeploy the forces.

> ## Kurdish Political Parties
>
> ### Kurdistan Democratic Party
>
> **KDP.** Kurdish secessionist party led by Massoud Barzani. Tribal-based, with a large militia (pesh-merga).
>
> ### Patriotic Union of Kurdistan
>
> **PUK.** Leftist splinter party of KDP led by Jalal Talabani and urban intelligentsia.

Figure 8.19 14th Infantry Regiment insignia.

CFSOCC and the Cease-Fire

With the Iraqi regime crumbling, the staff of Coalition Forces Special Operations Component Command faced significantly different issues than from the early days of the campaign: how to deal with the disin-

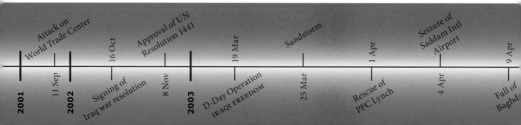

tegrating Iraqi Army and the numerous other elements coming under the custody of the American forces, how to manage the Kurdish population as Task Force Viking liberated the cities of Mosul and Kirkuk in northern Iraq, and how to support CJSOTF-west in its evolving role supporting the ground forces in their drive into Baghdad. One such case involved the Mujahedin-e Khalq (MeK), the division-sized formation of Iranian dissidents serving with Saddam's forces.

Mujahedin-e Khalq (MeK) *Iranian dissidents who supported Saddam Hussein. This well-equipped and well=trained force was a significant presence on the battlefield.*

When the MeK stopped fighting, the question as to its status arose. Was this surrender or just a cease-fire? There are significant legal ramifications in the categorizing of these events. For Navy Lieutenant Commander Garth Benson*, CFSOCC staff judge advocate, the final disposition of the MeK status impacted significantly on the U.S. forces who dealt with them. "CENTCOM pushed for capitulation. This meant that the MeK would surrender their weapons," said Benson, "Ultimately we negotiated a cease-fire which allowed the MeK to retain their weapons on the promise of occupying specific camps we set aside for them. Many of the MeK were schooled in the United States and still had families there. All these factors impacted on our eventual negotiated settlement."[58]

Questions of this nature, many dealing with the ambiguities of unconventional warfare and the role of Americans when working with indigenous troops, consumed a large part of Benson's time. As the campaign unfolded, legal issues relating to the status of enemy prisoners of war. and the application of the laws of armed conflict in relation to non-state terrorists required clarification. Often these questions found their way back to the Department of Defense for resolution.[59]

LIBERATION OF KIRKUK

The historically Kurdish-dominated city of Kirkuk proved to be as heavily contested as any in the fighting between the Iraqi Army and the Kurdish peshmerga in northern Iraq. On 8 April, Kurdish forces of the Patriotic Union of Kurdistan (PUK) and Kurdistan Democratic Party (KDP), working with Special Forces operational detachments from Advanced Operating Base 070, engaged in severe fighting for the Iraqi strongpoint positions along the Koni Domlan Ridge north of Kirkuk.[60]

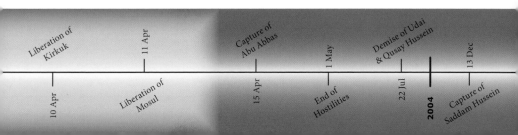

Liberation of Kirkuk · 10 Apr · 11 Apr · Liberation of Mosul · Capture of Abu Abbas · 15 Apr · 1 May · End of Hostilities · 22 Jul · Demise of Udai & Qusay Hussein · 2004 · 13 Dec · Capture of Saddam Hussein

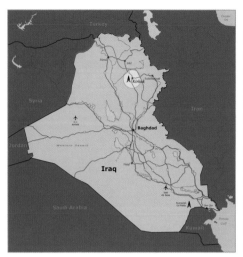

Figure 8.21 Map highlighting Kirkuk. *The battle for Kirkuk liberated the historically Kurdish city and secured the adjacent Zambo Oil Field.*

At the same time as AOB 070 attacked along Koni Domlan Ridge, elements of AOB 080 attacked the Jabal Bur ridge east of Kirkuk and the village of Laylan southeast of the city. In the course of the attack to capture the villages of Bidawah, Laylan, and the Zambo oil field, the PUK commander, out in front with the lead element, was killed while standing next to Captain Herrera*, ODA 084's team leader. Herrera immediately took charge of the assault, and with his detachment led the peshmerga to victory. Jabal Bur was the last piece of commanding terrain before entering Kirkuk and the ridge dominated the approaches to the city.[61]

Up on the ridgelines, the Special Forces troops observed the Iraqi lines spread out before them. "Every evening there would be mortar fire directly in front of the Iraqi positions, and sporadic gunfire within their defensive lines," remembers Staff Sergeant Adam Owens* of ODA 084. "Later, we found out that the senior Iraqi commanders were firing to the front of the lines and shooting at their own men to keep the conscripts in place and fighting."[62]

The Kurdish forces pushed the Iraqis back from the Green Line, in some cases as far as fifty kilometers to the last ridgelines, before entering the city of Kirkuk. AOB 080 and its ODAs, along with their peshmerga counterparts, attacked towards Kirkuk along three separate routes, specifically from the Jabal Bur ridgeline and along Highway 4 in the east, and through the small villages of Laylan and Daquq in the southeast. On the evening of 8 April, ODA 081 with five hundred peshmerga seized the city of Tuz, thirty-five kilometers south of Kirkuk along the main north–south highway. The seizure of Tuz proved to be as psychologically significant as it was tactically important. The village controlled the main line of communication between all the northern cities, including Kirkuk and Baghdad. Now the only way out of Kirkuk lay on the road west toward Tikrit. That evening, the Special Forces troops observed a column of approximately one hundred civilian vehicles leaving the city and reports indicated that stay-behind forces received instructions to hold out as long as possible.[63]

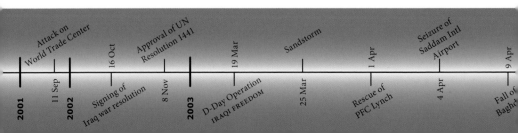

As the peshmerga exploited their operational successes and began surrounding the city, the Kurdish underground in Kirkuk began to take action to assist the Special Forces and peshmerga attacks. Many of the peshmerga actions relied on loose contact times and impromptu signals rather than direct communications with the underground elements. The events unfolding to the south in Baghdad indicated to many that the time was ripe for the underground to rise up and begin overt attacks against Iraqi forces. However, this caused the underground to take action sooner than Coalition forces could get into a position to attack the city.[64]

The situation on the eve of the attack on Kirkuk was tense. While the outcome seemed inevitable, too many of the variables could change at the last minute to allow Task Force 103 to relax. In the city of Kirkuk, the underground reported that the fedayeen were rounding up young men and shooting them in the streets. The underground uprising weakened by the day, even as the peshmerga fought along the ridges outside the city. Kurds were dying and the PUK grew impatient with, as they put it, "the Coalition's political sensitivities about the right way to prosecute the war."[65]

Figure 8.22 Members of AOB 080, FOB 103, attacking northwest to Kirkuk.

In addition to the PUK's impatience, AOB 070 also dealt with constant incursions by the KDP into PUK territory. The KDP wanted to ensure they played a part in the seizure of Kirkuk and the subsequent redrawing of the territorial boundaries. Any time KDP and PUK forces mixed on the battlefield, it was generally a recipe for disaster; fighting each other was never far from either faction's minds.

Nor were all elements for the attack in place. Although it was tasked to support the Special Forces/peshmerga assault, the 173rd Airborne Brigade (-) had a difficult time getting to the front. The United States believed that the sight of an American tank could cause considerable fear among the Iraqi defenders, and the 173rd tried to get its armor into the fight. However, the four M1A1 Abrams tanks brought by the 173rd experienced mechanical problems on the drive from the airfield to the frontlines. They were too late to join the battle, but Brigadier General James Parker had the unit position one of the vehicles in

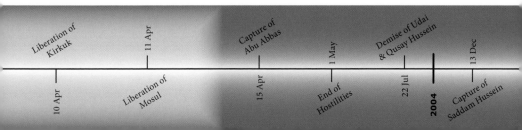

Liberation of Kirkuk — 10 Apr

Liberation of Mosul — 11 Apr

Capture of Abu Abbas — 15 Apr

End of Hostilities — 1 May

22 Jul — Demise of Udai & Qusay Hussein

2004 — 13 Dec — Capture of Saddam Hussein

the city and the other at the traffic control point entering the city, as a show of force. The next best option turned out to be having a PSYOP team broadcasting recordings of moving tanks; the sound of approaching armor tended to freeze the Iraqis in place.[66]

International politics also colored the pre-assault atmosphere. In

Figure 8.23 10th SFG soldiers on the Green Line. *Soldiers of the 10th SFG watch from their position on the Green Line as bombs fall on the Iraqi defenders.*

the early days of April, Turkey arrayed heavy units along the border—it wanted to be in a position to restore order in case the situation deteriorated into the ethnic infighting that the Turks had warned the Coalition about. The presence of the Turks, however, created great tension in the KDP sector as it diverted forces north to defend against a possible Turkish incursion. The Kurds regarded the Turks' mobilization a gesture of opportunism, and feared this historic enemy would move to seize new territory and control of the oil fields.

Mounting tension at the border caused the Coalition to fear that the U.S.-equipped peshmerga, a key ally in Operation IRAQI FREEDOM, would go to war against the forces of a NATO ally. As disastrous as such an encounter would be in the short-term, the long-term concern was that without the Kurds there could be no post-conflict peace in Iraq.

Finally, on 9 April, the day the statue of Saddam toppled in Baghdad, the Iraqi forces in Kirkuk began to collapse under the combined weight of panic and popular uprising. Early that morning, fighting erupted on both the eastern and northern ridges, and the Special Forces troops realized that the peshmerga planned to take the city that day. In light of these new developments, new orders to FOB 103 directed the unit to get as many Americans as possible into the city and attempt to restrain any inappropriate behavior.[67]

The Iraqi military withdrew via the western side of Kirkuk as U.S. and peshmerga forces entered from the north, south, and east. The Special Forces soldiers found the outer perimeter of the city ringed with destroyed Iraqi vehicles and abandoned uniforms. Thousands of people lined the city streets cheering the arrival of the American and Kurdish forces. On liberation day, the Special Forces personnel from FOB 103 deliberately wore U.S. flags on their uniforms and vehicles. They worked diligently to make it look like many more Americans liberated the city than the nine ODAS and Headquarters' personnel

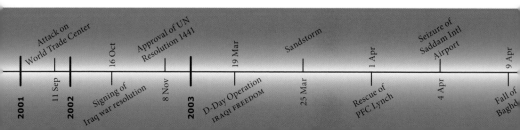

2001
Attack on World Trade Center
11 Sep
2002
16 Oct
Signing of Iraq war resolution
Approval of UN Resolution 1441
8 Nov
2003
19 Mar
D-Day Operation IRAQI FREEDOM
25 Mar
Sandstorm
Rescue of PFC Lynch
1 Apr
4 Apr
Seizure of Saddam Intl Airport
9 Apr
Fall of Baghd

that comprised the forward operating base. The U.S. troops passed out hundreds of small U.S. flags throughout the city. When they encountered media personnel, the "quiet professionals" made a concerted effort to be noticed. When asked questions that were off limits, like "How many Americans are in the city?" the ODA team members routinely answered, "About two to three thousand . . . a whole U.S. paratrooper brigade. Didn't you see them just come through here?" By mid-afternoon, FOB 103 personnel reached the center of Kirkuk just as its residents were toppling their city's own Saddam statue. Kirkuk became the first major city in the north to be taken by Coalition soldiers, and the scene remained jubilant and celebratory, despite the large number of armed groups still present.[68]

As people celebrated, numerous individuals wearing colored arm- or headbands ran around the city carrying rifles they had picked up. They now claimed to be part of the peshmerga. These mobs posed a great concern to all sides. The organized peshmerga represented the rule of law, and they knew that any atrocities and looting against Arabs would only exacerbate the long-term problems facing the region. For this reason, the PUK actually blocked the roads from the Green Line to prevent Kurdish families from resettling back into their old homes and most likely taking revenge on the Arabs who currently occupied those areas. Saddam Hussein went to great lengths to install Arabs in Kirkuk during the 1990s. The Kurdish leadership and the Americans went to great lengths to prevent clashes between those Arabs and the Kurds who had been displaced.

The establishment of FOB 103 in the center of the city brought a tremendously calming effect on the populous. The people in Kirkuk and most of the rival entities at the time did not know how few Americans had actually entered the city. Most of the ethnic groups did not trust each other and looked to the Americans to maintain order. In some cases, people tried to take advantage of the chaos for their own advantage. Owens recalled a man who came to the Americans complaining that

Figure 8.24 Map showing the advance to Kirkuk. *With news that Kirkuk would soon fall, the peshmerga and thousands of Kurdish civilians rushed to the city, many to reclaim houses seized by Saddam in the 1991 war.*

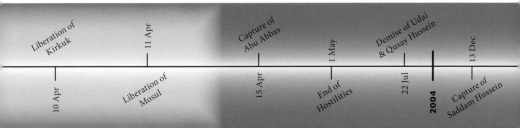

his car was stolen. "When we questioned about the car, he couldn't describe it, but he said if we came with him he would point it out when he saw it," Owens said. The same sort of problem frequently occurred when Kurds tried to usurp Arab houses.[69]

For the first twenty-four hours after the collapse of the city, Lieutenant Colonel Kenneth Tovo, commander of FOB 103, became the de facto mayor of Kirkuk. All parties involved accepted this and contributed to the restoration of order in the city. Almost immediately, the ODAS began patrols to show a visible U.S. presence and develop situational awareness throughout the city. As night fell, local groups began bringing in groups of men accused of being Saddam Fedayeen or Baath Party loyalists. While a number of these men turned out to be innocent civilians, approximately forty were detained and evacuated to Irbil. Many of these detainees turned out to be of Syrian and Palestinian origin, in Iraq to join the "anti-American jihad." This rounding up of potential insurgents demonstrated acceptance of the Coalition forces as the local authority, and for the most part, the population remained calm.[70]

Figure 8.25 Lieutenant Colonel Kenneth Tovo and Brigadier General James Parker in the Governor's Mansion in Kirkuk.

One of the biggest challenges for Tovo lay with the numerous entities bidding for control in the city. The PUK and KDP represented the major Kurdish factions, but the city contained significant populations of Arabs, Shiites, Sunnis, Turkoman, and Assyrians. Brigadier General Parker hosted a meeting in the mayor's office with the representatives of the various factions at which he discussed the liberation of the city and emphasized the necessity of removing the peshmerga fighters from the city. Within twenty-four hours of occupying the city, FOB 103 established a Civil Military Operations Center in the center of the city. The former governor's building became the focal point for all issues, complaints, and grievances. By immediately opening a multi-ethnic venue for complaints and instituting town hall meetings, the U.S. elements quelled rumors and sorted out crises before they became armed conflicts. The local residents immediately possessed a voice in the future of their city. This dialogue led to perhaps the most successful aspect of the entire campaign. The locals

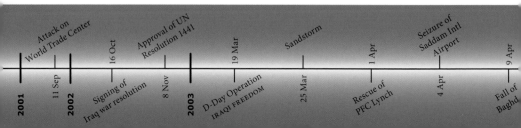

told the center's personnel exactly where the problems in the city existed, and as a result, seventy-five percent of the water and power was up and running within forty-eight hours. The importance of returning infrastructure to a fully operational state could not be over emphasized; the city calmed down virtually overnight.[71]

Figure 8.26 EUCOM HRC/MRC BFV. *An HRC/ MRC BFV with a Special Forces soldier in Kirkuk.*

The Khasah River divides the city in half from north to south. AOB 070 controlled the western half, staging out of Chemical Ali's former house. AOB 080 operated in the eastern sector, headquartered out of the former Baath Party headquarters. The task force headquarters was initially established in the Iraqi Internal Security Services headquarters building, but later moved to the former Iraqi Air Defense headquarters at the airfield. Each advanced operating base took care to interact with members of its respective communities.[72]

On the morning of 10 April, the 173rd advance party arrived in Kirkuk to link up with elements of FOB 103. Units of one airborne battalion arrived at the airfield at approximately noon. The 173rd then positioned one battalion on the Baba Gurga Oil Field and one battalion at the airfield itself. As the 173rd gradually moved into the city, the ODAs kept up their constant patrols, maintaining a high profile.[73]

The Special Forces personnel assumed a tremendous amount of risk by making a specific effort to be highly visible to the local population. Ever alert, they spent the majority of the time patrolling the streets in pairs of Land Rovers. The ODAs made an effort to engage the locals at every opportunity. For most of the people, this meeting was their first contact with Americans. Later, the teams began orienting the 173rd elements to the key local contacts the Special Forces troops had developed and to the most important areas downtown. By 18 April, Kirkuk represented the most stable city in all of Iraq, and FOB 103 handed over full control to the 173rd Airborne Brigade (-), so the Special Forces soldiers could move on to other missions.[74]

Liberation of Kirkuk

10 Apr

Liberation of Mosul

11 Apr

Capture of Abu Abbas

15 Apr

End of Hostilities

1 May

22 Jul

Demise of Udai & Qusay Hussein

2004

13 Dec

Capture of Saddam Hussein

THE LIBERATION OF MOSUL

Through the second week of April, Forward Operating Base 102, 2nd Battalion, 10th SFG, pushed forward with its peshmerga allies to capture the key northern city of Mosul. By conducting attacks from the west, north, and east of Iraq's third largest city, the outnumbered and outgunned American and Kurdish forces kept constant pressure on the Iraqi 5th Corps. The small Special Forces detachments effectively used their superior air support to decimate the Iraqi morale by calling in around-the-clock B-52 air strikes. Lieutenant Colonel Robert Waltemeyer, 2nd Battalion commander, orchestrated an encirclement of the 5th Corps with his ODAs working side-by-side with ten thousand Kurdish peshmerga fighters. As the resistance began to collapse, Waltemeyer balanced the disparate interests of the Coalition, the Kurdistan Democratic Party, the surrendering Iraqi forces, and the local population, coordinating a reasonably smooth transfer of power in the midst of an extremely volatile situation.[75]

Beginning on 9 April, Advanced Operating Base 050, formed from B Company, 2nd Battalion, 10th SFG, and 9,200 peshmerga, unleashed a punishing attack using close air support, direct-fire weapons systems, and mortar fire against the three Iraqi divisions arrayed before them across a forty-kilometer front. In the face of Iraqi artillery fire and several counterattacks, the combined American-Kurdish force massed enough firepower to push the Iraqis twenty kilometers south to the outskirts of Mosul.[76]

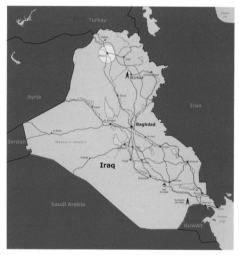

Figure 8.27 Map highlighting Mosul. *FOB 102 was instrumental in the capture of the city of Mosul.*

On 10 April, after a tough fight with two Iraqi mechanized brigades, AOB 040 (A Company, 2nd Battalion, 10th SFG) and AOB 370 (A Company, 3rd Battalion, 3rd SFG) pushed through Debecka Pass and secured the Makloub Mountain ridgeline, overlooking Mosul from the south. Through a well-coordinated effort, the Special Forces with their peshmerga allies and Coalition strike aircraft defeated the well-entrenched Iraqi troops. Brigadier General Parker directed AOB 370 to secure the oil fields to the south of the city and provide a

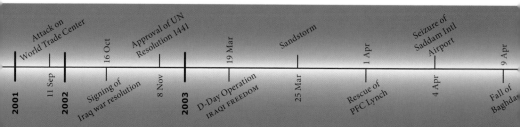

screen for the forces approaching Mosul. By 10 April, FOB 102 cleared the axis of advance toward Mosul and connected all three AOB sectors to form a combined front for the attack on Mosul.[77]

With the fall of Baghdad and Kirkuk, the Iraqi 5th Corps commander understood the futility of his fight. When presented with a surrender demand from General Parker, CFSOCC deputy commander, he opted for a less deadly course of action than continued resistance, convincing the local sheik to broker the surrender. On 11 April, the KDP leaders first learned of the imminent defeat of the 5th Corps and rushed toward the city to claim victory. Waltemeyer had no choice but to take his small entourage of Special Forces troops and follow. Kurds by the thousands were streaming toward the city in any vehicles they could get their hands on. Luckily, in the midst of the "million-man march on Mosul," a massive traffic jam afforded Waltemeyer time to confer with his subordinates and take steps to bring some control to a very volatile situation.[78]

Figure 8.28 The rush to Mosul. *With the word of the fall of Baghdad spreading, thousands of Kurds group up for the "Million-man March on Mosul."*

Receiving an order to link up with his battalion commander, Captain Mark Donaldson*, team leader for ODA 051, departed Dahuk and raced to the grid coordinates provided by the forward operating base. As his team approached the area, Donaldson witnessed a gridlock of vehicles containing thousands of peshmerga from the KDP, all trying to inch towards Mosul. Finally spotting his commander and Colonel Cleveland, Donaldson snaked his way through the traffic to their vehicle. Donaldson huddled with his bosses atop the hood of Waltemeyer's vehicle, trying to devise a way to gain control of the situation.[79]

Quickly formulating a plan, Waltemeyer had ODA 051 escort the command element and several attached officers of the Judge Advocate General Corps into town. Placing a large American flag on his vehicle, Waltemeyer told the Kurds along the road to "stay behind the flag." Everyone fell in behind Waltemeyer's vehicle and they set off for the city. A local Arab leader led the convoy. In order to avoid being surprised, Donaldson kept a KDP leader familiar with Mosul close by. Not knowing what to expect or having much in the way of a clear

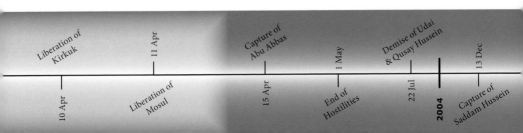

Liberation of Kirkuk

11 Apr

Capture of Abu Abbas

1 May

Demise of Udai & Qusay Hussein

13 Dec

10 Apr

Liberation of Mosul

15 Apr

End of Hostilities

22 Jul

2004

Capture of Saddam Hussein

plan, the Special Forces soldiers followed their intuition and exploited their ability to mingle with the locals to successfully enter the city at the front of the mob.[80]

As the convoy entered the city, it was apparent that widespread looting had occurred in the Arab part of town following the withdrawal of the Iraqi military. Soon the convoy turned down a one-way street and stopped. Waltemeyer and Cleveland went into a building that housed the local sheik, to make him aware of the situation. The sheik proved to be a minor entity in the big scheme of things, and could do little to assist them. They soon departed, accompanied by their peshmerga security element. Ten minutes later, the convoy worked its way into the center of town.[81]

In the city square, the commanders entered a large government building. After meeting with local officials of various ranks and positions, the commanders exited the building, leaving a Special Forces communications sergeant to set up satellite radios to communicate with CFSOCC headquarters. While the American leadership gathered to discuss things outside the building, Donaldson and his team sergeant, Master Sergeant Ty Forth*, dispatched the peshmerga to the rooftops and emplaced snipers to provide security. The sound of distant gunfire, which had provided background noise since their entry into the city, suddenly came closer. The next thing that Donaldson heard was a bullet zinging past his helmet. The captain looked over to his right and screamed at the two colonels, "We have incoming sniper fire!" Waltemeyer looked up, not registering the danger until Forth yelled, "Let's get the hell out of here!" Snapping out of their reveries, everyone immediately loaded into vehicles, and the KDP leader directed them out of town to the airfield.[82]

The airport terminal had been ransacked; broken glass was everywhere, and the plumbing had been ripped out. Forth set up a perimeter with the limited peshmerga forces remaining, again placing snipers on the rooftops. When ODA 056 called in and reported that the team and its peshmerga forces were eighteen kilometers away, its forward operating base directed the group to go to the airfield. By now, it was night. After regrouping at the airfield, Cleveland declared it was time to conduct a presence patrol to get some situational awareness and let the population know that the Americans were still present. At approximately 2230 local time, ODA 051 loaded into its vehicles and

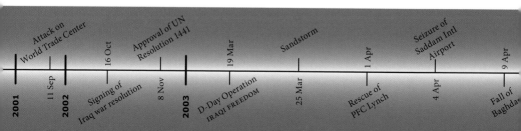

headed into "Indian country," not knowing the streets or the situation.[83]

Cleveland rode with Donaldson, while Sergeant First Class Holbrook* pulled rear security in the back of the civilian vehicle they occupied, with the detachment vehicles flanking them. As the Special Forces soldiers drove through the city, they could see that the people had started taking steps to defend their homes and businesses. On every street corner were bunkers and debris piled up to serve as checkpoints. As the ODA team members rode through in civilian vehicles, the soldiers made a particular effort to say, "Hello, USA, how are you?" trying to identify themselves as Americans.

Figure 8.29 AOB 040 at the Mosul Airport. *AOB 040 personnel and equipment resting the morning after the nighttime movement to the city and before establishing its own headquarters.*

Generally, the force was well received, but several rounds in their direction reminded them that the city was not totally safe.[84]

As the convoy approached a section of town where numerous tires were burning, the lead vehicle stopped out of Donaldson's sight. He heard one of his sergeants yelling, "No, No, No, USA!" An obviously frightened man was pointing a gun at the vehicle, and the sergeant was desperately trying to defuse the situation. At the same moment, a ten-year-old boy approached Donaldson's vehicle from behind a pillar to the right and aimed an AK-47 at Cleveland. With a flurry of hand gestures, the situation was quickly resolved. "The maturity of the [Special Forces] guys and their ability to deal with these types of situations was key to our success. These guys are pros," said Cleveland. The patrol headed back to the airfield, arriving around midnight. As ODA 051 unloaded its vehicles, ODAS 056 and 065 arrived. Waltemeyer quickly dispatched the two ODAs to do the same type of presence patrols throughout the remainder of the night.[85]

The afternoon of 12 April, Cleveland received word that the Iraqi 5th Corps commander was in town and ready to capitulate. He grabbed ODA 051, now designated the quick reaction force, and with Waltemeyer followed the Iraqi contingent into the city. After driving to the northeast side of Mosul, they were disappointed with the results of the parley. Instead of the 5th Corps commander and top Baath party official they had expected, Cleveland and Waltemeyer met with their surrogates. The Iraqis attempted to secure amnesty and

Figure 8.30 Marines of the 26th MEU take up a defensive position in Mosul.

compensation for their role in the surrender, both items outside of Cleveland's authority to grant. The group returned to the airfield, and at this point, Cleveland left tactical control of the city to Waltemeyer and FOB 102. The next day, Brigadier General Parker ordered the 3rd SFG contingent with its attached 2nd Battalion, 14th Infantry, from the 10th Mountain Division, and the 26th Marine Expeditionary Unit, all part of Task Force Viking, under Colonel Cleveland, to reinforce FOB 102 in Mosul.[86]

In the weeks that followed, constant mounted patrols through the war-torn streets of Mosul by 2nd Battalion maintained the U.S. presence and began the transition to civilian control of the city. The Special Forces soldiers demonstrated their versatility as peacemakers and civil administrators, in addition to their combat skills. They worked tirelessly with the local civic and political leadership to bring peace to the politically unstable city. This combined effort set the conditions to rejuvenate the civil infrastructure, including the reestablishment of the water and electricity supplies. FOB 102 captured over forty weapons and ammunition caches, as well as what appeared to be a mobile biological weapons production laboratory. When FOB 102 left Mosul, its influence was still felt long after the city rebuilt along peaceful lines.[87]

TIGER TEAM TO MOSUL

The 16 April daily targeting meeting at CJSOTF-North was near its end when the commander entered the tent. Colonel Cleveland sat down. "We're pretty much done," said the J-5 (plans officer), "Do you want us to go through this again or do you have anything to add?" "Don't worry about going through it again," Cleveland replied, as he stood up turning to face the crowd. The first thing that the Task Force Viking Information Operations officer, Lieutenant Colonel Paul Gallo, noticed was that the commander was not smiling. Cleveland asked the intelligence and security officer and the staff judge advocate a few questions, paused a few seconds, then said "The IO [Information Operations] campaign in Mosul is a failure. Where's Gallo?" "Here

2001   Attack on World Trade Center   11 Sep   2002   Signing of Iraq war resolution   16 Oct   Approval of UN Resolution 1441   8 Nov   2003   D-Day Operation IRAQI FREEDOM   19 Mar   25 Mar   Sandstorm   Rescue of PFC Lynch   1 Apr   4 Apr   Seizure of Saddam Intl Airport   9 Apr   Fall of Baghdad

Sir," responded Gallo. "Paul, get a team together and get down to Mosul and help the FOB commander get a handle on the information situation. Its going crazy down there," ordered Cleveland, and with that, he left the meeting.[88]

Gallo knew that Cleveland had gone to Mosul with Waltemeyer's FOB 102 and entered the city with the first FOB 102 soldiers. With the sudden withdrawal of Iraqi regular forces from the city, as Cleveland later put it, the city "was like something out of the movie *Escape from New York*." Looting was rampant. In some neighborhoods, groups were protecting their homes armed with anything they could get their hands on, while other neighborhoods were settling old grudges. A small Special Forces convoy entered the city, but when it attempted to set up at the governor's office downtown, it came under sniper fire and one soldier was wounded. Waltemeyer withdrew his thirty-man force to the Mosul Airport. That night, Cleveland patrolled part of the city with one of his ODAs; the situation at night was no better than it had been during the day.[89]

The next day, the Americans returned to reclaim the governor's office. While there, Cleveland witnessed a large anti-Coalition demonstration. A large firefight broke out between the mob and a group of Marines from the 26th Marine Expeditionary Unit, and several armed Iraqis were killed and wounded. Some ill-informed reporters would later call this a "massacre," despite the fact that the people on the ground were armed with AK-47s. Later the same day, Cleveland returned to his headquarters just in time for the daily targeting meeting.[90]

After a quick brainstorming session with the Information Operations staff, Gallo formed his team, which public affairs officer Major Timothy dubbed the IO Tiger Team.

Figure 8.31 IO Tiger Team. *The Information Operations Tiger Team and its interpreter in Mosul.*

(Tiger Team is a Vietnam-era Army term for a group of experts pulled together to solve a specific problem.) Gallo selected six soldiers with various specialties: Major Timothy, Task Force Viking public affairs officer; Major Jude Oscar*, commander, A Company, 9th PSYOP Battalion; Major Fred Vance*, Task Force Viking IO officer; Captain Jeff Rogers*, Task Force Viking staff judge advocate; Staff Sergeant Joel LaBuff, PSYOP team sergeant, A Company, 9th

Psyop Battalion; and Specialist Brock*, Task Force Viking communications specialist. Early the next morning, 17 April, the IO Tiger Team moved as fast as it could in a two-vehicle convoy to Mosul.[91]

The IO Tiger Team arrived at the FOB 102 headquarters at Mosul Airport and immediately reviewed the situation with Waltemeyer. Waltemeyer saw the problem as an information vacuum. The media was fully controlled by the Baath Party; when Mosul fell, party officials fled or hid and the television and radio stations went off the air. While FOB 102 conducted preliminary Information Operations with its PSYOP detachment, the Coalition IO message did not filter down to the people. In the information vacuum, the large Arab minority in Mosul got its information from rumors that spread across the city in a matter of hours. Sporadic challenges to U.S. authority occurred as a result, and two confrontations at the governor's office threatened goodwill and stability. And, just to add to FOB 102's already full plate, the international media's coverage of these confrontations focused worldwide attention on Mosul.[92]

Waltemeyer already had a concept plan; he just needed the Tiger Team's expertise to execute it. The mission quickly came into focus for the team; in order to gain and maintain popular support in Mosul, FOB 102 had to gain control of the television station. A combination of public affairs, PSYOP, Civil Affairs, and Special Forces face-to-face interaction with the people and international media would reinforce the television broadcasts. Waltemeyer immediately tasked the Tiger Team to coordinate the Information Operations campaign, to draft and coordinate an address by General Franks to the people of Mosul, and to write and synchronize television broadcasts.

The IO Tiger Team quickly synchronized and implemented Waltemeyer's intent. Working together, they designed a comprehensive IO execution matrix built on three themes calculated to influence, persuade, and inform the people and key leaders of Mosul. The themes were:

1. Iraqi civic responsibility:
   U.S. Forces are not here to occupy the city, but to assist in setting the conditions for a secure and stable environment.
2. Conflict is counterproductive:
   Nothing is to be gained from fighting. "Can't we all just get along?"
3. Mosul self-governance:

Iraqis will be responsible for governing themselves [93]

Only a few hours after getting to Mosul, the IO Tiger Team watched as Waltemeyer's first television address to the people of Mosul was broadcast later that same day. A Special Forces team and Tactical PSYOP Detachment 910 secured and assumed control of Mosul's Channel 9/TV Ninevah earlier in the week. The first address was rebroadcast on 18 April, after which Waltemeyer began recording and broadcasting a daily television spot in support of Coalition stabilization operations. The IO Tiger Team produced five television broadcasts providing a direct-information forum to Mosul's people regarding U.S. activities. Immediate feedback from the people indicated that the broadcasts directly contributed to the establishment of security and stability in the city of Mosul.

A major success in the Tiger Team's Information Operations campaign involved retired Iraqi officers. On 19 and 20 April, Waltemeyer made two separate televised appeals (as part of his daily TV addresses) for former Iraqi Army officers in Mosul to attend the inaugural meeting of the Iraqi Retired Officers Committee for Reconstruction to discuss rebuilding issues. Waltemeyer stressed that the officers had an obligation to help their city and country. As a clear measure of effectiveness, on 21 April, over one thousand former Iraqi officers, including forty retired generals, arrived at Mosul Airport to attend the first meeting. The officers waited with their cars parked for over half a mile on both sides of the road to the Mosul Airport. In fact, the response was so great that the meeting was postponed until a venue large enough to accommodate everyone could be found.[94]

Figure 8.32 Street to Mosul Airport. *On 21 April 2003, Iraqi civilian vehicles parked on both sides of the street leading to Mosul Airport, clear indication that the FOB 102 commander's message was received by the population.*

Figure 8.33 Broadcasting at Mosul Airport. *TPD 910 with its loudspeakers in front of the Mosul Airport communicate with the retired former Iraqi army officers who had come forward following Lieutenant Colonel Robert Waltemeyer's televised appeal.*

Waltemeyer's FOB 102 was faced with a possible civil war in Mosul. Although short in duration, the five-day IO Tiger Team concept was later used as an example for future Information Operations. On 25 April, the 101st Airborne Division assumed control of Mosul

Liberation of Kirkuk

11 Apr

Capture of Abu Abbas

1 May

Demise of Udai & Qusay Hussein

13 Dec

10 Apr

Liberation of Mosul

15 Apr

End of Hostilities

22 Jul

2004

Capture of Saddam Hussein

from FOB 102. Using assets from the 318th Tactical PSYOP Company, the 101st Airborne Division continued to use television information spots to keep the people of Mosul informed and aware. [95]

TRANSITION TO STABILITY OPERATIONS IN THE NORTH

Forward Operating Base 102's Special Forces soldiers at Mosul Airport engaged in a variety of missions to facilitate the establishment of a stable, local government and a safe and peaceful environment for the citizens of Mosul. Some peshmerga fighters took advantage of being the only sizable armed force in Mosul after the Iraqi 5th Corps collapsed. The peshmerga abuses within Mosul enraged much of the Arab population there. The general perception remained that the United States worked exclusively alongside the peshmerga; therefore, the Americans condoned all peshmerga actions. As peshmerga forces took over security for key sites around the city, Arab citizens witnessed what they interpreted as the American-sanctioned transfer of power to the Kurdish population in the area. To minimize tensions between Kurds and Arabs in the region, the Special Forces soldiers repositioned peshmerga troops outside the city.[96]

Walking a fine line between establishing a strong presence in the city and reducing tensions between factions, Lieutenant Colonel Waltemeyer facilitated negotiations and administration of Mosul, focusing on stabilizing a city of over one million people using a force of less than two thousand U.S. soldiers. All of his available assets, both Special Forces and Marines, concentrated on establishing presence patrols, security operations, restoring basic services, and establishing urban area coordination centers to support the Office of Reconstruction and Humanitarian Assistance.

The 101st Airborne Division relieved FOB 102 and the Marine Expeditionary Unit at Mosul Airport on 23 April. The Marines returned to the USS *Boxer,* and the forward operating base repositioned to Irbil. Major General David Petraeus, 101st Airborne Division commander, capitalized on the cordial relationships that Waltemeyer and his soldiers had established with the people of Mosul, even as he brought more muscle to the area.[97]

In addition to providing security and basic services in Kirkuk and Mosul, the CJSOTF reached agreements with Kurdish leaders on

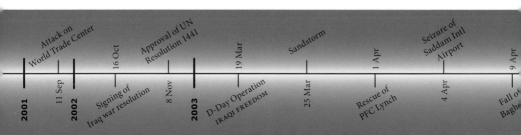

the disposition of their forces. In Irbil on 23 April, Colonel Cleveland signed a memorandum of understanding with the two major Kurdish political factions, the Kurdistan Democratic Party and the Patriotic Union of Kurdistan, that specified the number and type of military forces the Kurds were allowed to maintain west and south of the former Green Line. The 10th SFG soldiers began monitoring the agreement to ensure that enthusiastic Kurds did not jeopardize the Coalition success by initiating any conflict with the local Arabs or Turks. These operations and others maintained a balance that allowed Coalition authorities to assert control in a stable northern Iraq.[98]

404TH CAB IN NORTHERN IRAQ

The 404th Civil Affairs Battalion (Special Operations) from Fort Dix, New Jersey, arrived in northern Iraq with the 10th SFG in early April 2003. This single battalion was tasked with giving Civil Affairs support to CJSOTF-North throughout its area of operations, which stretched from Sulaimaniyah in the east to Dahuk in the north. The 404th concentrated its efforts on Kirkuk and Mosul until May, when it spread its four companies between Kirkuk and the Sulaimaniyah, Irbil, and Dahuk governates.[99]

When Kirkuk and Mosul were liberated by Coalition forces, on 10 and 11 April respectively, all 404th Civil Affairs teams moved to those cities to begin civil military operations, leaving the battalion's headquarters element in Irbil with CJSOTF-North headquarters. In Irbil, the 404th established a Civil Military Operations Center in the Ainkawa neighborhood on 12 April. As U.S., UN, and nongovernmental organizations descended on Irbil, the center was instrumental in coordinating aid and reconstruction efforts for northern Iraq.

Figure 8.34 Civil Military Operations Center meeting in Kirkuk.

Among the center's more significant accomplishments in April and May were coordinating the reopening of Irbil's Hawler Airfield for operations on 7 May; coordinating the delivery of fifty tons of humanitarian supplies to Irbil, largely via Hawler Airfield; organizing the international effort to remove mines and unexploded

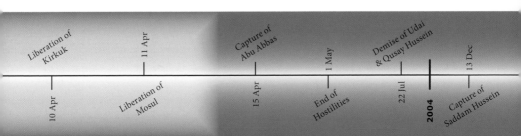

Liberation of Kirkuk — 10 Apr

11 Apr — Liberation of Mosul

Capture of Abu Abbas — 15 Apr

1 May — End of Hostilities

Demise of Udai & Qusay Hussein — 22 Jul

2004

13 Dec — Capture of Saddam Hussein

ordnance throughout northern Iraq; participating in Coalition efforts to care for the estimated 800,000 internally displaced persons living in northern Iraq; and successfully implementing a weapons control policy in conjunction with the Kurdistan Regional Government. The Civil Military Operations Center also addressed the needs of individual Iraqis who approached the center with problems. As battalion commander Lieutenant Colonel Harry Schute stated, "The purpose of this facility is to give the community a place to go to interact with the military."[100]

Figure 8.35 404th CAB insignia.

A Company of the 404th concentrated its initial efforts in Kirkuk and Mosul. Schute described the situation when Kirkuk fell to Coalition forces:

> I went into Kirkuk with that first six-man assessment team. We got there and the first thing that was apparent was a water crisis. They hadn't had any water for three days, as the power was out. In the short term, we had to get water into Kirkuk. I directed my Bravo Company down here to find out where all the electricity was provided. That next morning, we had 700,000 liters of water delivered to Kirkuk. The [logistics officer] and my guys contracted with a local company to truck it down. We had power on within four days. The water was flowing after three days, and the delivered water was stopped at that time.[101]

A Company's public health team worked with local emergency services personnel in Mosul to coordinate efforts to fight hazardous sulfur fires at and near the Musharaq Sulfur Mining and Manufacturing Facility. The public health team also assessed Mosul's hospitals, and tested water quality not only at the hospitals, but also throughout the city. The team's recommendations for improving the water treatment facilities improved water quality and increased availability to city residents as summer approached. In Kirkuk, the public health team surveyed the city's agricultural and livestock storage provisions and made sure that fresh food continued to be distributed to the population.

A confluence of Kurdish, Arab, Turkish, and Assyrian influence, Kirkuk presented the 404th with a tenuous political situation. While the 10th SFG technically governed Kirkuk, both CJSOTF-North and the 404th soon realized that the local leaders needed to be consulted if Kirkuk was to be returned to local control and responsibility. Schute

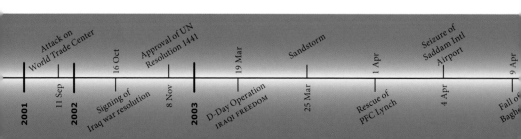

Attack on World Trade Center

Approval of UN Resolution 1441

16 Oct

19 Mar

Sandstorm

1 Apr

Seizure of Saddam Intl Airport

9 Apr

2001   11 Sep   2002   Signing of Iraq war resolution   8 Nov   2003   D-Day Operation IRAQI FREEDOM   25 Mar   Rescue of PFC Lynch   4 Apr   Fall of Baghd

explained the situation: "When we first got here, we found out about a political council that was going to be held. Our initial orders were to stop the meeting so that the role of the U.S. Army as the ultimate local power would be reinforced. We had to change that over time and support the actions of the council. We held a council meeting where each ethnic group could have six representatives, and then we worked through that group. It takes time to make things happen through a political process." Major Derek Storino*, commander of D Company, 96th CAB, which was also helping rebuild northern Iraq, added that the situation in Kirkuk did not fit Civil Affairs doctrine. "Our doctrine calls for us to go in and recognize an established government; but here, there is no government. We are walking a fine line between getting the city up and running versus showing the power of the U.S. Army. We have to maintain a very balanced approach."[102]

Figure 8.36 96th CAB insignia.

Captain Troy Roscoe* led B Company's SO-31, which was tasked with restoring city government functions to Kirkuk. After surveying the demographic and ethnic layout of the city, SO-31 helped establish the multi-ethnic Emergency Council, to govern the city until the 26 May election of an interim government. As the Emergency Council reestablished government services, SO-31 worked to convince former government workers to return to their jobs.[103]

The 404th CAB was instrumental in preventing humanitarian crises in northern Iraq. Although the battalion was only able to begin its work in mid-April, it continued to work on a multitude of fronts to rebuild northern Iraq throughout 2003 and well into 2004. The 404th's efforts supported Coalition forces—both SOF and conventional—in the touchy political and security situation of northern Iraq, and provided a base for further rehabilitation efforts.

MUJAHEDIN-E KHALQ CEASE-FIRE OPERATIONS

As the situation in Kirkuk stabilized, the atmosphere north of Baghdad was anything but calm. AOB 090, its ODAs, and their peshmerga counterparts continued to attack enemy units as they moved south into the Iraqi 2nd Corps' area. The formation pushed nearly a hundred kilometers south to liberate the town of Mandali from the last enemy unit to stand and fight—the Mujahedin-e Khalq. The MEK was composed of Iranian dissidents who fled Iran after the Shah's fall in 1979, and hated the current Iranian government. In the same fashion,

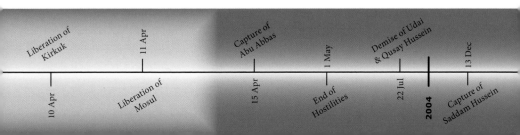

Liberation of Kirkuk

11 Apr

Capture of Abu Abbas

1 May

Demise of Udai & Qusay Hussein

13 Dec

10 Apr

Liberation of Mosul

15 Apr

End of Hostilities

22 Jul

2004

Capture of Saddam Hussein

Saddam used his elite Republican Guard to watch the Army, he used the меk to watch the Republican Guard. Better equipped than any other units in Iraq, the меk brigades were extremely well trained and disciplined. Chief Warrant Officer 3 Mack Mellers* and his team from ODA 095, 3rd Battalion, 10th SFG, observed the меk at close quarters: "The меk [was] the most disciplined and organized unit in Iraq. Their English language skills were good. A high percentage of their people had doctorates and master's degrees from American universities. In many cases, their families were in the United States, and the men divorced themselves from them to go fight for the cause. They were the only unit the [peshmerga] were really afraid of."[104]

With a troop strength thought at one time to be as high as ten thousand, this elite militia fielded over two thousand tanks, armored personnel carriers, artillery pieces, and air defense weapons, and posed a formidable threat. Its excellent fighting qualities were clearly evident when members of AOB 090 first encountered the меk's defenses in fighting around Jalula. FOB 103's only U.S. casualty in Operation IRAQI FREEDOM sustained his wounds from меk artillery fire. Yet, the меk astutely read the handwriting on the wall as it watched the Iraqi forces rapidly collapse.[105]

Figure 8.37 Map highlighting Mandali.

On 13 April, the меk sent a request for peace to Major Greg Tsouris*, C Company commander (AOB 090). Staff Sergeant Ralph McPherson* related that the меk pulled some vehicles up near the lines to initiate a dialogue. "We felt it was a big bluff," said McPherson. Mellers, McPherson, and members of the team drove down toward the vehicles expecting at any time to receive fire. It proved to be a genuine request for a parley.[106]

The next day, Lieutenant Colonel Kenneth Tovo, Tsouris, and a small group of staff met with the меk representatives. The меk claimed it had contacted the U.S. government months before the commencement of hostilities with an offer to fight on the side of the Coalition during any invasion. After two days of intense negotiations, the меk agreed to the cease-fire terms set by Tovo.[107]

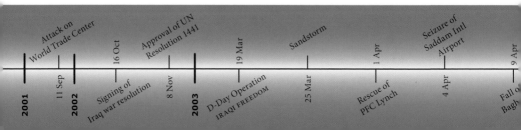

This arrangement prohibited the MEK from engaging in any hostilities toward the Coalition and confined them to five camps northeast of Baghdad. Sequestered in their camps, the four thousand MEK fighters were incapable of posing a threat to the Coalition. Securing the area around the far-flung camps was a trying task for the U.S. units. AOB 090's portion covered almost thirty-six thousand square kilometers, a huge area that required around-the-clock monitoring by the teams.[108]

After determining that the MEK was honoring the terms of the cease-fire agreement, FOB 103 deployed a field surgical team to assist with the treatment of combat casualties. This gesture brought immediate gratitude and additional cooperation from the MEK. The amicable resolution with the MEK provided residual benefits, as the MEK later passed on a great deal of quality information about Iran, which it had gathered from its extensive intelligence networks throughout the country.[109]

A CHANGE OF MISSION FOR *FOB 103: PHASE IV*

As the major combat phase of the war ended, several problems linked to the transition to a new Iraqi government arose. The Patriotic Union of Kurdistan, the dominant political force in Kirkuk, was very interested in pursuing the remnants of the Baath Party before the former Hussein henchmen could organize any resistance. Many former Iraqi military leaders contacted the PUK requesting amnesty in exchange for their support of the Kurdish effort. The handling of these individuals presented a dilemma for FOB 103. When the cooperation option was presented to V Corps, the response was that any remaining Baath officials or military leaders were to be given only two options: surrender or die.[110]

The role of the Special Forces troops in the transition phase also received considerable scrutiny. There was some consideration given to using the Special Forces to train the new army and police forces, and to assist in integrating the peshmerga into the future Iraqi military (potentially as a regional home guard or border guard). The Special Forces then could remain as advisors to new Iraqi battalions as they executed counterinsurgency missions. In the end, neither of these options was chosen.[111]

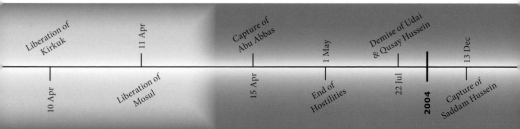

By 15 April, FOB 103's elements began a rapid transition to stability and support operations. That included the handover of Kirkuk to the 173rd Airborne Brigade (-), and the employment of Civil Affairs crisis action teams. The FOB also provided a Special Forces liaison element to the 4th ID to facilitate the handover of the Mujahedin-e Khalq forces.[112]

The individual Special Forces teams performed a wide variety of missions in the stability phase of operations: providing security details for diplomats; liaisons with the various factions; and the continued effort to demonstrate American presence and resolve in the period following the cessation of hostilities. On 29 April, a variety of sources in the Halabja area reported that the Ansar al-Islam had conducted a meeting in Iran and agreed to disband due to the American presence and current disposition of the PUK in the region. This was a tribute to the 10th SFG's 3rd Battalion's successful fight against Ansar al-Islam in the early days of the war. On 11 May, the 4th ID assumed the responsibility of monitoring the MEK. With this major mission now out of its hands, the forward operating base began the task of redeploying the forces. Lieutenant Colonel Tovo repositioned his battalion to Irbil, and began redeployment on 15 May.[113]

CJSOTF-West

CJSOTF-west continued a myriad of operations across western, southern, and central Iraq. By mid-April it had established a tactical headquarters at recently renamed Baghdad International Airport. As conventional units occupied the airport, the war slowly transitioned to stability and security operations by the end of April.[114]

FOB 51 effectively controlled western Iraq. Its ODAs continued to roam the western desert, securing, and in some cases destroying arms caches and abandoned artillery pieces. The mission also included interdicting lines of communication. The ODAs set up checkpoints with infantry squads in hopes of capturing Saddam loyalists attempting to escape into Syria. On 15 April, Iraqi forces in Al Qaim and Ar Ramadi surrendered to ODAs from FOB 51. The Civil Affairs and PSYOP elements attached to FOB 51 conducted humanitarian assistance missions in Ar Rutba and other cities.[115]

Lieutenant Colonel Christopher Conner's FOB 52 had a number of complex missions to accomplish. While many of the ODA's continued

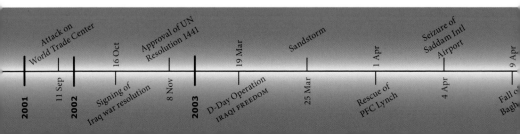

liaison missions with the conventional Army and Marine forces, others began conducting stability and support operations in the southern cities. ODA 551, fresh from its special reconnaissance mission, assisted in the Shiite pilgrimage to Karbala—the first in over a decade. Perhaps the most trying mission was supporting the Free Iraqi Forces units that moved into the region.[116]

Figure 8.38 Security duty. *Soldiers from FOB 53 provide security while teammates talk to locals in the west side of Baghdad.*

FOB 53 moved north from Kuwait temporarily setting up its headquarters at Baghdad International Airport. Before the FOB's arrival, several of its ODAs provided timely intelligence while operating inside Baghdad before the conventional forces arrived. With the seizure of the city, ODAs continued conducting stability and security operations throughout the Baghdad area with an emphasis on intelligence gathering.[117]

In the month of April, the special operations soldiers of CJSOTF-west oversaw the transition from war to an uneasy peace. Already the plan for the transition to widespread stability and security operations throughout all of Iraq was coming into fruition. Soon elements transferred authority in their areas to conventional units and pulled back to the pre-hostility staging areas.

ODA 542 AND THE FREE IRAQI FORCES

The constant roar of aircraft taking off and landing at Kuwait's Ali As-Salim Air Base was a regular reminder to Captain Mike King* that he and his team were on the sidelines of the big show. The 2nd Battalion, 5th SFG, was sending teams on missions throughout southern Iraq, but King and ODA 542 had been left behind. ODA 542 had been selected to serve as an area support team to assist with the myriad supply details and operations coordination required for such a large-scale operation. King and the others took scant comfort in knowing that they were performing duties critical to the battalion's success. Between area support duties, the men of ODA 542 spent whatever time they could keeping their individual and team skills sharp for the day they, too, would be sent on a mission. Finally, on 10 April, ODA 542

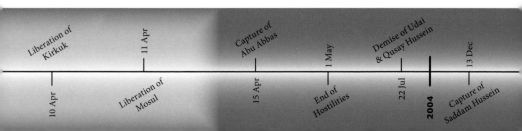

moved by MC-130 to Tallil Air Base, where it was detailed to train and work with members of the Free Iraqi Forces.

In early April, Ahmed Chalabi, Chairman of the Iraqi National Congress Executive Council, and more than six hundred Iraqi volunteers flew into Nasiriya to assist with the overthrow of Saddam Hussein's regime. Most were Iraqi expatriates who had fled the regime over the past decade. The Free Iraqi Forces volunteers had varying levels of military experience. The U.S. Defense Department championed Chalabi and the Free Iraqi Forces, and saw them as a transitional force to be used in lieu of the police. The State Department, on the other hand, saw the Free Iraqi Forces as nothing more than the military arm of the Iraqi National Congress. Whatever the disagreements in Washington DC, the Free Iraqi Forces were on the ground and Central Command had to find them a job.[118]

The original plan called for ODA 542 to train and employ a platoon-sized element of the Free Iraqi Forces. In the first week, however, one hundred men arrived for training. Some of the local recruits were rumored to be fedayeen, which led ODA 542 to take those individuals into custody and turn them over to the counterintelligence section for questioning. Once possible infiltrators were culled, the team set about organizing the trainees. The Free Iraqi Forces reported en masse, with no apparent internal leadership organization. Master Sergeant Theodore Ruggins*, Staff Sergeant Frank Findley*, and Staff Sergeant Steve Means* acted as primary trainers, and organized the Free Iraqi Forces into three platoons. The Special Forces trainers used basic infantry small unit tactics, drills, and patrolling exercises to identify those Free Iraqi Forces soldiers with natural leadership ability; these soldiers were then appointed as squad and platoon leaders. In the course of teaching the volunteers basic weapons proficiency, the Special Forces identified the best marksmen and designated them as machine gunners.[119]

As the tactical organization and assessment of the Free Iraqi Forces's skills continued, ODA 542 also addressed administrative and supply

Figure 8.39 Map showing route from Tallil Air Base to Al Kut.

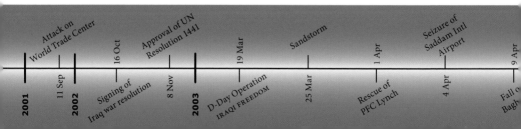

issues such as identification documents, pay, food, and ammunition. Using a digital camera, the team made each Free Iraqi Forces volunteer a photo identification card printed with an English transcription of the soldier's name. The paymaster arrived on 14 April to pay the troops—each volunteer receiving an impressive $150 per month. Until the Special Forces team could contract for local food, members of ODA 542 opened Meals Ready-to-Eat (MREs) and removed the culturally inappropriate items before distributing them to the Free Iraqi Forces soldiers. The shortage of AK-47 ammunition was finally solved when team members found a local source.[120]

Figure 8.40 Ahmed Chalabi.

As the training progressed, both the Special Forces and Free Iraqi Forces soldiers were restless and eager to get into the fight. On 16 April, they were finally ordered to report to the Marine Task Force Tarawa in Al Kut, where the Free Iraqi Forces would receive their first test by fire. After the Baath Party leaders had fled Al Kut, Sheik Said Ahmed, an Iranian sympathizer, had claimed the mayoral position and had begun working to restore civil services. While members of ODA 542 assessed Al Kut, they gathered some interesting information on Said Ahmed from conversations with local residents. Evidently the Iranian government was funding the mayor, and he was using Iranian money to purchase food and other items for exclusive distribution to the Shia faithful. Said Ahmad was also reported to have stolen food from civic storage facilities and similarly distributed it under his name. The mayor was responsible for posting anti-American and pro-Iranian posters throughout the city, and hiring people to conduct weekly protests at the Marine headquarters. The team passed all such intelligence to the commander of Task Force Tarawa, as well as the fact that Said Ahmed spent his off hours at the former Saddam Hussein General Hospital. The Marines acted on the information and gave Said Ahmed an ultimatum: stop the anti-American propaganda or get out of Al Kut.[121]

On the 25 April, Said Ahmed decided to capitulate to the Marines' demands and leave town—but not without a fight. That afternoon, heavy fire broke out in Al Kut, warning the members of ODA 542 to either return to their safe house (which was located near the hospital), or hunker down with the Marines at Tarawa House. All afternoon and into the evening, gunfire increased and spread, targeting task force compounds and drawing closer to the team's safe house and the hospital. In response, King scrambled a forty-man Free Iraqi Forces

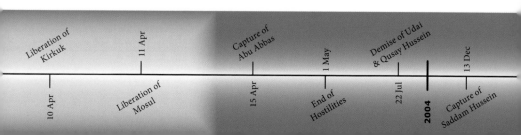

Liberation of Kirkuk — 11 Apr — Capture of Abu Abbas — 1 May — Demise of Udai & Qusay Hussein — 13 Dec

10 Apr — Liberation of Mosul — 15 Apr — End of Hostilities — 22 Jul — 2004 — Capture of Saddam Hussein

platoon and twelve American troops and rushed to secure the hospital. The team rolled into the hospital not a minute too soon, and Free Iraqi Forces Colonel Ali Hasan and Ruggins hastily positioned the Free Iraqi Forces soldiers in defensive perimeter. Within five minutes

Figure 8.41 Free Iraqi Forces. *Free Iraqi Forces gather at Tallil Air Base before deploying into Iraq. Special Forces had the responsibility for training and advising the Free Iraqi Forces.*

of their arrival, the AK-47 and machine gunfire directed at the hospital intensified. As fire came from all sides, it seemed that the insurgents were probing the perimeter to locate a weak spot; the perimeter held. As the battle continued into the night, the electricity went out. To keep the enemy at bay, Staff Sergeant James Cook* called on a nearby Marine mortar unit to fire illumination rounds for the Free Iraqi Forces. Meanwhile King and the rest of the Americans cleared and secured the hospital itself. The firing continued sporadically for about three hours, then tapered off. Insurgent casualties coming in to the hospital replaced rounds, and the wounded eventually outnumbered attackers.[122]

Back at the safe house, Chief Warrant Officer 2 Bill Shoemaker* and Staff Sergeant Bob Flood* shored up defenses with reinforcements from a nearby Marine unit and the remaining team members. At the same time the hospital came under attack, the safe house began receiving automatic weapons fire from several directions. The fire did not appear to be directed at anything in particular and while the buildings received several hits, no team member was injured. The team members returned fire, but could not ascertain effectiveness. Ultimately, the attack ceased and the insurgents departed Al Kut.[123]

The firefight at the hospital was the turning point for ODA 542 and the Free Iraqi Forces in Al Kut. Much to the delight of both the doctors and the patients, King left a Free Iraqi Forces security force in place to discourage looters. Over the next few days, word spread of the protection being provided and the number of people seeking medical care increased dramatically. Word of the role the Free Iraqi Forces had played in saving the hospital also spread throughout Al Kut, and soon other facilities and businesses in town asked for Free Iraqi Forces security details. King developed a list of key facilities

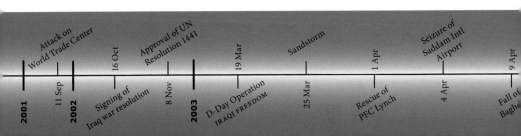

and locations for the Free Iraqi Forces to secure: the hospitals, banks, water treatment plant, and propane filling station.[124]

With Said Ahmed and the Iranian influence gone, the anti-American protestors also disappeared. Once common, random firing was now rarely heard. During their first night on security detail, the Free Iraqi Forces added to their reputation by thwarting two attempted robberies. The security presence encouraged people who feared for their safety to come out in public and return to their normal pursuits. King said the transition was remarkable: "Almost overnight, it went from a ghost town to Times Square."[125]

Mission complete, on the morning of 15 May, ODA 542 and the Free Iraqi Forces returned to Tallil Air Base; the team to take another assignment, and the Free Iraqi Forces to demobilize. While a good idea, the Free Iraqi Forces had outlived their usefulness, and resources needed to be allocated elsewhere. Five extra dollars were added to the volunteers' pay in order to facilitate their journey home, and each was given a certificate of service. Allegations of corruption had certainly hastened their demobilization, but they had also accomplished some good in Al Kut, and could be proud of their service.

As for the men of ODA 542, on 17 May, they loaded their vehicles one last time in Iraq, and headed south for the return journey to Ali As-Salim Air Base. As the dust swirled behind its convoy and Al Kut disappeared in its rearview mirrors, the team felt both a sense of satisfaction and regret. It had helped thwart Iranian efforts to influence postwar politics in Al Kut, and had worked to restore a sense of security and normalcy for the general population. It could be proud of those accomplishments. Working with the Free Iraqi Forces, however, brought mixed emotions. The training and supervision of the Free Iraqi Forces had been both rewarding and frustrating, as the team struggled to turn a motley group of recruits with diverse motivations into a professional fighting force. ODA 542 could not complain too much, though—it had finally received a combat mission in Iraq.

ODA 544 IN NAJAF: POWER POLITICS

Politics, like nature, abhor a vacuum. As Saddam Hussein's corrupt regime began to fall, ODA 544 found itself involved in political and religious infighting reminiscent of a story from the *Arabian Nights*. Najaf had a laundry list of factions, all vying for power—some with the

Figure 8.42 Muqtada al-Sadr.

backing of organizations outside Iraq. In addition to the former Saddam-appointed sheiks, a number of Iran-backed groups attempted to frustrate ODA 544's efforts to bring stability to the city. The major anti-Coalition groups in Najaf were the Supreme Council for the Islamic Revolution in Iraq, Hezbollah, the Badr Corps, and a rapidly growing group led by a renegade Shiite cleric named Muqtada al-Sadr.[126]

Muqtada al-Sadr would prove to be especially troublesome for ODA 544 in the days ahead. He was the sole surviving son of Grand Ayatollah Mohammed Sadiq al-Sadr, the highly respected head of the al-Hawza, the Center for Shia Instruction in Najaf. In 1999, Saddam Hussein's secret police murdered the Grand Ayatollah and two of his sons. As Saddam's regime crumbled, Muqtada al-Sadr saw a chance to restore his family's place in Iraq, and emerged to oppose the Coalition and to promote the establishment of an Iran-style Islamic government dominated by clerics. He refused to recognize or participate in the Coalition-appointed Iraqi Governing Council, and established his own shadow cabinet. Despite his nonviolent rhetoric, he formed a paramilitary militia, the al-Mahdi Army, to fight for his vision of Iraq.[127]

In direct opposition to radicals like Muqtada al-Sadr were moderate Muslims like Abdul Majid al-Khoei. When Saddam ruthlessly crushed the Shiite uprising in southern Iraq after Operation DESERT STORM, Majid al-Khoei fled into exile in the United Kingdom in March 1991. Saddam put all male members of al-Khoei's family to death. In London, al-Khoei established an Iraqi resistance group called the al-Khoei Foundation. Knowing that he was a key communicator, the United States brought al-Khoei to Najaf to help bring order to the large Shiite population in southern Iraq.[128]

Returning to Najaf in early April, al-Khoei quickly became involved in negotiating a deal to peacefully clear Saddam loyalists from the Imam Ali Mosque, where they had taken refuge. The voice of reconciliation, al-Khoei urged Iraqis to let go of the past and avoid the chaos and turmoil that revenge killings would bring. He also spoke in favor of a secular,

Figure 8.43 Map highlighting Najaf.

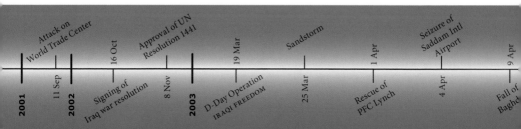

2001
11 Sep   Attack on World Trade Center
2002
Signing of Iraq war resolution
16 Oct
8 Nov   Approval of UN Resolution 1441
2003
19 Mar
D-Day Operation IRAQI FREEDOM
25 Mar   Sandstorm
Rescue of PFC Lynch
1 Apr
4 Apr   Seizure of Saddam Intl Airport
9 Apr   Fall of Baghdad

inclusive, post-Saddam government, a vision that was in direct contradiction to the views of the Iran-backed Shiite radicals. Cognizant of the risk he faced, al-Khoei was escorted by ODA 544 and other U.S. forces as he moved about the city.[129]

Figure 8.44 Abdul Majid al-Khoei.

By 10 April, it appeared that the standoff at the Imam Ali Mosque would end. Abdul Majid al-Khoei and Haider al-Kadar, Saddam Hussein's former minister of religion, went to the Imam Ali Mosque to conduct a ceremony of reconciliation. Al-Khoei declined an escort for the ceremony, saying, "The people will protect me." Helpless in the face of its protectee's confidence, ODA 544 continued with other work. Later that same day, the team learned that al-Khoei had been murdered. A group of Muqtada al-Sadr's followers, intent on avenging al-Sadr's father by killing al-Kadar, had trailed al-Khoei and al-Kadar into the mosque. The assassins broke into the meeting armed with knives and swords, attacking both al-Khoei and al-Kadar. Hearing noises of the attack, a group of al-Khoei's followers broke into the meeting and carried the wounded al-Khoei out of the mosque. However, the assailants were intent on murder and followed the rescuers outside, where they finally succeeded in killing al-Khoei.[130]

Muqtada al-Sadr immediately held a press conference denying all knowledge of the murder. Nevertheless, within days, two of the assassins were identified as al-Sadr bodyguards, whom the cleric claimed to have recently fired. The men of ODA 544 believed that al-Sadr had arranged for al-Khoei's assassination to eliminate his long-time rival, opening the way for greater influence and power.[131]

Although shocked by al-Khoei's murder, ODA 544 still had a mission. For the next month, the soldiers continued with security assistance and stability operations in Najaf. The destabilizing effect of the Iranian influence and the volatility of the political-religious environment of the city were not lost on the ODA. They discovered that Iranian-backed groups like the Supreme Council for the Islamic Revolution in Iraq and Hezbollah were in every neighborhood—especially the lower income areas—recruiting unemployed Iraqi males between the ages of eighteen and twenty-four and organizing them into militias. Chief Warrant Officer 3 Sidney Schwarz* predicted a dire future for the city: "I think things will flare up. If we don't get active, we will lose the fight." In the case of al-Sadr, his prediction was accurate.[132]

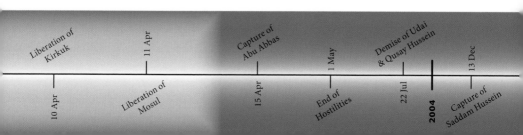

Liberation of Kirkuk

11 Apr

Capture of Abu Abbas

1 May

Demise of Udai & Qusay Hussein

13 Dec

10 Apr

Liberation of Mosul

15 Apr

End of Hostilities

22 Jul

2004

Capture of Saddam Hussein

WIRING RADWANIYA PALACE FOR COMMUNICATION

The nine soldiers from C Company, 112th Special Operations Signal Battalion, who supported Special Forces FOB 53 spent the early weeks of the war at Ali As-Salim Air Base, where they had been stationed since January. As combat continued and Coalition forces moved into Baghdad, everybody in FOB 53—including C Company—anxiously awaited the order to move forward and assist conventional forces in rooting out Saddam loyalists. The order came in mid-April, and C Company prepared to move to Baghdad International Airport.[133]

Figure 8.45 Imam Ali Mosque, Najaf.

Getting the TSC-93E V(2) satellite package to Baghdad took some doing. Because the satellite van (a HMMWV with shelter mounted on the back) was too tall to fit on a C-130, and the equipment was too sensitive for convoy transport, Staff Sergeant Melvin Pelham* and Specialist Albert Acord* had to take a detour in order to catch a C-17. Pelham recounted, "I took myself and one of my guys and we took the shelter to Kuwait International Airport, while the rest of the crew and everybody else stayed back at Ali As-Salim." Pelham, Acord, and their vehicle, along with another signal detachment from the 3rd Battalion, 5th SFG, and its satellite van, "sat at Kuwait International Airport for three days. We slept on the tarmac, just waiting for a plane to come in." After waiting on the flight line in Kuwait for three days, Acord, Pelham, and the satellite van finally arrived at Baghdad International Airport on 17 April, the first elements of C Company to arrive in Baghdad.[134]

Twelve hours after Pelham and Acord landed in Baghdad, three C-130s carrying C Company personnel and equipment began arriving at the airport. Specialist Josh Kinlaw's* recollection of the journey in on the C-130 was that it was: "Pretty neat. It was blackout [conditions] the whole way. We were inside the vehicle, and as soon as we touched ground they dropped the back and we started [unloading]." Private First Class Brenda Meter* was slightly less enthusiastic about her trip in a C-130: "It was different. They didn't have any room for me in the seats, so I sat in the Humvee the whole time."[135]

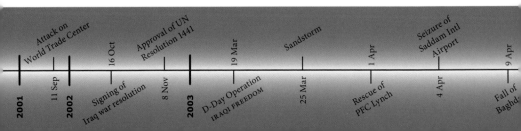

While most of the signal soldiers made the journey to Baghdad by air in a matter of hours, Sergeant Bob Petty* and a few other C Company soldiers were left to get the remaining ammunition and equipment to Baghdad the old-fashioned way: by truck. As part of a thirteen-vehicle convoy comprised primarily of FOB 53 personnel, Petty made the monotonous, two-day journey at an average rate of twenty miles-per-hour. Aside from minor roadside repairs, the convoy proceeded without incident along the pipeline road to Baghdad, arriving on 21 April.[136]

FOB 53's new home, and therefore the signal soldiers' new duty station, was Saddam's Radwaniya Palace complex, located approximately twenty minutes from the airport. Surrounded on three sides by a man-made lake and on the fourth by a hunting preserve, the complex was not an ideal location for communications, but the signal team managed. As Pelham put it, "We're kind of in an awkward place here, just because of the terrain. But it gets the job done. That's kind of what we do—we improvise."[137]

Figure 8.46 112th SOSB insignia.

Once the entire signal section supporting FOB 53 arrived at Radwaniya Palace, it was immediately put to work setting up its communication systems. Before First Lieutenant Kyle Ruger* even had time to put down his rucksack, the 3rd Battalion's executive officer requested a timeline for setting up the signal package: "Lieutenant, how long before you have your systems up?" Caught by surprise, Ruger gave a safe estimate: "Forty-eight hours, Sir." Not impressed, the executive officer forcefully responded, "Not good enough! You've got twenty-four hours and time started when you left the airport!" Ruger knew a challenge when he heard one, and he and his crew rose to the occasion.[138]

Pulling together, the 112th Signal personnel worked through the night to get the job done. Exemplifying Pelham's observation that improvisation is part of their job description, the signalers dealt with the challenges inherent in wiring the palace. Standing procedure for laying communications wire in a building was to drill the necessary holes in plaster and drywall to allow wires to pass through walls, saving wire and creating a minimum of disturbance to foot traffic. Unfortunately, Radwaniya Palace's walls were made of solid marble a foot thick; the signal soldiers laid a lot of wire that night. Just as the sun rose the next morning, the last of the signal systems were installed, checked, and declared operational. Ruger was pleased to

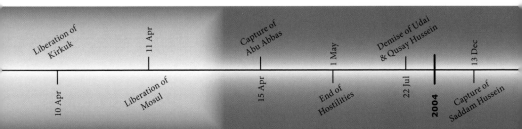

Liberation of Kirkuk — 11 Apr — Capture of Abu Abbas — 1 May — Demise of Uday & Qusay Hussein — 13 Dec

10 Apr — Liberation of Mosul — 15 Apr — End of Hostilities — 22 Jul — 2004 — Capture of Saddam Hussein

Figure 8.47 Radwaniya Palace Complex, Baghdad.

report to a surprised Special Forces battalion executive officer that his communications were up and running.[139]

While living conditions at the palace were better than what most soldiers were enduring at that time, the 112th soldiers still dealt with less than ideal circumstances. Aside from the odd building conditions, the climate was hot and humid. The canals and lakes surrounding the palace were ideal breeding grounds for clouds of ravenous mosquitoes. When the soldiers were not breathing bugs, they were inhaling unsavory smells and acrid smoke from the city. The air was also filled with the sounds of gunfire and explosions, which were especially audible at night. Ruger's pragmatic attitude regarding the unexplained sources of the noise was, "If you aren't in the kill zone, it doesn't matter." Perhaps Meter's assessment of the situation best described the soldiers' sentiments: while she thought it was "pretty cool" to be living in an ornate palace with marble floors and two swimming pools, "We were still eating MREs and had no air-conditioning."[140]

OTHER ARSOF

The missions for the Joint Special Operations Task Force did not stop with the fall of Baghdad. The JSOTF established a tactical headquarters and staging area at Baghdad International Airport to conduct operations in the Baghdad area. Part of the JSOTF remained at the H-1 Airfield and continued conducting line-of-communication interdiction missions focusing on capturing high-value targets—not only the fleeing members of Saddam's regime, but also terrorists who found refuge in Iraq.

PERSISTENCE PAYS OFF: CAPTURE OF ABU ABBAS

The search for and capture of major regime figures was a priority for many special operations units. Because Iraq had long been a safe haven for Middle Eastern terrorists, several names became intelligence priorities. To capture these high-value targets, a task force was organized

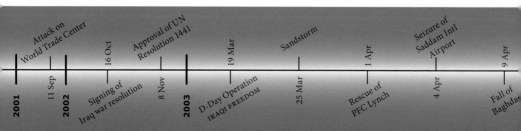

at the recently renamed Baghdad International Airport, combining various special operations forces—Rangers, Special Forces, and the Night Stalkers of the 160th SOAR—sometimes backed by conventional units. Acting on the available intelligence, the task force conducted raids throughout Iraq.

During one early morning raid, the SOF task force captured Palestinian terrorist Abu Abbas. Using combined helicopter assault and ground assault forces—the 1st Battalion, 160th SOAR, the 1st and 2nd Battalions, 75th Ranger Regiment, special forces troops, and mechanized infantry from the 3rd ID—launched on two very short-notice, time-sensitive, target locations. The combined force successfully captured its high-value target in a building complex in the center of Baghdad, an area that had not been secured by Coalition forces. The successive high-risk raids were a key objective of the Iraq campaign: to search for, capture, and drive out terrorists who found safe haven in Iraq.[141]

Figure 8.48 Abu Abbas.

Mohammed Abbas, better known to the world as Abu Abbas, was the key planner in the hijacking of the Italian cruise ship *Achille Lauro* in October 1985, and was responsible for murdering Leon Klinghoffer, a wheelchair-bound American, aboard the ship. An Italian court convicted Abbas in absentia and sentenced him to five life terms in prison. He fled to Tunisia and then Iraq and had been residing in Baghdad for the past several years. As the director of the Palestinian Liberation Front, designated a terrorist organization by the U.S. State Department, Abbas enjoyed the largesse of Saddam Hussein. The Coalition's encirclement around Baghdad in the first week of April prompted Abbas to try to escape to another safe haven, Syria. However, his several attempts to cross the border into Syria failed, and on 14 April, U.S. intelligence pinpointed his whereabouts.[142]

Early in the morning on 14 April, actionable intelligence indicated that Abbas was at a farm along the Tigris River in central Baghdad. One thing that all the special operations soldiers knew was that the high-value targets were constantly moving throughout the country, staying in one place only one or two days and then moving again, some moving twice a day. When the task force had good intelligence they had to act on it as fast as possible. SOF forces operating from a hangar at Baghdad International Airport formulated a plan, conducted a rapid-action briefing, and descended upon the farm location in an afternoon raid several hours after receiving notification.

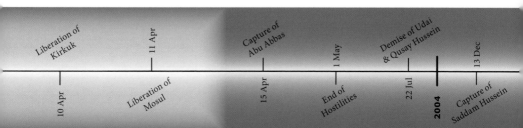

Liberation of Kirkuk

11 Apr

Capture of Abu Abbas

1 May

Demise of Udai & Qusay Hussein

13 Dec

10 Apr

Liberation of Mosul

15 Apr

End of Hostilities

22 Jul

2004

Capture of Saddam Hussein

Using a standardized plan with three elements—a Ranger ground assault force to set up blocking positions, a special forces assault team aboard MH-6 helicopters to approach as close possible, and AH-6 attack

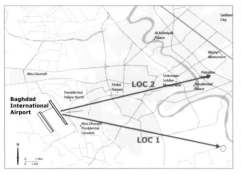

helicopters providing close fire support overhead—they left the airport. A Company, 2nd Battalion, 75th Ranger Regiment, departed shortly after the briefing in a ground assault convoy. Using Iraqi road maps for navigation, the Rangers established blocking positions to the north and south of the farm. In a carefully timed and well-orchestrated move, the helicopter assault force arrived simultaneously at the farm. Flying an AH-6, Chief Warrant Officer 4 Daniel Clement* directed the MH-6 flight into an alternate landing zone when he identified a flock of ostriches on the primary

Figure 8.49 Map showing an overview of the Abbas mission.

landing zone. Within seconds, four MH-6 Little Bird assault helicopters cycled into a field next to the main farm house, while a pair of AH-6 Little Bird gunships provided overhead protection. The Special Forces assault teams exited the helicopters and stormed the house. All elements executed their part of the plan precisely.[143]

Unfortunately, it was a dry hole—Abbas had left the farm just moments earlier in his black Range Rover. The Special Forces troops questioned people at the farm, confiscated Abbas's passport, and secured several weapons. The raiders remained at the site and waited for several hours for Abbas' return, but to no avail. No longer needed, the Night Stalker pilots returned to Baghdad International Airport. The remainder of the ground force returned to the airport aboard the Rangers' Ground Mobility Vehicles disappointed, but fully understanding that timing was everything. The task force had hit dry holes before. Some of the soldiers chalked it up as practice, a chance to improve techniques and refine mission execution. All knew there would be other chances to capture high-value targets.[144]

The chance came five hours later, when U.S. intelligence tracked Abbas to his new hiding place in eastern Baghdad. Coalition forces had not yet entered this part of the city; therefore, intelligence suggested that it was a semi-permissive environment at best. This added several new dimensions to the equation. Located deep within Baghdad, it would be a completely urban operation, with narrow streets

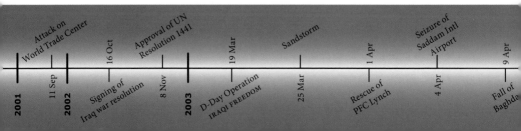

and tall buildings on both sides—a danger to the entire assault force. To some of the Rangers the setting was reminiscent of another sprawling city, Mogadishu.

The plan mirrored the earlier operation, but with a new wrinkle. As rehearsed, the first lift of the helicopter assault force landed as the Ranger ground assault force simultaneously seized blocking positions to isolate the objective area. The new twist for this mission was the addition of mechanized forces from the 3rd ID. M2 Bradley Fighting Vehicles and M113 armored personnel carriers carried the Rangers to their objectives. The special operations forces would air assault onto the objective while the Rangers of B Company, 1st Ranger Battalion (B/1/75th), searched and cleared buildings on the western side of the objective. The Rangers of B Company, 2nd Ranger Battalion (B/2/75th), isolated the objective, and by encirclement, prevented anyone from escaping or entering the area. Each of the Ranger companies directed its complement of BFVs and M113 armored personnel carriers. The helicopter assault force would launch once the mechanized force was at a checkpoint near the objective to preclude helicopters loitering or give advanced warning to the subjects in and around the target.[145]

Anticipating additional maneuver time, the ground assault forces departed in complete darkness at 0200 hours with the Rangers riding inside the armored vehicles. B/2/75th led the movement followed by a Ranger tactical command element and B/1/75th. The ground shook as the twenty-four BFVs, four M113s, and several GMVs rumbled out of Baghdad International Airport. The convoy rolled eastward past the brightly lit Palestine Hotel, the temporary home of the news media.

The entire convoy was filmed on its way to the target. The armored convoy easily bypassed several minor obstacles along the way and as it closed on the objective, the helicopter assault force launched from Baghdad International Airport.[146]

For the Night Stalkers, this was true urban navigation. The buildings had numerous wires and antennas protruding from the rooftops, which were difficult to see using night vision goggles. The pilots relied on road maps to fly through the city; helicopter navigations systems were a backup since the flying dis-

Figure 8.50 MH-6 Little Bird entering Baghdad.

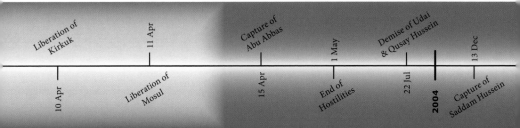

Liberation of Kirkuk

11 Apr

Capture of Abu Abbas

1 May

Demise of Udai & Qusay Hussein

13 Dec

10 Apr

Liberation of Mosul

15 Apr

End of Hostilities

22 Jul

2004

Capture of Saddam Hussein

tance was simply too short. The flight of seven Little Birds, five lift preceded by two gunships in the lead, raced past the buildings and apartments precisely as planned. Within a few minutes, Chief Warrant Officer 4 Doug Carter* was over the target building just as the Rangers came within a hundred meters of their blocking positions. He watched as seconds later, two MH-6s at a time landed in the parking lot north of the objective. It was an extremely tight fit but the SOAR pilots accomplished the landing without any problems. However, just as the second pair of MH-6s landed the aircraft shook from the concussion of explosions as the special operations forces breached the objective building. The MH-6's quickly pulled out and returned to Baghdad while the search on the ground continued. Carter's attack team circled over the objective.[147]

Just as the helicopters touched down, B/2/75th occupied its blocking positions. The lead BFVs carrying the 1st Platoon, B/1/75th, secured the northern blocking position isolating the objective. The BFVs carrying the remainder of the company continued on to the southern blocking position. The drivers, however, became disoriented and dropped the Rangers five hundred meters from the objective. Recognizing the mistake, the Ranger platoon leader reoriented the BFV commander, reloaded his Rangers, and moved into the correct intersection. At the blocking positions, the Rangers focused on the objective, cordoning the area and preventing any "squirters" from escaping the area. The BFVs positioned themselves to face away from the objective, to prevent any vehicle threats or reinforcements from entering the area. An attached tactical PSYOP team broadcasted a non-interference message in Arabic, warning the civilians of the Coalition forces' presence.[148]

Figure 8.51 The landing zone at the farm. *This location proved to be a "dry hole," but provided intelligence. The ostriches can be seen to the left of the landing zone.*

As B/2/75th occupied its blocking positions to isolate the area, B/1/75th began clearing the apartment complex and the block of buildings on the opposite (western) side of the street from the objective building. The B/1/75th Rangers met no resistance. The special operations forces cleared the objective building and then moved through the surrounding structures, but found nothing significant.[149]

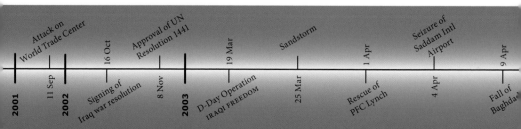

The process moved relatively quickly with some minor exceptions. There was one report of weapon fire from the east; however, it was ineffective and could not be positively identified. Bfvs at two of the blocking positions fired warning shots at vehicles attempting to enter the area. The drivers heeded the warning and quickly raced away in the opposite direction. The assault forces temporarily detained all males, and moved them to a designated Personnel Under Control site.[150]

As b/1/75th Rangers cleared its buildings, they made a discovery. One man stood out from the rest of the detainees. The Rangers had secured a six-foot tall, 220-pound man in a well-furnished apartment. He did not attempt to flee and nonchalantly opened the door when the Rangers knocked, emanating a very casual demeanor. It was not until he was at the Personnel Under Control site that the Rangers realized that they had captured the target—Abu Abbas. A further search of

Figure 8.52 Abu Abbas objective overview #2. *The Rangers sealed the area during the capture of Abu Abbas.*

the residence revealed a number of passports, several calling cards, an iridium satellite phone, and $35,000 in American currency. The ground assault force commander released the ah-6 gunships and the Night Stalkers returned to the airport. With the entire ground assault force aboard, the armored convoy rumbled home through Baghdad's streets with its prize securely in hand.[151]

The capture of Abu Abbas was the result of persistence and an unwavering commitment to mission success. Special operations forces rely on actionable intelligence to prosecute high-value target missions, but they also know that intelligence is time sensitive. Sof soldiers are uniquely trained and equipped to execute short notice missions, both day and night. Flexibility and adaptability enabled sof soldiers to use conventional assets to capture a renowned terrorist who had been enjoying a free life under Saddam Hussein's protection. The success of the mission provided notice to other terrorists in Iraq that they were no longer safe.

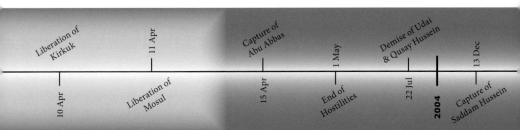

KEEPING THE BIRDS FLYING

The aviation mechanics of the 160th SOAR played a critical role in keeping the unit mission-ready. Drawing from their experiences during Operation ENDURING FREEDOM, the maintenance personnel adjusted the scheduling of the aircraft for major services and implemented procedures to improve aircraft performance in the dusty, hot climate of Iraq. The extreme environmental conditions and rapid pace of the operations placed a premium on aircraft maintenance.[152]

Figure 8.53 160th SOAR insignia.

This attention to aircraft preparation paid considerable dividends when the Night Stalkers arrived in the theater. The build-up of the aircraft from their dismantled transportation configuration went smoothly and no major assemblies were required to get the aircraft mission-ready. This proved to be a boon, as the flow of repair parts became choked off in the early days of the campaign as other cargo took priority in the airflow. The pre-mission preparation helped alleviate the shortage of supplies and allowed units like D Company, 2nd Battalion, to fly five months in Iraq without replacing an engine.[153]

Not only were the aircraft engines the subject of an intense maintenance program, but the weapons systems also needed constant attention in the corrosive environment of the Iraqi desert. The B Company, 1st Battalion, MH-60L Defensive Armed Penetrators were armed with the Gau 19—a three-barreled, .50 caliber machine gun—which proved to be extremely sensitive to the vagaries of the environment. Sergeant First Class Colt Deckert*, the armaments platoon sergeant, lived by the axiom "a dry gun is a happy gun" when dealing with the Gau. After some initial problems, he hit upon a dry lubrication program that reduced weapon malfunctions to zero over the course of the campaign.[154]

The breadth of talent among Night Stalker maintenance personnel manifested itself in many ways. When the winch on an Air Force C-17 broke with equipment on board, two 160th mechanics repaired the winch and kept the equipment off-load moving while the Air Force wanted to wait for a maintenance specialist to arrive. Specialist Jacob Gibbons* of F Company, 1st Battalion, replaced a complex electrical component in an MH-60L that normally required a factory contract representative to install. One avionics mechanic rewired the entire FLIR system in an MH-47E in fifteen hours, meticulously hand-soldering every wire. The mechanics often worked alone on their particular

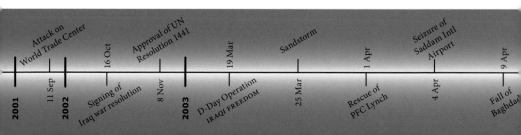

2001

Attack on World Trade Center

11 Sep

2002

16 Oct

Signing of Iraq war resolution

Approval of UN Resolution 1441

8 Nov

2003

D-Day Operation IRAQI FREEDOM

19 Mar

25 Mar

Sandstorm

Rescue of PFC Lynch

1 Apr

4 Apr

Seizure of Saddam Intl Airport

9 Apr

Fall of Baghdad

specialties, many times away from their units as they moved around the battlefield to work on the aircraft on-site. For Staff Sergeant Stephen Meyers*, his jump to the airfield at H-1 came when he was told to: "Grab your toolbox quick. We'll have you back in ten hours." He returned twelve days later.[155]

SUMMARY

By the end of April, Iraq was in the hands of the Coalition, with the exception of a few isolated areas. In less than a month, Coalition forces had virtual control of all key Iraqi cities, including Baghdad, Basra, Mosul, Kirkuk, and Tikrit. V Corps set up its operations center at Baghdad International Airport controlling the city with the 3rd ID and attached elements of the 101st Airborne and 2nd Armored Cavalry Regiment. Although Saddam Hussein's government was no longer in control, there was no official regime surrender. Units transitioned, depending on their location, from combat operations to stability and support operations. Then the main Coalition emphasis switched to humanitarian assistance.[156]

While combat wound down, both Civil Affairs and PSYOP units worked overtime throughout the country. Especially troublesome was Baghdad. V Corps was now responsible for the city of over five million people. To cover the city, the 352nd Civil Affairs Command assigned both the 308th Civil Affairs Brigade, supporting V Corps, and the 354th Civil Affairs Brigade, fresh from supporting the British in Basra, responsibility for the city. In turn subordinate units, the 422nd CAB, and elements from the 414th and 431st CABs received responsibility for the sections of the city that their supported units had been assigned during combat operations. With the movement of the Office of Reconstruction and Humanitarian Assistance to Baghdad in the last week of April, some planning staffs, perhaps wishfully, prepared to turn over all responsibility for running the country to the newly created organization. The primary focus of Operation IRAQI FREEDOM had been the downfall of the regime, but as Phase IV approached, the Office of Reconstruction and Humanitarian Assistance planning began in earnest.[157]

The transition to Phase IV of IRAQI FREEDOM was significant to the special operations forces. When conditions permitted, many of the

special operations contingents in Iraq would return home. The duties of an occupation force could be performed by conventional units. However, as late as mid-April, many of the Civil Affairs and PSYOP units were still in Kuwait or en route from Fort Bragg. Elements of the 75th Ranger Regiment and 160th SOAR began to redeploy at the end of April to prepare for other Global War on Terrorism contingencies as well as ENDURING FREEDOM in Afghanistan. Combined Forces Special Operations Command Component planned to transition Colonel Mulholland's CJSOTF-west to special operations units in Iraq into the organization dubbed CJSOTF–Arabian Peninsula.[158]

Chapter Nine

War Transitions

D+43 (1 May)–end of June

*T*HE COMBINED POWER OF Coalition air and ground forces simultaneously applied on five fronts overwhelmed the Iraqi military and led to the rapid collapse of the Saddam Hussein regime in Iraq. Capturing Baghdad, the capital and "center of gravity" of the country in less than five weeks of major combat created a well-earned sense of euphoria among Coalition forces. The very dynamic and hard-hitting offense had worked. The offensive drive "snowballed" as the push for Baghdad became dominant and large areas of resistance—whole cities—were simply bypassed to be dealt with afterward. A false sense of calm descended over most of Iraq when President George W. Bush declared an end to major combat operations on 1 May 2003.

It all happened so quickly that Central Command planners had given little thought to the military operations transition from Phase III to Phase IV. While Coalition forces had captured Baghdad, they did not control the entire country (much like the British burning Washington during the War of 1812). The media chose to interpret the presidential declaration to mean the end of Phase III. To the press, the war was over. Embedding controls no longer applied. Many active military and Coalition force leaders felt that they had done the hard part—the warfighting. It was time to begin redeploying home. "Post-war" missions in Iraq belonged to the civil military types, the State

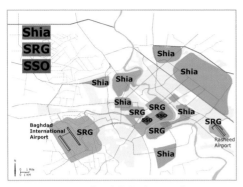

Figure 9.1 Map of Baghdad. *This map depicts Baghdad with various sections controlled by the State Security Organization, Special Republican Guard, and Shia militias.*

Department, and international organizations.

In the midst of the tranquility there was major turmoil as the major commands tried to accomplish missions for which they had not planned. And the Time-Phased Force Deployment Data continued to flow forces into Iraq. Feeling short-changed, many of these units were looking for a fight. One Civil Affairs officer was assigned to help write the V Corps' post-conflict plan in June 2003, a month and half after Baghdad had been captured.[1]

During this transition period, Special Operations Command Central consolidated the Special Forces assets in Iraq under a single Combined Joint Special Operations Task Force–Arabian Peninsula in Baghdad effective 1 May. As the Coalition Forces Land Component Command conventional forces took control of more areas throughout Iraq, active Army special operations forces elements were drawn down and redeployed to the United States. Conventional forces with attached Civil Affairs and Psychological Operations units (Army Reserve and National Guard) would conduct security and stability operations. The Global War on Terrorism was ongoing and Army SOF had worldwide missions to support.[2]

CONVENTIONAL OPERATIONS

Figure 9.2 1st Armored Division shoulder patch.

Security and stability operations continued through May and June 2003. The 1st Armored Division assumed responsibility for Baghdad in early May, relieving the 3rd ID. While the operations had definitely moved toward Phase IV, Coalition forces continued to encounter pockets of fedayeen resistance; however, Iraqi regular forces surrendered formally or simply disintegrated. Coalition forces continued the search for weapons of mass destruction and conventional weapons caches. The latter were found in large numbers throughout the country. Schools were a favorite hiding place. All military forces tried to minimize looting. Humanitarian aid needs were constantly assessed. If the presidential declaration marked the "end" of the war, the transi-

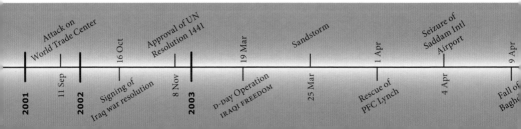

2001 | 11 Sep — Attack on World Trade Center | 2002 | 16 Oct — Signing of Iraq war resolution | Approval of UN Resolution 1441 | 8 Nov | 2003 | 19 Mar — D-Day Operation IRAQI FREEDOM | 25 Mar — Sandstorm | Rescue of PFC Lynch | 1 Apr | 4 Apr — Seizure of Saddam Intl Airport | 9 Apr — Fall of Baghdad

tion period was not clean. The first two months of this transition indicated that stability operations would entail combat for quite a while.

PSYCHOLOGICAL OPERATIONS IN BAGHDAD

The 315th Tactical Psyop Company from Upland, California, mobilized for Iraq on 28 February 2003. The company left for Kuwait on 12 April, but did not arrive until the 15th. After another week waiting for its equipment to arrive by sea, the 315th convoyed to Baghdad International Airport on 2 May. Various tactical psyop teams that had preceded the 315th were subsequently attached to the company upon arrival. The 315th TPC replaced C Company, 9th Psyop Battalion, which was supporting the 3rd ID. It performed that mission and joined the 1st Armored Division when it assumed responsibility for Baghdad in early June. What the 315th encountered in the first two months set the tone for its entire tour.[3]

Figure 9.3 315th TPC insignia.

The 315th TPC arrival in Baghdad did not begin on a high note. Less than a week before the company rolled into Baghdad ready to assume its mission, C Company, 9th Psyop Battalion, lost everything in a fire. C Company went from directing around-the-clock operations to scrounging uniforms and toothbrushes. The fire had left the 315th with nothing to begin work: no products, no equipment, no plan, and no place to work. It had to start from scratch.[4]

Worse than no equipment was no psyop guidance. The 315th TPC concentrated on supporting the 3rd ID's transition to low-intensity operations. The company leaders found space to live and work in the main passenger terminal of the airport. Using a single, one-color-at-a-time copier, the production development detachment began producing handbills. A single run of 10,000 low-resolution, single-sided handbills took three hours. After running the copier almost continuously to cover the 5.6 million people who lived in Baghdad, the plastic components of the copier (in the non–air conditioned terminal) literally melted with the 100,000th copy. Nineteen three-man tactical psyop teams then distributed them throughout the city by hand.[5]

The 3rd ID had no psyop plan. The Office of Reconstruction and Humanitarian Assistance and the subsequent Coalition Provisional Authority had no psyop plan, and the Central Command Joint Psychological Operations Task Force forward in Qatar, had redeployed to Fort Bragg, North Carolina. Major Donald Thomas*, the 315th TPC

*Pseudonyms have been used for all military personnel with a rank lower than lieutenant colonel.

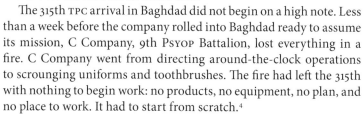

15 Apr | ...ture of ...ou Abbas | 1 May | End of Hostilities | CJSOTF-AP stands up in Baghdad | 2 May | 23 May | Recovery of Mi-17 Hip | 11 Jun | Raid on Rawah Terrorist Camp | 22 Jul | Demise of Udai & Qusay Hussein | 2004 | Capture of Saddam Hussein | 13 Dec

commander explained, "There was no plan to fall in on. There was nothing from higher coming down. You would get these short suspenses to execute on a topic. That is not a campaign plan. There was no synchronization matrix that said 'Here is our plan for the next three months, and here is what you need to start developing.' Every PSYOP company was essentially running its own PSYOP campaign plan." Although each division coordinated PSYOP plans internally there was no opportunity for external coordination.[6]

Each tactical PSYOP detachment commander had to establish a relationship with his assigned brigade. In the beginning, the 3rd ID and 1st Armored Division expectations outstripped the capabilities of the detachments. Captain Ron Castle*, commander of Tactical PSYOP Detachment 1210, explained, "When we first got [to Baghdad], these maneuver guys were demanding a real quick turnaround, [but] we weren't able to supply that." The combat brigades and battalions responded by designing and distributing their own Information Operations products. Then, the tactical PSYOP detachments had to convince the commanders to use the PSYOP products instead of their Information Operations products. The detachments tried to anticipate brigade commanders' needs and to develop products accordingly.[7]

Maneuver commanders focused on troop safety. They did not initially understand nor appreciate the long-term goals of PSYOP. The commanders wanted products that would enhance security now instead of products that would lead to long-lasting changes in Iraqi culture or behavior. Thomas summarized the issue:

> *When you have maneuver guys that are not PSYOP trained, they tend to have a short-term view. It's fine to address an immediate need, but it doesn't address the psychological, long-term goal that you are trying to achieve. We were constantly battling with maneuver commanders, saying, 'I know that our soldiers are getting killed, and that is something that is very important to you. But, you know what, the target audience doesn't care about our soldiers much. We need to address topics that are important to them on a long-term basis, because we are trying to change the culture of the country.' We constantly battled this. What they would want was a short-term product. All they cared about was a handbill that talks about rockets, a handbill that*

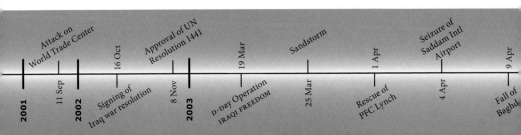

talks about IEDS *[improvised explosive devices]. And that is not* PSYOP.[8]

Captain Marvin Holiday*, commander of TPD 1220, agreed: "At least for us, that was one of the hardest parts about [product] dissemination. Some of the products being generated or pushed by the maneuver commander appeared to be self-serving. 'We're going to focus on IEDS. Well, only Americans are getting killed by IEDS. The Americans only want IEDS to stop because they are killing Americans. You're not helping Iraqis. Tell us how you are going to help us, and maybe we'll report this information.'" The 315th TPC tried to balance products that addressed the commanders' short-term concerns with products that addressed long-term PSYOP goals, such as those emphasizing progress in rebuilding a better Iraq.[9]

Figure 9.4 *Bagdad Now* distribution. *A soldier of the 315th TPC distributes the* Baghdad Now *newspaper.*

At times the PSYOP teams had to show the maneuver commanders that in psychological operations, often no news was good news. Captain Chambers* described the maneuver soldiers' attitudes: "The infantry officer or the armor officer is used to putting steel on a target and seeing an immediate effect. 'I fired my weapon and I killed something.' The long-term, residual effect of a PSYOP product is going to be delayed. You may never see a reaction to a product you've disseminated in the area." But the cumulative effects of the PSYOP messages become evident over time. It was difficult for maneuver commanders to understand that PSYOP effectiveness can often be calculated in terms of negative activity. Thomas recounted, "What we'd have to do is get into these Socratic philosophical discussions. [The commanders would say], 'We want to know what you guys are doing.' 'Well, here's what we're doing: Are you seeing mass demonstrations?' 'Well, no.' 'Are you seeing negative attitudes towards Coalition forces?' 'Well, no.' 'That's where PSYOP comes in.'"[10]

Once the brigade combat teams understood the capabilities of the tactical PSYOP teams, the units worked effectively together. TPT 1214 worked with the 1st Platoon, Hawk Troop, 1st Cavalry Regiment, 3rd Brigade Combat Team, from 10–31 May. Hawk Troop controlled the distribution of scarce propane gas. When Hawk Troop began its mis-

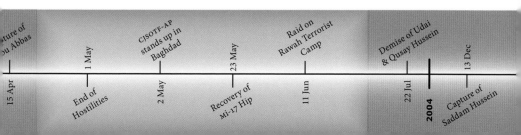

sion, Iraqi civilians would riot at the distribution stations, sometimes in groups of more than three hundred. On five occasions, the riots grew so large that TPT 1214 had to shut down the loudspeakers and help the Hawk Troop soldiers employ riot control measures. However, the PSYOP team's primary weapon against the rioters was its loudspeakers. By daily broadcasting messages explaining the propane distribution system and encouraging cooperation, the team reduced the number and severity of the riots.[11]

One of the 315th's early missions was to disseminate safety information to the residents of Baghdad. The city's usual modes of communication—radio, television, and telephone—were so badly disrupted that the U.S. Army had to rely on old-fashioned means to spread its message: paper. One part of the safety campaign involved educating the public about the presence and danger of unexploded ordnance and munitions throughout the city. The product development detachment designed and produced two-sided leaflets with pictures of different ordnance and instructions on how to report mines and weapons caches. The TPTs then distributed the leaflets by hand to the public taking the opportunity to interact with Iraqis on the street. Sergeant Reed Costner* summarized: "Our mission is basically encouraging mine and unexploded ordnance awareness through leaflets, posters, and face-to-face communication."[12]

Another PSYOP campaign was against electrical wire theft. "No sooner would they put up new wire than it would be gone the next day." Thomas described the thrust of the PSYOP effort:

> We had to constantly try to correlate the actions of the individual to the greater good. People were more focused on gaining whatever money they could by stealing and reselling electrical wire and had no interest in the bigger problem. When the locals were confronted with the situation there responses was: 'Oh, if I steal from my neighborhood, we won't have power. You're absolutely right.' If they did understand the implication, they would simply go steal from another neighborhood, not caring that they were causing problems for the entire city.[13]

One detachment commander encountered a woman who simply did not care about anybody else:

> This lady told me straight up that she didn't care about anybody that did not live in her little neighborhood which

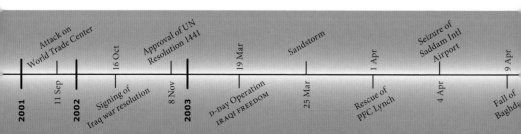

> *had a Baath Party headquarters. They used to get electric-*
> *ity twenty-four hours a day. So, when they started to push*
> *[electricity] out to everyone, causing temporary blackouts,*
> *she told me, 'I don't care. If that's the way it is, then the*
> *Americans need to go out and buy generators for every-*
> *one in this apartment building. Unless we get that, I'm not*
> *going to be happy.'*[14]

Frustrating as it was, by the end of the PSYOP campaign, looting of wire had been considerably reduced.

Psychological operations in Baghdad were not all paper and hand-shakes. More than one tactical PSYOP team encountered violence, and all five of the 315th tactical PSYOP detachments participated in cordon and search operations and raids. While raids were usually conducted in conjunction with conventional forces, on one occasion the PSYOP soldiers acted alone. On 27 April, TPD 1280 surrounded a residence and broadcast a surrender appeal to the six men inside, who were systematically robbing the house while wait-ing for the owner—a former member of the Baath Party—to return home so they could murder him. All six heavily armed men sur-rendered without a fight. While two soldiers guarded the criminals, two PSYOP soldiers cleared the house. TPD 1280 confiscated the thugs' stolen pickup truck, several grenades, an RPK machine gun, six AK-47s, six pistols, and ammunition.[15]

Earlier in May, teams from TPD 1230 had converged to help prevent a riot around Abu Hanifa Mosque in the Aadhamiyah District

Figure 9.5 Abu Hanifa Mosque, Baghdad.

of northwest Baghdad. Using their loudspeakers to call for peace-ful behavior, distributing leaflets with similar messages, and simply engaging demonstrators in conversation, the PSYOP teams helped prevent a potentially violent confrontation between insurgents, civil-ians, and Coalition troops. The scenario was repeated often in the days and weeks following the fall of Baghdad. The TPT response to riot situations was to broadcast appeals for nonviolence, identify key personalities in the crowds, and address the people's grievances as best it could.[16]

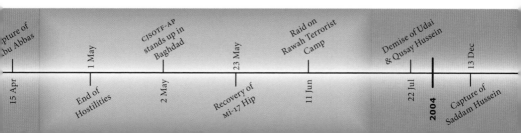

One TPT had the opportunity to use its PSYOP equipment in its defense. A TPT 1213 vehicle was hit by an IED while distributing handbills in Al Hara, Baghdad. The vehicle was damaged by the explosion, but not completely disabled. The team quickly grabbed its most effective weapon—the loudspeaker—to defend themselves. As soon as they started broadcasting, several Iraqis came forward and told them about two more IEDs along the convoy route. With this information, TPT 1213 was able to safely route help to them.[17]

The vast majority of the 315th TPC products were designed internally. Thomas said: "Our guys, who had never done this before, designed [almost] every product that we put out." Since the Joint PSYOP Task Force forward at Qatar, the endpoint for the much-touted "reach-back system" of the 4th PSYOP Group, had redeployed to Fort Bragg, the Army Reserve PSYOP units in Iraq were on their own. Using photo editing and design software, the soldiers of the product development detachment translated ideas from the field into realities that were quickly sent back for distribution. As TPTs and TPDs saw needs and obtained feedback from civilians, they sent them back to the product development team. Situation reports from the TPTs were often very clear: "Stop using this product, because it's just pissing them off!" Once turned into a viable PSYOP design, the product was given to a locally contracted printer. They were able to produce four-color handbills or posters on demand, which cut product turnaround to a matter of days.[18]

Circumstances—no printing equipment—caused the 315th to resort to contracting local printers. While the mission was to distribute hundreds of thousands of PSYOP handbills, it had no capability to produce them. Major Chip West*, chief of the product development detachment, explained how the company solved the problem:

One of the teams came back and said 'Hey, we met this printer.' Because I had contracting experience, I went and found the division contracting officer. We discussed [the requirement] and established a Blanket Purchasing Agreement rather than a service contract. The 1st Armored Division started dumping money into it; . . . fortunately, the G-8 [comptroller] was a former Special Forces guy who understood special operations. He said, 'This is all the information that I need.' In order to have competition, I found another three printers. There are four printing contracts that run through the BPA." The purchasing agreement meant that the 315th did not have to bid each

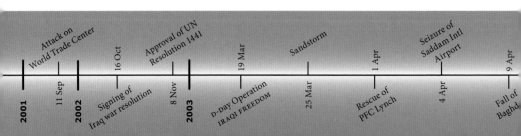

Figure 9.6 *Baghdad Now* cover.

Figure 9.7 Children reading *Baghdad Kids.*

Figure 9.8 *Baghdad Kids* cover.

print job; rather, it simply placed orders with the contracted printers and received good, timely service. Thomas added, "In an emergency, we could [produce] 200,000 handbills, double-sided, four-color, in roughly twenty-four to forty-eight hours." Access to four local printers enabled the 315th to design and distribute about 1.2 million handbills and posters a week if necessary.[19]

The 315th's abilities to produce PSYOP products in-house and to get them professionally printed were key to future successes. By July, the company was publishing the biweekly newspaper *Baghdad Now.* It provided both Coalition and Iraqi news in Arabic and English. Some Iraqi teachers used *Baghdad Now* in their English classes. In January 2004, the company published its first issue of *Baghdad Kids*, a comic strip offshoot of *Baghdad Now* aimed at the city's youth. Distributed free of charge by the TPTs, these newspapers gave the tactical teams an additional way to interact positively with the citizens of Baghdad.

Baghdad Humanitarian Assistance Coordination Center

As chief of operations for the 354th Civil Affairs Brigade's Humanitarian Assistance Coordination Center, Lieutenant Colonel Daniel Robey was the U.S. Army interface in Baghdad during the early months of Operation IRAQI FREEDOM. He was the critical link between the Iraqi people, Coalition forces, the international aid community, and the numerous U.S. government agencies tasked with rebuilding Iraq. Robey's mission was unusual for Army Civil Affairs, but its scale and broad scope took the 354th Civil Affairs Brigade into

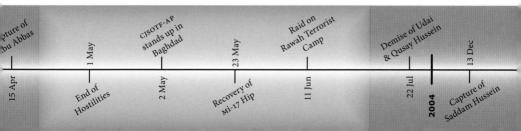

Figure 9.9 Start-up meeting at the Baghdad HACC. *Major Del Kravert* is briefing various nongovernmental organizations on the role of the HACC.

Figure 9.10 354th Civil Affairs Brigade insignia.

Figure 9.11 422nd CAB insignia.

uncharted territory. The work was demanding, the pace relentless, and guidance from higher mostly nonexistent; but, if the job was difficult, Robey's tireless diligence was equal to the challenge.[20]

Robey spoke with boundless enthusiasm about the Humanitarian Assistance Coordination Center projects, which ranged from empowering local leaders to persuading an international organization to fix a broken sewer system. He ran the HACC from a simple office cubicle just down the street from one of Saddam Hussein's palaces. The building "was literally a furniture warehouse," Robey explained matter-of-factly about the former Republican Guard facility. A cluster of throne-like chairs and gilded sofas outside his office were reminders of the building's past purpose. Robey's twenty-person team arrived in Baghdad on 23 April 2003, and immediately got down to the business of rebuilding the beleaguered capital.[21]

The concept for HACC operations did not come with an instruction manual. Existing Civil Affairs doctrine helped to define the mission by couching it in familiar terms. The HACC would function like a Civil Military Operations Center described in Field Manual 41-10, but on a much larger scale. "Think of it as baking a cake for six," said Robey, "and now you're baking a cake for sixty." Operating as an oversized Civil Military Operations Center, the HACC would facilitate and coordinate between the international aid organizations and the Iraqi people. In a city of nearly six million, more than a central center was needed. Battalions of the 354th Civil Affairs Brigade attached to maneuver units established satellite centers in each of Baghdad's nine political districts. In less than two months, six local facilities were operational.[22]

Robey attributed the rapid success of the HACC to the solid foundation built by the 422nd Civil Affairs Battalion. As soon as it arrived in Baghdad the battalion commander had begun daily meetings with international and nongovernmental organizations. They called their operation a Civil Military Assistance Center, another term alien to Civil Affairs doctrine like the HACC. Regardless, the 422nd Civil Mili-

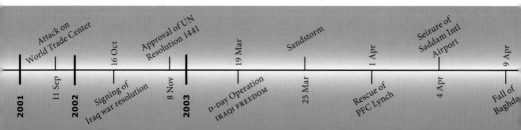

2001   11 Sep   2002   Signing of Iraqi war resolution   8 Nov   2003   D-Day Operation IRAQI FREEDOM   25 Mar   Rescue of PFC Lynch   4 Apr   Fall of Baghdad

Attack on World Trade Center   16 Oct   Approval of UN Resolution 1441   19 Mar   Sandstorm   1 Apr   Seizure of Saddam Intl Airport   9 Apr

tary Assistance Center established vital links to the nongovernmental and international organizations communities in Baghdad. "Had [the 422nd] not done such good work to start with," remarked Robey, "we would have been way behind the power curve."[23]

The HACC team prepared for its mission by observing the Humanitarian Operations Center in Kuwait City. They watched the British-run center in action for three days, taking notes on daily operations. That experience gave the team a model for operations. It also provided a valuable Lieutenant Colonel Stuart Gordon, who later relocated to Baghdad to establish another center called the Iraqi Assistance Center.

Figure 9.12 Interim government meeting. *Ambassador L. Paul Bremer III, newly appointed head of the Office of Reconstruction and Humanitarian Affairs, addresses the media on 18 May about issues of interim government development and displaced persons, during his familiarization tour of northern Iraq. Also pictured are: Ghanim Al Basso (far left), mayor of Mosul and Nineveh Province, and Major General David Petraeus (immediate left), commander, 101st Airborne Division.*

Running at full speed, the HACC officially completed 116 actions in just over six weeks. Although the HACC was equipped to manage a heavy workload; Robey's goal was to eliminate the HACC in Baghdad. "Our measure of success was putting ourselves out of business," he commented. The 354th Civil Affairs Brigade lacked the expertise and resources to manage large-scale humanitarian projects alone. The HACC's job was to identify projects and make sure that they were handled by the appropriate agencies. Consequently, the HACC devoted much of its time to coordinating with humanitarian organizations that were better equipped to identify the needs of the Iraqi people.[24]

Despite the presidential declaration that major combat operations were finished on 1 May 2003, many in the international aid community were hesitant to enter Baghdad because of safety concerns. To build confidence, Robey's team started the "Adopt a Neighborhood" program to lure nongovernmental organizations into less permissive areas of the capital. In fifteen-minute presentations given by the battalion Civil Military Operations Centers at the HACC, they provided aid workers with a "virtual" tour of a Baghdad neighborhood, using digital photos, giving character sketches of local leaders, and identifying three to five critical projects in each neighborhood. The program was simply designed to introduce the human dimension into mundane repair and reconstruction jobs.

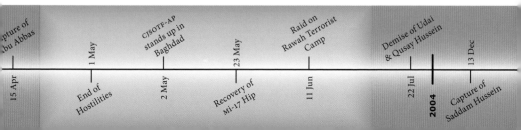

Capture of Abu Abbas · 15 Apr · End of Hostilities · 1 May · 2 May · CJSOTF-AP stands up in Baghdad · 23 May · Recovery of MI-17 Hip · 11 Jun · Raid on Rawah Terrorist Camp · 22 Jul · Demise of Udai & Qusay Hussein · 2004 · Capture of Saddam Hussein · 13 Dec

The HACC tried to "deconflict" all humanitarian agency meetings in the city to maximize the international and nongovernmental organizations presence. "We [were] all trying to figure out the best use of our assets," said Robey "because we [were] all on the same team; we [were] all in this together." Committed to that philosophy, Robey rescheduled HACC meetings with nongovernmental organizations on Tuesdays when he learned that the United Nations was holding its meetings at the same time. He announced all meetings to include the Nongovernmental Coordination Center in Iraq, a group that was opposed to military involvement. "Our mission [was] to support humanitarian assistance in Baghdad," says Robey. "If that [meant] supporting an NGO [nongovernmental organization] that [had snubbed] us then [we'd] do it."[25]

When Robey was not meeting with international agencies, he was busy enlisting the help of maneuver commanders. Meetings with combat arms commanders often yielded important leads on local leaders who were eager to participate in the rebuilding process. The commander of the 4th Battalion, 64th Armor Regiment, 3rd ID, said a Mr. Mustafa was a unifying force in his area. Robey passed this information on to the Office of Coalition Provisional Authority, the civilian agency charged with rebuilding Iraq. Within a week, Mr. Mustafa had met with the Authority officials to discuss rehabilitating his neighborhood. Starting a dialogue with community leaders was the first step empowering the residents of Baghdad.

During its short time in the Iraqi capital, the HACC saw a decline in its daily business. According to Robey, this was a positive trend. Larger humanitarian agencies like the U.S. Agency for International Development had stepped in with money to award contracts for rehabilitation projects. As the HACC moved to transition out of Baghdad, its information on local business people was passed on to the Office of Coalition Provisional Authority and the Agency for International Development in hopes that some loyal Iraqis would receive contracts. Although the HACC's role in Baghdad wound down, Robey and his team never turned anyone away. "These groups [of Iraqis] come in and if we simply turn them away we lose affirmative contact with them forever," believed Robey. The ability to recognize how small actions affected the big picture was the source of the HACC's success amid the confusion of civil military relations in postwar Baghdad.[26]

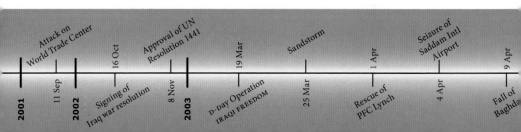

MASS GRAVES

The tragic events of 11 September were quite vivid for Army Reserve Lieutenant Colonel Edward Burley. Looking out the window of his office in Washington DC, Burley saw the smoke rising from the Pentagon and knew his life, like many others, was about to change. What he did not know on that day was that his role in the Global War on Terrorism would require not only his strengths as a citizen soldier, but his civilian expertise as well. Burley was a U.S. prosecuting attorney—his strong background in murder investigations and forensic science became invaluable in Iraq.[27]

In the days following major combat operations in Iraq, Burley and his civilian team of British and Australian forensic anthropologists began the tragic process of identifying the dead from the mass murders perpetrated by Saddam Hussein's terrible regime. Attached to the Office of Reconstruction and Humanitarian Assistance, Burley coordinated the efforts of a civilian team specially trained in the excavation and evaluation of mass graves. The Institute for Forensic Excellence and Investigation of Genocide team was controlled by the Office of Human Rights. The Institute charter went well beyond the basics of exhuming graves. It had become heavily involved in crosschecking lists compiled by local citizens that identified possible assassination victims.

Figure 9.13 Mass graves. *Iraqi workers dig for the remains of Iraqis from a mass grave in al-Musayyib, 75 kilometers southwest of Baghdad. The victims are thought to be from among some 2,000 persons reported missing after the 1991 uprising against the Iraqi government.*

Internationally, the scope of the work was staggering. In Bosnia, the estimated number of people buried in mass graves is 30,000; after nine years, only about 9,000 persons have been located. In Iraq, the lowest estimate was 290,000, and the highest estimate was close to 3 million regime victims buried in mass graves. The mission of the team was to identify bodies and gather evidence to prosecute the perpetrators for war crimes or international crimes against humanity.[28]

Burley and his thirty-person team had to work within a complex set of cultural and religious rules. Despite the age of many of the sites, Burley's team made sure that any body exhumed during the day was reburied by nightfall in accordance with Islamic custom. Women on

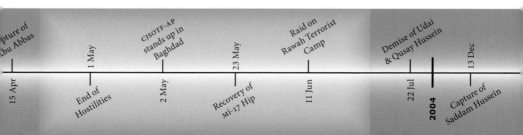

...pture of ..bu Abbas

15 Apr

1 May

End of Hostilities

CJSOTF-AP stands up in Baghdad

2 May

23 May

Recovery of Mi-17 Hip

Raid on Rawah Terrorist Camp

11 Jun

Demise of Udai & Qusay Hussein

22 Jul

2004

13 Dec

Capture of Saddam Hussein

the team were careful to keep their heads covered while working at the various sites. Grieving survivors were given access to the sites in order to mourn for the missing. Clerics and religious leaders were continuously consulted to ensure appropriate respect was accorded as the team continued its grim work.

Civil military issues occasionally arose. Despite having good relationships with U.S. military commanders in areas where they worked, some senior military and civilian leaders were uncomfortable with the mass graves mission. The issue was about who should be directing the effort. This problem ended when the mandate for the British/Australian forensic team ended and Burley passed control of the mass graves investigation to a civilian office in the newly formed Coalition Provisional Authority. Still, the team had made a good start on the investigations. Much more remained to be done, but it would be carried out by Iraqis seeking justice for their citizenry. The U.S. prosecuting attorney, Burley, knew how that part worked.

CFSOCC/SOCCENT

From the Coalition Forces Special Operations Component Command perspective, the ground war ended when the planned objectives of the campaign were achieved. CJSOTF-North with its Kurdish allies occupied the key northern cities of Mosul and Kirkuk. CJSOTF-West had followed the conventional forces into Baghdad and established its base of operations in the capital. According to Colonel Patrick Higgins, CFSOCC operations officer, special operations forces were major contributors to the successful Coalition effort: "We had success on all fronts. We got inside their decision cycle and stayed there. SOF enabled that in a very big way."[29]

As part of the transition after the declared end to major ground combat, CFSOCC established the CJSOTF-West headquarters in Baghdad. The new CJSOTF-AP (Arabian Peninsula) reflected the ongoing nature of the Global War on Terrorism and the SOF role in that conflict. The 10th Special Forces Group, the core of Task Force Viking, was designated an advanced operating base to remain in the north and provide situational awareness in that sector. CFSOCC issued CJSOTF-AP a new mission order outlining its responsibilities. "We crafted an order that narrowed the scope of the mission. This was

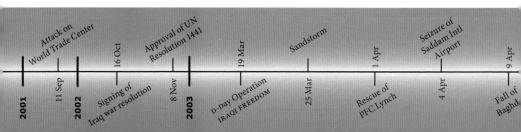

reflective of the priorities of a War on Terror mission set and supported the special operations force structure available to SOCCENT," recounted Higgins.[30]

CJSOTF-AP

During the transition between Phase III and Phase IV, the combined Special Forces assets in Iraq were consolidated under the CJSOTF-AP. On 1 May 2003, CJSOTF-AP assumed operational control over the majority of SOF in Iraq. In mid-May, Brigadier General Gary Harrell redeployed with the CFSOCC staff and main body to Tampa, Florida.[31]

Figure 9.14 CJSOTF-AP logo.

The CFSOCC plan for Phase IV had been to draw down SOF assets in Iraq from three special operations task forces (CJSOTF-west, CJSOTF-north, and the Naval Task Force), to an appropriately sized command based on the conditions. This force, named CJSOTF-AP, could increase or decrease SOF forces depending upon the conditions. This gave the commander more flexibility to meet requirements. Between May and July, the SOF commitment was reduced from three task forces to one task force. CJSOTF-north redeployed its headquarters and then Forward Operating Bases 103 and 33. FOB 102 initially assumed control of the northern zone before passing that responsibility to AOB 050 and its four to six operational detachments alphas (ODAS). The SOF forces assigned to each zone were based on conditions; it was not a "cookie cutter" approach. Because conditions varied throughout the country, so did the requirement for SOF forces. But if one area needed additional combat power to handle its mission, ODAS could be shifted to support it. By June, CJSOTF-AP had three advanced operating bases—AOBS 570 and 580 from FOB 53, and AOB 050 from 10th SFG—to work with the peshmerga of the Patriotic Union of Kurdistan and Kurdistan Democratic Party in the northern region. The three to five ODAS were assigned a variety of missions from liaison to special reconnaissance and direct action.[32]

Because FOB 53 would be the core of the new CJSOTF-AP headquarters, it needed staff augmentation. CJSOTF-west and CJSOTF-north had been built around Special Forces group Headquarters' staffs, and had joint staff augmentees from various Joint Manning Documents. Instead of building the CJSOTF-AP around the entire 5th SFG staff, it had been formed around a Special Forces battalion staff. This was

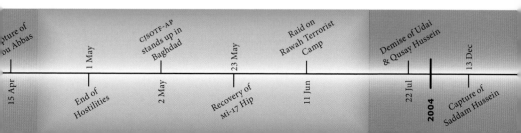

Figure 9.15 Radwaniya Palace Complex, Baghdad. *CJSOTF-AP made the Radwaniya Palace Complex its home in Iraq.*

quite different from CJSOTF-Afghanistan as well. Only small detachments of Civil Affairs and PSYOP were attached to the SOF headquarters. The majority of the Civil Affairs and Psychological Operations units remained under the control of conventional forces in their assigned zones. The staff section requiring the most augmentation was the CJSOTF-AP operation to maintain around-the-clock situational awareness of the country.

The CJSOTF-AP commanded and synchronized the Special Forces operating throughout Iraq. These Special Forces units conducted unconventional warfare, counter-insurgency, and advanced special operations. The ODAS conducted integrated operations with conventional units and Coalition SOF, but often operated independently. Special Forces ODAS developed target intelligence packets and did accelerated mission planning for high-value target–related cordon and search missions. The ODAS then shared the intelligence packets and conducted planning with conventional units. The direct action element from CJSOTF-AP would conduct the search portion of the operation while conventional units performed the cordon around the objective. Thus, manpower and firepower were maximized. Afterward, the ODAS would perform sensitive-site exploitation and tactical interrogation of detainees on the target.[33]

To further enhance rapport with the conventional forces in Iraq, CJSOTF-AP placed liaison officers at Combined Joint Task Force–7 and with each division headquarters. The liaison officers proved critical since there were no formal command and control relationships between Special Forces and the conventional units. The liaison officers not only deconflicted and synchronized operations, but also acted as special operations subject matter experts to the conventional commanders. Information flow worked both ways as the liaison officers also kept the CJSOTF informed of conventional operations.[34]

Additional support was needed in special staff elements and soldiers came from a wide variety of units including the U.S. Army Special Operations Command headquarters, the U.S. Army John F. Kennedy Special Warfare Center and School, the U.S. Army Infantry

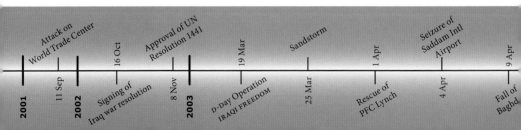

School, and the National Guard units from several states. One interesting addition was a command psychologist.

FOCUSING THE HIGH-VALUE TARGET HUNT

As discussed earlier, psychologists had demonstrated their value to the two CJSOTFs during earlier operations in Iraq. Profiling military and civilian personalities, Iraqi military leadership, and culture had proved quite valuable. When CJSOTF-west transitioned to CJSOTF-AP in Baghdad, Lieutenant Colonel John Chin volunteered to continue as the command psychologist. With the authority of Colonel Hector Pagan, the new 5th SFG commander and CJSOTF-AP commander, Chin began to refine his cultural profile of Saddam Hussein and family to give better focus to the high-value target hunt. Input from others was needed.

The deputy commander, Lieutenant Colonel Kirk Burton, was tasked by Pagan to manage a part-time work group/think tank made up of selected CJSOTF-AP staff officers and personnel from two National Guard Special Operations Detachments (Special Operations Detachment–Joint Forces Command and Special Operations Detachment–Korea). Chin served as the moderator/facilitator during the daily sessions of the group, stimulating thought, analysis, and discussion among the participants. It began as a CJSOTF-AP initiative, but word about this effort eventually leaked out. The group's written products attracted outside interest, and Chin had to expand the "need to know" circle with other elements. As far as Chin was concerned, the fact that others were interested and doing more thinking about specific high-value targets, helped to give the group a necessary focus.[35]

How successful this CJSOTF-AP think tank profiling effort was can be judged by what happened in November and December 2003. Chin had already returned to the United States and was on terminal leave pending retirement when Saddam Hussein was captured. Less than twelve hours after the capture of Saddam was announced, Chin was back in uniform being flown to Baghdad. Thirty days later he returned home to again start terminal leave. The value of an experienced psychologist on the staff of a joint SOF command had been proved most convincingly. Also of vital importance to sustaining operations were small logistics and signal elements from the 528th Special Operations Support Battalion and 112th Special Operations Signal Battalion.[36]

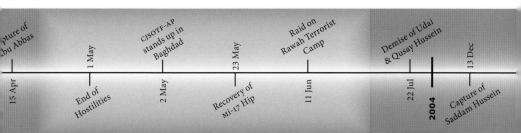

SUSTAINING OPERATIONS

In early May 2003, Alpha Forward Support Company, 528th Special Operations Support Battalion, organized a platoon-sized forward support element to support the CFSOCC advance headquarters in Baghdad. The support element included mechanics, cooks, water purification teams, fuel teams, and engineers commanded by First Lieutenant Robert Winston*. With no dedicated aircraft to get to Baghdad International Airport, it took the forward support element almost two weeks of "strap-hanging" to get the entire element out of H-5.[37]

Once in Baghdad, Winston's forward support element quickly set up the standard bare-base amenities, albeit in one of Saddam Hussein's seventy palaces. Among the more popular improvements the element brought were hot food and showers. The CJSOTF soldiers had been eating a combination of locally contracted food and Meals Ready-to-Eat. The forward support element set up its mobile kitchen and started serving American-style hot meals twice daily. Because the water was out in the palace, the element also set up three shower units. The engineers built everything from privies to planning tables, chart easels, and other staff necessities. They also used their Bobcats and mini-dozers to create berms and bunkers around the headquarters to improve force protection.[38]

Figure 9.16 528th SOSB insignia.

When CJSOTF-West transitioned to CJSOTF-AP, the support mission was transferred to another 528th element. Replacing Winston and his soldiers after nearly eight months was a forward support element from the newly activated Charlie Forward Support Company, which deployed intertheater from Afghanistan to Iraq. This element had National Guardsmen from several states.[39]

Among the soldiers assigned to support CJSOTF-AP were a dozen Tennessee Army National Guardsmen from the 777th Maintenance Company, attached to C Company, 528th Special Operations Support Battalion. After a four-month tour in Afghanistan supporting the CJSOTF in Bagram, the Guardsmen went to Iraq for a second overseas assignment in less than six months. Throughout Afghanistan, Sergeant Justin McCleary*, a light wheeled–vehicle mechanic, had worked on everything and anything that had an engine in the remote special forces firebases. McCleary and the other mechanics worked long hours to keep vehicles running. It was no different in Baghdad.

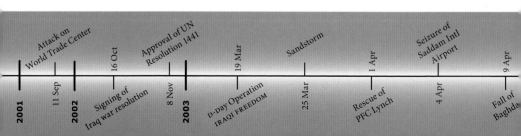

2001

Attack on World Trade Center

11 Sep

2002

Signing of Iraq war resolution

16 Oct

Approval of UN Resolution 1441

8 Nov

2003

D-Day Operation IRAQI FREEDOM

19 Mar

25 Mar

Sandstorm

Rescue of PFC Lynch

1 Apr

4 Apr

Seizure of Saddam Intl Airport

9 Apr

Fall of Baghdad

Sometimes this meant ordering commercial parts directly from the United States and waiting to receive them in the mail. More often than not, however, the experienced mechanics and soldiers relied on old-fashioned "horse trading" for needed parts with other units in Baghdad—anything to keep the vehicles functioning after months of hard use in Iraq. Specialist Josh Carlton, a Tennessee generator mechanic, worked long hours to make sure the CJSOTF-AP had uninterrupted power.[40]

What the Guardsmen also brought with them when mobilized were their civilian skills. Three soldiers—McCleary, Sergeant Timmons*, and Specialist Fitts*—had civilian welding experience, although this was not an military occupational specialty–qualified skill in their records. In fact, Timmons was a certified welder in Tennessee with many years of experience. The three Guardsmen solved a force protection problem for the headquarters with characteristic ingenuity. The Radwaniya Palace complex contained numerous perimeter guard towers that were simply bare platforms with no protection for the guards. Employing techniques used by ship welders on freighter hulls, the three welders created individual, suspended work platforms to hang from the tops of the towers. Each day they would lower themselves with a block and tackle assembly while seated on their work platforms with welding torches and acetylene tanks. In less than two weeks the three men fabricated and installed protective steel "skirts" or barriers from local materials around the tower platforms. These were further reinforced with sandbags to protect the guards.

Figure 9.17 Construction of guard tower platform skirts.

Another welding task, to improve unit morale, was the fabrication of four barbecue grills from concertina wire stakes and 55-gallon drums. These were built to help the hard-working mess section. In the beginning, the mess section had prepared all meals using its mobile kitchen trailer. Combine the 110-degree heat of Iraq with the cooking heat in a confined trailer and one can see the importance of the alternate outside grills. They were finished in time to have an old-fashioned barbecue on Memorial Day. While small in the overall scope of

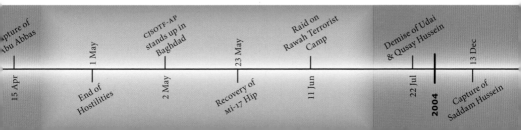

Capture of Abu Abbas · 15 Apr · 1 May · End of Hostilities · 2 May · CJSOTF-AP stands up in Baghdad · 23 May · Recovery of MI-17 Hip · 11 Jun · Raid on Rawah Terrorist Camp · 22 Jul · 2004 · Demise of Udai & Qusay Hussein · Capture of Saddam Hussein · 13 Dec

Operation IRAQI FREEDOM, the soldiers supporting CJSOTF-AP made a difference to the new headquarters.[41]

OTHER ARSOF

Figure 9.18 Saddam Hussein as the ace of spades card.

Other Army SOF continued operations in Iraq, but at a reduced level. The 75th Ranger Regiment and the 160th Special Operations Aviation Regiment reconfigured the size of the Joint Special Operations Task Force and consolidated forces at Baghdad International Airport. Eighty percent of the task force redeployed by the end of May. Most of the 2nd Ranger Battalion and a small aviation detachment from the 160th SOAR remained at Baghdad International Airport. The mission set for the Joint Special Operations Task Force narrowed to raiding high-value target locations and capturing the "deck of cards"—high-value personnel from the former regime that included Saddam and his inner circle. The ability of that task force to quickly plan and execute a direct action mission made it invaluable to security and stability operations.[42]

FLASH TO BANG: A WELL-ORCHESTRATED ASSAULT

One of the capabilities that make the ARSOF units so lethal is their ability to rapidly act on current intelligence. The Night Stalkers of the 160th SOAR can deliver SOF assault teams swiftly and on target. They pride themselves on their ability to accomplish this precisely within plus or minus thirty seconds of the appointed time. Combine that with the ferocious strike capability of the Army Rangers and it is possible to eradicate a terrorist training camp.

On the evening of 11 June 2003, the Rangers of B Company, 2nd Battalion, 75th Ranger Regiment, attacked and killed more than seventy Islamic terrorists at a training camp thirty miles east of the Syrian border in the vicinity of Rawah, Iraq. During the carefully coordinated assault on the camp—Objective Reindeer—two Ranger platoons and a command element infiltrated on four MH-60K Black Hawks and two MH-47E Chinooks to attack the camp from the east. A third Ranger platoon with a battalion mortar team drove 175 miles overland to arrive simultaneously with the air assault. They established several blocking positions and a mortar position. The AH-6 attack helicopters from the 160th SOAR provided close air support through-

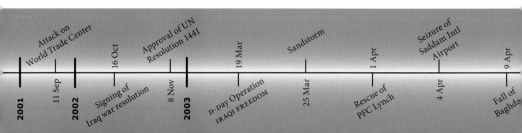

out the operation. The mission guidance was very clear: destroy all terrorists in and around the camp to prevent attacks against Coalition forces—a textbook mission for the Rangers and Night Stalkers.

The night before, Major John McGinnis*, 2nd Battalion operations officer, and Captain Mel Everett*, assistant operations officer, had received a warning order at 2200 to begin planning for a combat assault on a terrorist camp. The 101st Airborne Division (Air Assault) had been planning an operation for several days when V Corps received new information that suggested an attack on Coalition forces from the terrorist camp was imminent. The Screaming Eagles wanted several more days to prepare. Therefore, V Corps asked if the 75th Ranger Regiment could conduct an

Figure 9.19 Map highlighting Rawah. *The 160th soar inserted a Ranger force at Rawah to destroy a terrorist training camp.*

immediate strike. McGinnis and Everett and the B Company commander, Captain George Hunter*, prepared an operational concept that night. This collaborative planning process (including the company commander in the development of the battalion plan) greatly reduced the time necessary to complete troop-leading procedures. Hunter devised a simple scheme of maneuver with blocking positions to ensure that no terrorists escaped. Concentrated fires on the objective were designed to ensure no escapes. Within hours, McGinnis forwarded the plan through command channels to V Corps stating that the Ranger platoon could strike within twenty-four hours. At this point, McGinnis still believed that the 101st would retain the mission.[43]

Objective Reindeer was a sunken wadi, 35 feet deep, 500 feet long, and 60–150 feet wide, adjacent to a large streambed with steep, rocky sides. Two smaller wadis channeled into Reindeer. The objective was divided into

Figure 9.20 Objective Reindeer. *The Objective Reindeer areas and the platoon avenues of attack.*

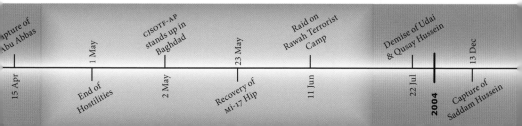

three separate objectives: Dasher, Rudolf, and Comet. Having sub-mitted their concept, Hunter issued his operations order at 0900 the next day (11 June) to his platoon leaders: the 1st Platoon would insert by helicopter, to isolate and clear Objectives Dasher and Rudolf; the 2nd Platoon would insert by helicopter, isolate and clear Objective Comet; and the 3rd Platoon would simultaneously establish blocking positions west of the objective to prevent any terrorist escapees after driving overland to the objective. Shortly afterward, McGinnis told Hunter that it looked like the mission would not take place after all. Despite this warning, Hunter used the opportunity to run his platoon leaders through a planning exercise based on the mission scenario. This proved to be wise because at 1100, McGinnis informed him that the mission was a "go" that night. The platoon leaders briefed their elements while Hunter and his fire support officer finalized close air support with the 160th SOAR planners. The final air mission briefing and a rock drill rehearsal were completed by 1700.[44]

Figure 9.21 3rd Armored Cavalry insignia.

The ground assault force left Baghdad International Airport at 1545 hours, crossing several damaged bridges as it moved along Highway 12. The convoy went through Ar Ramadi and Hit to a road junction south of Rawah. Along the way, the ground assault force linked up near Haditha with two M3 Bradley Fighting Vehicles carrying a 3rd Armored Cavalry Regiment infantry platoon. A forward arming and refueling point had been established near the highway south of Rawah. After quickly refueling, the ground assault force awaited the signal to move to the objective: the commencement of pre-assault fires by the 160th SOAR. On that signal, the ground assault force headed straight to the objective, leaving the infantry platoon and Bradley Fighting Vehicles to secure the refueling point and reinforce the ground assault force, if needed.

The helicopter assault force departed Baghdad International Air-port and refueled at another airfield at 2030. When one MH-60K Black Hawk failed to start minutes before the scheduled departure time, the "bump plan" (a contingency to cross-load key individuals or groups in the event of an aircraft breakdown) was implemented, leaving a Ranger squad at the airfield. The helicopter assault force departed two and one-half minutes late, but speeded up to arrive on time for H-HOUR: 2200. Sequencing in to hit their target, the first pair of AH-6 gunships suppressed the enemy fighters that had survived six Joint Direct Attack Munitions that had exploded as airbursts on Objec-

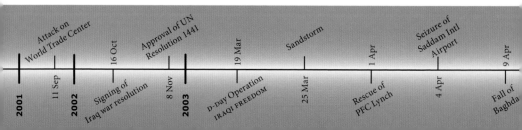

tive Dasher. Then an AC-130 Spectre Gunship raked the area with its 105mm cannon and 40mm chain guns.[45]

First Lieutenant Peter Korenek*, 1st Platoon, was riding in the lead MH-60K Black Hawk. With the side doors open he saw fires burning in the vicinity of Sparrow, his helicopter landing zone. Having lost his reference with the ground, Chief Warrant Officer 4 Travis Davis*, the pilot, touched down hard in a cloud of dust. Oblivious to the dangerous

Figure 9.22 AC-130 Spectre gunship.

landing, the Rangers leaped clear of the helicopter and raced into the dusty darkness as a pair of AH-6 Little Bird gunships strafed a nearby enemy position with 7.62mm minigun rounds and 2.75 inch rockets. Enemy fighters shot rocket-propelled grenades (RPGs) wildly as the Little Birds streaked by.

Having landing several hundred meters short of Sparrow because of an AH-6 gun run, Staff Sergeant Mitchell Burn* got his squad oriented toward Objective Dasher and ran across the flat surface of the wadi with Korenek. The Ranger squad reached a draw as Chief Warrant Officer 3 James Nattier*, the MH-47E Chinook flight lead, touched down on Sparrow with the rest of the 1st Platoon. At the same time, just south of Korenek's position, a second Black Hawk landed at Helicopter Landing Zone Wren with Staff Sergeant Alexander Weis* and his squad. They seized the high ground near the gulch to overwatch Objective Rudolph. The cacophony of sounds, acrid smells, small burning fires, and whoosh of RPGs convinced the Rangers that this event was genuine, and the enemy was, in fact, trying to kill them. While realizing this, the second wave of the assault flew in.[46]

The 2nd Platoon came into Helicopter Landing Zones Napier and Emu aboard a Black Hawk and a Chinook respectively. Sergeant Roger Mueller* and his weapons squad left the Chinook first, followed by the command element headed toward Objective Comet. Mueller and his two Ranger machine gun teams established a blocking position and prepared to clear through Comet. The remainder of the 2nd Platoon moved from Napier into blocking positions, facing Objective Reindeer from the north. En route to their positions, the Rangers engaged and killed three enemy fighters using their rifles and grenades. First Sergeant Philip Roemer* led the last element off the Chinook. Roemer,

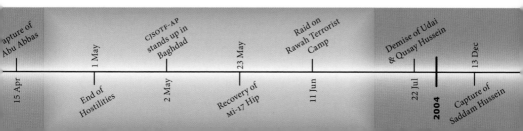

Capture of Abu Abbas — 15 Apr

End of Hostilities — 1 May

2 May

CJSOTF-AP stands up in Baghdad

Recovery of Mi-17 Hip — 23 May

11 Jun

Raid on Rawah Terrorist Camp

Demise of Udai & Qusay Hussein — 22 Jul

2004 — Capture of Saddam Hussein

13 Dec

Figure 9.23 Objective Reindeer helicopter landing zones.

Corporal Ralph Antonio*, his radio operator, and Sergeant Brad Gillis*, the senior medic, were to establish a casualty collection point in the smaller east–west wadi leading to Objective Dasher. As they approached the wadi, two terrorists opened fire on them, shooting Antonio's rucksack strap off his right shoulder. Gillis and Antonio spun and shot their assailants who were concealed in a nearby ditch.[47]

Meanwhile, the ground assault force had arrived and established its blocking positions and the mortar firing points. En route the mortar vehicle became stuck in a small wadi. The mortar team switched vehicles and still managed to be operational in less than ten minutes. The company executive officer and ground assault force commander, First Lieutenant Dirk Nester*, radioed an update to Hunter and moved closer to Objective Reindeer. All the supporting fires were oriented down into the wadi from both the east and west sides, reducing the potential for fratricide. Soon, the mortar team began executing fire missions in concert with the AH-6 Little Bird gunships to support the 1st Platoon.[48]

Burn and his squad moved into the gulch on the 3rd Platoon's right flank, locating a huge weapons cache of RPGs, RPK machine guns, SA-7 surface-to-air-missiles, and all types of munitions. Burn marked it for destruction and pressed forward. The squad comprising the platoon's main effort, led by Staff Sergeant Roger Duncan*, cleared the high ground south of Objective Dasher, killing five combatants, before the squad moved down into the wadi. Staff Sergeant Bradley Talbert* and his squad guarded the 3rd Platoon's left flank from the high ground overlooking Objective Rudolph.[49]

Above the objective, Chief Warrant Officer 4 Mark Willington* coordinated the rotation of AH-6s through the forward arming and refueling point. This enabled the Little Bird pilots to continuously provide close air support over the objective. The air cover proved crucial as the ground combat intensified.[50]

Korenek and Sergeant First Class Clint Anderson*, platoon sergeant for the 2nd Platoon, coordinated their simultaneous entry into the wadi to clear it from both sides. As Duncan maneuvered his squad down the wadi, they encountered twelve terrorists and killed them. In

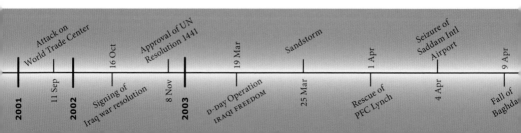

response to fire from two terrorists on a shelf just below the edge of the cliff, Korenek dropped a fragmentation grenade over the side. The grenade did not stop the firing, so he climbed over the edge to a point where he could get a clear shot at the enemy and killed them both. A burning vehicle in the center of the wadi limited the effectiveness of the night vision goggles of Burn and his squad, so they continued concentrating on the wadi to the west.[51]

As the 2nd Squad pushed south into the wadi, the Rangers were backlit by the burning truck. Sergeant Mark Walters*, the lead team leader, spotted an RPG team and shouted, "RPG!" firing as he did. The enemy gunner fired simultaneously, blowing off Walters' leg below the knee. In spite of this devastating injury, and further injury to his left elbow and thumb, Walters emptied a full magazine into the RPG position, killing the gunner, all the while shouting fire commands to his team. The platoon medic, Specialist Garcia*, stabilized Walters, expertly treating his wounds while under fire. With Walters stabilized and packaged on a Skedco (rescue sled), Sergeant First Class Oscar Weimer* had several Rangers carry Walters to Sparrow for evacuation. En route they met Roemer and Gillis making their way to the landing zone. Weimer gave Walters' equipment to the first sergeant, and returned to the fight. Hunter called in the casualty evacuation helicopter that was air loitering nearby. Thirty seconds later Chief Warrant Officer 3 Mark Teske* landed his Chinook and Walters was loaded aboard for the trip to a medical aircraft.[52]

In the meantime, Duncan pinpointed another fleeing RPG gunner and his assistant with his infrared laser. They were quickly dispatched by Talbert's machine gunners. Having spotted other enemy fighters fleeing into the tall grass of the wadi, Korenek attempted to clear the grass by fire with M240s and squad automatic weapons then set it afire using incendiary grenades, flares, and burning debris, but the grass was too damp. By then, the platoon sector was clear and the 1st Platoon Rangers began exploitation of the area.[53]

The 2nd Platoon advanced on line through Objective Comet with Mueller's squad, clearing the west side of the wadi and Weimer's men clearing the east side by fire. Mueller saw two enemy fighters drop down onto a ledge just two feet away from his platoon sergeant. As he engaged the enemy with his M4 carbine, Anderson dropped down and threw several hand grenades into the position. The threat was eliminated. As the 2nd Platoon continued to clear the wadi moving

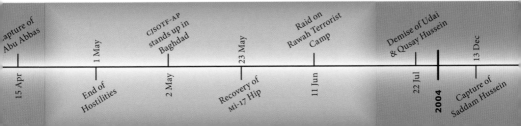

toward the burning vehicles, it methodically engaged terrorists, all the while paying close attention to the 1st Platoon approaching from the opposite direction.[54]

After approximately forty minutes, the two platoons linked up. Initial reports were fifteen terrorists killed, but during the follow-on exploitation, that number quickly grew to seventy bodies. With their night vision goggles in place, what the Rangers had thought were burning debris and sandbags were, in fact, body parts scattered throughout Objective Rudolph by the six Joint Direct Attack Munitions. Confident that the objective was clear, Hunter and McGinnis ordered the 1st and 2nd Platoons to prepare for egress. The Night Stalkers arrived at 0400 and extracted the two platoons of Rangers and flew back to the Baghdad International Airport. The 3rd Platoon remained to conduct a sensitive-site exploitation of the area in daylight.[55]

Sergeant First Class Barry Fontes*, the 3rd Platoon sergeant, started the sensitive-site exploitation of the objective at daybreak on 12 June. While two squads examined the wadi, one squad remained in a blocking position for security. While documenting the site with

pictures, the Rangers were surprised to find a wounded enemy fighter near Objective Comet. The medic treated the terrorist and prepared him for evacuation. He noted that the enemy's body had been shaved, and his beard was trimmed, possibly in anticipation of a suicide attack and martyrdom. The site exploitation lasted several hours as the Rangers waited for a 101st Airborne Division relief-in-place force to arrive. The battle at Rawah, however, was far from over.[56]

Figure 9.24 AH-64 Apache gunships.

The relief element from C Company, 1st Battalion, 327th Infantry arrived in three lifts of helicopters. While Nester was briefing the company commander, the four AH-64 Apache gunships that had flown cover for the troop carriers began firing from a stationary hover to the northwest of the objective. Suddenly a RPG exploded against one of the gunships. The Apache helicopter slammed into the ground and caught fire. Quickly reacting to the crash, Fontes sent two squads of Rangers in their Ground Mobility Vehicles (GMVs) to the site. The subsequent fight to secure the crash

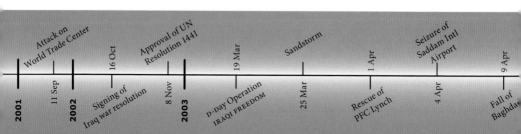

2001 — Attack on World Trade Center — 11 Sep
2002 — 16 Oct — Signing of Iraq war resolution — Approval of UN Resolution 1441 — 8 Nov
2003 — 19 Mar — D-Day Operation IRAQI FREEDOM — Sandstorm — 25 Mar — 1 Apr — Rescue of PFC Lynch — Seizure of Saddam Intl Airport — 4 Apr — 9 Apr — Fall of Baghdad

site and defeat several enemy counterattacks became known as the battle for Objective Vixen.[57]

Sergeant Daniel Height*, the weapons squad leader of the 3rd Platoon in the first GMV, maneuvered to engage the enemy with an M240B machine gun and a Carl-Gustaf M3 recoilless rifle. Height sent Private First Class Alberto Nieves* and Corporal Jacob Oliver*, a team leader, in a GMV to an overwatch position. As their vehicle crested a small knoll, Oliver observed the two pilots getting out of the AH-64, oblivious to the enemy fire they were receiving. Responding to the situation, Oliver and Nieves headed the GMV toward the pilots, using the vehicle to shield them from enemy fire. Oliver tried to suppress the enemy with his turret-mounted M2 .50 caliber machine gun as Nieves closed on the crashed helicopter. Rounds were impacting all around the dazed pilots and others buzzed past Oliver's head. The two Rangers managed to get the pilots safely away from the burning helicopter shortly before its ordnance began to explode.[58]

Having dropped the pilots in the safety of a 327th observation post, Nieves and Oliver turned back to the crash site. As they approached, Oliver surprised four terrorists trying to get to the downed helicopter, killing two and wounding another with his .50 caliber machine gun. As he dealt with that threat, two more terrorists opened fire, wounding Nieves in the hand. Oliver told Nieves to pull back as he swung the M2 to cover their withdrawal. Hidden in another wadi, Oliver treated Nieves' wound and summoned the platoon medic, Corporal Bob Holcomb*, and asked for a new driver. After handing Nieves his pistol to protect himself, Oliver rejoined the firefight with two other GMVs on top of a knoll. This combined firepower on the enemy allowed a Ranger assault element to slip within five meters of the enemy's position to destroy it.[59]

Moving at top speed toward the burning helicopter wreck, the small Ranger assault element led by Fontes was quickly taken under small arms fire by the terrorists. Covered by his men, Fontes worked his way toward an enemy position less than fifty meters away. Within hand grenade range, he lobbed one into the position. With this accomplished, the ad hoc assault element consisting of Holcomb, the platoon medic, Sergeant Derron Zack*, Corporal James Urich*, the platoon radioman, and Corporal Carl Vasser* charged forward. They no sooner had cleared the position than they began receiving fire from another group a hundred meters away. To deal with this threat, Fontes

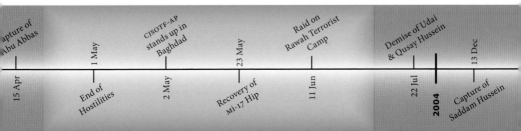

and his element established a heavy base of fire in a deep wadi to pin the enemy down. Then they proceeded to hammer the enemy with everything they had available: 81mm and 60mm mortars, 40mm high explosive grenades, .50 caliber machine gunfire, and small arms.[60]

When it became clear that the gaps in the terrain did not support an assault by the other two squads, Fontes led the final assault with his ad hoc element. While executing fire and movement, his M4 malfunctioned, but he courageously continued forward. Three remaining terrorists threw hand grenades and fired their weapons as the Rangers closed to within fifteen meters. As they made to assault, Fontes dove out of the way of a grenade that landed directly in front of him. Then Fontes charged forward tossing his remaining fragmentation grenades while his Rangers assaulted, killing the last two terrorists at point blank range.[61]

The Rangers demonstrated their bravery and resourcefulness while fighting a very tenacious enemy, killing fourteen terrorists in and around Objective Vixen, nine in close quarters combat. The Rangers rescued the two aviators from capture. Once the fighting was over and the area secured, the Rangers evacuated their casualties along with the enemy wounded to the casualty evacuation airfield. The attack on Reindeer had eliminated seventy terrorists and netted two thousand RPGs, fifty RPK machine guns, eighty-seven SA-7 surface-to-air missiles, and a huge stockpile of munitions. The fighting at Vixen sent another fourteen terrorists to martyrdom. After an eighteen-hour day, the ground assault force returned to Baghdad International Airport without further incident.

The late night raid by Army SOF prevented at least one terrorist attack on Coalition forces in Iraq. The rescue of the Apache pilots saved them from captivity. As is normal, many factors contributed to the success of these missions. Several Rangers and Night Stalkers commented that the operation played out like a multilateral training exercise, and that "everything went like clockwork." The force's previous combat experience also refined the Rangers and the 160th SOAR's planning processes, enabling them to execute a complex operation in hours instead of days. Finally, in the case of the assault on Objective Reindeer, a highly skilled force demonstrated how a well-executed, simple plan employing shock and violent action was able to destroy a tenacious enemy. This fight revealed the fanaticism of terrorists fighting a jihad. Americans have not fought an enemy like this since they

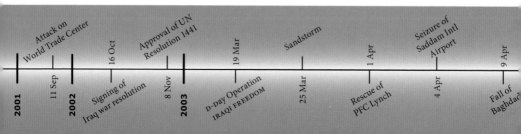

2001 — 11 Sep — Attack on World Trade Center
2002 — 16 Oct — Signing of Iraq war resolution — Approval of UN Resolution 1441 — 8 Nov
2003 — 19 Mar — D-Day Operation IRAQI FREEDOM — 25 Mar — Sandstorm — 1 Apr — Rescue of PFC Lynch — 4 Apr — Seizure of Saddam Intl Airport — 9 Apr — Fall of Baghdad

faced the Japanese in the Pacific whose banzai charges and kami-kaze attacks during World War II had to be defeated at close quarters—whether by Navy gunners firing on suicide planes before they hit their ships to infantrymen in the islands using bayonets to break the momentum of last ditch Japanese infantry assaults. And these terrorists had been hammered by six Joint Direct Attack Munitions, one AC-130 gunship, and several AH-6 attack helicopters. In the end, Army SOF dealt a fatal blow to a significant terrorist threat.

HARVESTING A CHOPPER FROM A DATE PALM TREE

Part of Saddam Hussein's defensive deception plan was to hide various types of aircraft in the western deserts of Iraq and among the palm groves along the Tigris River. After finding a Soviet-manufactured MI-17 Hip medium transport helicopter thirty miles north of Baghdad, the Joint Special Operations Task Force ordered the exploitation of the aircraft. The ensuing recovery operation was not without drama as a combined force of Army Rangers, 160th SOAR aviators, and Special Forces worked for several days to retrieve the helicopter. Neither interference by the local population nor a sudden sandstorm prevented the SOF troops from completing the mission.

Returning from a night mission in mid-May 2003, an AH-6 Little Bird gunship pilot spotted a fleet of about twenty MI-17 Hip helicopters in a grove of date palm trees along the Tigris River. The grove was just thirty miles north of Baghdad. The Iraqi military had parked them in and around palm trees, coated the bodies with mud, and used camouflage netting to further hide them. Piled neatly nearby were the removed rotor blades. According to intelligence sources, Baath Party members had threatened local inhabitants with death if anyone tampered with the Hips. Senior SOF leadership saw the value of having a Soviet Hip for training or possible use in future operations. The 160th SOAR was tasked to recover a working MI-17. Chief Warrant Officer 3 Derek Falcon* of A Company, 2nd Battalion, was charged with the mission.[62]

Figure 9.25 Mi-17 Hip in a palm grove. *The Hussein regime went to great lengths to conceal helicopters and other weapons systems from the Coalition.*

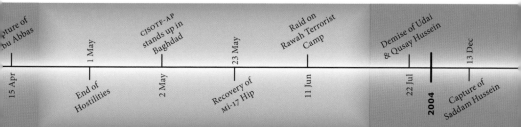

pture of
bu Abbas

15 Apr

1 May

End of
Hostilities

CJSOTF-AP
stands up in
Baghdad

2 May

23 May

Recovery of
Mi-17 Hip

Raid on
Rawah Terrorist
Camp

11 Jun

Demise of Udai
& Qusay Hussein

22 Jul

2004

Capture of
Saddam Hussein

13 Dec

Figure 9.26 Second Mi-17 Hip located under the palm trees. *The Ranger security force is moving into position while the Night Stalkers evaluate the aircraft for transport.*

Falcon, an MH-47E Chinook flight lead, formed a planning cell to gather pertinent data about the Hip from available intelligence sources. After accumulating the information, he developed a recovery plan. The key to success was obtaining an accurate weight of the Mi-17 in its current configuration. In order assess the Mi-17's condition, Falcon wanted to do an onsite inspection.

Falcon assembled his recovery team. It consisted of a Ranger platoon for security, SOF explosive ordnance disposal personnel to remove booby traps, and 160th SOAR maintenance personnel to evaluate the maintenance condition of the Hip. Falcon led the flight of two MH-47E Chinooks carrying the team to the date palm grove. A flight of two AH-6 Little Bird gunships accompanied the Chinooks, providing aerial escort en route and overhead protection while the helicopters were inspected. Before landing, Falcon and his team visually scanned the helicopters for good candidates. Landing next to a Hip that outwardly appeared to be in good shape, the crew exited the Chinook, inspected it for booby traps, quickly checked it over and deemed it to be a good find. As a backup, Falcon checked another helicopter "boneyard" nearby that the Little Bird pilots had identified. The first site seemed to be the best choice. The plan was to come back the next day and extract it.[63]

Upon their return to the airport, the maintenance teams from D Company, 160th SOAR, began stripping the MH-47E assigned to lift the Hip. Removing all the ballistic protection, armament, nonessential mission equipment, and as many unneeded parts as possible, the crew made the Chinook as light as anyone had ever seen it. A lull in operational tempo allowed the lift operation to proceed, since the "stripped down" MH-47E was no longer fully mission capable. Falcon knew that even with a short break in the action, the SOF senior leaders would only tolerate a stripped bird for a very short time, so the crew worked quickly. By late afternoon, the recovery team was ready to go.[64]

The next day, Falcon again led the Chinook flight to the palm grove with a pair of Little Birds for overhead protection. At the location, the Rangers established security positions while the explosive ordnance

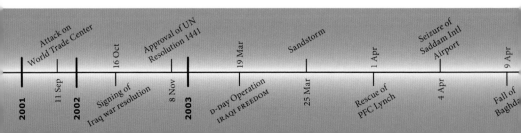

disposal team rechecked the helicopter identified for recovery. The D Company maintenance crew began loading the rotor blades found nearby, but after loading one blade, all work ceased. Having spotted the Americans surveying the Hip the day before, the locals realized that the helicopter was not booby-trapped. While the Americans were gone, the locals had ransacked the MI-17. They had removed numerous parts from the helicopter and had wrecked whatever they could not unscrew or unbolt, damaging gauges, smashing windows out, and flattening tires. Disheartened, but also kicking themselves for not guarding the helicopter, everyone returned to Baghdad International Airport and reworked the plan. It was a week before the leadership approved another "strip down" to recover a new helicopter.[65]

To prevent the locals from vandalizing the chosen Hip, the team planned to locate, clear, and recover the MI-17 on the same day. By using a series of reconnaissance flights, Falcon planned to find another Hip, insure that it had no booby-traps, evaluate it, and begin preparations with the first flight. He then planned to return to the airport with the rotor blades, leaving the security element and maintenance team in place while he brought in another stripped-down Chinook carrying the minimum amount of fuel to save weight. He would then extract the Hip with the second flight. The mission had to be executed on 23 May because the MH-47E needed to be built back up to a fully mission capable condition by the 24th.[66]

Figure 9.27 Loading the rotor blades for transport back to Baghdad International Airport.

With the mission planned and the team prepared, the weather threw a monkey wrench into the operation. A sandstorm swept through the area that day, causing poor visibility. Still, it was decided that the mission could continue. After a detailed briefing, the first flight proceeded to look for a likely candidate. A flight of two AH-6 Little Birds, one Chinook, and an MH-60K Black Hawk set out at mid-afternoon, flying in the suspended dust. The team felt that it had sufficient time to prepare the site, return with the MI-17 rotor blades, and still extract the Hip by dusk.[67]

Leading the search pack, Little Bird pilots Chief Warrant Officers 4 Tony Clement* and David Croaker* spotted what appeared to be

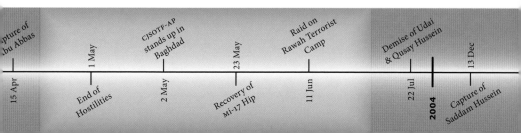

a viable helicopter and landed. Clement cautiously approached the Hip, and after a brief inspection, radioed to Falcon that it looked like a good airframe. Falcon had the Black Hawk pilots bring in the explosive ordnance disposal crew while Falcon landed his Chinook nearby. The Rangers established a security perimeter. Once their explosive ordnance disposal crew had cleared the helicopter, Falcon and his maintenance team, led by test pilot Chief Warrant Officer 3 Aaron Garrote*, began preparing the Mi-17 Hip for extraction. The MH-60K departed, leaving Falcon's Chinook and the two Little Birds on the ground. In thirty minutes the explosive ordnance disposal and maintenance troops had the rotor blades loaded aboard the Chinook in transport cradles. As the maintenance and explosive ordnance disposal crews concentrated on the final preparations around the pickup area, the Little Bird pilots kept watch on the small crowd of Iraqis gathering nearby. The presence of the Rangers kept them at a distance. Anticipating a forty-minute round trip, Falcon left for Baghdad International Airport with the helicopter blades while Garrote's team feverishly worked to meet the timeline; a delay at the palm grove could

Figure 9.28 Mi-17 Hip carried in sling-load.

cause mission failure since the time on station for the "stripped down" and minimally fueled Chinook was limited.[68]

Landing near the refuel point at the airport, Falcon switched seats with Chief Warrant Officer 2 Barry Littleton*, who was waiting at the refuel point in the "stripped down" recovery aircraft. Falcon was now flying with Chief Warrant Officer 2 Elliot Brietzke* because both were experienced slinging heavy loads. Littleton followed him in the second Chinook, accompanied by a flight of two AH-6 Little Bird gunships led by Chief Warrant Officer 4 Timothy Parkens*. When they arrived at the palm grove, the hook-up crew on the ground was not ready. Because they had no manual on how rig a Hip for a sling load, Garrote had to be sure to get things right the first time. In the end, he relied on experience and a lot of ingenuity.[69]

As dusk descended over the area, Garrote finally signaled Falcon to hover over the load. To clear the lift area, the maintenance team had cut down an adjacent palm tree. Now, the debris began to kick

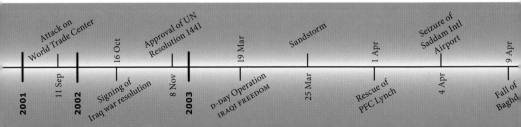

Attack on World Trade Center

16 Oct

Approval of UN Resolution 1441

19 Mar

Sandstorm

1 Apr

Seizure of Saddam Intl Airport

9 Apr

11 Sep

Signing of Iraq war resolution

8 Nov

D-Day Operation IRAQI FREEDOM

25 Mar

Rescue of PFC Lynch

4 Apr

Fall of Baghd

2001

2002

2003

up as the big Chinook hovered over the Hip. Garrote was standing atop the Mi-17 to attach a clevis (shackle) to the MH-47E's center hook as Falcon carefully inched his helicopter down over the load. Once attached, Falcon's crewchief told him to begin increasing power slowly to take the slack out of the 120 feet of nylon lifting straps before picking up the Hip. Then, Falcon carefully applied torque to his engines to start the lift, and at 101 percent of rated torque, the Hip finally lifted clear of the ground and started to slide up the side of a nearby palm tree. The engine torque indicated

Figure 9.29 Mi-17 Hip in a BIAP hangar awaiting repair.

that the Mi-17 Hip weighed over twenty thousand pounds, slightly more than the planning data for an MH-47E. Now, operating at the maximum gross weight for the Chinook, Falcon pushed forward on the cyclic to achieve effective translational lift—a condition of flying in uninterrupted air necessary to provide an effective climbing capability. In the rotor wash, the Hip swung clear of the palm tree. Falcon had successfully "harvested" the Soviet helicopter and he headed for Baghdad International Airport. The ground detail boarded the second Chinook, and Littleton easily caught up with the lumbering Chinook carrying the Mi-17 as the night closed in.[70]

Five AH-6 gunships covered the two Chinooks as the flight traversed a vast, agricultural area heading toward the lights of Baghdad. The suspended dust reduced visibility even further. Not anticipating a night flight, Falcon and his crew had no night vision goggles. To fly "unaided" in a dust storm at night was an uncomfortable situation at best, and to add to the challenge, the Iraqi power lines were strung high across the river to allow ship passage underneath. As the Night Stalkers closed on the Tigris River, they climbed higher to clear the power lines. Falcon had switched flying duties with Brietzke soon after getting the Hip airborne. Now, operating at such a high gross weight, Brietzke applied all the remaining power to climb, and hoped for the best. Meanwhile, "[Parkens] was radioing about every five minutes [saying], 'Cut the load away, cut the load away,'" said Falcon. From Parkens' position behind, it looked like the Hip was getting out of control, but was in fact, simply trying to "fly" using the aerodynamics of the airframe. Falcon had complete confidence in his flight

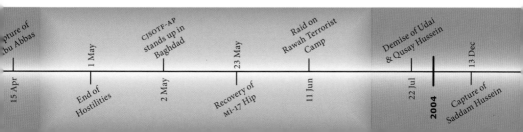

engineer, Staff Sergeant Mark Nugent*, to make the decision to "cut away" the load because Nugent was monitoring the sling load from Chinook's center cargo hole. He had his hand on the quick release lever, ready to "punch the load" if it became a threat to his aircraft or the crew aboard.[71]

Having barely cleared the Tigris power lines, Falcon radioed the tower at Baghdad International Airport with his intent to land near the Night Stalker hanger. Brietzke transferred the flight controls back to Falcon for the landing. With a large crowd watching the unusual feat, Falcon came to a stationary hover, gently descended, and lowered the Hip while Nugent provided height and drift corrections. As the MI-17 wheels touched the ground, the struts flexed and the helicopter began to roll. Nugent immediately told Falcon to lift it back up. Falcon imagined that the Hip was rolling forward but in reality the Hip was actually tipping over on its side. Quickly reacting to the danger, Falcon recovered the MI-17 and prevented damage to their prize. On his second attempt the helicopter stabilized and remained upright long enough for a ground crew to place chalks under its wheels and unshackle the sling. After Falcon had safely parked his Chinook, the nervous tension began to drain away.[72]

The Night Stalkers accomplished a task that had started with a low probability of success. Neither interference by local Iraqis nor a sandstorm prevented the small contingent of ARSOF troops from completing its mission. The MI-17 Hip helicopter was now available for training or other uses by the SOF community. The well-coordinated and executed mission exemplified the flexibility, determination, and mission of all involved.

SUMMARY

Combat operations in Iraq were far from complete as Coalition forces found themselves in transition between Phase III and Phase IV. The major fighting had lasted less than five weeks instead of the ninety days envisioned by planners. The CFLCC campaign plan lacked specifics as to missions during the interim and no Phase IV plan of action had ever been approved. The Time-Phased Force Deployment Data kept sending forces into Kuwait and Iraq. Latecomers arrived ready for Phase III, but major combat operations had been declared ended

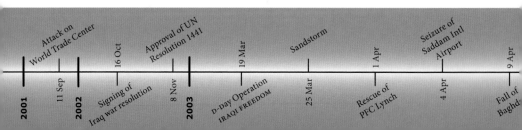

by the President. Instead of accepting the security and stability operations mission, some chose to confront Iraq as if it were a foreign internal defense environment.

CFSOCC had never intended to stay since the SOF commands had accomplished their missions. Special operations forces were consolidated under a new CJSOTF, Arabian Peninsula, and the size had been tailored for security and stability operations. It was a time of confusion and change as conventional forces moved to control many of the major cities throughout Iraq. Army Reserve Civil Affairs units attached to conventional divisions and regiments were being tasked to manage civil military operations with little or no guidance from higher commands. Reserve PSYOP units faced the same dilemma but the early redeployment of the Combined Joint Psychological Operations Task Force forward in Qatar cut access to the 4th PSYOP Group. The Reserve PSYOP units had no one to "reach back" to for product support.

While these dilemmas clouded the situation in Iraq, Army SOF soldiers and units never stopped trying to accomplish their assigned missions. In the midst of the disorder and confusion, Army Reserve Civil Affairs units like the HACC persevered for all the right reasons. Psychological Operations companies led by majors and below accomplished what they could at the tactical level. Rangers and Night Stalkers continued to take fight to the terrorists to eliminate their strongholds. This last combat vignette illustrated the tenacity and dedication of fanatical fighters imbued with jihad and seeking martyrdom. The U.S. military had not dealt with this level of fanaticism since fighting the Japanese in the Pacific in World War II—and battleship guns had hammered the Japanese on Saipan and Okinawa for days before the assaults there had begun. In the end, whether in World War II or Iraq, infantrymen must close with a determined enemy to destroy him. These Rangers did exactly that and defeated the most determined fighters in Iraq. And not to be forgotten, a CJSOTF-AP special staff officer helped focus the hunt for Saddam Hussein and other high-value targets.

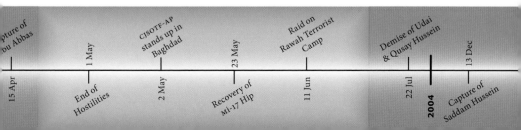

Turkey

Syria

Jordan

Saudi Arabia

Dahuk

Aqrah
Ayn Sifni
Irbil
Airfield
Mosul
Irbil

Bashur
Airfield

Sulaimaniyah
Airfield

Kirkuk
Sulaimaniyah

Halabjah

Sargat

K-2
Airfield

Tikrit

Iran

Rawah
Al Qadisiyah
Reservoir

Tharthar
Lake

Haditha

H-1
Airfield

Baquba

H-2
Airfield

Ar Ramadi

Fallujah

Baghdad

Ar Rutba

Baghdad
International
Airport

Rasheed
Air Base

Aziziyah

H-3
Airfield

Western Desert

al-Musayyib

Mudaysis

Karbala

Hindiya
Hilla

Al Kut

Amarah

Nukhayb

Iraq

Kifl

Najaf

Diwaniya

Samawah

Wadi al Khirr
Airfield

Nasiriya

Talil
Air Base

Basra

Umm Qasr

Rumaylah
Oil Fields

Al Fa

Per
Gu

N

Kuwait

Ali As-Salim
Air Base

0   100 Miles
0   100 KM

Chapter Ten

Conclusion

*T*HE PURPOSE OF *All Roads Lead to Baghdad* was to explain what the various Army special operations elements accomplished during the U.S.-led Coalition offensive to collapse the regime of Saddam Hussein in Iraq. Special Forces, Rangers, Special Operations Aviation, Civil Affairs, Psychological Operations, and Special Operations Support (Signal and Combat Support) are part of the ARSOF spectrum. The U.S. Army Reserve and Army National Guard provide a good portion of ARSOF: two Army National Guard Special Forces groups, the majority (90 percent) of Psychological Operations and Civil Affairs, and round out combat service support units. Not all are "gunfighters" but all are Army SOF soldiers. All contributed to the successes achieved by the ARSOF team in Iraq, just as they did in Afghanistan, the Philippines, Colombia, and Kosovo.

While this book was only a five-month snapshot of the war in Iraq, it did cover those phases of Operation IRAQI FREEDOM during which ARSOF was most active. To provide context, the book began by answering the question, "Why Iraq?" The military architecture in Iraq, foreign and domestic, and a short cultural background followed a thumbnail geopolitical sketch. Saddam Hussein was identified and U.S. involvement with Iraq from the first Gulf War was explained through Operation ENDURING FREEDOM. The operational planning by the various commands showed how multiple levels—strategic, operational, and tactical—developed their command guidance, concept of operations, command and control, and organized for battle with coordination throughout. The issues facing the Army and joint SOF commands were identified and explained before preparations were detailed. This was the second major campaign in America's Global War on Terrorism. And it was to be conducted while sustaining operations in Afghanistan, the Philippines, Colombia, and the Balkans. Special Operations Command Central established two Combined Joint Special Operations Task Forces and a Naval Task Force to execute its SOF campaign in support of the Central Command conventional air and ground offensives. The presentation format was expanded to explain the conventional fight before the actions of CJSOTF-North, CJSOTF-West, and other ARSOF were presented. A chronological sequence, highlighted on each page, carried current operations forward into June 2002.

As one would expect, the major combat operations phase contained the best soldier stories. They spanned the ARSOF spectrum from PSYOP before the offensive to Army special operations attack helicopter teams knocking out border observation posts to inserting Special Forces special reconnaissance teams to watch key terrain critical to the conventional force. Rangers parachute assaulted far behind enemy lines while Signalers provided command and control to Combat Supporters building base camps and supplying the troops and Civil Affairs teams kept electricity flowing at Haditha Dam. The variety of missions was wide and the range enormous—from the western desert to the oil fields of northern Iraq. Army special operations forces demonstrated again why they are so dynamic and versatile. Army SOF truly owned the night. The majority of the missions were executed at night on very short notice. There were periods of great danger and there were heroic moments. Commanders took calculated risks, persevered, and acted like professionals. But the successes achieved by ARSOF elements in Iraq, as they were in Afghanistan before, are directly attributed to majors, captains, warrant officers, and sergeants leading tactical teams and aircrews.

The selected historical vignettes told the story of ARSOF in Iraq. There was a conscious effort to present an equitable balance of stories that covered all ARSOF elements within security constraints. The Special Operations Command Central commander, two Special Forces group commanders, and two ARSOF regimental commanders identified their best stories to research. Multiple views—top, middle, bottom, and Coalition—were sought to gain perspective. Still, the soldier stories were "his story"—the true origin of the word or term history. Soldiers explained (in their words) how they prepared for missions, which skill sets and tactics were used, what special capabilities SOF-unique equipment provided, how they determined success, and what they sought to achieve. By considering all these aspects together, the true strength of ARSOF was revealed—highly trained, motivated, and dedicated soldiers. Technology provided an edge to Army SOF, but it took multiskilled, determined soldiers and well-trained elements to capitalize on those advantages.

The great majority of *All Roads Lead to Baghdad* was written using classified materials as primary sources. The vignettes were based primarily on recorded classified interviews, after-action reports, personal journals, and operations center logs. Classified portions of the narrative and vignettes were carefully "sanitized" by the writers. Because the Global War on Terrorism is ongoing and Army SOF soldiers are involved in combat operations in Afghanistan and Iraq today, only 90 percent of the ARSOF story could be presented. The Army SOF soldiers understand, accept, and expect these constraints. After all, they are and will be the ones at risk while continuing to do their duty in harm's way in Iraq and Afghanistan today, tomorrow, and in the future.

By ignoring the acronyms and focusing on the narrative and the soldiers' stories—the vignettes—the reader obtained the essence of this current history. Since this represented ARSOF operations through June 2003, it was more than sufficient to grasp the varied missions and the quality of soldiers that make up this dynamic military force. Because the authors knew that they could not fool the players, the readers got the "real deal" as soldiers like to say.

On 1 May 2003, when President George W. Bush, following the recommendation of General Tommy Franks, the Operation IRAQI FREEDOM commander, announced the end of major combat operations in Iraq, the U.S.-led Coalition forces had toppled the regime of Saddam Hussein. The nexus of power, Baghdad (wherein all roads lead), had been captured in a little over four weeks of fighting. Cities and large areas of the country had simply been bypassed in the rush to the capital. The Iraqi war had reached a transitory period. Late-arriving conventional forces still wanted their piece of the action, few combat commanders wanted any part of civil military duty, tactical air commands were withdrawing to Kuwait because close air support requirements were vanishing, and long-committed forces—U.S. and Coalition—focused on rotating home.

This turbulent, unsettled time was also when the Iraqi people, controlled by terror for more than twenty years, needed structure in their daily lives. The Iraqi people were highly literate and concentrated in large urban centers much like the Germans that Adolf Hitler dominated for twelve years. While Saddam did not have a Heinrich Himmler, he used television and radio to manage and terror to control the people for more than twenty years—an entire generation.

The scope of this book covered ARSOF in Iraq into June 2003, after the international press had made the premature post-conflict declarations. The project focused on the early part of the second Iraq war when ARSOF was most involved. A timely account of the war can only be written while it is still fresh. That is what you have.

Observations based on official documents and interviews with participants at all levels, including Coalition personnel, follow. Reflections are situational assessments made by active and retired ARSOF officers who served in Iraq and participated in the ARSOF in Operation IRAQI FREEDOM history project.

Chapter Eleven

Observations and Reflections

*T*HE PURPOSE OF *All Roads Lead to Baghdad* was to explain what Army special operations elements accomplished during the U.S.-led Coalition offensive to collapse the regime of Saddam Hussein in Iraq. A five-month snapshot of Operation IRAQI FREEDOM, the book covers the period of major combat operations when Army special operations forces were the most active. This current operations history was not intended to capture operational lessons learned (a doctrinal S-3/G-3/J-3 function), resolve special warfare doctrine issues, nor clarify definitions for Army special operations. *All Roads Lead to Baghdad* did achieve its purpose. The advantage to having a current operations project compiled by retired Army SOF personnel is that they, unlike active duty ARSOF deeply immersed in the war, can get "above the fray" and access leaders, staff, and soldiers at all levels. This provides a better overall view, especially when clarified by insightful, candid, confidential interviews. These professional soldiers would be remiss if they did not share their insights and analysis.

The observations and reflections, based on official documents and interviews with Operation IRAQI FREEDOM participants at all levels from all services and allies, are non-attributable. They cover planning and preparations for 1003V and the conduct of the Iraqi war from the early spring of 2002 through June 2003. They are not intended to be criticisms of a successfully executed U.S.-led Coalition campaign to topple the regime of Saddam Hussein in Iraq. The successful accomplishments in this epilogue are not presented to give any of the Army SOF elements "the lion's share of the credit." Success was the result of an ARSOF team effort that supported the main conventional offensive. There are always shortfalls and problems and that is why leaders and managers are needed. Those identified should not be a surprise to the participants. Many continue to plague Army special operations forces today (late 2005) because the situation in Iraq is far from being settled.

THE ARMY FIELD ORDER

To simply present the observations and reflections, they have been organized to fit the five paragraphs of the Army field order:

Situation	*what is known about the enemy and what the enemy is most likely to do.*
Mission	*what is to be accomplished by the allied forces in general terms.*
Execution	*who will do what tasks and how things will be accomplished—as well as planning and preparations.*
Administration	*how all combat forces will be supported—including mobilization, resourcing, legal, and logistics issues.*
Command and Control	*who is in charge of what, when that responsibility is to be transferred, and how communications will take place—including how orders and plans will be issued.*

Not all topics of discussion fit smoothly into this format, however they will be presented as they applied to the various commands in a descending rank order, i.e., Central Command (CENTCOM), then Special Operations Command Central (SOCCENT), and the Combined Joint Special Operations Task Forces (CJSOTFs), where applicable. Since the epilogue is short, only the most significant issues are summarized at the end.

SITUATION

FRIENDLY

Unlike a typical warfighting field order where only the enemy situation is presented, it is important to remember the friendly situation. The key to understanding and appreciating ARSOF planning and preparations for Operation IRAQI FREEDOM is the necessity to weigh an event or action in relation to previous commitments and lessons from

Afghanistan—putting it in the proper context. Lessons learned or experiences in Operation ENDURING FREEDOM prompted commanders at all levels to initiate corrective action. Some of the initiatives addressed major issues that affected all Army SOF, like casualties from friendly fire (fratricide) and compatible equipment for Army Reserve and National Guard. Most importantly, ARSOF responded to the 1003V missions based on ENDURING FREEDOM in Afghanistan, operations in Kosovo, and training in the Philippines and Colombia.

Toppling the Taliban regime in Afghanistan during ENDURING FREEDOM had been a major achievement for ARSOF, but combat costs in materiel, equipment, and mobilization had been high. Sustaining the Army SOF commitment in Afghanistan had serious impacts on the availability and readiness of ARSOF units. Having left its vehicles (military and nonstandard tactical) and heavy weapons systems to support the CJSOTF-Afghanistan, the 5th Special Forces Group had to be refitted with replacement Ground Mobility Vehicles and weapons while radios and computer equipment underwent extensive maintenance and refurbishing. With Army National Guard Special Forces groups and Army Reserve Civil Affairs and Psychological Operations elements assuming more ARSOF missions as round-out units and backfills for active elements, these force multipliers needed compatible radios, small arms, computer systems, Ground Mobility Vehicles, and heavy weapons systems.

Major aircraft inspections and scheduled maintenance had to be performed as the 160th Special Operations Aviation Regiment supported operations in Afghanistan and the Philippines. Operation ENDURING FREEDOM battle-damaged aircraft and losses had to be repaired and replaced. More ammunition was needed to qualify the active force on heavy weapons systems before deployment and the mobilizations of Army National Guard and Reserve units required pre-deployment small arms qualifications and vehicle-mounted, crew-served weapons familiarization as part of combat immediate action drills. Training munitions for the Philippines and Colombia were already six months behind schedule.

Individual Reservists mobilized shortly after 9/11 to fill Joint Manning Documents throughout the Department of Defense were already in their second year. Most operationally ready Psychological Operations and Civil Affairs battalions had already been mobilized for ENDURING FREEDOM. The realities of operational readiness in Army Reserve and Army National Guard elements caused commanders to fill requirements for units by cross-leveling from all available assets—essentially gutting units to "slow roll" the problem. With roles unspecified (supported versus supporting) unconstrained planning continued and Central Command and European Command competed equally for resources. More than ten years had elapsed since Order of Battle was a high intelligence priority and operational readiness had been analyzed.

ENEMY

The Iraqi military was a formidable foe with large quantities of modern equipment. They had mobile theater ballistic (SCUD) missiles, sophisticated air defense missile systems, mechanized and motorized divisions with heavy tanks, and commandos. Weapons of mass destruction (chemical) and laser weapons had been used on the Iranians and Kurds. Saddam Hussein supported a mechanized brigade of more than 5,000 Mujahedin-e Khalq—non-secular Iranian dissidents—as well as another brigade of several thousand Badr Corps fighters, Iraqi Shias.

The Iraqi people were highly literate and the population was concentrated in large urban centers much like the Germans that Adolf Hitler dominated for twelve years. While Saddam did not have a Heinrich Himmler, he used mass media to control the people and terror to dominate them for more than twenty years. An entire generation had been raised in this tightly controlled environment. The Iraqi people had never lived under any semblance of democratic government. Power had determined politics. Iraqis considered themselves "Iraq-unique Arabs." Concepts of human and civil rights were something read about in western newspapers.

MISSION

The mission of CENTCOM was to remove Saddam Hussein and the Baath party regime from power in Iraq and to secure Baghdad. The national strategic goal was to establish a stable, secure, prosperous, peaceful, and democratic Iraqi nation that would be a viable member of the community of nations. Removal from power included killing or capturing key leadership.

The mission was to be accomplished in four phases: *Phase I—Preparation* set conditions to neutralize Iraqi forces; *Phase II—Shape the Battlespace* required posturing Coalition forces to conduct sustained combat operations, degrading Iraqi command and control systems and border security forces, seizing key terrain, and countering theater ballistic missiles and weapons of mass destruction operations; *Phase III—Decisive Operations* included the Coalition air campaign, preparatory ground operations, and the conventional attack north to Baghdad. This phase of Operation IRAQI FREEDOM technically ended when Saddam Hussein and the Baath regime were removed from power and Baghdad was secured; *Phase IV—Post-Hostility or Stability Operations* covered the transition from major combat to security and stability operations including humanitarian assistance and reconstruction.

The CENTCOM military mission was accomplished in a little more than four weeks of decisive offensive operations. The Iraqi military had simply been overwhelmed by the U.S.-led Coalition air and ground forces. Before preparations could be effected to transition to the next phase, General Tommy Franks convinced President George W. Bush to publicly declare "the end of major combat operations" in Iraq. Confusion would be the best description of the response among commanders and soldiers in Iraq. Large sections of the country, including major cities, had been bypassed in the drive to capture Baghdad—the "center of gravity" of Saddam Hussein's regime. There was still much to be done to gain control of Iraq.

EXECUTION

Planning and preparations were interdependent and conducted simultaneously at all levels—from battalions to regional combatant commands and the service departments in the Pentagon—to create a sense of orderly parallel chaos. Correcting problems encountered in Afghanistan was important. Sustaining worldwide Army SOF commitments determined the elements available to support a second Global War on Terrorism campaign. Time proved to be a constant foe.

CENTRAL COMMAND

Operational Plan 1003 went from the planned middle-of-the-road to the Victor option (1003v) between the "Generated Start" of 1003 with its pre-planned Time-Phased Force Deployment Data and the "Running Start" option to something more akin to a "Running Start" in the execution. To capitalize on surprise the air and ground offensives were launched almost simultaneously. The deployment process, the Time-Phased Force Deployment Data computerized system, once started, "drove the train." But, it was the "Generated Start" train with some tweaking.

Draft strategic and operational plans for civil military operations were never approved. In the absence of specific guidance, Civil Affairs planners (primarily Army Reserve) reverted to what they knew—experience in the semi-permissive environment of the Balkans and training missions that called for humanitarian civil assistance. By focusing only on Phase IV post-conflict stability operations when the military was no longer in charge, Civil Affairs effectively planned itself out of any role in the war. Lacking strategic and operational guidance and plans during Phase I through III, tactical Civil Affairs was done "on the fly" and the quality depended on the experience and initiative of battalion and company commanders. Most Army Reserve units attached to conventional forces simply reverted to basic Civil Affairs tasks until the Iraqi people finally complained, "Every new Coalition force that comes through does assessments, when do we see results?"

The 8th Psychological Operations Battalion commander served as the Joint Psyop Task Force commander for CENTCOM. The JPOTF was originally formed to support ENDURING FREEDOM in Afghanistan. With the start of 1003 planning in February 2002, its mission was expanded to plan and execute all PSYOP in theater while supporting Operation ENDURING FREEDOM. A lieutenant colonel was responsible for supporting PSYOP in two major Global War on Terrorism campaigns with a joint staff of Reservists from all services. Access to the J-2 (intelligence), J-3 (operations), and General Franks was very difficult for a lieutenant colonel who did not have the "clout" of a colonel PSYOP commander. The Department of Defense was responsible for the PSYOP campaign in Iraq in Phases I through III, but there was no transition plan between Phases III and IV. The JPOTF forward in Qatar was pulled back to Fort Bragg, North Carolina, cutting the PSYOP theater "reach-back" link to the 4th Psyop Group and the JPOTF in Tampa was drawn down shortly after the President had made his announcement. The bag of command guidance, and strategic and operational plans given to Army Reserve PSYOP units arriving to backfill active elements was empty. The commanders did what their Reserve Civil Affairs counterparts had done—basic tactical PSYOP learned in semipermissive environments.

The strategic Information Operations plan proposed by the Secretary of Defense garnered little support in Washington DC. Operational and tactical Information Operations depended on the quality and experience of the staff officers in the field commands. Information Operations guidance and strategic and operational plans from CENTCOM could not be found. Even these efforts ceased after 1 May 2003, when the Iraqi people most needed that media information structure. Saddam Hussein had used mass media to control the Iraqi people and had dominated them with terror for more than twenty years. An entire generation had grown up in this media-controlled environment.

SPECIAL OPERATIONS COMMAND CENTRAL

The Special Operations Command Central commander was the SOF warfighter for Operation IRAQI FREEDOM. The special operations commander provided commander's guidance and SOCCENT wrote the SOF campaign plan to support 1003v with input from supporting commands. In theater, the special operations commander executed the SOF campaign that supported the Coalition Forces Air Component Command and the Coalition Forces Land Component Command with two Combined Joint Special Operations Task Forces and a Naval Task Force. During the planning phase, SOCCENT set priorities for Special Operations Command, Joint Forces Command joint staff training and augmentation. The CENTCOM crisis reaction element was held in reserve for regional emergencies. Regional special operations detachments provided by U.S. Special Operations Command were assigned base operations, enemy prisoners of war, liaison, and special operations command and control element missions.

Psychologists and artillery forward observers were assigned to CJSOTFs to promulgate effects-based planning and British and Australian officers were embedded in key staff positions in the CJSOTFs. The Australian component commander served as the senior liaison to Brigadier General Gary Harrell. Control of Blue Force Tracker Systems was assigned to SOCCENT. Embedded media worked well until the presidential declaration. The staff judge advocate dealt with a myriad of operational law issues which ranged from rules of engagement to cease-fire versus surrender connotations, to handling enemy prisoners of war while actively participating in joint fires planning.

Special Operations Command Europe Brigadier General Mike Jones coordinated forward basing the 10th Special Forces Group in Constanta, Romania, while serving primarily as the European Command special operations forces advisor and senior staff officer. The liaison role that he performed with SOCCENT was understated. General Jones succeeded in making this critical command-to-command relationship transparent.

With Brigadier General James Parker as his deputy SOCCENT, General Harrell could concentrate on the whole SOF campaign while Parker handled "stray command and control voltage" that had developed in northern Iraq. The operational control attachment of the 173rd Airborne Brigade (-) to CJSOTF-North by CFSOCC prompted European Command to send a senior liaison element headed by a brigadier general to northern Iraq. The Secretary of Defense mandated a defense attaché mission to liaison with the Free Iraqi Forces leadership. Having placed a SOF general officer on the northern front reinforced the U.S. commitment to Kurdish forces and defined the supporting and supported command relationships. Brigadier General Parker was an effective "lightning rod" for both commands. The value of a general officer as the deputy special operations commander was demonstrated in Iraq.

There were several unresolved issues. Why does the commander of CFSOCC, as the joint special operations component commander, not have the authority to override air mission cancellations or denials by the joint special operations air component commander, his subordinate service component? Why do U.S. Air Force peacetime rules for airfield surveys prior to landing apply to Air Force special operations aircraft (MC-130 Combat Talon) in combat? Will the C-17 Globemaster III be tactically employed in combat?

SPECIAL OPERATIONS COMMAND, JOINT FORCES COMMAND

Special Operations Command, Joint Forces Command fulfilled the Joint Forces Command charter with U.S. Special Operations Command to provide joint staff training to SOCCENT, the two Special Forces group staffs, and the Naval Special Warfare Group 2. While acting as the JSOTF for Millennium Challenge 02, the special operations command staff validated the capability of the 20th SFG staff to serve as CJSOTF-Afghanistan. Both CJSOTFs received experienced joint staff officers as augmentees during IRAQI FREEDOM. Special Operations Command, Joint Forces Command arranged the inter-service resolution of Joint Fire Controls during the Joint Expeditionary Force Exercise 02 at Nellis Air Force Base, Nevada, during Millennium Challenge 02. Close air support fire protocols were developed and validated between the 9th Air Force, Navy, and Marines, and the 5th and 10th SFGs to correct a major problem from ENDURING FREEDOM.

Unresolved joint issues are truly joint command and control of air assets and a joint air planning process rather than a U.S. Air Force–dominated air mission planning cycle that is locked at seventy-two hours with a service-controlled final approval authority for air missions. If the special operations commander is the regional joint SOF component commander, why is the joint special operations air component commander not subordinate to that command like the other services and corresponding Joint Special Operations Air Detachments not subordinate to Joint Special Operations Task Force commanders? Coalition, conventional Army, and U.S. Marine forces were subordinated to CJSOTF-North.

Further specifications in the definitions of supporting and supported are a legal response. Collaboration between commands usually worked at the general officer level. It rarely worked between staffs from staff directors and lower. Part of the issue is the ad hoc nature of the wartime joint staffs. At company level and below, issues regarding the supported and supporting relationships rarely surfaced, regardless of service and Coalition differences. How do conventional force commanders and staffs learn the capabilities of a JSOTF?

JOINT EXERCISES

The regional joint combined exchange training proved very beneficial to the 5th and 19th SFGs. The number and locations were not sufficient to pre-position the majority of ARSOF supporting 1003V in theater. Joint combined exchange training enabled the 10th SFG to execute Flintlock Reborn in Germany and Turkey in April 2002. While the Millennium Challenge 02 experiment served to validate the 20th SFG headquarters to serve as the CJSOTF-Afghanistan, Joint Expeditionary Force Exercise 02 was used to develop, test, and validate Joint Fire Control protocols at Nellis Air Force Base. The vast joint experiment did little to address civil military operations in any phase of combat operations. Requests came into the Joint Forces Command staff very late in the planning and were not elevated to the highest level. Internal Look 02 enabled CENTCOM to establish its forward operations center and exercise the battle staff and service component staffs using a Middle East contingency. Establishing the computer-based command and control systems with linkage to all staffs was a major task. The "final bugs" in Joint Fire Control operating procedures and protocols were worked out in Internal Look 02. A coterie of retired general officer mentors interfaced with all component commanders during the exercise. Civil military operations were not addressed in the CENTCOM command post exercise. The focus of warfighting was oriented on conducting the first three phases of war. Transition to Phase IV was only discussed in general terms.

COALITION SUPPORT

For the first time, British and Australian forces were operational control to the special operations commander and CJSOTF-west. The British "leased" Blue Force Tracker Systems for its forces while SOCCENT arranged to have U.S. Air Force Special Tactics Squadron personnel carrying Blue Force Trackers work with the Australians. British and Australian officers were embedded in key positions of CJSOTF-west and the intelligence fusion staff of CJSOTF-north. Despite large monetary investments in background investigations by both countries to upgrade individual security clearances, access to the classified operational computer network and the secure compartmented intelligence facility for the embedded Coalition staff officers and force commanders was relegated to CJSOTF commanders, just as it was for Afghanistan. Australia and Great Britain are our closest allies. Both Coalition forces had national command elements in theater. The Australians beefed up their command and liaison elements, support package, and brought C-130 transports and CH-47 Chinook helicopters. Based on Operation IRAQI FREEDOM success, the Australians will fully adopt the U.S. Joint Fire Control system. Working with the Marines and British 1st Armoured Division proved frustrating for the advanced operating bases and operational detachment alphas of 5th SFG.

CJSOTFs

The two CJSOTFs operated fully integrated, effects-based planning cells with operations, intelligence, joint fires, staff judge advocate, psychologist, PSYOP, and Civil Affairs participating. The presence of Brigadier General Parker, the deputy SOCCENT, in northern Iraq alleviated the supporting versus supported issue with the 173rd Airborne Brigade (-) and the European Command liaison. Unilateral cancellation of air missions and support requests by the joint special operations air component commander were constant problems. Even CFSOCC lacked appeal authority. The embedded media effort worked well until the presidential declaration that major combat in Iraq had ended. Staff judge advocates worked operational law issues ranging from enemy prisoners of war handling to cease-fire and surrender to rules of engagement as well as joint fires planning. The psychologists contributed profiles—individual, organizational, cultural—to assist commanders and staff at all levels and covered enemy prisoners of war interrogations demonstrating their value added to CJSOTF staffs.

ARMY SPECIAL OPERATIONS FORCES

Active Army SOF elements think of themselves as nine-one-one forces that should rotate home as soon as major combat has ended in order to prepare for the next fight or sustain commitments in Afghanistan, the Philippines, Colombia, Kosovo, etc. This happened in Afghanistan starting in early December 2002. The transition period between major combat and post-conflict operations for Afghanistan and Iraq began before Phase III had ended and Phase IV had started. Redeployment planning proved more important than planning smooth battle hand-offs to prevent consolidation and reorganization of remaining enemy forces.

Which command(s) has/have the responsibility to provide strategic and operational Civil Affairs and PSYOP guidance and planning that covers all phases of war? What and how do Army Reserve Civil Affairs and PSYOP units prepare for their mission in Phase I? What command(s) should provide tactical Civil Affairs and PSYOP guidance? Is it different for active versus Army Reserve and Army National Guard elements? How do deployed Army Reserve units reach-back for PSYOP support when JPOTF connectivity is broken by the departure of active forces and receiving arrangements have not been pre-coordinated with conventional Corps–level signal assets in theater?

U.S. Army Special Operations Command ceased to be solely a force provider during Operation ENDURING FREEDOM. It became the de facto Army SOF component of CENTCOM. What are the Global War on Terrorism and general war roles of the major command and its major subordinate commands—U.S. Army Special Forces Command, U.S. Civil Affairs and Psychological Operations Command, and U.S. Army John F. Kennedy Special Warfare Center and School—today?

ARSOF Elements

Special Forces, in conjunction with Special Operations Command, Joint Forces Command and the 9th Air Force, fixed the Joint Fire Control problems of ENDURING FREEDOM. The Ranger Regiment and battalions demonstrated their capability to simultaneously command and control several long-range combined arms operations involving the High Mobility Artillery Rocket System, M1 Abrams tanks, and the 160th Special Operations Aviation Regiment and support Information Operations missions. A joint direct action mission was successfully conducted in virtual textbook fashion against a large terrorist training camp less than twenty-four hours after receiving a warning order. Rangers have demonstrated the maturity and discipline to successfully execute direct action missions against high-value targets. Ranger commanders had no problem with the supporting versus supported concept and operational control relationships. The only shortfall in the successful Haditha Dam mission was the late employment of Civil Affairs and PSYOP assets on this critical strategic target. The use of MH-60L Defensive Armed Penetrators to escort MH-47E Chinooks was carried over from ENDURING FREEDOM. MH-6 and AH-6 Little Birds successfully teamed together as they did during Operation PRIME CHANCE. The 3rd Battalion, 160th Special Operations Aviation Regiment, combat-validated the effectiveness of the hybrid MH-60L Defensive Armed Penetrator with strap-on/strap-off weapon systems. The availability of heavy caliber ammunition, 2.75 inch rockets, and weapon systems will determine whether the concept is continued. The employment of kevlar protective blankets inside MH-47s and oversized Ground Mobility Vehicles ("Swamper") tires reduced aircraft internal carry capabilities.

JPOTF product delivery communications from Fort Bragg to Tampa and Tampa to Qatar were sufficient to handle large files. The JPOTF–Qatar link to Iraq, like it was/is to Afghanistan, proved to be the chokepoint for Army Reserve units lacking communications compatible with active PSYOP units. The speed associated with the 4th PSYOP Group reach-back was nullified by the lack of capacity in country to download a large product with sufficient resolution to be enlarged for field use. JPOTF connectivity to conventional Corps-level systems is essential to support the Army Reserve elements effectively.

The Department of Defense and CENTCOM controlled PSYOP in Iraq during Phases I–III. What prevents active PSYOP from establishing an in country "footprint" during these phases? PSYOP products for CJSOTF-North revealed that little research had been done on the Gulf War debriefs of senior enemy prisoners of war in Iraq concerning PSYOP effectiveness. What function does the senior active duty PSYOP group commander serve in wartime if he is not also the JPOTF commander?

Civil Affairs tactical plans were hard to develop without strategic and operational guidance and plans or operations plans annexes that covered all phases of the war. The 1003 Time-Phased Force Deployment Data "drove the train" on Civil Affairs unit deployments regardless of when the unit they were to support arrived. The push was to get as many Civil Affairs units in theater as quickly as possible. Some Civil Affairs units sat in Kuwait for months waiting to join their assigned unit.

Operation IRAQI FREEDOM served to validate the 528th forward support team concept of employment for CJSOTFs. The assignment of the senior ARSOF logistics commander (Special Operations Support Command) to the Coalition Forces Land Component Command J-4 (logistics) as the SOF "trouble shooter" between conventional and SOF logisticians proved invaluable and validated the role of Special Operations Support Command in war. Mobilization of combat service support units from the Army Reserve and National Guard enabled the 528th Support Battalion to continue its forward support team support to Afghanistan while focused on Iraq. By partnering the 112th Signal Battalion with the joint communications signal element, CFSOCC could command and control two CJSOTFs and a Naval Task Force as well as Coalition forces.

ADMINISTRATION AND LOGISTICS

Mobilization to fill headquarters wartime Table of Distribution and Allowances and Joint Manning Documents (individuals) and to augment the active Army with Special Forces, Civil Affairs, and PSYOP units exposed the raw realities of Army Reserve and National Guard operational readiness. Volunteers fill the "One Army" of Active, Reserve, and National Guard units. Even with incentives, the competition for recruits has become heavy. The other services are also competing in the volunteer pool.

Traditional levels of funding that date back to the end of World War II have sustained Army Reserve and Army National Guard units at operational ready rates of 70 percent, 20 percentage points below the 90 percent standard required for overseas deployment. Funding dictates how much equipment is provided, how many soldiers are school trained, and how much training can be done annually—individual and collective. The several measures of operational readiness are interdependent: number of assigned personnel, available and operationally ready equipment, and state of training (individual and unit). The lowest common denominator determines overall readiness.

Ad hoc Army Reserve and National Guard battalions and companies have been created to meet ARSOF requirements in Iraq and Afghanistan. Unit cohesion has been lost in the gutting of commands and camaraderie has been fragmented. Mobilization of both National Guard Special Forces groups for Operation ENDURING FREEDOM ensured that those battalions would be used up by 2006. How long they remain "on the shelf"—three to five years—will depend on the number of experienced individual volunteers who are recruited to fill ad hoc Guard Special Forces battalions for Afghanistan and other commitments.

Army Reserve Civil Affairs and PSYOP unit mobilizations have been done at Fort Bragg without funding since the stand-up of the U.S. Army Civil Affairs and Psychological Operations Command in 1992. Fort Bragg was designated a Force Projection Platform by the Army in 2005, pending funding. Civil Affairs and PSYOP mobilizations will be funded "out of hide" until Forces Command and the Army solve the problem. The U.S. Army Special Operations Command has the distinction of being the first major command to deal with the mobilization realities. As the numbers of Army Reserve and Army National Guard combat, combat support, and combat service support units continue to grow to fill Afghanistan and Iraq rotations, the issue will be exponentially magnified.

Significant progress was made in equipping the Army Reserve and National Guard elements of ARSOF with compatible vehicles, small arms and heavy weapons systems, communications equipment, and body armor. Medical and dental coverage for family members has been made available as an individual insurance option. Use of military commissaries and post exchanges has expanded to accommodate mobilized Reservists, Guardsmen, and their families. Dental care before overseas deployment is still limited to emergency treatments.

U.S. Special Operations Command funds distribution was necessary to refit the 5th SFG with Ground Mobility Vehicles, heavy weapons systems, computers, and refurbished communications. It covered the nonstandard mobility requirements of the 10th SFG. Army, Army Reserve, National Guard Bureau, and U.S. Army Special Operations Command funds were used to procure compatible equipment and cover some mobilization training requirements.

COMMAND AND CONTROL

Issues revolved around supporting and supported relationships between CENTCOM and European Command because that designation was never delineated by the Secretary of Defense as was done for General Norman Schwartzkopf in the Gulf War. Positioning the deputy CFSOCC, Brigadier General Parker, in northern Iraq to handle the "stray command and control voltage" and reinforce the U.S. commitment to the Kurds proved very wise. Airflow priorities to support the 173rd Airborne Brigade (-) parachute jump delayed the entry of CJSOTF-North forces into northern Iraq; most importantly it delayed the Ground Mobility Vehicle–mobile 3rd Battalion, 3rd SFG, when the 2nd and 3rd Battalions, 10th SFG, Land Rovers had become stuck in Turkey.

Transition and the problems of rotation warfare reared up in Iraq after the presidential declaration, much like they did after the fall of Kabul and Kandahar in Afghanistan. The irony was that CENTCOM planners were working on 1003 options when that transition came to head during Operation ANACONDA. When the president declared an end of major combat operations during Phase III, General Franks had no designated receivers downfield. The hand-off can be best described as trying to "pass off a nuclear warhead." Fear of contamination had the members of the CENTCOM warfighting team scattering in all directions. The Office of Reconstruction and Humanitarian Assistance, over 150 newcomers, was sitting on the bench with the wrong playbook, and it was incomplete. They only had a concept plan for Phase IV; there was nothing for Phase III.

Warfighting, as evidenced by the response of CENTCOM combat commanders, ended with the collapse of the Saddam Hussein regime and the capture of Baghdad. That premise was reinforced with the presidential declaration. To compound matters, late-arriving combat division commanders wanted a piece of whatever fight was left. Only the active Army SOF committed to CJSOTF–Arabian Peninsula were focusing on foreign internal defense and development while the remaining fedayeen, insurgents, and criminals consolidated and reorganized in the ensuing turmoil. A nine-one-one mentality had pervaded all the active duty warfighters including SOF.

Few preparations had been made for this transitional period and the accompanying rotation warfare factors—summer permanent changes of station and changes of command in the Army, thirty- to ninety-day personnel rotation policies in some services, relocation of Joint Special Operations Air Detachments to Kuwait, Coalition troop hand-offs and drawdowns, and shifting warships on station. The few existing operational and tactical Information Operations initiatives ground down just as the embedded U.S. media inadvertently started an Iraqi Information Operations campaign that lent further credence to Arab television coverage. The U.S.-led Coalition military were still in charge of PSYOP, Civil Affairs, and Information Operations, but had no approved strategic, operational, and tactical plans. Guidance had been minimal. There was little to cover battle hand-offs. In the false calm after repeated successes, euphoria led to diminished force protection as commanders worked to provide creature comforts for the victorious soldiers. Burger King was colocated in the 1st Armored Division headquarters complex. By the time Saddam Hussein's sons were killed and he was captured in Tikrit, the foreign internal defense and development environment had morphed into counterinsurgency. The "COIN word" with all its negative Vietnam connotations has had to be accepted.

SUMMARY

The last three paragraphs of Command and Control are considered to be the most telling observations and reflections. Transition, active military warfighting, and rotational warfare have plagued ARSOF in the past, do today, and will tomorrow. Because this epilogue has been provided from non-attributable sources, I accept responsibility for these observations and reflections on Army SOF planning and preparations for 1003V, and ARSOF combat operations in Iraq that go beyond July 2003.

C.H. Briscoe

Figure 11.1 Coalition special operations forces. *Coalition SOF from the United States, Australia, and the United Kingdom arrayed after operations.*

Chapter Notes

Chapter 1 Notes

1   Anthony H. Cordesman, *The Iraq War: Strategy, Tactics, and Military Lessons* (Washington, D.C.: CSIS Press, 2003), 20, 40–52; *Combined Forces Special Operations Component Command Yearbook*, 2003, 29; Shlomo Brom, "The Strike against Iraq: A Military Overview," *Strategic Assessment*, Volume 5, No. 3, November 2002, 1–2, http://www.tau.ac.il/jcss/sa/v5n3p2Bro.html; Jane's Information Group, "Jane's Sentinel Security Assessment—The Gulf States," September 2005, http://sentinel.janes.com/subscribe/sentinel/country_report_doc.jsp?Prod_Name=GULFS&…, 178.

2   Jane's, "The Gulf States," 101; Cordesman, *The Iraq War*, 409.

3   Jane's, "The Gulf States," 97; Charles Tripp, *A History of Iraq* (London: Cambridge University Press, 2002), 71; William R. Polk, *Understanding Iraq* (New York: Harper Collins, 2005), 99.

4   Tripp, *A History of Iraq*, 8; Polk, *Understanding Iraq*, 32.

5   Helen Chapin Metz, ed., *Iraq, a Country Study* (Washington, DC: U.S. Government Printing Office, 1990), 7.

6   Metz, *Iraq, a Country Study*, 21–25.

7   Metz, *Iraq, a Country Study*, 26; Jane's, 13; Yitzhak Nakash, *The Shi'is of Iraq* (Princeton: Princeton University Press, 1994), 14.

8   Tripp, *A History of Iraq*, 12.

9   Tripp, *A History of Iraq*, 271.

10 Polk, *Understanding Iraq*, 63–64; Metz, *Iraq, a Country Study*, 29.

11 Tripp, *A History of Iraq*, 41; Metz, *Iraq, a Country Study*, 32.

12 Tripp, *A History of Iraq*, 43–44; Metz, *Iraq, a Country Study*, 36.

13 Tripp, *A History of Iraq*. 47–49.

14 David McDowall, *A Modern History of the Kurds* (New York: I.B. Tauris, 2005), 134–35.

15 Metz, *Iraq, a Country Study*, 40–49.

16 Polk, *Understanding Iraq*, 127.

17 Jane's, 10–11; Tripp, 253; "Biography of Saddam Hussein of Tikrit," *The Iraq Foundation*, http://www.iraqfoundation.org/research/bio.html; "Saddam Hussein," *Encyclopedia of the Orient*, http://i-cias.com/e.o/sad_huss.htm.

18 Tommy Franks, *American Soldier* (New York: Regan Books, 2004), 429.

19 Polk, *Understanding Iraq*, 21, 27; Tripp, *A History of Iraq*, 181.

20 Lieutenant Colonel Paul Chin, Combined Joint Special Operations Task Force-Arabian Pennisula Psychologist, "Saddam Hussein al-Majid al-Tikriti, A Psychological Profile," n.d., copy in USASOC History Office Classified Files, Fort Bragg, NC.

21 Eric H. Cline, "Saddam Hussein and History 101," *By George! Online*, 4 March 2003, http://www.gwu.edu/~bygeorge/030403/clineedit.html.

22 Jackie Craven, "Saddam's Babylonian Palace," *About Architecture*, http://architecture.about.com/cs/countriescultures/a/saddamspalace.htm.

Chapter 2 Notes

1   George W. Bush, "Address to the Joint Session of Congress and the American People," 20 September 2001, http://whitehouse.gov/news/2001/09/print/20010920-8.html.

2   Tommy Franks, *American Soldier* (New York: Regan Books, 2004), 333–35.

3   Franks, *American Soldier*, 339–40.

4   Franks, *American Soldier*, 349–52.

5   Franks, *American Soldier*, 361–66.

6   Franks, *American Soldier*, 366–67.

7   Franks, *American Soldier*, 367–69, 389.

8   Franks, *American Soldier*, 385–89.

9   Franks, *American Soldier*, 389–91.

10 Franks, *American Soldier*, 395–97.

11 United Nations Security Resolution 1441, 8 November 2002, http://www.un.int/usa/sres-iraq.htm; U.S. Congress, Public Law 107-243, dated 16 October 2002, http://www.c-span.org/resources/pdf/hjres114.pdf.

12 Charles H. Briscoe, "Rescuing the Burnhams: The Unspoken SOCPAC Mission," *Special Warfare*, September 2004, 46–51; Charles H. Briscoe, "Balikatan Exercise Spearheaded ARSOF Operations in the Philippines," *Special Warfare*, September 2004, 16–17.

13 Colonel Patrick Higgins, Headquarters, U.S. Special Operation Command Central, interview by Lieutenant Colonel Michael A. Ceroli, 30 April 2003, MacDill Air Force Base, FL, tape recording, USSOCOM History Office Classified Files, MacDill Air Force Base, FL.

14 Major General Gary L. Harrell, U.S. Special Operations Command Central, interview by Dr. Charles H. Briscoe, 22 July 2005, Fort Bragg, NC, tape recording, USASOC History Office Classified Files, Fort Bragg, NC.

15 Brigadier General Gary M. Jones, U.S. Army Special Forces Command, interview by Dr. Charles H. Briscoe, 9 March 2004, Fort Bragg, NC, tape recording, USASOC History Office Classified Files, Fort Bragg, NC.

16 JULLS Number 42938-48113, "JPOTF Integration with USCENTCOM," submitted by CCJ3, Operation IRAQI FREEDOM, conducted by U.S. Central Command, 27 April 2003, USASOC History Office Classified Files, Fort Bragg, NC.

17 Colonel Kevin B. Rue, 352nd Civil Affairs Command, interview by Lieutenant Colonel Dennis J. Cahill, 3 June 2003, Camp Doha, Kuwait, tape recording, USASOC History Office Classified Files, Fort Bragg, NC.

18 The 4th Psychological Operations Group, "Operations ENDURING FREEDOM and IRAQI FREEDOM Consolidated Psychological Operations Lessons Learned," 24 September 2003, USASOC History Office Classified Files, Fort Bragg, NC.

19 Brigadier General Gary M. Jones, U.S. Army Special Forces Command, interview by Dr. Charles H. Briscoe, 2 April 2004, Fort Bragg, NC, tape recording, USASOC History Office Classified Files, Fort Bragg, NC; Jones interview, 2 April 2004.

20 Colonel John F. Mulholland, 5th Special Forces Group, interview by Dr. Charles H. Briscoe, 4 August 2003, Fort Bragg, NC, tape recording, USASOC History Office Classified Files, Fort Bragg, NC.

21 Colonel Charles T. Cleveland, U.S. Army Special Operations Command, interview by Dr. Charles H. Briscoe, 4 August 2003, Fort Bragg, NC, tape recording, USASOC History Office Classified Files, Fort Bragg, NC.

22 Major General Geoffrey C. Lambert, U.S. Army John F. Kennedy Special Warfare Center and School, interview by Dr. Charles H. Briscoe, 7 May 2004, Fort Bragg, NC, tape recording, USASOC History Office Classified Files, Fort Bragg, NC.

23 Cleveland interview, 4 August 2003.

24 Cleveland interview, 4 August 2003.

25 Lambert interview.

26 Colonel Charles T. Cleveland, U.S. Army Special Operations Command, interview by Dr. John Brener and Dr. Charles H. Briscoe, 20 February 2004, Fort Bragg, NC, tape recording, USASOC History Office Classified Files, Fort Bragg, NC.

27 Cleveland interview, 20 February 2004.

Chapter 3 Notes

1 Tommy Franks, *American Soldier* (New York: Regan Books, 2004), 409–10.

2 Franks, *American Soldier*, 413–16, 475–76.

3 Secretary of State Colin Powell, Address to the U.N. Security Council, 5 February 2003, transcript, http://www.whitehouse.gov/news/releases/2003/02/20030205-1.html.

4 Colonel Patrick Higgins, Headquarters, U.S. Special Operations Command Central, interview by Dr. John Partin, 22 October 2002, MacDill Air Force Base, FL, digital recording, USSOCOM History Office Classified Files, MacDill Air Force Base, FL; Colonel Patrick Higgins, Headquarters, U.S. Special Operations

Command Central, interview by Lieutenant Colonel Michael A. Ceroli, 30 April 2003, MacDill Air Force Base, FL, digital recording, USSOCOM History Office Classified Files, MacDill Air Force Base, FL.

5 Lieutenant Colonel Jay Santiago, U.S. Special Operations Command Central, interview by Lieutenant Colonel Robert W. Jones Jr., 12 August 2003, MacDill Air Force Base, FL, tape recording, USASOC History Office Classified Files, Fort Bragg, NC; Colonel James Lien, Joint Communications Signal Element, interview by Dr. Charles H. Briscoe, 13 August 2003, MacDill Air Force Base, FL, tape recording, USASOC History Office Classified Files, Fort Bragg, NC.

6 Colonel Morgan Banks, U.S. Army Special Operations Command, interview by Dr. Charles H. Briscoe, 1 August 2005, Fort Bragg, NC, tape recording, USASOC History Office Classified Files, Fort Bragg, NC.

7 Banks interview.

8 Lieutenant Colonel John Chin, Combined Joint Special Operations Task Force–Arabian Peninsula, interview by Dr. Charles H. Briscoe, 2 July 2003, Baghdad, Iraq, tape recording, USASOC History Office Classified Files, Fort Bragg, NC; John Chin interview by Dr. Charles H. Briscoe, 1 October 2004, Fort Bragg, NC, digital recording, USASOC History Office Classified Files, Fort Bragg, NC; Banks interview; Colonel John F. Mulholland, 5th Special Forces Group, interview by Dr. Charles H. Briscoe, 4 August 2003, Fort Bragg, NC, tape recording, USASOC History Office Classified Files, Fort Bragg, NC.

9 Chin interview, 1 October 2004.

10 Chin interview, 1 October 2004.

11 Chin interview, 1 October 2004; Mulholland interview.

12 Colonel Thomas J. Williams, U.S. Army War College, interview by Dr. Charles H. Briscoe, 16 March 2005, Carlisle Barracks, PA, digital recording, USASOC History Office Classified Files, Fort Bragg, NC.

13 Williams interview.

14 Williams interview.

15 Brigadier General Joseph Votel, Deputy Chief of Staff, Operations, Department of the Army, interview by Dr. Charles H. Briscoe, 18 February 2005, Washington DC, tape recording, USASOC History Office Classified Files, Fort Bragg, NC.

16 "Australia Increases Military Commitment to Iraq," http://www.centcom.mil/operations/Coalition/Coalition_pages/Australia.htm.

17 Major General Duncan Lewis, Special Operations Commander Australia, interview by Dr. Charles H. Briscoe, 17 September 2003, Fort Bragg, NC, tape recording, USASOC History Office Classified Files, Fort Bragg, NC.

18 Lewis interview.

19 United Kingdom Ministry of Defense report, *Operations in Iraq: Lessons for the Future* (London: 2003) 7.

20 Mulholland interview; Lewis interview.

21 Lewis interview.

22 Lewis interview; United Kingdom Ministry of Defense report, *Operations in Iraq: Lessons for the Future,* 36.

23 United Kingdom Ministry of Defense report,*Operations in Iraq: Lessons for the Future,* 53.

24 United Kingdom Ministry of Defense report, *Operations in Iraq: Lessons for the Future,* 5; United Kingdom Ministry of Defense report, *Operations in Iraq: Lessons for the Future,* 3; "Australia Increases Military Commitment to Iraq."

25 Lieutenant General Philip R. Kensinger Jr., U.S. Army Special Operations Command, interview by Dr. Charles H. Briscoe, 7 May 2004, Fort Bragg, NC, tape recording, USASOC History Office Classified Files, Fort Bragg, NC.

26 Kensinger interview, 7 May 2004.

27 Annex G (Civil Affairs), CFLCC OPLAN COBRA II, HQ, CFLCC, U.S. Army Forces CENTCOM, Camp Doha, Kuwait, 13 January 2003, USASOC History Office Classified Files, Fort Bragg, NC.

28 Annex G.

29 Annex G.

30 Annex G; Major General Herbert A. Altshuler, U.S. Army Civil Affairs and Psychological Operations Command,

interview by Dr. Charles H. Briscoe, 25 May 2004, Fort Bragg, NC, tape recording, USASOC History Office Classified Files, Fort Bragg, NC.

31   Harrell interview.

32   Colonel Patrick Higgins, Headquarters, U.S. Special Operations Command Central, interview by Dr. Charles H. Briscoe, 14 August 2003, MacDill Air Force Base, FL, tape recording, USASOC History Office Classified Files, Fort Bragg, NC.

33   Major General Geoffrey C. Lambert, U.S. Army John F. Kennedy Special Warfare Center and School, interview by Dr. Charles H. Briscoe, 7 May 2004, Fort Bragg, NC, tape recording, USASOC History Office Classified Files, Fort Bragg, NC.

34   Altshuler interview, 25 May 2004.

35   Altshuler interview, 25 May 2004.

36   Altshuler interview, 25 May 2004; Major General Herbert A. Altshuler, U.S. Army Civil Affairs and Psychological Operations Command, interview by Dr. Charles H. Briscoe, 20 July 2004, Fort Bragg, NC, tape recording, USASOC History Office Classified Files, Fort Bragg, NC.

37   Altshuler interview, 25 May 2004.

38   Altshuler interview, 25 May 2004.

39   528th Support Battalion integrated most of these elements by specialties into A and B Companies. After a short orientation personnel with critical skills—vehicle mechanics and repairmen—were deployed overseas on forward support teams to fill Combined Joint Special Operations Task Force–Afghanistan requirements. Some, having completed their Afghan assignments, were then shipped to Iraq. The artillerymen of C Battery, 3rd Battalion, 115th Field Artillery became the U.S. Army Special Operations Command internal security force.

40   General Bryan D. Brown, interview by Dr. Charles H. Briscoe, 26 May 2005, MacDill Air Force Base, FL, digital recording, USASOC History Office Classified Files, Fort Bragg, NC.

41   Brown interview.

42   Colonel Richard Polcyznski, U.S. Special Operations Command, interview by Dr.

Charles H. Briscoe, 5 April 2004, MacDill Air Force Base, FL, tape recording, USASOC History Office Classified Files, Fort Bragg, NC.

43   Brigadier General Howard Yellen, U.S. Army Special Operations Command, interview by Dr. Charles H. Briscoe, 26 July 2004, Fort Bragg, NC, tape recording, USASOC History Office Classified Files, Fort Bragg, NC.

44   Polcynski interview.

45   Higgins interview, 22 October 2002.

46   Mulholland interview.

47   Colonel Robert Green, U.S. Army John F. Kennedy Special Warfare Center and School, interview by Dr. Charles H. Briscoe, 26 April 2004, Fort Bragg, NC, tape recording, USASOC History Office Classified Files, Fort Bragg, NC.

48   "News from USJFCOM: Joint Expeditionary Force Experiment '02 begins," http:// www.jfcom.mil/newslink/storyarchive/2002/no072402.htm.

49   "News from USJFCOM: Joint Expeditionary Force Experiment '02 begins."

50   Higgins interview, 14 August 2003.

51   Colonel Michael Findlay, U.S. Special Operations Command, Joint Forces Command, interview by Dr. Charles H. Briscoe, 3 May 2004, Norfolk, VA, tape recording, USASOC History Office Classified Files, Fort Bragg, NC.

52   David Stephenson, U.S. Special Operations Command, Joint Forces Command, interview by Dr. Charles H. Briscoe, 5 May 2004, Norfolk, VA, tape recording, USASOC History Office Classified Archives, Fort Bragg, NC.

53   Mulholland interview.

54   Mulholland interview; Green interview.

55   Colonel Charles T. Cleveland, U.S. Army Special Operations Command, interview by Dr. Charles H. Briscoe, 20 August 2004, Fort Bragg, NC, tape recording, USASOC History Classified Files, Fort Bragg, NC.

56   Lieutenant Commander Mathew Banks and Lieutenant Colonel Paul Wida, U.S. Special Operations Command, Joint Forces Command, interview by Dr. Charles H. Briscoe, 4 May 2004, Norfolk, VA, tape recording, USASOC History Office Classified Archives, Fort Bragg, NC.

57 Findlay interview.

58 Findlay interview.

59 Major General Geoffrey C. Lambert, interview by Lieutenant Colonel Christopher K. Haas, 15 January 2005, Tampa, FL, tape recording, USASOC History Office Classified Files, Fort Bragg, NC.

60 Colonel Joseph Celeski, 3rd Special Forces Group, interview by Dr. Charles H. Briscoe, 21 July 2004, Fort Bragg, NC, tape recording, USASOC History Office Classified Files, Fort Bragg, NC.

61 Lambert interview, 7 May 2004; Altshuler interview, 25 May 2004.

62 Lambert interview, 5 May 2004.

63 "Internal Look," http://www.globalsecurity.org/military/ops/internal-look.htm and "U.S. Military Will Conduct War Games in Qatar," http://www.globalsecurity.org/wmd/library/news/iraq/2002/iraq-021204-usia01.htm.

64 Higgins interview, 30 April 2003.

65 Harrell interview.

66 Higgins interview, 22 October 2002; Michael Bennett, U.S. Special Operations Command, Joint Forces Command, interview by Dr. Charles H. Briscoe, 5 May 2004, Norfolk, VA, tape recording, USASOC History Office Classified Archives, Fort Bragg, NC.

67 Higgins interview, 30 April 2003.

68 Findlay interview, 3 May 2004.

Chapter 4 Notes

1 Tommy Franks, *American Soldier* (New York: Regan Books, 2004), 428–29.

2 Franks, *American Soldier*, 429.

3 All information concerning rules of engagement from: Lieutenant Commander Garth Benson*, U.S. Navy, interview by Dr. Charles H. Briscoe and Dr. Kenneth Finlayson, 12 August 2003, MacDill Air Force Base, FL, tape recording, USASOC History Office Classified Files, Fort Bragg, NC.

4 Colonel Patrick Higgins, Headquarters, U.S. Special Operations Command Central, interview by Lieutenant Colonel Michael A. Ceroli, 30 April 2003, MacDill Air Force Base, FL, recording, USSOCOM History Office Classified Files, MacDill Air Force Base, FL.

5 Colonel John F. Mulholland, 5th Special Forces Group, interview by Dr. Charles H. Briscoe, 4 August 2003, Fort Bragg, NC, recording, USASOC History Office Classified Files, Fort Bragg, NC.

6 Mulholland interview.

7 Colonel Charles T. Cleveland, U.S. Army Special Operations Command, interview by Dr. Charles H. Briscoe, 20 August 2004, Fort Bragg, NC, tape recording, USASOC History Office Classified Files, Fort Bragg, NC.

8 Cleveland interview, 20 August 2004; Colonel Charles T. Cleveland, U.S. Army Special Operations Command, interview by Dr. John Brener and Dr. Charles H. Briscoe, 4 August 2003, Fort Bragg, NC, tape recording, USASOC History Office Classified Files, Fort Bragg, NC.

9 Cleveland interview, 20 August 2004; Cleveland interview, 4 August 2003.

10 Brigadier General Gary M. Jones, U.S. Army Special Forces Command, interview by Dr. Charles H. Briscoe, 2 April 2004, Fort Bragg, NC, tape recording, USASOC History Office Classified Files, Fort Bragg, NC; Colonel Charles T. Cleveland, U.S. Army Special Operations Command, interview by Dr. Charles H. Briscoe, 4 October 2004, Fort Bragg, NC, tape recording, USASOC History Office Classified Files, Fort Bragg, NC.

11 Cleveland interview, 4 October 2004.

12 Cleveland interview, 20 August 2004; Cleveland interview, 4 August 2003.

13 Cleveland interview, 20 August 2004; Cleveland interview, 4 August 2003.

14 Major Tad Woodcock*, telephone interview by A. Dwayne Aaron, 8 July 2004, interview notes, USASOC History Office Classified Files, Fort Bragg, NC.

15 Woodcock interview.

16 Woodcock interview.

17 Woodcock interview.

18 Mark Edwards, interview by A. Dwayne Aaron, 14 July 2004, Fort Bragg, NC, digital recording, USASOC History Office Classified Files, Fort Bragg, NC.

19 Woodcock interview; Edwards interview, 14 July 2004.

20 Woodcock interview.

21 Woodcock interview.

22 Woodcock interview.

23 Edwards interview, 14 July 2004.

24 Edwards interview, 14 July 2004; Woodcock interview.

25 Woodcock interview.

26 Woodcock interview.

27 Woodcock interview.

28 Woodcock interview.

29 Edwards interview, 14 July 2004.

30 Sergeant Major Caleb Ballard*, 528th Special Operations Support Battalion, interview by A. Dwayne Aaron, 13 May 2004, Fort Bragg, NC, interview notes, USASOC History Office Classified Files, Fort Bragg, NC.

31 Major Richard Geery*, B Company, 528th Special Operations Support Battalion, interview by A. Dwayne Aaron, 9 June 2003, interview notes, USASOC History Office Classified Files, Fort Bragg, NC; Chief Warrant Officer 3 Fern Roads*, First Lieutenant Carl Hancock*, Sergeant First Class Hal Andrews*, Staff Sergeant Dan Pulham*, Specialist Jeremy Thurston*, Specialist Dustin Crews*, Sergeant Arthur Bingham*, Specialist Walt Masters*, and Private First Class Jay Gomez*, 528th Special Operations Support Battalion, interview by A. Dwayne Aaron, 18 June 2003, Fort Bragg, NC, tape recording, USASOC History Office Classified Files, Fort Bragg, NC, hereafter cited as 528th interview.

32 528th interview.

33 Lieutenant Colonel Mark Edwards, U.S. Special Operations Support Command, interview by A. Dwayne Aaron, 5 June 2003, Fort Bragg, NC, recording, USASOC History Office Classified Files, Fort Bragg, NC.

34 Edwards interview, 5 June 2003.

35 528th interview.

36 Sergeant Ethan Gibson*, Specialist Cameron Owens*, Sergeant Chad Martin*, Staff Sergeant Mitchell Davis*, Sergeant Joshua London*, and Sergeant Don Travis*, B Company, 528th Special

Operations Support Battalion, interview by A. Dwayne Aaron, 27 August 2003, Fort Bragg, NC, tape recording, USASOC History Office Classified Files, Fort Bragg, NC, hereafter cited as BFSC interview.

37 Edwards interview, 5 June 2003.

38 528th interview.

39 BFSC interview.

40 Mulholland interview; 5th Special Forces Group, Narrative Justification for the Presidential Unit Citation, n.d., USASOC History Office Classified Files, Fort Bragg, NC.

41 First Sergeant Darryl Vaught*, 1st Battalion, 5th Special Forces Group, interview by Major Michael Schellhammer, 7 March 2003, Iraq, digital recording, USASOC History Office Classified Files, Fort Bragg, NC; Lieutenant Colonel Christopher K. Haas and Major Patrick Roberts*, 1st Battalion, 5th Special Forces Group, interview by Major Michael Schellhammer, 8 March 2003, Iraq, digital recording, USASOC History Office Classified Files, Fort Bragg, NC.

42 Captain Jeff Nuttal* and First Sergeant Nate Hunt*, Group Support Company, 5th Special Forces Group, interview by Major Michael Schellhammer, 10 March 2003, Iraq, digital recording, USASOC History Office Classified Files, Fort Bragg, NC; 5th Special Forces Group, Narrative Justification for the Presidential Unit Citation.

43 Haas interview.

44 Major Carl Mitchell*, 3rd Battalion, 5th Special Forces Group, interview by Lieutenant Colonel Dennis P. Mroczkowski, 15 April 2003, Iraq, digital recording, USASOC History Office Classified Files, Fort Bragg, NC.

45 Lieutenant Colonel Christopher Conner, 2nd Battalion, 5th Special Forces Group, interview by Lieutenant Colonel Dennis P. Mroczkowski, 22 May 2003, Kuwait, digital recording, USASOC History Office Classified Files, Fort Bragg, NC.

46 Sergeant Jared Sayre*, B Company, 1st Battalion, 152nd Infantry Regiment, Indiana Army National Guard, interview by Lieutenant Colonel Dennis P. Mroczkowski, 20 April 2003, Iraq, digital recording, USASOC History Office Classified Files, Fort Bragg, NC; Lieuten-

ant Colonel Nathan Lowrey, "2-14th Infantry with TF Viking in Northern Iraq," n.d., USSOCOM History Office Classified Files, MacDill Air Force Base, FL.

47 5th Special Forces Group, Narrative Justification for the Presidential Unit Citation.

48 Major Chris Parker*, B Company, 9th Psychological Operations Battalion, interview by Major Michael Schellhammer, 14 March 2003, digital recording, USASOC History Office Classified Files, Fort Bragg, NC.

49 Parker interview; Major Karl Hedges*, Tactical Psychological Operations Detachment 960, 301st Psychological Operations Company, interview by Lieutenant Colonel Dennis P. Mroczkowski, 15 April 2003, Iraq, digital recording, USASOC History Office Classified Files, Fort Bragg, NC.

50 Parker interview.

51 Parker interview.

52 Parker interview.

53 Colonel Richard Polzcynski, 160th Special Operations Aviation Regiment, interview by Dr. Charles H. Briscoe, 29 April 2004, MacDill Air Force Base, FL, tape recording, USASOC History Office Classified Files, Fort Bragg, NC.

54 Sergeant First Class Tim Hill*, Headquarters Company, 3rd Battalion, 160th Special Operations Aviation Regiment, interview by Lieutenant Colonel Robert W. Jones Jr., 8 March 2005, Hunter Army Airfield, GA, digital recording, USASOC History Office Classified Files, Fort Bragg, NC.

55 Hill interview.

56 Staff Sergeant Fred Gillespie*, Headquarters Company, 3rd Battalion, 160th Special Operations Aviation Regiment, interview by Lieutenant Colonel Robert W. Jones Jr., 8 March 2005, Hunter Army Airfield, GA, digital recording, USASOC History Office Classified Files, Fort Bragg, NC.

57 Sergeant First Class Sean Holdman*, Headquarters Company, 3rd Battalion, 160th Special Operations Aviation Regiment, interview by Lieutenant Colonel Robert W. Jones Jr., 8 March 2005, Hunter Army Airfield, GA, digital

recording, USASOC History Office Classified Files, Fort Bragg, NC.

58 Lieutenant Colonel Robert Welch, 3rd Battalion, 160th Special Operations Aviation Regiment, interview by Lieutenant Colonel Richard Perkins, 19 March 2003, H-5 Airfield, tape recording, USASOC History Office Classified Files, Fort Bragg, NC; Major Monty Bremen*, A Company, 3rd Battalion, 160th Special Operations Aviation Regiment, interview by Lieutenant Colonel Robert W. Jones Jr., 8 March 2005, Hunter Army Airfield, GA, digital recording, USASOC History Office Classified Files, Fort Bragg, NC.

59 "Operation Desert Spring," http://www.globalsecurity.org/military/ops/desert_spring.htm.

60 Thomas M. Joyce, "SOCCE-Kuwait: Establishing Long-Term Military-to-Military Relationships," *Special Warfare*, August 2003, 20.

61 Master Sergeant Frank Holbrook*, A Company, 1st Battalion, 19th Special Forces Group, interview by Lieutenant Colonel Dennis P. Mroczkowski, 15 April 2003, Baghdad, Iraq, digital recording, USASOC History Office Classified Files, Fort Bragg, NC.

62 Linda Robinson, *Masters of Chaos: The Secret History of the Special Forces* (New York: PublicAffairs Books, 2004), 245–273; Sergeant First Class George Wester*, A Company, 1st Battalion, 19th Special Forces Group, e-mail to Lieutenant Colonel Robert W. Jones Jr., 4 February 2005, USASOC History Office Classified Files, Fort Bragg, NC.

63 Thomas E. Ricks, "Special Operations Units Already in Iraq; Weapons Defectors, Communications Links Sought," *The Washington Post*, 13 February 2003, sec. A, 1; Department of the Army, *Special Forces Operations*, Field Manual 3-05.20, June 2001, 1–19; William Matthews, "Lethal Envoys," *National Guard Magazine,* September 2003, http://ngaus.org/ngmagazine/lethalenvoys903.asp.

64 Sergeant First Class John-Paul Levert*, A Company, 1st Battalion, 19th Special Forces Group, interview by Lieutenant Colonel Robert W. Jones Jr., 2 October 2004, Buckley, WA, digital recording,

USASOC History Office Classified Files, Fort Bragg, NC.

65 Colonel Kevin Leonard, U.S. Special Operations Support Command, interview by A. Dwayne Aaron, 24 June 2003, Fort Bragg, NC, tape recording, USASOC History Office Classified Files, Fort Bragg, NC.

66 Leonard interview; Lieutenant Colonel Michael Bird, U.S. Special Operations Support Command, interview by A. Dwayne Aaron, 2 June 2003, Fort Bragg, NC, tape recording, USASOC History Office Classified Files, Fort Bragg, NC.

67 Lieutenant Colonel Michael Saulnier, Commander, 528th Special Operations Support Battalion, interview by A. Dwayne Aaron, 11 May 2004, Fort Bragg, NC, digital recording, USASOC History Office Classified Files, Fort Bragg, NC; Leonard interview; Major Wes Wickham*, U.S. Special Operations Support Command, interview by A. Dwayne Aaron, 2 June 2003, Fort Bragg, NC, tape recording, USASOC History Office Classified Files, Fort Bragg, NC.

68 Leonard interview; Wickham interview.

69 Leonard interview.

70 Leonard interview; Saulnier interview, 11 May 2004.

71 Leonard interview.

72 Wickham interview.

73 Captain Roger Campbell*, 8th Psychological Operations Battalion, 4th Psychological Operations Group, interview by Lieutenant Colonel Robert W. Jones Jr., 23 June 2003, Fort Bragg, NC, tape recording, USASOC History Office Classified Files, Fort Bragg, NC.

74 Campbell interview.

75 Paul Hart, "The Most Deployed Unit in the Air National Guard," The Voice of the Quiet Professionals of AFSOC, http://www.spectrumwd.com/c130/articles/193rdsog.htm.

76 Lieutenant Colonel Michael Schellhammer, "Psychological Operations (PSYOP) in Joint Special Operations Area–West," USSOCOM History Office Classified Files, MacDill Air Force Base, FL, 9.

77 Schellhammer, 9.

78 Schellhammer, 9.

79 Schellhammer, 9.

80 Rick Rogers, "Psy-war: Old tactic, new technique; unit aims to confuse, convince," Daily Press (Newport News, VA), 15 April 2003.

81 Schellhammer, 34.

82 Schellhammer, 34.

83 David A. Converse, Operation IRAQI FREEDOM, Psychological Operations Field Collection Team, "Operational Assessment," n.d., USASOC History Office Classified Files, Fort Bragg, NC, 33.

Chapter 5 Notes

1 "President's speech to the nation," 19 March 2003, http://www.whitehouse.gov/news/releases/2003/03/print/20030319-7.html.

2 Tommy Franks, *American Soldier* (New York: Regan Books, 2004), 436.

3 Franks, *American Soldier*, 436–39, 471.

4 Franks, *American Soldier*, 471.

5 Franks, *American Soldier*, 471.

6 Gregory Fontenot, E.J. Degen, and David Tohn, *On Point: The United States Army in Operation IRAQI FREEDOM* (Fort Leavenworth, KS: Combat Studies Institute Press, 2004), 115–21.

7 Franks, *American Soldier*, 479–83.

8 Franks, *American Soldier*, 485–87.

9 Fontenot et al., *On Point*, 133–35.

10 Daniel Williams, "U.S. Troops Working With Kurdish Fighters," *The Washington Post*, 17 March 2003, A14.

11 Williamson Murray and Robert H. Scales Jr., *The Iraq War: A Military History* (Cambridge, MA: Belknap Press of Harvard University Press, 2003), 187.

12 Dennis Brewer, "352nd Special Operations Group 'Silent Professionals' make noise with command, Air Force awards," *The Marauder*, 23 April 2004, 7; "Department of the Air Force, Distinguished Flying Cross Citation for Captain Justin R. Hoffman," 352nd Special Operations Group.

13 Captain David McDougal*, ODA 062, 2nd Battalion, 10th Special Forces Group,

interview by Lieutenant Colonel Robert W. Jones Jr., 25 June 2003, Fort Carson, CO, tape recording, USASOC History Office Classified Files, Fort Bragg, NC.

14 McDougal interview.

15 Warrant Officer 1 Thomas Zolitck*, ODA 062, 2nd Battalion, 10th Special Forces Group, interview by Lieutenant Colonel Robert W. Jones Jr., 25 June 2003, Fort Carson, CO, tape recording, USASOC History Office Classified Files, Fort Bragg, NC.

16 Zolitck interview.

17 Staff Sergeant Earl Carter*, ODA 075, 3rd Battalion, 10th Special Forces Group, interview by Lieutenant Colonel Robert W. Jones Jr., 25 June 2003, Fort Carson, CO, tape recording, USASOC History Office Classified Files, Fort Bragg, NC.

18 Sergeant First Class Curtis Yates*, ODA 085, 3rd Battalion, 10th Special Forces Group, interview by Lieutenant Colonel Robert W. Jones Jr., 25 June 2003, Fort Carson, CO, tape recording, USASOC History Office Classified Files, Fort Bragg, NC.

19 Sergeant First Class Carson Jones*, ODA 094, 3rd Battalion, 10th Special Forces Group, interview by Lieutenant Colonel Robert W. Jones Jr., 25 June 2003, Fort Carson, CO, tape recording, USASOC History Office Classified Files, Fort Bragg, NC.

20 Jones interview.

21 Captain Patrick Flood, "Special Ops Signal Bn provides special support for Operations Iraqi Freedom," *Army Communicator*, Fall 2003, http://www.gordon.army.mil/AC/Fall%2003/FALL_03_online.pdf.

22 First Sergeant Floyd Granger*, Captain Kyle Ruger*, and Staff Sergeant Donald Tripp*, 112th Special Operations Signal Battalion, interview by A. Dwayne Aaron, 20 April 2004, Fort Bragg, NC, notes, USASOC History Office Classified Files, Fort Bragg, NC, hereafter cited as Granger interview.

23 Granger interview.

24 Granger interview.

25 Granger interview.

26 Granger interview.

27 Granger interview.

28 Granger interview.

29 Lieutenant Colonel Michael Schellhammer, *The Air-Ground Team in Combined Joint Special Operations Task Force–West during Operation Iraqi Freedom*, USSOCOM History Office Classified Files, MacDill Air Force Base, FL.

30 Lieutenant Colonel Christopher Conner, 2nd Battalion, 5th Special Forces Group, interview by Dr. Kenneth Finlayson, 10 September 2003, Fort Campbell, KY, tape recording, USASOC History Office Classified Files, Fort Bragg, NC; Linda Robinson, *Masters of Chaos: The Secret History of the Special Forces* (New York: PublicAffairs Books, 2004), 224–225.

31 Sergeant First Class Buck Spruce*, ODA 553, 2nd Battalion, 5th Special Forces Group, interview by Lieutenant Colonel Dennis P. Mroczkowski, 30 May 2003, Ali As-Salim Air Base, Kuwait, digital recording, USASOC History Office Classified Files, Fort Bragg, NC.

32 Lieutenant Colonel James C. Slife, 20th Special Operations Squadron, interview by Lieutenant Colonel Dennis P. Mroczkowski, 30 March 2003, Ali As-Salim Air Base, Kuwait, digital recording, USASOC History Office Classified Files, Fort Bragg, NC; Robinson, *Masters of Chaos*, 277; Spruce interview.

33 Conner interview; Major Boyd Sinclair*, Advanced Operating Base 570, 2nd Battalion, 5th Special Forces Group, interview by Lieutenant Colonel Dennis P. Mroczkowski, 4 May 2003, Baghdad, Iraq, digital recording, USASOC History Office Classified Files, Fort Bragg, NC.

34 Major Jack Gray*, Advanced Operating Base 520, 1st Battalion, 5th Special Forces Group, interview by Dr. Kenneth Finlayson, 10 September 2003, Fort Campbell, KY, tape recording, USASOC History Office Classified Files, Fort Bragg, NC.

35 Department of the Army, *Special Forces Operations, Field Manual 3-05.20*, June 2001, 3–26; Gray interview.

36 Robinson, *Masters of Chaos*, 195; Gray interview.

37 Gray interview.

38 Gray interview.

39 Gray interview.

40 Franks, *American Soldier*, 433–34; Murray and Scales, *The Iraq War*, 186; Schellhammer, The Air-Ground Team in Combined Joint Special Operations Task Force–West during Operation Iraqi Freedom; Bob Woodward, "Attack Was 48 Hours Old When It 'Began,'" *The Washington Post*, 23 March 2003, A1; Tim Ripley, "Iraq's western desert a special forces playground," Jane's Defense Weekly, 3 April 2003, http://www.janes.com/regional_news/africa_middle_east/news/jdw/jdw030403_1_n.shtml.

41 Gray interview.

42 Staff Sergeant Jesse Dundee*, C Company, 1st Battalion, 124th Infantry Regiment, Florida Army National Guard, interview by Major Michael Schellhammer, 30 March 2003, H-5 Airfield, recording, USASOC History Office Classified Files, Fort Bragg, NC; Captain Wayne Pelham*, C Company, 1st Battalion, 124th Infantry Regiment, Florida Army National Guard, interview by Major Michael Schellhammer, 30 March 2003, H-5 Airfield, recording, USASOC History Office Classified Files, Fort Bragg, NC.

43 Private Noel Platz*, C Company, 1st Battalion, 124th Infantry Regiment, Florida Army National Guard, interview by Major Michael Schellhammer, 30 March 2003, H-5 Airfield, recording, USASOC History Office Classified Files, Fort Bragg, NC; Pelham interview.

44 Pelham interview.

45 Gray interview.

46 Robinson, *Masters of Chaos*, 198; Gray interview; John Pike, "H-3 Airfield," http://www.globalsecurity.org/military/world/iraq/h-3-new.htm.

47 ODA 523, 1st Battalion, 5th Special Forces Group, group interview by Lieutenant Colonel Richard Perkins, 15 April 2003, Ar Rutba, Iraq, digital recording, USASOC History Office Classified Files, Fort Bragg, NC.

48 ODA 522, 1st Battalion, 5th Special Forces Group, group interview by Lieutenant Colonel Richard Perkins, 18 April 2003, Ar Rutba, Iraq, recording, USASOC History Office Classified Files, Fort Bragg, NC.

49 ODA 522 interview.

50 Robinson, *Masters of Chaos*, 200–205; Lieutenant Colonel Richard Perkins, "SOF Infiltration of Western Iraq and the Battle of Ar Rutba," 25 July 2003, USSOCOM History Office Classified Files, MacDill Air Force Base, FL.

51 Robinson, *Masters of Chaos*, 200–205; Perkins, "SOF Infiltration of Western Iraq."

52 ODA 524, 1st Battalion, 5th Special Forces Group, group interview by Lieutenant Colonel Richard Perkins, 15 April 2003, Ar Rutba, Iraq, digital recording, USASOC History Office Classified Files, Fort Bragg, NC; Robinson, *Masters of Chaos*, 200–205; Perkins; Staff Sergeant Fred Sawolski*, ODA 525, interview by Lieutenant Colonel Richard Perkins, 16 April 2003, Irbil, Iraq, digital recording, USASOC History Office Classified Files, Fort Bragg, NC; Sergeant First Class Alex Bingham*, ODA 525, interview by Lieutenant Colonel Richard Perkins, 15 April 2003, Irbil, Iraq, digital recording, USASOC History Office Classified Files, Fort Bragg, NC; Captain Mark Pointer*, ODA 525, interview by Lieutenant Colonel Richard Perkins, 15 April 2003, Irbil, Iraq, digital recording, USASOC History Office Classified Files, Fort Bragg, NC; Captain Jay Green*, ODA 525, interview by Lieutenant Colonel Richard Perkins, 16 April 2003, Irbil, Iraq, digital recording, USASOC History Office Classified Files, Fort Bragg, NC.

53 Robinson, *Masters of Chaos*, 205–206; Gray interview.

54 Schellhammer, *The Air-Ground Team*, 18–20.

55 Lieutenant Colonel Christopher Conner, 2nd Battalion, 5th Special Forces Group, interview by Lieutenant Colonel Dennis P. Mroczkowski, 22 May 2003, Ali As-Salim Air Base, Kuwait, digital recording, USASOC History Office Classified Files, Fort Bragg, NC.

56 First Lieutenant Chris Hill*, 23rd Special Tactics Squadron, U.S. Air Force, interview by Lieutenant Colonel Dennis P. Mroczkowski, 25 March 2003, Ali As-Salim Air Base, Kuwait, digital recording, USASOC History Office Classified Files, Fort Bragg, NC.

57 Advanced Operating Base 570 Commander's Concept Briefing.

58 Captain Doug Hoffman*, ODA 574, 2nd Battalion, 5th Special Forces Group, interview by Lieutenant Colonel Dennis P. Mroczkowski, 5 May 2003, Baghdad, Iraq, digital recording, USASOC History Office Classified Files, Fort Bragg, NC.

59 Master Sergeant James Robins*, 23rd Special Tactics Squadron, U.S. Air Force, interview by Lieutenant Colonel Dennis P. Mroczkowski, 25 May 2003, Ali As-Salim Air Base, Kuwait, digital recording, USASOC History Office Classified Files, Fort Bragg, NC.

60 Pike, "H-3 Airfield."

61 Robins interview.

62 First Lieutenant Wayne West*, 23rd Special Tactics Squadron, U.S. Air Force, interview by Lieutenant Colonel Dennis P. Mroczkowski, 25 March 2003, Ali As-Salim Air Base, Kuwait, digital recording, USASOC History Office Classified Files, Fort Bragg, NC; Sergeant Major Thad Berino*, ODB 570, 2nd Battalion, 5th Special Forces Group, interview by Lieutenant Colonel Dennis P. Mroczkowski, Baghdad, Iraq, 12 April 2003, digital recording, USASOC History Office Classified Files, Fort Bragg, NC.

63 Berino interview.

64 Robins interview.

65 Hoffman interview; Hill interview.

66 West interview.

67 Berino interview.

68 Hill interview.

69 Robins interview.

70 Robins interview.

71 Master Sergeant Bill Dayton*, 23rd Special Tactics Squadron, U.S. Air Force, interview by Lieutenant Colonel Dennis P. Mroczkowski, 25 March 2003, Ali As-Salim Air Base, Kuwait, digital recording, USASOC History Office Classified Files, Fort Bragg, NC.

72 Sergeant First Class Bruce Kroll*, ODB 570, 3rd Battalion, 5th Special Forces Group, interview by Lieutenant Colonel Dennis P. Mroczkowski, Baghdad, Iraq, 12 April 2003, digital recording, USASOC History Office Classified Files, Fort Bragg, NC.

73 Berino interview.

74 Robins interview.

75 Hoffman interview.

76 West interview.

77 Dayton interview.

78 Berino interview.

79 Hill interview.

80 Berino interview.

81 Sinclair interview.

82 Sergeant First Class Tim Kreiler*, ODA 544, 2nd Battalion, 5th Special Forces Group, interview by Lieutenant Colonel Dennis P. Mroczkowski, 15 May 2003, Najaf, Iraq, digital recording, USASOC History Office Classified Files, Fort Bragg, NC.

83 Clinger interview.

84 Chief Warrant Officer 3 Sidney Schwarz-kopf*, ODA 544, 2nd Battalion, 5th Special Forces Group, interview by Lieutenant Colonel Dennis P. Mroczkowski, 15 May 2003, Najaf, Iraq, digital recording, USASOC History Office Classified Files, Fort Bragg, NC; Kreiler interview; Robinson, *Masters of Chaos*, 253.

85 Schwarzkopf interview.

86 Kreiler interview.

87 Kreiler interview.

88 Kreiler interview.

89 Kreiler interview.

90 Sergeant First Class Mark Combs*, ODA 544, 2nd Battalion, 5th Special Forces Group, interview by Lieutenant Colonel Dennis P. Mroczkowski, 15 May 2003, Najaf, Iraq, digital recording, USASOC History Office Classified Files, Fort Bragg, NC.

91 Combs interview.

92 Combs interview.

93 Combs interview.

94 Kreiler interview.

95 Senior Airman Sergio Manchini*, 23rd Tactical Squadron attached to ODA 544, 2nd Battalion, 5th Special Forces Group, interview by Lieutenant Colonel Dennis P. Mroczkowski, 4 April 2003, Najaf, Iraq, digital recording, USASOC History Office Classified Files, Fort Bragg, NC.

96 Schwarzkopf interview.

97 Combs interview.

98   Combs interview.

99   Schwarzkopf interview.

100   Manchini interview; Kreiler interview; Sergeant First Class Tad Holley*, ODA 544, 2nd Battalion, 5th Special Forces Group, interview by Lieutenant Colonel Dennis P. Mroczkowski, 4 April 2003, Najaf, Iraq, digital recording, USASOC History Office Classified Files, Fort Bragg, NC.

101   Captain Don Raintree*, ODA 551, B Company, 2nd Battalion, 5th Special Forces Group, interview by Lieutenant Colonel Dennis P. Mroczkowski, 18 May 2003, Ali As-Salim Air Base, Kuwait, digital recording, USASOC History Office Classified Files, Fort Bragg, NC.

102   Raintree interview; Bernard Weinraub, "All eyes are on the Karbala Gap," *The Deseret News*, 28 March 2003, sec. A, 5.

103   Chief Warrant Officer 2 Clyde Hawks*, ODA 551, B Company, 2nd Battalion, 5th Special Forces Group, interview by Lieutenant Colonel Dennis P. Mroczkowski, 18 May 2003, Ali As-Salim Air Base, Kuwait, digital recording, USASOC History Office Classified Files, Fort Bragg, NC.

104   Raintree interview; Hawks interview.

105   Staff Sergeant Charles Godfrey*, ODA 551, B Company, 2nd Battalion, 5th Special Forces Group, interview by Lieutenant Colonel Dennis P. Mroczkowski, 18 May 2003, Ali As-Salim Air Base, Kuwait, digital recording, USASOC History Office Classified Files, Fort Bragg, NC; Sergeant First Class John Spencer*, ODA 551, B Company, 2nd Battalion, 5th Special Forces Group, interview by Lieutenant Colonel Dennis P. Mroczkowski, 18 May 2003, Ali As-Salim Air Base, Kuwait, digital recording, USASOC History Office Classified Files, Fort Bragg, NC; Raintree interview.

106   Thomas E. Ricks, "Special Operations Units Already in Iraq; Weapons Defectors, Communications Links Sought," *The Washington Post*, 13 February 2003, A1; Levert interview.

107   Raintree interview.

108   "FalconView," www.falconview.org/FAQ_FVW330.htm; Raintree interview; Spencer interview.

109   Godfrey interview.

110   Raintree interview; Robinson, *Masters of Chaos*, 248; Hawks interview.

111   Raintree interview; Lieutenant Colonel Vince Reed, 3rd Battalion, 160th Special Operations Aviation Regiment, interview by Lieutenant Colonel Richard Perkins, 22 March 2003, tape recording, USASOC History Office Classified Files, Fort Bragg, NC.

112   Hawks interview; Fred J. Pushies, *Night Stalkers: 160th Special Operations Aviation Regiment (Airborne)* (St. Paul, MN: Zenith Press, 2005), 80–81, 98–101; "MH-60L Direct Action Penetrator (DAP)/AH-60L," Global Security.Org, www.globalsecurity.org/military/systems/aircraft/mh-60l-dap.htm; Raintree interview.

113   Hawks interview; Spencer interview.

114   Hawks interview; Raintree interview.

115   Major Jerry Baxter*, Advanced Operating Base 560, 2nd Battalion, 5th Special Forces Group, interview by Dr. Kenneth Finlayson, 10 September 2003, Fort Campbell, KY, digital recording, USASOC History Office Classified Files, Fort Bragg, NC.

116   Major Jerry Baxter*, Advanced Operating Base 560, 2nd Battalion, 5th Special Forces Group, interview by Lieutenant Colonel Dennis P. Mroczkowski, 23 May 2003, Ali As-Salim Air Base, Kuwait, digital recording, USASOC History Office Classified Files, Fort Bragg, NC; Murray and Scales, *The Iraq War*, 68.

117   Baxter interview, 23 May 2003; Murray and Scales, *The Iraq War*, 117–18.

118   Baxter interview, 10 September 2003; Advanced Operating Base 560, "Post Mission Report: Operation IRAQI FREEDOM," 22 May 2003, USASOC History Office Classified Files, Fort Bragg, NC.

119   Captain Jeff Davis*, ODA 544, 2nd Battalion, 5th Special Forces Group, interview by Lieutenant Colonel Dennis P. Mroczkowski, 19 May 2003, Ali As-Salim Air Base, Kuwait, digital recording, USASOC History Office Classified Files, Fort Bragg, NC.

120   Robinson, *Masters of Chaos*, 227; Master Sergeant Mitch Semmes*, ODA 554, 2nd Battalion, 5th Special Forces Group,

interview by Lieutenant Colonel Dennis P. Mroczkowski, 19 May 2003, Ali As-Salim Air Base, Kuwait, digital recording, USASOC History Office Classified Files, Fort Bragg, NC.

121 Davis interview; Semmes interview.

122 Robinson, *Masters of Chaos*, 229–31; Semmes interview.

123 Robinson, *Masters of Chaos*, 229–31; Semmes interview; Davis interview.

124 Davis interview; Semmes interview.

125 Semmes interview.

126 Semmes interview; Davis interview.

127 Baxter interview, 23 May 2003.

128 Baxter interview, 23 May 2003.

129 Baxter interview, 23 May 2003.

130 Master Sergeant John Kape*, ODB 560, 2nd Battalion, 5th Special Forces Group, interview by Lieutenant Colonel Dennis P. Mroczkowski, 23 May 2003, Ali As-Salim Air Base, Kuwait, digital recording, USASOC History Office Classified Files, Fort Bragg, NC.

131 Captain Paul Hampton*, ODB 560, 2nd Battalion, 5th Special Forces Group, interview by Lieutenant Colonel Dennis P. Mroczkowski, 23 May 2003, Ali As-Salim Air Base, Kuwait, digital recording, USASOC History Office Classified Files, Fort Bragg, NC.

132 Baxter interview, 23 May 2003; Captain Gale Cobb*, ODA 565, 2nd Battalion, 5th Special Forces Group, interview by Lieutenant Colonel Dennis P. Mroczkowski, 21 May 2003, Ali As-Salim Air Base, Kuwait, digital recording, USASOC History Office Classified Files, Fort Bragg, NC.

133 Baxter interview, 23 May 2003; Hampton interview, 23 May 2003; Robinson, *Masters of Chaos*, 236.

134 Hampton interview.

135 Baxter interview, 23 May 2003; Robinson, *Masters of Chaos*, 236.

136 Semmes interview.

137 Baxter interview, 23 May 2003; Murray and Scales, *The Iraq War*, 146.

138 Baxter interview, 23 May 2003; Hampton interview; Davis interview.

139 Baxter interview, 23 May 2003.

140 Cobb interview; Davis interview.

141 First Lieutenant Robert Winston*, A Company, 528th Special Operations Support Battalion, interview by A. Dwayne Aaron, 28 June 2004, Fort Bragg, NC, digital recording, USASOC History Office Classified Files, Fort Bragg, NC; Captain Earl Jensen*, 528th Special Operations Support Battalion, interview by A. Dwayne Aaron, 26 May 2004, Fort Bragg, NC, digital recording, USASOC History Office Classified Files, Fort Bragg, NC.

142 Winston interview; Lieutenant Colonel Michael Saulnier, 528th Special Operations Support Battalion, interview by A. Dwayne Aaron, 18 June 2003, Fort Bragg, NC, digital recording, USASOC History Office Classified Files, Fort Bragg, NC.

143 Saulnier interview, 18 June 2003; Jensen interview.

144 Winston interview.

145 Winston interview; Jensen interview.

146 Winston inteview.

147 Winston interview.

148 Winston interview; Saulnier interview, 11 May 2004.

149 Winston interview.

150 Winston interview.

151 Winston interview.

152 Winston interview; Jensen interview.

153 Private First Class Brenda Meter* and Specialist Josh Kinlaw*, C Company, 112th Special Operations Signal Battalion, interview by Chief Warrant Officer 3 Yul C. Yurcaba, 30 June 2003, Baghdad, Iraq, tape recording, USASOC History Office Classified Files, Fort Bragg, NC.

154 Granger interview.

155 Granger interview; Staff Sergeant Dale Durham*, C Company, 112th Special Operations Signal Battalion, interview by Chief Warrant Officer 3 Yul C. Yurcaba, 30 June 2003, Baghdad, Iraq, tape recording, USASOC History Office Classified Files, Fort Bragg, NC.

156 Meter and Kinlaw interview.

157 Chief Warrant Officer 3 Travis Walter*, C Company, 1st Battalion, 160th Special Operations Aviation Regiment, interview by James Schroder, 29 April 2004, Fort

Campbell, KY, tape recording, USASOC History Office Classified Files, Fort Bragg, NC.

158 Walter interview.

159 Walter interview.

160 Walter interview.

161 Walter interview.

162 Chief Warrant Officer 4 Doug Carter*, B Company, 1st Battalion, 160th Special Operations Aviation Regiment, interview by James Schroder, 17 March 2004, Fort Campbell, KY, tape recording, USASOC History Office Classified Files, Fort Bragg, NC.

163 Carter interview.

164 Chief Warrant Officer 4 Daniel Clement*, A Company, 1st Battalion, 160th Special Operations Aviation Regiment, interview by Dr. Charles H. Briscoe, 10 September 2003, Fort Campbell, KY, tape recording, USASOC History Office Classified Files, Fort Bragg, NC.

165 Clement interview.

166 Clement interview.

167 Chief Warrant Officer 4 Randall Ramsey*, Headquarters Company, 1st Battalion, 160th Special Operations Aviation Regiment, interview by James Schroder, 17 March 2004, Fort Campbell, KY, tape recording, USASOC History Office Classified Files, Fort Bragg, NC.

168 Clement interview.

169 Major Mark Mohan*, B Company, 1st Battalion, 160th Special Operations Aviation Regiment, interview by James Schroder, 17 March 2004, Fort Campbell, KY, tape recording, USASOC History Office Classified Files, Fort Bragg, NC; Carter interview.

170 Lieutenant Colonel Robert Welch, 3rd Battalion, 160th Special Operations Aviation Regiment, interview by Lieutenant Colonel Richard Perkins, 19 March 2003, Middle East, tape recording and transcripts, USASOC History Office Classified Files, Fort Bragg, NC.

171 "Operational summary and mission briefing, 3rd Battalion 160th SOAR, 19 March 2003," copy in USASOC History Office Classified Files, Fort Bragg, NC.

172 "Operational summary and mission briefing, 3rd Battalion, 160th SOAR, 19 March 2003."

173 Welch interview.

174 Robert W. Black, *Rangers in World War II* (New York: Random House), 113–14,146–48.

175 Major Ralph Morgenstern*. 18th Field Artillery Brigade, interview by Steven D. Cage, 12 April 2003, H-1 Airfield, Iraq, tape recording, USASOC History Office Classified Files, Fort Bragg, NC; Lockheed Martin, http://www.missilesandfirecontrol.com/our_products/firesupport/HIMARS/product-HIMARS.html.

176 Captain Stan Knell*, 18th Field Artillery Brigade, interview by Lieutenant Colonel Robert W. Jones Jr., 28 March 2005, Fort Bragg, NC, digital recording, USASOC History Office Classified Files, Fort Bragg, NC.

177 General Bryan D. Brown, U.S. Special Operations Command, interview by Dr. Charles H. Briscoe and Dr. John Partin, 26 May 2005, MacDill Air Force Base, FL, digital recording, USASOC History Office Classified Files, Fort Bragg, NC.

178 Colonel Joseph Votel, 75th Ranger Regiment, interview by Steven D. Cage, 25 April 2003, H-1 Airfield, Iraq, tape recording, USASOC History Office Classified Files, Fort Bragg, NC; Morganstern interview.

179 Captain Stan Knell*, 18th Field Artillery Brigade, interview by Steven D. Cage, 12 April 2003, H-1 Airfield, Iraq, tape recording, USASOC History Office Classified Files, Fort Bragg, NC.

180 Knell interview, 12 April 2003.

181 Knell interview, 12 April 2003; Master Sergeant James Bradley*, B Company, 3rd Ranger Battalion, 75th Ranger Regiment, interview by Dr. Charles H. Briscoe, 16 June 2003, Fort Benning, GA, tape recording, USASOC History Office Classified Files, Fort Bragg, NC.

182 Sergeant First Class Christopher Marrow*, 3rd Ranger Battalion, 75th Ranger Regiment, interview by Sergeant First Class Patrick Jennings, 8 November 2003, Fort Benning, GA, tape recording and transcripts, USASOC History Office Classified Files, Fort Bragg, NC.

183 Marrow interview; Bradley interview; Knell interview, 28 March 2005.

184 Marrow interview; Bradley interview; Knell interview, 28 March 2005.

185 Morganstern interview; Knell interview, 12 April 2003.

186 Captain James Estrich*, 3rd Ranger Battalion, 75th Ranger Regiment, interview by Sergeant First Class Patrick Jennings, 23 October 2003, Fort Benning, GA, tape recording, USASOC History Office Classified Files, Fort Bragg, NC.

187 Knell interview, 28 March 2005.

188 Estrich interview; Marrow interview.

189 Marrow interview; Knell interview, 28 March 2005; Bradley interview.

Chapter 6 Notes

1   General Bryan D. Brown, "Testimony of General Bryan D. Brown, U.S. Army, Commander, U.S. Special Operations Command, before the United States House of Representatives Committee on Armed Services, Subcommittee on Terrorism, Unconventional Threats and Capabilities," 11 March 2004, http://armedservices. house/openingstatementsandpressre-leases/10.../04-03-11brown.htm

2   Tommy Franks, *American Soldier* (New York: Regan Books, 2004), 503–504.

3   Gregory Fontenot, E.J. Degen, and David Tohn, *On Point: The United States Army in Operation IRAQI FREEDOM* (Fort Leavenworth, KS: Combat Studies Institute Press, 2004), 221–22.

4   Fontenot et al., *On Point*, 202–209.

5   Fontenot et al., *On Point*, 212–13.

6   Fontenot et al., *On Point*, 215–19.

7   Fontenot et al., *On Point*, 222–29; The 173rd Airborne Brigade (-) had two airborne infantry battalions, an artillery battery, and support units assigned in 2003.

8   Fontenot et al., *On Point*, 229; Patrick Warren and Keith Barclay, "Operation Northern Dragon, Northern Iraq," *Military Review*, November–December 2003, 11–14.

9   Linda Robinson, *Masters of Chaos: The Secret History of the Special Forces* (New York: PublicAffairs Books, 2004), 245–53; "Special Operations Forces, Operation Iraqi Freedom," U.S. Special Operations Command, May 2003, 22–23, USASOC History Office Classified Files, Fort Bragg, NC.

10 Colonel John F. Mulholland, 5th Special Forces Group, interview by Dr. Charles H. Briscoe, 4 August 2003, Fort Bragg, NC, tape recording, USASOC History Office Classified Files, Fort Bragg, NC; 5th Special Forces Group, Narrative Justification for the Presidential Unit Citation, n. d., USASOC History Office Classified Files, Fort Bragg, NC.

11 Fontenot et al., *On Point*, 221–22; John D. Gresham, "Special Operations Forces in Operation Iraqi Freedom," Operation Iraqi Freedom, 74.

12 Colonel Charles T. Cleveland, 10th Special Forces Group, interview by Dr. Kenneth Finlayson, 26 June 2003, Fort Carson, CO, tape recording, USASOC History Office Classified Files, Fort Bragg, NC; Major Michael Giroux*, 3rd Battalion, 10th Special Forces Group, interview by Dr. Kenneth Finlayson and Lieutenant Colonel Robert W. Jones Jr, 23 June 2003, Fort Carson, CO, tape recording, USASOC History Office Classified Files, Fort Bragg, NC; Robinson, *Masters of Chaos*, 299–301.

13 Cleveland interview, 26 June 2003.

14 Lieutenant Colonel Kenneth Tovo, 3rd Battalion, 10th Special Forces Group, comments on early draft of article, 4 January 2005, copy in USASOC History Office Classified Files, Fort Bragg, NC.

15 Tovo comments; Major Greg Tsouris*, 3rd Battalion, 10th Special Forces Group, interview by Dr. Kenneth Finlayson, 24 June 2003, Fort Carson, CO, tape recording, USASOC History Office Classified Files, Fort Bragg, NC.

16 Tovo comments.

17 Tovo comments; Tsouris interview.

18 Sergeant First Class Mitch Greenlaw*, C Company, 3rd Battalion, 10th Special Forces Group, interview by Dr. Kenneth Finlayson, 24 June 2003, Fort Carson, CO, tape recording, USASOC History Office Classified Files, Fort Bragg, NC.

19 Captain Blake Ranier*, ODA 081, C Company, 3rd Battalion, 10th Special

Forces Group, interview by Dr. Kenneth Finlayson, 24 June 2003, Fort Carson, CO, tape recording, USASOC History Office Classified Files, Fort Bragg, NC.

20 Giroux interview.

21 Tovo comments; Giroux interview.

22 Tovo comments.

23 Sergeant Wayne Allred* and Specialist Randy Brown*, Bravo Forward Support Company, 528th Special Operations Support Battalion, interview by A. Dwayne Aaron, 7 July 2004, Fort Bragg, NC, digital recording, USASOC History Office Classified Files, Fort Bragg, NC; Staff Sergeant James Urich*, Bravo Forward Support Company, 528th Special Operations Support Battalion, interview by A. Dwayne Aaron, 15 July 2004, Fort Bragg, NC, digital recording, USASOC History Office Classified Files, Fort Bragg, NC.

24 Allred and Brown interview; Urich interview.

25 Allred and Brown interview; Urich interview.

26 Allred and Brown interview; Urich interview.

27 Allred and Brown interview; Urich interview.

28 Sergeant Ethan Gibson*, Specialist Cameron Owens*, Sergeant Chad Martin*, Staff Sergeant Mitchell Davis*, Sergeant Joshua London*, and Sergeant Don Travis*, Bravo Forward Support Company, 528th Special Operations Support Battalion, interview by A. Dwayne Aaron, 27 August 2003, Fort Bragg, NC, tape recording, USASOC History Office Classified Files, Fort Bragg, NC, hereafter cited as BFSC interview.

29 BFSC interview.

30 Allred and Brown interview.

31 Allred and Brown interview; Urich interview.

32 Allred and Brown interview; Urich interview.

33 Allred and Brown interview; Urich interview.

34 Department of the Army, 404th Civil Affairs Battalion, "Memorandum to the Commander, Combined Joint Task Force

7, Camp Victory, Baghdad, Iraq, Subject: Submission of Army Meritorious Unit Citation," n.d., USASOC History Office Classified Files, Fort Bragg, NC.

35 Lieutenant Colonel Harry Schute Jr. and Major Derek Storino*, 40th Civil Affairs Battalion and D Company, 96th Civil Affairs Battalion, Combined Joint Special Operations Task Force–North, interview by Lieutenant Colonel John Katz, 16 April 2003, Kirkuk Airfield, Iraq, summary transcript, USASOC History Office Classified Files, Fort Bragg, NC; 404th Civil Affairs Battalion "Memorandum."

36 Williamson Murray and Robert H. Scales Jr., *The Iraq War: A Military History* (Cambridge, MA: Belknap Press of Harvard University Press, 2003), 186; Schute and Storino interview.

37 404th Civil Affairs Battalion "Memorandum;" Schute and Storino interview.

38 Murray and Scales, *The Iraq War*, 186; Thom Shanker and Eric Schmitt, "Special Operations forces penetrate Iraq—Some rally Kurdish fighters—others save oil wells, POWs," *The Ventura County Star*, 6 April 2003, sec. A, 14; Robinson, *Masters of Chaos*, 245.

39 Robinson, *Masters of Chaos*, 245; Captain Don Raintree*, ODA 551, B Company, 2nd Battalion, 5th Special Forces Group, interview by Dr. Kenneth Finlayson, 11 September 2003, Fort Campbell, KY, tape recording, USASOC History Office Classified Files, Fort Bragg, NC.

40 Sergeant First Class John Spencer*, ODA 551, B Company, 2nd Battalion, 5th Special Forces Group, interview by Lieutenant Colonel Dennis P. Mroczkowski, 18 May 2003, Ali As-Salim Airfield, Kuwait, digital recording, USASOC History Office Classified Files, Fort Bragg, NC; Captain Don Raintree*, ODA 551, B Company, 2nd Battalion, 5th Special Forces Group, interview by Lieutenant Colonel Dennis P. Mroczkowski, 18 May 2003, Ali As-Salim Airfield, Kuwait, digital recording, USASOC History Office Classified Files, Fort Bragg, NC.

41 Chief Warrant Officer 2 Clyde Hawks*, ODA 551, B Company, 2nd Battalion, 5th Special Forces Group, interview by Lieutenant Colonel Dennis P. Mroczkowski, 18 May 2003, Ali As-Salim

Airfield, Kuwait, digital recording, USASOC History Office Classified Files, Fort Bragg, NC; Raintree interview, 18 May 2003; Master Sergeant Albert Bones*, ODA 551, B Company, 2nd Battalion, 5th Special Forces Group, interview by Lieutenant Colonel Dennis P. Mroczkowski, 18 May 2003, Ali As-Salim Airfield, Kuwait, digital recording, USASOC History Office Classified Files, Fort Bragg, NC.

42 Raintree interview, 18 May 2003.

43 Raintree interview, 18 May 2003.

44 Hawks interview.

45 Robinson, *Masters of Chaos*, 245; Ryan Chilcote, "Technology links 101st on the battlefield," CNN.com, 19 March 2003, http://cnn.worldnews.printthis.clickability.com/pt/cpt?action=cpt&title=CNN.com+-+Tech...

46 Hawks interview; Robinson, *Masters of Chaos*, 249–50; Raintree interview, 11 September 2003.

47 Staff Sergeant Charles Godfrey*, ODA 551, B Company, 2nd Battalion, 5th Special Forces Group, interview by Lieutenant Colonel Dennis P. Mroczkowski, 18 May 2003, Ali As-Salim Airfield, Kuwait, digital recording, USASOC History Office Classified Files, Fort Bragg, NC.

48 Bones interview.

49 Hawks interview; Raintree interview, 11 September 2003.

50 Godfrey interview.

51 Hawks interview; Spencer interview; Raintree interview, 18 May 2003; Fontenot et al., *On Point*, 150.

52 Bones interview; Spencer interview.

53 Hawks interview; Sergeant First Class John-Paul Levert*, ODA 916, A Company, 1st Battalion, 19th Special Forces Group, interview by Lieutenant Colonel Robert W. Jones Jr., 2 October 2004, Buckley, WA, digital recording, USASOC History Office Classified Files, Fort Bragg, NC.

54 Raintree interview, 18 May 2003.

55 Chief Warrant Officer 3 Richard Hoyt*, C Company, 1st Battalion, 160th Special Operations Aviation Regiment, interview by Dr. Charles H. Briscoe, 11 September 2003, Fort Campbell, KY, tape recording, USASOC History Office Classified Files, Fort Bragg, NC.

56 Hoyt interview.

57 Chief Warrant Officer 4 Thomas Brady*, C Company, 1st Battalion, 160th Special Operations Aviation Regiment, interview by Dr. Kenneth Finlayson, 29 April 2004, Fort Campbell, KY, tape recording, USASOC History Office Classified Files, Fort Bragg, NC.

58 Chief Warrant Officer 4 Bradley Elliot*, A Company, 1st Battalion, 160th Special Operations Aviation Regiment, interview by James Schroder, 30 April 2004, Fort Campbell, KY, tape recording, USASOC History Office Classified Files, Fort Bragg, NC.

59 Elliot interview; Chief Warrant Officer 3 Walter Moeschet*, A Company, 1st Battalion, 160th Special Operations Aviation Regiment, interview by James Schroder, 30 April 2004, Fort Campbell, KY, tape recording, USASOC History Office Classified Files, Fort Bragg, NC.

60 Captain Theodore Shaffer*, C Company, 1st Battalion, 160th Special Operations Aviation Regiment, interview by James Schroder, 16 March 2004, Fort Campbell, KY, tape recording, USASOC History Office Classified Files, Fort Bragg, NC.

61 Shaffer interview.

62 Elliot interview.

63 Chief Warrant Officer 2 Barry Littleton*, A Company, 2nd Battalion, 160th Special Operations Aviation Regiment, interview by James Schroder, 3 May 2004, Fort Campbell, KY, tape recording, USASOC History Office Classified Files, Fort Bragg, NC.

64 Staff Sergeant Marty Milner*, A Company, 2nd Battalion, 160th Special Operations Aviation Regiment, interview by Dr. Kenneth Finlayson, 27 April 2004, Fort Campbell, KY, tape recording, USASOC History Office Classified Files, Fort Bragg, NC.

65 Littleton interview.

66 Elliot interview.

67 Brady interview.

68 Chief Warrant Officer 3 James Nattier*, A Company, 2nd Battalion, 160th Special Operations Aviation Regiment, interview

by James Schroder, 26 April 2004, Fort Campbell, KY, tape recording, USASOC History Office Classified Files, Fort Bragg, NC.

69   Nattier interview; Hoyt interview; Brady interview.

70   Nattier interview; Hoyt interview; Brady interview.

71   Major Charles Vasek*, 1st Battalion, 75th Ranger Regiment, interview by Dr. Charles H. Briscoe, 21 October 2003, Savannah, GA, tape recording, USASOC History Office Classified Files, Fort Bragg, NC.

72   Captain Daniel Gutierrez*, A Company, 1st Battalion, 75th Ranger Regiment, interview by Dr. Charles H. Briscoe, 20 October 2003, Savannah, GA, tape recording, USASOC History Office Classified Files, Fort Bragg, NC.

73   Gutierrez interview.

74   Gutierrez interview; Sergeant First Class Charles Lander*, A Company, 1st Battalion, 75th Ranger Regiment, interview by Dr. Charles H. Briscoe, 22 October 2003, Savannah, GA, tape recording, USASOC History Office Classified Files, Fort Bragg, NC.

75   Gutierrez interview; Lander interview.

76   Vasek interview.

77   Captain Jeffery Roche*, C Company, 1st Battalion, 75th Ranger Regiment, interview by Lieutenant Colonel Robert W. Jones Jr., 20 October 2003, Savannah, GA, tape recording, USASOC History Office Classified Files, Fort Bragg, NC; Sergeant First Class Christopher Barron*, C Company, 1st Battalion, 75th Ranger Regiment, interview by Lieutenant Colonel Robert W. Jones Jr., 20 October 2003, Savannah, GA, tape recording, USASOC History Office Classified Files, Fort Bragg, NC.

78   Roche interview.

79   Roche interview.

80   Roche interview.

81   Vasek interview.

82   Gutierrez interview.

83   Chief Warrant Officer 3 George Caper*, B Company, 1st Battalion, 160th Special Operations Aviation Regiment, interview

by Dr. Charles H. Briscoe, 10 September 2003, Fort Campbell, KY, tape recording, USASOC History Office Classified Files, Fort Bragg, NC.

84   Caper interview; Gutierrez interview.

85   Gutierrez interview; Vasek interview.

86   Staff Sergeant Jack Barker*, A Company, 3rd Battalion, 75th Ranger Regiment, interview by Lieutenant Colonel Robert W. Jones Jr., 22 October 2003, Fort Benning, GA, tape recording, USASOC History Office Classified Files, Fort Bragg, NC; Sergeant First Class Ronald Redmond*, A Company, 3rd Battalion, 75th Ranger Regiment, interview by Staff Sergeant Patrick Jennings, 22 October 2003, Fort Benning, GA, tape recording, USASOC History Office Classified Files, Fort Bragg, NC; Staff Sergeant Lamont Lawson*, A Company, 3rd Battalion, 75th Ranger Regiment, interview by Lieutenant Colonel Robert W. Jones Jr., 22 October 2003, Fort Benning, GA, tape recording, USASOC History Office Classified Files, Fort Bragg, NC.

87   Redmond interview; Barker interview.

88   Captain David Hess*, A Company, 3rd Battalion, 75th Ranger Regiment, interview by Lieutenant Colonel Robert W. Jones Jr., 22 October 2003, Fort Benning, GA, tape recording, USASOC History Office Classified Files, Fort Bragg, NC.

89   Barker interview.

90   David A. Converse, Operation IRAQI FREEDOM, Psychological Operations Field Collection Team, "Operational Assessment," n.d., USASOC History Office Classified Files, Fort Bragg, NC, 40.

91   Joel Hobbs*, former member B Company, 2nd Battlion, 75th Ranger Regiment, interview by Sergeant Landon Mavrelis, 18 May 2003, Hilla, Iraq, digital recording, USASOC History Office Classified Files, Fort Bragg, NC; Andrew Urvina*, former member B Company, 2nd Battlion, 75th Ranger Regiment, interview by Sergeant Landon Mavrelis, 18 May 2003, Hilla, Iraq, digital recording, USASOC History Office Classified Files, Fort Bragg, NC; Matt Ortega*, former member B Company, 2nd Battlion, 75th Ranger Regiment, interview by Sergeant Landon Mavrelis, 18 May 2003, Hilla, Iraq, digital recording,

USASOC History Office Classified Files, Fort Bragg, NC.

92 Converse, 40

93 Converse, 40; Richard S. Lowry, "The Battle of An Nasiriyah," *Military.com,* 28 April 2004, www.military.com/NewContent/0,13190,042804_Nasiriyah, 00.html? ESRC=army-a.nl.

94 Ellen Knickmeyer, "Allies Face Tough Battles at An Nasiriyah," *Associated Press,* 23 March 2003, www.drumbeat.mlaterz. net/March%202003/Allies%20face%20toug h%20battle%20at; Hobbs interview; General Vincent Brooks, U.S. Central Command, Operation Iraqi Freedom Briefing, 26 March 2003, www.centcom. mil/CENTCOMNews/Transcripts/20030326.htm.

95 "A story of An Nasiriyah," *GIReports.com,* www.gireports.com/page.cfm?Awards.

96 Hobbs interview; Urvina interview; Ortega interview.

97 Hobbs interview.

98 Hobbs interview.

99 Urvina interview.

100 Ortega interview.

101 Ortega interview.

102 Ortega interview.

103 Urvina interview.

104 Ortega interview.

105 "A story of An Nasiriyah."

106 Converse, 42.

107 Converse, 42.

108 Converse, 43.

109 Converse, 43.

110 Converse, 43.

111 General Tommy Franks, U.S. Central Command, transcript of 30 March 2003 Central Command briefing, Operational Update, www.centcom.mil/CENTCOMNews/News_Release. asp?NewsRelease=20030396.txt.

Chapter 7 Notes

1   Gregory Fontenot, E.J. Degen, and David Tohn, *On Point: The United States Army in Operation IRAQI FREEDOM* (Fort Leavenworth, KS: Combat Studies Institute Press, 2004), 262–65.

2   Fontenot et al., *On Point,* 267–73.

3   Fontenot et al., *On Point,* 273–76.

4   Fontenot et al., *On Point,* 276–77.

5   Fontenot et al., *On Point,* 277–82.

6   Fontenot et al., *On Point,* 282–87.

7   Fontenot et al., *On Point,* 287–93.

8   Fontenot et al., *On Point,* 294–95.

9   Fontenot et al., *On Point,* 294–99.

10 Fontenot et al., *On Point,* 299–304.

11 Fontenot et al., *On Point,* 310–11.

12 Fontenot et al., *On Point,* 312–21.

13 Royal Scots Dragoon Guards, "The SCOTS DG Battle Group during Op TELIC," http://www.army.mod.uk/scotsdg/ serving_regiment/serving_recent_ deployments.htm.

14 David J. Lynch, "HQ applauds Marines' advance," *USA Today,* 3 April 2003.

15 Evan Osnos and Hugh Dellios, "U.S. fights off Iraqi attacks," *Chicago Tribune,* 9 April 2003; Fontenot et al., *On Point,* 336.

16 Captain Gary Caldwell*, B Company, 2nd Battalion, 10th Special Forces Group, interview by Dr. Kenneth Finlayson, 24 June 2003, Fort Carson, CO, tape recording, USASOC History Office Classified Files, Fort Bragg, NC.

17 Caldwell interview, 24 June 2003.

18 Master Sergeant Peter Quinlan*, B Company, 2nd Battalion, 10th Special Forces Group, interview by Dr. Kenneth Finlayson, 24 June 2003, Fort Carson, CO, tape recording, USASOC History Office Classified Files, Fort Bragg, NC.

19 Quinlan interview

20 Captain Monty Dennings*, B Company, 2nd Battalion, 10th Special Forces Group, interview by Lieutenant Colonel Robert W. Jones Jr., 25 June 2003, Fort Carson, CO, tape recording, USASOC History Office Classified Files, Fort Bragg, NC.

21 "After Action Report," B Company, 2nd Battalion, 10th Special Forces Group, n.d., copy in USASOC History Office Classified Files, Fort Bragg, NC.

22 Captain Gary Caldwell*, B Company, 2nd Battalion, 10th Special Forces Group, interview by Dr. Kenneth Finlayson, 25 June 2003, Fort Carson, CO, tape recording, USASOC History Office Classified Files, Fort Bragg, NC.

23 Sergeant Major Sean Roark*, B Company, 2nd Battalion, 10th Special Forces Group, interview by Dr. Charles H. Briscoe, 3 July 2003, Fort Carson, CO, tape recording, USASOC History Office Classified Files, Fort Bragg, NC.

24 Dennings interview.

25 Dennings interview.

26 Caldwell interview, 25 June 2003.

27 "After Action Report," B Company, 2nd Battalion, 10th Special Forces Group.

28 Lieutenant Colonel Robert Waltemeyer, 3rd Battalion, 10th Special Forces Group, interview by Lieutenant Colonel Nathan Lowrey, 29 March 2003, Irbil, Iraq, digital recording, USASOC History Office Classified Files, Fort Bragg, NC; Major Myron Cassidy*, interview by Lieutenant Colonel Nathan Lowrey, 24 April 2003, Irbil, Iraq, digital recording, USASOC History Office Classified Files, Fort Bragg, NC; Major Fred Beaumont*, interview by Lieutenant Colonel Nathan Lowrey, 14 April 2003, Mosul, Iraq, digital recording, USASOC History Office Classified Files, Fort Bragg, NC.

29 Beaumont interview; Waltemeyer interview; Sergeant Major Travis Street*, interview by Lieutenant Colonel Nathan Lowrey, 16 April 2003, Mosul, Iraq, digital recording, USASOC History Office Classified Files, Fort Bragg, NC; Sergeant Major Jerry Tolman*, interview by Lieutenant Colonel Nathan Lowrey, 14 April 2003, Mosul, Iraq, digital recording, USASOC History Office Classified Files, Fort Bragg, NC.

29 Cassidy interview; Beaumont interview.

30 Sergeant First Class Thad Shelton*, interview by Lieutenant Colonel Nathan Lowrey, 16 April 2003, Mosul, Iraq, digital recording, USASOC History Office Classified Files, Fort Bragg, NC.

31 Shelton interview.

32 Shelton interview; Captain Ed Wood* and Chief Warrant Officer 2 Mel McArthur*, interview by Lieutenant Colonel Nathan Lowrey, 27 April 2003, Irbil, Iraq, digital recording, USASOC History Office Classified Files, Fort Bragg, NC; Major Earl Hoffman*, interview by Lieutenant Colonel Nathan Lowrey, 16 April 2003, Mosul, Iraq, digital recording, USASOC History Office Classified Files, Fort Bragg, NC.

33 Wood and McArthur interview; Shelton interview; Captain Marcus Sommers* and Master Sergeant Kyle Tippets*, interview by Lieutenant Colonel Nathan Lowrey, 27 April 2003, Irbil, Iraq, digital recording, USASOC History Office Classified Files, Fort Bragg, NC; Hoffman interview; Major Craig Houston*, interview by Lieutenant Colonel Nathan Lowrey, 27 April 2003, Irbil, Iraq digital recording, USASOC History Office Classified Files, Fort Bragg, NC; Captain Drake Fowler*, interview by Lieutenant Colonel Nathan Lowrey, 17 April 2003, Mosul, Iraq, digital recording, USASOC History Office Classified Files, Fort Bragg, NC; Captain Justin Spindler* and Master Sergeant Michael Cook*, interview by Lieutenant Colonel Nathan Lowrey, 28 April 2003, Irbil, Iraq, digital recording, USASOC History Office Classified Files, Fort Bragg, NC; Master Sergeant Boyd Innsbruck* and Sergeant First Class Neil Rain*, interview by Lieutenant Colonel Nathan Lowrey, 28 April 2003, Irbil, Iraq, digital recording, USASOC History Office Classified Files, Fort Bragg, NC.

34 Sommers and Tippets interview; Shelton interview; Hoffman interview; Major Earl Hoffman*, personal communication with Lieutenant Colonel Nathan Lowrey, 10 May 2003, transcript, USASOC History Office Classified Files, Fort Bragg, NC.

35 Spindler and Cook interview; Innsbruck and Rain interview.

36 Spindler and Cook interview; Innsbruck and Rain interview.

37 Shelton interview; Wood and McArthur interview; Sommers and Tippets interview.

38 Sommers and Tippets interview; Wood and McArthur interview.

39 Shelton interview; Wood and McArthur interview.

40 Shelton interview.

41 Shelton interview; Sommers and Tippets interview; Wood and McArthur interview.

42 Shelton interview; Wood and McArthur interview.

43 Shelton interview; Wood and McArthur interview; Sommers and Tippets interview.

44 Shelton interview; Wood and McArthur interview; Sommers and Thompson interview.

45 Hoffman interview; Sommers and Thompson interview; Shelton interview; Wood and McArthur interview.

46 Wood and McArthur interview.

47 Wood and McArthur interview; Shelton interview; Captain Ryan Barge*, interview by Lieutenant Colonel Nathan Lowrey, 16 April 2003, Mosul, Iraq, digital recording, USASOC History Office Classified Files, Fort Bragg, NC; Houston interview.

48 Wood and McArthur interview; Sommers and Thompson interview; Shelton interview.

49 Sommers and Thompson interview; Houston interview.

50 Forward Operating Base 102 SITREP #055, 6 April 2003, USASOC History Office Classified Files, Fort Bragg, NC; Shelton interview; Hoffman interview; Wood and McArthur interview.

51 Sommers and Thompson interview; Houston interview; Wood and McArthur interview; Sergeant Major Jack Watkins*, interview by Lieutenant Colonel Nathan Lowrey, 4 May 2003, Irbil, Iraq, digital recording, USASOC History Office Classified Files, Fort Bragg, NC.

52 Sergeant Ethan Gibson*, Specialist Cameron Owens*, Sergeant Chad Martin*, Staff Sergeant Mitchell Davis*, Sergeant Joshua London*, and Sergeant Don Travis*, Bravo Forward Support Company, 528th Special Operations Support Battalion, interview by A. Dwayne Aaron, 27 August 2003, Fort Bragg, NC, tape recording, USASOC History Office Classified Files, Fort Bragg, NC, hereafter cited as BFSC interview.

53 BFSC interview.

54 BFSC interview.

55 BFSC interview.

56 BFSC interview; Sergeant Major Chris Bond*, 528th Special Operations Support Battalion, interview by A. Dwayne Aaron, 13 May 2004, Fort Bragg, NC, recording, USASOC History Office Classified Files, Fort Bragg, NC.

57 BFSC interview.

58 BFSC interview.

59 Major Richard Geery*, "Operation Iraqi Freedom," Operations Summary for Bravo Forward Support Company, 528th Special Operations Support Battalion, 6 June 2003; Bond interview.

60 Chief Warrant Officer 3 Fern Roads*, First Lieutenant Carl Hancock*, Sergeant First Class Hal Andrews*, Staff Sergeant Dan Pulham*, Specialist Jeremy Thurston*, Specialist Dustin Crews*, Sergeant Arthur Bingham*, Specialist Walt Masters*, and Private First Class Jay Gomez, 528th Special Operations Support Battalion, interview by A. Dwayne Aaron, 18 June 2003, Fort Bragg, NC, tape recording, USASOC History Office Classified Files, Fort Bragg, NC.

61 Sergeant First Class Malcolm Gaston*, ODA 041, A Company, 2nd Battalion, 10th Special Forces Group, interview by Dr. Kenneth Finlayson, 25 June 2003, Fort Carson, CO, tape recording, USASOC History Office Classified Files, Fort Bragg, NC.

62 Gaston interview.

63 Gaston interview.

64 Lieutenant Colonel Michael Schellhammer, "Psychological Operations in Joint Special Operations Area–West," 2003, USSOCOM History Office, copy in USASOC History Office Classified Files, Fort Bragg, NC.

65 Schellhammer, "Psychological Operations."

66 Schellhammer, "Psychological Operations."

67 Schellhammer, "Psychological Operations."

68 Schellhammer, "Psychological Operations."

69 Schellhammer, "Psychological Operations."

70 Schellhammer, "Psychological Operations."

71 Colonel Jerry Vaughn, interview by Dr. Kenneth Finlayson, 13 August 2003, MacDill Air Force Base, FL, tape recording, USASOC History Office Classified Files, Fort Bragg, NC.

72 Lieutenant Colonel David Knapp, "Task Force Seminole," 2003, manuscript, USASOC History Office Classified Files, Fort Bragg, NC.

73 Knapp, "Task Force Seminole."

74 Vaughn interview.

75 Knapp, "Task Force Seminole."

76 Vaughn interview.

77 Christian Lowe, "Secret Mission revealed—Florida Guard fought alongside Special Forces as war began," *Army Times,* 15 September 2003, 22.

78 Lowe, "Secret Mission revealed," 22.

79 Lowe, "Secret Mission revealed ," 22.

80 Major Boyd Sinclair*, Advanced Operating Base 570, 3rd Battalion, 5th Special Forces Group, interview by Lieutenant Colonel Dennis Mroczkowski, 4 May 2003, Baghdad, Iraq, digital recording, USASOC History Office Classified Files, Fort Bragg, NC.

81 Lieutenant Colonel Timothy Williams, 3rd Battalion, 5th Special Forces Group, interview by Lieutenant Colonel Dennis P. Mroczkowski, 11 April 2003, Baghdad, Iraq, digital recording, USASOC History Office Classified Files, Fort Bragg, NC.

82 Sinclair interview; Williams interview.

83 Sinclair interview; Captain Al Pollard*, ODA 572, 3rd Battalion, 5th Special Forces Group, interview by Lieutenant Colonel Dennis P. Mroczkowski, 13 April 2003, Baghdad, Iraq, digital recording, USASOC History Office Classified Files, Fort Bragg, NC.

84 Pollard interview; Sergeant First Class Wilson Wynn*, ODB 570, 3rd Battalion, 5th Special Forces Group, interview by Lieutenant Colonel Dennis P. Mroczkowski, 12 April 2003, Baghdad, Iraq, digital recording, USASOC History Office Classified Files, Fort Bragg, NC.

85 SSG Juan Nahuel*, Advanced Operating Base 570, 3rd Battalion, 5th Special Forces Group, interview by Lieutenant Colonel Dennis Mroczkowski, 4 May 2003, Baghdad, Iraq, digital recording, USASOC History Office Classified Files, Fort Bragg, NC; Sinclair interview.

86 Sergeant First Class Louis Kowalski*, ODA 572, 3rd Battalion, 5th Special Forces Group, interview by Lieutenant Colonel Dennis P. Mroczkowski, 14 April 2003, Baghdad, Iraq, digital recording, USASOC History Office Classified Files, Fort Bragg, NC.

87 Sergeant First Class Jacob Vasili*, ODA 572, 3rd Battalion, 5th Special Forces Group, interview by Lieutenant Colonel Dennis P. Mroczkowski, 14 April 2003, Baghdad, Iraq, digital recording, USASOC History Office Classified Files, Fort Bragg, NC; Sergeant First Class Lee Forrest*, ODB 570, 3rd Battalion, 5th Special Forces Group, interview by Lieutenant Colonel Dennis P. Mroczkowski, 12 April 2003, Baghdad, Iraq, digital recording, USASOC History Office Classified Files, Fort Bragg, NC.

88 Staff Sergeant Joel Percy*, ODA 572, 3rd Battalion, 5th Special Forces Group, interview by Lieutenant Colonel Dennis P. Mroczkowski, 13 April 2003, Baghdad, Iraq, digital recording, USASOC History Office Classified Files, Fort Bragg, NC.

89 Warrant Officer 1 Bill Brande*, ODA 572, 3rd Battalion, 5th Special Forces Group, interview by Lieutenant Colonel Dennis P. Mroczkowski, 14 April 2003, Baghdad, Iraq, digital recording, USASOC History Office Classified Files, Fort Bragg, NC; Percy interview.

90 Vasili interview.

91 Forrest interview; Sergeant Major Thad Berino*, ODB 570, 3rd Battalion, 5th Special Forces Group, interview by Lieutenant Colonel Dennis P. Mroczkowski, 12 April 2003, Baghdad, Iraq, digital recording, USASOC History Office Classified Files, Fort Bragg, NC.

92 Kowalski interview; Forrest interview.

93 Kowalski interview; Brande interview.

94 Vasili interview; Brande interview.

95 Wynn interview.

96 Sergeant First Class Bruce Kroll*, ODB 570, 3rd Battalion, 5th Special Forces Group, interview by Lieutenant Colonel Dennis P. Mroczkowski, 12 April 2003, Baghdad, Iraq, digital recording, USASOC History Office Classified Files, Fort Bragg, NC.

97 Brande interview.

98 Kowalski interview.

99 Nahuel interview.

100 Forrest interview.

101 Nahuel interview; Pollard interview.

102 Kowalski interview; Brande interview; Berino interview; Nahuel interview.

103 Sinclair interview.

104 Berino interview.

105 Berino interview; Percy interview.

106 Kowalski interview.

107 Pollard interview; Berino interview.

108 Brande interview.

109 Wynn interview.

110 Wynn interview; Berino interview.

111 Forrest interview.

112 Forrest interview.

113 Kowalski interview.

114 Wynn interview.

115 Kroll interview; Berino interview.

116 Brande interview; Vasili interview.

117 Brande interview.

118 Brande interview; Nahuel interview.

119 Pollard interview; Vasili interview.

120 Forrest interview; Wynn interview.

121 Sinclair interview; Berino interview; Wynn interview.

122 John Keegan, *The Iraq War* (New York: Alfred A. Knopf, 2004), 177; Major Jerry Baxter*, AOB 560, 2nd Battalion, 5th Special Forces Group, interview by Lieutenant Colonel Dennis P. Mrocz-kowski, 23 May 2003, Ali As-Salim Air Base, Kuwait, digital recording, USASOC History Office Classified Files, Fort Bragg, NC; Williamson Murray and Robert H. Scales Jr., *The Iraq War: A Military History* (Cambridge, MA: Belknap Press of Harvard University Press, 2003), 147.

123 Baxter interview.

124 Baxter interview; Murray and Scales, *The Iraq War*, 145, 150–51.

125 Baxter interview.

126 Lieutenant Colonel Christopher Conner, 2nd Battalion, 5th Special Forces Group, interview by Lieutenant Colonel Dennis P. Mroczkowski, 22 May 2003, Ali As-Salim Air Base, Kuwait, digital recording, USASOC History Office Classified Files, Fort Bragg, NC; Baxter interview.

127 Conner interview; Baxter interview.

128 Fontenot et al., *On Point*, 215–17; Chief Warrant Officer 3 Sidney Schwarzkopf*, ODA 544, 2nd Battalion, 5th Special Forces Group, interview by Lieutenant Colonel Dennis P. Mroczkowski, 15 May 2003, Najaf, Iraq, digital recording, USASOC History Office Classified Files, Fort Bragg, NC; Captain Roy Clinger*, ODA 544, 2nd Battalion, 5th Special Forces Group, interview by Lieutenant Colonel Dennis P. Mroczkowski, 15 May 2003, Najaf, Iraq, digital recording, USASOC History Office Classified Files, Fort Bragg, NC; Charles Recknagel, "Iraq: Washington Arrests U. S.-Appointed Mayor of Al-Najaf for Abuse of Power," Radio Free Europe/Radio Liberty, www.rferl.org; Linda Robinson, *Masters of Chaos: The Secret History of the Special Forces* (New York: PublicAffairs Books, 2004), 253–59.

129 Schwarzkopf interview; Clinger interview.

130 Clinger interview.

131 Schwarzkopf interview; Tom Hundley, "Iraq's Destiny Tied to Mosque Politics," *Chicago Tribune*, 18 May 2003; Sergeant First Class Mark Combs*, ODA 544, 2nd Battalion, 5th Special Forces Group, interview by Lieutenant Colonel Dennis P. Mroczkowski, 15 May 2003, Najaf, Iraq, digital recording, USASOC History Office Classified Files, Fort Bragg, NC; Clinger interview.

132 Sergeant First Class Tim Kreiler*, ODA 544, 2nd Battalion, 5th Special Forces Group, interview by Lieutenant Colonel Dennis P. Mroczkowski, 15 May 2003, Najaf, Iraq, digital recording, USASOC History Office Classified Files, Fort Bragg, NC; Combs interview; Schwarzkopf interview; Clinger interview.

133 Clinger interview.

134 Schwarzkopf interview; Clinger interview.

135 Schwarzkopf interview; Clinger interview; Robinson, *Master of Chaos*, 263.

136 Clinger interview.

137 Clinger interview; Schwarzkopf interview.

138 Clinger interview; Schwarzkopf interview.

139 Schwarzkopf interview.

140 Clinger interview; Schwarzkopf interview.

141 Clinger interview.

142 Schwarzkopf interview.

143 Combs interview.

144 Clinger interview.

145 Clinger interview; Recknagel, "Iraq: Washington Arrest U.S.-Appointed Mayor of Al-Najaf for Abuse of Power;" Coalition Provisional Authority, "Press Release: Interim Governor of Najaf," 30 June 2003, PR No. 008, www.iraqcoalition.org/ pressreleases/30June03PR8Najaf.html; Rajiv Chandrasekaran and Peter Finn, "'Sidewinder' seeks Saddam loyalists," *The Washington Post,* 1 July 2003; "Najaf's mayor ousted by U.S.," *Baltimore Sun,* 1 July 2003.

146 Murray and Scales, *The Iraq War,* 204; John Keegan, *The Iraq War,* 189; 3rd Battalion, 75th Ranger Regiment, "Battle Summary for Objective Lynx (Haditha Dam), 31 March–9 April 2003," 17 April 2003, USASOC History Office Classified Files, Fort Bragg, NC.

147 Captain Dirk Dillard*, B Company, 3rd Battalion, 75th Ranger Regiment, interview by Sergeant First Class Patrick Jennings, 23 October 2003, Fort Benning, GA, digital recording, USASOC History Office Classified Files, Fort Bragg, NC.

148 Dillard interview.

149 Dillard interview.

150 Dillard interview; Sergeant First Class James Lauder*, B Company, 3rd Battalion, 75th Ranger Regiment, interview by Sergeant First Class Patrick Jennings, 23 October 2003, Fort Benning, GA, digital recording, USASOC History Office Classified Files, Fort Bragg, NC.

151 First Lieutenant Gary Whittle*, B Company, 3rd Battalion, 75th Ranger Regiment, interview by Lieutenant Colonel Robert W. Jones Jr., 23 October 2003, Fort Benning, GA, tape recording, USASOC History Office Classified Files, Fort Bragg,
NC; Captain Jake Humbolsky*, B Company, 3rd Battalion, 75th Ranger Regiment, interview by Lieutenant Colonel Robert W. Jones Jr., 20 July 2005, Fort Bragg, NC, interview notes, USASOC History Office Classified Files, Fort Bragg, NC.

152 Chief Warrant Officer 4 Mark Willington*, B Company, 1st Battalion, 160th Special Operations Aviation Regiment, interview by James Schroder, 16 March 2004, Fort Campbell, KY, tape recording and transcripts, USASOC History Office Classified Files, Fort Bragg, NC.

153 Chief Warrant Officer 3 George Caper*, B Company, 1st Battalion, 160th Special Operations Aviation Regiment, interview by Dr. Charles H. Briscoe, 10 September 2003, Fort Campbell, KY, tape recording and transcripts, USASOC History Office Classified Files, Fort Bragg, NC.

154 Whittle interview.

155 Staff Sergeant James Narrow*, B Company, 3rd Battalion, 75th Ranger Regiment, interview by Dr. Charles H. Briscoe, 23 October 2003, Fort Benning, GA, tape recording, USASOC History Office Classified Files, Fort Bragg, NC.

156 Narrow interview; Whittle interview.

157 Whittle interview.

158 Whittle interview.

159 Narrow interview.

160 Narrow interview.

161 Narrow interview; Dillard interview.

162 Captain Josh Truman*, C Company, 3rd Battalion, 75th Ranger Regiment, interview by Dr. Charles H. Briscoe, 23 October 2003, Fort Benning, GA, tape recording, USASOC History Office Classified Files, Fort Bragg, NC.

163 Truman interview.

164 Truman interview.

165 Humbolsky interview; Lauder interview.

166 Lauder interview; Humbolsky interview.

167 Humbolsky interview.

168 Humbolsky interview; Lauder interviews.

169 Dillard interview.

170 Dillard interview.

171 Truman interview.

172 Lauder interview; Humbolsky interview.

173 Dillard interview.

174 Lauder interview.

175 Captain Timothy Donald*, A Company, 2nd Battalion, 160th Special Operations Aviation Regiment, interview by Dr. Charles H. Briscoe, 12 September 2003, Fort Campbell, KY, tape recording, USASOC History Office Classified Files, Fort Bragg, NC; Joyce Shannon, "Neighbors seek to help soldier injured in combat in Iraq," *Tribune-Review*, 26 May 2003.

176 Dillard interview.

177 Chief Warrant Officer 4 Doug Carter*, B Company, 1st Battalion, 160th Special Operations Aviation Regiment, interview by James Schroder, 17 March 2003, Fort Campbell, KY, tape recording, USASOC History Office Classified Files, Fort Bragg, NC.

178 Willington interview.

179 Caper interview.

180 Willington interview; Caper interview.

181 Willington interview; Caper interview.

182 Willington interview; Caper interview.

183 Willington interview; Caper interview.

184 Willington interview; Caper interview.

185 Willington interview; Caper interview.

186 Willington interview; Caper interview.

187 U.S. Central Command Operation Iraqi Freedom Briefing, 2 April 2003, transcript available at http://www.centcom.mil/ CENTCOMNews, Release Number 03-04-25.

188 World Commission on Dams, "Dam Statistics: Africa and the Middle East Regions," December 1999, www.dams.org/ kbase/consultations/afrme/dam_stats_ eng.htm.

189 Sergeant First Class Karl Compton*, Sergeant First Class Charles Atlas*, Sergeant First Class Earl Hampton*, and Sergeant First Class Kevin Goodin*, E Company, 96th Civil Affairs Battalion, interview by Michael R. Mullins, 23 February 2004, Fort Bragg, NC, tape recording, USASOC History Office Classified Files, Fort Bragg, NC, hereafter cited as 96th CAB interview.

190 96th CAB interview.

191 96th CAB interview.

192 96th CAB interview.

193 96th CAB interview.

194 96th CAB interview.

195 U.S. Army Corps of Engineers, "Corps 'TeleEngineering' Contributes to the War Fight," www.usace.army.mil/inet/ functions/cw/hot_topics/teleengineering. htm.

196 96th CAB interview.

197 Fontenot et al., *On Point*, 154–59.

198 Dana Priest, William Booth, and Susan Schmidt, "A Broken Body, a Broken Story, Pieced Together," http://www.washington-post.com/ac2/wp-dyn/A2760-2003Jun?la; Chief Warrant Officer 4 Jason Holt* and Captain Theodore Shaffer*, 1st Battalion, 160th Special Operations Aviation Regiment, interview by James Schroder and Dr. Kenneth Finlayson, 16 March 2004, Fort Campbell, KY, tape recording, USASOC History Office Classified Files, Fort Bragg, NC.

199 Major Duncan Norman*, 2nd Battalion, 5th Special Forces Group, telephone interview by Dr. Kenneth Finlayson, 9 November 2005, Fort Bragg, NC, notes, USASOC History Office Classified Files, Fort Bragg, NC.

200 Master Sergeant Mark Wohl*, ODA 553, 2nd Battalion, 5th Special Forces Group, interview by Lieutenant Colonel Dennis P. Mroczkowski, 3 May 2003, Baghdad, Iraq, digital recording, USASOC History Office Classified Files, Fort Bragg, NC; Sergeant First Class Buck Spruce*, ODA 553, 2nd Battalion, 5th Special Forces Group, interview by Lieutenant Colonel Dennis P. Mroczkowski, 3 May 2003, Baghdad, Iraq, digital recording, USASOC History Office Classified Files, Fort Bragg, NC; Chief Warrant Officer 4 Randall Ramsey*, 1st Battalion, 160th Special Operations Aviation Regiment, interview by James Schroder and Dr. Kenneth Finlayson, 30 April 2004, Fort Campbell, KY, tape recording, USASOC History Office Files, Fort Bragg, NC.

201 Ramsey interview.

202 Ramsey interview.

203 Major Mark Mohan*, 1st Battalion, 160th Special Operations Aviation Regiment, interview by James Schroder and Dr. Kenneth Finlayson, 30 April 2004, Fort

Campbell, KY, tape recording, USASOC History Office Classified Files, Fort Bragg, NC; Colonel Joseph Votel, 75th Ranger Regiment, interview by Steven D. Cage, 25 April 2003, Baghdad, Iraq, tape recording, USASOC History Office Classified Files, Fort Bragg, NC.

204 Chief Warrant Officer 4 Daniel Clement*, 1st Battalion 160th Special Operations Aviation Regiment, interview by Dr. Charles H. Briscoe, 11 September 2003, Fort Campbell, KY, tape recording, USASOC History Office Classified Files, Fort Bragg, NC.

205 Ramsey interview; Clement interview.

206 Mohan interview.

207 Mohan interview.

208 Holt and Shaffer interview.

209 Holt and Shaffer interview.

210 Brigadier General Vincent Brooks, U.S. Central Command Press Briefing, Doha, Qatar, 2 April 2003, transcript, USASOC History Office, Fort Bragg, NC.

211 Chief Warrant Officer 4 Thomas Brady*, 1st Battalion, 160th Special Operations Aviation Regiment, interview by Dr. Kenneth Finlayson, 29 April 2004, Fort Campbell, KY, tape recording, USASOC History Office Classified Files, Fort Bragg, NC.

212 Brady interview.

213 "E-3 Sentry Aircraft Fact Sheet," http://www.af.mil/factsheets/factsheet_print.asp?fsID=98&page=1

214 Brady interview.

215 Chief Warrant Officer 3 Richard Hoyt*, 1st Battalion, 160th Special Operations Aviation Regiment, interview by Dr. Charles H. Briscoe, 11 September 2003, Fort Campbell, KY, tape recording, USASOC History Office Classified Files, Fort Bragg, NC.

216 Sergeant Jeffery Landis*, 1st Battalion, 160th Special Operations Aviation Regiment, interview by James Schroder, 29 April 2004, Fort Campbell, KY, tape recording USASOC History Office Classified Files, Fort Bragg, NC.

217 Brady interview.

218 Hoyt interview.

219 Chief Warrant Officer 4 Walter Florenson*, 1st Battalion, 160th Special Operations Aviation Regiment, interview by Dr. Charles H. Briscoe, 11 September 2003, Fort Campbell, KY, tape recording, USASOC History Office Classified Files, Fort Bragg, NC.

220 Brady interview.

221 Brady interview.

222 Hoyt interview.

223 Robert W. Black, *Rangers in World War II* (New York: Random House, 1992), 113.

224 Fontenot et al., *On Point*, 225; Lieutenant Colonel Patrick Warren and Major Keith Barclay, "Operation Airborne Dragon, Northern Iraq," *Military Review*, November–December 2003, 11–14.

225 Votel interview; Captain Sean Carlson*, C Company, 2nd Battalion, 70th Armor Regiment, interview by Steven D. Cage, 13 April 2003, Mission Support Site Grizzly, Iraq, tape recording, USASOC History Office Classified Files, Fort Bragg, NC.

226 Captain Sean Carlson*, C Company, 2nd Battalion, 70th Armor Regiment, interview by Lieutenant Colonel Robert W. Jones Jr., 5 October 2004, Seattle, WA, digital recording, USASOC History Office Classified Files, Fort Bragg, NC.

227 C Company, 2nd Battalion, 70th Armor Regiment, is normally assigned to the 3rd Brigade, 1st Armored Division, at Fort Riley, Kansas; however, prior to the start of Operation IRAQI FREEDOM, the 2nd Battalion, 70th Armor Regiment, deployed to Kuwait and was attached to the 3rd Infantry Division until it was attached to the 75th Ranger Regiment.

228 Sergeant Abe Thomas*, C Company, 2nd Battalion, 70th Armor Regiment, interview by Steven D. Cage, 13 April 2003, Mission Support Site Grizzly, Iraq, tape recording, USASOC History Office Classified Files, Fort Bragg, NC.

229 Fontenot et al., *On Point*, 253.

230 Thomas interview; Carlson interview, 5 October 2004.

231 Mike Heronemus, "Valor earns medals," *Fort Riley Post*, Vol. 47, No. 15, 16 April 2004, 1–2.

232 Carlson interview, 13 April 2003.

233 75th Ranger Regiment Briefing, "Attack on OBJ Badger," 26 August 2003, USASOC History Office Classified Files, Fort Bragg, NC; Heronemus, "Valor earns medals," 1–2.

234 Votel interview.

235 Chief Warrant Officer 3 James Nattier*, 2nd Battalion, 160th Special Operations Aviation Regiment, interview by James Schroder, 26 April 2004, Fort Campbell, KY, tape recording, USASOC History Office Classified Files, Fort Bragg, NC.

236 Nattier interview.

237 Nattier interview.

238 Nattier interview.

239 Nattier interview; Chief Warrant Officer 2 Barry Littleton*, 2nd Battalion, 160th Special Operations Aviation Regiment, interview by James Schroder, 3 May 2004, Fort Campbell, KY, tape recording, USASOC History Office Classified Files, Fort Bragg, NC; Chief Warrant Officer 3 Stanley Branson*, 2nd Battalion, 160th Special Operations Aviation Regiment, interview by Dr. Kenneth Finlayson, 29 April 2004, Fort Campbell, KY, tape recording, USASOC History Office Classified Files, Fort Bragg, NC.

240 Nattier interview; Littleton interview.

241 Branson interview.

242 Nattier interview; Littleton interview.

243 Chief Warrant Officer 2 Steve Bozeman*, 2nd Battalion, 160th Special Operations Aviation Regiment, interview by James Schroder, 28 April 2004, Fort Campbell, KY, tape recording, USASOC History Office Classified Files, Fort Bragg, NC.

244 Nattier interview; Littleton interview.

245 Bozeman interview.

246 Nattier interview; Littleton interview; Bozeman interview.

Chapter 8 Notes

1 Gregory Fontenot, E.J. Degen, and David Tohn, *On Point: The United States Army in Operation IRAQI FREEDOM* (Fort Leavenworth, KS: Combat Studies Institute Press, 2004), 339–340.

2 Command Sergeant Major Jake Lincoln*, U.S. Special Operations Command Central, interview by Dr. Kenneth Finlayson, 12 August 2003, MacDill Air Force Base, FL, digital recording, USASOC History Office Classified Files, Fort Bragg, NC; Staff Sergeant David Agua*, ODA 912, A Company, 1st Battalion, 19th Special Forces Group, interview by Lieutenant Colonel Robert W. Jones Jr., 2 October 2004, Buckley, WA, digital recording, USASOC History Office Classified Files, Fort Bragg, NC.

3 Agua interview.

4 Lincoln interview.

5 Secretary of Defense, "Public Affairs Guidance on Embedding Media During Possible Future Operations/Deployments in the U.S. Central Command Area of Responsibility," 10 February 2003, USASOC History Office Classified Files, Fort Bragg, NC.

6 Secretary of Defense, "Public Affairs Guidance."

7 Lieutenant Commander Kyle Andersen*, interview by Dr. Charles H. Briscoe and Dr. Kenneth Finlayson, 12 August 2003, Tampa, FL, tape recording, USASOC History Office Classified Files, Fort Bragg, NC.

8 Lieutenant Commander Kyle Andersen*, "SOCCENT PAO Briefing," 12 August 2003, copy in USASOC History Office Classified Files, Fort Bragg, NC.

9 Andersen interview.

10 Lieutenant Colonel Tim Nye, interview by Dr. Charles H. Briscoe, 12 August 2003, Tampa, FL, tape recording, USASOC History Office Classified Files, Fort Bragg, NC.

11 Andersen interview.

12 Nye interview.

13 Andersen interview; Donald H. Rumsfeld and General Richard B. Myers, "DOD News Briefing," 21 March 2003, 1036PST; James Dao, "Navy Seals Easily Seize Two Oil Sites," *The New York Times,* 22 March 2003.

14 Nye interview.

15 "Marines advance into Tikrit," *CNN.com/ World,* 13 April 2003, http://www.cnn.com/2003/WORLD/meast/04/13/sprj.irq.

tikrit/; Rajiv Chandrasekaran, "Major Combat Is 'Over' as Tikrit Falls—Mission Shifts To Restoring Order, Finding Militiamen," *The Washington Post*, 15 April 2003, sec. A, 1.

16 Jim Garamone, "Coalition Focuses on Pockets of Resistance," *American Forces Information Service,* 15 April 2003, http://www.defenselink.mil/news/Apr2003/n04152003_200304151.html; Jim Garamone, "Coalition Forces Still Conducting Operations," *American Forces Information Service,* 16 April 2003, http://www.defenselink.mil/news/Apr2003/n04162003_200304164.html; Jim Garamone, "Another Regime Leader Captured; Coalition Forces Transition," *American Forces Information Service,* 18 April 2003, http://www.defenselink.mil/news/Apr2003/n04182003_200304181.html; Peter Baker, "U.S. Forces Will Redeploy Into 3 Zones—Marines to Occupy Southern Iraq as Army Takes Over North—General Will Oversee Capital," *The Washington Post,* 16 April 2003, sec. A, 31; "U.S. Army Special Operations Command: Crisis Action Team Update 29 April 2003," CD-ROM, 29 April 2003, USASOC History Office Classified Files, Fort Bragg, NC.

17 Major Dustin Hilburn*, 422nd Civil Affairs Battalion, interview by Lieutenant Colonel Dennis J. Cahill, 11 May 2003, Baghdad, Iraq, summary transcription, USASOC History Office Classified Files, Fort Bragg, NC.

18 Major Bronson*, Captain Tailor*, Sergeant First Class Wes Henderson*, Staff Sergeant Ahmen*, Sergeant Colton*, and Specialist Addison*, Direct Support Team 3, 422nd Civil Affairs Battalion, interview by Lieutenant Colonel Dennis J. Cahill, May 2003, Baghdad, Iraq, summary transcription, USASOC History Office Classified Files, Fort Bragg, NC, hereafter cited as DST 3 interview.

19 DST 3 interview.

20 DST 3 interview.

21 DST 3 interview.

22 DST 3 interview; Captain Merino*, Direct Support Team 4, 422nd Civil Affairs Battalion, interview by Lieutenant Colonel Dennis J. Cahill, 12 May 2003, Baghdad, Iraq, summary transcription, USASOC

History Office Classified Files, Fort Bragg, NC; Hilburn interview.

23 DST 3 interview.

24 Specialist Mason T. Lowery, "Civil Affairs team locates massive Iraqi weapons cache," *USASOC News Service*, Release 030401-01, 1 April 2003, www.soc.mil/News/releases/03APR/030401-01.htm.

25 DST 3 interview.

26 DST 3 interview.

27 Hilburn interview; Merino interview.

28 Merino interview.

29 Hilburn interview; Lieutenant Colonel R. Alan King, "422nd Soldiers Receive Bronze Star Medals with 'V,'" *Scroll & Sword: The Journal and Newsletter of the Civil Affairs Association,* Vol. 56, Issue 3 (Winter 2003), 8; Michael R. Gordon, "Seeking Calm in the Chaos," *CNN.com/WORLD,* 12 April 2003, www.cnn.com/2003/WORLD/meast/04/12/nyt.gordon/index.html.

30 King, "422nd Soldiers Receive Bronze Star;" Gordon, "Seeking Calm in the Chaos;" Lieutenant Colonel R. Alan King, 422nd Civil Affairs Battalion, interview by Staff Sergeant Patrick Jennings, 1 May 2003, Baghdad, Iraq, digital recording, USASOC History Office Classified Files, Fort Bragg, NC.

31 Lieutenant Colonel Gerard Healy, "Greensboro Fire Captain Evaluates Baghdad's Fire Dept," *Defend America,* 30 April 2003, www.defendamerica.mil/articles/apr2003/a043003b.html; Major Bob Glass*, 422nd Civil Affairs Battalion, interview by Major Paul Landry, 13 May 2003, Baghdad, Iraq, digital recording, USASOC History Office Classified Files, Fort Bragg, NC.

32 Glass interview.

33 Sergeant Frank N. Pellegrini, "Army Reserve Civil Affairs Trains New Baghdad Police," *Defend America,* 13 May 2003, www.defendamerica.mil/articles/may2003/a051303c.html; Major Baughn Christian*, 422nd Civil Affairs Battalion, interview by Major Paul Landry, 12 May 2003, Baghdad, Iraq, digital recording, USASOC History Office Classified Files, Fort Bragg, NC.

34 Pellegrini; Druin interview.

35 Hilburn interview.

36 Hilburn interview; Jim Garamone, "Civil Affairs Teams Help Put Baghdad Back Together," *American Forces Information Service*, 4 May 2003, www.defenselink. mil/news/May2003/n05042003_200305042.html.

37 Sergeant Chris Mercer*, 422nd Civil Affairs Battalion, interview by Sergeant First Class Dan Moriarty, 28 April 2003, Baghdad, Iraq, digital recording, USASOC History Office Classified Files, Fort Bragg, NC; Hamil R. Harris, "From Md Law To Postwar Iraq Lawlessness," *The Washington Post*, 28 April 2003, sec. B, 1.

38 Colonel Warner J. Anderson, Public Health Team, 352nd Civil Affairs Command, interview by Major Paul Landry, 1 May 2003, Baghdad, Iraq, digital recording and transcript, USASOC History Office Classified Files Archives, Fort Bragg, NC.

39 Anderson interview.

40 Anderson interview.

41 Anderson interview.

42 Anderson interview.

43 Anderson interview.

44 Anderson interview.

45 Major Jim Downing*, B Company, 13th Psychological Operations Battalion (EPW/CI), interview by Lieutenant Colonel Charles P. Pierett, 1 June 2003, Camp Bucca, Umm Qasr, Iraq, summary transcription, USASOC History Office Classified Files, Fort Bragg, NC.

46 Downing interview; Coalition Forces Land Component Command Public Affairs Office, "Enemy Prisoner of War Camps Named for FDNY 9/11 Heroes," *Defend America*, 1 May 2003, www.defendamerica.mil/articles/may2003/a050103c.html.

47 David Josar, "Psyops unit works to win trust, get information from enemy POWs," *Stars and Stripes European Edition*, 15 April 2003.

48 Josar, "Psyops unit works to win trust."

49 Downing interview.

50 Specialist Craig Meyers*, U.S. Army Reserve public affairs officer, "U.S. Army Spc. Ben Watkins: Desert DJ plays for Iraqi POWs," *Defend America*, www.defendamerica.mil/profiles/apr2003/pro43003a.html; Saul Hudson, "Captive

Soldiers Riot Almost Daily," *Information Clearing House*, www.informationclearinghouse.info/article2929.htm; Information Paper, "Defining the Critical Role and Versatility of Enemy Prisoner of War/Civilian Internee (EPW/CI) PSYOP Forces," n.d., USASOC History Office Classified Files, Fort Bragg, NC, 5–6.

51 Information Paper, "Defining the Critical Role," 5; Downing interview.

52 Josar, "PSYOPs unit works to win trust;" Information Paper, "Defining the Critical Role," 5.

53 13th Psychological Operations Battalion, "EPW Interview Summaries," n.d., copy in USASOC History Office Classified Files, Fort Bragg, NC.

54 Information Paper, "Defining the Critical Role," 5.

55 Downing interview.

56 "Freed Iraqi POWs leave camp bashing Saddam and cheering Bush," *The Associated Press*, 28 April 2003, www.charleston.net/stories/042803/ter_28pows.shtml.

57 Michael Ware, "The Turks Enter Iraq," *Time.com*, 24 April 2003; David Rohde, "U.S. Says Turks Tried to Smuggle Arms into Northern Iraq City," *The New York Times*, 27 April 2003.

58 Lieutenant Commander Garth Benson*, Headquarters, U.S. Special Operations Command Central, interview by Dr. Kenneth Finlayson, 12 August 2003, MacDill Air Force Base, FL, tape recording, USASOC History Office Classified Files, Fort Bragg, NC.

59 Benson interview.

60 Major Michael Giroux*, 3rd Battalion, 10th Special Forces Group, "FOB 103 Operations Summary," n.d., USASOC History Office Classified Files, Fort Bragg, NC.

61 Giroux, "FOB 103 Operations Summary."

62 Giroux, "FOB 103 Operations Summary;" Staff Sergeant Adam Owens*, ODA 084, 3rd Battalion, 10th Special Forces Group, interview by Dr. Kenneth Finlayson, 24 June 2003, Fort Carson, CO, tape recording, USASOC History Office Classified Files, Fort Bragg, NC.

63 Giroux, "FOB 103 Operations Summary."

64 Giroux, "FOB 103 Operations Summary."

65   Giroux, "FOB 103 Operations Summary."

66   Giroux, "FOB 103 Operations Summary."

67   Giroux, "FOB 103 Operations Summary."

68   Giroux, "FOB 103 Operations Summary."

69   Giroux, "FOB 103 Operations Summary;" Owens interview.

70   Giroux, "FOB 103 Operations Summary."

71   Giroux, "FOB 103 Operations Summary."

72   Giroux, "FOB 103 Operations Summary."

73   Giroux, "FOB 103 Operations Summary."

74   Giroux, "FOB 103 Operations Summary."

75   2nd Battalion, 10th Special Forces Group, "Recommendation for Valorous Unit Award," 2003, USASOC History Office Classified Files, Fort Bragg, NC.

76   2nd Battalion, 10th Special Forces Group, "Recommendation for Valorous Unit Award."

77   2nd Battalion, 10th Special Forces Group, "Recommendation for Valorous Unit Award."

78   Chief Warrant Officer 3 Seth Folsom*, ODA 042, A Company, 2nd Battalion, 10th Special Forces Group, interview by Dr. Kenneth Finlayson, 25 June 2003, Fort Carson, CO, tape recording, USASOC History Office Classified Files, Fort Bragg, NC.

79   Captain Mark Donaldson*, ODA 051, B Company, 2nd Battalion, 10th Special Forces Group, interview by Lieutenant Colonel Nathan Lowery, 17 April 2003, Mosul, Iraq, tape recording, USASOC History Office Classified Files, Fort Bragg, NC.

80   Donaldson interview.

81   Donaldson interview.

82   Donaldson interview.

83   Donaldson interview.

84   Donaldson interview.

85   Colonel Charles T. Cleveland, 10th Special Forces Group, interview by Dr. Kenneth Finlayson, 26 June 2003, Fort Carson, CO, tape recording, USASOC History Office Classified Files, Fort Bragg, NC.

86   Cleveland interview, 26 June 2003.

87   Donaldson interview.

88   Lieutenant Colonel Paul Gallo, 10th Special Forces Group, interview by Lieutenant Colonel Robert W. Jones Jr., 20 November 2004, Raleigh, NC, digital recording, USASOC History Office Classified Files, Fort Bragg, NC.

89   Colonel Charles T. Cleveland, 10th Special Forces Group, interview by Dr. Charles H. Briscoe, 20 February 2004, Fort Bragg, NC, tape recording, USASOC History Office Classified Files, Fort Bragg, NC.

90   Cleveland interview; Paul Watson, "U.S. Troops in Mosul Battle Mob," *Los Angeles Times*, 16 April 2003, sec. A, 3; Gallo interview; Nye interview.

91   Gallo interview; 10th Special Forces Group, "Task Force Viking Information Operations After Action Review," 16 June 2003, Fort Carson, CO; Nye interview.

92   10th Special Forces Group, "Task Force Viking;" Rajiv Chandrasekaran, "Major Combat Is 'Over' as Tikrit Falls."

93   Gallo interview; 10th Special Forces Group, "Task Force Viking."

94   Gallo interview; 10th Special Forces Group, "Task Force Viking;" Mary Beth Sheridan, "For Help in Rebuilding Mosul, U.S. Turns to Its Former Foes—40 Retired Iraqi Generals Enlisted In Northern City," *The Washington Post*, 25 April 2003, sec. A, 10.

95   Major John Freeburg and Sergeant First Class Jess Todd, "The 101st Airborne Division in Iraq: Televising Freedom," *Military Review*, November–December 2004, 39–41.

96   10th Special Forces Group, "Valorous Unit Award Narrative," 16 June 2003, CD, USASOC History Office Classified Files, Fort Bragg, NC; Captain Arnaldo Colon, "U.S. Marines in Northern Iraq A Certain Force," CD, USASOC History Office Classified Files, Fort Bragg; Sheridan, "For Help Rebuilding Mosul."

97   10th Special Forces Group, "Valorous Unit Award Narrative;" Colon, "Certain Force;" Sheridan, "For Help Rebuilding Mosul."

98   10th Special Forces Group, "Valorous Unit Award Narrative;" Colon, "Certain Force;" Christine Spolar, "Mosul Taking Path Toward New Stability," *Chicago Tribune*, 14 May 2003.

99   Unless otherwise noted, all information regarding 404th Civil Affairs Battalion activities in northern Iraq are taken from:

404th Civil Affairs Battalion, "Memorandum for Commander, CJTF-7, Subject: Submission of Meritorious Unit Commendation," 2004, copy in USASOC History Office Classified Files, Fort Bragg, NC.

100 Ken Dilanian, "A challenge for U.S. in oil-rich Kirkuk," *The Miami Herald,* 21 April 2003, http://www.miami.com/mld/miamiherald/news/special_packages/iraq/dispatche/5679000....

101 Lieutenant Colonel Harry Schute, 404th Civil Affairs Battalion, interview by Lieutenant Colonel Robert Walsh, 12 May 2003, Irbil, Iraq, summary transcript, USASOC History Office Classified Files, Fort Bragg, NC.

102 Lieutenant Colonel Harry Schute, 404th Civil Affairs Battalion, and Major Derek Storino*, D Company, 96th Civil Affairs Battalion, interview by Lieutenant Colonel John Katz, 16 April 2003, Kirkuk, Iraq, summary transcript, USASOC History Office Classified Files, Fort Bragg, NC.

103 Sabrina Tavernise, "Kurds Mobilize to Elect One of Their Own in City of Kirkuk," *The New York Times Online,* 28 May 2003.

104 "FOB 103 Operations Summary;" Chief Warrant Officer 3 Mack Mellers*, ODA 090, 3rd Battalion, 10th Special Forces Group, interview by Lieutenant Colonel Robert W. Jones Jr., 24 June 2003, Fort Carson, CO, tape recording, USASOC History Office Classified Files, Fort Bragg, NC.

105 U.S. Central Command, "Coalition Iraqi Police Work to Make Iraq Secure," News Release 03-05-57, 17 May 2003, copy in USASOC History Office Classified Files, Fort Bragg, NC.

106 Staff Sergeant Ralph McPherson*, ODB 090, 3rd Battalion, 10th Special Forces Group, interview by Lieutenant Colonel Robert W. Jones Jr., 24 June 2003, Fort Carson, CO, tape recording, USASOC History Office Classified Files, Fort Bragg, NC.

107 Giroux, "FOB 103 Operations Summary;" Arnaud de Borchgrave, "Old Forces Unleashed in War's Aftermath," *The Washington Times,* 1 May 2003, 19.

108 Mellers interview.

109 Giroux, "FOB 103 Operations Summary;" U.S. Central Command, News release: 03-05-57.

110 Giroux, "FOB 103 Operations Summary."

111 Giroux, "FOB 103 Operations Summary."

112 Giroux, "FOB 103 Operations Summary;" Kevin Dougherty, "Army 'Mayor' Plans for Diversity in Kirkuk's Future," *Stars and Stripes,* 5 May 2003.

113 Giroux, "FOB 103 Operations Summary."

114 Colonel John F. Mulholland, 5th Special Forces Group, interview with Dr. Charles H. Briscoe, 4 August 2003, Fort Bragg, NC, USASOC History Office Classified Files, Fort Bragg, NC.

115 Major Jack Gray*, Advanced Operating Base 520, 1st Battalion, 5th Special Forces Group, interview by Dr. Kenneth Finlayson, 10 September 2003, Fort Campbell, KY, tape recording, USASOC History Office Classified Files, Fort Bragg, NC; Lieutenant Colonel Christopher K. Haas, 1st Battalion, 5th Special Forces Group, interview by Dr. Kenneth Finlayson, 10 September 2003, Fort Campbell, KY, tape recording, USASOC History Office Classified Files, Fort Bragg, NC.

116 Lieutenant Colonel Christopher Conner, 2nd Battalion, 5th Special Forces Group, interview by Dr. Kenneth Finlayson, 10 September 2003, Fort Campbell, KY, tape recording, USASOC History Office Classified Files, Fort Bragg, NC.

117 Lieutenant Colonel Timothy Williams, 3rd Battalion, 5th Special Forces Group, interview by Lieutenant Colonel Dennis P. Mroczkowski, 11 April 2003, Baghdad, Iraq, digital recording, USASOC History Office Classified Files, Fort Bragg, NC; Colonel Patrick Higgins, Headquarters, U.S. Special Operations Command Central, interview by Lieutenant Colonel Michael A. Ceroli, 30 April 2003, Baghdad, Iraq, digital recording, USASOC History Office Classified Files, Fort Bragg, NC; Major Carl Mitchell*, 3rd Battalion, 5th Special Forces Group, interview by Lieutenant Colonel Dennis P. Mroczkowski, 15 April 2003, Baghdad, Iraq, digital recording, USASOC History Office Classified Files, Fort Bragg, NC.

118 "The Little Man that would," SMH.COM.
     AU, 18 April 2003, www.smh.com.au/
     articles/2003/04/17/1050172705937.html.

119 Staff Sergeant Steve Means*, ODA 542, B
     Company, 2nd Battalion, 5th Special
     Forces Group, interview by Lieutenant
     Colonel Dennis P. Mroczkowski, 25 May
     2003, Ali As-Salim Airfield, Kuwait,
     digital recording, USASOC History Office
     Classified Files, Fort Bragg, NC; Staff
     Sergeant James Cook*, ODA 542, B
     Company, 2nd Battalion, 5th Special
     Forces Group, interview by Lieutenant
     Colonel Dennis P. Mroczkowski, 24 May
     2003, Ali As-Salim Airfield, Kuwait,
     digital recording, USASOC History Office
     Classified Files, Fort Bragg, NC.

120 Master Sergeant Theodore Ruggins*, ODA
     542, B Company, 2nd Battalion, 5th Special
     Forces Group, interview by Lieutenant
     Colonel Dennis P. Mroczkowski, 24 May
     2003, Ali As-Salim Airfield, Kuwait,
     digital recording, USASOC History Office
     Classified Files, Fort Bragg, NC; Captain
     Mike King*, ODA 542, B Company, 2nd
     Battalion, 5th Special Forces Group,
     interview by Lieutenant Colonel Dennis P.
     Mroczkowski, 24 May 2003, Ali As-Salim
     Airfield, Kuwait, digital recording,
     USASOC History Office Classified Files,
     Fort Bragg, NC.

121 Chief Warrant Officer 2 Bill Shoemaker*,
     ODA 542, B Company, 2nd Battalion, 5th
     Special Forces Group, interview by
     Lieutenant Colonel Dennis P. Mrocz-
     kowski, 24 May 2003, Ali As-Salim
     Airfield, Kuwait, digital recording,
     USASOC History Office Classified Files,
     Fort Bragg, NC; King interview.

122 Cook interview; King interview; Staff
     Sergeant Frank Findley*, ODA 542, B
     Company, 2nd Battalion, 5th Special
     Forces Group, interview by Lieutenant
     Colonel Dennis P. Mroczkowski, 25 May
     2003, Ali As-Salim Airfield, Kuwait,
     digital recording, USASOC History Office
     Classified Files, Fort Bragg, NC.

123 Shoemaker interview.

124 King interview.

125 King interview.

126 Chief Warrant Officer 3 Sidney Schwarz-
     kopf*, ODA 544, 2nd Battalion, 5th Special
     Forces Group, interview by Lieutenant
     Colonel Dennis P. Mroczkowski, 15 May

2003, Najaf, Iraq, digital recording,
USASOC History Office Classified Files,
Fort Bragg, NC.

127 "Who is Muqtada al-Sadr?,"*CNN.com*, 6
     April 2004, http://www.cnn.com/2004/
     WORLD/meast/04/06/shiite.leaders/.

128 Abdul Majid al-Khoei, exiled Shiite cleric,
     interview by Lieutenant Colonel Dennis P.
     Mroczkowski, 5 April 2003, Najaf, Iraq,
     digital recording, USASOC History Office
     Classified Files, Fort Bragg, NC.

129 Sergeant First Class Tim Kreiler*, ODA
     544, 2nd Battalion, 5th Special Forces
     Group, interview by Lieutenant Colonel
     Dennis P. Mroczkowski, 15 May 2003,
     Najaf, Iraq, digital recording, USASOC
     History Office Classified Files, Fort Bragg,
     NC; Glenn Frankel and Nora Boustany,
     "Mob Kills 2 Clerics At Shiite Shrine," *The
     Washington Post*, 11 April 2003, sec. A, 32;
     Michael Wood, "Abdul Majid al-Khoei,"
     The Guardian Unlimited, 12 April 2003,
     http://www.guardian.co.uk/Iraq/
     Story/0,2763,935242,00.html.

130 Joshua Hammer, "Murder at the Mosque,"
     MSNBC.com, 19 May 2003, http://msnbc.
     com/id/3068555/print/1/display-
     mode/1098/; Sergeant First Class Mark
     Combs*, ODA 544, 2nd Battalion, 5th
     Special Forces Group, interview by
     Lieutenant Colonel Dennis P. Mrocz-
     kowski, 15 May 2003, Najaf, Iraq, digital
     recording, USASOC History Office
     Classified Files, Fort Bragg, NC; Linda
     Robinson, *Masters of Chaos: The Secret
     History of the Special Forces* (New York:
     PublicAffairs Books, 2004), 261; Frankel
     and Boustany, "Mobs Kills 2 Clerics."

131 Robinson, *Masters of Chaos*, 261–62;
     Captain Roy Clinger*, ODA 544, 2nd
     Battalion, 5th Special Forces Group,
     interview by Lieutenant Colonel Dennis P.
     Mroczkowski, 15 May 2003, Najaf, Iraq,
     digital recording, USASOC History Office
     Classified Files, Fort Bragg, NC.

132 Schwarzkopf interview.

133 Specialist Albert Acord* and Sergeant Bob
     Petty*, C Company, 112th Special
     Operations Signal Battalion, interview by
     Chief Warrant Officer 3 Yul C. Yurcaba, 30
     June 2003, Baghdad, Iraq, tape recording,
     USASOC History Office Classified Files,
     Fort Bragg, NC.

134 Acord and Petty interview; Captain Patrick Flood, "Special Ops Signal Bn provides special support for Operation Iraqi Freedom," *Army Communicator*, Fall 2003, 22.

135 Private First Class Brenda Meter* and Specialist Josh Kinlaw*, C Company, 112th Special Operations Signal Battalion, interview by Chief Warrant Officer 3 Yul C. Yurcaba, 30 June 2003, Baghdad, Iraq, tape recording, USASOC History Office Classified Files, Fort Bragg, NC.

136 Acord and Petty interview.

137 Staff Sergeant Melvin Pelham*, C Company, 112th Special Operations Signal Battalion, interview by Sergeant Major Michael Barnes, 30 June 2003, Baghdad, Iraq, tape recording, USASOC History Office Classified Files, Fort Bragg, NC.

138 Captain Kyle Ruger*, First Sergeant Floyd Granger*, and Staff Sergeant Donald Tripp*, C Company, 112th Special Operations Signal Battalion, interview by A. Dwayne Aaron, 20 April 2004, Fort Bragg, NC, digital recording, USASOC History Office Classified Files, Fort Bragg, NC, hereafter cited as Granger interview.

139 Granger interview, 20 April 2004.

140 Meter and Kinlaw interview; Granger interview.

141 Brigadier General Vincent Brooks, U.S. Central Command Press Briefing, 16 April, 2003, Camp Doha, Qatar, copy in USASOC History Office Classified Files, Fort Bragg, NC.

142 Merle D, Kellerhals, "U.S. Forces Capture Terrorist Abu Abbas in Baghdad," Department of State Washington File: EPF306 04/16/2003, (http:usinfo.state.gov); David Ensor, "U.S. captures mastermind of Achille Lauro hijacking," *CNN.com*, 16 April 2003, http://www.cnn.com/2003/WORLD/meast/04/15/sprj.irq.abbas.arrested/.

143 1st Battalion, 160th Special Operations Aviation Regiment, "After action and mission summary briefing," n.d., USASOC History Office Classified Files, Fort Bragg, NC.

144 Chief Warrant Officer 4 Doug Carter*, B Company, 1st Battalion, 160th Special Operations Aviation Regiment, interview by James Schroder, 17 March 2004, Fort Campbell, KY, tape recording, USASOC History Office Classified Files, Fort Bragg, NC.

145 B Company , 2nd Ranger Battalion, 75th Ranger Regiment, "Battle Summary—Objective Cat, 14 April 2003," n.d., USASOC History Office Classified Files, Fort Bragg, NC.

146 B/2/75, "Battle Summary—Objective Cat;" Captain Paul Kasper*, B Company, 2nd Battalion, 75th Ranger Regiment, interview by Dr. Charles H. Briscoe, 16 October 2003, Fort Lewis, WA, tape recording, USASOC History Office Classified Files, Fort Bragg, NC.

147 Carter interview.

148 B/2/75, "Battle Summary—Objective Cat."

149 B/2/75, "Battle Summary—Objective Cat."

150 B/2/75, "Battle Summary—Objective Cat."

151 B/2/75, "Battle Summary—Objective Cat."

152 Major Ernest Bascomb*, F Company, 1st Battalion, 160th Special Operations Aviation Regiment, interview by James Schroder, 17 March 2003, Fort Campbell, KY, tape recording, USASOC History Office Classified Files, Fort Bragg, NC.

153 Sergeant Thomas Montgomery*, D Company, 2nd Battalion, 160th Special operations Aviation Regiment, interview by Dr. Kenneth Finlayson, 17 March 2003, Fort Campbell, KY, tape recording, USASOC History Office Classified Files, Fort Bragg, NC.

154 Sergeant First Class Colt Decker*, B Company, 1st Battalion, 160th Special Operations Aviation Regiment, interview by Dr. Kenneth Finlayson, 17 March 2003, Fort Campbell, KY, tape recording, USASOC History Office Classified Files, Fort Bragg, NC.

155 Staff Sergeant Stephen Meyers*, C Company, 1st Battalion, 160th Special Operations Aviation Regiment, interview by Dr. Kenneth Finlayson, 29 April 2003, Fort Campbell, KY, tape recording, USASOC History Office Classified Files, Fort Bragg, NC; Bascomb Interview.

156 Anthony H. Cordesman, Center for Strategic and International Studies, "The Lessons of the Iraq War: Main Report," Eleventh Working Draft, 21 July 2003, 105–106

157 Higgins interview; Lieutenant Colonel
     Mark Yanaway, 308th Civil Affairs
     Brigade, interview by Lieutenant Colonel
     Robert W. Jones Jr., 6 August 2004, Fort
     Bragg, NC, interview notes, USASOC
     History Office Classified Files, Fort Bragg,
     NC.

158 Higgins interview; Mitchell interview.

Chapter 9 Notes

1   Lieutenant Colonel Mark Yanaway, 308th
    Civil Affairs Brigade, interview by
    Lieutenant Colonel Robert W. Jones Jr., 6
    August 2004, Fort Bragg, NC, digital
    recording, USASOC History Office
    Classified Files, Fort Bragg, NC.

2   Colonel Patrick Higgins, Headquarters,
    U.S. Special Operations Command
    Central, interview by Lieutenant Colonel
    Michael A. Ceroli, 30 April 2003, Baghdad,
    Iraq, digital recording, USASOC History
    Office Classified Files, Fort Bragg, NC;
    "U.S. Army Special Operations Command:
    Crisis Action Team Update," 15 May 2003,
    CD-ROM, USASOC History Office
    Classified Files, Fort Bragg, NC; Major
    Kaleb Holmes*, Headquarters, Coalition
    Joint Special Operations Task Force–
    Arabian Peninsula, interview by Dr.
    Charles H. Briscoe, 4 July 2003, Baghdad,
    Iraq, tape recording, USASOC History
    Office Classified Files, Fort Bragg, NC.

3   Major Donald Thomes*, Sergeant Travis
    Fletcher*, Major Chip West*, Captain Alex
    Donovan*, Captain Ron Castle*, and
    Captain Marvin Holiday*, 315th Tactical
    Psychological Operations Company,
    interview by Lieutenant Colonel Robert W.
    Jones Jr., and Dr. Cherilyn A. Walley, 12
    March 2004, Fort Bragg, NC, digital
    recording, USASOC History Office
    Classified Files, Fort Bragg, NC, hereafter
    cited as 315th TPC interview; 315th
    Psychological Operations Company,
    "Meritorious Unit Citation Packet," 22
    December 2003, copy in USASOC History
    Office Classified Files, Fort Bragg, NC.

4   Major David A. Converse, "Operation
    IRAQI FREEDOM Psychological
    Operations Field Collection Team
    Operational Assessment," 2004, 58–59,

USASOC History Office Classified Files,
Fort Bragg, NC.

5   315th TPC interview.

6   315th TPC interview.

7   315th TPC interview.

8   315th TPC interview.

9   315th TPC interview.

10 315th TPC interview.

11 315th Psychological Operations Company,
    "Meritorious Unit Citation Packet."

12 Specialist Chad D. Wilkerson, "315th
    PSYOPS keep communication lines open,"
    Defend America, June 2003.

13 315th TPC interview.

14 315th TPC interview.

15 315th Psychological Operations Company,
    "Meritorious Unit Citation Packet."

16 315th Psychological Operations Company,
    "Meritorious Unit Citation Packet."

17 315th Psychological Operations Company,
    "Meritorious Unit Citation Packet."

18 315th TPC interview.

19 315th TPC interview.

20 Lieutenant Colonel Daniel L. Robey, 354th
    Civil Affairs Brigade, interview by
    Sergeant Landon Mavrelis, 15 June 2003,
    Baghdad, Iraq, tape recording, USASOC
    History Office Classified Files, Fort Bragg,
    NC.

21 Robey interview.

22 Robey interview.

23 Robey interview.

24 Robey interview.

25 Robey interview.

26 Robey interview.

27 Lieutenant Colonel Edward Burley, 352nd
    Civil Affairs Command, interview by Staff
    Sergeant Patrick Jennings, 26 July 2003,
    Baghdad, Iraq, digital recording, USASOC
    History Office Classified Files, Fort Bragg,
    NC.

28 Nick Hawton, "Bosnia's largest mass
    grave," *BBC News*, 30 July 2003, http://
    news.bbc.uk/go/pr/fr/-/1/hi/world/
    europe/3111189.stm; "Forensic Scientists at
    Work in the Iraq War Zone," The Institute
    for Forensic Excellence and Investigation
    of Genocide, http://www.inforce.org.uk/
    archives.htm.

29 Colonel Patrick Higgins, Headquarters, U.S. Special Operations Command Central, interview by Dr. Kenneth Finlayson, 14 August 2003, MacDill Air Force Base, FL, tape recording, USASOC History Office Classified Files, Fort Bragg, NC.

30 Higgins interview, 14 August 2003.

31 Higgins interview, 30 April 2003; Holmes interview; "Crisis Action Team Update."

32 Lieutenant Colonel Timothy Williams, 3rd Battalion, 5th Special Forces Group, interview by Lieutenant Colonel Dennis P. Mroczkowski, 11 April 2003, Baghdad, Iraq, digital recording, USASOC History Office Classified Files, Fort Bragg, NC; Major Carl Mitchell*, 3rd Battalion, 5th Special Forces Group, interview by Lieutenant Colonel Dennis P. Mrocz-kowski, 15 April 2003, Baghdad, Iraq, digital recording, USASOC History Office Classified Files, Fort Bragg, NC.

33 Center for Army Lessons Learned, "Stability Operations, Support Operations: Operation Iraqi Freedom, Initial Impressions Report," December 2003, 71–72.

34 Center for Army Lessons Learned, "Stability Operations;" "Crisis Action Team Update."

35 Dr. John Chin, interview by Dr. Charles H. Briscoe, 1 October 2004, Fort Bragg, NC, digital recording, USASOC History Office Classified Files, Fort Bragg, NC.

36 Chin interview.

37 First Lieutenant Robert Winston*, Alpha Forward Support Company, 528th Special Operations Support Battalion, interview by A. Dwayne Aaron, 28 June 2004, Fort Bragg, NC, digital recording, USASOC History Office Classified Files, Fort Bragg, NC; Captain Earl Jensen*, 528th Special Operations Support Battalion, interview by A. Dwayne Aaron, 26 May 2004, Fort Bragg, NC, digital recording, USASOC History Office Classified Files, Fort Bragg, NC.

38 Winston interview.

39 Jensen interview; Lieutenant Colonel Michael Saulnier, Commander, 528th Special Operations Support Battalion, interview by A. Dwayne Aaron, 6 June 2003, Fort Bragg, NC, digital recording, USASOC History Office Classified Files, Fort Bragg, NC.

40 Sergeant Justin McCleary*, 777th Maintenance Company, Tennessee Army National Guard, interview by Dr. Charles H. Briscoe, 30 June 2003, Baghdad, Iraq, tape recording, USASOC History Office Classified Files, Fort Bragg, NC.

41 McCleary interview.

42 "Crisis Action Team Update."

43 Major John McGinnis*, 2nd Battalion, 75th Ranger Regiment, e-mail to Lieutenant Colonel Robert W. Jones Jr., 18 November 2004, USASOC History Office Classified Files, Fort Bragg, NC; Captain Mel Everett*, 2nd Battalion, 75th Ranger Regiment, interview by Dr. Charles H. Briscoe, 16 October 2003, Fort Lewis, WA, tape recording, USASOC History Office Classified Files, Fort Bragg, NC.

44 First Lieutenant Peter Korenek*, 2nd Battalion, 75th Ranger Regiment, interview by Dr. Charles H. Briscoe, 16 October 2003, Fort Lewis, WA, tape recording, USASOC History Office Classified Files, Fort Bragg, NC; First Sergeant Philip Roemer*, 2nd Battalion, 75th Ranger Regiment, interview by Dr. Charles H. Briscoe, 16 October 2003, Fort Lewis, WA, tape recording, USASOC History Office Classified Files, Fort Bragg, NC.

45 Chief Warrant Officer 3 James Nattier*, interview by James Schroder, 26 April 2004, Fort Campbell, KY, tape recording, USASOC History Office Classified Files, Fort Bragg, NC; Chief Warrant Officer 4 Mark Willington*, interview by James Schroder, 16 March 2004, Fort Campbell, KY, tape recording, USASOC History Office Classified Files, Fort Bragg, NC.

46 Korenek interview; Nattier interview; Willington interview.

47 Roemer interview; Sergeant Roger Mueller*, 2nd Battalion, 75th Ranger Regiment, interview by Dr. Charles H. Briscoe, 16 October 2003, Fort Lewis, WA, tape recording, USASOC History Office Classified Files, Fort Bragg, NC.

48 Everett interview.

49 "Objective Reindeer Debrief, 13 June 2003," USASOC History Office Classified Files, Fort Bragg, NC.

50 Korenek interview.

51 Korenek interview.

52 Roemer interview.

53 "Objective Reindeer Debrief."

54 "Objective Reindeer Debrief."

55 Korenek interview.

56 "Objective Reindeer Debrief."

57 "Bronze Star Award Narrative for SFC Barry Fontes*," CD-ROM, USASOC History Office Classified Files, Fort Bragg, NC.

58 The Multi-Role Anti-Armor Anti-Personnel Weapon System (MAAWS) consists of the shoulder fired M3 Carl Gustaf recoilless rifle system and a family of 84mm munitions; "Silver Star Award Narrative for CPL Jacob Oliver*," CD-ROM, USASOC History Office Classified Files, Fort Bragg, NC.

59 Oliver Narrative.

60 Fontes Narrative.

61 Fontes Narrative.

62 Chief Warrant Officer 3 Derek Falcon*, interview by James Schroder, 4 May 2004, Fort Campbell, KY, tape recording, USASOC History Office Classified Files, Fort Bragg, NC.

63 Falcon interview; Chief Warrant Officer 2 Elliot Brietzke*, interview by James Schroder, 3 May 2004, Fort Campbell, KY, tape recording, USASOC History Office Classified Files, Fort Bragg, NC.

64 Chief Warrant Officer 3 Aaron Garrote*, interview by James Schroder, 28 April 2004, Fort Campbell, KY, tape recording, USASOC History Office Classified Files, Fort Bragg, NC.

65 Falcon interview; Brietzke interview; Garrote interview.

66 Falcon interview; Brietzke interview; Garrote interview.

67 Falcon interview; Brietzke interview; Garrote interview.

68 Chief Warrant Officer 4 David Croaker*, interview by Dr. Kenneth Finlayson, 30 April 2004, Fort Campbell, KY, tape recording, USASOC History Office Classified Files, Fort Bragg, NC; Falcon interview; Brietzke interview; Garrote interview.

69 Chief Warrant Officer 2 Barry Littleton*, by James Schroder 3 May 2004, Fort Campbell, KY, tape recording, USASOC History Office Classified Files, Fort Bragg, NC; Falcon interview; Brietzke interview: Garrote interview.

70 Falcon interview; Brietzke interview; Garrote interview; Littleton interview.

71 Falcon interview; Brietzke interview.

72 Falcon interview; Brietzke interview.

Glossary

(-) *indicates less than full modified table of organization and equipment strength*

(L) *indicates a non-mechanized (light) unit*

(R) *retired*

A

A-Day *day air operations are initiated*

AFSB *alpha forward support battalion*

AH *attack helicopter*

Ansar al-Islam *Islamic terrorist group with links to Iran that operates in northern Iraq*

AOB *advanced operating base*

AP *Arabian Peninsula*

ARSOF *U.S. Army special operations forces*

ATV *all-terrain vehicle*

B

BCT *brigade combat team*

BFSB *bravo forward support battalion*

BFV *Bradley Fighting Vehicle*

BIAP *Baghdad International Airport*

BMP *Soviet-designed armored personnel carrier*

C

CA *Civil Affairs*

CAB *Civil Affairs battalion*

CAC *Civil Affairs company*

CAS *close air support*

CAT-A *Civil Affairs Team–A*

CAT-B *Civil Affairs Team–B*

CENTCOM *U.S. Central Command*

CFACC *Coalition Forces Air Component Command*

CFLCC *Coalition Forces Land Component Command*

CFSOCC *Combined Forces Special Operations Component Command*

CH *cargo helicopter*

CJSOTF *combined joint special operations task force*

CJSOTF-North *Combined Joint Special Operations Task Force–Northern Iraq*

JSOTF-West *Combined Joint Special Operations Task Force–Western Iraq*

CMO *civil military operations*

CWO *chief warrant officer*

D

DAP *defensive armed penetrator*

DART *downed aircraft recovery team*

dinar *Iraqi monetary denomination*

DSN *defense switched network*

DST *direct support team*

E

EOD *explosive ordnance disposal*

EPW *enemy prisoner of war*

ETAC *enlisted terminal air controller*

EUCOM *U.S. European Command*

F

FARP *forward arming and refueling point*

Fedayeen *term used to describe irregular forces in Iraq, sponsored by the Iraqi Government*

FIF *Free Iraqi Forces*

FOB *forward operating base*

FSB *forward support base/forward support battalion*

FSSP *fuel system supply point*

G

G-Day *day major ground combat operations are initiated*

GMV *ground mobility vehicle (M1113 HMMWV for special operations forces)*

GOPLATS *gas oil platforms*

GPS *global positioning system*

H

HDR *humanitarian daily ration*

HEMTT *heavy expanded mobility tactical truck*

H-Hour *hour attack is initiated*

HIMARS *High Mobility Artillery Rocket System*

HMMWV *High-Mobility Multipurpose Wheeled Vehicle*

HVT *high-value target*

I

ID *infantry division*

IO *Information Operations*

J

JDAMS *Joint Direct Attack Munitions System*

JOC *Joint Operations Center*

JPOTF *Joint Psychological Operations Task Force*

JSOA *Joint Special Operations Area*

JSOAD *Joint Special Operations Air Detachment*

JSOTF *Joint Special Operations Task Force*

JSOTF-North *Joint Special Operations Task Force–Northern Iraq*

JSOTF-West *Joint Special Operations Task Force–Western Iraq*

JTF *Joint Task Force*

K

KDP *Kurdish Democratic Party*

kHz *kilohertz*

km *kilometer*

L

LMTV *Light Medium Tactical Vehicle*

M

MEF *Marine expeditionary force*

MIL/mm *millimeter*

MOPP *mission oriented protective posture*

MP *military police*

MRE *meal ready-to-eat*

MTLB *Soviet-design armored personnel carrier*

N

NATO *North Atlantic Treaty Organization*

NIPRNET *Non-secure Internet Protocol Router Network*

NOD *night observation device*

NSV *nonstandard vehicle*

NVG *night vision goggles*

O

ODA *operational detachment alpha*

ODB *operational detachment bravo*

OEF *Operation ENDURING FREEDOM*

OIF *Operation IRAQI FREEDOM*

OPLAN *operations plan*

P

PAO *public affairs officer*

Peshmerga *Kurdish freedom fighters*

POB *Psychological Operations battalion*

POC *Psychological Operations company*

POG *Psychological Operations group*

PSYOP *Psychological Operations*

PUK *Patriotic Union of Kurdistan*

Q

R

RCT *regimental combat team*

ROE *Rules of Engagement*

RPG *rocket-propelled grenade*

S

SCAMPI *secure communication system providing access to several intelligence agency networks*

SCUD *generic term for land-based missiles used as a weapon of mass destruction*

SF *Special Forces*

SFG *Special Forces group*

SFLE *Special Forces liaison element*

SIPRNET *Secure Internet Protocol Router Network*

SOAR *Special Operations Aviation Regiment*

SOCCE *special operations command and control element*

SOCCENT *U.S. Special Operations Command Central*

SOCOM *U.S. Special Operations Command*

SOF *special operations forces*

SOSB *Special Operations Signal Battalion or Special Operations Support Battalion*

SOSCOM *Special Operations Support Command*

SOW *Special Operations Wing, U.S. Air Force*

supay *Kurdish battalion*

T

TLAM *Tomahawk Land Attack Missile*

TOC *tactical operations center*

TOE *Table of Organization and Equipment*

TPC *Tactical Psychological Operations company*

TPD *Tactical Psychological Operations detachment*

TPT *Tactical Psychological Operations team*

U

U.S. *United States*

UH *utility helicopter*

UN *United Nations*

USACAPOC *U.S. Army Civil Affairs and Psychological Operations Command*

USAJFKSWCS *U.S. Army John F. Kennedy Special Warfare Center and School*

USASFC *U.S. Army Special Forces Command*

USASOC *U.S. Army Special Operations Command*

USNS *U.S. naval ship*

USS *U.S. ship*

USSOCOM *U.S. Special Operations Command*

UW *unconventional warfare*

V

W

wadi *a gully in the desert*

WMD *weapon of mass destruction*

X

Y

Z

ZULU *Greenwich Mean Time*

Contributors

Dr. Charles H. Briscoe has been the U.S. Army Special Operations Command Historian since 2000. He is a retired airborne infantry and Special Forces officer who served overseas in the Dominican Republic, Vietnam, Italy, and Panama. Dr. Briscoe earned a PhD in history from the University of South Carolina in 1996. He is the author of *La Fuerza Interamerica de Paz* (1999, 2000) and *Trienta Años Después* (2001). Dr. Briscoe taught military and Latin American history at Campbell University and Methodist College. He has contributed articles to *Veritas: The Journal of ARSOF History* and *Special Warfare Magazine*. He was the editor and a contributor to *Weapon of Choice: Army Special Operations in Afghanistan*.

Dr. Kenneth Finlayson is the Command Historian for the U.S. Army John F. Kennedy Special Warfare Center and School. He graduated and received a commission from Colorado State University in 1978. He served on active duty as an Infantry officer until 1992 and retired from the Army Reserve in 2004. He received his PhD in history from the University of Maine in 1996. His first book, *An Uncertain Trumpet: The Evolution of U.S. Army Infantry Doctrine, 1919–1942*, was published in July 2001. He has contributed articles to *Veritas: The Journal of ARSOF History* and *Special Warfare Magazine*.

Robert W. Jones Jr. is a historian at the USASOC History Office and a Lieutenant Colonel in the Army Reserve. He graduated and received a commission from the University of Washington in 1982 and served in Infantry, Psychological Operations, and Civil Affairs assignments in the United States, Panama, and Bosnia and deployed to Afghanistan as a historian. LTC Jones earned an MA from Duke University and an MS from Troy State University and has contributed articles to *Veritas: The Journal of ARSOF History*.

Dr. Cherilyn A. Walley received her PhD in Agricultural History and Rural Studies from Iowa State University in 2003. She worked for the USASOC History Office from September 2003 through October 2005, serving as a historian, writer, and as the editor of *Veritas: The Journal of ARSOF History*. Dr. Walley has contributed articles to *Veritas, Special Warfare Magazine*, and *Sword and Scroll: The Newsletter of the Civil Affairs Association*.

A. Dwayne Aaron is a retired Special Forces officer and 1971 graduate of the United States Military Academy at West Point. His military career includes assignments with the 82nd Airborne Division, 509th Airborne Battalion Combat Team, XVIII Airborne Corps, and the 5th Special Forces Group. He is a veteran of Operations JUST CAUSE and DESERT STORM. In his last assignment, he commanded the 3rd Battalion, 1st Special Warfare Training Group. He is a graduate of the Command and General Staff College and earned an MS from the University of West Alabama. Mr. Aaron has contributed articles to *Infantry Magazine, Veritas: The Journal of ARSOF History,* and *Special Warfare Magazine*.

Michael R. Mullins is a former Marine Infantryman and retired Army Civil Affairs officer. He primarily served in Sub-Saharan Africa and Eastern Europe with the 96th Civil Affairs Battalion (Airborne). He has served as a Civil Affairs Team Leader, Company Commander, and Battalion Executive Officer in the 96th CAB. He served as a senior Civil Affairs advisor in the Combined Joint Special Operations Task Force–Afghanistan during Operation ENDURING FREEDOM. He is a graduate of the Command and General Staff College and earned a BA in Political Science and an MS in International Relations. Mr. Mullins has contributed articles to *Veritas: The Journal of ARSOF History.*

James A. Schroder earned an MBA at Murray State University. A retired aviation chief warrant officer, he previously served seven years with the 160th Special Operations Aviation Regiment as an MH-47E Chinook pilot and flight lead. He also served in military intelligence, Special Forces, and aviation units in the United States and overseas, and earned two Air Medals piloting CH-47D Chinook helicopters in Operation DESERT STORM. Mr. Schroder has contributed articles to *Veritas: The Journal of ARSOF History* and *Special Warfare Magazine* and was a previous contributor to *Weapon of Choice: Army Special Operations in Afghanistan.*

Wendy Nielsen is the managing editor of *Veritas: The Journal of ARSOF History* and publications specialist for the USASOC History Office. She earned a BS in Statistics and an MBA from Brigham Young University. Ms. Nielsen has brought her skill and attention to detail to the varied aspects of designing, editing, and publishing *Veritas* and *All Roads Lead to Baghdad.*

Earl J. Moniz is the digital information specialist with the USASOC History Office. After retiring as a Special Forces noncommissioned officer, he earned his MLS degree from North Carolina Central University. He has contributed articles to *Veritas: The Journal of ARSOF History* and produced the ARSOF history posters: Veritas, Colonel Aaron Bank, and ARSOF in OEF. He served as the photo editor for *All Roads Lead to Baghdad.*

Frank E. Allen is a retired U.S. Army graphics illustrator who spent eight years as an M60A3 and M1 tank crewman before serving in the 4th Psychological Operations Group, 751st Military Intelligence Battalion, in Korea and in the 5th Special Forces Group in Afghanistan and Iraq. His art credits, before designing the cover and making the chapter sketches for *All Roads Lead to Baghdad,* have spanned the spectrum: a Special Forces sniper print, a 4th PSYOP Group poster, a Golden Knights poster, an Evolution of Special Forces print, Special Forces wall murals, Army aviation unit patches, unit coins, a Task Force Dagger in Iraq print, airbrushed motorcycle artwork, and etched glass Volkswagen awards. His next print, "Army Special Operations Forces in Iraq," will contain the sketches created for this book and appear at the beginning of every chapter.

Index

Vaughn, Colonel Jerry   267, 269
Votel, Colonel Joseph   65, 71, 179, 309

W

Wadi al Khirr, Iraq   123, 134–139, 142,
    144–145, 147, 151, 269, 271, 288
Wallace, Lieutenant General William   76
Williams, Colonel Thomas   45, 47–48

X

XVIII Airborne Corps   29, 70

Y

Yazidis   10
Yellen, Brigadier General Howard   60
Yuma Proving Ground, Nevada   68

Z

Zalm Valley, Iraq   197
Zambo Oil Field   366

ISBN 0-16-075364-3

9 780160 753640

ISBN 0-16-075364-3